THE ENCYCLOPEDIA
OF THE
ARAB-ISRAELI
CONFLICT

A Political, Social, and Military History

THE ENCYCLOPEDIA OF THE ARAB-ISRAELI CONFLICT

A Political, Social, and Military History

VOLUME IV: Documents

Dr. Spencer C. Tucker

Volume Editor

Dr. Priscilla Roberts

Editor, Documents Volume

Dr. Paul G. Pierpaoli Jr.

Associate Editor

Major General David Zabecki, USAR (retired)

Dr. Sherifa Zuhur

Assistant Editors

FOREWORD BY

General Anthony C. Zinni, USMC (retired)

A B C · C L I O

Santa Barbara, California   Denver, Colorado   Oxford, England

Copyright © 2008 by ABC-CLIO, Inc.

Cataloging-in-Publication Data is on file with the Library of Congress

ISBN 978-1-85109-841-5 (hard copy : alk. paper) — ISBN 978-1-85109-842-2 (ebook)

10 09 08 07 06 05   10 9 8 7 6 5 4 3 2 1

This book is also available on the World Wide Web as an ebook.
Visit abc-clio.com for details.

ABC-CLIO, Inc.
130 Cremona Drive, P.O. Box 1911
Santa Barbara, California 93116–1911

This book is printed on acid-free paper ∞ .
Manufactured in the United States of America

Contents

List of Documents

Documents

1. Lord Palmerston to Viscount Beauvale, June 28, 1839

Introduction

By the 1830s, European powers realized that the Ottoman Empire was in decline. Ottoman Turkey's weakness quickly became a factor in international power politics. After a long and bitter rebellion, in 1832 the Greeks won independence from the Ottoman Empire, an event that encouraged other states to seek to partition the Ottoman Empire. Czarist Russia, which considered itself the spiritual heir of the Byzantine Empire, sought to enhance its position in the Caucasus and the Middle East. Russian leaders cherished designs of regaining the former Byzantine capital of Istanbul (Constantinople), which controlled the strategic Bosporus Straits, the only maritime passage from the Russian-dominated Black Sea to the Mediterranean. France, too, sought special rights in the Middle East in Lebanon, Syria, Egypt, and Palestine. The Austrian Empire, whose Balkan provinces shared borders with the Ottoman Empire, also hoped to enhance its territorial position. Alarmed by the ambitions of their European rivals, whose power they did not wish to strengthen, British statesmen decided that the preservation of the Ottoman Empire was in their own country's interests. In an 1839 letter to Viscount Beauvale, the British ambassador in Vienna (capital of the Austrian Empire), Lord Palmerston, then British foreign secretary and later a Conservative prime minister, enunciated this position. Protection of the territorial integrity of the Ottoman Empire would remain British foreign policy for at least four decades and was a major reason for Britain's intervention in the 1854–1856 Crimean War.

Primary Source

The general view which Her Majesty's Government, as at present informed, entertain of the affair in question, may be stated as follows:

The Great Powers are justified in interfering in these matters, which are, in fact, a contest between a sovereign and his subject, because this contest threatens to produce great and imminent danger to the deepest interests of other Powers, and to the general peace of Europe. Those interests and that peace require the maintenance of the Turkish Empire; and the maintenance of the Turkish Empire is, therefore, the primary object to be aimed at. This object cannot be secured without putting an end to future chances of collision between the Sultan and Mehemet Ali. But as long as Mehemet Ali continues to occupy Syria, there will be danger of such collision. Mehemet Ali cannot hold Syria without a large military force constantly stationed there. As long as there is an Egyptian force in Syria, there must necessarily be a Turkish army in that part of Asia Minor which borders on Syria. Each party might agree at present to reduce those forces to a given amount, but neither could be sure that the other was not, after a time, secretly increasing his amount of force; and each party would, beyond a doubt, gradually augment his own force; and thus at no distant period, the same state of things which has existed of late, would again recur: for the motives and passions which have led to it would still be in action. Mehemet Ali, or Ibrahim, would still desire to add more territory to their Pashalics; the Sultan would still burn to drive them back into Egypt.

It appears then to Her Majesty's Government, that there can be no end to the danger with which these affairs menace the peace of Europe until Mehemet Ali shall have restored Syria to the direct authority of the Sultan; shall have retired into Egypt; and shall have interposed the Desert between his troops and authorities and the troops and authorities of the Sultan. But Mehemet Ali could not be expected to consent to this, unless some equivalent advantage were granted to him; and this equivalent advantage might be hereditary succession in his family to the Pashalic of Egypt: Mehemet Ali and his descendants being secured in the Government of that Province in the same way that a former Pasha of Scutari and his family were so secured; the Pasha continuing to be the vassal of the Porte, paying a reasonable tribute, furnishing a contingent of men, and being bound like any other Pasha by the treaties which his sovereign might make. Such an arrangement would appear to be equitable between the parties, because, on the one hand, it would secure the Sultan against many dangers and inconveniences which arise from the present occupation of Syria by the Pasha; while, on the other hand, it would afford to the Pasha that security as to the future fate of his family, his anxiety about which, he has often declared to be the main cause of his desire to obtain some final and permanent arrangement.

It appears to Her Majesty's Government that if the Five Powers were to agree upon such a plan, and were to propose it to the two parties, with all the authority which belongs to the Great Powers of Europe, such an arrangement would be carried into effect, and through its means, Europe would be delivered from a great and imminent danger.

Source: United Kingdom, *Parliamentary Papers* (1841), 29:117–119.

2. Definitive Concession for the Construction of the Suez Canal [Excerpt], January 5, 1856

Introduction

From the early 19th century onward, successive French governments demonstrated special interest in Egypt. Among the more ambitious projects contemplated by French leaders from Emperor Napoleon I onward was the construction of a canal to link the Mediterranean Sea with the Red Sea, thereby making it unnecessary for ships traveling from Europe to Asia to circumnavigate the continent of Africa. The British government, which feared that such a strategically significant waterway would become an international flash point rivaling the Bosporus Straits, opposed all such French schemes. In 1854 Said Pasha, the new governor of Egypt, nonetheless awarded the concession to build such a canal to Ferdinand de Lesseps, a former French diplomat. The agreement was finalized in 1856. Work on the canal began in 1859, and despite fierce British opposition, the waterway was completed and opened in 1869. The new canal quickly revolutionized international trade. In 1875 Britain bought Egypt's shares in the Suez Canal Company from the financially straitened Ismail Pasha, who had succeeded Said Pasha, although the French government still remained the majority shareholder. British officials soon came to regard the canal as a major strategic interest of their country, a route that greatly facilitated sea communications with India, their greatest imperial possession.

Primary Source

We, Mohammed Said Pasha, Viceroy of Egypt.

In view of our Act of Concession dated November 30, 1854, by which we gave to our friend, Mr. Ferdinand de Lesseps, exclusive power for the purpose of establishing and directing a universal company to cut through the Isthmus of Suez, to operate a passage suitable for large vessels, to establish or adapt two adequate entrances, one on the Mediterranean, the other on the Red Sea, and to establish one or two ports:

Mr. Ferdinand de Lesseps having represented to us that, in order to establish the aforementioned company in the form and under the conditions generally adopted for companies of this nature, it

is desirable to stipulate in advance, in a more detailed and more complete act, on the one hand, the responsibilities, obligations, and charges to which such company will be subject and, on the other hand, the concessions, immunities, and advantages to which it shall be entitled, as well as the facilities that will be granted to it for its administration.

We have laid down as follows the conditions for the concession which forms the subject of these presents.

OBLIGATIONS

Art. I. The company founded by our friend, Mr. Ferdinand de Lesseps, by virtue of our grant of November 30, 1854, must execute at its own expense, risk, and peril, all work, including construction, necessary for the establishment of:

(1) A canal for large seagoing vessels, between Suez on the Red Sea and the Bay of Pelusium in the Mediterranean Sea;
(2) An irrigation canal also suitable for use by Nile shipping, connecting the river with the maritime canal above-mentioned;
(3) Two irrigation and feeder branches leading off from the above-mentioned canal and flowing in the two directions of Suez and Pelusium.

The work will be carried out so as to be finished within a period of six years, except in the event of hindrances and delays resulting from *force majeure.*

II. The company shall be empowered to carry out the work with which it is charged by itself under State supervision or to cause it to be carried out by contractors through competitive bids or on an agreed-price basis. In all cases at least four-fifths of the workmen employed in this work are to be Egyptians.

III. The canal suitable for large seagoing vessels shall be dug to the depth and width fixed by the program of the International Scientific Commission.

[…]

VII. The maritime canal and ports belonging to it, as well as the canal connecting with the Nile and the lead-off canal, shall at all times be kept in good condition by the company, at its expense.

[…]

CONCESSIONS
[…]

XIV. We solemnly declare, for ourselves and our successors, subject to ratification by His Imperial Majesty the Sultan, that the great maritime canal from Suez to Pelusium and the ports belonging to it shall be open forever, as neutral passages, to every merchant vessel crossing from one sea to the other, without any distinction, exclusion, or preference with respect to persons or nationalities, in consideration of the payment of the fees, and compliance with the regulations established by the universal company, the concession-holder, for the use of the said canal and its appurtenances.

XV. In consequence of the principle laid down in the foregoing article, the universal company holding the concession may not, in any case, give to any vessel, company, or private party any advantage or favor not given to all other vessels, companies, or private parties on the same terms.

XVI. The life of the company is fixed at 99 years, counting from the completion of the work and the opening of the maritime canal to large vessels.

At the expiration of that period, the Egyptian Government will resume possession of the maritime canal constructed by the company, and it shall be its responsibility, in this case, to take over all materials and supplies used in the company's maritime service and, in return, to pay the company the value to be fixed, either by amicable agreement or on the basis of an opinion of experts.

Nevertheless, should the company retain the concession for successive periods of 99 years, the levy for the benefit of the Egyptian Government stipulated in Article XVIII below shall be increased for the second period to 20 percent, for the third period to 25 percent, and so on, at the rate of 5 percent for each period; but such levy shall, however, never exceed 35 percent of the net profits of the company.

XVII. In order to compensate the company for the expenses of construction, maintenance, and operation for which it is made responsible by these presents, we authorize it, henceforth and for its entire term of possession, as specified in paragraphs 1 and 3 of the foregoing article, to establish and collect, for passage in the canals and the ports belonging thereto, navigation, pilotage, towage, and anchorage fees, according to rate-schedules which it may change at any time, subject to the express condition that it shall:

(1) Collect these fees without exception or favor from all vessels, under the same terms.

[...]

XVIII. At the same time, in view of the land grants and other advantages accorded the company in the foregoing articles, we shall make, for the benefit of the Egyptian Government, a levy of 15 percent of the net profits for each year as determined and apportioned at the general meeting of shareholders.

XIX. The list of charter members who contributed by their work, their studies, and their capital to the accomplishment of the undertaking, before the founding of the company, shall be prepared by us.

After deduction of the amount levied for the Egyptian Government stipulated in Article XVIII above, 10 percent of the annual net profits of the enterprise is to be allotted to the charter members or their heirs or assigns.

XX. Independently of the time necessary for the execution of the work, our friend and representative, Mr. Ferdinand de Lesseps, will preside over and direct the company as first founder for ten years from the time when the period of the enjoyment of the 99-year concession begins, under the terms of article XVI above.

[...]

Source: U.S. Department of State, *The Suez Canal Problem: July 26–September 22, 1956* (Washington, DC: U.S. Government Printing Office, 1956).

3. Bilu Group Manifesto, January 1, 1882

Introduction

In the later 19th century, Zionist sentiment burgeoned rapidly among young Jewish people. This development was in part a reflection of the pervasive growth of nationalism during the entire century, as numerous ethnic groups in Europe and beyond affirmed their rights to their own nation or state. In the case of the Jews, rising Zionism was also a response to the escalating violence of anti-Jewish pogroms within the czarist Russian Empire, which drove hundreds of thousands of Jews to immigrate to other European nations and especially to the United States. The Bilu groups were established in 1882 in the wake of a particularly strong wave of Russian anti-Semitic violence the previous year. Taking their name from the first letters of Chapter 2, Verse 5, of the biblical Book of Isaiah, "House of Jacob, Come, Let us Go," they urged Jews to leave Russia and settle in Palestine, the biblical Holy Land. The Biluim, as they were known, consisted of approximately 500 young people, most from the Kharkov region of Russia. This manifesto, issued by a Bilu group near Constantinople, envisaged obtaining permission from the Ottoman sultan to establish a Jewish homeland in Palestine. The Biluim were only part of the broader grouping of Hovevei Zion (Lovers of Zion) that developed in Russia in the early 1880s and envisaged the establishment of a Jewish homeland. Some at least achieved their ambition of moving to Palestine, where—with the financial assistance of such wealthy Jews as Lord Rothschild—they established agricultural settlements. The Jewish desire to reestablish the state of Israel, which had been destroyed almost 19 centuries earlier, caught the imagination of many Western intellectuals and was one of the inspirations for the British novelist George Eliot's work *Daniel Deronda* (1876).

Primary Source

To our brothers and sisters in Exile!

"If I do not help myself, who will help me?"

Nearly two thousand years have passed since, in an evil hour, after an heroic struggle, the glory of our Temple vanished in fire and our kings and chieftains exchanged their crowns and diadems for the chains of exile. We lost our country where our beloved ancestors had lived. Into the Exile we took with us, of all our glories, only a spark of the fire by which our Temple, the abode of the Great One, was engirdled, and this little spark kept us alive while the towers of our enemies crumbled into dust, and this spark leapt into the celestial flame and illuminated the heroes of our race and inspired them to endure the horrors of the dance of death and the tortures of the autos-da-fé. And this spark is again kindling and will shine for us, a true pillar of fire going before us on the road to Zion, while behind us is a pillar of cloud, the pillar of oppression threatening to destroy us. Are you asleep, O our nation? What have you been doing until 1882? Sleeping and dreaming the false dream of assimilation. Now thank God, you have awaked from your slothful slumber. The pogroms have awakened you from your charmed sleep. Your eyes are open to recognize the obscure and delusive hopes. Can you listen in silence to the taunts and mocking of your enemies? . . .

Where is your ancient pride, your old spirit? Remember that you were a nation possessing a wise religion, a law, a constitution, a celestial Temple who[se] wall is still a silent witness to the glories of the past. . . .

Your state in the West is hopeless: the star of your future is gleaming in the East. Deeply conscious of all the foregoing, and inspired by the true teaching of our great master, Hillel, "If I do not help myself, who will help me?" we propose to form the following society for national ends:

1. The society will be named 'BILU', according to the motto, "House of Jacob, come let us go." It will be divided into local branches according to the numbers of its members.
2. The seat of the Committee will be Jerusalem.
3. Donations and contributions shall be unfixed and unlimited.

WE WANT:

1. A home in our country. It was given to us by the mercy of God; it is ours as registered in the archives of history.
2. To beg it of the Sultan himself, and if it be impossible to obtain this, to beg that we may at least possess it as a state within a larger state; the internal administration to be ours, to have our civil and political rights, and to act with the Turk-

ish Empire only in foreign affairs, so as to help our brother Ishmael in his time of need.

We hope that the interests of our glorious nation will rouse the national spirit in rich and powerful men, and that everyone, rich or poor, will give his best labors to the holy cause.

Greetings dear brothers and sisters!

HEAR! O ISRAEL! The Lord is our God, the Lord is one, and our land Zion is our only hope.

GOD be with us! The Pioneers of BILU

> **Source:** "Bilu Manifesto," http://www.zionism-israel.com/hdoc/Bilu_Manifesto_1882/htm.

4. Convention Respecting the Free Navigation of the Suez Maritime Canal [Excerpt], October 29, 1888

Introduction

After British forces occupied Egypt in 1882, the British government sought to establish guidelines for the smooth operation at all times of the Suez Canal, now so vital to British imperial communications. In 1888 the British put forward a convention governing the waterway's administration under the supervision of an international commission, a provision that would, however, only come into effect after the British military occupation had ended. In time of war, foreign warships would only be allowed limited stays in the canal and would be barred from unloading either troops or munitions, while commerce was to continue uninterrupted. Measures taken for the defense of Egypt were not affected by this convention. Austria, Germany, Italy, the Netherlands, the Ottoman Empire, Russia, Spain, Britain, and France signed the convention in 1888, but the French initially objected to the reservation regarding British military occupation of Egypt. The convention eventually came into effect in 1904 and remained in force until 1956. During the 1956 Suez Crisis, after Egypt nationalized the canal, Britain and France claimed that their subsequent military intervention was intended only to restore free passage of all ships under this agreement.

Primary Source

ARTICLE I

The Suez Maritime Canal shall always be free and open, in time of war as in time of peace, to every vessel of commerce or of war, without distinction of flag.

Consequently, the High Contracting Parties agree not in any way to interfere with the free use of the Canal, in time of war as in time of peace.

The Canal shall never be subjected to the exercise of the right of blockade.

ARTICLE II

The High Contracting Parties, recognizing that the Fresh-Water Canal is indispensable to the Maritime Canal, take note of the engagements of His Highness the Khedive towards the Universal Suez Canal Company as regards the Fresh-Water Canal; which engagements are stipulated in a Convention bearing the date of 18th March, 1863, containing an *exposé* and four Articles.

They undertake not to interfere in any way with the security of that Canal and its branches, the working of which shall not be exposed to any attempt at obstruction.

ARTICLE III

The High Contracting Parties likewise undertake to respect the plant, establishments, buildings, and works of the Maritime Canal and of the Fresh-Water Canal.

ARTICLE IV

The Maritime Canal remaining open in time of war as a free passage, even to the ships of war of belligerents, according to the terms of Article I of the present Treaty, the High Contracting Parties agree that no right of war, no act of hostility, nor any act having for its object to obstruct the free navigation of the Canal shall be committed in the Canal and its ports of access, as well as within a radius of three marine miles from those parts, even though the Ottoman Empire should be one of the belligerent Powers.

Vessels of war of belligerents shall not revictual or take in stores in the Canal and its ports of access, except in so far as may be strictly necessary. The transit of the aforesaid vessels through the Canal shall be effected with the least possible delay, in accordance with the Regulations in force, and without any other intermission than that resulting from the necessities of the service.

Their stay at Port Said and in the roadstead of Suez shall not exceed twenty-four hours, except in cases of distress. In such case they shall be bound to leave as soon as possible. An interval of twenty-four hours shall always elapse between the sailing of a belligerent ship from one of the ports of access and the departure of a ship belonging to the hostile Power.

ARTICLE V

In time of war belligerent Powers shall not disembark nor embark within the Canal and its ports of access either troops, munitions, or materials of war. But in case of an accidental hindrance in the Canal, men may be embarked or disembarked at the ports of access by detachments not exceeding 1,000 men, with a corresponding amount of war material.

ARTICLE VI

Prizes shall be subjected, in all respects, to the same rules as the vessels of war of belligerents.

ARTICLE VII

The Powers shall not keep any vessel of war in the waters of the Canal (including Lake Timsah and the Bitter Lakes).

Nevertheless, they may station vessels of war in the ports of access of Port Said and Suez, the number of which shall not exceed two for each Power.

This right shall not be exercised by belligerents.

ARTICLE VIII

The Agents in Egypt of the Signatory Powers of the present Treaty shall be charged to watch over its execution. In case of any event threatening the security or the free passage of the Canal, they shall meet on the summons of three of their number under the presidency of their Doyen, in order to proceed to the necessary verifications. They shall inform the Khedivial Government of the danger which they may have perceived, in order that that Government may take proper steps to insure the protection and the free use of the Canal. Under any circumstances, they shall meet once a year to take note of the due execution of the Treaty.

The last-mentioned meetings shall take place under the presidency of a Special Commissioner nominated for that purpose by the Imperial Ottoman Government. A Commissioner of the Khedive may also take part in the meeting, and may preside over it in case of the absence of the Ottoman Commissioner.

They shall especially demand the suppression of any work or the dispersion of any assemblage on either bank of the Canal, the object or effect of which might be to interfere with the liberty and the entire security of the navigation.

ARTICLE IX

The Egyptian Government shall, within the limits of its powers resulting from the Firmans, and under the conditions provided for in the present Treaty, take the necessary measures for insuring the execution of the said Treaty.

In case the Egyptian Government shall not have sufficient means at its disposal, it shall call upon the Imperial Ottoman Government, which shall take the necessary measures to respond to such appeal; shall give notice thereof to the Signatory Powers of the Declaration of London of the 17th March, 1885; and shall, if necessary, concert with them on the subject.

The provisions of Articles IV, V, VII, and VIII shall not interfere with the measures which shall be taken in virtue of the present Article.

ARTICLE X

Similarly, the provisions of Articles IV, V, VII, and VIII shall not interfere with the measures which His Majesty the Sultan and His Highness the Khedive, in the name of His Imperial Majesty, and within the limits of the Firmans granted, might find it necessary to take for securing by their own forces the defence of Egypt and the maintenance of public order.

In case His Imperial Majesty the Sultan, or His Highness the Khedive, should find it necessary to avail themselves of the exception for which this Article provides, the Signatory Powers of the Declaration of London shall be notified thereof by the Imperial Ottoman Government.

It is likewise understood that the provisions of the four Articles aforesaid shall in no case occasion any obstacle to the measures which the Imperial Ottoman Government may think it necessary to take in order to insure by its own forces the defence of its other possessions situated on the eastern coast of the Red Sea.

ARTICLE XI

The measures which shall be taken in the cases provided for by Articles IX and X of the present Treaty shall not interfere with the free use of the Canal. In the same cases, the erection of permanent fortifications contrary to the provisions of Article VIII is prohibited.

ARTICLE XII

The High Contracting Parties, by application of the principle of equality as regards the free use of the Canal, a principle which forms one of the bases of the present Treaty, agree that none of them shall endeavour to obtain with respect to the Canal territorial or commercial advantages or privileges in any international arrangements which may be concluded. Moreover, the rights of Turkey as the territorial Power are reserved.

ARTICLE XIII

With the exception of the obligations expressly provided by the clauses of the present Treaty, the sovereign rights of His Imperial Majesty the Sultan and the rights and immunities of His Highness the Khedive, resulting from the Firmans, are in no way affected.

ARTICLE XIV

The High Contracting Parties agree that the engagements resulting from the present Treaty shall not be limited by the duration of the Acts of Concession of the Universal Suez Canal Company.

[...]

Source: D. C. Watt, *Documents on the Suez Crisis: 26 July to 6 November 1956* (London: Royal Institute of International Affairs, 1957).

5. Theodor Herzl, *The Jewish State* [Excerpt], 1896

Introduction

The most influential early theoretician and publicist of Zionism was Theodor Herzl (1860–1904), a Hungarian Jew who earned a law degree from the University of Vienna. A journalist who spent much of his life working in Paris, Herzl was greatly affected by the famous Dreyfus case of 1894 in which a Jewish French Army captain, Alfred Dreyfus, was wrongly accused of treason. The popular anti-Semitism that this episode stirred up convinced Herzl that ineradicable prejudice meant that Jews could not be assimilated into Western nations but instead must establish a nation of their own. In 1896 he published the book *Der Judenstaat* (*The Jewish State*) setting forth these views and proposing that Jews from around the world raise funds and set up a company to work to create a separate Jewish state, a suggestion that ultimately resulted in the formation of the Zionist Organization. Herzl's call resonated with many relatively poor Jews in Eastern Europe who quickly became dedicated supporters, although the wealthy Jewish leaders such as Baron Hirsch and Baron Rothschild whose backing he had hoped for were far less enthusiastic. In August 1897 Herzl followed up his book by summoning a Zionist Congress, which met in Basel, Switzerland. The delegates founded the World Zionist Organization (WZO) and adopted a resolution demanding the establishment of a Jewish national homeland in Palestine. This was the first of six annual Zionist Congresses that Herzl summoned before his untimely death in 1904, a demise many attributed to exhaustion caused by overwork in the Zionist cause.

Primary Source

[...]

The Jewish question still exists. It would be foolish to deny it. It is a remnant of the Middle Ages, which civilized nations do not even yet seem able to shake off, try as they will. They certainly showed a generous desire to do so when they emancipated us. The Jewish question exists wherever Jews live in perceptible numbers. Where it does not exist, it is carried by Jews in the course of their migrations. We naturally move to those places where we are not persecuted, and there our presence produces persecution. This is the case in every country, and will remain so, even in those highly civilized—for instance, France—until the Jewish question finds a solution on a political basis. The unfortunate Jews are now carrying the seeds of Anti-Semitism into England; they have already introduced it into America.

I believe that I understand Anti-Semitism, which is really a highly complex movement. I consider it from a Jewish standpoint, yet without fear or hatred. I believe that I can see what elements there are in it of vulgar sport, of common trade jealousy, of inherited prejudice, of religious intolerance, and also of pretended self-defense. I think the Jewish question is no more a social than a religious one, notwithstanding that it sometimes takes these and other forms. It is a national question, which can only be solved by making it a political world-question to be discussed and settled by the civilized nations of the world in council.

We are a people—one people.

We have honestly endeavored everywhere to merge ourselves in the social life of surrounding communities and to preserve the faith of our fathers. We are not permitted to do so. In vain are we loyal patriots, our loyalty in some places running to extremes; in vain do we make the same sacrifices of life and property as our fellow-citizens; in vain do we strive to increase the fame of our native land in science and art, or her wealth by trade and commerce. In countries where we have lived for centuries we are still cried down as strangers, and often by those whose ancestors were not yet domiciled in the land where Jews had already had experience of suffering. The majority may decide which are the strangers; for this, as indeed every point which arises in the relations between nations, is a question of might. I do not here surrender any portion of our prescriptive right, when I make this statement merely in my own name as an individual. In the world as it now is and for an indefinite period will probably remain, might precedes right. It is useless, therefore, for us to be loyal patriots, as were the Huguenots who were forced to emigrate. If we could only be left in peace. . . .

But I think we shall not be left in peace.

Oppression and persecution cannot exterminate us. No nation on earth has survived such struggles and sufferings as we have gone through. Jew-baiting has merely stripped off our weaklings; the strong among us were invariably true to their race when persecution broke out against them. This attitude was most clearly apparent in the period immediately following the emancipation of the Jews. Those Jews who were advanced intellectually and materially entirely lost the feeling of belonging to their race. Wherever our political well-being has lasted for any length of time, we have assimilated with our surroundings. I think this is not discreditable. Hence, the statesman who would wish to see a Jewish strain in his nation would have to provide for the duration of our political well-being; and even a Bismarck could not do that.

For old prejudices against us still lie deep in the hearts of the people. He who would have proofs of this need only listen to the people where they speak with frankness and simplicity: proverb and fairy-tale are both Anti-Semitic. A nation is everywhere a great child, which can certainly be educated; but its education would, even in most favorable circumstances, occupy such a vast amount of time that we could, as already mentioned, remove our own difficulties by other means long before the process was accomplished.

Assimilation, by which I understood not only external conformity in dress, habits, customs, and language, but also identity of feeling and manner—assimilation of Jews could be effected only by intermarriage. But the need for mixed marriages would have to be felt by the majority; their mere recognition by law would certainly not suffice.

[. . .]

No one can deny the gravity of the situation of the Jews. Wherever they live in perceptible numbers, they are more or less persecuted. Their equality before the law, granted by statute, has become practically a dead letter. They are debarred from filling even moderately high positions, either in the army, or in any public or private capacity. And attempts are made to thrust them out of business also: "Don't buy from Jews!"

Attacks in Parliaments, in assemblies, in the press, in the pulpit, in the street, on journeys—for example, their exclusion from certain hotels—even in places of recreation, become daily more numerous. The forms of persecution varying according to the countries and social circles in which they occur. In Russia, imposts are levied on Jewish villages; in Rumania, a few persons are put to death; in Germany, they get a good beating occasionally; in Austria, Anti-Semites exercise terrorism over all public life; in Algeria, there are traveling agitators; in Paris, the Jews are shut out of the so-called best social circles and excluded from clubs. Shades of anti-Jewish feeling are innumerable. But this is not to be an attempt to make out a doleful category of Jewish hardships.

I do not intend to arouse sympathetic emotions on our behalf. That would be a foolish, futile, and undignified proceeding. I shall content myself with putting the following questions to the Jews: Is it not true that, in countries where we live in perceptible numbers, the position of Jewish lawyers, doctors, technicians, teachers, and employees of all descriptions becomes daily more intolerable? Is it not true, that the Jewish middle classes are seriously threatened? Is it not true, that the passions of the mob are incited against our wealthy people? Is it not true, that our poor endure greater sufferings than any other proletariat? I think that this external pressure makes itself felt everywhere. In our economically upper classes it causes discomfort, in our middle classes continual and grave anxieties, in our lower classes absolute despair.

Everything tends, in fact, to one and the same conclusion, which is clearly enunciated in that classic Berlin phrase: "Juden Raus" (Out with the Jews)!

I shall now put the Question in the briefest possible form: Are we to "get out" now and where to?

Or, may we yet remain? And, how long?

Let us first settle the point of staying where we are. Can we hope for better days, can we possess our souls in patience, can we wait in pious resignation till the princes and peoples of this earth are more mercifully disposed towards us? I say that we cannot hope for a change in the current of feeling. And why not? Even if we were as near to the hearts of princes as are their other subjects, they could not protect us. They would only feel popular hatred by showing us too much favor. By "too much," I really mean less than is claimed as a right by every ordinary citizen, or by every race. The nations in whose midst Jews live are all either covertly or openly Anti-Semitic.

The common people have not, and indeed cannot have, any historic comprehension. They do not know that the sins of the Middle Ages are now being visited on the nations of Europe. We are what the Ghetto made us. We have attained pre-eminence in finance, because mediaeval conditions drove us to it. The same process is now being repeated. We are again being forced into finance, now it is the stock exchange, by being kept out of other branches of economic activity. Being on the stock exchange, we are consequently exposed afresh to contempt. At the same time we continue to produce an abundance of mediocre intellects who find no outlet, and this endangers our social position as much as does our increasing wealth. Educated Jews without means are now rapidly becoming Socialists. Hence we are certain to suffer very severely in the struggle between classes, because we stand in the most exposed position in the camps of both Socialists and capitalists.

[...]

Source: Theodor Herzl, *A Jewish State: An Attempt at a Modern Solution of the Jewish Question* (New York: Maccabæan Publishing Company, 1904).

6. Declaration of the First Zionist Congress, Basel, Switzerland, August 1897

Introduction

The First Zionist Congress was held in Basel, Switzerland, in August 1897. Summoned by Theodor Herzl, the leading proponent and publicist of a separate Jewish state, it gathered in the Basel Municipal Casino's Concert Hall for three days, August 29–31, 1897. Around 200 delegates from 17 countries attended. Sixty-nine of these represented specific Zionist organizations, and the remainder had been invited in their personal capacity. The organization established the World Zionist Organization (WZO), electing Herzl as its first president. Its objectives, as stated in the declaration of the congress, were to encourage settlement and the creation of a national Jewish homeland in the territory of Palestine and to foster cooperation among all Jews. The WZO became the most prominent group working for the establishment of a Jewish state. For the first five years the Zionist Congresses met annually, and from 1903 until 1939 they met every two years. The WZO provided the focal point and institutional underpinning for the Zionist movement, conducting extensive lobbying and propaganda campaigns and coordinating Zionist efforts to assist beleaguered Jews and win a Jewish national home. Many wealthier and more conservative Jews, however, regarded it with some distrust, considering its membership and campaigns

overly radical and extreme and fearing that its activities would discredit well-established Jewish communities in states where they had won acceptance as a respected minority.

Primary Source

The aim of Zionism is to create for the Jewish people a home in Palestine secured by public law. The Congress contemplates the following means to the attainment of this end:

1. The promotion, on suitable lines, of the colonization of Palestine by Jewish agricultural and industrial workers.
2. The organization and binding together of the whole of Jewry by means of appropriate institutions, local and international, in accordance with the laws of each country.
3. The strengthening and fostering of Jewish national sentiment and consciousness.
4. Preparatory steps towards obtaining government consent, where necessary, to the attainment of the aim of Zionism.

Source: Walter Laqueur and Barry Rubin, eds., *The Israel-Arab Reader: A Documentary History of the Middle East Conflict* (New York: Penguin, 2001), 9–10.

7. Negib Azoury, Program of the League of the Arab Fatherland, 1905

Introduction

By 1905, nationalist Arab sentiment was already growing within the Ottoman Empire, the product in part of the same forces that propelled the growth of Zionism and numerous other 19th-century separatist ethnic movements. As was often the case, nationalist activists were frequently forced to become exiles living outside their own country. One of the earliest Arab nationalists was Negib Azoury, a Maronite Christian journalist who based himself in Paris, France, where he edited the journal *L'Indépendence Arabe* (Arab Independence). He helped to found the League of the Arab Fatherland, on whose behalf in 1905 he published the article "Réveil de la Nation Arabe dans l'Asie Turqu" (Appeal to the Arab Nation in Turkish Asia). Azoury urged all Arabs to work to establish a Pan-Arab state, or empire, to be headed by any member of the family of the khedive of Egypt who was prepared to devote himself to its interests. The state that Azoury envisaged was to be based on liberal constitutional principles, with "freedom of all the religions and the equality of all citizens before the law." Unlike some Arab nationalists, who merely sought greater autonomy within the Ottoman Empire, Azoury envisaged total secession from the Arabs' existing overlords and even rejected Arab union with Egypt on the grounds that most Egyptians were not genuine Arabs. When no suitable Egyptian khedival prince heeded his appeal, Azoury apparently shifted his support to the sharif of Mecca, Hussein ibn Ali of the

Hejaz, and his family, endorsing their World War I rebellion against Ottoman rule.

Primary Source

THERE IS NOTHING more liberal than the league's program.

The league wants, before anything else, to separate the civil and the religious power, in the interest of Islam and the Arab nation, and to form an Arab empire stretching from the Tigris and the Euphrates to the Suez Isthmus, and from the Mediterranean to the Arabian Sea.

The mode of government will be a constitutional sultanate based on the freedom of all the religions and the equality of all the citizens before the law. It will respect the interests of Europe, all the concessions and all the privileges which had been granted to her up to now by the Turks. It will also respect the autonomy of the Lebanon, and the independence of the principalities of Yemen, Nejd, and Iraq.

The league offers the throne of the Arab Empire to that prince of the Khedivial family of Egypt who will openly declare himself in its favor and who will devote his energy and his resources to this end.

It rejects the idea of unifying Egypt and the Arab Empire under the same monarchy, because the Egyptians do not belong to the Arab race; they are of the African Berber family and the language which they spoke before Islam bears no similarity to Arabic. There exists, moreover, between Egypt and the Arab Empire a natural frontier which must be respected in order to avoid the introduction, in the new state, of the germs of discord and destruction. Never, as a matter of fact, have the ancient Arab caliphs succeeded for any length of time in controlling the two countries at the same time.

The Arab fatherland also offers the universal religious caliphate over the whole of Islam to that sherif (descendant of the Prophet) who will sincerely embrace its cause and devote himself to this work. The religious caliph will have as a completely independent political state the whole of the actual vilayet of Hijaz, with the town and the territory of Medina, as far as Aqaba. He will enjoy the honors of a sovereign and will hold a real moral authority over all the Muslims of the world.

One of the principal causes of the fall of the vast empire of the Arabs was the centralization in a single hand of the civil and the religious powers. It is also for this reason that the caliphate of Islam has become today so ridiculous and so contemptible in the hands of the Turks. The successor of the Prophet of Allah must enjoy an incontestable moral prestige; his whole life must be of unblemished honor, his authority suffering no diminution, his majesty independent [of anything other than itself]. His power also will be universal; from his residence he will rule morally over all the Muslims of the universe who will hurry in pilgrimage to the sanctuaries of Mohammed.

[*About the position of the caliph, Azoury offers a word of explanation.*]

The caliph of Islam must be either the sovereign of all the Muslims of the earth united in a single state, which has always proved impossible, even under the first caliphs, or, quite simply, the sovereign of a country entirely Islamic. There is indeed no country more Islamic than the Hijaz, and there are no towns more suitable than Medina and Mecca to receive the Supreme Head of the believers.

Source: Sylvia G. Haim, *Arab Nationalism, an Anthology* (Berkeley and Los Angeles: University of California Press, 1962), 81–82.

8. Resolution of the Arab-Syrian Congress at Paris [Excerpt], June 21, 1913

Introduction

Like other ethnic groups around the world, the Arabs demonstrated a new nationalist consciousness and sentiment during the 19th century, which may be ascribed in part to that era's new emphasis on identification along the lines of national groupings. By the turn of the century, Arab nationalism had developed rapidly, the product in part of a revitalization of national pride and culture encouraged by French and American missionaries in the Lebanon. The growing use of the Arabic language and texts in education helped to spread nationalist sentiment throughout Syria, Iraq (then known as Mesopotamia), and Egypt. In much of the Ottoman Empire, Arab nationalism, although centering on opposition to unadulterated Ottoman rule, often advocated greater Arab autonomy within the empire rather than total independence. Such demands were given additional force when modernizing young military officers took over the Ottoman government in 1909 and launched a program of secular reforms. In Egypt, by contrast, dual Franco-British control and the later British occupation became the focus for Arab protests and resentment. In June 1913, 24 Arab delegates from Syria, Lebanon, Iraq, and the United States met in an Arab-Syrian Congress, held in Paris, and passed resolutions demanding that the Ottoman government grant the Arabs and Armenians of Syria, Iraq, and Lebanon more autonomy and recognize Arabic as an official language. The meeting was evidence of a burgeoning sense of a specifically Arab identity that transcended the boundaries of particular Arab provinces.

Primary Source

1. Radical and urgent reforms are needed in the Ottoman Empire.
2. It is important to guarantee the Ottoman Arabs the exercise of their political rights by making effective their participation in the central administration of the Empire.

3. It is important to establish in each of the Syrian and Arab vilayets a decentralized regime suitable to their needs and aptitudes.

4. The vilayet of Bayrut having formulated its claims in a special project adopted on 31 January 1913 by an ad hoc General Assembly and based on the double principle of the extension of the powers of the general council of the vilayet and the nomination of foreign councilors, the Congress requests the execution of the above project.

5. The Arabic language must be recognized in the Ottoman Parliament and considered as an official language in Syrian and Arab countries.

6. Military service shall be regional in Syrian and Arab vilayets, except in case of extreme necessity.

7. The Congress expresses the wish that the Ottoman Imperial Government provide the *mutasarriflik* [autonomous provincial district] of Lebanon with the means of improving its financial situation.

8. The Congress affirms that it favors the reformist and decentralizing demands of the Armenian Ottomans.

9. The present resolution shall be communicated to the Ottoman Imperial Government.

10. These resolutions shall also be communicated to the Powers friendly to the Ottoman Empire.

[. . .]

Source: J. D. Hurewitz, *The Middle East and North Africa in World Politics: A Documentary Record*, Vol. 1, *European Expansion, 1535–1914*, 2nd rev. ed. (New Haven, CT: Yale University Press, 1975), 566–567.

9. Sultan Mehmed, Turkey Declares War on the Allies, October 29, 1914

Introduction

After almost three months of wavering and an initial halfhearted attempt at neutrality, in late October 1914 Turkey finally opted to enter World War I as an ally of the Central Powers, Germany and Austria-Hungary. This decision did not surprise the Allies, but it meant that they now felt free to reach agreements among themselves as to the future disposition of various Turkish-ruled territories in the Near and Middle East and in Europe. In secret treaties that the Russian Bolshevik government that came to power in late 1917 afterward published, the British and French governments quickly promised Russia Constantinople (the Ottoman capital) and control of the strategic Bosporus and Dardanelles straits, something the Russian government had long coveted. France and Britain also reached agreements with each other over the division of Ottoman Turkey's Middle Eastern territories. Intervention in the war would initially bring humiliating Allied military defeats, including the disastrous Gallipoli Campaign of 1915 and the fall of the city of Kut, in present-

day Iraq, in April 1916. It also, however, precipitated the Arab Revolt and the permanent loss of the Ottoman Empire's provinces in Syria, Mesopotamia, and Palestine, developments that brought the final downfall of the Ottoman sultanate in the early 1920s.

Primary Source

To my army! To my navy!

Immediately after the war between the Great Powers began, I called you to arms in order to be able in case of trouble to protect the existence of empire and country from any assault on the part of our enemies, who are only awaiting the chance to attack us suddenly and unexpectedly as they have always done.

While we were thus in a state of armed neutrality, a part of the Russian fleet, which was going to lay mines at the entrance of the straits of the Black Sea, suddenly opened fire against a squadron of our own fleet at the time engaged in maneuvers.

While we were expecting reparation from Russia for this unjustified attack, contrary to international law, the empire just named, as well as its allies, recalled their ambassadors and severed diplomatic relations with our country.

The fleets of England and France have bombarded the straits of the Dardanelles, and the British fleet has shelled the harbor of Akbah on the Red Sea. In the face of such successive proofs of wanton hostility we have been forced to abandon the peaceful attitude for which we always strove, and now in common with our allies, Germany and Austria, we turn to arms in order to safeguard our lawful interests.

The Russian Empire during the last three hundred years has caused our country to suffer many losses in territory, and when we finally arose to that sentiment of awakening and regeneration which would increase our national welfare and our power, the Russian Empire made every effort to destroy our attempts, either with war or with numerous machinations and intrigues. Russia, England, and France never for a moment ceased harboring ill-will against our Caliphate, to which millions of Mussulmans, suffering under the tyranny of foreign dominations, are religiously and wholeheartedly devoted, and it was always these powers that started every misfortune that came upon us.

Therefore, in this mighty struggle which now we are undertaking, we once for all will put an end to the attacks made from one side against the Caliphate, and from the other against the existence of our country.

The wounds inflicted, with the help of the Almighty, by my fleet in the Black Sea, and by my army in the Dardanelles, in Akbah, and on the Caucasian frontiers against our enemies, have strengthened in us the conviction that our sacred struggle for a right cause will triumph. The fact, moreover, that today the countries and armies of our enemies are being crushed under the heels of our allies is a good sign, making our conviction as regards final success still stronger.

My heroes! My soldiers! In this sacred war and struggle, which we began against the enemies who have undermined our religion and our holy fatherland, never for a single moment cease from strenuous effort and from self-abnegation.

Throw yourselves against the enemy as lions, bearing in mind that the very existence of our empire, and of 300,000,000 Moslems whom I have summoned by sacred Fetva to a supreme struggle, depend on your victory.

The hearty wishes and prayers of 300,000,000 innocent and tortured faithful, whose faces are turned in ecstasy and devotion to the Lord of the universe in the mosques and the shrine of the Kasbah, are with you.

My children! My soldiers! No army in the history of the world was ever honored with a duty as sacred and as great as is yours. By fulfilling it, show that you are the worthy descendants of the Ottoman Armies that in the past made the world tremble, and make it impossible for any foe of our faith and country to tread on our ground, and disturb the peace of the sacred soil of Yemen, where the inspiring tomb of our prophet lies. Prove beyond doubt to the enemies of the country that there exist an Ottoman army and navy which know how to defend their faith, their country and their military honor, and how to defy death for their sovereign!

Right and loyalty are on our side, and hatred and tyranny on the side of our enemies, and therefore there is no doubt that the Divine help and assistance of the just God and the moral support of our glorious Prophet will be on our side to encourage us. I feel convinced that from this struggle we shall emerge as an empire that has made good the losses of the past and is once more glorious and powerful.

Do not forget that you are brothers in arms of the strongest and bravest armies of the world, with whom we now are fighting shoulder to shoulder. Let those of you who are to die a martyr's death be messengers of victory to those who have gone before us, and let the victory be sacred and the sword be sharp of those of you who are to remain in life.

Source: Charles F. Horne and Walter F. Austin, eds., *Great Events of the Great War* (Washington, DC: National Alumni, 1920), 2:382–384.

10. Letter from Sir Henry McMahon to Hussein ibn Ali, October 24, 1915

Introduction

As the Turkish sultanate lost its hold on the territories of the Ottoman Empire and exacerbated Muslim sensibilities by allying itself with Christian Germany in World War I, Hussein ibn Ali, the high priest or sharif of the Islamic territory of the Hejaz, which contains the holy cities of Medina and Mecca, moved more aggressively toward independence. He was encouraged by British officials, including Sir Henry McMahon, British high commissioner in Egypt, who promised him and his three sons, Ali, Faisal, and Abdullah, recognition and financial and military assistance if they were willing to rebel against Ottoman rule. Arab nationalists regarded McMahon's pledge as a promise of immediate and complete independence. The territorial delimitations described in McMahon's letter were ambiguous and left unclear whether or not they included what was then Palestine, present-day Israel. The British later claimed that Palestine, which was not mentioned, was implicitly excluded from the regions promised to Hussein. Arab nationalists argued that the territories pledged to them included Palestine and that the subsequent British Sykes-Picot Agreement with France over the partition of the Ottoman Empire and the 1917 Balfour Declaration promising Jews a national homeland in Palestine contravened McMahon's letter.

Primary Source

The two districts of Mersina and Alexandretta and portions of Syria lying to the west of the districts of Damascus, Homs and Aleppo cannot be said to be purely Arab, and should be excluded from the limits demanded (by the Arabs).

With the above modification, and without prejudice to our existing treaties with Arab chiefs, we accept those limits.

As for those regions lying within these frontiers wherein Great Britain is free to act without detriment to the interests of her ally, France, I am empowered in the name of the government of Great Britain to give the following assurances and make the following reply to your letter.

1) Subject to the above modifications, Great Britain is prepared to recognise and support the independence of the Arabs in the regions within the limits demanded by the Sherif of Mecca.

2) Great Britain will recognise the Holy Places against all external aggression and will recognise their inviolability.

3) When the situation admits, Great Britain will give to the Arabs her advice and will assist them to establish what may appear to be the most suitable forms of government in those various territories.

4) On the other hand, it is understood that the Arabs have decided to seek the advice and guidance of Great Britain only, and that such European advisors and officials as may be required for the formation of a sound administration will be British.

5) With regards to the vilayets of Baghdad and Basra, the Arabs will recognise that the established position and interests of

Great Britain necessitate special administrative arrangements in order to secure these territories from foreign aggression to promote the welfare of the local populations and to safeguard our mutual economic interests.

I am convinced that this declaration will assure you beyond all possible doubt of the sympathy of Great Britain towards the aspirations of her friends the Arabs and will result in a firm and lasting alliance, the immediate results of which will be the expulsion of the Turks from Arab countries and the freeing of the Arab peoples from the Turkish yoke, which for so many years has pressed heavily upon them.

Source: United Kingdom, Parliament, *Husain-McMahon Correspondence*, Miscellaneous No. 3., Cmd. 5957, 1939.

11. Sykes-Picot Agreement [Excerpt], 1916

Introduction

As Turkish power crumbled in the Middle East, British and French officials reached tentative agreement as to how to divide influence within that region between their two nations. On May 9, 1916, French foreign minister Paul Cambon wrote to British foreign secretary Sir Edward Grey formally proposing a disposition of the Middle East between France and Britain, along lines already agreed to by junior French and British diplomats in the area. Grey replied, first briefly and then at greater length. Britain recognized French predominance in Syria, Lebanon, and Palestine (later exchanged for portions of Iraq) in return for French acceptance of British control of Iraq and Jordan. The British and French envisaged permitting Arab states in these former Ottoman provinces, but only on the condition that their governments recognize British or French overlordship. At the subsequent 1919 Paris Peace Conference, Britain and France retained control of these regions, which were defined as mandates under the new League of Nations. This was a great disappointment to the Arab nationalists, who had hoped to establish independent states free of Western colonial rule. During the 1920s resentment of Anglo-French domination continued to simmer in the newly established kingdoms of Iraq and Transjordan and in the states of Syria and Lebanon.

Primary Source

Sir Edward Grey to Paul Cambon, May 15, 1916

I shall have the honour to reply in a further note to your Excellency's note of the 9th instant, relative to the creation of an Arab State, but I should meanwhile be grateful if your Excellency could assure me that in those regions which, under the conditions recorded in that communication, become entirely French, or in which French interests are recognised as predominant, any existing British concessions, rights of navigation or development, and the rights and

privileges of any British religious, scholastic, or medical institutions will be maintained.

His Majesty's Government are, of course, ready to give a reciprocal assurance in regard to the British area.

Sir Edward Grey to Paul Cambon, May 16, 1916

I have the honour to acknowledge the receipt of your Excellency's note of the 9th instant, stating that the French Government accept the limits of a future Arab State, or Confederation of States, and of those parts of Syria where French interests predominate, together with certain conditions attached thereto, such as they result from recent discussions in London and Petrograd on the subject.

I have the honour to inform your Excellency in reply that the acceptance of the whole project, as it now stands, will involve the abdication of considerable British interests, but, since His Majesty's Government recognise the advantage to the general cause of the Allies entailed in producing a more favourable internal political situation in Turkey, they are ready to accept the arrangement now arrived at, provided that the co-operation of the Arabs is secured, and that the Arabs fulfil the conditions and obtain the towns of Homs, Hama, Damascus, and Aleppo.

It is accordingly understood between the French and British governments:

1. That France and Great Britain are prepared to recognize and protect an independent Arab State or a confederation of Arab states (A) and (B) marked on the annexed map, under the suzerainty of an Arab chief. That in area (A) France, and in area (B) Great Britain, shall have priority of right of enterprise and local loans. That in area (A) France, and in area (B) Great Britain, shall alone supply advisers or foreign functionaries at the request of the Arab state or confederation of Arab states.

2. That in the blue area France, and in the red area Great Britain, shall be allowed to establish such direct or indirect administration or control as they desire and as they may think fit to arrange with the Arab State or Confederation of Arab States.

3. That in the brown area there shall be established an international administration, the form of which is to be decided upon after consultation with Russia, and subsequently in consultation with the other Allies, and the representatives of the Shereef of Mecca.

4. That Great Britain be accorded (1) the ports of Haifa and Acre, (2) guarantee of a given supply of water from the Tigris and Euphrates in area (A) for area (B). His Majesty's government, on their part, undertake that they will at no time enter into negotiations for the cession of Cyprus to any third Power without the previous consent of the French Government.

5. That Alexandretta shall be a free port as regards the trade of the British Empire, and that there shall be no discrimination in port charges or facilities as regards British shipping and British goods; that there shall be freedom of transit for British goods through Alexandretta and by railway through the blue area, whether those goods are intended for or originate in the red area, or (B) area, or area (A); and there shall be no discrimination, direct or indirect, against British goods on any railway or against British goods or ships at any port serving the areas mentioned.

That Haifa shall be a free port as regards the trade of France, her dominions and protectorates, and there shall be no discrimination in port charges or facilities as regards French shipping and French goods. There shall be freedom of transit for French goods through Haifa and by the British railway through the brown area, whether those goods are intended for or originate in the blue area, area (A), or area (B), and there shall be no discrimination, direct or indirect, against French goods on any railway, or against French goods or ships at any port serving the areas mentioned.

6. That in area (A) the Baghdad railway shall not be extended southwards beyond Mosul, and in area (B) northwards beyond Samarra, until a railway connecting Baghdad and Aleppo via the Euphrates valley has been completed, and then only with the concurrence of the two governments.

7. That Great Britain has the right to build, administer, and be sole owner of a railway connecting Haifa with area (B), and shall have a perpetual right to transport troops along such a line at all times.

It is to be understood by both Governments that this railway is to facilitate the connexion of Baghdad with Haifa by rail, and it is further understood that, if the engineering difficulties and expense entailed by keeping this connecting line in the brown area only make the project unfeasible, that the French government shall be prepared to consider that the line in question may also traverse the polygon Banias-Keis Marib-Salkhad Tell Otsda-Mesmie before reaching area (B).

8. For a period of twenty years the existing Turkish customs tariff shall remain in force throughout the whole of the blue and red areas, as well as in areas (A) and (B), and no increase in the rates of duty or conversions from ad valorem to specific rates shall be made except by agreement between the two Powers.

There shall be no interior customs barriers between any of the above-mentioned areas. The customs duties leviable on goods destined for the interior shall be collected at the port of entry and handed over to the administration of the area of destination.

9. It shall be agreed that the French Government will at no time enter into any negotiations for the cession of their rights and will not cede such rights in the blue area to any third Power, except the Arab State or Confederation of Arab States without the previous agreement of His Majesty's Government, who, on their part, will give a similar undertaking to the French Government regarding the red area.

10. The British and French Governments, as the protectors of the Arab State, shall agree that they will not themselves acquire and will not consent to a third power acquiring territorial possessions in the Arabian peninsula, nor consent to a third power installing a naval base either on the east coast, or on the islands, of the Red Sea. This, however, shall not prevent such adjustment of the Aden frontier as may be necessary in consequence of recent Turkish aggression.

11. The negotiations with the Arabs as to the boundaries of the Arab State or Confederation of Arab States shall be continued through the same channel as heretofore on behalf of the two powers.

12. It is agreed that measures to control the importation of arms into the Arab territories will be considered by the two Governments.

[…]

Source: *British Documents on Foreign Affairs: Reports and Papers from the Foreign Office Confidential Print, Series H, the First World War, 1914–1918*, Vol. 2 (Bethesda, MD: University Publications of America, an Imprint of CIS, 1989). Reprinted by permission of LexisNexis.

12. King Hussein of Hejaz, Proclamation of War, June 27, 1916

Introduction

In June 1916 the long-contemplated Arab Revolt finally broke out, under the leadership of Sharif Hussein of Mecca and his three sons, Ali, Faisal, and Abdullah. The sharif published a lengthy proclamation accusing the Ottoman overlords of having jettisoned Islamic principles by installing a secular government in Constantinople. This document was widely circulated around the Arab world. Whereas Turkey, then and after World War I, continued on a secularist and modernizing course, for the rest of the 20th century Arab states would remain largely wedded to a traditional Islamic political and social outlook, something that Hussein's proclamation foreshadowed. Such staunch adherence to Muslim principles would later help to promote pervasive Arab and Islamic distaste and suspicion of Western societies and would contribute to the fervor with which Arab leaders and peoples resented Jewish claims on Palestine and, once it was established, the State of Israel.

Primary Source

Translation of proclamation published in Mecca by the Sherif and distributed by him in June–July 1916:

In the name of God, the Merciful, the Compassionate.

This is our general proclamation to all our Moslem brothers.

O God, judge between us and our people in truth: Thou art the Judge.

The world knoweth that the first of all Moslem princes and rulers to acknowledge the Turkish Government were the Emirs of Mecca the Blessed. This they did to bind together and make strong the congregation of Islam, as they saw the Sultans of the House of Osman (may the dust of their tombs be blessed, and may they dwell in Paradise), how they were upright, and how they fulfilled all the commandments and ordinances of the faith and of the Prophet (prayers be upon him) perfectly. Therefore they were obedient to them at all times.

For a token of this, remember how in 1327 I, with my Arabs, helped them against the Arabs, to save Ebhah from those who were besieging it, and to preserve the name of the Government in honour; and remember how again in the next year I helped them with my armies, which I entrusted to one of my sons: for indeed we were one with the Government until the Committee of Union and Progress rose up and strengthened itself and laid its hands on power. Consider how since then ruin has overtaken the State, and its possessions have been torn from it, and its place in the world has been lost, until now it has been drawn into this last and most fatal war.

All this they have done, being led away by shameful appetites, which are not for me to set forth, but which are open and a cause for sorrow to the Moslems of the whole world, who have seen this greatest and most noble Moslem Power broken in pieces and led down to ruin and utter destruction. Our lament is also for so many of its subjects, Moslems and others alike, whose lives have been sacrificed without fault on their part. Some have been treacherously put to death, others cruelly driven from their homes, as though the calamities of war were not enough. Of these calamities the heaviest share has fallen upon the Holy Land. The poor, and even the families of substance, have been made to sell their doors and windows, yea, even the wooden frames of their houses, for bread, after they had lost their furniture and all their goods.

Not even so was the lust of the Union and Progress fulfilled. They laid bare all the measure of their wicked design and broke the only bond that endured between them and the true followers of Islam. They departed from their obedience to the precepts of the Book.

With the countenance of the Grand Vizier of the Ottoman Empire, the Sheikh-ul-Islam, the Ulema, the Ministers and the notables, one of their papers called the 'Ijtihad' published in Constantinople unworthy things about the Prophet (the Prayer and Peace of God be upon him) and spoke evil of him (God forbid). Then the Union and

Progress rejected God's word 'A man shall have twice a woman's share' and made them equal. They went further, and removed one of the five corner stones of the faith, even the fast in Ramadan, by causing the soldiers in garrison in Mecca, Medina and Damascus to break their fast for new and foolish reasons, taking no account of the ordinance of God saying: 'Those of you who are sick or on a journey. . . .' Yea, they went further. They made weak the person of the Sultan, and robbed from him his honour, forbidding him to choose for himself the chief of his personal cabinet. Other like things they did to sap the foundation of the Khalifate.

For this it had been clearly our part and our necessary duty to separate ourselves from them and renounce them and their obedience. Yet we would not believe their wickedness, and tried to think that they were the imaginings of evil doers to make a division between us and the Government. We bore with them until it was open to all men that the rulers in Turkey were Enver Pasha, Jemal Pasha and Talaat Bey, who were doing whatsoever they pleased. They made their guilt manifest when they wrote to the Judge of the Sacred Court in Mecca, traducing the verses in the Cow, and laying upon him to reject the evidence of believers outside the court, and to consider only the deeds and contracts engrossed within the court. They made manifest their guilt when they hanged in one day twenty-one of the most honourable and enlightened Moslems, among them Emir Omar El Jezairi, Emir Arif El Shehabi, Shefik Bey Moayad, Shukri Bey El Asli, Abdel Wahab, Tewfik El Bassat, Abdel Hamid El Zahrawi, Abdel Ghani El Areisi and their learned companions.

To destroy so many, even of cattle, at one time would be hard for men void of all natural affection or mercy. And, if we suppose they had some excuse for this evil deed, by what right did they carry away to strange countries the innocent and most miserable families of those ill-fated men? Children, old men and delicate women, bereaved of their natural protectors, were subjected in exile to all foul usage, and even to tortures, as though the woes they had already suffered were not chastisement enough. Did not God say: 'No punishment shall be inflicted on anyone for the sins of another'? Let us suppose they found for themselves some reason for ill-treating the harmless families of their victims. But why did they rob them of their properties and possessions that alone remained to keep them from death by famine? And, if we suppose for this evil deed also an excuse or reason, how shall we find pardon for their shattering the tomb of our most righteous and upright Lord and Brother, El Sayed El Sherif Abd El Kader El Jazairi El Hassani, whose bones they have polluted and whose dust they have scattered abroad?

We leave the judgment of these misdeeds, which we have touched on so briefly, to the world in general and to Moslems in particular. What stronger proof can we desire of the faithlessness of their inmost hearts to the religion and their feelings towards the Arabs than their bombardment of that ancient House, which God had chosen for His House, saying: 'Keep My House pure for all who come to it'—a House so venerated by all Moslems? From their fort of Jyad when the revolt began they shelled it. The first shot struck a yard and a half above the Black Stone. The second fell three yards short of it, so that the flame leapt up and took hold upon the Kiswa, which, when they saw, the thousands and thousands of Moslems first raised a lamentable cry, running to and fro, and then shouted in fierce anger, and rushed to save it. They had to burst open the door and mount upon the roof before they could quench the flames. Yet a third shell fell upon the tomb of Abraham, and other shells fell in and about the precincts, which they made a target for their guns, killing every day three or four who were at prayer within the mosque till they prevented the people coming near to worship. This will show how they despised His House and denied it the honour given it by believers.

We leave all this to the Moslem world for judgment.

Yes, we can leave the judgment to the Moslem world, but we may not leave our religion and our existence as a people to be the plaything of the Unionists. God (blessed be He) has made open for us the attainment of freedom and independence, and has shown us a way of victory, to cut off the hand of the oppressors, and to cast out their garrison from our midst. We have attained independence—an independence of the rest of the Ottoman Empire, which is still groaning under the tyranny of our enemy. Our independence is complete, absolute, not to be laid hands on by any foreign influence or aggression, and our aim is the preservation of Islam, and the uplifting of its standard in the world. We fortify ourselves on the noble religion, which is our only guide and advocate in the principles of administration and of justice. We are ready to accept all things in harmony with the faith, and all that leads to the Mountain of Islam, and in particular to uplift the mind and spirit of all classes of the people in so far as we have the strength and ability.

This is what we have done, in accord with the dictates of our religion, and on our part we trust that our brethren in all parts of the world will each do his duty also, as is incumbent upon him, that the bonds of brotherhood in Islam may be confirmed.

We beseech the Lord of Lords for the sake of the Prophet of Him who giveth all things, to grant us prosperity, and to direct us in the right way for the welfare of the faith and of the faithful.

We depend upon God the all-powerful, whose defence is sufficient for us.

(Signed) Sherif and Emir of Mecca, HUSSEIN.

Source: *British Documents on Foreign Affairs: Reports and Papers from the Foreign Office Confidential Print, Series H, the First World War, 1914–1918,* Vol. 2 (Bethesda, MD: University Publications of America, an Imprint of CIS, 1989). Reprinted by permission of LexisNexis.

13. Balfour Declaration, 1917

Introduction

World War I gave considerable impetus to Zionist demands for the establishment of a Jewish state or homeland in Palestine, then part of the Ottoman Empire. At least some British statesmen were sympathetic, in part because of the romantic fascination that the Zionist idea exercised upon some individuals, notably British foreign secretary Arthur James Balfour. More practical considerations also impelled them. British leaders were anxious to win support from Jewish elements in countries with which they were at war. They also sought to win over the politically influential Jewish lobby in the United States, initially a key neutral state and eventually a vital ally whose economic and manpower resources proved crucial in bringing about an Allied victory. Lobbying efforts by Chaim Weizmann, a leading Zionist and biochemist whose scientific research was of great value to the Allied efforts, also proved persuasive to British leaders. On November 2, 1917, Balfour wrote an official letter to Lord Rothschild, a prominent British Zionist figure. Although its terms were somewhat ambivalent, this brief communication offered Jews a homeland in Palestine, a development that eventually led to the creation of the State of Israel in 1948. Correctly or not, Sharif Hussein of Mecca, a key Arab leader and British ally in the revolt against Turkey, believed that he too had been promised this territory, a source of lasting bitterness among Arab leaders and peoples. After World War I, Palestine would become a British mandate under the League of Nations, and Arab and Jewish settlers would begin a lengthy struggle over which element should predominate in this territory.

Primary Source

November 2, 1917

Dear Lord Rothschild,

I have much pleasure in conveying to you, on behalf of His Majesty's Government, the following declaration of sympathy with Jewish Zionist aspirations which has been submitted to, and approved by, the Cabinet.

His Majesty's Government view with favour the establishment in Palestine of a national home for the Jewish people, and will use their best endeavours to facilitate the achievement of this object, it being clearly understood that nothing shall be done which may prejudice the civil and religious rights of existing non-Jewish communities in Palestine, or the rights and political status enjoyed by Jews in any other country.

I should be grateful if you would bring this declaration to the knowledge of the Zionist Federation.

Signed: Arthur James Balfour

Source: "Letter of Foreign Minister Balfour to Lord Rothschild," *The Times* (London), November 2, 1917.

14. Agreement between Emir Faisal and Chaim Weizmann, January 3, 1919

Introduction

In the aftermath of the Balfour Declaration, whose promulgation by the British government in 1918 owed much to the lobbying efforts of the scientist and prominent Zionist Chaim Weizmann, Jewish and Arab leaders initially made efforts to reconcile their respective ambitions for Palestine. In 1918 the British government appointed Weizmann head of a Zionist commission that it dispatched to Palestine to make recommendations on the area's future. During his stay he met with Emir Faisal, son of Sharif Husain Ibn Ali of the Hejaz and the central figure in the Arab Revolt against Ottoman rule. As the Paris Peace Conference began in January 1919, the two men met again in the French capital and reached an understanding, envisaging the development of both an Arab state and a separate Jewish national homeland in Palestine. This accord was reached at the urging of the British government, which was to arbitrate any differences arising between the two parties. Faisal made his signature conditional on the fulfillment by the British government of its earlier pledges to him and his father to establish an Arab state, something on which Faisal felt the British subsequently reneged. Although he became king of Iraq in 1921, his realm only encompassed part of the territory he believed had been promised him, and he therefore repudiated his agreement with Weizmann. Ten years later Faisal even made an official proclamation that he had no memory of ever signing this document. The fact that he did so was, nonetheless, strong evidence that at the end of World War I neither Jews nor Arabs considered each other's territorial claims in the Middle East to be irreconcilable.

Primary Source

His Royal Highness the Emir Feisal, representing and acting on behalf of the Arab Kingdom of Hedjaz, and Dr. Chaim Weizmann, representing and acting on behalf of the Zionist Organization, mindful of the racial kinship and ancient bonds existing between the Arabs and the Jewish people, and realizing that the surest means of working out the consummation of their natural aspirations is through the closest possible collaboration in the development of the Arab State and Palestine, and being desirous further of confirming the good understanding which exists between them, have agreed upon the following:

Article I

The Arab State and Palestine in all their relations and undertakings shall be controlled by the most cordial goodwill and understanding, and to this end Arab and Jewish duly accredited agents shall be established and maintained in the respective territories.

Article II

Immediately following the completion of the deliberations of the Peace Conference, the definite boundaries between the Arab State and Palestine shall be determined by a Commission to be agreed upon by the parties hereto.

Article III

In the establishment of the Constitution and Administration of Palestine, all such measures shall be adopted as will afford the fullest guarantees for carrying into effect the British Government's Declaration of the 2nd of November, 1917.

Article IV

All necessary measures shall be taken to encourage and stimulate immigration of Jews into Palestine on a large scale, and as quickly as possible to settle Jewish immigrants upon the land through closer settlement and intensive cultivation of the soil. In taking such measures the Arab peasant and tenant farmers shall be protected in their rights and shall be assisted in forwarding their economic development.

Article V

No regulation or law shall be made prohibiting or interfering in any way with the free exercise of religion; and further, the free exercise and enjoyment of religious profession and worship, without discrimination or preference, shall forever be allowed. No religious test shall ever be required for the exercise of civil or political rights.

Article VI

The Mohammedan Holy Places shall be under Mohammedan control.

Article VII

The Zionist Organization proposes to send to Palestine a Commission of experts to make a survey of the economic possibilities of the country, and to report upon the best means for its development. The Zionist Organization will place the aforementioned Commission at the disposal of the Arab State for the purpose of a survey of the economic possibilities of the Arab State and to report upon the best means for its development. The Zionist Organization will use its best efforts to assist the Arab State in providing the means for developing the natural resources and economic possibilities thereof.

Article VIII

The parties hereto agree to act in complete accord and harmony on all matters embraced herein before the Peace Congress.

Article IX

Any matters of dispute which may arise between the contracting parties shall be referred to the British Government for arbitration.

Given under our hand at London, England, the third day of January, one thousand nine hundred and nineteen.

Chaim Weizmann   Feisal Ibn-Hussein

Reservation by the Emir Feisal

If the Arabs are established as I have asked in my manifesto of 4 January, addressed to the British Secretary of State for Foreign Affairs, I will carry out what is written in this agreement. If changes are made, I cannot be answerable for failing to carry out this agreement.

Source: "The Weizmann-Feisal Agreement, 3 Jan 1919," Israel Ministry of Foreign Affairs, http://www.israel-mfa.gov.il/MFA.

15. Statement of the Zionist Organization regarding Palestine [Excerpt], February 3, 1919

Introduction

As the Paris Peace Conference proceeded, the Zionist Organization mounted intensive lobbying efforts to persuade Allied leaders to endorse their claim for a Jewish homeland in Palestine. Claiming to seek to fulfill the pledges of the Balfour Declaration, the British government sought authority from the Peace Conference to establish a mandate over Palestine, a request that the Zionists supported. This would give the British the right to administer Palestine, under the supervision of the new League of Nations, for an indefinite period until it finally became possible at some undefined point in the future to hand the territory over to the local inhabitants. At Paris, Zionist leaders sought to ensure that the area subsumed in the Palestine mandate be as substantial as possible, ideally stretching from Sidon in the north to Aqaba on the Egyptian border in the south and beyond the Jordan River to Amman. They also urged that the mandatory power should encourage Jewish immigration in order to establish a Jewish national home in Palestine, as promised by the Balfour Declaration. The Zionists pointed to the existing accomplishments of Jewish settlers in the area in developing modern agricultural practices and urged all Jews to give generous financial support to enhance such efforts in the future and to develop transportation and commercial facilities. Although they promised that the rights of all races and religions would be respected, they imagined Palestine as being largely administered by a Jewish Council. Again, although the final form of government once British supervision was withdrawn was to be decided democratically, with all inhabitants enjoying equal rights "irrespective of race or faith," the authors clearly envisaged that the country would finally become a Jewish state.

Primary Source

[...]

The Zionist Organization respectfully submits the following draft resolutions for the consideration of the Peace Conference:

1. The High Contracting Parties recognise the historic title of the Jewish people to Palestine and the right of the Jews to reconstitute in Palestine their National Home.
2. The boundaries of Palestine shall be as declared in the Schedule annexed hereto.
3. The sovereign possession of Palestine shall be vested in the League of Nations and the Government entrusted to Great Britain as Mandatory of the League.
4. (Provision to be inserted relating to the application in Palestine of such of the general conditions attached to mandates as are suitable to the case.)
5. The mandate shall be subject also to the following special conditions:
   I. Palestine shall be placed under such political, administrative and economic conditions as will secure the establishment there of the Jewish National Home and ultimately render possible the creation of an autonomous Commonwealth, it being clearly understood that nothing shall be done which may prejudice the civil and religious rights of existing non-Jewish communities in Palestine or the rights and political status enjoyed by Jews in any other country.
   II. To this end the Mandatory Power shall *inter alia*:
      a. Promote Jewish immigration and close settlement on the land, the established rights of the present non-Jewish population being equitably safeguarded.
      b. Accept the cooperation in such measures of a Council representative of the Jews of Palestine and of the world that may be established for the development of the Jewish National Home in Palestine and entrust the organization of Jewish education to such Council.
      c. On being satisfied that the constitution of such Council precludes the making of private profit, offer to the Council in priority any concession for public works or for the development of natural resources which it may be found desirable to grant.
   I. The Mandatory Power shall encourage the widest measure of self-government for localities practicable in the conditions of the country.
   II. There shall be for ever the fullest freedom of religious worship for all creeds in Palestine. There shall be no discrimination among the inhabitants with regard to citizenship and civil rights, on the grounds of religion, or of race.

[...]

Statement.
The historic title
The claims of the Jews with regard to Palestine rest upon the following main considerations:

1. The land is the historic home of the Jews; there they achieved their greatest development; from that centre, through their

agency, there emanated spiritual and moral influences of supreme value to mankind. By violence they were driven from Palestine, and through the ages they have never ceased to cherish the longing and the hope of a return.

2. In some parts of the world, and particularly in Eastern Europe, the conditions of life of millions of Jews are deplorable. Forming often a congested population, denied the opportunities which would make a healthy development possible, the need of fresh outlets is urgent, both for their own sake and in the interest of the population of other races, among whom they dwell. Palestine would offer one such outlet. To the Jewish masses it is the country above all others in which they would most wish to cast their lot. By the methods of economic development to which we shall refer later, Palestine can be made now as it was in ancient times, the home of a prosperous population many times as numerous as that which now inhabits it.

3. Palestine is not large enough to contain more than a proportion of the Jews of the world. The greater part of the fourteen millions or more scattered through all countries must remain in their present localities, and it will doubtless be one of the cares of the Peace Conference to ensure for them, wherever they have been oppressed, as for all peoples equal rights and humane conditions. A Jewish National Home in Palestine will, however, be of high value to them also. Its influence will permeate the Jewries of the world; it will inspire these millions, hitherto often despairing, with a new hope; it will hold out before their eyes a higher standard; it will help to make them even more useful citizens in the lands in which they dwell.

4. Such a Palestine would be of value also to the world at large, whose real wealth consists in the healthy diversities of its civilisations.

5. Lastly the land itself needs redemption. Much of it is left desolate. Its present condition is a standing reproach. Two things are necessary for that redemption—a stable and enlightened government, and an addition to the present population which shall be energetic, intelligent, devoted to the country, and backed by the large financial resources that are indispensable for development. Such a population the Jews alone can supply.

Inspired by these ideas, Jewish activities particularly, during the last thirty years, have been directed to Palestine within the measure that the Turkish administrative system allowed. Some millions of pounds sterling have been spent in the country, particularly in the foundation of Jewish agricultural settlements. These settlements have been for the most part highly successful.

With enterprise and skill the Jews have adopted modern scientific methods and have shown themselves to be capable agriculturists. Hebrew has been revived as a living language: it is the medium of instruction in the schools and the tongue is in daily use among the rising generation. The foundations of a Jewish University have been laid at Jerusalem and considerable funds have been contributed for the creation of its building and for its endowment. Since the British occupation, the Zionist Organization has expended in Palestine approximately £50,000 a month upon relief, education and sanitation. To promote the future development of the country great sums will be needed for drainage, irrigation, roads, railways, harbours and public works of all kinds, as well as for land settlement and house building. Assuming a political settlement under which the establishment of a Jewish National Home in Palestine is assured, the Jews of the world will make every effort to provide the vast sums of money that will be needed.

Hundreds of thousands of Jews pray for the opportunity speedily to begin life anew in Palestine. Messengers have gone out from many places, and groups of young Jewish men proceeding on foot have already reached Trieste and Rome on their weary pilgrimage to Zion.

The historic title of the Jews to Palestine was recognised by the British Government in its Declaration of November 2nd 1917, addressed by the British Secretary of State for Foreign Affairs to Lord Rothschild.

[...]

Source: "Statement of the Zionist Organization regarding Palestine," United Nations Information System on the Question of Palestine, http://domino.un.org.

16. Statement to the Peace Conference by Prominent U.S. Jews, March 4, 1919

Introduction

By no means were all American Jews enthusiastic Zionists. This was particularly true of those who were well established and assimilated in the United States. As Zionist leaders put forward their aims at the Paris Peace Conference, other prominent American Jews made their objections known. Many felt that support for the Zionist cause would undercut Jewish efforts to assimilate and be accepted as full citizens in the countries in which they resided and would encourage anti-Semitism in those nations. They also feared that a state organized along Jewish religious lines would effectively segregate and divide Jews from all other peoples. They believed too that it would be impossible to define the boundaries of Palestine and that the effort to do so would alienate both Arabs and Christians who resided there. In March 1919 a number of prominent American anti-Zionist Jewish leaders—including Henry Morgenthau Sr., former ambassador to Turkey; Adolf Ochs, publisher of *The New York Times;* several well-known rabbis and academics; and numerous others—signed a statement that Congressman Julius Kahn presented to President Woodrow Wilson. While affirming their commitment to opposing anti-Semitism and improving the conditions of oppressed

Jews in Eastern Europe and Russia, the anti-Zionists uncompromisingly declared: "We do not wish to see Palestine, either now or at any time in the future, organized as a Jewish State."

Primary Source

As a future form of government for Palestine will undoubtedly be considered by the approaching Peace Conference, we, the undersigned citizens of the United States, unite in this statement, setting forth our objections to the organization of a Jewish State in Palestine as proposed by the Zionist Societies in this country and Europe and to the segregation of the Jews as a nationalistic unit in any country. We feel that in so doing we are voicing the opinion of the majority of American Jews born in this country and of those foreign-born who have lived here long enough to thoroughly assimilate American political and social conditions. The American Zionists represent, according to the most recent statistics available, only a small proportion of the Jews living in this country, about 150,000 out of 3,500,000 (American Jewish Year Book, 1918, Philadelphia).

At the outset we wish to indicate our entire sympathy with the efforts of Zionists which aim to secure for Jews at present living in lands of oppression a refuge in Palestine or elsewhere, where they may freely develop their capabilities and carry on their activities as free citizens.

But we raise our voices in warning and protest against the demand of the Zionists for the reorganization of the Jews as a national unit, to whom, now or in the future, territorial sovereignty in Palestine shall be committed. This demand not only misrepresents the trend of the history of the Jews, who ceased to be a nation 2,000 years ago, but involves the limitation and possible annulment of the larger claims of Jews for full citizenship and human rights in all lands in which those rights are not yet secure. For the very reason that the new era upon which the world is entering aims to establish government everywhere on principles of true democracy, we reject the Zionistic project of a "national home for the Jewish people in Palestine."

Zionism arose as a result of the intolerable conditions under which Jews have been forced to live in Russia and Rumania. But it is evident that for the Jewish population of these countries, variously estimated at from 6,000,000 to 10,000,000, Palestine can become no homeland. Even with the improvement of the neglected condition of this country, its limited area can offer no solution. The Jewish question in Russia and Rumania can be settled only within those countries by the grant of full rights of citizenship to Jews.

We are all the more opposed to the Zionists, because they, themselves, distinctly repudiate the solely ameliorative program. They demand and hail with delight the "Balfour Declaration" to establish "a national home for the Jewish people in Palestine," i.e., a home not merely for Jews living in countries in which they are oppressed, but for Jews universally. No Jew, wherever he may live, can consider himself free from the implications of such a grant.

The willingness of Jews interested in the welfare of their brethren to aid in redeeming Palestine from the blight of centuries of Turkish misrule, is no acceptance of the Zionist project to segregate Jews as a political unit and to reinstitute a section of such a political unit in Palestine or elsewhere.

At the present juncture in the world's affairs when lands that have hitherto been subjected to foreign domination are to be recognized as free and independent States, we rejoice in the avowed proposal of the Peace Congress to put into practical application the fundamental principles of democracy. That principle, which asserts equal rights for all citizens of a State, irrespective of creed or ethnic descent, should be applied in such a manner as to exclude segregation of any kind, be it nationalistic or other. Such segregation must inevitably create differences among the sections of the population of a country. Any such plan of segregation is necessarily reactionary in its tendency, undemocratic in spirit and totally contrary to the practices of free government, especially as these are exemplified by our own country. We therefore strongly urge the abandonment of such a basis for the reorganization of any State.

Against such a political segregation of the Jews in Palestine or elsewhere we object:

1. Because the Jews are dedicated heart and soul to the welfare of the countries in which they dwell under free conditions. All Jews repudiate every suspicion of a double allegiance, but to our minds it is necessarily implied in and cannot by any logic be eliminated from the establishment of a sovereign State for the Jews in Palestine.

   By the large part taken by them in the great war, the Jews have once and for all shattered the base aspersions of the anti-Semites which charged them with being aliens in every land, incapable of true patriotism and prompted only by sinister and self-seeking motives. Moreover, it is safe to assume that the overwhelming bulk of the Jews of America, England, France, Italy, Holland, Switzerland and the other lands of freedom, have no thought whatever of surrendering their citizenship in these lands in order to resort to a "Jewish homeland in Palestine". As a rule those who favor such a restoration advocate it not for themselves but for others. Those who act thus, and yet insist on their patriotic attachment to the countries of which they are citizens, are self-deceived in their profession of Zionism and under the spell of an emotional romanticism or of a religious sentiment fostered through centuries of gloom.

2. We also object to political segregation of Jews for those who take their Zionistic professions seriously as referring not to others, but to themselves. Granted that the establishment of a sovereign Jewish State in Palestine would lead many to emigrate to that land, the political conditions of the millions who would be unable to migrate for generations to come, if

ever, would be made far more precarious. Rumania—despite the pledges of the Berlin Treaty—has legally branded her Jews as aliens, though many are descended from families settled in that country longer than the present Rumanian government has existed. The establishment of a Jewish State will manifestly serve the malevolent rulers of that and other lands as a new justification for additional repressive legislation. The multitudes who remain would be subject to worse perils, if possible, even though the few who escape might prosper in Palestine.

3. We object to the political segregation also of those who might succeed in establishing themselves in Palestine. The proposition involves dangers which, it is manifest, have not had the serious consideration of those who are so zealous in its advocacy. These dangers are adverted to in a most kindly spirit of warning by Sir George Adam Smith, who is generally acknowledged to be the greatest authority in this world on everything connected with Palestine either past or present. In a recent publication, "Syria and the Holy Land," he points out that there is absolutely no fixity to the boundaries of Palestine. These have varied greatly in the course of the centuries. The claims to various sections of this undefined territory would unquestionably evoke bitter controversies. "It is not true," says Sir George, "that Palestine is the national home of the Jewish people and of no other people. It is not correct to call its non-Jewish inhabitants 'Arabs' or to say that they have left no image of their spirit and made no history except in the great Mosque. Nor can we evade the fact that Christian communities have been as long in possession of their portion of this land as ever the Jews were. These are legitimate questions," he says, "stirred up by the claims of Zionism, but the Zionists have not yet fully faced them."

To subject the Jews to the possible recurrence of such bitter and sanguinary conflicts which would be inevitable, would be a crime against the triumphs of their whole past history and against the lofty and world-embracing visions of their great prophets and leaders.

4. Though these grave difficulties be met, still we protest against the political segregation of the Jews and the re-establishment in Palestine of a distinctively Jewish State as utterly opposed to the principles of democracy which it is the avowed purpose of the World's Peace Conference to establish.

Whether the Jews be regarded as a "race" or as a "religion," it is contrary to the democratic principles for which the world war was waged to found a nation on either or both of these bases. America, England, France, Italy, Switzerland and all the most advanced nations of the world are composed of representatives of many races and religions. Their glory lies in the freedom of conscience and worship, in the liberty of thought and custom which binds the followers of many faiths and varied civilizations in the common bonds of political union. A Jewish State involves fundamental limitations as to race and religion, else the term "Jewish" means nothing. To unite Church and State, in any form, as under the old Jewish hierarchy, would be a leap backward of 2,000 years.

"The rights of other creeds and races will be respected under Jewish dominance," is the assurance of Zionism, but the keynotes of democracy are neither condescension nor tolerance, but justice and equality. All this applies with special force to a country like Palestine. That land is filled with associations sacred to the followers of three great religions, and as a result of migrating movements of many centuries contains an extraordinary number of different ethnic groups, far out of proportion to the small extent of the country itself. Such a condition points clearly to a reorganization of Palestine on the broadest possible basis.

We object to the political segregation of the Jews because it is an error to assume that the bond uniting them is of a national character. They are bound by two factors: First, the bond of common religious beliefs and aspirations and, secondly, the bond of common traditions, customs, and experiences, largely, alas, of common trials and sufferings. Nothing in their present status suggests that they form in any real sense a separate nationalistic unit.

The reorganization of Palestine as far as it affects the Jews is but part of a far larger issue, namely, the constructive endeavor to secure the emancipation of the Jews in all the lands in which they dwell. This movement, inaugurated in the eighteenth century and advancing with steady progress through the western lands, was checked by such reactionary tendencies as caused the expulsion of the Poles from Eastern Prussia and the massacre of Armenians in Turkey. As directed against Jews these tendencies crystallized into a political movement called anti-Semitism, which had its rise in Germany. Its virulence spread (especially) throughout Eastern Europe and led to cruel outbreaks in Rumania and elsewhere, and to the pogroms of Russia with their dire consequences.

To guard against such evils in the future we urge that the great constructive movement, so sadly interrupted, be reinstituted and that efficient measures be taken to insure the protection of the law and the full rights of citizenship to Jews in every land. If the basis of the reorganization of Governments is henceforth to be democratic, it cannot be contemplated to exclude any group of people from the enjoyment of full rights.

As to the future of Palestine, it is our fervent hope that what was once a "promised land" for the Jews may become a "land of promise" for all races and creeds, safeguarded by the League of Nations which, it is expected, will be one of the fruits of the Peace Conference to whose deliberations the world now looks forward so anxiously and so full of hope. We ask that Palestine be constituted as a free and independent state, to be governed under a democratic form of government, recognizing no distinctions of creed or race or ethnic descent, and with adequate power to protect the country against oppression of any kind. We do not wish to see Palestine, either now or at any time in the future, organized as a Jewish State.

Source: "Protest to Wilson against Zionist State," *New York Times*, March 5, 1919.

17. Winston Churchill, White Paper, June 3, 1922

Introduction

By 1922, opposition to Zionist ambitions for Palestine was growing. Plans to make the area a Jewish homeland alarmed both existing Muslim and Christian inhabitants, who submitted complaints to the British government. In 1920 and 1921 Arabs in Palestine launched anti-Jewish riots. Emir Hussein ibn Ali's sons Faisal and Abdullah, who had led the Arab Revolt, also resented the omission of Palestine—as well as the new French Mandate for Syria—from the territory that Britain and France permitted their family to rule once World War I had ended. Faced with increasing dissent and controversy, British colonial secretary Winston Churchill reviewed the status of Palestine, and eventually, in June 1922, the British government issued a White Paper on the subject. This document stated that although Palestine was to serve as a Jewish national home, this did not mean that all Palestine would constitute such a home. Although the Jews were to be encouraged to continue to develop their religion and culture in the mandate, the Jews were to be only one of the various religious and ethnic communities in Palestine. Arab inhabitants would not be disadvantaged, and their rights would be respected. Immigration into Palestine must remain within reasonable limits, under regulation by the British government, so as not to strain the territory's resources, and "persons who [were] politically undesirable" would be denied entry. Self-government would only gradually be granted. While affirming that Palestine was not included in the territories promised to the Arabs by the 1915 McMahon letter, Churchill excluded the area of Transjordan (later Jordan)—which many Zionists coveted—from Palestine, and it was established as a separate kingdom under Faisal's brother Abdullah. The Churchill White Paper was a compromise that sought to please all parties involved. Like many such attempts, however, it left most of those affected somewhat disgruntled, with a lasting grievance against the British government.

Primary Source

The Secretary of State for the Colonies has given renewed consideration to the existing political situation in Palestine, with a very earnest desire to arrive at a settlement of the outstanding questions which have given rise to uncertainty and unrest among certain sections of the population. After consultation with the High Commissioner for Palestine [Sir Herbert Samuel] the following statement has been drawn up. It summarizes the essential parts of the correspondence that has already taken place between the Secretary of State and a delegation from the Moslem Christian Society of Palestine, which has been for some time in England, and it states the further conclusions which have since been reached.

The tension which has prevailed from time to time in Palestine is mainly due to apprehensions, which are entertained both by sections of the Arab and by sections of the Jewish population. These apprehensions, so far as the Arabs are concerned, are partly based upon exaggerated interpretations of the meaning of the Balfour Declaration favouring the establishment of a Jewish National Home in Palestine, made on behalf of His Majesty's Government on 2nd November, 1917.

Unauthorized statements have been made to the effect that the purpose in view is to create a wholly Jewish Palestine. Phrases have been used such as that Palestine is to become "as Jewish as England is English." His Majesty's Government regard any such expectation as impracticable and have no such aim in view. Nor have they at any time contemplated, as appears to be feared by the Arab delegation, the disappearance or the subordination of the Arabic population, language, or culture in Palestine. They would draw attention to the fact that the terms of the Declaration referred to do not contemplate that Palestine as a whole should be converted into a Jewish National Home, but that such a Home should be founded 'in Palestine.' In this connection it has been observed with satisfaction that at a meeting of the Zionist Congress, the supreme governing body of the Zionist Organization, held at Carlsbad in September, 1921, a resolution was passed expressing as the official statement of Zionist aims "the determination of the Jewish people to live with the Arab people on terms of unity and mutual respect, and together with them to make the common home into a flourishing community, the upbuilding of which may assure to each of its peoples an undisturbed national development."

It is also necessary to point out that the Zionist Commission in Palestine, now termed the Palestine Zionist Executive, has not desired to possess, and does not possess, any share in the general administration of the country. Nor does the special position assigned to the Zionist Organization in Article IV of the Draft Mandate for Palestine imply any such functions. That special position relates to the measures to be taken in Palestine affecting the Jewish population, and contemplates that the organization may assist in the general development of the country, but does not entitle it to share in any degree in its government.

Further, it is contemplated that the status of all citizens of Palestine in the eyes of the law shall be Palestinian, and it has never been intended that they, or any section of them, should possess any other juridical status.

So far as the Jewish population of Palestine are concerned it appears that some among them are apprehensive that His Majesty's Government may depart from the policy embodied in the Declaration of 1917. It is necessary, therefore, once more to affirm that these fears are unfounded, and that that Declaration, reaffirmed by the Conference of the Principal Allied Powers at San Remo and again in the Treaty of Sèvres, is not susceptible of change.

During the last two or three generations the Jews have recreated in Palestine a community, now numbering 80,000, of whom about one fourth are farmers or workers upon the land. This community has its own political organs; an elected assembly for the direction of its domestic concerns; elected councils in the towns; and an organization for the control of its schools. It has its elected Chief Rabbinate and Rabbinical Council for the direction of its religious affairs. Its business is conducted in Hebrew as a vernacular language, and a Hebrew Press serves its needs. It has its distinctive intellectual life and displays considerable economic activity. This community, then, with its town and country population, its political, religious, and social organizations, its own language, its own customs, its own life, has in fact "national" characteristics. When it is asked what is meant by the development of the Jewish National Home in Palestine, it may be answered that it is not the imposition of a Jewish nationality upon the inhabitants of Palestine as a whole, but the further development of the existing Jewish community, with the assistance of Jews in other parts of the world, in order that it may become a centre in which the Jewish people as a whole may take, on grounds of religion and race, an interest and a pride. But in order that this community should have the best prospect of free development and provide a full opportunity for the Jewish people to display its capacities, it is essential that it should know that it is in Palestine as of right and not on sufferance. That is the reason why it is necessary that the existence of a Jewish National Home in Palestine should be internationally guaranteed, and that it should be formally recognized to rest upon ancient historic connection.

This, then, is the interpretation which His Majesty's Government place upon the Declaration of 1917, and, so understood, the Secretary of State is of opinion that it does not contain or imply anything which need cause either alarm to the Arab population of Palestine or disappointment to the Jews.

For the fulfilment of this policy it is necessary that the Jewish community in Palestine should be able to increase its numbers by immigration. This immigration cannot be so great in volume as to exceed whatever may be the economic capacity of the country at the time to absorb new arrivals. It is essential to ensure that the immigrants should not be a burden upon the people of Palestine as a whole, and that they should not deprive any section of the present population of their employment. Hitherto the immigration has fulfilled these conditions. The number of immigrants since the British occupation has been about 25,000.

It is necessary also to ensure that persons who are politically undesirable be excluded from Palestine, and every precaution has been and will be taken by the Administration to that end.

It is intended that a special committee should be established in Palestine, consisting entirely of members of the new Legislative Council elected by the people, to confer with the administration upon matters relating to the regulation of immigration. Should any difference of opinion arise between this committee and the Administration, the matter will be referred to His Majesty's Government, who will give it special consideration. In addition, under Article 81 of the draft Palestine Order in Council, any religious community or considerable section of the population of Palestine will have a general right to appeal, through the High Commissioner and the Secretary of State, to the League of Nations on any matter on which they may consider that the terms of the Mandate are not being fulfilled by the Government of Palestine.

With reference to the Constitution which it is now intended to establish in Palestine, the draft of which has already been published, it is desirable to make certain points clear. In the first place, it is not the case, as has been represented by the Arab Delegation, that during the war His Majesty's Government gave an undertaking that an independent national government should be at once established in Palestine. This representation mainly rests upon a letter dated the 24th October, 1915, from Sir Henry McMahon, then His Majesty's High Commissioner in Egypt, to the Sherif of Mecca, now King Hussein of the Kingdom of the Hejaz. That letter is quoted as conveying the promise to the Sherif of Mecca to recognise and support the independence of the Arabs within the territories proposed by him. But this promise was given subject to a reservation made in the same letter, which excluded from its scope, among other territories, the portions of Syria lying to the west of the District of Damascus. This reservation has always been regarded by His Majesty's Government as covering the vilayet of Beirut and the independent Sanjak of Jerusalem. The whole of Palestine west of the Jordan was thus excluded from Sir Henry McMahon's pledge.

Nevertheless, it is the intention of His Majesty's government to foster the establishment of a full measure of self-government in Palestine. But they are of the opinion that, in the special circumstances of that country, this should be accomplished by gradual stages and not suddenly. The first step was taken when, on the institution of a Civil Administration, the nominated Advisory Council, which now exists, was established. It was stated at the time by the High Commissioner that this was the first step in the development of self-governing institutions, and it is now proposed to take a second step by the establishment of a Legislative Council containing a large proportion of members elected on a wide franchise. It was proposed in the published draft that three of the members of this Council should be non-official persons nominated by the High Commissioner, but representations having been made in opposition to this provision, based on cogent considerations, the Secretary of State is prepared to omit it. The Legislative Council would then consist of the High Commissioner as President and twelve elected and ten official members. The Secretary of State is of the opinion that before a further measure of self-government is extended to Palestine and the Assembly placed in control over the Executive, it would be wise to allow some time to elapse. During this period the institutions of the country will have become well established; its financial credit will be based on firm foundations, and the Palestinian officials will have been enabled to gain experience of sound methods of government. After a few years the situation will be again reviewed, and if the experience of the working of the constitution now to be established so warranted, a larger share of authority would then be extended to the elected representatives of the people.

The Secretary of State would point out that already the present administration has transferred to a Supreme Council elected by the Moslem community of Palestine the entire control of Moslem Religious endowments (Waqfs), and of the Moslem religious Courts. To this Council the Administration has also voluntarily restored considerable revenues derived from ancient endowments which have been sequestrated by the Turkish Government. The Education Department is also advised by a committee representative of all sections of the population, and the Department of Commerce and Industry has the benefit of the cooperation of the Chambers of Commerce which have been established in the principal centres. It is the intention of the Administration to associate in an increased degree similar representative committees with the various Departments of the Government.

The Secretary of State believes that a policy upon these lines, coupled with the maintenance of the fullest religious liberty in Palestine and with scrupulous regard for the rights of each community with reference to its Holy Places, cannot but commend itself to the various sections of the population, and that upon this basis may be built up a spirit of cooperation upon which the future progress and prosperity of the Holy Land must largely depend.

Source: "The Churchill White Paper," United Nations Information System on the Question of Palestine, http://domino.un.org.

18. Council of the League of Nations, British Mandate for Palestine [Excerpt], July 24, 1922

Introduction

Not until April 1920 did the delegates attending the peace conferences following World War I decide which Allied powers would obtain League of Nations mandates over former Ottoman imperial territories in the Middle East. Under the Sykes-Picot Agreement,

the British and French had already tentatively agreed to divide control of these areas between themselves. Considerable hard bargaining took place over the precise demarcation of each power's sphere of influence during which the French agreed to allow the British to administer Palestine, even though the 1916 Sykes-Picot Agreement had originally assigned it to France. Meeting at San Remo, Italy, in April 1920, British and French officials agreed that Britain would obtain mandates over Iraq, Transjordan (present-day Jordan), and Palestine, while France would take Syria and Lebanon. The French suppressed an abortive effort by Emir Faisal to establish himself as king of Syria, and in 1921 the British made him king of Iraq, while his brother Abdullah became king of Transjordan. Zionist leaders had hoped that the Palestine mandate would include Transjordan and resented its separation from the Palestine mandate, but that area was undoubtedly included in the territory that Britain promised to Emir Hussein in 1915 under the McMahon agreement. So, too, was Syria, which the British assigned to France, one reason that Faisal repudiated his earlier agreement with Zionist leader Chaim Weizmann. In July 1922 the League of Nations formally announced the final text of the agreement granting the British a mandate over Palestine. The document clearly stated that one objective in doing so was to enable the British to fulfill their pledges of establishing "a national home for the Jewish people in Palestine," something that it was to accomplish while doing nothing "which might prejudice the civil and religious rights of existing non-Jewish communities in Palestine." The mandate agreement called for the establishment of an "appropriate Jewish agency" that would work with and advise the British administration of Palestine on matters affecting the Jewish population and help develop the country. The mandatory power was also instructed to encourage Jewish immigration to Palestine and to facilitate the acquisition of Palestinian citizenship by such immigrants. English, Arabic, and Hebrew were to be the official languages of the mandate. In most respects, the mandate met the demands that Zionist leaders had enunciated at the beginning of the Paris Peace Conference.

Primary Source

Whereas the Principal Allied Powers have agreed, for the purpose of giving effect to the provisions of article 22 of the Covenant of the League of Nations, to entrust to a Mandatory selected by the said Powers the administration of the territory of Palestine, which formerly belonged to the Turkish Empire, within such boundaries as may be fixed by them; and

Whereas the Principal Allied Powers have also agreed that the Mandatory should be responsible for putting into effect the declaration originally made on the 2nd November, 1917, by the Government of His Britannic Majesty, and adopted by the said Powers, in favor of the establishment in Palestine of a national home for the Jewish people, it being clearly understood that nothing should be done which might prejudice the civil and religious rights of existing non-Jewish communities in Palestine, or the rights and political status enjoyed by Jews in any other country; and

Whereas recognition has thereby been given to the historical connection of the Jewish people with Palestine and to the grounds for reconstituting their national home in that country; and

Whereas the Principal Allied Powers have selected His Britannic Majesty as the Mandatory for Palestine; and

Whereas the mandate in respect of Palestine has been formulated in the following terms and submitted to the Council of the League for approval; and

Whereas His Britannic Majesty has accepted the mandate in respect of Palestine and undertaken to exercise it on behalf of the League of Nations in conformity with the following provisions; and

Whereas by the afore-mentioned article 22 (paragraph 8), it is provided that the degree of authority, control or administration to be exercised by the Mandatory, not having been previously agreed upon by the Members of the League, shall be explicitly defined by the Council of the League Of Nations;

Confirming the said Mandate, defines its terms as follows:

ARTICLE 1
The Mandatory shall have full powers of legislation and of administration, save as they may be limited by the terms of this mandate.

ARTICLE 2
The Mandatory shall be responsible for placing the country under such political, administrative and economic conditions as will secure the establishment of the Jewish national home, as laid down in the preamble, and the development of self-governing institutions, and also for safeguarding the civil and religious rights of all the inhabitants of Palestine, irrespective of race and religion.

ARTICLE 3
The Mandatory shall, so far as circumstances permit, encourage local autonomy.

ARTICLE 4
An appropriate Jewish agency shall be recognised as a public body for the purpose of advising and co-operating with the Administration of Palestine in such economic, social and other matters as may affect the establishment of the Jewish national home and the interests of the Jewish population in Palestine, and, subject always to the control of the Administration, to assist and take part in the development of the country.

The Zionist Organization, so long as its organization and constitution are in the opinion of the Mandatory appropriate, shall be recognised as such agency. It shall take steps in consultation with His Britannic Majesty's Government to secure the co-operation of all Jews who are willing to assist in the establishment of the Jewish national home.

ARTICLE 5
The Mandatory shall be responsible for seeing that no Palestine territory shall be ceded or leased to, or in any way placed under the control of, the Government of any foreign Power.

ARTICLE 6
The Administration of Palestine, while ensuring that the rights and position of other sections of the population are not prejudiced, shall facilitate Jewish immigration under suitable conditions and shall encourage, in co-operation with the Jewish agency referred to in Article 4, close settlement by Jews on the land, including State lands and waste lands not required for public purposes.

ARTICLE 7
The Administration of Palestine shall be responsible for enacting a nationality law. There shall be included in this law provisions framed so as to facilitate the acquisition of Palestinian citizenship by Jews who take up their permanent residence in Palestine.

ARTICLE 8
The privileges and immunities of foreigners, including the benefits of consular jurisdiction and protection as formerly enjoyed by Capitulation or usage in the Ottoman Empire, shall not be applicable in Palestine.

Unless the Powers whose nationals enjoyed the aforementioned privileges and immunities on 1st August, 1914, shall have previously renounced the right to their re-establishment, or shall have agreed to their non-application for a specified period, these privileges and immunities shall, at the expiration of the mandate, be immediately re-established in their entirety or with such modifications as may have been agreed upon between the Powers concerned.

ARTICLE 9
The Mandatory shall be responsible for seeing that the judicial system established in Palestine shall assure to foreigners, as well as to natives, a complete guarantee of their rights.

Respect for the personal status of the various peoples and communities and for their religious interests shall be fully guaranteed. In particular, the control and administration of Waqfs shall be exercised in accordance with religious law and the dispositions of the founders.

ARTICLE 10
Pending the making of special extradition agreements relating to Palestine, the extradition treaties in force between the Mandatory and other foreign Powers shall apply to Palestine.

ARTICLE 11
The Administration of Palestine shall take all necessary measures to safeguard the interests of the community in connection with the

development of the country, and, subject to any international obligations accepted by the Mandatory, shall have full power to provide for public ownership or control of any of the natural resources of the country or of the public works, services and utilities established or to be established therein. It shall introduce a land system appropriate to the needs of the country, having regard, among other things, to the desirability of promoting the close settlement and intensive cultivation of the land.

The Administration may arrange with the Jewish agency mentioned in Article 4 to construct or operate, upon fair and equitable terms, any public works, services and utilities, and to develop any of the natural resources of the country, in so far as these matters are not directly undertaken by the Administration. Any such arrangements shall provide that no profits distributed by such agency, directly or indirectly, shall exceed a reasonable rate of interest on the capital, and any further profits shall be utilised by it for the benefit of the country in a manner approved by the Administration.

ARTICLE 12

The Mandatory shall be entrusted with the control of the foreign relations of Palestine and the right to issue exequaturs to consuls appointed by foreign Powers. He shall also be entitled to afford diplomatic and consular protection to citizens of Palestine when outside its territorial limits.

ARTICLE 13

All responsibility in connection with the Holy Places and religious buildings or sites in Palestine, including that of preserving existing rights and of securing free access to the Holy Places, religious buildings and sites and the free exercise of worship, while ensuring the requirements of public order and decorum, is assumed by the Mandatory, who shall be responsible solely to the League of Nations in all matters connected herewith, provided that nothing in this article shall prevent the Mandatory from entering into such arrangements as he may deem reasonable with the Administration for the purpose of carrying the provisions of this article into effect; and provided also that nothing in this mandate shall be construed as conferring upon the Mandatory authority to interfere with the fabric or the management of purely Moslem sacred shrines, the immunities of which are guaranteed.

ARTICLE 14

A special commission shall be appointed by the Mandatory to study, define and determine the rights and claims in connection with the Holy Places and the rights and claims relating to the different religious communities in Palestine. The method of nomination, the composition and the functions of this Commission shall be submitted to the Council of the League for its approval, and the Commission shall not be appointed or enter upon its functions without the approval of the Council.

ARTICLE 15

The Mandatory shall see that complete freedom of conscience and the free exercise of all forms of worship, subject only to the maintenance of public order and morals, are ensured to all. No discrimination of any kind shall be made between the inhabitants of Palestine on the ground of race, religion or language. No person shall be excluded from Palestine on the sole ground of his religious belief.

The right of each community to maintain its own schools for the education of its own members in its own language, while conforming to such educational requirements of a general nature as the Administration may impose, shall not be denied or impaired.

ARTICLE 16

The Mandatory shall be responsible for exercising such supervision over religious or eleemosynary bodies of all faiths in Palestine as may be required for the maintenance of public order and good government. Subject to such supervision, no measure shall be taken in Palestine to obstruct or interfere with the enterprise of such bodies or to discriminate against any representative or member of them on the ground of his religion or nationality.

ARTICLE 17

The Administration of Palestine may organize on a voluntary basis the forces necessary for the preservation of peace and order, and also for the defense of the country, subject, however, to the supervision of the Mandatory, but shall not use them for purposes other than those above specified save with the consent of the Mandatory. Except for such purposes, no military, naval or air forces shall be raised or maintained by the Administration of Palestine.

Nothing in this article shall preclude the Administration of Palestine from contributing to the cost of the maintenance of the forces of the Mandatory in Palestine.

The Mandatory shall be entitled at all times to use the roads, railways and ports of Palestine for the movement of armed forces and the carriage of fuel and supplies.

ARTICLE 18

The Mandatory shall see that there is no discrimination in Palestine against the nationals of any State member of the League of Nations (including companies incorporated under its laws) as compared with those of the Mandatory or of any foreign State in matters concerning taxation, commerce or navigation, the exercise of industries or professions, or in the treatment of merchant vessels or civil aircraft. Similarly, there shall be no discrimination in Palestine against goods originating in or destined for any of the said States, and there shall be freedom of transit under equitable conditions across the mandated area.

Subject as aforesaid and to the other provisions of this mandate the Administration of Palestine may, on the advice of the Mandatory, impose such taxes and customs duties as it may consider necessary, and take such steps as it may think best to promote the development of the natural resources of the country and to safeguard the interests of the population. It may also, on the advice of the Mandatory, conclude a special customs agreement with any State the territory of which in 1914 was wholly included in Asiatic Turkey or Arabia.

[…]

ARTICLE 22
English, Arabic and Hebrew shall be the official languages of Palestine. Any statement or inscription in Arabic on stamps or money in Palestine shall be repeated in Hebrew and any statement or inscription in Hebrew shall be repeated in Arabic.

ARTICLE 23
The Administration of Palestine shall recognize the holy days of the respective communities in Palestine as legal days of rest for the members of such communities.

[…]

ARTICLE 25
In the territories lying between the Jordan and the eastern boundary of Palestine as ultimately determined, the Mandatory shall be entitled, with the consent of the Council of the League of Nations, to postpone or withhold application of such provisions of this mandate as he may consider inapplicable to the existing local conditions, and to make such provision for the administration of the territories as he may consider suitable to those conditions, provided that no action shall be taken which is inconsistent with the provisions of Articles 15, 16 and 18.

[…]

Source: U.S. Department of State, *The Palestine Mandate: Collected United States Documents Relating to the League of Nations Mandate for Palestine, to the Possible Future Independence of Palestine and to the Need for the Creation of a Separate Jewish State* (Salisbury, NC: Documentary Publications, 1977).

19. Reich Citizenship Law, September 15, 1935

Introduction

In 1933 a government headed by National Socialist Party (Nazi) chancellor Adolf Hitler came to power in Germany. By the end of the year, the Nazis had seized power and overthrown the democratic system that had ruled Germany since the end of World War I. The Nazi Party and Hitler were committed to a racist ideology that claimed that Anglo-Saxons (or Aryans) constituted a master race, with all others being at varying levels of inferiority. Jews were not merely placed on the lowest level of this hierarchy but instead were characterized as evil parasites whose blood and machinations had corrupted the purity and functioning of the German nation and people (*Volk*) and who were to be persecuted and eradicated from the German body politic. German Jews were immediately dismissed from public positions and subjected to physical and mental harassment, humiliation, and torture. The Nazi government soon passed legislation putting into effect its theories that Jews were inferior and were not entitled to German citizenship. Under the Nuremberg decrees of September–November 1935, German Jews were denied citizenship and could not hold public office. They were also forbidden to marry German nationals. One Jewish grandparent sufficed to define a person as a Jew. The citizenship law came into force on September 30, 1935. For the next six years, German restrictions on Jews became ever tighter. Those who could or would not flee the country were maltreated, restricted to ghettoes, and eventually deported eastward, with those who survived ultimately shipped to concentration and extermination camps.

Primary Source

The Reichstag has unanimously enacted the following law, which is promulgated herewith:

§ 1
A subject of the State is a person who enjoys the protection of the German Reich and who in consequence has specific obligations towards it.

The status of subject of the State is acquired in accordance with the provisions of the Reich and State Citizenship Law.

§ 2
A Reich citizen is a subject of the State who is of German or related blood, who proves by his conduct that he is willing and fit faithfully to serve the German people and Reich.

Reich citizenship is acquired through the granting of a Reich Citizenship Certificate.

The Reich citizen is the sole bearer of full political rights in accordance with the Law.

§ 3
The Reich Minister of the Interior, in coordination with the Deputy of the Führer, will issue the Legal and Administrative orders required to implement and complete this Law.

Law for the Protection of German Blood and German Honor
September 15, 1935

Moved by the understanding that purity of the German Blood is the essential condition for the continued existence of the German people, and inspired by the inflexible determination to ensure the existence of the German Nation for all time, the Reichstag has unanimously adopted the following Law, which is promulgated herewith:

Article 1.

1) Marriages between Jews and subjects of the state of German or related blood are forbidden. Marriages nevertheless concluded are invalid, even if concluded abroad to circumvent this law.

2) Annulment proceedings can be initiated only by the State Prosecutor.

Article 2.

Extramarital intercourse between Jews and subjects of the state of German or related blood is forbidden.

Article 3.

Jews may not employ in their households female subjects of the state of German or related blood who are under 45 years old.

Article 4.

1) Jews are forbidden to fly the Reich or National flag or to display the Reich colors. They are, on the other hand, permitted to display the Jewish colors. The exercise of this right is protected by the State.

Article 5.

(1) Any person who violates the prohibition under § 1 will be punished by a prison sentence with hard labor.

(2) A male who violates the prohibition under § 2 will be punished with a prison sentence with or without hard labor.

(3) Any person violating the provisions under § 3 or § 4 will be punished with a prison sentence of up to one year and a fine, or with one or the other of these penalties.

Article 6.

The Reich Minister of the Interior, in coordination with the Deputy of the Führer and the Reich Minister of Justice, will issue the Legal and Administrative regulations required to implement and complete this Law.

Article 7.

The Law takes effect on the day following promulgations except for § 3, which goes into force on January 1, 1936.

Nuremberg, September 15, 1935 at the Reich Party Congress of Freedom

First Supplementary Decree of November 14, 1935

On the basis of Article III of the Reich Citizenship Law of September 15, 1935, the following is hereby decreed:

ARTICLE 2.

(2) An individual of mixed Jewish blood is one who is descended from one or two grandparents who, racially, were full Jews, insofar that he is not a Jew according to Section 2 of Article 5. Full-blooded Jewish grandparents are those who belonged to the Jewish religious community.

ARTICLE 3.

Only citizens of the Reich, as bearers of full political rights, can exercise the right of voting in political matters, and have the right to hold public office. The Reich Minister of the Interior, or any agency he empowers, can make exceptions during the transition period on the matter of holding public office. The measures do not apply to matters concerning religious organizations.

ARTICLE 4.

(1) A Jew cannot be a citizen of the Reich. He cannot exercise the right to vote; he cannot hold public office. (2) Jewish officials will be retired as of December 31, 1935. In the event that such officials served at the front in the World War either for Germany or her allies, they shall receive as pension, until they reach the age limit, the full salary last received, on the basis of which their pension would have been computed. They shall not, however, be promoted according to their seniority in rank. When they reach the age limit, their pension will be computed again, according to the salary last received on which their pension was to be calculated.

ARTICLE 5.

(1) A Jew is an individual who is descended from at least three grandparents who were, racially, full Jews. . . . (2) A Jew is also an individual who is descended from two full-Jewish grandparents if: (a) he was a member of the Jewish religious community when this law was issued, or joined the community later; (b) when the law was issued, he was married to a person who was a Jew, or was subsequently married to a Jew; (c) he is the issue from a marriage with a Jew, in the sense of Section I, which was contracted after the coming into effect of the Law for the Protection of German Blood and Honor of September 15, 1935; (d) he is the issue of an extramarital relationship with a Jew, in the sense of Section I, and was born out of wedlock after July 31, 1936.

ARTICLE 7.

The Führer and Chancellor of the Reich is empowered to release anyone from the provisions of these administrative decrees.

Source: "Documents Relating to the Holocaust War Crimes and Genocide," University of West England, http://www.ess.uwe.ac.uk/genocide/docments.htm.

20. Colonel H. R. P. Dickson, Report to George Rendel, October 28, 1937

Introduction

The Arab Revolt of 1936–1939, encouraged by Haj Amin al-Husseini, the grand mufti of Jerusalem, disrupted normal life in Palestine, making the mandate increasingly expensive for the British to hold. It also won the Palestinian Arabs widespread support from other Arab leaders, including those of Saudi Arabia and Iraq. Ibn Saud, the monarch of Saudi Arabia, showed considerable interest in the mandate and offered to mediate a settlement, good offices that, since the terms he envisaged would have ended all Jewish immigration to Palestine and granted Arab rioters an amnesty, the British government found unacceptable. Anxious to rid themselves of an increasingly burdensome responsibility, in 1936 the British government appointed a Royal Commission headed by Lord Peel to suggest ways of settling the Palestine problem. Peel's report, published in July 1937, suggested that the grievances between the Arabs and Jews in Palestine had become so intractable and irreconcilable that the only feasible solution was to divide Palestine into separate Jewish and Arab states. The Jewish state would consist of the area around the city of Tel Aviv, including Galilee, the Yezreel Valley, and part of the coastal plain, about 20 percent of the country. Most of the rest, constituting Arab Palestine, would be united with Transjordan. The British government would retain a small mandatory area including the Holy Places of Islamic, Jewish, and Christian religions comprising Jerusalem, Bethlehem, and possibly Nazareth and the Sea of Genezareth. The Zionist Congress accepted this plan, although a considerable and vocal minority of Zionists were not in favor. Arab leaders were more intransigent. In a 90-minute meeting with King Ibn Saud, former British official Colonel H. R. P. Dickson sought his views on the Peel plan. Dickson's report, submitted to the British Foreign Office but not circulated because its contents were considered so inflammatory, made it clear that Ibn Saud was adamantly opposed to the partition of Palestine and would have preferred long-term British rule to any such division. Ibn Saud implied that if the British sought to pressure him on the subject, he and other Arab leaders might well turn to Britain's enemies—Italy, Germany, and Turkey—and launch a military attack on Palestine. Once again, he urged the British to ban all further Jewish immigration into Palestine. The episode was an index of the degree to which other Arab rulers in the Middle East were taking an interest in the question of Palestine's future, further restricting Britain's options at a time of growing international tensions in Europe and Asia. The British eventually rejected the option of partition and in a 1939 White Paper largely tailored to appease Arab sensibilities also declared that it was the policy of the British government that Palestine would never become a Jewish state. They also tightly restricted further Jewish immigration into Palestine.

Primary Source

His Majesty early on turned to the subject obviously close to his heart, namely the Palestine tangle, and for close on an hour and a half delivered himself as follows. He spoke for the most part in [a] low earnest voice as though his words were not intended for his Counsellors sitting round and he continually kept placing his hand on my arm as though to emphasize his meaning.

(Here I shall use the King's words as near as possible using the first person plural for the most part.)

'We are aware O Dickson that you are no longer a Government Official, but as you have held high and honourable post under His Majesty's government for many years, we know also that you are trusted by your Government, and so not only do we make you doubly welcome, but we feel we can open our heart to you, and we are glad that you have been able to visit us in our capital.

'We are most anxious that the British Government should send us every eight months or so an experienced officer whom they trust, or equally well an ex-official like yourself, who can listen personally to what we have on our minds, and what troubles our hearts, for times are deeply serious and full of danger these days. We feel that personal contact of such a nature will be far more efficacious, than any amount of letter writing or telegraph representations. The latter though well enough in themselves must nearly always fail to convey the full meaning of our thoughts and anxieties, and if anything will tend rather to breed misunderstanding and misconception than remove same. But such a person, if and when he is sent us must be thoroughly conversant with our language (Arabic), and must understand the wider meaning of our beautiful tongue which is so full of parable and expressive phrase. It is no use sending a man who has to listen to what we have to say through the medium of an interpreter. The person sent should know and understand our Arab psychology, be conversant if possible with our Arabian manners and customs, and above all should be acquainted with our Arab pride and our hopes, and have read something of God's Holy Word, as vouchsafed to us in our Blessed Qur'an.

'O Dickson when will your London Government realize that we Arabs by our very nature can be bought body and soul by an act of kindness, and vice versa become implacable enemies for all time of those who treat us harshly or deal unjustly with us.

'Today we and our subjects are deeply troubled over this Palestine question, and the cause of our disquiet and anxiety is the strange attitude of your British Government, and the still more strange hypnotic influence which the Jews, a race accursed by God according to His Holy Book, and destined to final destruction and eternal damnation hereafter, appear to wield over them and the English people generally.

'God's Holy Book (the Qur'an) contains God's own word and divine ordinance, and we commend to His Majesty's Government to read and carefully peruse that portion which deals with the Jews and especially what is to be their fate in the end. For God's words are unalterable and must be.

'We Arabs believe implicitly in God's revealed word and we know that God is faithful. We care for nothing else in this world but our belief in the One God, His Prophet and our Honour, everything else matters nothing at all, not even death, nor are we afraid of hardship, hunger, lack of this world's goods etc, etc. and we are quite content to eat camel's meat and dates to the end of our days, provided we hold to the above three things.

'Our hatred for the Jews dates from God's condemnation of them for their persecution and rejection of Isa (Jesus Christ), and their subsequent rejection later of His chosen Prophet. It is beyond our understanding how your Government, representing the first Christian power in the world today, can wish to assist and reward these very same Jews who maltreated your Isa (Jesus).

'We Arabs have been the traditional friends of Great Britain for many years, and I, Bin Sa'ud, in particular have been your Government's firm friend all my life, what madness then is this which is leading on your Government to destroy this friendship of centuries, all for the sake of an accursed and stiffnecked race which has always bitten the hand of everyone who has helped it since the world began.

'It were far preferable from every point of view if Great Britain were to make Palestine a British Possession and rule it for the next 100 years, rather than to partition it in the way they propose: such partition cannot possibly solve the difficulty but must only perpetuate it and lead to war and misery. Some people seem to think that I, Bin Sa'ud, have an eye on Palestine myself, and would like to benefit by the disturbed state of affairs existing there, to step in and offer to take it over myself. That certainly would be a solution, but God forbid that this should happen, for I have enough and to spare as it is.

'Today I am the 'Imam' or 'Spiritual Leader' as well as the Temporal Ruler of the greater part of Arabia. I also have not a little influence in all the great Muslim countries of the world. I am being placed in the most difficult and most invidious of all positions by the British Government my friends. On the one hand I am being appealed to by means of myriads of letters and telegrams by day and night from all quarters of the Muslim world to step in and save Palestine for the Arabs. I am even urged by my own people of Najd, and all good Muslims in the outer world to break with the English and save Palestine for its people by war. On the other hand I see that it would be utterly futile to break with my old friends the English, for to do so would bring untold woe on the world, and would be to play right into the hands of the Jews, the enemies of Arabia as well as of England.

'I definitely shall not wage war against you English and I have told my people this, because I am the only man among them who can see far ahead and I know that by so doing I should lose the one potential ally I now have. For are not Italy, Germany and Turkey (especially the latter) like ravening wolves today seeking whom they may devour. They are all flirting with me at the present moment, but I know they will wish to devour me later. A friendly England will, I believe, always prevent them from accomplishing their ends. Hence, though as a Muslim I have no particular love for any Christian European nation, political interest demands that I keep in with the best of them, that is, England.

'The difficulty is my Arabs and the Ikhwan tribes of Najd—Over this Palestine business their senses are only in their eyes, and they cannot see one cubit ahead. They even now blame me for wavering and obeying the orders of the English, and yet your Government should remember that I am the Arabs' religious leader and so am the interpreter of the scriptures. God's word to them cannot be got round.

'Verily the word of God teaches us, and we implicitly believe this O Dickson, that for a Muslim to kill a Jew, or for him to be killed by a Jew ensures him an immediate entry into Heaven and into the august presence of God Almighty. What more then can a Muslim want in this hard world, and that is what my people are repeatedly reminding me of? Most assuredly your government is placing me in the same dilemma that they did in 1929–30 which ended in the Ikhwan going out in rebellion against me.

'The Jews are of course your enemies as well as ours though they are cleverly making use of you now. Later your Government will see and feel their teeth. For the present they (the Jews) prefer biding their time. Perhaps your Government does not know that the Jews contemplate as their final aim not only the seizure of all Palestine but the land south of it as far as Medina. Eastward also they hope some day to extend to the Persian Gulf. They cozen certain imperialistic-minded Englishmen with stories of how a strong Jewish and Pro-British State stretching from the Mediterranean to the Persian Gulf will safeguard England's communications with the East, saying that the Arabs are England's enemies and will always be so. At the same time they play on the minds of the sentimental British masses, by telling them that the Old Testament prophets foretold how they, the Jews, would eventually return to their Promised Land, or again that they, the persecuted and wandering Bani Israel, should not be denied a small place in the world where to lay their weary heads. Now, O Dickson, would the people of Wales like it if you English suddenly gave the Jews their country? But no, it is easier to give away other people's countries and not so dangerous.

'That the Jews of Palestine are even now straining every nerve to cause a permanent split between the English people and the Arabs can be proved to the hilt by the recent murders of officials in Palestine. It is as clear as daylight to me that the Godless Arab gunmen, hired from abroad, who committed those vile deeds were hired and paid for by Jewish money. We state this to be an absolute fact, for did not the Grand Mufti of Jerusalem swear to us in the 'Haram' of Mecca by the Holy Kaaba that he would never resort to any but constitutional methods in opposing the Zionist machinations in Palestine? And I believe him even today.

'What we fear so greatly and what Great Britain must not allow to come to pass is the turning of the Arabs of Arabia and neighboring Arab countries into enemies of England. Once this happens then an irreparable crime will have been committed, for, as we said above, the Arabs will never forget an injury, and will bide their opportunity to take revenge for a hundred years if need be. Enemies of England would not be slow to take advantage of this, and an England in difficulties, or engaged elsewhere in war, would then be the signal for the Arabs to act.

'The very thought of the above happening is hateful to me Abdul Aziz, yet be assured the Partition in Palestine will bring this about in spite of all your misdirected efforts. And after all I cannot help you forever as I cannot live more than a few years more. I repeat then that the only solution that I can see is for your Government to rule Palestine herself. The Zionists of course will not like this, but their views must not be asked. The Arabs will agree to this solution and those who do not must be made to agree by such people as myself.

'The main thing at all costs is to prevent the Jews from having an independent state of their own sliced out of Arab territory with no one to guide their future acts and policy. For from such will come a perpetual struggle with the Arabs living round them. Firstly because the Jews are determined to expand, will intrigue from the very beginning, and not rest until they have created discord between Great Britain and us Arabs, out of which they will hope to benefit. Secondly, they, having the money, will create a highly effective though perhaps small mechanized Army and Air Force, which they will assuredly use one day for aggressive purposes against the Arabs, seeing that their aim is the whole of Palestine, Trans-jordan and their old stronghold Medina—the land they went to when driven out of Palestine and dispersed after the Romans destroyed Jerusalem.

'On top of this your Government must at once restrict further immigration of Jews into Palestine leaving alone all those already there but allowing no more to come in.'

I here took advantage of a pause in the King's rather forcible harangue to try and explain His Majesty's Government's point of view on the lines suggested by Rendel when I saw him recently in London. But before I had gone very far the King in vigorous fash-

ion checked and rather overwhelmed me with the words, 'By God, your Government has no point of view, except the willful committing of an injustice. Every God-fearing man be he Muslim or Christian knows that it cannot be right to do a wrong, however cleverly the committing may be served up to the people. If I, an ignorant Badawin Arab of Arabia can see, as clearly as I see the sun rise, that the proposed partition of Palestine is wicked and wrong in God's sight, surely the more clever Western politicians, if they fear God at all, can see this also. Thank God I believe in God and his Oneness, and I know that it is this very belief of mine that makes me see things as clearly as I do. I am firmly convinced that I am right, and that God has opened my eyes to the right, as I believe that God will punish me if I lie to him. Therefore there is *no other side* to this question except bargaining with Satan.'

Source: Elie Kedourie, *Islam in the Modern World* (New York: Holt, Rinehart and Winston, 1980).

21. British Government's Position regarding Palestine, November 1938

Introduction

The British government considered at some length the recommendations of the Peel Commission, put forward in July 1937, that Palestine be divided into two states, a small Jewish entity centered on Tel Aviv and a larger Arab one. Besides discussing these proposals with various Arab leaders, including the kings of Iraq and Saudi Arabia, the latter of whom was particularly vehement in his opposition to them, the British government established a second body, the Woodhead Commission, to consider the feasibility of partition. The second commission's members visited Palestine and considered three potential partition plans, all of which they rejected. The grounds given were, as the British government stated in November 1938, that since the Jewish state would run a substantial budgetary surplus while the Arab state and the remaining mandate territory under British rule would suffer from financial deficits, such schemes were impossible given the need for each to be independent of the other. The underlying reason for British rejection of partition was probably the unwavering opposition of Arab leaders outside Palestine, who were supporting the Arab Revolt there both out of genuine sympathy and as a means of bolstering their own political standing within their countries and the broader Arab world. The British government's statement appealed, in rather vague terms, for negotiations that would promote greater understanding and cooperation between the Arab and Jewish communities in Palestine. With partition abandoned as a feasible solution, the British government would increasingly embark on policies whose primary objective was damage limitation, seeking to damp down tensions within Palestine by curtailing further Jewish immigration and discountenancing all calls for a separate Jewish state.

Primary Source

PALESTINE

STATEMENT BY HIS MAJESTY'S GOVERNMENT IN THE UNITED KINGDOM

1. The Royal Commission, presided over by the late Earl Peel, published its report in July, 1937, and proposed a solution of the Palestine problem by means of a scheme of partition under which independent Arab and Jewish States would be established while other areas would be retained under mandatory administration. In their statement of policy following upon the publication of the report, His Majesty's Government in the United Kingdom announced their general agreement with the arguments and conclusions of the Royal Commission, and expressed the view that a scheme of partition on the general lines recommended by the Commission represented the best and most hopeful solution of the deadlock.

2. The proposal of the Commission was framed in the light of the information available at the time, and it was generally recognized that further detailed examination would be necessary before it could be decided whether such a solution would prove practicable. This proposal was subsequently discussed in Parliament and at meetings of the Permanent Mandates Commission and the Council and Assembly of the League of Nations, when His Majesty's Government received authority to explore the practical application of the principle of partition. A despatch of 23rd December, 1937, from the Secretary of State for the Colonies to the High Commissioner for Palestine, announced the intention of His Majesty's Government to undertake the further investigations required for the drawing up of a more precise and detailed scheme. It was pointed out that the final decision could not be taken in merely general terms and that the further enquiry would provide the necessary material on which to judge, when the best possible partition scheme had been formulated, its equity and practicability. The despatch also defined the functions and terms of reference of the technical Commission who were appointed to visit Palestine for the purpose of submitting in due course to His Majesty's Government proposals for such a detailed scheme.

3. His Majesty's Government have now received the report of the Palestine Partition Commission who have carried out their investigations with great thoroughness and efficiency, and have collected material which will be very valuable in the further consideration of policy. Their report is now published, together with a summary of their conclusions. It will be noted that the four members of the Commission advise unanimously against the adoption of the scheme of partition outlined by the Royal Commission. In addition to the Royal Commission's scheme, two other schemes described as plans B and C are examined in the report. One member prefers plan B. Two other members, including the Chairman, consider that plan C is the best scheme of partition which, under the terms of reference, can be devised. A fourth member, while agreeing that plan C is the best that can be devised under the terms of reference,

regards both plans as impracticable. The report points out that under either plan, while the budget of the Jewish State is likely to show a substantial surplus, the budgets of the Arab State (including Trans-Jordan) and of the Mandated Territories are likely to show substantial deficits. The Commission reject as impracticable the Royal Commission's recommendation for a direct subvention from the Jewish State to the Arab State. They think that, on economic grounds, a customs union between the States and the Mandated Territories is essential and they examine the possibility of finding the solution for the financial and economic problems of partition by means of a scheme based upon such a union. They consider that any such scheme would be inconsistent with the grant of fiscal independence to the Arab and Jewish States. Their conclusion is that, on a strict interpretation of their terms of reference, they have no alternative but to report that they are unable to recommend boundaries for the proposed areas which will afford a reasonable prospect of the eventual establishment of self-supporting Arab and Jewish States.

4. His Majesty's Government, after careful study of the Partition Commission's report, have reached the conclusion that this further examination has shown that the political, administrative and financial difficulties involved in the proposal to create independent Arab and Jewish States inside Palestine are so great that this solution of the problem is impracticable.

5. His Majesty's Government will therefore continue their responsibility for the government of the whole of Palestine. They are now faced with the problem of finding alternative means of meeting the needs of the difficult situation described by the Royal Commission which will be consistent with their obligations to the Arabs and the Jews. His Majesty's Government believe that it is possible to find these alternative means. They have already given much thought to the problem in the light of the reports of the Royal Commission and of the Partition Commission. It is clear that the surest foundation for peace and progress in Palestine would be an understanding between the Arabs and the Jews, and His Majesty's Government are prepared in the first instance to make a determined effort to promote such an understanding. With this end in view, they propose immediately to invite representatives of the Palestinian Arabs and of neighbouring States on the one hand and of the Jewish Agency on the other, to confer with them as soon as possible in London regarding future policy, including the question of immigration into Palestine. As regards the representation of the Palestinian Arabs, His Majesty's Government must reserve the right to refuse to receive those leaders whom they regard as responsible for the campaign of assassination and violence.

6. His Majesty's Government hope that these discussions in London may help to promote agreement as to future policy regarding Palestine. They attach great importance, however, to a decision being reached at an early date. Therefore, if the London discussions should

not produce agreement within a reasonable period of time, they will take their own decision in the light of their examination of the problem and of the discussions in London, and announce the policy which they propose to pursue.

7. In considering and settling their policy His Majesty's Government will keep constantly in mind the international character of the Mandate with which they have been entrusted and their obligations in that respect.

Source: United Kingdom, "Statement by His Majesty's Government in the United Kingdom," United Nations, http://domino.un.org.

22. Haj Amin al-Husseini, Summons to a Jihad against Britain, May 10, 1941

Introduction

British efforts to conciliate Arab leaders in Palestine during the 1930s proved unavailing. In 1921 Haj Amin al-Husseini became the grand mufti of Jerusalem, the preeminent Islamic religious figure in Palestine, a position he won in part thanks to British influence. Al-Husseini soon became one of the strongest voices urging Arab opposition to the growing Jewish presence in Palestine, a major force behind the Arab riots of 1929 and the Arab Revolt of 1936–1939. Al-Husseini was a leading member of the Higher Arab Committee that directed the Arab Revolt. In the autumn of 1937, after he and others in the group were implicated in the murder of the British high commissioner for Galilee, al-Husseini fled Palestine for Lebanon and then Iraq. He was among those who helped to plan the May 1941 coup whereby four Iraqi generals overthrew the pro-British regent of Iraq and installed a military government friendly to Germany in the hope that this would allow them to win full Iraqi independence from Britain, as opposed to the limited independence granted in 1937. On May 10, 1941, al-Husseini also proclaimed a fatwa (religious ruling) calling on Muslims throughout the world to launch a jihad, or holy war, against Britain and British imperialism. His message was broadcast throughout the Middle East and Europe by Iraqi and German radio stations. Six months later, in November 1941, al-Husseini met with German chancellor Adolf Hitler, an encounter in which the grand mufti expressed his strong support for Hitler's anti-Jewish policies and requested German aid for the Arabs in their efforts to win complete independence from Western colonial rule. Hitler promised that as and when the military situation permitted, he would turn German forces to the task of eliminating Jewish elements in the Middle East and particularly Palestine. Al-Husseini was reputedly related to the later Palestinian leader Yasser Arafat, and the grand mufti's views allegedly had a considerable influence upon Arafat's thinking.

Primary Source

In the name of Merciful and Almighty God.

I invite all my Moslem brothers throughout the whole world to join in the Jihad for Allah, for the defense of Islam and her lands against her enemy. O Faithful, obey and respond to my call.

O Moslems!

Proud 'Iraq has placed herself in the vanguard of this Holy Struggle, and has thrown herself against the strongest enemy of Islam certain that God will grant her victory.

The English have tried to seize this Arab-Moslem land, but she has risen, full of dignity and pride to defend her safety, to fight for her honor and to safeguard her integrity. 'Iraq fights the tyranny which has always had as its aim the destruction of Islam in every land. It is the duty of all Moslems to aid 'Iraq in her struggle and to seek every means to fight the enemy, the traditional traitor in every age and every situation.

Whoever knows the history of the East has everywhere seen the hand of the English working to destroy the Ottoman Empire and to divide the Arab countries. British politics toward the Arab people is masked under a veil of Hypocrisy. The minute she sees her chance, England squeezes the prostrate country in her Imperialist grasp, adding futile justifications. She creates discord and division within a country and while feeding it in secret openly she assumes the role of advisor and trusted friend.

The time when England could deceive the peoples of the East is passed. The Arab Nation and the Moslem people have awakened to fight British domination. The English have overthrown the Ottoman Empire, have destroyed Moslem rule in India, inciting one community against another; they stifled the Egyptian awakening, the dream of Mohammed Ali, colonizing Egypt for half a century. They took advantage of the weakening of the Ottoman Empire to stretch out their hands and use every sort of trick to take possession of many Arab countries as happened to Aden, the 9 Districts, the Hadramut, Oman, Masqat and the Emirates of the Persian Gulf and Transjordania.

The vivid proof of the imperialistic designs of the British is to be found in Moslem Palestine which, although promised by England to Sheriff Hussein has had to submit to the outrageous infiltration of Jews, shameful politics designed to divide Arab-Moslem countries of Asia from those of Africa. In Palestine the English have committed unheard of barbarisms; among others, they have profaned the el-Aqsa Mosque and have declared the most unyielding war against Islam, both in deed and in word. The Prime Minister at that time told Parliament that the world would never see peace as long as the Koran existed. What hatred against Islam is stronger than that which publicly declares the Sacred Koran an enemy of human kind? Should such sacrilege go unpunished?

After the dissolution of the Moslem Empire in India and of the Ottoman Caliphate, England, adhering to the policy of Gladstone, pursued her work of destruction to Islam depriving many Islamic States both in the East and in the West of their freedom and independence. The number of Moslems who today live under the rule of England and invoke liberation from their terrible yoke exceeds 220,000,000.

Therefore I invite you, O Brothers, to join in the War for God to preserve Islam, your independence and your lands from English aggression. I invite you to bring all your weight to bear in helping 'Iraq that she may throw off the shame that torments her. O Heroic 'Iraq, God is with Thee, the Arab Nation and the Moslem World are solidly with Thee in Thy Holy Struggle!

Source: "The Palestinian Grand Mufti Haj Amin el Husseini: Fatwa—Holy War against Britain—1941," Zionism and Israel Information Center, http://www.zionism-israel.com/hdoc/Mufti_Fawa_1941.htm.

23. The Final Solution: The Wannsee Protocol, January 20, 1942

Introduction

Between 1939 and 1941, German troops overran most of Europe and a substantial part of Russia. In January 1942 top German officials met at Wannsee to discuss the best means for exterminating Jews throughout Europe. The officials listed not only those Jews then resident in Germany and territories occupied by Germany but also those in countries allied with Germany, neutral, or not yet conquered. In their discussion, the officials contemplated first the forcible deportation of Jews to territories in the East; their employment in labor camps, where many of them were expected to die of "natural causes"; and then a "final solution" to remove the remainder permanently from European life. In all, these discussions envisaged disposing of more than 11 million Jews throughout Europe. Where persons of mixed blood were concerned some latitude might be allowed, especially if combined with forcible sterilization. Effectively, the meeting sanctioned genocide on a massive scale, to be implemented where possible by methods adapted from industrial processes designed to handle large quantities of raw materials or animals. German actions were responsible for the deaths of approximately 6 million European Jews during World War II. At first, Allied leaders found it difficult to accept that genocide on this scale had genuinely occurred, but the discovery at the end of the war of the concentration and extermination camps to which Jews were consigned en masse made it only too clear that even as they were waging war, German officials had made massive efforts to murder all Europe's Jews. These revelations helped predispose postwar leaders to sympathize with Zionist demands for a Jewish homeland in Palestine.

Primary Source

TOP SECRET
Minutes of Meeting
I.
The following persons took part in the discussion about the final solution of the Jewish question which took place in Berlin, am Grossen Wannsee No. 56/58 on 20 January 1942:

Gauleiter Dr. Meyer and Reichsamtleiter Dr. Leibbrandt of the Ministry for the Occupied Eastern Territories; Dr. Stuckart, Secretary of State of the Ministry for the Interior; Secretary of State Neumann, Plenipotentiary for the Four Year Plan; Dr. Freisler, Secretary of State of the Ministry of Justice; Dr. Bühler, Secretary of State of the Office of the General Government; Dr. Luther, Under Secretary of State of the Foreign Office; SS-Oberführer Klopfer of the Party Chancellery; Ministerialdirektor Kritzinger of the Reich Chancellery; SS-Gruppenführer Hofmann of the Race and Settlement Main Office; SS-Gruppenführer Müller and SS-Obersturmbannführer Eichmann of the Reich Main Security Office; SS-Oberführer Dr. Schöngarth of the Security Police, Security Department, Commander of the Security Police, Security Department (SD) of the General Government; SS-Sturmbannführer Dr. Lange of the Security Police, Security Department, Commander of the Security Police and the Security Department for the General-District of Latvia, in his capacity as deputy to the Commander of the Security Police and the Security Department for the Reich Commissariat "Eastland."

II.
At the beginning of the discussion Chief of the Security Police and of the SD, SS-Obergruppenführer Heydrich, reported that the Reich Marshal [Hermann Göring] had appointed him delegate for the preparations for the final solution of the Jewish question in Europe and pointed out that this discussion had been called for the purpose of clarifying fundamental questions. The wish of the Reich Marshal to have a draft sent to him concerning organizational, factual and material interests in relation to the final solution of the Jewish question in Europe makes necessary an initial common action of all central offices immediately concerned with these questions in order to bring their general activities into line. The Reichsführer-SS [Heinrich Himmler] and the Chief of the German Police (Chief of the Security Police and the SD) [Reinhard Heydrich] were entrusted with the official central handling of the final solution of the Jewish question without regard to geographic borders. The Chief of the Security Police and the SD then gave a short report of the struggle which has been carried on thus far against this enemy, the essential points being the following:

a) the expulsion of the Jews from every sphere of life of the German people
b) the expulsion of the Jews from the living space of the German people

In carrying out these efforts, an increased and planned acceleration of the emigration of the Jews from Reich territory was started, as the only possible present solution.

By order of the Reich Marshal, a Reich Central Office for Jewish Emigration was set up in January 1939 and the Chief of the Security Police and SD was entrusted with the management. Its most important tasks were:

a) to make all necessary arrangements for the preparation for an increased emigration of the Jews,
b) to direct the flow of emigration,
c) to speed the procedure of emigration in each individual case.

The aim of all this was to cleanse German living space of Jews in a legal manner.

All the offices realized the drawbacks of such enforced accelerated emigration. For the time being they had, however, tolerated it on account of the lack of other possible solutions of the problem.

The work concerned with emigration was, later on, not only a German problem, but also a problem with which the authorities of the countries to which the flow of emigrants was being directed would have to deal. Financial difficulties, such as the demand by various foreign governments for increasing sums of money to be presented at the time of the landing, the lack of shipping space, increasing restriction of entry permits, or the canceling of such, increased extraordinarily the difficulties of emigration. In spite of these difficulties, 537,000 Jews were sent out of the country between the takeover of power and the deadline 31 October 1941. Of these there were:

In Germany proper on 30 January 1933 approximately 360,000
In Austria (Ostmark) on 15 March 1939 approximately 147,000
In the Protectorate of Bohemia and Moravia on 15 March 1939 approximately 30,000.

The Jews themselves, or their Jewish political organizations, financed the emigration. In order to avoid impoverished Jews remaining behind, the principle was followed that wealthy Jews have to finance the emigration of poor Jews; this was arranged by imposing a suitable tax, i.e., an emigration tax, which was used for financial arrangements in connection with the emigration of poor Jews and was imposed according to income.

Apart from the necessary Reichsmark exchange, foreign currency had to be presented at the time of landing. In order to save foreign exchange held by Germany, the foreign Jewish financial organizations were—with the help of Jewish organizations in Germany—made responsible for arranging an adequate amount of foreign currency. Up to 30 October 1941, these foreign Jews donated a total of around 9,500,000 dollars.

In the meantime the Reichsführer-SS and Chief of the German Police had prohibited emigration of Jews due to the dangers of an emigration in wartime and due to the possibilities of the East.

III.

Another possible solution of the problem has now taken the place of emigration, i.e., the evacuation of the Jews to the East, provided that the Führer gives the appropriate approval in advance.

These actions are, however, only to be considered provisional, but practical experience is already being collected which is of the greatest importance in relation to the future final solution of the Jewish question.

Approximately 11 million Jews will be involved in the final solution of the European Jewish question, distributed as follows among the individual countries:

[The document proceeds to list the number of Jews living not only in states such as France, Hungary, and Rumania already currently under German occupation or control, but also in countries at war with Germany including Britain and Russia; allied with it, such as Italy; sympathetic but neutral, such as Spain and Portugal; and simply neutral, including Ireland, Sweden, and Switzerland.]

Under proper guidance, in the course of the final solution the Jews are to be allocated for appropriate labor in the East. Able-bodied Jews, separated according to sex, will be taken in large work columns to these areas for work on roads, in the course of which action doubtless a large portion will be eliminated by natural causes. The possible final remnant will, since it will undoubtedly consist of the most resistant portion, have to be treated accordingly, because it is the product of natural selection and would, if released, act as the seed of a new Jewish revival (see the experience of history).

In the course of the practical execution of the final solution, Europe will be combed through from west to east. Germany proper, including the Protectorate of Bohemia and Moravia, will have to be handled first due to the housing problem and additional social and political necessities.

The evacuated Jews will first be sent, group by group, to so-called transit ghettos, from which they will be transported to the East.

SS-Obergruppenführer Heydrich went on to say that an important prerequisite for the evacuation as such is the exact definition of the persons involved.

It is not intended to evacuate Jews over 65 years old, but to send them to an old-age ghetto—Theresienstadt is being considered for this purpose.

In addition to these age groups—of the approximately 280,000 Jews in Germany proper and Austria on 31 October 1941, approximately 30% are over 65 years old—severely wounded veterans and Jews with war decorations (Iron Cross I) will be accepted in the old-age ghettos. With this expedient solution, in one fell swoop many interventions will be prevented.

The beginning of the individual larger evacuation actions will largely depend on military developments. Regarding the handling of the final solution in those European countries occupied and influenced by us, it was proposed that the appropriate expert of the Foreign Office discuss the matter with the responsible official of the Security Police and SD.

In Slovakia and Croatia the matter is no longer so difficult, since the most substantial problems in this respect have already been brought near a solution. In Rumania the government has in the meantime also appointed a commissioner for Jewish affairs. In order to settle the question in Hungary, it will soon be necessary to force an adviser for Jewish questions onto the Hungarian government.

With regard to taking up preparations for dealing with the problem in Italy, SS-Obergruppenführer Heydrich considers it opportune to contact the chief of police with a view to these problems.

In occupied and unoccupied France, the registration of Jews for evacuation will in all probability proceed without great difficulty.

Under Secretary of State Luther calls attention in this matter to the fact that in some countries, such as the Scandinavian states, difficulties will arise if this problem is dealt with thoroughly and that it will therefore be advisable to defer actions in these countries. Besides, in view of the small numbers of Jews affected, this deferral will not cause any substantial limitation.

The Foreign Office sees no great difficulties for southeast and western Europe.

SS-Gruppenführer Hofmann plans to send an expert to Hungary from the Race and Settlement Main Office for general orientation at the time when the Chief of the Security Police and SD takes up the matter there. It was decided to assign this expert from the Race and Settlement Main Office, who will not work actively, as an assistant to the police attaché.

IV.

[Intermarriages between Jews and non-Jews could give rise to problems in defining precisely who qualified as a Jew, and here it was proposed to follow the guidelines given in the earlier Nuremberg Laws of the 1930s, though in many cases exceptions and exemptions for meritorious conduct or the reverse were at least theoret-

ically possible, as were forcible sterilization and the involuntary dissolution of mixed marriages.]

With regard to the issue of the effect of the evacuation of Jews on the economy, State Secretary Neumann stated that Jews who are working in industries vital to the war effort, provided that no replacements are available, cannot be evacuated.

SS-Obergruppenführer Heydrich indicated that these Jews would not be evacuated according to the rules he had approved for carrying out the evacuations then underway.

State Secretary Dr. Bühler stated that the General Government would welcome it if the final solution of this problem could be begun in the General Government, since on the one hand transportation does not play such a large role here nor would problems of labor supply hamper this action. Jews must be removed from the territory of the General Government as quickly as possible, since it is especially here that the Jew as an epidemic carrier represents an extreme danger and on the other hand he is causing permanent chaos in the economic structure of the country through continued black market dealings. Moreover, of the approximately 2 1/2 million Jews concerned, the majority is unfit for work.

State Secretary Dr. Bühler stated further that the solution to the Jewish question in the General Government is the responsibility of the Chief of the Security Police and the SD and that his efforts would be supported by the officials of the General Government. He had only one request, to solve the Jewish question in this area as quickly as possible.

In conclusion the different types of possible solutions were discussed, during which discussion both Gauleiter Dr. Meyer and State Secretary Dr. Bühler took the position that certain preparatory activities for the final solution should be carried out immediately in the territories in question, in which process alarming the populace must be avoided.

The meeting was closed with the request of the Chief of the Security Police and the SD to the participants that they afford him appropriate support during the carrying out of the tasks involved in the solution.

Source: "Wannsee Protocol," Harold B. Lee Library, Brigham Young University, http://eudocs.lib.byu.edu/index.php/Wannsee_Protocol.

24. Biltmore Declaration, May 11, 1942
Introduction

Despite British efforts to close Palestine to Jewish immigration, World War II, especially German chancellor Adolf Hitler's persecution of

European Jews, gave a new impetus to Zionist efforts to establish a Jewish state there. American Zionists in particular now envisaged this as providing a sanctuary for Jewish refugees who sought to escape Nazi oppression, and the Zionists felt that only a state, not merely a homeland, would suffice for this purpose. The change in policy emphasis from seeking a homeland to a state required endorsement by the World Zionist Congress, but given wartime conditions, this was seen as almost impossible. American Zionists formed the American Emergency Committee of Zionist Affairs, which convened the Extraordinary Zionist Conference, held at the Biltmore Hotel in New York City in May 1942. The conference attracted 600 delegates, who included Zionists drawn from 18 countries, including such widely respected figures as Chaim Weizmann, one of the fathers of the Balfour Declaration, and David Ben-Gurion, chairman of the Executive of the Jewish Agency in Palestine. The conference adopted eight resolutions, generally known as the Biltmore Program. These reaffirmed the conference's faith in the pledges of the Balfour Declaration and President Woodrow Wilson that Palestine would be a "Jewish Commonwealth"; rejected the 1939 British White Paper and demanded free and unlimited Jewish immigration into Palestine, under the control of the Jewish Agency; and demanded "that Palestine be established as a Jewish Commonwealth integrated in the structure of the new democratic world." The Biltmore Program also celebrated the achievements of Jewish settlers in developing Palestine and demanded that Jews be allowed to form a separate military force to fight in the war against the Axis powers. The conference marked a new sense of assertiveness on the part of American and international Zionists, a refusal to acquiesce in or be satisfied with earlier compromise solutions.

Primary Source

Declaration adopted by the Extraordinary Zionist Conference at the Biltmore Hotel of New York City, May 11, 1942.

The following programme was approved by a Zionist Conference held in the Biltmore Hotel, New York City:

1. American Zionists assembled in this Extraordinary Conference reaffirm their unequivocal devotion to the cause of democratic freedom and international justice to which the people of the United States, allied with the other United Nations, have dedicated themselves, and give expression to their faith in the ultimate victory of humanity and justice over lawlessness and brute force.

2. This Conference offers a message of hope and encouragement to their fellow Jews in the Ghettos and concentration camps of Hitler-dominated Europe and prays that their hour of liberation may not be far distant.

3. The Conference sends its warmest greetings to the Jewish Agency Executive in Jerusalem, to the Va'ad Leumi, and to the whole Yishuv in Palestine, and expresses its profound admiration for their steadfastness and achievements in the face of peril and great difficulties. . . .

4. In our generation, and in particular in the course of the past twenty years, the Jewish people have awakened and transformed their ancient homeland; from 50,000 at the end of the last war their numbers have increased to more than 500,000. They have made the waste places to bear fruit and the desert to blossom. Their pioneering achievements in agriculture and in industry, embodying new patterns of cooperative endeavour, have written a notable page in the history of colonization.

5. In the new values thus created, their Arab neighbours in Palestine have shared. The Jewish people in its own work of national redemption welcomes the economic, agricultural and national development of the Arab peoples and states. The Conference reaffirms the stand previously adopted at Congresses of the World Zionist Organization, expressing the readiness and the desire of the Jewish people for full cooperation with their Arab neighbours.

6. The Conference calls for the fulfillment of the original purpose of the Balfour Declaration and the Mandate which, "recognizing the historical connection of the Jewish people with Palestine," was to afford them the opportunity, as stated by President Wilson, to found there a Jewish Commonwealth.

The Conference affirms its unalterable rejection of the White Paper of May 1939 and denies its moral or legal validity. The White Paper seeks to limit, and in fact to nullify Jewish rights to immigration and settlement in Palestine, and, as stated by Mr. Winston Churchill in the House of Commons in May 1939, constitutes "a breach and repudiation of the Balfour Declaration." The policy of the White Paper is cruel and indefensible in its denial of sanctuary to Jews fleeing from Nazi persecution; and at a time when Palestine has become a focal point in the war front of the United Nations, and Palestine Jewry must provide all available manpower for farm and factory and camp, it is in direct conflict with the interests of the allied war effort.

7. In the struggle against the forces of aggression and tyranny, of which Jews were the earliest victims, and which now menace the Jewish National Home, recognition must be given to the right of the Jews of Palestine to play their full part in the war effort and in the defense of their country, through a Jewish military force fighting under its own flag and under the high command of the United Nations.

8. The Conference declares that the new world order that will follow victory cannot be established on foundations of peace, justice and equality, unless the problem of Jewish homelessness is finally solved.

The Conference urges that the gates of Palestine be opened; that the Jewish Agency be vested with control of immigration into Palestine and with the necessary authority for upbuilding the country, including the development of its unoccupied and uncultivated lands; and that Palestine be established as a Jewish Commonwealth integrated in the structure of the new democratic world.

Then and only then will the age-old wrong to the Jewish people be righted.

> **Source:** "Declaration Adopted by the Extraordinary Zionist Conference at the Biltmore Hotel of New York City, 11 May 1942," United Nations Information System on the Question of Palestine, http://unispal.un.org.

25. Foreign Petroleum Policy of the United States, April 11, 1944

Introduction

By early 1944, concern about future access to overseas oil supplies was sufficiently strong to impel the U.S. State Department to seek to formulate guidelines for U.S. international policy on oil. Several plans for governmental acquisition of stakes in major British and American oil companies' overseas concessions in Saudi Arabia and Iran to construct pipelines in the Persian Gulf area and to reach agreement with the British government on petroleum policy around the globe proved abortive. These ventures nonetheless led State Department officials, whom the demands of war made ever more conscious that U.S. military readiness and the civilian economy both depended heavily on plentiful oil supplies, to draft guidelines on oil policy. These envisaged ensuring U.S. access on equal terms to oil supplies, conserving the Western Hemisphere's oil resources and discouraging exports of these outside the Western Hemisphere, and facilitating U.S. access to and development of Middle Eastern oil reserves, if necessary by negotiating an understanding with Great Britain to ensure maximal exploitation of these resources. U.S. officials were anxious to prevent the transfer of any American-owned Middle Eastern oil concessions to nationals of other countries and to encourage Americans to cultivate such concessions to their full potential. State Department officials also thought it desirable that European needs for oil be met from Middle Eastern rather than Western Hemisphere sources, effectively enabling the United States to retain its hemispheric oil supplies for its own use. The guidelines gave striking proof that the U.S. government was fully conscious that petroleum was a valuable and essential international commodity, one that was vital to the effective functioning of the U.S. civilian and military economy, and that State Department officials were determined, in the interests of national security, to encourage U.S. businesses to obtain and develop to their own and their

country's maximum advantage as large a share as possible of global petroleum reserves.

Primary Source

I. Objectives of United States Foreign Petroleum Policy

1. The "equal access" clause of the Atlantic Charter should be implemented in respect of petroleum.

2. General recognition should be achieved of the principle of equal opportunity for American enterprise in exploration for additional sources of supply of petroleum, and in the development of whatever reserves may be found in the future.

3. A broad policy of conservation of Western Hemisphere petroleum reserves should be adopted in the interest of hemispheric security, in order to assure the adequacy for military and civilian requirements of strategically available reserves. This broad policy would need to be implemented by measures of domestic as well as foreign policy. The appropriate foreign policy should include these three elements:
   a. Curtailment, in so far as practicable, of the flow of petroleum and its products from Western Hemisphere sources to Eastern Hemisphere markets. This change in the flow of trade in Western Hemisphere oil should be accompanied by reasonable safeguards for the interests of Western Hemisphere producing countries having established market outlets in the Eastern Hemisphere.
   b. Facilitation, by international agreement and otherwise, of substantial and orderly expansion of production in Eastern Hemisphere sources of supply, principally in the Middle East, to meet increasing requirements of post-war markets.
   c. Removal, by international agreement and otherwise, of impediments to the exploitation of Middle Eastern concessions held by United States nationals.

4. In order that adequate supplies of Eastern Hemisphere petroleum may be available to the United States to permit it to take appropriate part in a system of collective security, steps should be taken to safeguard existing concessions held abroad by United States nationals. These steps are:
   a. To use diplomatic assistance where necessary to assure against alienation of those concessions.
   b. To arrive at an international understanding concerning the development of Middle Eastern petroleum resources free from unilateral political intervention.

5. This Government should endeavor to assure maximum economic benefits to the foreign areas in which petroleum is located.

II. Application of the Policy to Middle Eastern Petroleum
Consideration has been given to the question of whether the accelerating depletion of United States oil reserves necessitates formulation

of a program for Government-sponsored net imports of petroleum from the Middle East to the United States, either for current consumption or stockpiling or both. The evidence of the necessity for such a program is not conclusive. Furthermore, the complex political and economic difficulties that would be involved render the program unwise.

A broad policy of conservation of Western Hemisphere reserves, however, does call for curtailment, in so far as practicable, of the flow of petroleum and its products from Western Hemisphere sources to Eastern Hemisphere markets. The logical and natural source of supply for these latter markets is the Eastern Hemisphere terminus of the oil axis, i.e., the broad area of sedimentary basins contiguous to the Black, Caspian and Red Seas, the Persian Gulf and the eastern end of the Mediterranean. These geologic regions include the great developed oilfields of Russia, Roumania, Iraq, Iran and the Arabian Peninsula as well as the potential petroleum resources of Turkey, the Levantine Coastal areas, Afghanistan and Baluchistan. These latter areas are as yet almost entirely undeveloped. Russian oil production, unless the tempo of exploitation is greatly accelerated, will probably continue to be barely adequate for Russia's expanding industrial requirements. Roumania has historically been a significant supplier of the European market and presumably will continue to be such; but Roumania cannot supply more than a fraction of Europe's requirements.

It is then, toward the remainder of this geologic region that the Eastern Hemisphere should logically turn for oil supplies—toward the Middle East—toward Iran, Iraq, and the Arabian peninsula including Saudi Arabia proper and the Sheikhdoms of Kuwait, Bahrein, Qatar and Trucial Oman. It is primarily with respect to these Middle Eastern areas, then that United States policy must be formulated and implemented.

The key points in that policy must be (a) development, and (b) assurance of adequate American participation in that development.

Prompt, full and orderly development of the known reserves of the area should be achieved in order to permit annual Middle Eastern production to supply the expanding net import requirements of Europe, Africa and such parts of Asia as are not more economically supplied from the East Indies. This in turn will conserve Western Hemisphere oil reserves for Western Hemisphere peace-time uses and as a security reserve in the event of War. Moreover, such development will create a potential outside source of supply for the United States in the event that the recent unfavorable curve of domestic discoveries should not take a turn for the better.

In so far as such development is delayed by existing conflicts of short-run interest between the United States and the United Kingdom, and is impeded by existing political and contractual restrictions upon United States companies having concession rights and proprietary interests in the Middle East, a close understanding with the British is most desirable in order to effectuate the basic United States policy.

American participation in the development of Middle Eastern petroleum is equitable because American interests hold a large percentage of proven reserves in that area and participate only to a minor extent in current production. Such participation is desirable because there will then be greater assurance that the tempo of exploitation will be adequate in relation to the desired conservation of Western Hemisphere oil reserves. Furthermore, and of greater importance, United States policy should, in general, aim to assure to this country, in the interest of security, a substantial and geographically diversified holding of foreign petroleum resources in the hands of United States nationals. This would involve the preservation of the absolute position presently obtaining, and therefore vigilant protection of existing concessions in United States hands coupled with insistence upon the Open Door principle of equal opportunity for United States companies in new areas.

The United States petroleum policy in the Middle East, then, must be predicated upon these two overall objectives: (a) full development of Middle Eastern Petroleum production, and (b) the stabilization and safeguarding of American concession rights. The more specific policy objectives are as follows:

1. An intergovernmental understanding with the United Kingdom should be reached immediately on broad principles governing petroleum development and distribution with particular reference to a development program for the Middle Eastern area. This understanding should provide for the establishment of a joint Anglo-American Petroleum Commission, the functions of which are summarized in Part IV hereof.

This bilateral understanding with the United Kingdom should be preliminary to the early negotiation of a multilateral agreement establishing an International Petroleum Council with appropriate representation for producing and consuming countries.

2. A second specific policy objective should be to provide protection against alienation of American-held concessions into non-American hands. To accomplish this it is necessary to forestall those factors that might operate in the direction of alienating American-controlled concessions. They include:
   a. Failure to exploit such concessions fully with the resultant failure to confer upon the countries granting the concessions those benefits which they legitimately anticipated as a consequence of discovery of oil within their domains;
   b. Failure to foresee and guard against political complications that might develop.

Any proposal of American-owned companies to transfer, in whole or in part, assets in foreign-held petroleum reserves should be subject to prior approval by this Government.

3. A third specific policy objective should be to influence the flow of world trade in petroleum products in such manner as to substitute Middle Eastern oil for Western Hemisphere oil in Eastern Hemisphere markets with due regard for the legitimate interests of the Western Hemisphere. This substitution may come about in consequence of natural economic forces once Middle Eastern production has been adequately stimulated.

4. A fourth objective should be to eliminate the unilateral political intervention that has characterized Middle Eastern petroleum affairs heretofore. This will come about necessarily after the negotiation of the proposed multilateral agreement and the establishment of the proposed International Petroleum Council. In the meanwhile, the preliminary bilateral understanding with the Government of the United Kingdom should include reciprocal assurances that petroleum development, processing and marketing shall not be impeded either by restrictions imposed unilaterally by either Government or by intercompany arrangements.

5. In implementation of the equal access clause of the Atlantic Charter, any international agreements should guarantee equality of treatment to all purchasers in respect of prices, quantities, and terms and conditions of sale. In this connection, it would be desirable to reach an agreed definition of the equal access concept as applicable to petroleum supplies which would assure outside buyers of continuing opportunity to purchase oil at a price based upon true cost plus a reasonable profit.

III. Relation of the Policy to Latin American Petroleum

The effect of the change in the flow chart of world petroleum trade, contemplated by the foregoing policy objectives, on the established marketing interests of Latin American producing countries must receive full consideration. The maximum provision that might be made to safeguard these interests would be firm guarantees with respect to minimum quantities of Latin American petroleum to be absorbed annually by the United States market. This would immobilize the trade position of a particular segment in an industry subject to continuing change and would, therefore, be undesirable. It is, nevertheless, necessary to provide reasonable safeguards for the legitimate interests of Latin American producing countries. To this end, it is imperative that these countries be accorded an effective participation in the proposed International Petroleum Council.

IV. Implementation of the Policy

1. An immediate objective of the forthcoming conversations with the British, as indicated in Part II, is to reach an understanding with the Government of the United Kingdom on the broad principles governing petroleum development and distribution, with particular reference to the Middle East. To effectuate this understanding, provision establishing a joint Anglo-American Petroleum Commission should be included in the accord.

The agreement establishing this Commission should embody the principles enunciated in Parts I and II hereof. This agreement should be designed to accomplish, among other things, these ends:

   a. Schedule aggregate exports from the Middle Eastern area to meet expanding demand. To realize this end it is necessary to work out a flexible schedule of probable import requirements of Eastern Hemisphere markets. This schedule must make allowance for probable rate of annual increase in consumption, for indigenous production, and for probable imports from other sources of supply. The aggregate volume of export so determined should be allocated among the various producing countries on some equitable basis.

   b. Assure adequate representation of consuming countries in the determination of export schedules and price arrangements.

   c. Consider problems arising in connection with the distribution of Middle Eastern petroleum, all conclusions reached to be consistent with any relevant international understandings.

   d. Assure equitably distributed economic benefits to all the producing areas affected.

   e. Abolish restrictions on production, refining, transportation and exports of petroleum from concession reserves held solely or jointly by American and/or non-American interests, in so far as inconsistent with the terms of the contemplated agreement.

   f. Provide that the two countries will make their petroleum resources available to each other and to all friendly countries in emergencies or for security reasons, consistently with whatever collective security arrangements may be established.

2. Furthermore, the understanding should include the following:

   a. That the two Governments will propose to other interested countries a multilateral petroleum convention based upon the principles adopted in the bilateral agreement; and

   b. That this multilateral convention will establish an International Petroleum Council, and indicate the views of the two Governments concerning the appropriate composition, functions and purposes of such a Council.

Source: U.S. Department of State, *Foreign Relations of the United States, Diplomatic Papers, 1944*, Vol. 5, *The Near East, South Asia, and Africa, the Far East* (Washington, DC: U.S. Government Printing Office, 1965), 27–33.

26. Alexandria Protocol [Excerpt], October 7, 1944

Introduction

During World War II several Arab states, most notably Syria and Lebanon, seized the opportunity available to them to win full independence from colonial overlordship, and all in all the experience of war encouraged and strengthened nationalist forces. Seeking to maximize both their leverage on the Western powers and their international weight, in late September and early October 1944 delegates from Egypt, Iraq, Transjordan, Saudi Arabia, Syria, Lebanon, and Yemen met in Alexandria, Egypt, for a conference on Arab unity. Observers from Palestine, Morocco, Tunisia, and Algeria also attended. The conferees drafted a protocol establishing the League of Independent Arab States to encourage cooperation on political, social, cultural, and economic matters. They specifically affirmed their support for the rights of the Arabs of Palestine and called for a cessation of Jewish immigration to Palestine and the establishment of an independent Arab state there. On March 22, 1945, all the participating states except Yemen, which joined two months later, signed the pact. As they gained independence, other Arab states would subsequently join the organization. From its inception onward, the Arab League formed a bloc self-consciously committed to protecting the interests of the Arabs of Palestine. This outlook meant that without the acquiescence of its member states, reaching a permanent settlement of the Palestine question and subsequently the Arab-Israeli question would be almost impossible.

Primary Source

The undersigned, chiefs and members of Arab delegations at the Preliminary Committee of the General Arab Conference, viz:

The President of Preliminary Committee
H.E. Mustafa al-Nahhas Pasha, Egyptian Prime Minister and Minister of Foreign Affairs; head of the Egyptian delegation;

Syrian Delegation
H.E. Sa'dallah al-Jabiri, Syrian Prime Minister and head of the Syrian delegation;
H.E. Jamil Mardam Bey, Minister of Foreign Affairs;
H E. Dr. Nagib al-Armanazi, Secretary General of the Presidency of the Syrian Republic;
H.E. M. Sabri al-'Asali, deputy of Damascus;

Trans-Jordanian Delegation
H.E. Tawfiq Abu al-Huda Pasha, Trans-Jordanian Prime Minister and Minister of Foreign Affairs, head of the Trans-Jordanian delegation;
H.E. Sulayman al-Sukkar Bey, Financial Secretary of the Ministry of Foreign Affairs;

Iraqi Delegation
H.E. Hamdi al-Bahjaji, Iraqi Prime Minister and head of the Iraqi delegation;
H.E. Arshad al-'Umari, Minister of Foreign Affairs;
H.E. Nuri al-Sa'id, former Iraqi Prime Minister;
H. E. Tahsin al-'Askari, Iraqi Minister Plenipotentiary in Egypt;

Lebanese Delegation
H.E. Riyad al-Sulh Bey, Lebanese Prime Minister and head of the Lebanese delegation;

H.E. Salim Taqla Bey, Minister of Foreign Affairs;
H.E. Musa Mubarak, Chief of the Presidential Cabinet;

Egyptian Delegation
H.E. Nagib al-Hilali Pasha, Minister of Education;
H.E. Muhammad Sabri Aub-'Alam Pasha, Minister of Justice;
H.E. Muhammad Salah-al-din Bey, Under Secretary of State of the Ministry of Foreign Affairs,

Anxious to strengthen and consolidate the ties which bind all Arab countries and to direct them toward the welfare of the Arab world, to improve its conditions, insure its future, and realize its hopes and aspirations.

And in response to Arab public opinion in countries,
Have met at Alexandria from Shawwal 8, 1363 (September 25, 1944) to Shawwal 20,1363 (October 7,1944) in the form of a Preliminary Committee of the General Arab Conference, and have agreed as follows:

1. League of Arab States
A League will be formed of the independent Arab States which consent to join the League. It will have a council which will be known as the "Council of the League of Arab States" in which all participating states will be represented on an equal footing.

The object of the League will be to control the execution of the agreements which the above states will conclude; to hold periodic meetings which will strengthen the relations between those states; to coordinate their political plans so as to insure their cooperation, and protect their independence and sovereignty against every aggression by suitable means; and to supervise in a general way the affairs and interests of the Arab countries.

The decisions of the Council will be binding on those who have accepted them except in cases where a disagreement arises between two member states of the League in which the two parties shall refer their dispute to the Council for solution. In this case the decision of the Council of the League will be binding.

In no case will resort to force to settle a dispute between any two member states of the League be allowed. But every state shall be free to conclude with any other member state of the League, or other powers, special agreements which do not contradict the text or the present dispositions.

In no case will the adoption of a foreign policy which may be prejudicial to the policy of the League or an individual member state be allowed.

The Council will intervene in every dispute which may lead to war between a member state of the League and any other member state or power, so as to reconcile them.

A subcommittee will be formed of the members of the Preliminary Committee to prepare a draft of the statutes of the Council of the League and to examine the political questions which may be the object of agreement among Arab States.

2. Cooperation in Economic, Cultural, Social, and Other Matters

A. The Arab States represented on the Preliminary Committee shall closely cooperate in the following matters:

(1) Economic and financial matters, i.e., commercial exchange, customs, currency, agriculture, and industry.
(2) Communications, i.e., railways, roads, aviation, navigation, posts and telegraphs.
(3) Cultural matters.
(4) Questions of nationality, passports, visas, execution of judgments, extradition of criminals, etc.
(5) Social questions.
(6) Questions of public health.

[...]

4. Special Resolution Concerning Lebanon

The Arab States represented on the Preliminary Committee emphasize their respect of the independence and sovereignty of Lebanon in its present frontiers, which the governments of the above States have already recognized in consequence of Lebanon's adoption of an independent policy, which the Government of that country announced in its program of October 7, 1943, unanimously approved by the Lebanese Chamber of Deputies.

5. Special Resolution Concerning Palestine

A. The Committee is of the opinion that Palestine constitutes an important part of the Arab World and that the rights of the Arabs in Palestine cannot be touched without prejudice to peace and stability in the Arab World.

The Committee also is of the opinion that the pledges binding the British Government and providing for the cessation of Jewish immigration, the preservation of Arab lands, and the achievement of independence for Palestine are permanent Arab rights whose prompt implementation would constitute a step toward the desired goal and toward the stabilization of peace and security.

The Committee declares its support of the cause of the Arabs of Palestine and its willingness to work for the achievement of their legitimate aims and the safeguarding of their just rights.

The Committee also declares that it is second to none in regretting the woes which have been inflicted upon the Jews of Europe by European dictatorial states. But the question of these Jews should not be confused with Zionism, for there can be no greater injustice and aggression than solving the problem of the Jews of Europe by another injustice, i.e., by inflicting injustice on the Arabs of Palestine of various religions and denominations.

B. The special proposal concerning the participation of the Arab Governments and peoples in the "Arab National Fund" to safeguard the lands of the Arabs of Palestine shall be referred to the committee of financial and economic affairs to examine it from all its angles and to submit the result of that examination to the Preliminary Committee in its next meeting.

[...]

Pact of the League of Arab States
March 22, 1945

Article 1.—The League of Arab States shall be composed of the independent Arab States that have signed this Pact.

Every Independent Arab State shall have the right to adhere to the League. Should it desire to adhere, it shall present an application to this effect which shall be filed with the permanent General Secretariat and submitted to the Council at its first meeting following the presentation of the application.

Article 2.—The purpose of the League is to draw closer the relations between member States and co-ordinate their political activities with the aim of realizing a close collaboration between them, to safeguard their independence and sovereignty, and to consider in a general way the affairs and interests of the Arab countries.

It also has among its purposes a close co-operation of the member States with due regard to the structure of each of these States and the conditions prevailing therein, in the following matters:

(a) Economic and financial matters, including trade, customs, currency, agriculture and industry.
(b) Communications, including railways, roads, aviation, navigation, and posts and telegraphs.
(c) Cultural matters.
(d) Matters connected with nationality, passports, visas, execution of judgments and extradition.
(e) Social welfare matters.
(f) Health matters.

Article 3.—The League shall have a Council composed of the representatives of the member States. Each State shall have one vote, regardless of the number of its representatives.

The Council shall be entrusted with the function of realizing the purpose of the League and of supervising the execution of the agreements concluded between the member States on matters referred to in the preceding article or on other matters.

It shall also have the function of determining the means whereby the League will collaborate with the international organizations which may be created in the future to guarantee peace and security and organize economic and social relations.

[...]

Article 5.—The recourse to force for the settlement of disputes between two or more member States shall not be allowed. Should there arise among them a dispute that does not involve the independence of a State, its sovereignty or its territorial integrity, and should the two contending parties apply to the Council for the settlement of this dispute, the decision of the Council shall then be effective and obligatory.

In this case, the States among whom the dispute has arisen shall not participate in the deliberations and decisions of the Council.

The Council shall mediate in a dispute which may lead to war between two member States or between a member State and another State in order to conciliate them.

The decisions relating to arbitration and mediation shall be taken by a majority vote.

[...]

Article 7.—The decisions of the Council taken by a unanimous vote shall be binding on all the member States of the League; those that are reached by a majority vote shall bind only those that accept them.

In both cases the decisions of the Council shall be executed in each State in accordance with the fundamental structure of that State.

Article 8.—Every member State of the League shall respect the form of government obtaining in the other States of the League, and shall recognize the form of government obtaining as one of the rights of those States, and shall pledge itself not to take any action tending to change that form.

[...]

Article 18.—If one of the member States intends to withdraw from the League, the Council shall be informed of its intention one year before the withdrawal takes effect.

The Council of the League may consider any State that is not fulfilling the obligations resulting from this Pact as excluded from the League, by a decision taken by a unanimous vote of all the States except the State referred to.

[...]

Source: "Text of the Alexandria Protocol," *Department of State Bulletin* 16 (411) (1947): 966–967. "Pact of the League of Arab States," *United Nations Treaty Series* 70(241) (March 22, 1945).

27. United Nations General Assembly Resolution 181, Future Government of Palestine [Excerpt], November 29, 1947

Introduction

After lengthy debate, on November 29, 1947, the United Nations (UN) General Assembly voted on the plan to partition Palestine into independent Arab and Jewish states put forward in the report of the United Nations Special Committee on Palestine (UNSCOP). Both the Soviet Union and the United States voted in favor of UN General Assembly Resolution 181, which described this plan, as did 31 other UN member states. Thirteen member states, including all the Arab states, voted in opposition: Afghanistan, Cuba, Egypt, Greece, India, Iran, Iraq, Lebanon, Pakistan, Saudi Arabia, Syria, Turkey, and Yemen. Ten member states, including the United Kingdom and several Latin American states as well as Yugoslavia and China, abstained. Besides advocating the partition of Palestine into Arab and Jewish states and ending the British mandate no later than August 1948 (sooner if possible), Resolution 181 also supported the creation of a zone under international administration that would include the highly religiously significant towns of Jerusalem and Bethlehem. The Jewish state included a substantial Arab minority, 45 percent of the total population, whereas only 1 percent of the inhabitants of the proposed Arab state would be Jewish. The bulk of Jews and Jewish groups in Palestine supported the partition, whereas it was highly unpopular with the Arabs within Palestine, most of whom refused to accept it. Arab attacks on Jewish individuals and businesses began almost immediately. Other Arab nations also declined to endorse the plan, sought to challenge it in the International Court of Justice, and passed resolutions at November and December 1947 meetings of the Arab League that envisaged taking military action to prevent fulfillment of the resolution. The British government, still the mandatory power, declined to try to implement partition on the grounds that it did not have the support of both parties involved and also refused to share the administration of Palestine with the UN Palestine Commission in the transitional period up to May 15, 1948. Jewish residents of areas in Palestine designated as part of the Arab state, together with inhabitants of Arab states elsewhere in the region, mostly fled to those regions earmarked to form the Jewish state, while Arab refugees likewise left what they feared would soon be hostile Jewish territories. All anticipated that as soon as the mandate ended, the bitter internecine Arab-Jewish fighting that began virtually as soon as Resolution 181 was passed would intensify, and that Arab nations would attack the new State of Israel.

Primary Source

The General Assembly,

[...]

Recommends to the United Kingdom, as the mandatory Power for Palestine, and to all other Members of the United Nations the adoption and implementation, with regard to the future Government of Palestine, of the Plan of Partition with Economic Union set out below;

Requests that

(a) The Security Council take the necessary measures as provided for in the plan for its implementation;

(b) The Security Council consider, if circumstances during the transitional period require such consideration, whether the situation in Palestine constitutes a threat to the peace. If it decides that such a threat exists, and in order to maintain international peace and security, the Security Council should supplement the authorization of the General Assembly by taking measures, under Articles 39 and 41 of the Charter, to empower the United Nations Commission, as provided in this resolution, to exercise in Palestine the functions which are assigned to it by this resolution;

(c) The Security Council determine as a threat to the peace, breach of the peace or act of aggression, in accordance with Article 39 of the Charter, any attempt to alter by force the settlement envisaged by this resolution;

(d) The Trusteeship Council be informed of the responsibilities envisaged for it in this plan;

Calls upon the inhabitants of Palestine to take such steps as may be necessary on their part to put this plan into effect;

Appeals to all Governments and all peoples to refrain from taking any action which might hamper or delay the carrying out of these recommendations;

[...]

PLAN OF PARTITION WITH ECONOMIC UNION
Part I.—Future Constitution and Government of Palestine
A. TERMINATION OF MANDATE, PARTITION AND INDEPENDENCE
1. The Mandate for Palestine shall terminate as soon as possible but in any case not later than 1 August 1948.

2. The armed forces of the mandatory Power shall be progressively withdrawn from Palestine, the withdrawal to be completed as soon as possible but in any case not later than 1 August 1948.

The mandatory Power shall advise the Commission, as far in advance as possible, of its intention to terminate the mandate and to evacuate each area.

The mandatory Power shall use its best endeavours to ensure that an area situated in the territory of the Jewish State, including a seaport and hinterland adequate to provide facilities for a substantial immigration, shall be evacuated at the earliest possible date and in any event not later than 1 February 1948.

3. Independent Arab and Jewish States and the Special International Regime for the City of Jerusalem, set forth in part III of this Plan, shall come into existence in Palestine two months after the evacuation of the armed forces of the mandatory Power has been completed but in any case not later than 1 October 1948. The boundaries of the Arab State, the Jewish State, and the City of Jerusalem shall be as described in Parts II and III below.

4. The period between the adoption by the General Assembly of its recommendation on the question of Palestine and the establishment of the independence of the Arab and Jewish States shall be a transitional period.

B. STEPS PREPARATORY TO INDEPENDENCE
1. A Commission shall be set up consisting of one representative of each of five Member States. The Members represented on the Commission shall be elected by the General Assembly on as broad a basis, geographically and otherwise, as possible.

2. The administration of Palestine shall, as the mandatory Power withdraws its armed forces, be progressively turned over to the Commission, which shall act in conformity with the recommendations of the General Assembly, under the guidance of the Security Council. The mandatory Power shall to the fullest possible extent coordinate its plans for withdrawal with the plans of the Commission to take over and administer areas which have been evacuated.
In the discharge of this administrative responsibility the Commission shall have authority to issue necessary regulations and take other measures as required.

The mandatory Power shall not take any action to prevent, obstruct or delay the implementation by the Commission of the measures recommended by the General Assembly.

3. On its arrival in Palestine the Commission shall proceed to carry out measures for the establishment of the frontiers of the Arab and Jewish States and the City of Jerusalem in accordance with the general lines of the recommendations of the General Assembly on the partition of Palestine. Nevertheless, the boundaries as described in part II of this Plan are to be modified in such a way that village areas as a rule will not be divided by state boundaries unless pressing reasons make that necessary.

4. The Commission, after consultation with the democratic parties and other public organizations of the Arab and Jewish States, shall select and establish in each State as rapidly as possible a Provisional Council of Government. The activities of both the Arab and Jewish Provisional Councils of Government shall be carried out under the general direction of the Commission.

[...]

7. The Commission shall instruct the Provisional Councils of Government of both the Arab and Jewish States, after their formation, to proceed to the establishment of administrative organs of government, central and local.

8. The Provisional Council of Government of each State shall, within the shortest time possible, recruit an armed militia from the residents of that State, sufficient in number to maintain internal order and to prevent frontier clashes.

This armed militia in each State shall, for operational purposes, be under the command of Jewish or Arab officers resident in that State, but general political and military control, including the choice of the militia's High Command, shall be exercised by the Commission.

9. The Provisional Council of Government of each State shall, not later than two months after the withdrawal of the armed forces of the mandatory Power, hold elections to the Constituent Assembly which shall be conducted on democratic lines.

The election regulations in each State shall be drawn up by the Provisional Council of Government and approved by the Commission. Qualified voters for each State for this election shall be persons over eighteen years of age who are: (a) Palestinian citizens residing in that State and (b) Arabs and Jews residing in the State, although not Palestinian citizens, who, before voting, have signed a notice of intention to become citizens of such State.

Arabs and Jews residing in the City of Jerusalem who have signed a notice of intention to become citizens, the Arabs of the Arab State and the Jews of the Jewish State, shall be entitled to vote in the Arab and Jewish States respectively.

Women may vote and be elected to the Constituent Assemblies.

During the transitional period no Jew shall be permitted to establish residence in the area of the proposed Arab State, and no Arab shall be permitted to establish residence in the area of the proposed Jewish State, except by special leave of the Commission.

10. The Constituent Assembly of each State shall draft a democratic constitution for its State and choose a provisional government to succeed the Provisional Council of Government appointed by the Commission. The Constitutions of the States shall embody Chapters 1 and 2 of the Declaration provided for in section C below and include, *inter alia,* provisions for:

(a) Establishing in each State a legislative body elected by universal suffrage and by secret ballot on the basis of proportional representation, and an executive body responsible to the legislature;

(b) Settling all international disputes in which the State may be involved by peaceful means in such a manner that international peace and security, and justice, are not endangered;

(c) Accepting the obligation of the State to refrain in its international relations from the threat or use of force against the territorial integrity or political independence of any State, or in any other manner inconsistent with the purposes of the United Nations;

(d) Guaranteeing to all persons equal and non-discriminatory rights in civil, political, economic and religious matters and the enjoyment of human rights and fundamental freedoms, including freedom of religion, language, speech and publication, education, assembly and association;

(e) Preserving freedom of transit and visit for all residents and citizens of the other State in Palestine and the City of Jerusalem, subject to considerations of national security, provided that each State shall control residence within its borders.

[...]

D. ECONOMIC UNION AND TRANSIT

1. The Provisional Council of Government of each State shall enter into an undertaking with respect to Economic Union and Transit. This undertaking shall be drafted by the Commission provided for in section B, paragraph 1, utilizing to the greatest possible extent the advice and cooperation of representative organizations and bodies from each of the proposed States. It shall contain provisions to establish the Economic Union of Palestine and provide for other matters of common interest. If by 1 April 1948 the Provisional Councils of Government have not entered into the undertaking, the undertaking shall be put into force by the Commission.

The Economic Union of Palestine

2. The objectives of the Economic Union of Palestine shall be:

(a) A customs union;

(b) A joint currency system providing for a single foreign exchange rate;

(c) Operation in the common interest on a non-discriminatory basis of railways; inter-State highways; postal, telephone and telegraphic services, and ports and airports involved in international trade and commerce;

(d) Joint economic development, especially in respect of irrigation, land reclamation and soil conservation;

(e) Access for both States and for the City of Jerusalem on a non-discriminatory basis to water and power facilities.

[...]

7. In relation to economic development, the functions of the Board shall be planning, investigation and encouragement of joint development projects, but it shall not undertake such projects except with the assent of both States and the City of Jerusalem, in the event that Jerusalem is directly involved in the development project.

8. In regard to the joint currency system, the currencies circulating in the two States and the City of Jerusalem shall be issued under the authority of the Joint Economic Board, which shall be the sole issuing authority and which shall determine the reserves to be held against such currencies.

9. So far as is consistent with paragraph 2(b) above, each State may operate its own central bank, control its own fiscal and credit policy, its foreign exchange receipts and expenditures, the grant of import licenses, and may conduct international financial operations on its own faith and credit. . . .

10. All economic authority not specifically vested in the Joint Economic Board is reserved to each State.

11. There shall be a common customs tariff with complete freedom of trade between the States, and between the States and the City of Jerusalem.

[...]

Freedom of Transit and Visit
18. The undertaking shall contain provisions preserving freedom of transit and visit for all residents or citizens of both States and of the City of Jerusalem, subject to security considerations; provided that each State and the City shall control residence within its borders.

Termination, Modification and Interpretation of the Undertaking
19. The undertaking and any treaty issuing therefrom shall remain in force for a period of ten years. It shall continue in force until notice of termination, to take effect two years thereafter, is given by either of the parties.

[...]

E. ASSETS
1. The movable assets of the Administration of Palestine shall be allocated to the Arab and Jewish States and the City of Jerusalem on an equitable basis. Allocations should be made by the United Nations Commission referred to in section B, paragraph 1, above.

Immovable assets shall become the property of the government of the territory in which they are situated.

[...]

F. ADMISSION TO MEMBERSHIP IN THE UNITED NATIONS
When the independence of either the Arab or the Jewish State as envisaged in this plan has become effective and the declaration and undertaking, as envisaged in this plan, have been signed by either of them, sympathetic consideration should be given to its application for admission to membership in the United Nations in accordance with article 4 of the Charter of the United Nations.

[...]

Part III.—City of Jerusalem
A. SPECIAL REGIME
The City of Jerusalem shall be established as a *corpus separatum* under a special international regime and shall be administered by the United Nations. The Trusteeship Council shall be designated to discharge the responsibilities of the Administering Authority on behalf of the United Nations.

B. BOUNDARIES OF THE CITY
The City of Jerusalem shall include the present municipality of Jerusalem plus the surrounding villages and towns, the most eastern of which shall be Abu Dis; the most southern, Bethlehem; the most western, Ein Karim (including also the built-up area of Motsa); and the most northern Shu'fat, as indicated on the attached sketch-map. . . .

C. STATUTE OF THE CITY
The Trusteeship Council shall, within five months of the approval of the present plan, elaborate and approve a detailed statute of the City which shall contain, *inter alia,* the substance of the following provisions:

1. *Government machinery; special objectives.* The Administering Authority in discharging its administrative obligations shall pursue the following special objectives:
   (a) To protect and to preserve the unique spiritual and religious interests located in the city of the three great monotheistic faiths throughout the world, Christian, Jewish and Moslem; to this end to ensure that order and peace, and especially religious peace, reign in Jerusalem;
   (b) To foster cooperation among all the inhabitants of the city in their own interests as well as in order to encourage and support the peaceful development of the mutual relations between the two Palestinian peoples throughout the Holy Land; to promote the security, well-being and any constructive measures of development of the residents having regard

to the special circumstances and customs of the various peoples and communities.

2. *Governor and administrative staff.* A Governor of the City of Jerusalem shall be appointed by the Trusteeship Council and shall be responsible to it. He shall be selected on the basis of special qualifications and without regard to nationality. He shall not, however, be a citizen of either State in Palestine.

The Governor shall represent the United Nations in the City and shall exercise on their behalf all powers of administration, including the conduct of external affairs. He shall be assisted by an administrative staff classed as international officers in the meaning of Article 100 of the Charter and chosen whenever practicable from the residents of the city and of the rest of Palestine on a non-discriminatory basis. A detailed plan for the organization of the administration of the city shall be submitted by the Governor to the Trusteeship Council and duly approved by it.

[...]

4. *Security measures.*
   (a) The City of Jerusalem shall be demilitarized; its neutrality shall be declared and preserved, and no para-military formations, exercises or activities shall be permitted within its borders.
   (b) Should the administration of the City of Jerusalem be seriously obstructed or prevented by the non-cooperation or interference of one or more sections of the population the Governor shall have authority to take such measures as may be necessary to restore the effective functioning of administration.
   (c) To assist in the maintenance of internal law and order, especially for the protection of the Holy Places and religious buildings and sites in the city, the Governor shall organize a special police force of adequate strength, the members of which shall be recruited outside of Palestine. The Governor shall be empowered to direct such budgetary provision as may be necessary for the maintenance of this force.

5. *Legislative organization.* A Legislative Council, elected by adult residents of the city irrespective of nationality on the basis of universal and secret suffrage and proportional representation, shall have powers of legislation and taxation. No legislative measures shall, however, conflict or interfere with the provisions which will be set forth in the Statute of the City, nor shall any law, regulation, or official action prevail over them. The Statute shall grant to the Governor a right of vetoing bills inconsistent with the provisions referred to in the preceding sentence. It shall also empower him to promulgate temporary ordinances in case the Council fails to adopt in time a bill deemed essential to the normal functioning of the administration.

[...]

8. *Freedom of transit and visit; control of residents.*

Subject to considerations of security, and of economic welfare as determined by the Governor under the directions of the Trusteeship Council, freedom of entry into, and residence within, the borders of the City shall be guaranteed for the residents or citizens of the Arab and Jewish States. Immigration into, and residence within, the borders of the city for nationals of other States shall be controlled by the Governor under the directions of the Trusteeship Council.

9. *Relations with the Arab and Jewish States.* Representatives of the Arab and Jewish States shall be accredited to the Governor of the City and charged with the protection of the interests of their States and nationals in connection with the international administration of the City.

10. *Official languages.* Arabic and Hebrew shall be the official languages of the city. This will not preclude the adoption of one or more additional working languages, as may be required.

11. *Citizenship.* All the residents shall become *ipso facto* citizens of the City of Jerusalem unless they opt for citizenship of the State of which they have been citizens or, if Arabs or Jews, have filed notice of intention to become citizens of the Arab or Jewish State respectively, according to Part 1, section B, paragraph 9, of this Plan.

The Trusteeship Council shall make arrangements for consular protection of the citizens of the City outside its territory.

12. *Freedoms of citizens.*
   (a) Subject only to the requirements of public order and morals, the inhabitants of the City shall be ensured the enjoyment of human rights and fundamental freedoms, including freedom of conscience, religion and worship, language, education, speech and press, assembly and association, and petition.
   (b) No discrimination of any kind shall be made between the inhabitants on the grounds of race, religion, language or sex.
   (c) All persons within the City shall be entitled to equal protection of the laws.
   (d) The family law and personal status of the various persons and communities and their religious interests, including endowments, shall be respected.
   (e) Except as may be required for the maintenance of public order and good government, no measure shall be taken to obstruct or interfere with the enterprise of religious or charitable bodies of all faiths or to discriminate against any representative or member of these bodies on the ground of his religion or nationality.

(f) The City shall ensure adequate primary and secondary education for the Arab and Jewish communities respectively, in their own languages and in accordance with their cultural traditions. The right of each community to maintain its own schools for the education of its own members in its own language, while conforming to such educational requirements of a general nature as the City may impose, shall not be denied or impaired. Foreign educational establishments shall continue their activity on the basis of their existing rights.

(g) No restriction shall be imposed on the free use by any inhabitant of the City of any language in private intercourse, in commerce, in religion, in the Press or in publications of any kind, or at public meetings.

13. *Holy Places.*

(a) Existing rights in respect of Holy Places and religious buildings or sites shall not be denied or impaired.

(b) Free access to the Holy Places and religious buildings or sites and the free exercise of worship shall be secured in conformity with existing rights and subject to the requirements of public order and decorum.

(c) Holy Places and religious buildings or sites shall be preserved. No act shall be permitted which may in any way impair their sacred character. If at any time it appears to the Governor that any particular Holy Place, religious building or site is in need of urgent repair, the Governor may call upon the community or communities concerned to carry out such repair. The Governor may carry it out himself at the expense of the community or communities concerned if no action is taken within a reasonable time.

(d) No taxation shall be levied in respect of any Holy Place, religious building or site which was exempt from taxation on the date of the creation of the City. No change in the incidence of such taxation shall be made which would either discriminate between the owners or occupiers of Holy Places, religious buildings or sites or would place such owners or occupiers in a position less favourable in relation to the general incidence of taxation than existed at the time of the adoption of the Assembly's recommendations.

14. *Special powers of the Governor in respect of the Holy Places, religious buildings and sites in the City and in any part of Palestine.*

(a) The protection of the Holy Places, religious buildings and sites located in the City of Jerusalem shall be a special concern of the Governor.

(b) With relation to such places, buildings and sites in Palestine outside the city, the Governor shall determine, on the ground of powers granted to him by the Constitution of both States, whether the provisions of the Constitution of the Arab and Jewish States in Palestine dealing therewith and the religious rights appertaining thereto are being properly applied and respected.

(c) The Governor shall also be empowered to make decisions on the basis of existing rights in cases of disputes which may arise between the different religious communities or the rites of a religious community in respect of the Holy Places, religious buildings and sites in any part of Palestine.

In this task he may be assisted by a consultative council of representatives of different denominations acting in an advisory capacity.

D. DURATION OF THE SPECIAL REGIME

The Statute elaborated by the Trusteeship Council on the aforementioned principles shall come into force not later than 1 October 1948. It shall remain in force in the first instance for a period of ten years, unless the Trusteeship Council finds it necessary to undertake a re-examination of these provisions at an earlier date. After the expiration of this period the whole scheme shall be subject to examination by the Trusteeship Council in the light of experience acquired with its functioning. The residents of the City shall be then free to express by means of a referendum their wishes as to possible modifications of the regime of the City.

[. . .]

Source: United Nations General Assembly Official Records, 2nd Sess., *Future Government of Palestine*, G.A. Res. 181 (II), November 29, 1947.

28. The Declaration of the Establishment of the State of Israel, May 14, 1948

Introduction

On May 14, 1948, a few hours before the withdrawal of British troops from the Palestine Mandate, the National Council, consisting of representatives of Palestine's Jewish inhabitants and of the Zionists, met in Tel Aviv and approved the declaration of independence of the new state of Israel, or Eretz Israel. The declaration began by recalling the historic ties of the Jewish people to the land of Israel and recounted the history of more than 50 years of Zionist efforts, beginning with Theodor Herzl's establishment of the First Zionist Congress and the Balfour Declaration, to establish the new state. The declaration invoked the sufferings of Jews in Europe during the Nazi Holocaust and the efforts of Jewish fighters during World War II. After recalling the endorsement that the United Nations (UN) had given to the creation of a Jewish state, the authors proclaimed the existence of the new State of Israel. From midnight that evening, the declaration established a Provisional State Council, based on the existing National Council, to hold authority until elections could be held under a constitution still to be drawn up. The new State of Israel declared itself ready to welcome all Jews as immigrants, to work closely with the UN, and to cooperate harmoniously with the Arab inhabitants of Palestine and with all Arab states. The declaration proclaimed Israel's intention of living in peace with all. The authors of this declaration nonetheless undoubtedly knew that the withdrawal of British troops would prove the signal for immediate attack by the armed forces of Transjordan, Egypt, Syria, and other neighboring Arab countries and that the attainment of peace would depend on their ability to wield the sword.

Primary Source

ERETZ-ISRAEL [(Hebrew)—the Land of Israel, Palestine] was the birthplace of the Jewish people. Here their spiritual, religious and political identity was shaped. Here they first attained to statehood, created cultural values of national and universal significance and gave to the world the eternal Book of Books.

After being forcibly exiled from their land, the people kept faith with it throughout their Dispersion and never ceased to pray and hope for their return to it and for the restoration in it of their political freedom.

Impelled by this historic and traditional attachment, Jews strove in every successive generation to re-establish themselves in their ancient homeland. In recent decades they returned in their masses. Pioneers, ma'pilim [(Hebrew)—immigrants coming to Eretz-Israel in defiance of restrictive legislation] and defenders, they made deserts bloom, revived the Hebrew language, built villages and towns, and created a thriving community controlling its own economy and culture, loving peace but knowing how to defend itself, bringing the blessings of progress to all the country's inhabitants, and aspiring towards independent nationhood.

In the year 5657 (1897), at the summons of the spiritual father of the Jewish State, Theodor Herzl, the First Zionist Congress convened and proclaimed the right of the Jewish people to national rebirth in its own country.

This right was recognized in the Balfour Declaration of the 2nd November, 1917, and reaffirmed in the Mandate of the League of Nations which, in particular, gave international sanction to the historic connection between the Jewish people and Eretz-Israel and to the right of the Jewish people to rebuild its National Home.

The catastrophe which recently befell the Jewish people—the massacre of millions of Jews in Europe—was another clear demonstration of the urgency of solving the problem of its homelessness by re-establishing in Eretz-Israel the Jewish State, which would open the gates of the homeland wide to every Jew and confer upon the Jewish people the status of a fully privileged member of the comity of nations.

Survivors of the Nazi holocaust in Europe, as well as Jews from other parts of the world, continued to migrate to Eretz-Israel, undaunted by difficulties, restrictions and dangers, and never ceased to assert their right to a life of dignity, freedom and honest toil in their national homeland.

In the Second World War, the Jewish community of this country contributed its full share to the struggle of the freedom- and peace-loving nations against the forces of Nazi wickedness and, by the blood of its soldiers and its war effort, gained the right to be reckoned among the peoples who founded the United Nations.

On the 29th November, 1947, the United Nations General Assembly passed a resolution calling for the establishment of a Jewish State in Eretz-Israel; the General Assembly required the inhabitants of Eretz-Israel to take such steps as were necessary on their part for the implementation of that resolution. This recognition by the United Nations of the right of the Jewish people to establish their State is irrevocable.

This right is the natural right of the Jewish people to be masters of their own fate, like all other nations, in their own sovereign State.

ACCORDINGLY WE, MEMBERS OF THE PEOPLE'S COUNCIL, REPRESENTATIVES OF THE JEWISH COMMUNITY OF ERETZ-ISRAEL AND OF THE ZIONIST MOVEMENT, ARE HERE ASSEMBLED ON THE DAY OF THE TERMINATION OF THE BRITISH MANDATE OVER ERETZ-ISRAEL AND, BY VIRTUE OF OUR NATURAL AND HISTORIC RIGHT AND ON THE STRENGTH OF THE RESOLUTION OF THE UNITED NATIONS GENERAL ASSEMBLY, HEREBY DECLARE THE ESTABLISHMENT OF A JEWISH STATE IN ERETZ-ISRAEL, TO BE KNOWN AS THE STATE OF ISRAEL.

WE DECLARE that, with effect from the moment of the termination of the Mandate being tonight, the eve of Sabbath, the 6th Iyar, 5708 (15th May, 1948), until the establishment of the elected, regular authorities of the State in accordance with the Constitution which shall be adopted by the Elected Constituent Assembly not later than the 1st October 1948, the People's Council shall act as a Provisional Council of State, and its executive organ, the People's Administration, shall be the Provisional Government of the Jewish State, to be called "Israel".

THE STATE OF ISRAEL will be open for Jewish immigration and for the Ingathering of the Exiles; it will foster the development of the country for the benefit of all its inhabitants; it will be based on freedom, justice and peace as envisaged by the prophets of Israel; it will ensure complete equality of social and political rights to all its inhabitants irrespective of religion, race or sex; it will guarantee freedom of religion, conscience, language, education and culture; it will safeguard the Holy Places of all religions; and it will be faithful to the principles of the Charter of the United Nations.

THE STATE OF ISRAEL is prepared to cooperate with the agencies and representatives of the United Nations in implementing the resolution of the General Assembly of the 29th November, 1947, and will take steps to bring about the economic union of the whole of Eretz-Israel.

WE APPEAL to the United Nations to assist the Jewish people in the building-up of its State and to receive the State of Israel into the comity of nations.

WE APPEAL—in the very midst of the onslaught launched against us now for months—to the Arab inhabitants of the State of Israel to preserve peace and participate in the upbuilding of the State on the basis of full and equal citizenship and due representation in all its provisional and permanent institutions.

WE EXTEND our hand to all neighbouring states and their peoples in an offer of peace and good neighbourliness, and appeal to them to establish bonds of cooperation and mutual help with the sovereign Jewish people settled in its own land. The State of Israel is prepared to do its share in a common effort for the advancement of the entire Middle East.

WE APPEAL to the Jewish people throughout the Diaspora to rally round the Jews of Eretz-Israel in the tasks of immigration and up-building and to stand by them in the great struggle for the realization of the age-old dream—the redemption of Israel.

PLACING OUR TRUST IN THE "ROCK OF ISRAEL", WE AFFIX OUR SIGNATURES TO THIS PROCLAMATION AT THIS SESSION OF THE PROVISIONAL COUNCIL OF STATE, ON THE SOIL OF THE HOMELAND, IN THE CITY OF TEL-AVIV, ON THIS SABBATH EVE, THE 5TH DAY OF IYAR, 5708 (14TH MAY, 1948).

David Ben-Gurion
Daniel Auster
Mordekhai Bentov
Yitzchak Ben Zvi
Eliyahu Berligne
Fritz Bernstein
Rabbi Wolf Gold
Meir Grabovsky
Yitzchak Gruenbaum
Dr. Abraham Granovsky
Eliyahu Dobkin
Meir Wilner-Kovner
Zerach Wahrhaftig
Herzl Vardi
Rachel Cohen
Rabbi Kalman Kahana
Saadia Kobashi
Rabbi Yitzchak Meir Levin

Meir David Loewenstein
Zvi Luria
Golda Myerson
Nachum Nir
Zvi Segal
Rabbi Yehuda Leib Hacohen Fishman
David Zvi Pinkas
Aharon Zisling
Moshe Kolodny
Eliezer Kaplan
Abraham Katznelson
Felix Rosenblueth
David Remez
Berl Repetur
Mordekhai Shattner
Ben Zion Sternberg
Bekhor Shitreet
Moshe Shapira
Moshe Shertok

Source: The Declaration of the Establishment of the State of Israel, May 14, 1948, Israel Ministry of Foreign Affairs, http://www.mfa.gov.il/MFA.

29. U.S. Recognition of Israel, May 14, 1948

Introduction

Between the world wars hundreds of thousands of Jews immigrated to Palestine, where the local Arab community deeply resented their presence. After World War II, Zionists, often citing the deaths of 6 million European Jews at the hands of Hitler's Germany, again took up the cause of an independent Jewish state. Against the advice of Secretary of State George Marshall, who feared that creating such an entity would permanently alienate Arab countries throughout the oil-rich Middle East, President Harry S. Truman supported its creation in the former British mandate. Truman, an avid reader of history, had a romantic respect for the Jewish people's dedication to the restoration of the ancient state of Israel and also felt that they deserved compensation for their wartime sufferings. As soon as the State of Israel came into existence, Truman recognized it. Israel was immediately confronted by a military attack from its Arab neighbors, both the United States and the Soviet Union, which had also recognized the new state, sent massive arms shipments as they competed for its allegiance. Caught between the passionate support that American Jews accorded Israel and their fear of further alienating resentful and oil-rich Arab states, whose anger might propel them toward the Soviets, in 1948 U.S. officials launched the first of many successive and still continuing efforts to negotiate a lasting Middle East peace settlement between Arabs and Israelis. Meanwhile, the powerful domestic Jewish lobby ensured that the small, beleaguered Israeli state quickly became the single-largest recipient of U.S. military and economic aid, a virtual U.S. client.

Primary Source

Text of Letter from the Agent of the Provisional Government of Israel to the President of the U.S.
[Released to the Press by the White House on May 15]
My Dear Mr. President:

I have the honor to notify you that the state of Israel has been proclaimed as an independent republic within frontiers approved by the General Assembly of the United Nations in its Resolution of November 29, 1947, and that a provisional government has been charged to assume the rights and duties of government for preserving law and order within the boundaries of Israel, for defending the state against external aggression, and for discharging the obligations of Israel to the other nations of the world in accordance with international law. The Act of Independence will become effective at one minute after six o'clock on the evening of 14 May 1948, Washington time.

With full knowledge of the deep bond of sympathy which has existed and has been strengthened over the past thirty years between the Government of the United States and the Jewish people of Palestine, I have been authorized by the provisional government of the new state to tender this message and to express the hope that your government will recognize and will welcome Israel into the community of nations.

Very respectfully yours,
Eliahu Epstein
Agent, Provisional Government of Israel

Statement by President Truman [Released to the press by the White House May 14]
This Government has been informed that a Jewish state has been proclaimed in Palestine, and recognition has been requested by the provisional government thereof.

The United States recognizes the provisional government as the *de facto* authority of the new State of Israel.

> **Source:** "Israel Proclaimed as an Independent Republic," *Department of State Bulletin* 18(464) (1948): 673.

30. Arab League Statement, May 15, 1948

Introduction

The same night that British forces withdrew from the Palestine mandate and the State of Israel was proclaimed, Arab League forces from Egypt, Syria, Lebanon, Iraq, and Transjordan invaded the new state. The Egyptian foreign minister informed the United Nations (UN) Security Council that their purpose in doing so was to restore law and order. On May 15, 1948, the Arab League issued a statement proclaiming that its forces were entering Palestine to protect the rights of its Arab inhabitants. The statement included a lengthy historical exposition of the Arab case and condemned the British for issuing the Balfour Declaration and allowing large numbers of Jews to enter and settle in Palestine over the previous 30 years. The Arab states demanded that Palestine should be governed by Arabs. They argued that a state of disorder, which might spread to Palestine's neighbors, currently prevailed there, with no existing governmental authority capable of restoring order, and that they were intervening to redress this situation and to establish a competent government and an independent Palestinian state. The UN condemned the Arab action, and Soviet foreign minister Andrei Gromyko even urged that in this case the UN should be particularly firm and clear in stating its views. Existing informal Israeli forces, the Haganah and Irgun, relatively quickly repelled the Syrian, Iraqi, and Lebanese invaders, although Jordanian forces initially captured East Jerusalem, and Israel gained additional portions of mandate territory west of the River Jordan. Egypt gained the small coastal corridor known as the Gaza Strip, while Jordan took Judea and Samaria, later known as the West Bank. The ability of Israel to withstand invasion by the united forces of its Arab enemies was a considerable humiliation to the Arabs.

Primary Source

1. Palestine was part of the former Ottoman Empire, subject to its law and represented in its parliament. The overwhelming majority of the population of Palestine were Arabs. There was in it a small minority of Jews that enjoyed the same rights and bore the same responsibilities as the [other] inhabitants, and did not suffer any ill-treatment on account of its religious beliefs. The holy places were inviolable and the freedom of access to them was guaranteed.

2. The Arabs have always asked for their freedom and independence. On the outbreak of the First World War, and when the Allies declared that they were fighting for the liberation of peoples, the Arabs joined them and fought on their side with a view to realizing their national aspirations and obtaining their independence. England pledged herself to recognize the independence of the Arab countries in Asia, including Palestine. The Arabs played a remarkable part in the achievement of final victory and the Allies have admitted this.

3. In 1917 England issued a declaration in which she expressed her sympathy with the establishment of a national home for the Jews in Palestine. When the Arabs knew of this they protested against it, but England reassured them by affirming to them that this would not prejudice the right of their countries to freedom and independence or affect the political status of the Arabs in Palestine. Not-

withstanding the legally void character of this declaration, it was interpreted by England to aim at no more than the establishment of a spiritual centre for the Jews in Palestine, and to conceal no ulterior political aims, such as the establishment of a Jewish State. The same thing was declared by the Jewish leaders.

4. When the war came to an end England did not keep her promise. Indeed, the Allies placed Palestine under the Mandate system and entrusted England with [the task of carrying it out], in accordance with a document providing for the administration of the country, in the interests of its inhabitants and its preparation for the independence which the Covenant of the League of Nations recognized that Palestine was qualified to have.

5. England administered Palestine in a manner which enabled the Jews to flood it with immigrants and helped them to settle in the country. [This was so] notwithstanding the fact that it was proved that the density of the population in Palestine had exceeded the economic capacity of the country to absorb additional immigrants. England did not pay regard to the interests or rights of the Arab inhabitants, the lawful owners of the country. Although they used to express, by various means, their concern and indignation on account of this state of affairs which was harmful to their being and their future, they [invariably] were met by indifference, imprisonment and oppression.

6. As Palestine is an Arab country, situated in the heart of the Arab countries and attached to the Arab world by various ties—spiritual, historical, and strategic—the Arab countries, and even the Eastern ones, governments as well as peoples, have concerned themselves with the problem of Palestine and have raised it to the international level; [they have also raised the problem] with England, asking for its solution in accordance with the pledges made and with democratic principles. The Round Table Conference was held in London in 1939 in order to discuss the Palestine question and to arrive at the just solution thereof. The Governments of the Arab States participated in [this conference] and asked for the preservation of the Arab character of Palestine and the proclamation of its independence. This conference ended with the issue of a White Paper in which England defined her policy towards Palestine, recognized its independence, and undertook to set up the institutions that would lead to its exercise of the characteristics of [this independence]. She [also] declared that her obligations concerning the establishment of a Jewish national home had been fulfilled, since that home had actually been established. But the policy defined in the [White] Paper was not carried out. This, therefore, led to the deterioration of the situation and the aggravation of matters contrary to the interests of the Arabs.

7. While the Second World War was still in progress, the Governments of the Arab States began to hold consultations regarding the reinforcement of their cooperation and the increasing of the means of their collaboration and their solidarity, with a view to safeguarding their present and their future and to participating in the erection of the edifice of the new world on firm foundations. Palestine had its [worthy] share of consideration and attention in these conversations. These conversations led to the establishment of the League of Arab States as an instrument for the cooperation of the Arab States for their security, peace and well-being.

The Pact of the League of Arab States declared that Palestine has been an independent country since its separation from the Ottoman Empire, but the manifestations of this independence have been suppressed due to reasons which were out of the control of its inhabitants. The establishment of the United Nations shortly afterwards was an event about which the Arabs had the greatest hopes. Their belief in the ideals on which that organization was based made them participate in its establishment and membership.

8. Since then the Arab League and its [member] Governments have not spared any effort to pursue any course, whether with the Mandatory Power or with the United Nations, in order to bring about a just solution of the Palestine problem; [a solution] based upon true democratic principles and compatible with the provisions of the Covenant of the League of Nations and the [Charter] of the United Nations, and which would [at the same time] be lasting, guarantee peace and security in the country and prepare it for progress and prosperity. But Zionist claims were always an obstacle to finding such a solution, [as the Zionists], having prepared themselves with armed forces, strongholds and fortifications to face by force anyone standing in their way, publicly declared [their intention] to establish a Jewish State.

9. When the General Assembly of the United Nations issued, on November 29, 1947, its recommendation concerning the solution of the Palestine problem, on the basis of the establishment of an Arab State and of another Jewish [state] in [Palestine] together with placing the City of Jerusalem under the trusteeship of the United Nations, the Arab States drew attention to the injustice implied in this solution [affecting] the right of the people of Palestine to immediate independence, as well as democratic principles and the provisions of the Covenant of the League of Nations and [the Charter] of the United Nations. [These States also] declared the Arabs' rejection of [that solution] and that it would not be possible to carry it out by peaceful means, and that its forcible imposition would constitute a threat to peace and security in this area.

The warnings and expectations of the Arab States have, indeed, proved to be true, as disturbances were soon widespread throughout Palestine. The Arabs clashed with the Jews, and the two [parties] proceeded to fight each other and shed each other's blood. Whereupon the United Nations began to realize the danger of recommending the partition [of Palestine] and is still looking for a way out of this state of affairs.

10. Now that the British mandate over Palestine has come to an end, without there being a legitimate constitutional authority in the country, which would safeguard the maintenance of security and respect for law and which would protect the lives and properties of the inhabitants, the Governments of the Arab States declare the following:

First: That the rule of Palestine should revert to its inhabitants, in accordance with the provisions of the Covenant of the League of Nations and [the Charter] of the United Nations and that [the Palestinians] should alone have the right to determine their future.

Second: Security and order in Palestine have become disrupted. The Zionist aggression resulted in the exodus of more than a quarter of a million of its Arab inhabitants from their homes and in taking refuge in the neighbouring Arab countries.

The events which have taken place in Palestine have unmasked the aggressive intentions and the imperialist designs of the Zionists, including the atrocities committed by them against the peace-loving Arab inhabitants, especially in Dayr Yasin, Tiberias and others. Nor have they respected the inviolability of consuls, as they have attacked the consulates of the Arab States in Jerusalem. After the termination of the British mandate over Palestine the British authorities are no longer responsible for security in the country, except to the degree affecting their withdrawing forces, and [only] in the areas in which these forces happen to be at the time of withdrawal as announced by [these authorities]. This state of affairs would render Palestine without any governmental machinery capable of restoring order and the rule of law to the country, and of protecting the lives and properties of the inhabitants.

Third: This state of affairs is threatening to spread to the neighbouring Arab countries, where feeling is running high because of the events in Palestine. The Governments of the Member States of the Arab League and the United Nations are exceedingly worried and deeply concerned about this state of affairs.

Fourth: These Governments had hoped that the United Nations would have succeeded in finding a peaceful and just solution of the problem of Palestine, in accordance with democratic principles and the provisions of the Covenant of the League of Nations and [the Charter] of the United Nations, so that peace, security and prosperity would prevail in this part of the world.

Fifth: The Governments of the Arab States, as members of the Arab League, a regional organization within the meaning of the provisions of Chapter VIII of the Charter of the United Nations, are responsible for maintaining peace and security in their area. These Governments view the events taking place in Palestine as a threat to peace and security in the area as a whole and [also] in each of them taken separately.

Sixth: Therefore, as security in Palestine is a sacred trust in the hands of the Arab States, and in order to put an end to this state of affairs and to prevent it from becoming aggravated or from turning into [a state of] chaos, the extent of which no one can foretell; in order to stop the spreading of disturbances and disorder in Palestine to the neighbouring Arab countries; in order to fill the gap brought about in the governmental machinery in Palestine as a result of the termination of the mandate and the non-establishment of a lawful successor authority, the Governments of the Arab States have found themselves compelled to intervene in Palestine solely in order to help its inhabitants restore peace and security and the rule of justice and law to their country, and in order to prevent bloodshed.

Seventh: The Governments of the Arab States recognize that the independence of Palestine, which has so far been suppressed by the British Mandate, has become an accomplished fact for the lawful inhabitants of Palestine. They alone, by virtue of their absolute sovereignty, have the right to provide their country with laws and governmental institutions. They alone should exercise the attributes of their independence, through their own means and without any kind of foreign interference, immediately after peace, security, and the rule of law have been restored to the country.

At that time the intervention of the Arab states will cease, and the independent State of Palestine will cooperate with the [other member] States of the Arab League in order to bring peace, security and prosperity to this part of the world.

The Governments of the Arab States emphasize, on this occasion, what they have already declared before the London Conference and the United Nations, that the only solution of the Palestine problem is the establishment of a unitary Palestinian State, in accordance with democratic principles, whereby its inhabitants will enjoy complete equality before the law, [and whereby] minorities will be assured of all the guarantees recognized in democratic constitutional countries and [whereby] the holy places will be preserved and the rights of access thereto guaranteed.

Eighth: The Arab States most emphatically declare that [their] intervention in Palestine was due only to these considerations and objectives, and that they aim at nothing more than to put an end to the prevailing conditions in [Palestine]. For this reason, they have great confidence that their action will have the support of the United Nations; [that it will be] considered as an action aiming at the realization of its aims and at promoting its principles, as provided for in its Charter.

Source: United Nations Security Council Official Records, S/745, May 15, 1948.

31. United Nations Security Council Resolution 62, November 16, 1948

Introduction

The Israeli War of Independence (1948–1949) was one of the earliest international crises to confront the new United Nations (UN). In June 1948 the UN called a one-month truce during which the Israel Defense Force (IDF) was established, and the IDF proved successful in beating back most of the invaders. By mid-November 1948 all parties could recognize that the war situation had become relatively static, and the UN sought to establish a permanent armistice agreement. The Security Council passed Resolution 62 calling for an armistice in all parts of Palestine. In the first half of 1949, UN negotiator Ralph Bunche negotiated separate armistice agreements between Israel and Egypt, Lebanon, Jordan, and Syria, delineating the territory under the control of each. Since Iraq and Saudi Arabia, even though they had sent troops against Israel, had no borders with Israel, they never signed armistice agreements. Israel gained additional portions of mandate territory west of the River Jordan. Egypt took the small coastal corridor known as the Gaza Strip, while Jordan won Judea and Samaria, later known as the West Bank. Long-running disputes and resentments over these areas would continue to embitter Israel's relations with its neighbors for decades and helped to give rise to new causes of contention. Demilitarized zones separating Israel and Syria proved to be a source of many subsequent military incidents and provocations on both sides. Although intended to be permanent, these settlements were once more destabilized during the 1967 and 1973 Arab-Israeli wars. Even so, Bunche won the Nobel Peace Prize for his efforts.

Primary Source

The Security Council,

Reaffirming its previous resolutions concerning the establishment and implementation of the truce in Palestine, and recalling particularly its resolution 54 (1948) of 15 July 1948 which determined that the situation in Palestine constitutes a threat to the peace within the meaning of Article 39 of the Charter of the United Nations,

Taking note that the General Assembly is continuing its consideration of the future government of Palestine in response to the request of the Security Council in its resolution 44 (1948) of 1 April 1948,

Without prejudice to the actions of the Acting Mediator regarding the implementation of Security Council resolution 61 (1948) of 4 November 1948,

1. *Decides* that, in order to eliminate the threat to the peace in Palestine and to facilitate the transition from the present truce to permanent peace in Palestine, an armistice shall be established in all sectors of Palestine;

2. *Calls upon* the parties directly involved in the conflict in Palestine, as a further provisional measure under Article 40 of the Charter, to seek agreement forthwith, by negotiations conducted either directly or through the Acting Mediator, with a view to the immediate establishment of the armistice, including:

    (a) The delineation of permanent armistice demarcation lines beyond which the armed forces of the respective parties shall not move;

    (b) Such withdrawal and reduction of their armed forces as will ensure the maintenance of the armistice during the transition to permanent peace in Palestine.

Source: United Nations Security Council Official Records, S.C. Res. 62, S/1080, November 16, 1948.

32. United Nations General Assembly Resolution 212 (III), Assistance to Palestine Refugees [Excerpt], November 19, 1948

Introduction

Among the bitterest legacies of the first Arab-Israeli war, and perhaps the most difficult to resolve, was the fate of those Palestine Arabs who fled from Israeli-controlled territories. Estimates of the number forced to become refugees varied between 500,000 and 1 million, with United Nations (UN) authorities who administered refugee camps eventually giving a figure of just over 700,000. By mid-November 1948, UN officials believed that at least 500,000 such individuals had already been forced out of Palestine. In the course of the fighting that took place both before and after partition, many Arab inhabitants of Palestine were compelled to flee. Other Arab inhabitants chose to flee, while Jewish inhabitants of areas occupied by invading Arab forces were either killed or expelled. During the war, irregular Haganah and Irgun guerrilla forces first established by the Zionists during the 1940s were particularly aggressive in seeking to expel Arabs from Israeli-held lands, in some cases staging massacres that terrorized Arabs into leaving, and as the war progressed the new Israeli government likewise sought to encourage Arabs to depart. Arab leaders also encouraged Palestinian Arabs to leave Palestine, at least for the duration of the war, and some community leaders set an example by themselves fleeing in terror. Seeking to address this humanitarian crisis, in November 1948 the UN appropriated almost $30 million to support such refugees and also called on the appropriate volunteer relief agencies for assistance.

Primary Source

Whereas the problem of the relief of Palestine refugees of all communities is one of immediate urgency and the United Nations Mediator on Palestine, in his progress report of 18 September 1948, part three, states that "action must be taken to determine the necessary measures [of relief] and to provide for their implementation" and that "the choice is between saving the lives of many thousands of people now or permitting them to die";

Whereas the Acting Mediator, in his supplemental report of 18 October 1948, declares that "the situation of the refugees is now critical" and that "aid must not only be continued but very greatly increased if disaster is to be averted";

Whereas the alleviation of conditions of starvation and distress among the Palestine refugees is one of the minimum conditions for the success of the United Nations to bring peace to that land,

The General Assembly

1. *Expresses* its thanks to the Governments and organizations which, and the individual persons who, have given assistance directly or in response to the Mediator's appeal;

2. *Considers,* on the basis of the Acting Mediator's recommendation, that a sum of approximately 29,500,000 dollars will be required to provide relief for 500,000 refugees for a period of nine months from 1 December 1948 to 31 August 1949; and that an additional amount of approximately 2,500,000 dollars will be required for administrative and local operational expenses;

3. *Authorizes* the Secretary General, in consultation with the Advisory Committee on Administrative and Budgetary Questions, to advance immediately a sum of up to 5,000,000 dollars from the Working Capital Fund of the United Nations, the said sum to be repaid before the end of the period specified in paragraph 2, from the voluntary governmental contributions requested under paragraph 4;

4. *Urges* all States Members of the United Nations to make as soon as possible voluntary contributions in kind or in funds sufficient to ensure that the amount of supplies and funds required is obtained, and states that, to this end, voluntary contributions of non-member States would also be accepted; contributions in funds may be made in currencies other than the United States dollar, in so far as the operations of the relief organization can be carried out in such currencies;

[. . .]

8. *Requests* the Secretary-General to take all necessary steps to extend aid to Palestine refugees and to establish such administrative organization as may be required for this purpose, inviting the assistance of the appropriate agencies of the several Governments, the specialized agencies of the United Nations, the United Nations International Children's Emergency Fund, the International Committee of the Red Cross, the League of Red Cross Societies and other voluntary agencies, it being recognized that the participation of voluntary organizations in the relief plan would in no way derogate from the principle of impartiality on the basis of which the assistance of these organizations is being solicited;

9. *Requests* the Secretary-General to appoint a Director of United Nations Relief for Palestine Refugees, to whom he may delegate such responsibility as he may consider appropriate for the overall planning and implementation of the relief programme;

10. *Agrees* to the convoking, at the discretion of the Secretary-General, of an *ad hoc* advisory committee of seven members to be selected by the President of the General Assembly, to which the Secretary-General may submit any matter of principle or policy upon which he would like the benefit of the committee's advice;

11. *Requests* the Secretary General to continue and to extend the implementation of the present programme, until the machinery provided for by the present resolution is set up;

12. *Urges* the World Health Organization, the Food and Agriculture Organization, the International Refugee Organization, the United Nations International Children's Emergency Fund, and other appropriate organizations and agencies, acting within the framework of the relief programme herein established, promptly to contribute supplies, specialized personnel and other services permitted by their constitutions and their financial resources, to relieve the desperate plight of Palestine refugees of all communities;

[. . .]

Source: United Nations General Assembly Official Records, 3rd Sess., *Assistance to Palestine Refugees*, G.A. Res. 212 (III), November 19, 1948.

33. United Nations General Assembly Resolution 194 (III), Palestine: Progress Report of the United Nations Mediator, December 11, 1948

Introduction

When the war ended, several hundred thousand Arab refugees were living outside Palestine. At the end of 1948, the Israeli government passed a law forbidding their return. In December 1948 the United Nations (UN) General Assembly, inspired in part by anger over the assassination of UN mediator Count Folke Bernadotte by members of the extremist Israeli Stern Gang, passed a resolution intended to facilitate the speedy return of such refugees to their homes and the payment of adequate compensation to those who chose not to return. It also placed Jerusalem, Nazareth, and Bethlehem—cities and towns sacred to Christians, Jews, and Muslims alike—under UN control. While Israel welcomed Jews from all sources, granting them virtually immediate citizenship, the provisions for the return of the Palestinians remained a dead letter. Recognizing that this was not a transitory problem, one year later UN General Assembly Resolution 302 established the UN Relief and Works Agency for Palestine Refugees to administer and supervise the refugee camps. Since other Arab states refused to accept Palestinian refugees in large numbers, the generally squalid and overcrowded camps became breeding grounds for vehemently anti-Israeli fanatics who sought revenge at all costs. Recruits from such sources not only undertook individual terrorist acts but later also became the backbone of such Arab guerrilla groups as the Palestinian Liberation Organization (PLO), Hezbollah, and Hamas.

Primary Source

The General Assembly,

Having considered further the situation in Palestine,

1. *Expresses* its deep appreciation of the progress achieved through the good offices of the late United Nations Mediator in promoting a peaceful adjustment of the future situation of Palestine, for which cause he sacrificed his life; and

Extends its thanks to the Acting Mediator and his staff for their continued efforts and devotion to duty in Palestine;

2. *Establishes* a Conciliation Commission consisting of three States Members of the United Nations which shall have the following functions:

   (a) To assume, in so far as it considers necessary in existing circumstances, the functions given to the United Nations Mediator on Palestine by resolution 182 (S-2) of the General Assembly of 14 May 1948;

   (b) To carry out the specific functions and directives given to it by the present resolution and such additional functions and directives as may be given to it by the General Assembly or by the Security Council;

   (c) To undertake, upon the request of the Security Council, any of the functions now assigned to the United Nations Mediator on Palestine or to the United Nations Truce Commission by resolutions of the Security Council; upon such request to the Conciliation Commission by the Security Council with respect to all the remaining functions of the United Nations Mediator on Palestine under Security Council resolutions, the office of the Mediator shall be terminated;

3. *Decides* that a Committee of the Assembly, consisting of China, France, the Union of Soviet Socialist Republics, the United Kingdom and the United States of America, shall present, before the end of the first part of the present session of the General Assembly, for the approval of the Assembly, a proposal concerning the names of the three States which will constitute the Conciliation Commission;

4. *Requests* the Commission to begin its functions at once, with a view to the establishment of contact between the parties themselves and the Commission at the earliest possible date;

5. *Calls upon* the Governments and authorities concerned to extend the scope of the negotiations provided for in the Security Council's resolution of 16 November 1948 and to seek agreement by negotiations conducted either with the Conciliation Commission or directly, with a view to the final settlement of all questions outstanding between them;

6. *Instructs* the Conciliation Commission to take steps to assist the Governments and authorities concerned to achieve a final settlement of all questions outstanding between them;

7. *Resolves* that the Holy Places—including Nazareth—religious buildings and sites in Palestine should be protected and free access to them assured, in accordance with existing rights and historical practice; that arrangements to this end should be under effective United Nations supervision; that the United Nations Conciliation Commission, in presenting to the fourth regular session of the General Assembly its detailed proposals for a permanent international régime for the territory of Jerusalem, should include recommendations concerning the Holy Places in that territory; that with regard to the Holy Places in the rest of Palestine the Commission should call upon the political authorities of the areas concerned to give appropriate formal guarantees as to the protection of the Holy Places and access to them; and that these undertakings should be presented to the General Assembly for approval;

8. *Resolves* that, in view of its association with three world religions, the Jerusalem area, including the present municipality of Jerusalem *plus* the surrounding villages and towns, the most eastern of which shall be Abu Dis; the most southern, Bethlehem; the most western, Ein Karim (including also the built-up area of Motsa); and the most northern, Shu'fat, should be accorded special and separate treatment from the rest of Palestine and should be placed under effective United Nations control;

Requests the Security Council to take further steps to ensure the demilitarization of Jerusalem at the earliest possible date;

Instructs the Conciliation Commission to present to the fourth regular session of the General Assembly detailed proposals for a permanent international régime for the Jerusalem area which will provide for the maximum local autonomy for distinctive groups consistent with the special international status of the Jerusalem area;

The Conciliation Commission is authorized to appoint a United Nations representative, who shall co-operate with the local authorities with respect to the interim administration of the Jerusalem area;

9. *Resolves* that, pending agreement on more detailed arrangements among the Governments and authorities concerned, the freest possible access to Jerusalem by road, rail or air should be accorded to all inhabitants of Palestine;

Instructs the Conciliation Commission to report immediately to the Security Council, for appropriate action by that organ, any attempt by any party to impede such access;

10. *Instructs* the Conciliation Commission to seek arrangements among the Governments and authorities concerned which will facilitate the economic development of the area, including arrangements for access to ports and airfields and the use of transportation and communication facilities;

11. *Resolves* that the refugees wishing to return to their homes and live at peace with their neighbours should be permitted to do so at the earliest practicable date, and that compensation should be paid for the property of those choosing not to return and for loss of or damage to property which, under principles of international law or in equity, should be made good by the Governments or authorities responsible;

Instructs the Conciliation Commission to facilitate the repatriation, resettlement and economic and social rehabilitation of the refugees and the payment of compensation, and to maintain close relations with the Director of the United Nations Relief for Palestine Refugees and, through him, with the appropriate organs and agencies of the United Nations;

12. *Authorizes* the Conciliation Commission to appoint such subsidiary bodies and to employ such technical experts, acting under its authority, as it may find necessary for the effective discharge of its functions and responsibilities under the present resolution;

The Conciliation Commission will have its official headquarters at Jerusalem. The authorities responsible for maintaining order in Jerusalem will be responsible for taking all measures necessary to ensure the security of the Commission. The Secretary-General will provide a limited number of guards for the protection of the staff and premises of the Commission;

13. *Instructs* the Conciliation Commission to render progress reports periodically to the Secretary-General for transmission to the Security Council and to the Members of the United Nations;

14. *Calls upon* all Governments and authorities concerned to co-operate with the Conciliation Commission and to take all possible steps to assist in the implementation of the present resolution;

15. *Requests* the Secretary-General to provide the necessary staff and facilities and to make appropriate arrangements to provide the necessary funds required in carrying out the terms of the present resolution.

Source: United Nations General Assembly Official Records, 3rd Sess., *Palestine-Progress Report of the United Nations Mediator*, G.A. Res. 194 (III), December 11, 1948.

34. Armistice between Israel and Lebanon [Excerpt], March 23, 1949

Introduction

The Israeli armistice agreement with Lebanon was one of four armistice agreements between Israel and hostile Arab states that United Nations (UN) representative Ralph Bunche negotiated in the first half of 1949. Under its terms, the international boundary separating Israel and Lebanon was reestablished as the border between the two states, and Israeli forces withdrew from territory they had seized in southern Lebanon. The relationship between the neighbors nonetheless remained difficult, in part because the recurrent weakness of Lebanese governments made the small country an easy host for irregular organizations hostile to Israel. Israeli forces subsequently felt free to intervene in Lebanon when that country served as a base for such groups, invading in spring 1983 to drive Palestinian Liberation Organization (PLO) members from Lebanon, shelling the southern region of the country in the spring of 1996 (Operation GRAPES OF WRATH) to attack Hezbollah guerrillas, and invading once again in July 2006 to strike against Hezbollah and Hamas operatives. Caught between stronger neighbors and often dominated by Syria, Lebanon several times fell victim to civil war, and assassinations of prominent and popular politicians were another factor that helped to destabilize successive governments.

Primary Source

PREAMBLE

The parties to the present agreement, responding to the Security Council resolution of 16 November 1948 calling upon them, as a further provisional measure under Article 40 of the Charter of the United Nations and in order to facilitate the transition from the present truce to permanent peace in Palestine, to negotiate an Armistice; having decided to enter into negotiations under United Nations Chairmanship concerning the implementation of the Security Council resolution 16 November 1948; and having appointed representatives empowered to negotiate and conclude an armistice agreement;

The undersigned representatives, having exchanged their full powers found to be in good and proper form, have agreed upon the following provisions:

Article I

With a view to promoting the return of permanent peace in Palestine and in recognition of the importance in this regard of mutual assurances concerning the future military operations of the Parties, the following principles, which shall be fully observed by both Parties during the Armistice, are hereby affirmed:

1. The injunction of the Security Council against resort to military force in the settlement of the Palestine question shall henceforth be scrupulously respected by both Parties.
2. No aggressive action by the armed forces—land, sea, or air—of either Party shall be undertaken, planned, or threatened against the people or the armed forces of the other; it being understood that the use of the term "planned" in this context has no bearing on normal staff planning as generally practised in military organizations.
3. The right of each Party to its security and freedom from fear of attack by the armed forces of the other shall be fully respected.
4. The establishment of an armistice between the armed forces of the two Parties is accepted as an indispensable step toward the liquidation of armed conflict and the restoration of peace in Palestine.

Article II

With a specific view to the implementation of the resolution of the Security Council of 16 November 1948, the following principles and purposes are affirmed:

1. The principle that no military or political advantage should be gained under the truce ordered by the Security Council is recognized.
2. It is also recognized that no provision of this Agreement shall in any way prejudice the rights, claims and positions of either Party hereto in the ultimate peaceful settlement of the Palestine question;
    (a) The provisions of this agreement being dictated exclusively by military considerations.

Article III

1. In pursuance of the foregoing principles and of the resolution of the Security Council of 16 November 1948, a general armistice between the armed forces of the two Parties—land, sea and air—is hereby established.

2. No element of the land, sea or air military or paramilitary forces of either Party, including non-regular forces, shall commit any warlike or hostile act against the military or paramilitary forces of the other Party, or against civilians in territory under the control of that Party; or shall advance beyond or pass over for any purpose whatsoever the Armistice Demarcation Line set forth in Article V of this Agreement; or enter into or pass through the air space of the other Party or through the waters within three miles of the coastline of the other Party.

3. No warlike act or act of hostility shall be conducted from territory controlled by one of the parties to this Agreement against the other Party.

Article IV

1. The line described in Article V of this Agreement shall be designated as the Armistice Demarcation Line and is delineated in pursuance of the purpose and intent of the resolutions of the Security Council of 16 November 1948.

2. The basic purpose of the Armistice Demarcation Line is to delineate the line beyond which the armed forces of the respective Parties shall not move.

3. Rules and regulations of the armed forces of the Parties, which prohibit civilians from crossing the fighting lines or entering the area between the lines, shall remain in effect after the signing of this Agreement with application to the Armistice Demarcation Line defined in Article V.

Article V

1. The Armistice Demarcation Line should follow the international boundary between Lebanon and Palestine.

2. In the region of the Armistice Demarcation Line the military forces of the Parties shall consist of defensive forces only as is defined in the Annex to this Agreement.

3. Withdrawal of forces to the Armistice Demarcation Line and their reduction to defensive strength in accordance with the preceding paragraph shall be completed within ten days of the signing of this Agreement. In the same way the removal of mines from mined roads and areas evacuated by either Party and the transmission of plans showing the location of such minefields to the other Party shall be completed within the same period.

Article VI

All prisoners of war detained by either Party to this Agreement and belonging to the armed forces, regular or irregular, of the other Party shall be exchanged.

[. . .]

Article VII

1. The execution of the provisions of this Agreement shall be supervised by a Mixed Armistice Commission composed of seven

members, of whom each Party to this Agreement shall designate three, and whose Chairman shall be the United Nations Chief of Staff of the Truce Supervision Organization or a senior officer from the Observer personnel of that Organization designated by him following consultation with both Parties to this Agreement.

2. The Mixed Armistice Commission shall maintain its headquarters at the frontier post North of Metulla and the Lebanese frontier post at En Naqoura, and shall hold its meetings at such places and at such times as it may deem necessary for the effective conduct of the work.

3. The Mixed Armistice Commission shall be convened in its first meeting by the United Nations Chief of Staff of the Truce Supervision Organization not later than one week following the signing of this Agreement.

4. Decisions of the Mixed Armistice Commission, to the extent possible, shall be based on the principle of unanimity. In the absence of unanimity, decisions shall be taken by a majority vote of the members of the Commission present and voting.

5. The Mixed Armistice Commission shall formulate its own rules of procedure. Meetings shall be held only after due notice to the members by the Chairman. The quorum for its meetings shall be a majority of its members.

6. The Commission shall be empowered to employ Observers, who may be from among the military organizations of the Parties or from the military personnel of the United Nations Truce Supervision Organization, or from both, in such numbers as may be considered essential to the performance of its functions. In the event United Nations Observers should be so employed, they shall remain under the command of the United Nations Chief of Staff of the Truce Supervision Organization. Assignments of a general or special nature given to United Nations Observers attached to the Mixed Armistice Commission shall be subject to approval by the United Nations Chief of Staff or his designated representative on the Commission, whichever is serving as Chairman.

7. Claims or complaints presented by either Party relating to the application of this Agreement shall be referred immediately to the Mixed Armistice Commission through its Chairman. The Commission shall take such action on all such claims or complaints by means of its observation and investigation machinery as it may deem appropriate, with a view to equitable and mutually satisfactory settlement.

[...]

Source: United Nations Security Council, S/1296, March 23, 1949.

35. United Nations General Assembly Resolution 303 (IV), Palestine: Question of an International Regime for the Jerusalem Area and the Protection of the Holy Places, December 9, 1949

Introduction

The original partition plan advanced by the United Nations (UN) in 1947 envisaged that the holy city of Jerusalem together with Bethlehem, which contained sites sacred to Jews, Muslims, and Christians, would be administered as an international city under UN supervision and sovereignty. By the end of hostilities, Jordan controlled all of Jerusalem, although Israel had at one time controlled the western half. Israel had initially accepted the principle of UN sovereignty and administration of Jerusalem, but at the end of the war the Israeli government rejected the idea on the grounds that the UN had made no effort to establish international control there or to ensure the safety of either its Arab or its Jewish inhabitants. In late 1949 the UN General Assembly nonetheless reaffirmed the principle that Jerusalem should come under UN jurisdiction. Even after Israel recaptured all of Jerusalem in the 1967 Six-Day War, the UN continued to adhere at least verbally to this proposal but made no real effort to enforce it, and officially Jerusalem remained a corpus separatum. Israel, however, proclaimed in 1950 that West Jerusalem was its capital and after 1967 added East Jerusalem to the city. Despite congressional resolutions to the contrary, the U.S. government has never recognized Jerusalem as part of Israel. The United States, Britain, and others have nonetheless in practice ignored UN affirmations of its own sovereignty over Jerusalem, regarding its status as a matter to be decided if and when Israel and its opponents ever reach a final settlement of their outstanding differences.

Primary Source

The General Assembly,

Having regard to its resolutions 181 (II) of 29 November 1947 and 194 (III) of 11 December 1948,

Having studied the reports of the United Nations Conciliation Commission for Palestine set up under the latter resolution,

I. *Decides*

In relation to Jerusalem,

Believing that the principles underlying its previous resolutions concerning this matter, and in particular its resolution of 29 November 1947, represent a just and equitable settlement of the question,

1. To restate, therefore, its intention that Jerusalem should be placed under a permanent international regime, which should envisage appropriate guarantees for the protection of the Holy Places, both within and outside Jerusalem, and to confirm specifically the following provisions of General Assembly Resolution 181 (II): (1) the City of Jerusalem shall be established as a *corpus separatum* under a special international regime and shall be administered by the United Nations; (2) the Trusteeship Council shall be designated to discharge the responsibilities of the Administering Authority . . . ; and (3) the City of Jerusalem shall include the present municipality of Jerusalem plus the surrounding villages and towns, the most eastern of which shall be Abu Dis; the most southern, Bethlehem; the most western, Ein Karim (including also the built-up area of Motsa); and the most northern, Shu'fat . . . ;

2. To request for this purpose that the Trusteeship Council at its next session, whether special or regular, complete the preparation of the Statute of Jerusalem, omitting the now inapplicable provisions, such as articles 32 and 39, and, without prejudice to the fundamental principles of the international regime for Jerusalem set forth in General Assembly resolution 181 (II) introducing therein amendments in the direction of its greater democratization, approve the Statute, and proceed immediately with its implementation. The Trusteeship Council shall not allow any actions taken by any interested Government or Governments to divert it from adopting and implementing the Statute of Jerusalem;

II. *Calls upon* the States concerned to make formal undertakings, at an early date and in the light of their obligations as Members of the United Nations, that they will approach these matters with good will and be guided by the terms of the present resolution.

Source: United Nations General Assembly Official Records, 4th Sess., *Palestine: Question of an International Regime for the Jerusalem Area and the Protection of the Holy Places*, G.A. Res. 303 (IV), December 9, 1949.

36. Israeli Law of Return [Excerpt], July 5, 1950

Introduction

In mid-1950 the Knesset (Israeli parliament) unanimously passed a law permitting any Jew, with the exception of those whose health was problematic or who posed a threat to the safety of the state, to obtain an immigration visa and settle in Israel. This legislation was a concrete expression of the longtime Zionist hope that Israel would serve as a physical homeland for all international Jewry. It was also an affirmation of the fact that Israel was fundamentally a Jewish state. Whereas Palestinian refugees were regarded as potentially disruptive and hazardous elements and were officially banned from

returning, the Israeli government readily welcomed any and all Jews, whatever their background, and granted them immediate citizenship. In 1949 and 1950, the entire Jewish population of Yemen, 49,000 in all, moved to Israel, as did the 114,000 Jewish inhabitants of Iraq, part of an influx of 700,000 Jews to Israel between 1948 and 1951 that doubled its Jewish population and meant that many of the new arrivals spent some time living in tents. Under the Law of Return, Jews were generally defined as anyone whose mother was Jewish. In 1970 the law was amended and expanded to cover the children and grandchildren of Jews and the spouses of Jews or their children or grandchildren. This may have been an effort to use demographics to increase the Jewish proportion of the population in relation to the still substantial numbers of Arabs in Israel, who generally had higher birthrates. The Law of Return helped to further harden the divisions between Israelis and Arabs while reinforcing Israel's predominantly Jewish identity.

Primary Source

1. Every Jew has the right to come to this country as an oleh.[*]

2. (a) Aliyah[*] shall be by oleh's visa.
   (b) An oleh's visa shall be granted to every Jew who has expressed his desire to settle in Israel, unless the Minister of Immigration is satisfied that the applicant
       (1) is engaged in an activity directed against the Jewish people; or
       (2) is likely to endanger public health or the security of the State.

3. (a) A Jew who has come to Israel and subsequent to his arrival has expressed his desire to settle in Israel may, while still in Israel, receive an oleh's certificate.
   (b) The restrictions specified in section 2(b) shall apply also to the grant of an oleh's certificate, but a person shall not be regarded as endangering public health on account of an illness contracted after his arrival in Israel.

4. Every Jew who has immigrated into this country before the coming into force of this Law, and every Jew who was born in this country, whether before or after the coming into force of this Law, shall be deemed to be a person who has come to this country as an oleh under this Law.

[. . .]

Source: Law of Return, July 5, 1950, Israel Ministry of Foreign Affairs, http://www.mfa.gov.il/MFA.

[*]Translator's Note: Aliyah means immigration of Jews, and oleh (plural: olim) means a Jew immigrating into Israel.

37. John Foster Dulles, Efforts toward Preserving Peace in the Near East [Excerpt], February 24, 1956

Introduction

By the mid-1950s the fluid situation in the volatile Middle East, where nationalist governments were coming to power and the Arab-Israeli antagonism was a continual sore point, was attracting the attention of the Cold War superpowers and major protagonists, the United States and the Soviet Union. Initially, both the United States and the Soviet Union were sympathetic to Israel's position, but this unusual united front proved short-lived, as developments in the Middle East were increasingly viewed in the context of the intensifying Cold War. In May 1950 the United States, Great Britain, and France issued a joint statement expressing their hopes for continuing peace and stability in the Middle East and their desire to avoid an ever-escalating arms race between the Arab states and Israel. The three powers also stated their intention of taking forcible action to prevent the outbreak of another conflict. The Arab League resented this assumption that the Middle East was effectively in a tutelary relationship to the three Western powers, who reserved the right to intervene there. Most Arab states were also suspicious when in February 1955 Iraq, Turkey, Pakistan, Iran, and the United Kingdom signed the Baghdad Pact, a mutual security agreement modeled on the North Atlantic Treaty Organization (NATO). The Soviet Union condemned the Baghdad Pact and increasingly aligned itself with Arab states against Israel. It also began to provide arms to nationalist Arab regimes such as that of Egypt, where a 1952 military coup had overthrown the previous monarchy and installed a modernizing radical government. Soviet officials warned Western powers against any kind of military intervention in the affairs of the Middle East. In response, U.S. secretary of state John Foster Dulles, speaking to the U.S. Senate's Foreign Relations Committee, reaffirmed the intention of the three Western powers to take action to prevent the eruption of any new conflict. He deplored Soviet arms sales to Arab states, but—at least in the short run—decided not to supply Israel with large quantities of U.S. arms since he feared that these might further inflame an already critical situation. While not ruling out future arms sales to either Israel or Arab states, Dulles recommended that Israel turn for protection primarily to the United Nations and to the earlier pledges that the three Western powers had made in 1950.

Primary Source

[. . .]

In a move consistent with the efforts of the United Nations, the United States joined with the United Kingdom and France on May 25, 1950, in the issuance of a joint declaration which set forth their deep interest in promoting the establishment and maintenance of peace and stability in the Near East. The three Governments there recognized that the Arab States and Israel all needed to maintain armed forces for the purposes of assuring their internal security and their legitimate self-defense and to permit them to play their part in the defense of the area as a whole. The three Governments reaffirmed at the same time their opposition to the development of an arms race between the Arab States and Israel. A third and vital part of the declaration of 1950 is contained in the statement of their unalterable opposition to the use of force or threat of force between any of the states in the Near East. The three Governments stated that, should they find that any of these states was preparing to violate frontiers or armistice lines, they would, consistently with their obligations as members of the United Nations, immediately take action, both within and without the United Nations, to prevent such violation.

During the past 6 months substantial amounts of Soviet-bloc arms have been sent to the area. The Soviet bloc has thus complicated the problem which the United Nations has sought to solve. Conditions for an arms race now exist as certain countries of the Near East vie with one another in the purchase of military items. Israel now wishes to obtain arms from the United States and elsewhere, and we have received similar requests from several of the Arab States which have not acquired arms from Russia or its satellites. While realizing that the introduction of large quantities of Soviet-bloc arms could upset the balance of arms within the area, we do not believe that a true peace can be based upon arms alone.

In requesting arms from the United States, representatives of Israel have expressed fear that their country's peaceful existence is threatened. It is natural that in the circumstances they would wish to increase their military capabilities. However, Israel, due to its much smaller size and population, could not win an arms race against Arabs having access to Soviet-bloc stocks. It would seem that Israel's security could be better assured, in the long run, through measures other than the acquisition of additional arms in circumstances which might exacerbate the situation.

These other measures include reliance on the United Nations, by which Israel was created and of which Israel and the Arab States are important members. The charter of the United Nations binds all of them not to threaten or use force. The United States, United Kingdom, and France, as I indicated earlier, announced their intentions in the declaration of 1950. More recently, President Eisenhower and Prime Minister Eden referred to this declaration and stated that they had made arrangements, in which the French have joined, for joint discussions as to the nature of measures to be taken in light of that declaration. All of these possible measures add up to a more effective deterrent than additional quantities of arms.

As I have indicated on previous occasions, the United States does not exclude the possibility of arms sales to Israel at a time when it will preserve the peace. We do not exclude the possibility of arms sales to the other Arab States under similar conditions.

[. . .]

Source: "Efforts toward Preserving Peace in the Near East," *Department of State Bulletin* 34(871) (1956): 368–369.

38. U.S. Statement on the Aswan High Dam, July 19, 1956

Introduction

In 1952 a coup led by revolutionary young military Free Officers overthrew the monarchy of King Farouk I in Egypt, replacing it with a self-consciously nationalist and anticolonial regime bent on modernization and determined to assert Egypt's independence. The new government introduced policies of land reform and other socialist measures. In 1954 one of the leading spirits among these officers, Colonel Gamal Abdel Nasser, became president of Egypt. He took a prominent role at the 1955 Bandung meeting of non-aligned nations that sought to remain aloof from the Cold War rivalries and was initially willing to accept assistance from both camps. Like many governments of the time, Nasser's Egypt embarked on ambitious developmental projects. The most extensive of these was the construction of a massive dam across the Nile at Aswan that was intended to generate hydroelectric power for all of Egypt and several surrounding countries. In December 1955 the United States, the United Kingdom, and the World Bank promised to provide much of the funding for this project. Seven months later, however, the United States, Britain, and the World Bank reversed course and withdrew their offers of funding. The stated reasons were simply that the undertaking was unfeasible and that expected progress had not been made. In reality, the denial of funding was due to Nasser's recent acceptance of large quantities of armaments from the Soviet Union. One reason for his eagerness to acquire such weapons was that Egypt's relations with Israel, Britain, and France were all reaching a flashpoint over issues related to Egyptian occupation of the Gaza Strip, seized from Israel in 1948, and the ownership and operation of the strategically and commercially important Suez Canal. These would soon become the center of a major Cold War and Middle Eastern crisis. The resulting Suez Crisis also drove Egypt closer to the Soviet Union, which eventually provided about one-third of the Aswan High Dam project's construction costs.

Primary Source

At the request of the Government of Egypt, the United States joined in December 1955 with the United Kingdom and with the World Bank in an offer to assist Egypt in the construction of a high dam on the Nile at Aswan. This project is one of great magnitude. It would require an estimated 12 to 16 years to complete at a total cost estimated at some $1,300,000,000, of which over $900,000,000 represents local currency requirements. It involves not merely the rights and interests of Egypt but of other states whose waters are contributory, including Sudan, Ethiopia, and Uganda.

The December offer contemplated an extension by the United States and United Kingdom of grant aid to help finance certain early phases of the work, the effects of which would be confined solely to Egypt, with the understanding that accomplishment of the project as a whole would require a satisfactory resolution of the question of Nile water rights. Another important consideration bearing upon the feasibility of the undertaking, and thus the practicability of American aid, was Egyptian readiness and ability to concentrate its economic resources upon this vast construction program.

Developments within the succeeding 7 months have not been favorable to the success of the project, and the U.S. Government has concluded that it is not feasible in present circumstances to participate in the project. Agreement by the riparian states has not been achieved, and the ability of Egypt to devote adequate resources to assure the project's success has become more uncertain than at the time the offer was made.

This decision in no way reflects or involves any alteration in the friendly relations of the Government and people of the United States toward the Government and people of Egypt.

The United States remains deeply interested in the welfare of the Egyptian people and in the development of the Nile. It is prepared to consider at an appropriate time and at the request of the riparian states what steps might be taken toward a more effective utilization of the water resources of the Nile for the benefit of the peoples of the region. Furthermore, the United States remains ready to assist Egypt in its effort to improve the economic condition of its people and is prepared, through its appropriate agencies, to discuss these matters within the context of funds appropriated by the Congress.

Source: "Aswan High Dam," *Department of State Bulletin* 35(892) (1956): 188.

39. Egyptian Law Nationalizing the Suez Canal Company [Excerpt], July 26, 1956

Introduction

One of the major reasons that Britain had taken over the administration of Egypt in the 1880s was to protect the then strategically and commercially vital Suez Canal waterway linking the Persian Gulf to the Mediterranean Sea. Ownership of this was vested in the Suez Canal Company, owned by the British and French governments, although the Egyptian government controlled access to the canal. The nationalist Egyptian government that came to power in 1952 found foreign ownership of the commercially valuable canal and its revenues a constant irritant. Even before then, use and operation of the canal had become internationally controversial. From the date of Israel's creation in 1948, Egypt had denied the use of the canal not just to Israeli vessels but also to ships bearing goods bound for Israel on the grounds that since Israel and Egypt—even after the 1949 armistice—were formally at war, the normal stipulations of free navigation by all nations did not apply. In September 1951 the United Nations (UN) Security Council passed Resolution 95 demanding that Egypt permit passage through the canal of Israeli ships and goods bound for Israel, a demand that successive Egyptian governments simply ignored. Under Gamal Abdel Nasser, who took power in 1954, demands that ownership of the canal and its revenues pass from the Suez Canal Company to the Egyptian government intensified and by early 1956 were reaching a crisis point. On the symbolically significant fourth anniversary of the Egyptian revolution, just a few days after Britain, the United States, and the World Bank withdrew their pledged funding for the construction of the Aswan High Dam, a project that Nasser regarded as inextricably linked to Egypt's international prestige, Nasser responded by seizing the physical property and administration of the Suez Canal and taking over not just its operation but all its revenues. Several other Arab neighboring states immediately applauded his audacity in facing up to what they considered neocolonial exploitation, and Nasser became a hero to nationalist movements around the world.

Primary Source

ARTICLE 1

The International Company of the Suez Maritime Canal (Egyptian Joint Stock Company) is hereby nationalized. Its assets and liabilities revert to the State and the councils and committees at present responsible for its administration are dissolved.

The shareholders and holders of founders' shares will be compensated for the stock and shares which they own on the basis of their closing price on the Paris Bourse immediately preceding the date on which this law enters into force.

Payment of this compensation will be made when all the assets of the nationalized company have been fully handed over to the State.

ARTICLE 2

The administration of traffic services through the Suez Canal will be carried out by an independent body with the legal status of a corporation; it will be attached to the Ministry of Commerce. An order of the President of the Republic will fix the composition of this body and the payment to be made to its members. This body will have full powers necessary for controlling this service and will not be subject to administrative routine and regulations.

[. . .]

ARTICLE 3

The funds of the nationalized company and its rights in Egypt and abroad are hereby frozen. Banks, institutions and private persons are forbidden to dispose of these assets in any way, to pay out any sum whatever or to meet claims for payment without previous sanction by the body envisaged in Article 2.

[. . .]

ARTICLE 5

Any breach of the terms of Article 3 will be punished with imprisonment and a fine equal to three times the value of the sum involved. Any breach of the terms of Article 4 will be punished with imprisonment; the offender will, in addition, be deprived of any right to a gratuity, pension or compensation.

[. . .]

Source: D. C. Watt, *Documents on the Suez Crisis: 26 July to 6 November 1956* (London: Royal Institute of International Affairs, 1957).

40. Sir Anthony Eden, Statement on the Anglo-French Communications to Egypt and Israel [Excerpt], October 30, 1956

Introduction

Western response to the Egyptian seizure of the Suez Canal was muted for several months, focusing publicly on negotiations among the Egyptian government, the United Nations (UN), the British and French governments, and the Suez Canal Users Association. In private, however, the British, French, and Israeli governments planned what they hoped would be a bold and daring operation that would not only regain the canal but would also enhance Israel's strategic position. Egypt used the Gaza Strip, seized from Israel in the Israeli War of Independence (1948–1949), for almost daily attacks against Israeli positions. Israel planned to respond with an invasion of Egypt, in the course of which Israeli troops would move toward the Suez Canal and appear to pose a threat to its operation. The British and French would then demand that Israel and Egypt end hostilities and that Israel withdraw and, when they refused to do so, would launch their own invasion and retake the canal. The hope was that presented with this fait accompli, other countries, including the United States, and the UN would acquiesce in the results. Israel would have regained the Gaza Strip and taken the strategically important Sinai area, and Britain and France would once more control the Suez Canal. Speaking in the British House of Commons immediately after issuing ultimata to both Egypt and Israel, British prime minister Sir Anthony Eden affirmed the intention of British and French forces to intervene within 12 hours to protect the Canal and restore order. The following day, British airplanes based in Cyprus bombed Egyptian airfields, causing the withdrawal of Egyptian forces from the Sinai, which Israeli troops quickly occupied. Anglo-French ground forces invaded Egypt on November 6 but one day later accepted a cease-fire negotiated by the UN.

Primary Source

With your permission, Mr. Speaker, and that of the House, I will make a statement.

As the House will know, for some time past the tension on the frontiers of Israel has been increasing. The growing military strength of Egypt has given rise to renewed apprehension, which the statements and actions of the Egyptian Government have further aggravated. The establishment of a Joint Military Command between Egypt, Jordan and Syria, the renewed raids by guerillas, culminating in the incursion of Egyptian commandos on Sunday night, had all produced a very dangerous situation.

Five days ago news was received that the Israel Government were taking certain measures of mobilisation. Her Majesty's Government at once instructed Her Majesty's Ambassador at Tel Aviv to make inquiries of the Israel Minister for Foreign Affairs and to urge restraint.

Meanwhile, President Eisenhower called for an immediate tripartite discussion between representatives of the United Kingdom, France and the United States. A meeting was held on 28th October, in Washington, and a second meeting took place on 29th October.

While these discussions were proceeding, news was received last night that Israel forces had crossed the frontier and had penetrated deep into Egyptian territory. Later, further reports were received indicating that paratroops had been dropped. It appears that the Israel spearhead was not far from the banks of the Suez Canal. From recent reports it also appeared that air forces are in action in the neighbourhood of the Canal.

During the last few weeks Her Majesty's Government have thought it their duty, having regard to their obligations under the Anglo-Jordan Treaty, to give assurances, both public and private, of their intention to honour these obligations. Her Majesty's Ambassador in Tel Aviv late last night received an assurance that Israel would not attack Jordan.

[…]

I must tell the House that very grave issues are at stake, and that unless hostilities can quickly be stopped free passage through the Canal will be jeopardised. Moreover, any fighting on the banks of the Canal would endanger the ships actually on passage. The number of crews and passengers involved totals many hundreds, and the value of the ships which are likely to be on passage is about £50 million, excluding the value of the cargoes.

Her Majesty's Government and the French Government have accordingly agreed that everything possible should be done to bring hostilities to an end as soon as possible. Their representatives in New York have, therefore, been instructed to join the United States representative in seeking an immediate meeting of the Security Council. This began at 4 p.m.

In the meantime, as a result of the consultations held in London today, the United Kingdom and French Governments have now addressed urgent communications to the Governments of Egypt and Israel. In these we have called upon both sides to stop all warlike action by land, sea and air forthwith and to withdraw their military forces to a distance of 10 miles from the Canal. Further, in order to separate the belligerents and to guarantee freedom of transit through the Canal by the ships of all nations, we have asked the Egyptian Government to agree that Anglo-French forces should move temporarily—I repeat temporarily—into key positions at Port Said, Ismailia and Suez.

The Governments of Egypt and Israel have been asked to answer this communication within 12 hours. It has been made clear to them that, if at the expiration of that time one or both have not undertaken to comply with these requirements, British and French forces will intervene in whatever strength may be necessary to secure compliance.

I will continue to keep the House informed of the situation.

> **Source:** Anthony Eden, "Statement on Anglo-French Communications to Egypt and Israel," Parliament, House of Commons. *House of Commons Debates*, 558, coll. 1274–1275.

41. Dwight D. Eisenhower, Radio and Television Report to the American People on the Developments in Eastern Europe and the Middle East [Excerpt], October 31, 1956

Introduction

When Israel, France, and Britain attacked Egypt in 1956, they had kept the U.S. government in ignorance of their plans, assuming that President Dwight D. Eisenhower and Secretary of State John Foster Dulles might offer verbal protests but would acquiesce in the outcome. In fact, U.S. officials deplored the Anglo-French-Israeli action. It came at a particularly embarrassing juncture, since a few days earlier the Soviet Union had sent troops to Hungary, one of its East European satellite states, to prevent that country from seceding from the Warsaw Pact and restore communist rule. The Eisenhower administration had strongly condemned the Soviet action and felt unable to acquiesce in its allies' military intervention in Egypt. The United States, moreover, sought to win the allegiance of anticolonialist and nationalist forces throughout the developing world in Asia, Africa, and the Middle East. If Eisenhower aligned his country with an Anglo-French invasion of Egypt and seizure of the Suez Canal, this would probably inflict irretrievable damage on all such efforts to attract Third World nationalists, to whom Gamal Abdel Nasser was already an inspiring hero. In addition, Eisenhower was running for reelection, and in early November the American people would be going to the polls. He particularly resented the fact that Britain and France had deceived him and other U.S. officials regarding their intentions and had then moved at such a domestically and internationally difficult time for him. Eisenhower therefore publicly repudiated the actions of Britain, France, and Israel and forcefully demanded that they cease all operations against Egypt and accept a cease-fire. Privately, he also cut off all U.S. economic and military assistance—including oil supplies and support for their currencies—to all three countries, drastic measures that quickly put so much financial pressure on those states that they were compelled to accept his demands within one week. The fact that Great Britain, half a century earlier the world's most powerful empire, was forced to accede to U.S. economic blackmail underlined the degree to which European states were now dependent on the United States and could not rival its economic or military strength.

Primary Source

[...]

I now turn to that other part of the world where, at this moment, the situation is somber. It is not a situation that calls for extravagant fear or hysteria. But it invites our most serious concern.

I speak, of course, of the Middle East. This ancient crossroads of the world was, as we all know, an area long subject to colonial rule. This rule ended after World War II, when all countries there won full independence. Out of the Palestinian mandated territory was born the new State of Israel.

These historic changes could not, however, instantly banish animosities born of the ages. Israel and her Arab neighbors soon found themselves at war with one another. And the Arab nations showed continuing anger toward their former colonial rulers, notably France and Great Britain.

The United States—through all the years since the close of World War II—has labored tirelessly to bring peace and stability to this area.

We have considered it a basic matter of United States policy to support the new State of Israel and—at the same time—to strengthen our bonds both with Israel and with the Arab countries. But, unfortunately through all these years, passion in the area threatened to prevail over peaceful purposes, and in one form or another, there has been almost continuous fighting.

This situation recently was aggravated by Egyptian policy including rearmament with Communist weapons. We felt this to be a misguided policy on the part of the Government of Egypt. The State of Israel, at the same time, felt increasing anxiety for its safety. And Great Britain and France feared more and more that Egyptian policies threatened their "life line" of the Suez Canal.

These matters came to a crisis on July 26th of this year, when the Egyptian Government seized the Universal Suez Canal Company. For ninety years—ever since the inauguration of the Canal—that Company has operated the Canal, largely under British and French technical supervision.

Now there were some among our allies who urged an immediate reaction to this event by use of force. We insistently urged otherwise, and our wish prevailed—through a long succession of conferences and negotiations for weeks—even months—with participation by the United Nations. And there, in the United Nations, only a short while ago, on the basis of agreed principles, it seemed that an acceptable accord was within our reach.

But the direct relations of Egypt with both Israel and France kept worsening to a point at which first Israel—then France and Great Britain also—determined that, in their judgment, there could be no protection of their vital interests without resort to force.

Upon this decision, events followed swiftly. On Sunday the Israeli Government ordered total mobilization. On Monday, their armed forces penetrated deeply into Egypt and to the vicinity of the Suez Canal, nearly one hundred miles away. And on Tuesday, the British and French Governments delivered a 12-hour ultimatum to Israel and Egypt—now followed up by armed attack against Egypt.

The United States was not consulted in any way about any phase of these actions. Nor were we informed of them in advance.

As it is the manifest right of any of these nations to take such decisions and actions, it is likewise our right—if our judgment so dictates—to dissent. We believe these actions to have been taken in error. For we do not accept the use of force as a wise or proper instrument for the settlement of international disputes.

To say this—in this particular instance—is in no way to minimize our friendship with these nations—nor our determination to maintain those friendships.

And we are fully aware of the grave anxieties of Israel, of Britain and of France. We know that they have been subjected to grave and repeated provocations.

The present fact, nonetheless, seems clear: the action taken can scarcely be reconciled with the principles and purposes of the United Nations to which we have all subscribed. And, beyond this, we are forced to doubt that resort to force and war will for long serve the permanent interest of the attacking nations.

Now—we must look to the future.

In the circumstances I have described, there will be no United States involvement in these present hostilities. I therefore have no plan to call the Congress in Special Session. Of course, we shall continue to keep in contact with Congressional leaders of both parties.

I assure you, your government will remain alert to every possibility of this situation, and keep in close contact and coordination with the Legislative Branch of this government.

At the same time it is—and it will remain—the dedicated purpose of your government to do all in its power to localize the fighting and to end the conflict.

We took our first measure in this action yesterday. We went to the United Nations with a request that the forces of Israel return to their own land and that hostilities in the area be brought to a close. This proposal was not adopted—because it was vetoed by Great Britain and by France.

The processes of the United Nations, however, are not exhausted. It is our hope and intent that this matter will be brought before the United Nations General Assembly. There—with no veto operating —the opinion of the world can be brought to bear in our quest for a just end to this tormenting problem. In the past the United Nations has proved able to find a way to end bloodshed. We believe it can and that it will do so again.

My fellow citizens, as I review the march of world events in recent years, I am ever more deeply convinced that the processes of the United Nations represent the soundest hope for peace in the world. For this very reason, I believe that the processes of the United Nations need further to be developed and strengthened. I speak particularly of increasing its ability to secure justice under international law.

In all the recent troubles in the Middle East, there have indeed been injustices suffered by all nations involved. But I do not believe that another instrument of injustice—war—is the remedy for these wrongs.

There can be no peace—without law. And there can be no law—if we were to invoke one code of international conduct for those who oppose us—and another for our friends.

The society of nations has been slow in developing means to apply this truth.

But the passionate longing for peace—on the part of all peoples of the earth—compels us to speed our search for new and more effective instruments of justice.

The peace we seek and need means much more than mere absence of war. It means the acceptance of law, and the fostering of justice, in all the world.

To our principles guiding us in this quest we must stand fast. In so doing we can honor the hopes of all men for a world in which peace will truly and justly reign.

[...]

Source: Dwight D. Eisenhower, *Public Papers of the Presidents of the United States: Dwight D. Eisenhower, 1956* (Washington, DC: U.S. Government Printing Office, 1958), 1060–1066.

42. Letter from Premier Nikolai Bulganin to Sir Anthony Eden, November 5, 1956

Introduction

Despite its preoccupation with separatist movements in both Hungary and Poland in Eastern Europe, the Soviet Union quickly took a position on the Suez Crisis. Predictably, Soviet officials were strongly pro-Egyptian and condemned the "unprovoked aggression" of Israel, Britain, and France as well as the Anglo-French blockade of access to the Suez Canal. Even before Britain and France intervened, on October 30 the Soviet Union submitted a resolution to the United Nations (UN) demanding the withdrawal of Israeli forces, and in public statements Soviet officials subsequently assailed the Anglo-French attacks. As days passed, the Soviets made suggestions that could be interpreted as thinly veiled threats of Soviet military action should the invaders not withdraw and end their campaigns. On November 4, the Soviet Union submitted a draft resolution to the UN threatening UN military intervention unless Britain, France, and Israel ceased their operations, although this was rejected. On November 5, Soviet prime minister Nikolai Bulganin addressed open letters to his British, French, and Israeli counterparts, Sir Anthony Eden, Guy Mollet, and David Ben-Gurion, and also wrote to U.S. president Dwight D. Eisenhower. Aligning his country with nationalist movements, Bulganin characterized the Suez operation as "a pretext for British and French aggression, which has other and far-reaching aims," a "predatory" attempt to squelch nationalist movements in the Middle East and restore "colonial slavery." Once again, he demanded the immediate cessation of operations and the withdrawal of the invading forces. Warning that the crisis had the potential to develop into a "third world war," Bulganin pointedly inquired of Eden, "In what situation would Britain find herself if she were attacked by stronger states, possessing all types of modern destructive weapons?" While Soviet threats to intervene in Egypt or take action elsewhere against Egypt's attackers may have been bluffs, they indicated dramatically how any such incident could only too easily escalate into a full-scale confrontation between nuclear-armed superpowers and added to the growing atmosphere of tension and crisis. To Eisenhower, Bulganin suggested that the Soviet Union and the United States, "great powers possessing all modern types of weapons, including atomic and hydrogen weapons," had "a special responsibility for stopping the war and restoring peace and tranquility in the area of the Near and Middle East." Reminding Eisenhower that both powers had powerful fleets and air forces in the area, Bulganin suggested that if necessary the two powers consider taking joint military action in Egypt under UN auspices. Bulganin's missive may have been intended primarily for propaganda purposes but may equally have represented an attempt to introduce Soviet forces into the Middle East and gain a military toehold in the area. The obvious Soviet interest in gaining an enhanced stake in this international strategic cockpit was likely to make Eisenhower even more eager to settle the Suez Crisis as expeditiously as possible.

Primary Source

Esteemed Mr. Prime Minister,

The Soviet government considers it necessary to draw your attention to the fact that the aggressive war engineered by Britain and France against the Egyptian state, in which Israel played the role of an instigator, is fraught with very dangerous consequences for universal peace.

The special emergency session of the General Assembly has adopted a decision on the immediate ending of hostilities and the withdrawal of foreign troops from Egyptian territory. Disregarding this, Britain, France and Israel are intensifying military operations, are continuing the barbarous bombing of Egyptian towns and villages, have landed troops on Egyptian territory, are reducing her inhabited localities to ruins and are killing civilians.

Thus, the government of Britain, together with the governments of France and Israel, has embarked upon unprovoked aggression against Egypt.

The motives cited by the British government in justifying the attack on Egypt are absolutely fallacious. First of all, the British government stated that it was intervening in the conflict between Israel and Egypt in order to prevent the Suez Canal from becoming a zone of military operations. Following the British and French interven-

tion, the Suez Canal area has become a zone of military operations and navigation through the canal has been disrupted, which harms the interests of nations using the canal.

Attempts to justify the aggression by reference to the interest of Britain and France in freedom of navigation through the Suez Canal are also fallacious. We understand your special interest in the canal. This, however, does not entitle you to conduct military operations against the Egyptian people. At the same time, the governments of Britain and France cannot assume the role of judges in the question of the means of securing freedom of navigation through the Suez Canal, since many other states that are denouncing the aggressive actions of Britain and France and demanding the maintenance of peace and tranquility in the Near and Middle East, have no less interest in it. Furthermore, it is well known that freedom of navigation through the Suez Canal was fully ensured by Egypt.

The Suez Canal issue was only a pretext for British and French aggression, which has other and far-reaching aims. It cannot be concealed that in actual fact an aggressive predatory war is now unfolding against the Arab peoples with the object of destroying the national independence of the states of the Near and Middle East and of reestablishing the regime of colonial slavery rejected by the peoples.

There is no justification for the fact that the armed forces of Britain and France, two great powers that are permanent members of the Security Council, have attacked a country which only recently acquired its national independence and which does not possess adequate means for self-defense.

In what situation would Britain find herself if she were attacked by stronger states, possessing all types of modern destructive weapons? And such countries could, at the present time, refrain from sending naval or air forces to the shores of Britain and use other means —for instance, rocket weapons. Were rocket weapons used against Britain and France, you would, most probably, call this a barbarous action. But how does the inhuman attack launched by the armed forces of Britain and France against a practically defenseless Egypt differ from this?

With deep anxiety over the developments in the Near and Middle East, and guided by the interests of the maintenance of universal peace, we think that the government of Britain should listen to the voice of reason and put an end to the war in Egypt. We call upon you, upon Parliament, upon the Labour Party, the trade unions, upon the whole of the British people: Put an end to the armed aggression; stop the bloodshed. The war in Egypt can spread to other countries and turn into a third world war.

The Soviet government has already addressed the United Nations and the President of the United States of America with the proposal to resort, jointly with other United Nations member-states, to the use of naval and air forces in order to end the war in Egypt and to curb aggression. We are fully determined to crush the aggressors by the use of force and to restore peace in the East.

We hope that at this critical moment you will show due common sense and draw the appropriate conclusions.

With sincere respect,

N. BULGANIN

Source: *Soviet News*, November 6, 1956.

43. White House Statement to Nikolai Bulganin, November 5, 1956

Introduction

U.S. president Dwight D. Eisenhower responded within hours to Soviet prime minister Nikolai Bulganin's suggestion that their two countries mount a joint military operation against Anglo-French and Israeli forces in Egypt. While deeply annoyed by his European allies' actions over Suez, Eisenhower had no desire to send American troops to fight British, French, and Israeli soldiers. He also profoundly distrusted Soviet motives in seeking to introduce their own forces in the area, particularly after their recent bloody suppression of the Hungarian uprising. Eisenhower wrote immediately to Bulganin and rejected the prime minister's proposal, and the White House also issued a statement on the subject. Eisenhower stressed that the United Nations (UN) was already dealing with the Suez Crisis, was fully capable of doing so, and should be left to tackle this job without further Soviet interference. He highlighted the fact that the Soviet Union had declined to vote in favor of the UN resolution on this subject the previous evening, calling for a cease-fire, the withdrawal of all foreign military forces, and the introduction of a UN peacekeeping force, and he urged the Soviet Union to accept and support this resolution. He warned that should Soviet forces enter the area they would be doing so in contravention of the UN mandate, and the United States would, if necessary, help in removing them. About half of the presidential statement was devoted to the situation in Hungary and condemned the fact that Soviet forces were still "brutally repressing the human rights of the Hungarian people." As the UN General Assembly had also urged the previous evening, the White House demanded that the Soviet Union end its military operations in Hungary and immediately withdraw all Soviet forces there.

Primary Source

The President has just received a letter from Chairman Bulganin which had been previously released to the press in Moscow. This letter—in an obvious attempt to divert world attention from the Hungarian tragedy—makes the unthinkable suggestion that the United States join with the Soviet Union in a bipartite employment of their military forces to stop the fighting in Egypt.

The Middle East question—in which there has been much provocation on all sides—is now before the United Nations. That world body has called for a cease-fire, a withdrawal of foreign armed forces, and the entry of a United Nations force to stabilize the situation pending a settlement. In this connection, it is to be regretted that the Soviet Union did not vote last night in favor of the organization of this United Nations force. All parties concerned, however, should accept these United Nations resolutions promptly and in good faith.

Neither Soviet nor any other military forces should now enter the Middle East area except under United Nations mandate. Any such action would be directly contrary to the present resolution of the United Nations, which has called for the withdrawal of those foreign forces which are now in Egypt. The introduction of new forces under these circumstances would violate the United Nations Charter, and it would be the duty of all United Nations members, including the United States, to oppose any such effort.

While we are vitally concerned with the situation in Egypt, we are equally concerned with the situation in Hungary. There, Soviet forces are at this very moment brutally repressing the human rights of the Hungarian people. Only last night the General Assembly in emergency session adopted a resolution calling on the Soviet Union to cease immediately its military operations against the Hungarian people and to withdraw its forces from that country. The Soviet Union voted against this resolution, just as it had vetoed an earlier resolution in the Security Council. The Soviet Union is, therefore, at this moment in defiance of a decision of the United Nations, taken to secure peace and justice in the world.

Under these circumstances, it is clear that the first and most important step that should be taken to insure world peace and security is for the Soviet Union to observe the United Nations resolution to cease its military repression of the Hungarian people and withdraw its troops. Only then would it be seemly for the Soviet Union to suggest further steps that can be taken toward world peace.

Since Chairman Bulganin has already released his letter to the President, it is proper now to release a letter written by the President yesterday to the Chairman about the situation in Hungary.

Source: "U.S. Rejects Soviet Proposal to Use Force in Egypt; Urges U.S.S.R. to Withdraw Troops from Hungary," *Department of State Bulletin* 35(908) (1956): 795–796.

44. David Ben-Gurion, Speech to the Knesset [Excerpt], November 7, 1956

Introduction

While Britain and France regarded the Suez operation as a humiliating fiasco and failure, for Israel it represented a considerable victory. By the time the war had ended, Israeli forces had regained the Gaza Strip and occupied the Sinai Peninsula, putting an end to Egyptian attacks on Israeli territory and also opening the Straits of Tiran to Israeli shipping from the port of Eilat in the Gulf of Aqaba. Speaking to the Knesset (Israeli parliament) as the United Nations (UN) cease-fire came into effect, Prime Minister David Ben-Gurion celebrated Israel's achievements. Israel initially intended to retain control of the Sinai. Eventually, in the spring of 1957 and under considerable U.S. pressure, Israeli forces withdrew but insisted that the area not be returned to Egypt but instead be handed over to the control of the UN Emergency Force (UNEF). Israel now expected the UNEF to prevent Egyptian fedayeen (peasants) from infiltrating into the Gaza Strip and mounting small-scale anti-Israeli operations there and warned that should the UNEF fail to do so, the Israeli government would consider this sufficient reason to move once more against the Sinai. Israeli officials also stated that should Egypt seek to close the Straits of Tiran to Israeli ships, this too would be a casus belli, or act justifying war. The Suez operation also helped to enhance Israel's image in the United States. Many U.S. congressmen, alarmed by Soviet pronouncements and eagerness to intervene during the Suez Crisis, now came to see Israel as a potential Cold War bulwark against Soviet designs on the Middle East. For Egypt, on the other hand, UN administration of the Sinai was a continuing sore point. The festering disagreements over Sinai would become one major factor precipitating the 1967 Six-Day War.

Primary Source

The glorious military operation which lasted a week and conquered the entire Sinai Peninsula of 60,000 square kilometers is an unprecedented feat in Jewish history and is rare in the world's history. The Army did not make an effort to occupy enemy territory in Egypt proper and limited its operations to free the area from northern Sinai to the tip of the Red Sea.

This heroic advance is a focal point not only for the consolidation of the State's security and internal tranquility but also for our external relations on the world scene. Our forces did not attack Egypt proper and I hope the Egyptian dictator will not compel Israelis to violate the Biblical injunction never to return to that country.

Three weeks ago, I told the Knesset of the increased gravity of the Czech arms deal which had supplied Egypt with a tremendous flow of heavy armaments—it is only a week ago that our forces discovered the astonishing quantity and first-rate quality of this copious supply of Soviet arms, only part of which had been dispatched to the Sinai Peninsula.

Neither the Egyptian dictator nor his peace-loving friends in Czechoslovakia had the least doubt about the purpose of these enormous quantities of heavy arms. Certainly neither the supplier nor the recipient meant them to fall into Israeli hands. On the contrary, they meant them to bring about the downfall of Israel.

The Suez crisis has aroused the whole world but it has not disturbed Israel to the same extent, not because Israel does not have [an] interest in freedom of navigation of this international waterway but because our right of free navigation was brutally and arbitrarily violated by Egypt's ruler several years ago, and this continued after the Security Council's decision in 1951 which was arrogantly defied.

The United States, Britain and, especially, the Soviet Union appeased Fascist, dictatorial Egypt at the expense of international law and the maintenance of the prestige of the Security Council and the United Nations Charter as long as Israel only was affected.

Israel has confined itself to safeguarding its rights in the international waterway, and world public opinion has supported this demand.

The injury inflicted and the danger posed to Israel by Egypt was not limited to the denial of our rights in the Suez Canal. For Israel's economy, both the present and the future freedom of navigation of the Red Sea from Elath is no less vital than Suez.

[...]

For centuries this island [Tiran] has been desolate, and only a few years ago the Egyptians occupied and garrisoned it for the purpose of interfering with Israeli shipping in the Gulf.

The Egyptian dictator, however, did not content himself with the maritime blockade of Israel and the organization of an economic blockade against Israel throughout the world.

He organized and built up in all the Arab countries special units of murderers who crossed the borders to sow terror among workers in the fields and civilians in their homes.

Nasser proclaimed time and again that Egypt was in a state of war with Israel, nor did he conceal that his central purpose was to attack Israel at the first suitable opportunity and wipe her off the earth.

It is no accident that among the large quantities of supplies captured by our forces in the Sinai desert we also found copies of Hitler's *Mein Kampf*.

Since my review to the Knesset 3 weeks ago, something happened which intensified the danger and compelled us immediately to adopt special vigorous precautionary measures. After the Jordanian elections, in which Egyptian bribery played a decisive role, a pro-Egyptian majority was elected, and immediately a tripartite military alliance was concluded among Egypt, Jordan, and Syria, under the terms of which the armed forces of those three countries were placed under Egyptian command, with one clear goal in view: War to the death against [Israel].

The Egyptian fedayeen who, during the Suez crisis, were ordered by the Egyptian dictator to suspend their murderous activities in Israel, were brought back into action as soon as it seemed to Abdel Nasser that the crisis had passed, resulting in the wounding of 28 Israeli soldiers.

There was no room left to doubt that the noose which had been prepared for us was tightening and would neglect no means serving to destroy us, and it was our duty to take urgent and effective measures for self-defense. We mobilized a number of reserve battalions to guard the eastern border against lightning attack from Jordan or Syria or both, and we mobilized a larger force of reserves, consisting especially of armor, on the southern border.

At the beginning of our mobilization, I received two messages from the President of the United States expressing concern over the mobilization of reserves.

In my reply to the President of October 29, I reminded him of his constant efforts for peace in the region for the past year, which I supported wholeheartedly, as well as the fact that it was the Egyptian dictator who sabotaged these efforts. I also informed the President of the increasing gravity of the situation arising from the dictator's expansionist aims, the extent of his rearmament and attempts to undermine the independence of the Arab countries, and above all his overt intention to destroy Israel, his establishing a military alliance with Jordan and Syria under Egyptian command, and the renewal of fedayeen activities.

I ended my reply with: "With Iraqi troops poised in great numbers on the Iraq-Jordanian border; with the creation of a joint command of Egypt, Syria, and Jordan; with the renewal of incursions into Israel by Egyptian gangs, my Government would be failing in its essential duty if it does not take all the necessary measures to insure that the declared Arab aim to eliminate Israel by force should not come about.

"My Government appealed to the people of Israel to combine alertness with calm, and I feel confident that with your vast military experience you appreciate to the full the crucial danger in which we find ourselves."

That same evening a number of our units set out to put an end to the nests of murderers which were part of the Egyptian Army and

to those bases from which they were planned and organized and the root forces whence the murderous gangs came. Into these engagements the Egyptians brought their air force and fierce battles developed—at the end of seven days the entire Egyptian force in Sinai was eliminated.

As I said previously, our forces were given strict orders not to cross the Suez Canal or to attack Egyptian territory proper, and remain entirely within the limits of the Sinai Peninsula. I am confident military histories will make a thorough study of this remarkable operation carried out by the Israeli Army in a few days in a vast desert area against an enemy armed and equipped down to the smallest detail with the finest, most modern weapons of the Soviet bloc and elsewhere.

It is only now, after the occupation of the Gaza Strip, Abu Ageila, El Arish, Nekhal, Mitlah, and the Eilat Gulf, that we have fully realized how great in quantity, how modern and excellent in quality were the Egyptian arms and equipment. They had heavy weapons, tanks, guns, first-class communications equipment, motor transport, armored cars, clothing supplies immeasurably superior to anything our forces possess.

In spite of all our previous information about the flow of heavy arms of all types which the Egyptian dictator received during the year, we had no real notion of the enormous quantities and superior quality of the arms and equipment he had received. The vast booty which fell into our hands proves that beyond all doubt Egypt's dictator squeezed Egypt's hungry masses to provide his army with everything they had, but all this was of no avail because there was no spirit in them.

About three divisions faced Israel's army, in addition to a number of units, copiously armed and equipped, scattered the length and breadth of Sinai. The Egyptian troops numbered over 30,000 men and heavy reinforcements arrived during the fighting, over two brigades. And this huge army was equipped with hundreds of Czech and British tanks and other armor, supported by an air force equipped with Vampire, Meteor, MIG jet planes, and the Egyptian Navy also came into action.

The first night of operations we took Kuntilla after 20 minutes of resistance, Ras el Naqeb near Elath after a brief engagement, and Kusseima after 45 minutes of resistance.

I know this dry description is not adequate for this extraordinary and truly heroic action which few would believe possible, but it did not come out of the blue; in the preliminary planning we kept two principal objectives in view: to insure speed of operation and to minimize the number of casualties.

I can say with deep satisfaction that both purposes were achieved more successfully than expected and our losses were about 150 killed.

Let us stand silent in glorious memory of our heroes. In deep grief and profound pride we send our love and respect to their parents.

I know that I express the feeling of the entire nation and the Jewish people throughout the world when I say that our love and admiration go out to the Israeli army on land, sea, and air. The whole nation is proud of you. You enhanced the prestige of our people in the world and powerfully reinforced Israel's security.

During the fighting I was profoundly concerned with the fate of the cities which might be bombed by Egyptian bombers, and we took special precautions to decrease the danger.

Referring to the international situation, I will not ask the United Nations why it did not take equally prompt action when the Arab countries in 1948 invaded our country, which we revived in accordance with the General Assembly's own recommendations.

There is not a people in the world so deeply concerned for the principles of peace and justice contained in the United Nations Charter than [as] the Jewish people, not only because these principles are part of our ancient spiritual heritage and were passed on by us to the civilized world, but because the entire future of our people depends largely on the rule of peace and justice in the world.

Israel will not consent, under any circumstances, that a foreign force—called whatever it may—take up positions whether on Israeli soil or in any area held by Israel. The armistice with Egypt is dead, as are the armistice lines, and no wizards or magicians can resurrect these lines which cloaked Egyptian murders and sabotage.

Israel has no quarrel with the Egyptian people. Farouk and Nasser incited the Egyptians, but there is no underlying enmity between Israel and Egypt or vice versa. The latter point is proven by the wholesale desertion of Egyptian officers in the Sinai Peninsula.

Israel wants peace and neighborly relations with Egypt under conditions of direct negotiations. It is to be hoped that all peace-loving and freedom-loving people will support Israel in this demand. We are also ready for peace negotiations with the other Arab states on condition that they respect the armistice lines. Israel will not attack the Arab states, but if attacked will strike back.

[...]

Source: "David Gen-Gurion Reviews Sinai Campaign (November 7, 1956)," Jewish Virtual Library, http://www.jewishvirtuallibrary .org/jsource/History/bgsinai.html.

45. Nikita Khrushchev, "We Will Bury You," Reported in *The Times*, November 19, 1956

Introduction

Nikita Khrushchev, who eventually succeeded Joseph Stalin as general secretary of the Soviet Communist Party and top Soviet leader, was less formidable than his predecessor but at times could be erratic. Khrushchev frequently expressed his hopes for peaceful coexistence with the West, believing that nonsocialist countries would either evolve into communist states or experience autonomous revolutions that were not fomented by Soviet operatives. Fearing the devastating potential impact of nuclear war, Khrushchev also sought to reach understandings on arms control. This did not, however, mean that he had abandoned his faith in communism, the political creed that he had embraced as a young factory worker before World War I. Khrushchev was also notorious for somewhat unpredictable behavior, especially when he had imbibed plentiful quantities of vodka. In mid-1956, shortly after Soviet troops brutally suppressed the Hungarian Revolution and before the resolution of the Suez Crisis that occurred when Israel, Great Britain, and France invaded Egypt and the United States exerted economic pressure to force the three powers to withdraw, Khrushchev attended receptions at the Kremlin and the Polish embassy. In remarks at both venues, he took the opportunity to condemn the Suez invasion while characterizing Soviet intervention in Hungary as a justifiable exercise in counterrevolution. Warning that "Fascist bands" sought to destroy Communist parties in Italy, France, and elsewhere outside the Soviet sphere, Khrushchev proclaimed that "history is on our side" and warned the Western diplomats present, "We will bury you." In practice the Russian words Khrushchev used were less menacing than they appeared in translation and in the original meant something close to "We will attend your funeral." Khrushchev, who around this time had also threatened Soviet intervention if the Suez situation should not be swiftly resolved, apparently meant that the Western powers would collapse of their own volition, but the journalists present reported a somewhat sensational version of his remarks. Indeed, some years later Khrushchev himself looked back on this episode and commented that he had "got into trouble for it" when he had only wished to say that the working classes of the Western states would themselves overthrow their rulers. Khrushchev's speech nonetheless impelled all the Western ambassadors to leave, and the episode was widely reported around the world as an instance of Khrushchev's bullying, blustering style and taken as a threat to the West. In the popular memory, "we will bury you" would become one of Khrushchev's best-remembered utterances.

Primary Source

Sir William Hayter, the British Ambassador, and diplomatic representatives of other North Atlantic Treaty Organization countries, walked out from a Kremlin reception last night in protest at a speech by Mr. Khrushchev, the Soviet Communist Party chairman, in which he used the words "Fascist" and "bandits" in referring to Britain and France and Israel.

The reception was in honour of Mr. Gomulka, who was concluding his visit to Moscow.

Out of courtesy to Mr. Gomulka, the N.A.T.O. ambassadors and representative of Israel waited until Mr. Gomulka had responded with a toast that was devoid of references to Egypt or Hungary and limited to advocating friendly ties with the Soviet Union based on equality and mutual benefit. Immediately on the conclusion of the translation into Russian of Mr. Gomulka's toast, read in Polish, the western diplomatists strode from the long white and gold St. George's Hall.

Mr. Khrushchev declared that the "bandit-like attack by Britain, France, and their puppet, Israel, on Egypt is a desperate attempt by colonializers to regain their lost positions, to frighten the peoples of dependent countries with force. But the time has passed when imperialists could seize weak countries with impunity. The freedom-loving people of Egypt have administered a fitting rebuff to the aggressors, and its just struggle against foreign invaders has evoked warm support all over the world."

Mr. Khrushchev, words tumbling from his lips in rapid fashion, continued by extending his accusations against other Powers besides Britain, France, and Israel. "Feverish activity is now in progress on the part of all the forces of reaction against the forces of Socialism and democracy. Fascist bands are making frenzied attacks on the advanced detachments of the working class, on the Communist parties of France, Italy, and other countries."

At a reception this evening at the Polish Embassy, Mr. Khrushchev delivered himself of a longer but more mildly worded address criticizing the western Powers. However, most western ambassadors, including Sir William Hayter, restricted themselves to wandering to an adjoining room while Mr. Khrushchev spoke.

Moscow, Nov. 18.—In his speech Mr. Khrushchev, who appeared to be directing his remarks to the western diplomatists, said: "We say this not only for the socialist States, who are more akin to us. We base ourselves on the idea that we must peacefully co-exist. About the capitalist States, it doesn't depend on you whether or not we exist. If you don't like us, don't accept our invitations and don't invite us to come to see you. Whether you like it or not, history is on our side. We will bury you."

There was applause from Mr. Khrushchev's colleagues, and Mr. Gomulka, who had been standing at one side rather glumly, laughed.

Mr. Khrushchev said that many mistakes had been made in building socialism in the Soviet Union because of the lack of examples and the lack of personnel. He continued: "If we could have the revolution over again we would carry it out more sensibly and with smaller losses; but history does not repeat itself. The situation is favourable for us. If God existed, we would thank him for this.

"We had Hungary thrust upon us. We are very sorry that such a situation exists there. We are sure that the Hungarian working class will find the strength to overcome the difficulties. But most important is that the counter-revolution must be shattered."

Turning to Mr. Gomulka, he said: "I am sorry to be making such a speech on the territory of a foreign State. The western Powers are trying to denigrate Nasser. He is not a Communist. Politically, he is closer to those who are waging war on him and he has even put Communists in gaol.

"We sent sharp letters to Britain, France, and Israel—well, Israel, that was just for form, because, as you know, Israel carries no weight in the world, and if it plays any role it was just to start a fight. If Israel hadn't felt the support of Britain, France, and others, the Arabs would have been able to box her ears and she would have remained at peace.

"The situation is serious and we are realists. The fire must be put out. I think the British and French will be wise enough to withdraw their forces, and then Egypt will emerge stronger than ever. We must seek a *rapprochement*. We must seek a settlement so that coexistence will be peaceful and advantageous."

Referring to the Soviet Government's latest disarmament plan, he said: "You say we want war, but you have now got yourselves into a position I would call idiotic. (Mr. Mikoyan interjected: "Let's say delicate.") But we don't want to profit by it.

"If you withdraw your troops from Germany, France, and Britain—I'm speaking of American troops—we will not stay one day in Poland, Hungary, and Rumania. But we, Mr. Capitalists, we are beginning to understand your methods. You have given us a lesson in Egypt. If we had a quarter of our present friendship for the Poles, Czechs, and Slovaks before the war, the war would never have started.

"Nobody should pretend to know the best methods of socialism. The Bulgarians, Poles, Yugoslavs, Rumanians, Czechs, and Soviets —all have their own; but, comrades, it is really better to hawk one's own wares, and if they are good, they will find a buyer on their own. So when our enemies try to bring us into conflict over which is the best method of socialism we reject this. It is not in the interests of socialism."

Source: "Ambassadors Walk Out," *London Times*, November 19, 1956. Reprinted with permission.

46. U.S. State Department, Statement on Withdrawal of British and French Forces from Egypt, December 3, 1956

Introduction

On November 7, 1956, the United Nations (UN) announced that all parties involved in the war against Egypt had accepted a cease-fire agreement. It was almost another month before Britain and France were willing to withdraw their forces, a decision they reached in part because the U.S. government continued to deny them economic assistance, including support for their currencies and foreign exchange reserves, and withheld oil supplies from both nations. The failure of their attempt at intervention was a major humiliation for both powers, seriously eroding what remained of their prestige in the Middle East. British prime minister Sir Anthony Eden resigned over what was widely perceived as his botched handling of the Suez affair. For many British officials, memories of U.S. behavior over Suez and what they saw as President Dwight D. Eisenhower's betrayal of an ally left a bitter and rankling legacy of resentment and distrust that would be invoked for decades to come. Although the United States had taken drastic action to force Gamal Abdel Nasser's two European opponents to end the Suez operation and leave Egypt, Eisenhower and Secretary of State John Foster Dulles still disliked and distrusted Nasser's radical nationalist regime and gave it little assistance. They sought instead to work with moderate and pro-Western governments throughout the Middle Eastern region, making Iran and Saudi Arabia pillars of their West Asian alliance system. They also encouraged the rulers of such states to turn to the United States for military and economic assistance should they be faced with radical opposition liable to destabilize their hold on power, a strategy that subsequent U.S. leaders would in their turn adopt.

Primary Source

The British and French Governments have now declared their purpose to comply with the U.N. resolution regarding withdrawal of their forces from Egypt. They have stated that they will work out with General Burns, Commander of the United Nations forces, a definite and early schedule for complete withdrawal.

The United States welcomes this decision. Its implementation will strengthen the capacity of the United Nations to deal with the other aspects of the Middle Eastern problems which are still unfinished business.

It will now, more than ever, become incumbent upon all members of the United Nations to insure that the remaining issues are dealt with justly and promptly. The United States has repeatedly said during this crisis in the Middle East that the United Nations cannot rightfully or prudently stop merely with maintaining peace. Under its charter it is obligated to deal with the basic sources of international friction and conflicts of interest. Only in this way can it attain the charter goal of peace with justice.

In keeping with this obligation the United States will continue fully to support the measures required to make the United Nations force adequate and effective for its mission. In carrying out his plans for this purpose the Secretary-General can count on the unstinting cooperation of the United States.

As the United Nations force replaces those of the United Kingdom and France, the clearance of the canal becomes imperative. Every day of delay in restoring the canal to normal use is a breach of the 1888 treaty and a wrong to the large number of nations throughout the world whose economies depend so heavily on its reliable operation.

The United Nations and the interested states should, we believe, promptly direct their attention to the underlying Middle East problems. The United States Government considers it essential that arrangements be worked out without delay to insure the operation of the canal in conformity with the six principles approved by the resolution of the Security Council on October 13, 1956.

The United States is equally determined, through the United Nations and in other useful ways, to assist in bringing about a permanent settlement of the other persistent conflicts which have plagued the Middle East over recent years. Repeatedly we have made clear our willingness to contribute for the purpose of bringing stability and just peace to this area. The present crisis is a challenge to all nations to work to this end.

Source: "Withdrawal of British and French Forces from Egypt," *Department of State Bulletin* 35(912) (1956): 951–952.

47. Judgment, Criminal Case No. 40/61, Trial of Adolf Eichmann, District Court of Jerusalem, Israel [Excerpt], December 11, 1961

Introduction

During the 1950s and 1960s, Israeli officials made strenuous efforts to track down former German and Austrian war criminals who had been responsible for killing and persecuting Jews from 1933 to 1945, when the German Nazi Party was in power under Adolf Hitler. Perhaps the most spectacular such operation came in 1960, when Israeli

Mossad (Secret Service) and Shabak (Security Service) agents captured Adolf Eichmann in Argentina and smuggled him to Israel to stand trial. Eichmann was an Austrian who joined the Nazi Party in 1932 and became a lieutenant colonel in the SS (Sicherheitspolizei, or Security Police). From the mid-1930s, he was responsible for dealing with German and Austrian Jews. At first he investigated the possibility of large-scale emigration to eliminate Jews from the German Reich but eventually decided that given the large numbers involved, this solution was not feasible. In the late 1930s and early 1940s, he handled the eastward deportation of hundreds of thousands of European Jews. Eichmann took notes at the 1942 Wannsee Conference that authorized the so-called Final Solution to destroy all European Jews and subsequently implemented many of its decisions, organizing with great efficiency the massive transportation effort involved in moving millions of Jews to death and labor camps. In Hungary in 1944 Eichmann directly supervised the deaths of 400,000 Jews. In 1945 even after SS head Heinrich Himmler ordered that Jewish extermination be halted and all evidence of the Final Solution destroyed, Eichmann continued his efforts in Hungary. Briefly captured by the U.S. Army in 1945, he then lived in hiding in Germany for some years, moving to Argentina in 1950. Israeli prime minister David Ben-Gurion announced Eichmann's sensational capture in May 1960, receiving a standing ovation in the Knesset. In April 1961 Eichmann's trial opened. The trial lasted 14 weeks and involved testimony from 100 prosecution witnesses, including 90 Nazi concentration camp survivors, while 1,500 documents were entered into evidence. Throughout the trial, Eichmann claimed that he was merely "following orders." In December 1961 the three judges, after lengthy deliberations, announced their verdict of guilty, which Israel's Supreme Court upheld the following May. Eichmann was hanged on June 1, 1962, the only civil execution in the history of Israel, which does not normally impose the death penalty for civil crimes. His discovery, trial, and death gave dramatic evidence of the lengths to which the Israeli government would go to avenge the Holocaust and bring to justice those responsible for it.

Primary Source

Adolf Eichmann has been brought to trial in this Court on charges of unsurpassed gravity—charges of crimes against the Jewish People, crimes against humanity, and war crimes. The period of the crimes ascribed to him, and their historical background, is that of the Hitler regime in Germany and in Europe, and the counts of the indictment encompass the catastrophe which befell the Jewish People during that period—a story of bloodshed and suffering which will be remembered to the end of time.

This is not the first time that the Holocaust has been discussed in court proceedings. It was dealt with extensively at the International Military Tribunal at Nuremberg during the Trial of the Major War Criminals, and also at several of the trials which followed; but this time it has occupied the central place in the Court proceedings, and it is this fact which has distinguished this trial from those which pre-

ceded it. Hence also the trend noticed during and around the trial, to widen its range. The desire was felt—understandable in itself—to give, within the trial, a comprehensive and exhaustive historical description of events which occurred during the Holocaust, and in so doing, to emphasize also the inconceivable feats of heroism performed by ghetto-fighters, by those who mutinied in the camps, and by Jewish partisans.

There are also those who sought to regard this trial as a forum for the clarification of questions of great import, some of which arose from the Holocaust, while others of long standing have now emerged once again in more acute form, because of the unprecedented sufferings which were visited upon the Jewish People and the world as a whole in the middle of the Twentieth Century.

How could this happen in the light of day, and why was it just the German people from which this great evil sprang? Could the Nazis have carried out their evil designs without the help given them by other peoples in whose midst the Jews dwelt? Would it have been possible to avert the Holocaust, at least in part, if the Allies had displayed a greater will to assist the persecuted Jews? Did the Jewish People in the lands of freedom do all in its power to rally to the rescue of its brethren and to sound the alarm for help? What are the psychological and social causes of the group-hatred which is known as anti-Semitism? Can this ancient disease be cured, and by what means? What is the lesson which the Jews and other nations must draw from all this, as well as every person in his relationship to others? There are many other questions of various kinds which cannot even all be listed.

2. In this maze of insistent questions, the path of the Court was and remains clear. It cannot allow itself to be enticed into provinces which are outside its sphere. The judicial process has ways of its own, laid down by law, and which do not change, whatever the subject of the trial may be. Otherwise, the processes of law and of court procedure are bound to be impaired, whereas they must be adhered to punctiliously, since they are in themselves of considerable social and educational significance, and the trial would otherwise resemble a rudderless ship tossed about by the waves.

It is the purpose of every criminal trial to clarify whether the charges in the prosecution's indictment against the accused who is on trial are true, and if the accused is convicted, to mete out due punishment to him. Everything which requires clarification in order that these purposes may be achieved, must be determined at the trial, and everything which is foreign to these purposes must be entirely eliminated from the court procedure. Not only is any pretension to overstep these limits forbidden to the court—it would certainly end in complete failure. The court does not have at its disposal the tools required for the investigation of general questions of the kind referred to above. For example, in connection with the description of the historical background of the Holocaust, a great amount of material was brought before us in the form of documents and evidence, collected most painstakingly, and certainly in a genuine attempt to delineate as complete a picture as possible. Even so, all this material is but a tiny fraction of all that is extant on this subject. According to our legal system, the court is by its very nature "passive," for it does not itself initiate the bringing of proof before it, as is the custom with an enquiry commission. Accordingly, its ability to describe general events is inevitably limited. As for questions of principle which are outside the realm of law, no one has made us judges of them, and therefore no greater weight is to be attached to our opinion on them than to that of any person devoting study and thought to these questions. These prefatory remarks do not mean that we are unaware of the great educational value, implicit in the very holding of this trial, for those who live in Israel as well as for those beyond the confines of this state. To the extent that this result has been achieved in the course of the proceedings, it is to be welcomed. Without a doubt, the testimony given at this trial by survivors of the Holocaust, who poured out their hearts as they stood in the witness box, will provide valuable material for research workers and historians, but as far as this Court is concerned, they are to be regarded as by-products of the trial. . . .

244. The indictment was formulated in considerable detail. The method generally followed by the Attorney General was to set out in each count the essence of the indictment in one of the paragraphs of the "particulars of offence," for example—in paragraph (a) of the first count (crime against the Jewish People by causing the death of Jews), in paragraph (b) of the third count (crime against the Jewish People by causing grave physical and mental harm), and in paragraph (a) of the seventh count (crime against humanity through the plunder of property). To this the Attorney General added a detailed factual description of part of the acts attributed to the Accused. This is particularly evident in counts 1–7 of the indictment. It is here stressed at the same time that the factual description is not exhaustive. Thus, in paragraph "g" of the first count, there is a partial description of the operations of the Einsatzgruppen (Operations Units) by the specification of the number of the victims during a given period; but it is clear from the opening words "the operations of these Units included inter alia the following operations, etc.", that the Attorney General merely sought to give instances and examples from among all the operations which were carried out by the Operations Units. Again, in the seventh count, various operations of plunder of property are enumerated, but it is stated that these were among the activities of the Accused.

We do not mean to criticize this way of wording the charge sheet. On the contrary, in the nature of things, the description could not be more exhaustive because of the vast dimensions of the activities with the execution of which the Accused was, together with others, charged, while the method of partial specification was apt to inform the Accused with greater clarity of the nature of the operations of which he was accused. But as we come now to convict the Accused,

we do not consider ourselves bound by this partial specification in the indictment. We shall adhere to the general framework of the indictment, insofar as it concerns the description of the statement of offence, and also those parts of the particulars of offence in which a general description of the nature of the offence appears. But, as regards all other details, we base the conviction of the Accused on the detailed description of the facts which we have given in this Judgment, and of which the principal ones have been recapitulated in the chapter containing the legal analysis of the facts. In the light of this detailed description, we will now comprise in the text of the conviction only that which appears to us essential in each of the counts of the indictment, insofar as they have been proved before us.

(1) We, therefore, convict the Accused, pursuant to the first count of the indictment, of a crime against the Jewish People, an offence under Section 1(a)(1) of the Nazis and Nazi Collaborators (Punishment) Law 5710-1950, in that during the period from August 1941 to May 1945, in Germany, in the territories of the Axis States, in the areas which were occupied by Germany and by the Axis States, and in the areas which were subject to the authority of Germany and the Axis States, he, together with others, caused the deaths of millions of Jews, with the purpose of implementing the plan which was known as the "Final Solution of the Jewish Question," with intent to exterminate the Jewish People.

We acquit the Accused of a crime against the Jewish People, by reason of the acts attributed to him in this count of the indictment during the period until August 1941. The criminal acts of the Accused until that time . . . will be included in the conviction for crimes against humanity, under paragraph (5) of the conviction, as set out below.

(2) We convict the Accused pursuant to the second count of the indictment of a crime against the Jewish People, an offence under Section 1(a)(1) of the above-mentioned law, in that during the period from August 1941 to May 1945, in the territories and areas mentioned in paragraph (1) of the conviction, as set out above, he, together with others, subjected millions of Jews to living conditions which were likely to bring about their physical destruction, in order to implement the plan which was known as the "Final Solution of the Jewish Question," with intent to exterminate the Jewish People.

We acquit the Accused of a crime against the Jewish People by reason of the acts attributed to him in this count during the period until August 1941.

(3) We convict the Accused, pursuant to the third count of the indictment, of a crime against the Jewish People, an offence under Section 1(a)(1) of the above-mentioned Law, in that during the period from August 1941 to May 1945, in the territories and areas mentioned in paragraph (1) of the conviction, as above, he, together with others, caused grave bodily and mental harm to millions of Jews, with intent to exterminate the Jewish People.

We acquit the Accused of a crime against the Jewish People attributed to him in this count during the period until August 1941.

(4) We convict the Accused, pursuant to the fourth count, of a crime against the Jewish People, an offence under Section 1(a)(1) of the above-mentioned Law, in that during the years 1943 and 1944 he took measures calculated to prevent births among Jews, by directing that births be banned and pregnancies terminated among Jewish women in the Terezin Ghetto, with intent to exterminate the Jewish People.

We acquit the Accused of having committed all other acts mentioned in the fourth count of the indictment.

(5) We convict the Accused, pursuant to the fifth count, of a crime against humanity, an offence under Section 1(a)(2) of the above-mentioned Law, in that during the period from August 1941 to May 1945, in the territories and areas mentioned in paragraph (1) of the conviction, as above, he, together with others, caused the murder, extermination, enslavement, starvation and deportation of the Jewish civilian population in those countries and in those areas.

We also convict the Accused of a crime against humanity, an offence under Section 1(a)(2) of the above-mentioned Law, in that he, together with others, caused during the period from March 1938 to October 1941, the expulsion of Jews from their homes in the territories of the Old Reich, Austria and the Protectorate of Bohemia-Moravia, by way of compulsory emigration through the Central Offices for Jewish Emigration in Vienna, Prague and Berlin.

We also convict the Accused of a crime against humanity, an offence under Section 1(a)(2) of the above-mentioned Law, in that during the period from December 1939 to March 1941 he, together with others, caused the deportation of Jews to Nisko and the deportation of Jews from areas in the East annexed to the Reich, and from the Reich area itself into the German-occupied area in the East and to France.

(6) We convict the Accused, pursuant to the sixth count, of a crime against humanity, an offence under Section 1(a)(2) of the above-mentioned Law, in that, when carrying out the activities mentioned in paragraphs 1–5 of the conviction, he persecuted Jews on national, racial, religious and political grounds.

(7) We convict the Accused, pursuant to the seventh count, of a crime against humanity, an offence under Section 1(a)(2) of the above-mentioned Law, in that, during the period from March 1938 to May 1945, in the territories and areas mentioned in paragraph (1) of the conviction, as above, he, together with others, caused the plunder of the property of millions of Jews through mass terror, linked with the murder, destruction, starvation and deportation of those Jews.

(8) We convict the Accused, pursuant to the eighth count, of a war crime, an offence under Section 1(a)(3) of the above-mentioned Law, in that he performed the acts of persecution, expulsion and murder mentioned in the preceding counts, so far as these were committed during the Second World War, against Jews from among the populations of the countries occupied by Germany and the other countries of the Axis.

(9) We convict the Accused, pursuant to the ninth count, of a crime against humanity, an offence under Section 1(a)(2) of the above-mentioned Law, in that he, together with others, during the years 1940–1942, caused the expulsion of a civilian population, namely hundreds of thousands of Poles, from their homes.

(10) We convict the Accused, pursuant to the tenth count, of a crime against humanity, an offence under Section 1(a)(2) of the above-mentioned Law, in that in 1941, he, together with others, caused the expulsion of a civilian population, namely more than fourteen thousand Slovenes, from their homes.

(11) We convict the Accused, pursuant to the eleventh count, of a crime against humanity, an offence under Section 1(a)(2) of the above-mentioned Law, in that during the Second World War, he, together with others, caused the expulsion of a civilian population, namely tens of thousands of Gypsies from Germany and German-occupied areas, and their transportation to the German-occupied areas in the East.

It has not been proved before us that the Accused knew that the Gypsies were being transported to extermination.

(12) We convict the Accused, pursuant to the twelfth count, of a crime against humanity, an offence under Section 1(a)(2) of the above-mentioned Law, in that in 1942, he, together with others, caused the expulsion of 93 of the children of the Czech village of Lidice. It has not been proved before us that the Accused is guilty of the murder of these children.

(13) We acquit the Accused of the charges of belonging to hostile organizations, under the thirteenth, fourteenth and fifteenth counts, with respect to the period until May 1940, because of the prescription of these offences.

(14) We convict the Accused, pursuant to the thirteenth count, of membership of a hostile organization, an offence under Section 3(a) of the above-mentioned Law, in that he was, as from May 1941, a member of the organization known as Schutzstaffeln der NSDAP (SS), which was declared a criminal organization by the International Tribunal which tried the Major War Criminals, and in that, as a member of such organization, he took part in acts that were declared criminal in Article 6 of the London Charter of 8 August 1945.

(15) We convict the Accused, pursuant to the fourteenth count, of membership of a hostile organization, an offence under Section 3(a) of the above-mentioned Law, in that, as from May 1941, he was a member of the organization known as Sicherheitsdienst des Reichsfuehrers-SS (SD) which was declared a criminal organization by the International Military Tribunal which tried the Major War Criminals, and as a member of such organization he took part in acts declared criminal in Article 6 of the London Charter of 8 August 1945.

(16) We convict the Accused, pursuant to the fifteenth count, of membership of a hostile organization, an offence under Section 3(a) of the above-mentioned Law, in that he was, from May 1940, a member of the organization known as the Geheime Staatspolizei, which was declared a criminal organization by the International Military Tribunal which tried the Major War Criminals, and as a member of such organization took part in acts which were declared criminal in Article 6 of the London Charter of 8 August 1945.

Source: "The Trial of Adolf Eichmann," The Nizkor Project, http://www.nizkor.org/.

48. Palestine Liberation Organization, Draft Constitution [Excerpt], 1963

Introduction

Well before World War II, other Arab states had shown deep interest in the situation in Palestine. The Israeli War of Independence (1948–1949), however, destroyed the independent Palestinian state that the United Nations (UN) partition plan had envisaged, as Palestinian Arabs were driven out of their homes and often confined to refugee camps. While the assorted Arab states still professed deep concern over the fate of the Palestinians and unrelenting hostility to Israel, Palestinians felt a need to establish their own organization. During the 1950s, various clandestine and unofficial guerrilla groups of young Palestinian refugees who pledged to attack Israel by all means possible emerged in Syria, Egypt, and Kuwait, the most prominent among them probably being Fatah (the Palestinian National Liberation Organization), a student organization founded in 1958 in Kuwait. At an Arab Summit Conference held in 1963, Egypt encouraged the formation of an official body to represent the interests of Palestinians, a decision that led to the creation of the Palestine Liberation Organization (PLO) in May 1964. The PLO's charter was drafted by Ahmed Shukairy, a lawyer whose original home was Palestine and who later served as a UN representative for both Saudi Arabia and Syria. The PLO was to represent Palestine officially in the Arab League and was to work for the liberation of Palestine. The PLO established a complicated and rather cumbrous system of institutions and committees, to be financed largely by sympathetic Arab states. The PLO's charter left it vague precisely what kind of ultimate territorial outcome it sought and whether the total destruction of Israel was its objective, although the latter was implied in Article 4. Article 19, which authorized the establishment of "[p]rivate Palestinian [military] contingents," effectively authorized armed struggle against Israel and its supporters, using terrorist tactics if necessary. The PLO became an umbrella organization for numerous and varied—though not all—Palestinian groups. After the 1967 Six-Day War, radical Palestinian elements led by Yasser Arafat, head of Fatah, a group committed to the eradication of Israel by violent means, came to dominate the PLO, which won the allegiance and support of the majority of Palestinians. The Palestinian National Covenant, promulgated in 1968, made it clear that the organization's objectives included the establishment of a Palestinian Arab state and the expulsion from what had been Palestine of all Jews and their descendants who had arrived there after 1917. In October 1973 the Arab League recognized the PLO as "the sole legitimate representative of the Palestinian people." Ironically, the PLO's ever more leftist, communist, and secularist orientation and in some cases its eagerness to provoke confrontations with Israel made the organization increasingly suspect in the eyes of most Arab states, and Jordan, home to numerous Palestinian refugees, expelled the PLO in 1970. Non-Arab states and Israel initially refused to recognize the PLO, refusing to deal with a body they considered a terrorist organization, but over time nearly all governments came to accord the PLO almost quasi-governmental status as representing the Palestinians. In 1973 the UN granted the PLO observer status, meaning that its representatives could attend the UN even though they were unable to vote. Although some Palestinian groups and factions were not included in the PLO and the organization was characterized by what were often savage ideological and personal rivalries and antagonisms, it ultimately won general recognition as the closest approach to a representative organization that the Palestinians possessed.

Primary Source

1. In accordance with this constitution, an organisation known as "The Palestine Liberation Organization" shall be formed, and shall launch its responsibilities in accordance with the principles of the National Charter and clauses of this constitution.

2. All the Palestinians are natural members in the Liberation Organization exercising their duty in the liberation of their homeland in accordance with their abilities and efficiency.

3. The Palestinian people shall form the larger base for this Organization; and the Organization, after its creation, shall work closely and constantly with the Palestine people for the sake of their organization and mobilization so they may be able to assume their responsibility in the liberation of their country.

4. Until suitable conditions are available for holding free general elections among all the Palestinians and in all the countries in which

they reside, the Liberation Organization shall be set up in accordance with the rules set in this constitution.

5. Measures listed in this constitution shall be taken for the convocation of a Palestinian General Assembly in which shall be represented all Palestinian factions, emigrants and residents, including organisations, societies, unions, trade unions and representatives of [Palestinian] public opinions of various ideological trends; this assembly shall be called The National Assembly of the Palestine Liberation Organization.

6. In preparation and facilitation of work of the assembly, the Palestinian representative at the Arab League [i.e., Ahmed Shukairy] shall, after holding consultations with various Palestinian factions, form:

a)—A Preparatory Committee in every Arab country hosting a minimum of 10,000 Palestinians; the mission of each one of these committees is to prepare lists according to which Palestinian candidates in the respective Arab country will be chosen as members of the assembly; these committees shall also prepare studies and proposals which may help the assembly carry out its work; these studies and proposals shall be presented to the Coordination Committee listed below.

b)—A Coordination Committee, with headquarters in Jerusalem; the mission of this committee shall be to issue invitations to the assembly, adopt all necessary measures for the holding of the assembly, and coordinate all proposals and studies as well as lists of candidates to the assembly, as specified in the clause above; also the committee shall prepare a provisional agenda—or as a whole, undertake all that is required for the holding and success of the assembly in the execution of its mission.

7. The National Assembly shall be held once every two years; its venue rotates between Jerusalem and Gaza; the National Assembly shall meet for the first time on May 14, 1964, in the city of Jerusalem.

[...]

18. The Arab states shall avail the sons of Palestine the opportunity of enlisting in their regular armies on the widest scale possible.

19. Private Palestinian contingents shall be formed in accordance with the military needs and plans decided by the Unified Arab Military Command in agreement and cooperation with the concerned Arab states.

20. A Fund, to be known as "The National Palestinian Fund," shall be established to finance operations of the Executive Committee: the Fund shall have a Board of Directors whose members shall be elected by the National Assembly.

21. Sources of the Fund are to be from:
a)—Fixed taxes levied on Palestinians and collected in accordance with special laws.
b)—Financial assistance offered by the Arab governments and people.
c)—A "Liberation Stamp" to be issued by the Arab states and be used in postal and other transactions.
d)—Donations on national occasions.
e)—Loans and assistance given by the Arabs or by friendly nations.

22. Committees, to be known as "Support Palestine Committees," shall be established in Arab and friendly countries to collect donations and to support the Liberation Organization.

23. The Executive Committee shall have the right to issue by-laws for fulfillment of provisions of this constitution.

24. This draft constitution shall be submitted to the National Assembly for consideration; what is ratified of it cannot be changed except by a two thirds majority of the National Assembly.

Source: Walter Laqueur and Barry Rubin, eds., *The Israel-Arab Reader: A Documentary History of the Middle East Conflict* (New York: Penguin, 2001), 93–96.

49. Declaration of Second Arab Summit Conference [Excerpt], September 13, 1964

Introduction

The decision of the First Arab Summit Conference to establish the Palestine Liberation Organization (PLO) in 1963 was only one indication that divisions between Israel and the Arab states remained unresolved and that reconciliation would be difficult, if not impossible, to achieve. Meeting in Alexandria, Egypt, in September 1964, Arab leaders from Jordan, Tunisia, Algeria, Sudan, Iraq, Saudi Arabia, Syria, Egypt, Yemen, Kuwait, Lebanon, Libya, and Morocco and the new PLO declared their commitment to eliminating Israel and implementing "the liberation of Palestine from Zionist colonialism." They approved plans to "establish a Palestinian Liberation Army," effectively a body that would undertake terrorist activities against Israel in support of Palestine's liberation. For their own part, the signatories agreed to take action to sabotage Israeli efforts to use water from the Sea of Galilee in nationwide irrigation projects by themselves diverting the waters of the Jordan River before they reached the Sea of Galilee. They also agreed to unify their military commands and increase their armed forces. The united front that the Arab states presented and the decisions reached at this meeting alarmed Israeli leaders sufficiently to impel them to complain to the United Nations (UN) that these initiatives contravened the UN Charter. Israel also took military action against Syrian efforts to divert the waters of the Jordan, bombing Syrian construction sites in July 1966 in raids that resulted in air battles that contributed to the escalating tensions that led to the 1967 Six-Day War.

Primary Source

The Council of the Kings and Heads of State of the Arab League held its second meeting, at Al-Montasah Palace, Alexandria, 5 to 11 September 1964.

[...]

The Council of Kings and Heads of State of the Arab League studied the report of the Secretary General of the Arab League on the resolutions and principles adopted by the first session of the Arab Summit Conference, the implementations of these resolutions and means of strengthening them.

The Council expressed its satisfaction with the unity of Arab ranks, with the progress of work on the resolutions of the first session, and with the initiation of collective constructive work for the advancement of the Arab people and for ensuring victory for the cause for which they are struggling.

In its second session, the Council achieved remarkable success in strengthening the solidarity of the Arab world and the joint Arab action and adopted resolutions augmenting and completing those of the first Summit Conference.

The Council was unanimous in defining national objectives for the liberation of Palestine from Zionist colonialism and in committing itself to a plan for joint Arab action both in the present stage for which plans have been made, and in the following stage.

The Council stressed the necessity of utilizing all Arab potentialities, and the mobilization of their resources and capabilities, in order to counter the challenge of colonialism and Zionism as well as Israel's continued aggressive policies and its insistence on denying the rights of the Arabs of Palestine to their homeland.

The Council adopted resolutions for the implementation of Arab plans, especially in the technical and military fields, including embarking on immediate work on projects for the exploitation of the waters of the River Jordan and its tributaries.

The Council welcomed the establishment of the Palestine Liberation Organization to consolidate the Palestine Entity, and as a vanguard for the collective Arab struggle for the liberation of Palestine. It approved the Organization's decision to establish a Palestinian Liberation Army and defined the commitments of the member States to assist it in its work.

The Council discussed the political and economic surveys and reports concerning the relations of the Arab countries with foreign countries. It discussed the results of the visits of the Arab Foreign Ministers to foreign countries.

The Council expressed its appreciation for the support given by foreign countries to Arab causes in general and the Palestine cause in particular. It decided on the continuation of these contacts with all countries of the world and the completion of studies as a prelude to the implementation of principles adopted in the First Summit Conference which called for the regulation of relations vis-à-vis foreign countries in accordance with their position regarding the Palestine question and other Arab causes.

The Council confirmed Arab determination to oppose anti-Arab forces, primarily British colonialist policy and its exploitation of wealth and acts of extermination now practised in the Occupied South in defiance of the Charter and principles of the United Nations and the right of the people to self-determination and the resolutions of the General Assembly and of the United Nations Special Committee with Regard to the Implementation of the Declaration on the Granting of Independence to Colonial Countries and Peoples.

The Council resolved to combat British imperialism in the Arab Peninsula and to provide assistance to the liberation movement in the Occupied South and Oman.

The Council devoted attention to consolidating Arab friendly relations with the amirates of the Arab Gulf to ensure the indivisible Arab freedom and to realize common interests.

The Council discussed means of consolidating unified Arab political, defence, economic and social action within the framework of the Arab League.

The Council placed special emphasis on the promotion of Arab economic co-operation and the implementation of all economic agreements since economic unity is the basic foundation on which Arab power and progress rests and the strongest bastion against foreign challenge. This, in addition to the fact that such unity is the primary objective of contemporary international groupings.

The Council stressed the necessity of stepping up co-operation and increasing the economic support to the States of the Arab Maghreb.

The Council agreed to form a joint Arab Council to undertake nuclear research for peaceful uses and to set up an Arab court of justice. It was also decided that the Council of Arab Kings and Heads of State should meet every year in September. It resolved that the Follow-Up Committee should continue to meet once every month at the present level, and once every four months at the level of Prime Ministers or Deputy Prime Ministers in one of the Arab States. The meeting at the level of Prime Ministers would assume the character of an executive authority for the Council of Kings and Heads of State, and would look into urgent matters in conformity with the resolutions of the Arab Kings and Heads of State. It will also be charged with executing and speeding up current plans. It is authorized to ask the Kings and Heads of State to hold extraordinary meetings in cases of urgent developments.

The Council welcomed the signing of the Joint Arab Defence Pact by the rest of the member States which has made the pact effective in every part of the Arab world from the Atlantic Ocean to the Arab Gulf. The Arab Kings and Heads of State emphasized that an attack on any Arab State will be regarded as an attack on all the Arab States which are committed to repelling it at once.

The Council, in its belief in Afro-Asian solidarity, supports the results of the Second African Summit Conference, held in Cairo in July 1964, and finds hope in the development of African unity and in the revelation that neo-colonialism is using Israel as a tool to realize its ambitions in the developing countries against their aspirations to attain progress, strength and unity, thus perpetuating illegal foreign exploitation.

The Council believes that the rights of the peoples for freedom, self-determination and elimination of colonialism and of racial discrimination, are an integral and an indivisible whole, and that Arab-African co-operation is a foundation of Arab policy by virtue of historical and geographical association and common interests and objectives. For this reason, the Council supports the struggle for independence of the peoples of Angola, Mozambique, Southern Rhodesia, South Africa, and so-called Portuguese Guinea, and condemns foreign intervention in the Democratic Republic of the Congo.

The Arab States believe that international co-operation and world peace constitute the basic foundations for world prosperity and the happiness of mankind and the Council therefore expresses its regret over recent imperialist shows of strength and the threat to use force in solving international disputes, contrary to the universal tendency prevailing in the past years towards policies affirming peaceful co-existence and the relaxation of international tension.

The Council confirms the need for liquidating imperialist bases which threaten the safety and security of Arab lands, particularly those in Cyprus and Aden.

The Council urges the major Powers to be inspired in their policies and actions by the will of the people and the principles of peace based on justice, and the right of nations to independence and self-determination.

[. . .]

Source: United Nations Security Council Official Records, Document S/6003, October 8, 1964.

50. Address of Gamal Abdel Nasser to the Egyptian National Assembly [Excerpt], May 29, 1967

Introduction

In the spring of 1967, tensions between Israel and neighboring Arab states rose dramatically. Fatah terrorist infiltrations into Israel targeted civilians, and from January onward clashes on the Syrian-Israeli border along the disputed Golan Heights escalated markedly. On May 14 Egyptian forces occupied the Sinai, ousting the United Nations Emergency Force (UNEF) that had held the area for the previous decade. One week later, Egyptian president Gamel Abdel Nasser took over the port of Sharm al-Sheikh and closed the Straits of Tiran to Israeli shipping, a move that Israeli leaders had warned 10 years earlier they would consider a reason for going to war. Nasser apparently still believed that he could take these actions without provoking war with Israel and was acting primarily to shore up his standing within the Arab world, where Syrian, Saudi, and Jordanian leaders were accusing him of indulging in loud rhetoric but failing to take effective measures open to him. In several speeches in late May, Nasser nonetheless used grandiloquent language, taunting Israel and warning those Middle Eastern states that claimed to be Israel's enemies, notably Saudi Arabia and Iran, to cease supplying Israel with oil. He claimed that Arab forces were willing and able to fight Israel and win, that they would welcome a war, and that they must defend and restore the rights of the Palestinians. Nasser may have believed that war could be avoided and that he could indulge in such saber rattling without provoking outright hostilities, but he was wrong. Israeli leaders, determined to deny Nasser the triumph of seeming to defy Israel with impunity, called his bluff with a pre-emptive strike. On June 5, 1967, Israel launched the Six-Day War, and within three hours Israeli attacks on Egyptian airfields had destroyed virtually the entire Egyptian Air Force. Israeli forces quickly occupied the entire Sinai Peninsula. Four days later, on June 9, a humiliated Nasser resigned. He confessed that Israel had inflicted "a stronger blow than we had expected," even though he claimed that this was largely due to assistance that Israel had received from Britain and the United States.

Primary Source

[. . .]

The circumstances through which we are now passing are in fact difficult ones because we are not only confronting Israel but also those who created Israel and who are behind Israel. We are confronting Israel and the West as well—the West, which created Israel and which despised us Arabs and which ignored us before and since

1948. They had no regard whatsoever for our feelings, our hopes in life, or our rights. The West completely ignored us, and the Arab nation was unable to check the West's course.

Then came the events of 1956—the Suez battle. We all know what happened in 1956. When we rose to demand our rights, Britain, France and Israel opposed us, and we were faced with the tripartite aggression. We resisted, however, and proclaimed that we would fight to the last drop of our blood. God gave us success and God's victory was great.

Subsequently we were able to rise and to build. Now, eleven years after 1956, we are restoring things to what they were in 1956. This is from the material aspect. In my opinion this material aspect is only a small part, whereas the spiritual aspect is the great side of the issue. The spiritual aspect involves the renaissance of the Arab nation, the revival of the Palestine question, and the restoration of confidence to every Arab and to every Palestinian. This is on the basis that if we were able to restore conditions to what they were before 1956, God will surely help and urge us to restore the situation to what it was in 1948.

Brothers, the revolt, upheaval and commotion which we now see taking place in every Arab country are not only because we have returned to the Gulf of Aqaba or rid ourselves of the UNEF, but because we have restored Arab honour and renewed Arab hopes.

Israel used to boast a great deal, and the Western Powers, headed by the United States and Britain, used to ignore and even despise us and consider us of no value. But now that the time has come—and I have already said in the past that we will decide the time and place and not allow them to decide—we must be ready for triumph and not for a recurrence of the 1948 comedies. We shall triumph, God willing.

Preparations have already been made. We are now ready to confront Israel. They have claimed many things about the 1956 Suez war, but no one believed them after the secrets of the 1956 collusion were uncovered—that mean collusion in which Israel took part. Now we are ready for the confrontation. We are now ready to deal with the entire Palestine question.

The issue now at hand is not the Gulf of Aqaba, the Straits of Tiran, or the withdrawal of the UNEF, but the rights of the Palestine people. It is the aggression which took place in Palestine in 1948 with the collaboration of Britain and the United States. It is the expulsion of the Arabs from Palestine, the usurpation of their rights, and the plunder of their property. It is the disavowal of all the UN resolutions in favour of the Palestinian people.

The issue today is far more serious than they say. They want to confine the issue to the Straits of Tiran, the UNEF and the right of passage. We demand the full rights of the Palestinian people. We say this out of our belief that Arab rights cannot be squandered because the Arabs throughout the Arab world are demanding these Arab rights.

We are not afraid of the United States and its threats, of Britain and its threats, or of the entire Western world and its partiality to Israel. The United States and Britain are partial to Israel and give no consideration to the Arabs, to the entire Arab nation. Why? Because we have made them believe that we cannot distinguish between friend and foe. We must make them know that we know who our foes are and who our friends are and treat them accordingly.

If the United States and Britain are partial to Israel, we must say that our enemy is not only Israel but also the United States and Britain and treat them as such. If the Western Powers disavow our rights and ridicule and despise us, we Arabs must teach them to respect us and take us seriously. Otherwise all our talk about Palestine, the Palestine people and Palestinian rights will be null and void and of no consequence. We must treat enemies as enemies and friends as friends.

I said yesterday that the States that champion freedom and peace have supported us. I spoke of the support given us by India, Pakistan, Afghanistan, Yugoslavia, Malaysia, the Chinese People's Republic and the Asian and African States.

After my statements yesterday I met the War Minister Shams Badran and learned from him what took place in Moscow. I wish to tell you today that the Soviet Union is a friendly Power and stands by us as a friend. In all our dealings with the Soviet Union—and I have been dealing with the USSR since 1955—it has not made a single request of us. The USSR has never interfered with our policy or internal affairs. This is the USSR as we have always known it. In fact, it is we who have made urgent requests of the USSR. Last year we asked for wheat and they sent it to us. When I also asked for all kinds of arms they gave them to us. When I met Shams Badran yesterday he handed me a message from the Soviet Premier Kosygin saying that the USSR supported us in this battle and would not allow any Power to intervene until matters were restored to what they were in 1956.

[...]

In the name of the UAR people, I thank the people of the USSR for their great attitude which is the attitude of a real friend. This is the kind of attitude that we expect. I said yesterday that we had not requested the USSR or any other State to intervene because we really want to avoid any confrontation which might lead to a world war and also because we really work for peace and advocate world peace. When we voiced the policy of non-alignment, our chief aim was world peace.

Brothers, we will work for world peace with all the power at our disposal, but we will also hold tenaciously to our rights with all the power at our disposal. This is our course.

[…]

Source: "Statement by President Nasser to Members of the Egyptian National Assembly, 29 May 1967," Israel Ministry of Foreign Affairs, http://www.mfa.gov.il/MFA.

51. Abba Eban, Speech to the UN Security Council [Excerpt], June 6, 1967

Introduction

The Six-Day War represented a stunning success for Israel. The United Nations (UN) almost immediately called for a cease-fire, but Arab states refused to accept this. Israeli officials also sought to delay this until they had accomplished their objectives of neutralizing their opponents and teaching a bloody lesson to each of the states that had employed fiery rhetoric and menacing threats against Israel. By the time King Hussein of Jordan had accepted a cease-fire on June 7, Israeli forces had taken Jerusalem and the West Bank of the Jordan River. They had also overrun the Sinai Peninsula before Egypt accepted a cease-fire on June 8. Syria signed a cease-fire agreement early on June 9, but Defense Minister Moshe Dayan nonetheless ordered a successful assault on the Golan Heights, which did not end until June 10. Speaking to the UN Security Council one day after the war began, Israeli foreign minister Abba Eban sought to justify Israel's preemptive strike on its enemies on the grounds that Egypt, Jordan, and Syria, besides supporting terrorist attacks on Israel, had massed their forces in preparation for an invasion of Israeli territory, and his country had therefore been acting in its own defense. He cited Egypt's actions in reentering the Sinai Peninsula and speeches by Egyptian leader Gamal Abdel Nasser and his military commander in chief in the Sinai as evidence that they were preparing for an all-out war to eliminate Israel. Drawing on still fresh emotional memories of the Nazi Holocaust against the Jews in Europe, Eban also reminded his listeners that Israel "was itself the last sanctuary of a people which had seen six million of its sons exterminated by a more powerful dictator two decades before."

Primary Source

I thank you, Mr. President for giving me this opportunity to address the Council. I have just come from Jerusalem to tell the Security Council that Israel, by its independent effort and sacrifice, has passed from serious danger to successful resistance.

Two days ago Israel's condition caused much concern across the humane and friendly world. Israel had reached a sombre hour. Let me try to evoke the point at which our fortunes stood.

An army, greater than any force ever assembled in history in Sinai, had massed against Israel's southern frontier. Egypt had dismissed the United Nations forces which symbolized the international interest in the maintenance of peace in our region. Nasser had provocatively brought five infantry divisions and two armored divisions up to our very gates; 80,000 men and 900 tanks were poised to move.

A special striking force, comprising an armored division with at least 200 tanks, was concentrated against Elath at the Negev's southern tip. Here was a clear design to cut the southern Negev off from the main body of our State. For Egypt had openly proclaimed that Elath did not form part of Israel and had predicted that Israel itself would soon expire. The proclamation was empty; the prediction now lies in ruin. While the main brunt of the hostile threat was focussed on the southern front, an alarming plan of encirclement was under way. With Egypt's initiative and guidance, Israel was already being strangled in its maritime approaches to the whole eastern half of the world. For sixteen years, Israel had been illicitly denied passage in the Suez Canal, despite the Security Council's decision of 1 September 1951 [resolution 95 (1951)]. And now the creative enterprise of ten patient years which had opened an international route across the Strait of Tiran and the Gulf of Aqaba had been suddenly and arbitrarily choked. Israel was and is breathing with only a single lung.

Jordan had been intimidated, against its better interest, into joining a defense pact. It is not a defense pact at all: it is an aggressive pact, of which I saw the consequences with my own eyes yesterday in the shells falling upon institutions of health and culture in the City of Jerusalem. Every house and street in Jerusalem now came into the range of fire as a result of Jordan's adherence to this pact; so also did the crowded and pathetically narrow coastal strip in which so much of Israel's life and population is concentrated.

Iraqi troops reinforced Jordanian units in area[s] immediately facing vital and vulnerable Israel communication centers. Expeditionary forces from Algeria and Kuwait had reached Egyptian territory. Nearly all the Egyptian forces which had been attempting the conquest of the Yemen had been transferred to the coming assault upon Israel. Syrian units, including artillery, overlooked the Israel villages in the Jordan Valley. Terrorist troops came regularly into our territory to kill, plunder and set off explosions; the most recent occasion was five days ago.

In short, there was peril for Israel wherever it looked. Its manpower had been hastily mobilized. Its economy and commerce were beating with feeble pulses. Its streets were dark and empty. There was an apocalyptic air of approaching peril. And Israel faced this danger alone.

We were buoyed up by an unforgettable surge of public sympathy across the world. The friendly Governments expressed the rather ominous hope that Israel would manage to live, but the dominant theme of our condition was danger and solitude.

Now there could be no doubt about what was intended for us. With my very ears I heard President Nasser's speech on 26 May. He said:

"We intend to open a general assault against Israel. This will be total war. Our basic aim will be to destroy Israel."

On 2 June, the Egyptian Commander in Sinai, General Murtagi, published his order of the day, calling on his troops to wage a war of destruction against Israel. Here, then, was a systematic, overt, proclaimed design at politicide, the murder of a State.

The policy, the arms, the men had all been brought together, and the State thus threatened with collective assault was itself the last sanctuary of people which had seen six million of its sons exterminated by a more powerful dictator two decades before.

[...]

I would say in conclusion that these are, of course, still grave times. And yet they may perhaps have fortunate issue. This could be the case if those who for some reason decided so violently, three weeks ago, to disrupt the status quo would ask themselves what the results and benefits have been. As he looks around him at the arena of battle, at the wreckage of planes and tanks, at the collapse of intoxicated hopes, might not an Egyptian ruler ponder whether anything was achieved by that disruption? What has it brought but strife, conflict with other powerful interests, and the stern criticism of progressive men throughout the world?

I think that Israel has in recent days proved its steadfastness and vigour. It is now willing to demonstrate its instinct for peace. Let us build a new system of relationships from the wreckage of the old. Let us discern across the darkness the vision of a better and a brighter dawn.

Source: United Nations Security Council Official Records, S/PV.1348, June 6, 1967.

52. Lyndon Johnson, Statement on Principles for Peace, June 19, 1967

Introduction

The Six-Day War gave Israel a new sense of confidence, greatly expanding the territory under its control and offering the possibility of redrawing Israel's frontiers so as to offer the nation greater security against its numerous surrounding enemies. U.S. president Lyndon Johnson was broadly sympathetic to Israel and had previously

authorized substantial U.S. armaments sales to the country that had undoubtedly contributed to its stunning military performance. The Six-Day War also energized the American Jewish community in support of Israel. Johnson did not, however, welcome the prospect of continuing tensions in the Middle East, which might precipitate yet more conflicts and encourage further Soviet involvement in the region. Ten days after the war ended, he therefore enunciated broad principles for a peace settlement. The first precondition, in the president's view, was that all the states involved should accept the right of the others to national existence, a position that meant that the Arab states would have to recognize that Israel was there to stay and cease their efforts to destroy it. Israel had already stated that unless and until it obtained acceptable peace agreements, it would not withdraw from the territory it had seized, a position that the United States officially endorsed. While stating that the United States was willing to accept territorial adjustments, Johnson nonetheless warned that mere conquest was not a justification for Israel to retain the lands it had seized and that there must be some good justification for any border adjustments. He also warned that the terms agreed to should be acceptable to all parties involved. He remained studiously vague as to the ultimate fate of Jerusalem, which the Israelis now controlled. He did, however, warn that after 20 years, some lasting solution of the festering Palestinian refugee problem was essential. He called for respect for maritime rights and for the Suez Canal and Tiran Straits to be left open to navigation by ships of all nations, including those of Israel. Lastly, he urged all nations in the Middle East to refrain from continuing their arms race. Although deliberately short on specifics, Johnson's prescriptions encapsulated the broad lines of U.S. policy on a Middle Eastern peace settlement for several decades to come.

Primary Source

Now, finally, let me turn to the Middle East—and to the tumultuous events of the past months.

Those events have proved the wisdom of five great principles of peace in the region.

The first and greatest principle is that every nation in the area has a fundamental right to live, and to have this right respected by its neighbors.

For the people of the Middle East, the path to hope does not lie in threats to end the life of any nation. Such threats have become a burden to the peace, not only of that region but a burden to the peace of the entire world.

In the same way, no nation would be true to the United Nations Charter, or to its own true interests, if it should permit military success to blind it to the fact that its neighbors have rights and its neighbors have interests of their own. Each nation, therefore, must accept the right of others to live.

Second, this last month, I think, shows us another basic requirement for settlement. It is a human requirement: justice for the refugees.

A new conflict has brought new homelessness. The nations of the Middle East must at last address themselves to the plight of those who have been displaced by wars. In the past, both sides have resisted the best efforts of outside mediators to restore the victims of conflict to their homes, or to find them other proper places to live and work. There will be no peace for any party in the Middle East unless this problem is attacked with new energy by all, and, certainly, primarily by those who are immediately concerned.

A third lesson from this last month is that maritime rights must be respected. Our Nation has long been committed to free maritime passage through international waterways, and we, along with other nations, were taking the necessary steps to implement this principle when hostilities exploded. If a single act of folly was more responsible for this explosion than any other, I think it was the arbitrary and dangerous announced decision that the Straits of Tiran would be closed. The right of innocent maritime passage must be preserved for all nations.

Fourth, this last conflict has demonstrated the danger of the Middle Eastern arms race of the last 12 years. Here the responsibility must rest not only on those in the area—but upon the larger states outside the area. We believe that scarce resources could be used much better for technical and economic development. We have always opposed this arms race, and our own military shipments to the area have consequently been severely limited.

Now the waste and futility of the arms race must be apparent to all the peoples of the world. And now there is another moment of choice. The United States of America, for its part, will use every resource of diplomacy, and every counsel of reason and prudence, to try to find a better course.

As a beginning, I should like to propose that the United Nations immediately call upon all of its members to report all shipments of all military arms into this area, and to keep those shipments on file for all the peoples of the world to observe.

Fifth, the crisis underlines the importance of respect for political independence and territorial integrity of all the states of the area. We reaffirmed that principle at the height of this crisis. We reaffirm it again today on behalf of all.

This principle can be effective in the Middle East only on the basis of peace between the parties. The nations of the region have had only fragile and violated truce lines for 20 years. What they now need are recognized boundaries and other arrangements that will give them security against terror, destruction, and war. Further, there

just must be adequate recognition of the special interest of three great religions in the Holy Places of Jerusalem.

These five principles are not new, but we do think they are fundamental. Taken together, they point the way from uncertain armistice to durable peace. We believe there must be progress toward all of them if there is to be progress toward any.

There are some who have urged, as a single, simple solution, an immediate return to the situation as it was on June 4. As our distinguished and able Ambassador, Mr. Arthur Goldberg, has already said, this is not a prescription for peace, but for renewed hostilities.

Certainly troops must be withdrawn, but there must also be recognized rights of national life, progress in solving the refugee problem, freedom of innocent maritime passage, limitation of the arms race, and respect for political independence and territorial integrity.

But who will make this peace where all others have failed for 20 years or more?

Clearly the parties to the conflict must be the parties to the peace. Sooner or later it is they who must make a settlement in the area. It is hard to see how it is possible for nations to live together in peace if they cannot learn to reason together.

But we must still ask, who can help them? Some say it should be the United Nations; some call for the use of other parties. We have been first in our support of effective peacekeeping in the United Nations, and we also recognize the great values to come from mediation.

We are ready this morning to see any method tried, and we believe that none should be excluded altogether. Perhaps all of them will be useful and all will be needed.

So, I issue an appeal to all to adopt no rigid view on these matters. I offer assurance to all that this Government of ours, the Government of the United States, will do its part for peace in every forum, at every level, at every hour.

Yet there is no escape from this fact: The main responsibility for the peace of the region depends upon its own peoples and its own leaders of that region. What will be truly decisive in the Middle East will be what is said and what is done by those who live in the Middle East.

They can seek another arms race, if they have not profited from the experience of this one, if they want to. But they will seek it at a terrible cost to their own people—and to their very long-neglected human needs. They can live on a diet of hate—though only at the cost of hatred in return. Or they can move toward peace with one another.

The world this morning is watching, watching for the peace of the world, because that is really what is at stake. It will look for patience and justice, it will look for humility and moral courage. It will look for signs of movement from prejudice and the emotional chaos of conflict to the gradual, slow shaping steps that lead to learning to live together and learning to help mold and shape peace in the area and in the world.

The Middle East is rich in history, rich in its people and its resources. It has no need to live in permanent civil war. It has the power to build its own life, as one of the prosperous regions of the world in which we live.

If the nations of the Middle East will turn toward the works of peace, they can count with confidence upon the friendship, and the help, of all the people of the United States of America.

In a climate of peace, we here will do our full share to help with a solution for the refugees. We here will do our full share in support of regional cooperation. We here will do our share, and do more, to see that the peaceful promise of nuclear energy is applied to the critical problem of desalting water and helping to make the deserts bloom.

Our country is committed—and we here reiterate that commitment today—to a peace that is based on five principles:

—first, the recognized right of national life ;
—second, justice for the refugees;
—third, innocent maritime passage;
—fourth, limits on the wasteful and destructive arms race; and
—fifth, political independence and territorial integrity for all.

This is a time not for malice, but for magnanimity; not for propaganda, but for patience; not for vituperation, but for vision.

On the basis of peace, we offer our help to the people of the Middle East. That land, known to every one of us since childhood as the birthplace of great religions and learning, can flourish once again in our time. We here in the United States shall do all in our power to help make it so.

Source: Lyndon B. Johnson, *Public Papers of the Presidents of the United States: Lyndon B. Johnson 1967,* Book 1 (Washington, DC: U.S. Government Printing Office, 1968), 632–634.

53. Protection of Holy Places Law, June 27, 1967

Introduction

From 1950 onward, Israel treated West Jerusalem as its capital, locating most government offices and ministries there. During the Six-Day War, Israel took East Jerusalem, which had previously been under Jordanian control. Although under the 1947 partition agreement Jerusalem, together with Bethlehem and Nazareth, had been assigned to the United Nations (UN) to administer as an international city, the Israeli government decided to keep all of Jerusalem. Israeli prime minister Levi Eshkol publicly pledged that Israel would maintain all the Holy Places, whether Christian, Jewish, or Muslim, and allow unfettered access to them by members of all faiths. That same day the Israeli Knesset passed a law to this effect. West Jerusalem was largely Israeli and was a major cultural and civic center, whereas East Jerusalem remained predominantly Arab and Muslim and was a source of continuing tensions, especially since the Palestinians claimed that Jerusalem would be their own future capital. Israeli authorities soon launched substantial rebuilding plans in the eastern Old City of Jerusalem, reestablishing a Jewish community there and developing several new neighborhoods. Even after 1967, most countries continued to locate their embassies in Tel Aviv, treating that city as Israel's capital, and the UN never officially recognized Israel's administration of Jerusalem.

Primary Source

1. The Holy Places shall be protected from desecration and any other violation and from anything likely to violate the freedom of access of the members of the different religions to the places sacred to them or their feelings with regard to those places.

2. (a) Whosoever desecrates or otherwise violates a Holy Place shall be liable to imprisonment for a term of seven years.

(b) Whosoever does anything likely to violate the freedom of access of the members of the different religions to the places sacred to them or their feelings with regard to those places shall be liable to imprisonment for a term of five years.

3. This Law shall add to, and not derogate from, any other law.

4. The Minister of Religious Affairs is charged with the implementation of this Law, and he may, after consultation with, or upon the proposal of, representatives of the religions concerned and with the consent of the Minister of Justice make regulations as to any matter relating to such implementation.

5. This Law shall come into force on the date of its adoption by the Knesset.

Levi Eshkol
Prime Minister

Zerach Warhaftig
Minister of Religious Affairs

Shneur Zalman Shazar
President of the State

Source: "Protection of Holy Places Law, 1967," Israel Ministry of Foreign Affairs, http://www.mfa.gov.il/MFA.

54. Prime Minister Levi Eshkol, Principles Guiding Israel's Policy in the Aftermath of the June 1967 War, August 9, 1967

Introduction

In the aftermath of the Six-Day War, Israeli officials were publicly somewhat evasive as to their plans for the extensive territories that Israeli forces had seized during the conflict. Privately, they hoped to retain as much of these lands as possible. Israeli prime minister Levi Eshkol nonetheless remained studiously noncommittal in his early statements on the subject, such as this one in August 1967 two months after the war had ended. While affirming Israel's desire to reach a lasting peace settlement with its Arab neighbors, to negotiate with any or all of them, to treat all the population of "the new areas" fairly and equitably, and to promote economic collaboration and regional planning with all states in the Middle East, Eshkol simply declined to address the subject of the future status of these areas. He merely promised full Israeli cooperation in dealing with the refugee problem. Eshkol did, however, stress Israel's need for additional immigration if it were not to stagnate, perhaps an indirect way of intimating that new Jewish immigrants would be able to settle in the territories that Israel had so recently gained.

Primary Source

(a) The Government of Israel will endeavour to achieve peace with the neighbouring Arab countries. We shall never permit a return to a situation of constant threat to Israel's security, of blockade and of aggression.

(b) The Government of Israel is prepared for direct negotiations with all the Arab States together, or with any Arab State separately.

(c) The State of Israel strives for economic cooperation and regional planning with all States in the Middle East.

(d) Israel will cooperate fully in the solution of the refugees problem . . . within the framework of an international and regional plan.

(e) The Government endeavours to maintain fair and equitable relations with the population in the new areas, while maintaining order and security.

After our military victory, we confront a fateful dilemma; immigration or stagnation. . . . By the end of the century, we must have five million Jews in Israel. We must work hard so that Israel may be able to maintain decent human, cultural, technical and economic standards. This is the test of Israel's existence as a Jewish State in the Middle East.

Source: *Israel Digest,* August, 25, 1967, reprinted in Yehuda Lukacs, ed., *The Israeli-Palestinian Conflict: A Documentary Record 1967–1990* (Cambridge: Cambridge University Press, 1992), 171; and Fuad E. Jabber, ed., *International Documents on Palestine, 1967* (Beirut: Institute on Palestine Studies, University of Kuwait, 1972), 156.

55. Khartoum Resolutions, September 1967

Introduction

In the aftermath of the 1967 Six-Day War and the Arab defeats, eight Arab heads of state met at Khartoum, Sudan, to decide on a united front policy toward Israel. They agreed that there should be "no peace with Israel, no recognition of Israel, no negotiations with it, and insistence on the rights of the Palestinian people in their own country." Since all were also in accord that they should bend their political and diplomatic efforts to regaining the territories lost in the Six-Day War, this stance effectively closed off many avenues. The leaders present discussed whether they should maintain the petroleum embargo they had imposed on Western states during the Six-Day War but decided that the revenue they received from such sales was at this time a more significant source of strength to them than maintaining the embargo would be. The heads of state also agreed to provide economic assistance to Egypt and Jordan, to help them to recover from the impact of war, and to end the civil war in Yemen. King Hussein of Jordan, who attended the Khartoum meeting, later recalled that from the standpoint of the conference the Khartoum Resolutions were considered relatively conciliatory since they did not call for a new war against Israel and that they were designed for public consumption and were not expected to preclude informal Arab negotiations with Israel and even de facto recognition. Syria and Libya were, it seems, the leading voices calling for no dealings with Israel. The apparently uncompromising Arab public stance nonetheless strengthened those hard-line individuals and political forces within Israel who sought to annex the conquered territories and establish Jewish settlements there, arguing that only such inescapable "facts on the ground" would pressure the Arab nations to make peace. It would be almost a decade before Egypt broke ranks and opened negotiations with Israel.

Primary Source

1. The conference has affirmed the unity of Arab ranks, the unity of joint action and the need for coordination and for the elimination of all differences. The Kings, Presidents and representatives of the other Arab Heads of State at the conference have affirmed their countries' stand by and implementation of the Arab Solidarity Charter which was signed at the third Arab summit conference in Casablanca.

2. The conference has agreed on the need to consolidate all efforts to eliminate the effects of the aggression on the basis that the occupied

lands are Arab lands and that the burden of regaining these lands falls on all the Arab States.

3. The Arab Heads of State have agreed to unite their political efforts at the international and diplomatic level to eliminate the effects of the aggression and to ensure the withdrawal of the aggressive Israeli forces from the Arab lands which have been occupied since the aggression of June 5. This will be done within the framework of the main principles by which the Arab States abide, namely, no peace with Israel, no recognition of Israel, no negotiations with it, and insistence on the rights of the Palestinian people in their own country.

4. The conference of Arab Ministers of Finance, Economy and Oil recommended that suspension of oil pumping be used as a weapon in the battle. However, after thoroughly studying the matter, the summit conference has come to the conclusion that the oil pumping can itself be used as a positive weapon, since oil is an Arab resource which can be used to strengthen the economy of the Arab States directly affected by the aggression, so that these States will be able to stand firm in the battle. The conference has, therefore, decided to resume the pumping of oil, since oil is a positive Arab resource that can be used in the service of Arab goals. It can contribute to the efforts to enable those Arab States which were exposed to the aggression and thereby lost economic resources to stand firm and eliminate the effects of the aggression. The oil-producing States have, in fact, participated in the efforts to enable the States affected by the aggression to stand firm in the face of any economic pressure.

5. The participants in the conference have approved the plan proposed by Kuwait to set up an Arab Economic and Social Development Fund on the basis of the recommendation of the Baghdad conference of Arab Ministers of Finance, Economy and Oil.

6. The participants have agreed on the need to adopt the necessary measures to strengthen military preparation to face all eventualities.

7. The conference has decided to expedite the elimination of foreign bases in the Arab States.

Source: "Khartoum Resolutions, September 1, 1967," Israel Ministry of Foreign Affairs, http://www.mfa.gov.il/MFA.

56. United Nations Security Council Resolution 242, November 22, 1967

Introduction

Five months after the Six-Day War ended, after lengthy discussions in the United Nations (UN) General Assembly and the Security Council, the latter body passed Resolution 242, which would form the basis of all subsequent peace plans. Effectively, the resolution called upon Israel to withdraw from most of the territory it had occupied during the war in return for a comprehensive peace settlement in which all states in the Middle East recognized each other's right to exist and agreed to respect each other's borders. It also called for "a just settlement of the refugee problem" without stating what this might imply. The resolution was largely drafted by the U.S. and British UN representatives, Arthur Goldberg and Lord Caradon, respectively, and all five Security Council permanent members voted for it. On U.S. insistence, the language of the resolution was tailored to permit some minor border adjustments so that Israel might negotiate to retain at least small but vitally significant areas. Both Israel and the Arab states as well as the Palestine Liberation Organization (PLO) claimed that the other was in breach of this resolution, justifying their own failure to observe its provisions: Israel because most Arab states were still nominally in a state of war and refused to recognize its own existence, and the Arab states and PLO because Israel had not withdrawn from the occupied territories. The refugee question also remained problematic, with Israel declining to accept the return of Palestinians to Israeli-controlled territory and in counterattack citing the Arab nations' failure to compensate Jews they expelled from their own countries. The PLO rejected Resolution 242 outright. Between 1967 and 1973, UN special envoy Gunnar Jarring held protracted but ultimately fruitless talks with Israel, Egypt, Jordan, and Lebanon (Syria refused even to participate) on the potential implementation of Resolution 242, negotiations dramatically concluded by the 1973 Yom Kippur War.

Primary Source

The Security Council,

Expressing its continuing concern with the grave situation in the Middle East,

Emphasizing the inadmissibility of the acquisition of territory by war and the need to work for a just and lasting peace in which every State in the area can live in security,

Emphasizing further that all Member States in their acceptance of the Charter of the United Nations have undertaken a commitment to act in accordance with Article 2 of the Charter,

1. *Affirms* that the fulfillment of Charter principles requires the establishment of a just and lasting peace in the Middle East which should include the application of both the following principles:
   (i)   Withdrawal of Israeli armed forces from territories occupied in the recent conflict;
   (ii) Termination of all claims or states of belligerency and respect for and acknowledgement of the sovereignty, territorial integrity and political independence of every State in the area and their right to live in peace within secure and recognized boundaries free from threats or acts of force;

2. *Affirms further* the necessity

   (a) For guaranteeing freedom of navigation through international waterways in the area;

   (b) For achieving a just settlement of the refugee problem;

   (c) For guaranteeing the territorial inviolability and political independence of every State in the area, through measures including the establishment of demilitarized zones;

3. *Requests* the Secretary-General to designate a Special Representative to proceed to the Middle East to establish and maintain contacts with the States concerned in order to promote agreement and assist efforts to achieve a peaceful and accepted settlement in accordance with the provisions and principles in this resolution;

4. *Requests* the Secretary-General to report to the Security Council on the progress of the efforts of the Special Representative as soon as possible.

   Source: United Nations Security Council Official Records, S.C. Res. 242, November 22, 1967.

57. PLO Statement Rejecting United Nations Resolution 242, November 23, 1967

Introduction

Defeat in the Six-Day War radicalized the Palestine Liberation Organization (PLO), which soon jettisoned its first head, Ahmed Shukairy, a lawyer better known for his rather florid rhetoric than executive ability, for the Fatah leader Yasser Arafat, a dedicated advocate of the use of violence to destroy Israel. From its headquarters in Cairo, Egypt, the PLO responded within one day to the passage of United Nations (UN) Security Council Resolution 242, rejecting it outright. Characterizing the document as a "British resolution," the PLO argued that it was merely a general statement of principles, giving Israeli leaders broad latitude to retain just as much occupied Arab territory as they wished. The PLO disagreed entirely with the provisions whereby Arab nations were expected to recognize Israel's right to exist, claiming that these not only ran counter to the Arab states' earlier Khartoum Summit Conference declaration but were also "fundamentally and gravely inconsistent with the Arab character of Palestine, the essence of the Palestine cause and the right of the Palestinian people to their homeland." The PLO also attacked the stipulations that the Suez Canal and the Gulf of Aqaba were international waterways that should be open to Israeli navigation. Overall the resolution was, PLO leaders claimed, "a political setback at the international level following the military setback which has befallen the Arab homeland." The dispatch to the states of a UN special envoy to facilitate implementation of the resolution would only give Israel additional opportunities to improve its position at Arab expense. The PLO's relentless hostility at this juncture to the very prospect of talks with or recognition of Israel, together with its sponsorship of terrorist attacks on Israeli citizens and property and also on others considered sympathetic to Israel, was one reason that Israeli leaders for many years simply declined to negotiate with PLO representatives.

Primary Source

Having studied the British resolution adopted by the Security Council on the Israeli aggression against Arab territories of June 1967, the Palestine Liberation Organization, in behalf of the Palestinian people, hereby defines its attitude to the said resolution as follows:

1. The resolution as a whole is in the nature of a political declaration of general principles, and is more like an expression of international intentions than the resolution of an executive power. Its treatment of the question of the withdrawal of Israeli forces is superficial, rather than being a decisive demand. It leaves Israel many loopholes to justify her continued occupation of Arab territories, and may be interpreted as permitting her to withdraw from such territories as she chooses to withdraw from and to retain such areas as she wishes to retain.

2. The resolution more than once refers to Israel's right to exist and to establish permanent, recognized frontiers. It also refers to Israel's safety and security and to her being freed from all threats, and in general to the termination of the state of belligerency with her. All this imposes on the Arab countries undertakings and a political and actual situation which are fundamentally and gravely inconsistent with the Arab character of Palestine, the essence of the Palestine cause and the right of the Palestinian people to their homeland. This resolution completely undermines the foundations of the principles announced by the Khartoum Summit Conference held after the aggression.

3. The resolution ignores the right of the refugees to return to their homes, dealing with this problem in an obscure manner which leaves the door wide open to efforts to settle them in the Arab countries and to deprive them of the exercise of their right to return, thereby annulling the resolutions adopted by the United Nations over the past twenty years.

4. The resolution recognizes the right of passage through international waterways, by which it means the Suez Canal and the Gulf of Aqaba. Granted that the Canal is an international waterway, this right cannot be exercised by a state which has engaged in usurpation and aggression, especially inasmuch as this usurpation and aggression were directed against an Arab country. The Gulf of Aqaba constitutes Arab internal waters, and its shores include a coastal area belonging to Palestine occupied by Israel through an act of usurpation and aggression. The principle of freedom of innocent passage is not applicable to the Gulf of Aqaba, especially as regards Israel.

5. The resolution includes provisions for the sending on a mission of a personal representative of the Secretary-General of the United Nations. This is no more than a repetition of unsuccessful attempts in the past, beginning with the dispatch of Count Bernadotte and ending with the formation of the International Conciliation Commission. All these attempts provided Israel with repeated opportunities to impose the *fait accompli* and to engage in further aggression and expansion.

6. The resolution as a whole validates Israel's attitude and her demands and disappoints the hopes of the Arab nation and ignores its national aspirations. The conflicting interpretations of the resolution made by members of the Security Council have weakened it even further, and it is not too much to say that the resolution is a political setback at the international level following the military setback which has befallen the Arab homeland.

For these reasons, the most important of which is that the Security Council ignores the existence of the Palestinian people and their right of self-determination, the Palestine Liberation Organization hereby declares its rejection of the Security Council resolution as a whole and in detail. In so doing it is not only confirming a theoretical attitude, but also declaring the determination of the Palestinian people to continue their revolutionary struggle to liberate their homeland. The Palestine Liberation Organization is fully confident that to achieve this sacred aim the Arab nation will meet its national responsibilities to mobilize all its resources for this battle of destiny, with the support of all forces of liberation throughout the world.

> **Source:** IPS Research and Documents Staff, *International Documents on Palestine, 1967* (Beirut: Institute for Palestine Studies, University of Kuwait, 1979), 290.

58. Palestine National Covenant, July 1968

Introduction

After the Six-Day War, the Palestine Liberation Organization (PLO) regrouped, jettisoning its first president Ahmed Shukairy, whom many considered a mere windbag and a mouthpiece for relatively moderate Arab leaders, for the charismatic Fatah activist Yasser Arafat, who was committed to violent revolutionary "armed struggle." Eighteen PLO delegates met in 1968 to draft a new covenant, or charter. Article 9 of their program uncompromisingly affirmed: "Armed struggle is the only way to liberate Palestine." The next article stated: "Commando action constitutes the nucleus of the Palestinian popular liberation war." The new covenant called for the "liberation" of Palestine, rejected the Balfour Declaration and the Palestine Mandate, and described the 1947 partition of Palestine and the establishment of Israel as "entirely illegal." The covenant

further called for the establishment of a Palestinian state and proclaimed that the Palestinians, "expressing themselves by the armed Palestine revolution, reject all solutions which are substitutes for the total liberation of Palestine and reject all proposals aiming at the liquidation of the Palestine problem, or its internationalization." Zionism was characterized as "an illegitimate movement" that should be outlawed everywhere in the world. The PLO claimed to be the only legitimate representative of the Palestine people in their struggle to realize these goals. The new Palestinian National Covenant implicitly rejected the entire approach of United Nations (UN) Security Council Resolution 242 that called for Arab recognition of Israel as the price of regaining the occupied territories. In 1993 when Arafat finally opened peace talks with Israel on behalf of the PLO, he declared that those provisions of this covenant that denied Israel's right to exist were no longer valid, a commitment he restated in 1998, and after considerable debate the organization repealed appropriate articles. Many Israelis, however, believed or feared that most PLO leaders and supporters still privately adhered to such principles and were only paying lip service to the new dispensation until a suitable opportunity arose for them to return to their original tenets.

Primary Source

Article 1

Palestine is the homeland of the Palestinian Arab people and an integral part of the great Arab homeland, and the people of Palestine is a part of the Arab nation.

Article 2

Palestine with its boundaries that existed at the time of the British mandate is an integral regional unit.

Article 3

The Palestinian Arab people possesses the legal right to its homeland, and when the liberation of its homeland is completed it will exercise self-determination solely according to its own will and choice.

Article 4

The Palestinian personality is an innate, persistent characteristic that does not disappear, and it is transferred from fathers to sons. The Zionist occupation, and the dispersal of the Palestinian Arab people as [a] result of the disasters which came over it, do not deprive it of its Palestinian personality and affiliation and do not nullify them.

Article 5

The Palestinians are the Arab citizens who were living permanently in Palestine until 1947, whether they were expelled from there or remained. Whoever is born to a Palestinian Arab father after this date, within Palestine or outside it, is a Palestinian.

Article 6

Jews who were living permanently in Palestine until the beginning of the Zionist invasion will be considered Palestinians.

Article 7

The Palestinian affiliation and the material, spiritual and historical tie with Palestine are permanent realities. The upbringing of the Palestinian individual in an Arab and revolutionary fashion, the undertaking of all means of forging consciousness and training the Palestinian, in order to acquaint him profoundly with his homeland, spiritually and materially, and preparing him for the conflict and the armed struggle, as well as for the sacrifice of his property and his life to restore his homeland, until the liberation—all this is a national duty.

Article 8

The phase in which the people of Palestine is living is that of the national struggle for the liberation of Palestine. Therefore, the contradictions among the Palestinian national forces are of a secondary order which must be suspended in the interest of the fundamental contradiction between Zionism and colonialism on the one side and the Palestinian Arab people on the other. On this basis, the Palestinian masses, whether in the homeland or in places of exile, organizations and individuals, comprise one national front which acts to restore Palestine and liberate it through armed struggle.

Article 9

Armed struggle is the only way to liberate Palestine and is therefore a strategy and not tactics. The Palestinian Arab people affirms its absolute resolution and abiding determination to pursue the armed struggle and to march forward toward the armed popular revolution, to liberate its homeland and return to it [to maintain] its right to a natural life in it, and to exercise its right of self-determination in it and sovereignty over it.

Article 10

Fedayeen action forms the nucleus of the popular Palestinian war of liberation. This demands its promotion, extension and protection, and the mobilization of all the mass and scientific capacities of the Palestinians, their organization and involvement in the armed Palestinian revolution, and cohesion in the national struggle among the various groups of the people of Palestine, and between them and the Arab masses, to guarantee the continuation of the revolution, its advancement and victory.

Article 11

The Palestinians will have three mottoes: national unity, national mobilization and liberation.

Article 12

The Palestinian Arab people believes in Arab unity. In order to fulfill its role in realizing this, it must preserve, in this phase of its national struggle, its Palestinian personality and the constituents thereof, increase consciousness of its existence and resist any plan that tends to disintegrate or weaken it.

Article 13

Arab unity and the liberation of Palestine are two complementary aims. Each one paves the way for realization of the other. Arab unity leads to the liberation of Palestine, and the liberation of Palestine leads to Arab unity. Working for both goes hand in hand.

Article 14

The destiny of the Arab nation, indeed the very Arab existence, depends upon the destiny of the Palestine issue. The endeavor and effort of the Arab nation to liberate Palestine follows from this sacred national aim.

Article 15

The liberation of Palestine, from an Arab viewpoint, is a national duty to repulse the Zionist, imperialist invasion from the great Arab homeland and to purge the Zionist presence from Palestine. Its full responsibilities fall upon the Arab nation, peoples and governments, with the Palestinian Arab people at their head.

For this purpose, the Arab nation must mobilize all its military, human, material and spiritual capacities to participate actively with the people of Palestine in the liberation of Palestine. They must, especially in the present stage of armed Palestinian revolution, grant and offer the people of Palestine all possible help and every material and human support, and afford it every sure means and opportunity enabling it to continue to assume its vanguard role in pursuing its armed revolution until the liberation of its homeland.

Article 16

The liberation of Palestine, from a spiritual viewpoint, will prepare an atmosphere of tranquillity and peace for the Holy Land, in the shade of which all the Holy Places will be safeguarded, and freedom of worship and visitation to all will be guaranteed, without distinction or discrimination of race, color, language or religion. For this reason, the people of Palestine looks to the support of all the spiritual forces in the world.

Article 17

The liberation of Palestine, from a human viewpoint, will restore to the Palestinian man his dignity, glory and freedom. For this, the Palestinian Arab people looks to the support of those in the world who believe in the dignity and freedom of man.

Article 18

The liberation of Palestine, from an international viewpoint, is a defensive act necessitated by the requirements of self-defense. For this reason, the people of Palestine, desiring to befriend all peoples, looks to the support of the states which love freedom, justice and peace in restoring the legal situation to Palestine, establishing security and peace in its territory, and enabling its people to exercise national sovereignty and national freedom.

Article 19

The partitioning of Palestine in 1947 and the establishment of Israel is fundamentally null and void, whatever time has elapsed, because it was contrary to the wish of the people of Palestine and its natural right to its homeland, and contradicts the principles embodied in the Charter of the United Nations, the first of which is the right of self-determination.

Article 20

The Balfour Declaration, the Mandate Document, and what has been based upon them are considered null and void. The claim of a historical or spiritual tie between Jews and Palestine does not tally with historical realities nor with the constituents of statehood in their true sense. Judaism, in its character as a religion of revelation, is not a nationality with an independent existence. Likewise, the Jews are not one people with an independent personality. They are rather citizens of the states to which they belong.

Article 21

The Palestinian Arab people, in expressing itself through the armed Palestinian revolution, rejects every solution that is a substitute for a complete liberation of Palestine, and rejects all plans that aim at the settlement of the Palestine issue or its internationalization.

Article 22

Zionism is a political movement organically related to world imperialism and hostile to all movements of liberation and progress in the world. It is a racist and fanatical movement in its formation; aggressive, expansionist and colonialist in its aims; and fascist and nazi in its means. Israel is the tool of the Zionist movement and a human and geographical base for world imperialism. It is a concentration and jumping-off point for imperialism in the heart of the Arab homeland, to strike at the hopes of the Arab nation for liberation, unity and progress.

Israel is a constant threat to peace in the Middle East and the entire world. Since the liberation of Palestine will liquidate the Zionist and imperialist presence and bring about the stabilization of peace in the Middle East, the people of Palestine looks to the support of all liberal men of the world and all the forces of good, progress and peace; and implores all of them, regardless of their different leanings and orientations, to offer all help and support to the people of Palestine in its just and legal struggle to liberate its homeland.

Article 23

The demands of security and peace and the requirements of truth and justice oblige all states that preserve friendly relations among peoples and maintain the loyalty of citizens to their homelands to consider Zionism an illegitimate movement and to prohibit its existence and activity.

Article 24

The Palestinian Arab people believes in the principles of justice, freedom, sovereignty, self-determination, human dignity and the right of peoples to exercise them.

Article 25

To realize the aims of this covenant and its principles the Palestine Liberation Organization will undertake its full role in liberating Palestine.

Article 26

The Palestine Liberation Organization, which represents the forces of the Palestinian revolution, is responsible for the movement of the Palestinian Arab people in its struggle to restore its homeland, liberate it, return to it and exercise the right of self-determination in it. This responsibility extends to all military, political and financial matters, and all else that the Palestine issue requires in the Arab and international spheres.

Article 27

The Palestine Liberation Organization will cooperate with all Arab States, each according to its capacities, and will maintain neutrality in their mutual relations in the light of, and on the basis of, the requirements of the battle of liberation, and will not interfere in the internal affairs of any Arab state.

Article 28

The Palestinian Arab people insists upon the originality and independence of its national revolution and rejects every manner of interference, guardianship and subordination.

Article 29

The Palestinian Arab people possesses the prior and original right in liberating and restoring its homeland and will define its position with reference to all states and powers on the basis of their positions with reference to the issue [of Palestine] and the extent of their support for [the Palestinian Arab people] in its revolution to realize its aims.

Article 30

The fighters and bearers of arms in the battle of liberation are the nucleus of the Popular Army, which will be the protecting arm of the gains of the Palestinian Arab people.

Article 31

This organization shall have a flag, oath and anthem, all of which will be determined in accordance with a special system.

Article 32

To this covenant is attached a law known as the fundamental law of the Palestine Liberation Organization, in which is determined the manner of the Organization's formation, its committees, institutions, the special functions of every one of them and all the requisite duties associated with them in accordance with this covenant.

Article 33

This covenant cannot be amended except by a two-thirds majority of all the members of the national council of the Palestine Liberation Organization in a special session called for this purpose.

Source: The Palestinian National Covenant—July 1968, Israel Ministry of Foreign Affairs, http://www.mfa.gov.il/MFA.

59. Abba Eban, The Nine-Point Peace Plan [Excerpt], October 8, 1968

Introduction

Speaking to the United Nations (UN) General Assembly in October 1968, Israeli foreign minister Abba Eban put forward his own country's views on an Arab-Israeli peace settlement. He prefaced this with a lengthy account of how Israel had, in effect, endured 20 years of war and attacks from Arab nations. Stating that the 1967 Six-Day War must be the last such war, he nonetheless warned that Israel must put its own security first and that "To prevent the renewal of these dangers is the first law of our policy." After describing the protracted negotiations for an Arab-Israeli peace settlement that UN special envoy Gunnar Jarring had already undertaken, to little if any effect, Eban set out his own country's "nine principles by which peace can be achieved." These envisaged the establishment of a permanent state of peace in which all countries in the region would have "secure and recognized boundaries" and guarantees of their security against attack. Frontiers and borders should be open, and navigation of all international waterways should be free and unhindered. Eban stated that even before peace negotiations began, Israel was willing to call a conference to work out a 5-year plan to deal with the refugee problem and to make special arrangements for the return of those refugees who had fled from the Israeli-occupied West Bank of the Jordan River during the recent hostilities. While remaining silent on the ultimate status of Jerusalem, he proclaimed Israel's willingness to share jurisdiction over the Islamic and Christian Holy Places there with members of those faiths. He also affirmed Israel's commitment to regional cooperation. Absent from Eban's speech was any suggestion as to the ultimate disposition of the occupied territories, an issue that lay at the heart of the peace process and of UN Security Council Resolution 242. He did, however, appeal to Arab governments to enter into negotiations and to state what peace terms would be acceptable to them and reiterated that Israel would be more than willing to open talks with any government willing

to do so. While Eban carefully reserved Israel's position on some of the most sensitive issues at stake, his address may well have represented a genuine overture to the Arab states. At this stage, however, none wished to reciprocate.

Primary Source

Mr. President, my Government has decided to give the members of the United Nations a detailed account of its views on the establishment of a just and lasting peace in the Middle East. Amidst the tumult of a rancorous public debate, the deeper motives of our policy have not always been clearly perceived. A structure of peace cannot, of course, be built by speeches at this rostrum. It may, however, be useful for the parties to clarify their intentions and to draw a picture of their policies beyond the routine vocabulary in which this discussion has been held down for sixteen months.

[…]

In discussing the reasons for the lack of substantive progress, we cannot fail to perceive that the discussion on peace has revolved too much around semantic expressions, too little around the solution of contentious issues. There is no instance in history in which a stubborn and complex conflict has been brought to an end by the mere recitation of texts without precise agreement on the issues of which the conflict is composed. Israel has accepted the Security Council's Resolution for the establishment of a just and lasting peace and declared its readiness to negotiate agreements on all the principles mentioned therein. We hold that the Resolution should be implemented through negotiation, agreement and the joint signature and application of appropriate treaty engagements.

When the parties accept a basis for settlement—their least duty is to clarify what they mean by their acceptance.

To make identical and laconic statements with diametrically opposed motives and interpretations would come dangerously close to international deceit. All parties must say what they mean, and mean what they say. And the heart of the problem is not what we say, but what we do. The construction of a peaceful edifice requires sustained action in order to bring the vital interests of the parties into an acceptable harmony. There is no such thing as peace by incantation. Peace cannot be advanced by recitations accompanied by refusal to negotiate viable agreements. The Security Council's Resolution has not been used as an instrument for peace. It has been invoked as an obstacle and alibi to prevent the attainment of peace.

In these conditions, my Government has given intensive consideration to the steps that we should now take. Our conclusion is this. Past disappointment should not lead to present despair. The stakes are too high. While the cease-fire agreements offer important security against large-scale hostilities, they do not represent a final state of peace. They must, of course, be maintained and respected until there is peace. They must be safeguarded against erosion by military assault and murderous incursion. But at the same time, the exploration of a lasting peace should be constant, unremitting, resilient and, above all, sincere. My Government deems the circumstances and atmosphere afforded by our presence here as congenial for a new attempt. We suggest that a new effort be made in the coming weeks to cooperate with Ambassador Jarring in his task of promoting agreements on the establishment of Peace.

It is important to break out of the declaratory phase in which the differences of formulation are secondary and in any case legitimate, in order to give tangible effect to the principles whereby peace can be achieved in conformity with the central purposes of the United Nations Charter or the Security Council Resolution and with the norms of international law. Instead of a war of words, we need acts of peace.

I come to enumerate the nine principles by which peace can be achieved:

1) The establishment of peace

The situation to follow the cease-fire must be a just and lasting peace, duly negotiated and contractually expressed.

Peace is not a mere absence of fighting. It is a positive and clearly defined relationship with far-reaching political, practical and juridical consequences. We propose that the peace settlement be embodied in treaty form. It would lay down the precise conditions of our co-existence, including a map of the secure and agreed boundary. The essence of peace is that it commits both parties to the proposition that their twenty-year-old conflict is at a permanent end. Peace is much more than what is called "non-belligerency." The elimination of belligerency is one of several conditions which compose the establishment of a just and lasting peace. If there had previously been peace between the States of our area and temporary hostilities had erupted, it might have been sufficient to terminate belligerency and to return to the previously existing peace. But the Arab-Israel area has had no peace. There is nothing normal or legitimate or established to which to return. The peace structure must be built from its foundations. The parties must define affirmatively what their relations shall be, not only what they will have ceased to be. The Security Council, too, called for the establishment of peace and not for any intermediate or ambiguous or fragmentary arrangement such as that which had exploded in 1967.

2) Secure and recognized boundaries

Within the framework of peace, the cease-fire lines will be replaced by permanent, secure and recognized boundaries between Israel and each of the neighbouring Arab States, and the disposition of forces will be carried out in full accordance with the boundaries under the final peace. We are willing to seek agreement with each Arab State on secure and recognized boundaries within the framework of a permanent peace.

It is possible to work out a boundary settlement compatible with the security of Israel and with the honour of Arab States. After twenty years, it is time that Middle Eastern States ceased to live in temporary "demarcation lines" without the precision and permanence which can come only from the definite agreement of the States concerned. The majority of the United Nations have recognized that the only durable and reasonable solutions are agreed solutions serving the common interests of our peoples. The new peace structure in the Middle East, including the secure and recognized boundaries, must be built by Arab and Israeli hands.

3) Security Agreements

In addition to the establishment of agreed territorial boundaries, we should discuss other agreed security arrangements designed to avoid the kind of vulnerable situation which caused a breakdown of the peace in the summer of 1967. The instrument establishing peace should contain a pledge of mutual non-aggression.

4) The open frontier

When agreement is reached on the establishment of peace with permanent boundaries, the freedom of movement now existing in the area, especially in the Israel-Jordan sector, should be maintained and developed. It would be incongruous if our peoples were to intermingle in peaceful contact and commerce only when there is a state of war and cease-fire—and to be separated into ghettos when there is peace. We should emulate the open frontier now developing within communities of States, as in parts of Western Europe. Within this concept, we include free port facilities for Jordan on Israel's Mediterranean coast and mutual access to places of religious and historic associations.

5) Navigation

Interference with navigation in the international waterways in the area has been the symbol of the state of war and, more than once, an immediate cause of hostilities. The arrangements for guaranteeing freedom of navigation should be unreserved, precise, concrete and founded on absolute equality of rights and obligations between Israel and other littoral States.

6) Refugees

The problem of displaced populations was caused by war and can be solved by peace. On this problem I propose:

One: A conference of Middle Eastern States should be convened, together with the Governments contributing to refugee relief and the specialized agencies of the United Nations, in order to chart a five-year plan for the solution of the refugee problem in the framework of a lasting peace and the integration of refugees into productive life. This conference can be called in advance of peace negotiations.

Two: Under the peace settlement, joint refugee integration and rehabilitation commissions should be established by the signatories in order to approve agreed projects for refugee integration in the Middle East, with regional and international aid.

Three: As an interim measure, my Government has decided, in view of the forthcoming winter, to intensify and accelerate action to widen the uniting of families scheme, and to process "hardship cases" among refugees who had crossed to the East Bank during the June 1967 fighting. Moreover, permits for return which had been granted and not used can be transferred to other refugees who meet the same requirements and criteria as the original recipients.

7) Jerusalem

Israel does not seek to exercise unilateral jurisdiction in the Holy Places of Christianity and Islam. We are willing in each case to work out a status to give effect to their universal character. We would like to discuss appropriate agreements with those traditionally concerned. Our policy is that the Christian and Moslem Holy Places should come under the responsibility of those who hold them in reverence.

8) Acknowledgement and recognition of sovereignty, integrity and right to national life

This principle, inherent in the Charter and expressed in the Security Council Resolution of November 1967, is of basic importance. It should be fulfilled through specific contractual engagements to be made by the Governments of Israel and of the Arab States to each other—by name. It follows logically that Arab Governments will withdraw all the reservations which they have expressed on adhering to international conventions, about the non-applicability of their signatures to their relations with Israel.

9) Regional cooperation

The peace discussion should examine a common approach to some of the resources and means of communication in the region in an effort to lay foundations of a Middle Eastern community of sovereign States.

Mr. President,

The process of exploring peace terms should follow normal precedents. There is no case in history in which conflicts have been liquidated or a transition effected from a state of war to a state of peace on the basis of a stubborn refusal by one State to meet another for negotiation. There would be nothing new in the experience and relationship of Israel and the Arab States for them to meet officially to effect a transition in their relationships. What is new and unprecedented is President Nasser's principle of "no negotiation."

In the meantime, we continue to be ready to exchange ideas and clarifications on certain matters of substance through Ambassador Jarring with any Arab Government willing to establish a just and lasting peace with Israel.

Mr. President,

I have expounded our views on peace in more detail than is usual in General Assembly debates. On each of these nine points we have elaborated detailed views and ideas which we would discuss with neighbouring States in a genuine exchange of views, in which we should, of course, consider comments and proposals from the other side.

No Arab spokesman has yet addressed himself to us in similar detail on the specific and concrete issues involved in peacemaking. Behind our proposals lie much thought and planning which can bear fruit when our minds and hearts interact with those of neighbouring States.

We ask friendly Governments outside the region to appraise the spirit as well as the content of the ideas which I have here outlined. We urge the Arab Governments to ponder them in a deliberate mood, and to explore their detailed implications with us in the normal and appropriate frameworks.

The solutions which I have outlined cover all the matters mentioned in the Security Council's Resolution and would constitute the effective fulfilment of its purposes.

We base ourselves on the integral and interdependent character of the points at issue. Nothing is less fruitful than an attempt to give separate identity or precedence to any single principle of international policy, thus destroying its delicate balance.

Moreover, the obligations of Israel and the Arab States to each other are not exhausted by any single text. They are also governed by the Charter, by the traditional precepts of international law, by constructive realism and by the weight of human needs and potentialities.

Lest Arab Governments be tempted out of sheer routine to rush into impulsive rejection, let me suggest that tragedy is not what men suffer but what they miss. Time and again Arab Governments have rejected proposals today—and longed for them tomorrow. The fatal pattern is drawn across the whole period since 1947—and before. There is nothing unrealistic about a negotiated peace inspired by a sense of innovation and constructed by prudent and flexible statecraft. Indeed, all other courses are unrealistic. The idea of a solution imposed on the parties by a concert of Powers is perhaps the most unrealistic of all. The positions of the Powers have not moved any closer in the last fifteen months than have the positions of the parties themselves. Moreover, the Middle East is not an international protectorate. It is an area of sovereign States which alone have the duty and responsibility of determining the conditions of their co-existence. When the parties have reached agreement, it would be natural for their agreement to receive international support. To the Arab States, we say: "For you and us alone, the Middle East is not a distant concern, or a strategic interest, or a problem of conflict, but the cherished home in which our cultures were born, in which our nationhood was fashioned and in which we and you and all our posterity must henceforth live together in mutuality of interest and respect."

It may seem ambitious to talk of a peaceful Middle Eastern design at this moment of tension and rancour. But there is such a thing in physics as fusion at high temperatures. In political experience, too, the consciousness of peril often brings a thaw in frozen situations. In the long run, nations can prosper only by recognizing what their common interest demands. The hour is ripe for the creative adventure of peace.

Source: "The Nine-Point Peace Plan—Statement to the General Assembly by Foreign Minister Eban—8 October 1968," Israel Ministry of Foreign Affairs, http://www.mfa.gov.il/MFA.

60. Abba Eban, Knesset Statement [Excerpt], May 13, 1969

Introduction

Speaking to the United Nations (UN) in the fall of 1968, Abba Eban was noncommittal as to which if any portions of the territories Israel intended to retain of those it had occupied during the Six-Day War. Addressing the Knesset (Israeli parliament) the following May, he was more forthright, listing three places that Israel considered vital to its interests. Even in these cases, however, some ambiguity remained, since Eban did not state that Israel intended to annex them outright. Instead, he called for Israel's "permanent presence at Sharm el-Sheikh," which could, for example, mean merely full or partial control or occupation; "a unified Jerusalem," under whose formal administration or sovereignty he declined to state; and the denial of the Golan Heights to Syria. While his statement may well have appeased hawks within the Knesset, in practice the ambiguities it contained left the foreign minister and his country substantial room to maneuver.

Primary Source

[. . .]

Three demands which Israel will not waive are a permanent presence at Sharm el-Sheikh, a unified Jerusalem despite concessions to Jordan over the Holy Places, and a Golan Heights for ever out of Syrian hands.

[. . .]

Source: *Jerusalem Post,* May 14, 1969.

61. William P. Rogers, A Lasting Peace in the Middle East: An American View [Excerpt], December 9, 1969

Introduction

When President Richard Nixon took office in January 1969, Middle Eastern policy was initially a fairly low priority. Policymaking in foreign affairs was dominated by Nixon and his charismatic national security adviser, Henry A. Kissinger, who wished to concentrate on the ongoing war in Vietnam and big-power diplomacy with the Soviet Union and China. They therefore left Middle Eastern policy largely to Secretary of State William Rogers. Seeking to resolve outstanding issues from the 1967 Six-Day War, in 1969 Rogers and Joseph Sisco, assistant secretary of state for Near Eastern and South Asian affairs, developed a peace plan envisaging Israeli withdrawal from occupied territories in return for evenhanded Soviet and U.S. policies toward both Arabs and Israel in the Middle East and a brokered peace settlement guaranteed by both big powers. Rogers sought a settlement on the lines of United Nations (UN) Security Council Resolution 242 under which Arab states would accept the right of Israel to exist in return for the restoration of most of the territory Israel had taken in 1967. He proposed that Palestinian refugees would be rehoused and that Israel and Jordan would jointly administer the city of Jerusalem, treating it as a unified city without barriers or checkpoints and granting access to all nationalities and faiths. Rogers's provisions largely resembled those that President Lyndon Johnson had advanced shortly after the war ended. Throughout 1969, Rogers pursued negotiations with the Soviets that were intended to reach a Middle Eastern settlement that they too would find acceptable. Kissinger, however, privately informed the Soviets in October 1969 that the White House had no real interest in this scheme, effectively sabotaging its chances of success. Like many other such efforts, the Rogers Plan was rejected by the Israelis. The Soviets later followed suit, while the Egyptians were also unenthusiastic. Rogers did, however, renew his efforts in 1970 after Israeli raids on Egypt led the Soviet Union to accede that March to Egyptian requests to send weapons, technicians, and combat personnel to Egypt in return for special rights over airbases and other installations. Rogers then launched an initiative to persuade Egypt, Jordan, and Israel to agree to Security Council Resolution 242 as a basis for negotiations, a proposal that the first two countries endorsed but that Israel only grudgingly accepted under duress. Even so, this was the first occasion on which an Israeli government had expressed itself willing to withdraw from any of the territory occupied in 1967.

Primary Source
[…]

I am going to speak tonight about the situation in the Middle East. I want to refer to the policy of the United States as it relates to that situation in the hope that there may be a better understanding of that policy and the reasons for it.

Following the third Arab-Israeli war in 20 years, there was an upsurge of hope that a lasting peace could be achieved. That hope has unfortunately not been realized. There is no area of the world today that is more important, because it could easily again be the source of another serious conflagration.

When this administration took office, one of our first actions in foreign affairs was to examine carefully the entire situation in the Middle East. It was obvious that a continuation of the unresolved conflict there would be extremely dangerous, that the parties to the conflict alone would not be able to overcome their legacy of suspicion to achieve a political settlement, and that international efforts to help needed support.

The United States decided it had a responsibility to play a direct role in seeking a solution.

Thus, we accepted a suggestion put forward both by the French Government and the Secretary General of the United Nations. We agreed that the major powers—the United States, the Soviet Union, the United Kingdom, and France—should cooperate to assist the Secretary General's representative, Ambassador Jarring, in working out a settlement in accordance with the resolution of the Security Council of the United Nations of November 1967. We also decided to consult directly with the Soviet Union, hoping to achieve as wide an area of agreement as possible between us.

These decisions were made in full recognition of the following important factors:

First, we knew that nations not directly involved could not make a durable peace for the peoples and governments involved. Peace rests with the parties to the conflict. The efforts of major powers can help, they can provide a catalyst, they can stimulate the parties to talk, they can encourage, they can help define a realistic framework for agreement; but an agreement among other powers cannot be a substitute for agreement among the parties themselves.

Second, we knew that a durable peace must meet the legitimate concerns of both sides.

Third, we were clear that the only framework for a negotiated settlement was one in accordance with the entire text of the U.N. Security Council resolution. That resolution was agreed upon after long and arduous negotiations; it is carefully balanced; it provides the basis for a just and lasting peace—a final settlement—not merely an interlude between wars.

Fourth, we believed that a protracted period of no war, no peace, recurrent violence, and spreading chaos would serve the interests of no nation, in or out of the Middle East.

U.S.-Soviet Discussions
[…]

On the one hand, the Arab leaders fear that Israel is not in fact prepared to withdraw from Arab territory occupied in the 1967 war.

On the other hand, Israeli leaders fear that the Arab states are not in fact prepared to live in peace with Israel.

Each side can cite from its viewpoint considerable evidence to support its fears. Each side has permitted its attention to be focused solidly and to some extent solely on these fears.

What can the United States do to help to overcome these roadblocks?

Our policy is and will continue to be a *balanced* one.

We have friendly ties with both Arabs and Israelis. To call for Israeli withdrawal as envisaged in the U.N. resolution without achieving agreement on peace would be partisan toward the Arabs. To call on the Arabs to accept peace without Israeli withdrawal would be partisan toward Israel. Therefore, our policy is to encourage the Arabs to accept a permanent peace based on a binding agreement and to urge the Israelis to withdraw from occupied territory when their territorial integrity is assured as envisaged by the Security Council resolution.

Basic Elements of the U.N. Resolution
In an effort to broaden the scope of discussion we have recently resumed four-power negotiations at the United Nations.

Let me outline our policy on various elements of the Security Council resolution. The basic and related issues might be described as peace, security, withdrawal, and territory.

Peace Between the Parties

The resolution of the Security Council makes clear that the goal is the establishment of a state of peace between the parties instead of the state of belligerency which has characterized relations for over 20 years. We believe the conditions and obligations of peace must be defined in specific terms. For example, navigation rights in the Suez Canal and in the Strait of Tiran should be spelled out. Respect for sovereignty and obligations of the parties to each other must be made specific.

But peace, of course, involves much more than this. It is also a matter of the attitudes and intentions of the parties. Are they ready to coexist with one another? Can a live-and-let-live attitude replace suspicion, mistrust, and hate? A peace agreement between the parties must be based on clear and stated intentions and a willingness to bring about basic changes in the attitudes and conditions which are characteristic of the Middle East today.

Security

A lasting peace must be sustained by a sense of security on both sides. To this end, as envisaged in the Security Council resolution, there should be demilitarized zones and related security arrangements more reliable than those which existed in the area in the past. The parties themselves, with Ambassador Jarring's help, are in the best position to work out the nature and the details of such security arrangements. It is, after all, their interests which are at stake and their territory which is involved. They must live with the results.

Withdrawal and Territory

The Security Council resolution endorses the principle of the non-acquisition of territory by war and calls for withdrawal of Israeli armed forces from territories occupied in the 1967 war. We support this part of the resolution, including withdrawal, just as we do its other elements.

The boundaries from which the 1967 war began were established in the 1949 armistice agreements and have defined the areas of national jurisdiction in the Middle East for 20 years. Those boundaries were armistice lines, not final political borders. The rights, claims, and positions of the parties in an ultimate peaceful settlement were reserved by the armistice agreements.

The Security Council resolution neither endorses nor precludes these armistice lines as the definitive political boundaries. However, it calls for withdrawal from occupied territories, the nonacquisition of territory by war, and the establishment of secure and recognized boundaries.

We believe that while recognized political boundaries must be established, and agreed upon by the parties, any changes in the preexist-

ing lines should not reflect the weight of conquest and should be confined to insubstantial alterations required for mutual security. We do not support expansionism. We believe troops must be withdrawn as the resolution provides. We support Israel's security and the security of the Arab states as well. We are for a lasting peace that requires security for both.

Issues of Refugees and Jerusalem

By emphasizing the key issues of peace, security, withdrawal, and territory, I do not want to leave the impression that other issues are not equally important. Two in particular deserve special mention: the questions of refugees and of Jerusalem.

There can be no lasting peace without a just settlement of the problem of those Palestinians whom the wars of 1948 and 1967 have made homeless. This human dimension of the Arab-Israeli conflict has been of special concern to the United States for over 20 years. During this period the United States has contributed about $500 million for the support and education of the Palestine refugees. We are prepared to contribute generously along with others to solve this problem. We believe its just settlement must take into account the desires and aspirations of the refugees and the legitimate concerns of the governments in the area.

The problem posed by the refugees will become increasingly serious if their future is not resolved. There is a new consciousness among the young Palestinians who have grown up since 1948 which needs to be channeled away from bitterness and frustration toward hope and justice.

The question of the future status of Jerusalem, because it touches deep emotional, historical, and religious wellsprings, is particularly complicated. We have made clear repeatedly in the past 2 1/2 years that we cannot accept unilateral actions by any party to decide the final status of the city. We believe its status can be determined only through the agreement of the parties concerned, which in practical terms means primarily the Governments of Israel and Jordan, taking into account the interests of other countries in the area and the international community. We do, however, support certain principles which we believe would provide an equitable framework for a Jerusalem settlement.

Specifically, we believe Jerusalem should be a unified city within which there would no longer be restrictions on the movement of persons and goods. There should be open access to the unified city for persons of all faiths and nationalities. Arrangements for the administration of the unified city should take into account the interests of all its inhabitants and of the Jewish, Islamic, and Christian communities. And there should be roles for both Israel and Jordan in the civic, economic, and religious life of the city.

It is our hope that agreement on the key issues of peace, security, withdrawal, and territory will create a climate in which these questions of refugees and of Jerusalem, as well as other aspects of the conflict, can be resolved as part of the overall settlement.

[. . .]

We remain interested in good relations with all states in the area. Whenever and wherever Arab states which have broken off diplomatic relations with the United States are prepared to restore them, we shall respond in the same spirit.

Meanwhile, we will not be deterred from continuing to pursue the paths of patient diplomacy in our search for peace in the Middle East. We will not shrink from advocating necessary compromises, even though they may and probably will be unpalatable to both sides. We remain prepared to work with others—in the area and throughout the world—so long as they sincerely seek the end we seek: a just and lasting peace.

Source: "A Lasting Peace in the Middle East: An American View," *Department of State Bulletin* 62(1593) (1970): 7–11.

62. Statement by the Israeli Government Embodying a Reaction to the Rogers Plan, December 11, 1969

Introduction

Within a day of learning the terms of the plan for an Arab-Israeli peace settlement put forward by U.S. secretary of state William Rogers, the Israeli government rejected them. Israel cited several years of fruitless negotiations by outside parties as proof that such efforts were futile. The first essential element of peace, the Israelis argued, was that the Arab governments must abandon their total hostility to Israel and their refusal to negotiate directly with Israel. Until they did so, it would be impossible to reach any kind of peace settlement. Efforts by other governments or institutions, including both the United States and the United Nations (UN), to mediate between Israel and its opponents only, the Israelis charged, encouraged the Arab states to believe that they could avoid dealing directly with Israel. The Israeli government also assailed Rogers's proposal that Jerusalem be under joint Israeli-Jordanian administration as an unacceptable attempt to preempt this sensitive issue. Shortly afterward, President Richard Nixon, reluctant to alienate the politically influential American supporters of Israel, privately informed Israeli prime minister Golda Meir that the United States would not press Israel to accept the Rogers Plan.

Primary Source

The Israel Government discussed in special session the political situation in the region and the latest speech of the U.S. Secretary of State on the Middle East.

The Government states that the tension in the Middle East referred to by Mr. Rogers derives from the aggressive policy of the Arab governments, the absolute refusal to make peace with Israel and the unqualified support of the Soviet Union for the Arab aggressive stand.

Israel is of the opinion that the only way to terminate the tension and the state of war in the region is by perpetual striving for a durable peace among the nations of the region, based on a peace treaty reached through direct negotiations which will take place without any prior conditions by any party. The agreed, secure and recognized boundaries will be fixed in the peace treaty. This is the permanent and stated peace policy of Israel and is in accordance with accepted international rules and procedures.

The Six Day War, or the situation created in its wake, cannot be spoken of in terms of expansion or conquest. Israel cried out against aggression which threatened its very existence, and used its natural right of national self-defence.

In his speech, Mr. Rogers said that states outside the region cannot fix peace terms; only states in the region are authorized to establish peace by agreement among themselves. The Government states regretfully that this principle does not tally with the detailed reference in the speech to peace terms, including territorial and other basic questions, among them Jerusalem. Jerusalem was divided following the conquest of part of the city by the Jordanian Army in 1948. Only now, after the unification of the city under Israel administration, does there exist freedom of access for members of all faiths to their holy places in the city.

The position of Israel is: The negotiations for peace must be free from prior conditions and external influences and pressures. The prospects for peace will be seriously marred if states outside the region continue to raise territorial proposals and suggestions on other subjects that cannot further peace and security.

When the Four Power talks began, the Government of Israel expressed its view on the harmful consequences involved in this move in its statement of March 27, 1969. The fears expressed then were confirmed.

Peace was not promoted. Arab governments were encouraged by the illusion that an arrangement could be reached by the exertion of external influences and pressures with no negotiations between the parties. In this period Egyptian policy reached the most extreme expressions, especially in President Nasser's speech in which he spoke of rivers flowing with blood and skies lit by fire. In this period, the region has not become tranquil. In an incessant violation of the cease-fire arrangement, fixed by the Security Council and accepted by all sides unconditionally and with no time limit, the Egyptians have intensified their attempts to disturb the cease-fire lines. Conveniently, Arab aggression in other sectors continued and terrorist acts, explicitly encouraged by Arab governments, were intensified. Even the Jarring mission to promote an agreement between the parties was paralyzed.

The focus of the problem as stated by Mr. Rogers lies in the basic intentions and positions of the governments of the region to the principle of peaceful coexistence. The lack of intention of the Arab governments to move towards peace with Israel is expressed daily in proclamations and deeds. The positions and intentions of the parties towards peace cannot be tested unless they agree to conduct negotiations as among states desiring peace. Only when there is a basic change in the Arab position, which denies the principle of negotiations for the signing of peace, will it be possible to replace the state of war by durable peace. This remains the central aim of the policy of Israel.

In his forthcoming talks with the Secretary of State, the Foreign Minister will explain in detail the position of the Government of Israel concerning the situation in the region.

Source: *Jerusalem Post,* December 12, 1969.

63. Leonid I. Brezhnev, Position on the 1973 War, October 9, 1973

Introduction

Arab states were determined to avenge their humiliation by Israel in the 1967 Six-Day War. Calls by Israeli hard-liners for the permanent retention of the territories occupied during that conflict and the ruling Labor Party's endorsement of this policy were an additional reason for seeking to reverse the outcome of the war. On October 6, 1973, the Jewish holy day of Yom Kippur (Day of Atonement), Egyptian and Syrian forces invaded Israel. Neither Israel nor the United States had expected the attack, which was prepared in secrecy. The war lasted two weeks. Initially, Arab units achieved stunning military success, with the Syrians overrunning the Golan Heights and the Egyptians advancing from the Suez Canal and breaking through the Israeli Bar-Lev Line. Seeking to enhance Soviet influence in the Middle East, Soviet general secretary Leonid Brezhnev expressed strong public support for Egypt and Syria, blaming the outbreak of the war on Israeli intransigence and armed raids on Syria, Egypt, and Lebanon. In a letter to Algerian president Hawari Boumédienne, a pillar of the Non-Aligned Movement and the Arab League, Brezhnev urged that Boumédienne use his influence and prestige to persuade other Arab states to take a united stand against Israel and support the Egyptian and Syrian war effort. Although Israeli forces subsequently reversed most of the initial Arab gains in the war, the early successes of Egyptian and Syrian troops were a source of great pride to all the Arab states proving that, when con-

ditions were right, they could defeat the Israeli military. Brezhnev's letter was almost certainly not the major reason that the Arab states soon imposed an embargo on oil sales to those Western nations that aided Israel, but it did imply that the Soviet Union would support them in such action.

Primary Source

President Hawari Boumedien [of Algeria] late last night received the USSR Ambassador, who handed him an important message from the CPSU Central Committee General Secretary on the Middle East situation. The message said:

The responsibility for the new military flare-up in the Middle East lies wholly and completely with the Tel Aviv leaders. While enjoying the support and protection of imperialist circles, Israel continues its aggression started in 1967 against the Arab countries, and foils every effort to establish a just peace in the Middle East and deliberately carries out provocations, including armed provocations, against Syria, Egypt and Lebanon, thus aggravating to the extreme the situation in this region.

I believe, dear comrade President, you agree that [in] the struggle at present being waged against Israeli aggression, for the liberation of Arab territories occupied in 1967 and the safeguarding of the legitimate rights of the Arab people of Palestine, Arab fraternal solidarity must, more than ever before, play a decisive role. Syria and Egypt must not be alone in their struggle against a treacherous enemy. There is an urgent need for the widest aid and support of the progressive regimes in these countries who, like Algeria, are the hope for progress and freedom in the Arab world.

The Central Committee of the CPSU and the Soviet Government are firmly convinced that the Algerian leaders, who are widely experienced in the anti-imperialist struggle, understand full well all the peculiarities of the present situation and that, guided by the ideals of fraternal solidarity, [they] will use every means and take every step required to give their support to Syria and Egypt in the tough struggle imposed by the Israeli aggressor.

Dear comrade President, your high personal prestige in the Third World countries which in particular contributed to the great success of the fourth non-aligned conference, clearly gives you the indisputable means to act with the Arab states with a view to bringing about a united stand in the face of the common danger.

As for the Soviet Union, it gives to the friendly Arab states multilateral aid and support in their just struggle against the imperialist Israeli aggression.

Source: Walter Laqueur and Barry Rubin, eds., *The Israel-Arab Reader: A Documentary History of the Middle East Conflict* (New York: Penguin, 2001), 142–143.

64. United Nations Security Council Resolution 338, October 22, 1973

Introduction

As both sides in the Yom Kippur War decided to agree to a cease-fire, the United Nations (UN) Security Council passed a resolution ordering the cessation of hostilities within 12 hours. In addition, the UN called upon all parties to begin peace negotiations using as a basis the earlier UN Security Council Resolution 242, which called upon the Arab states to recognize Israel's existence and make lasting peace with that country in exchange for the return of most of the territories Israel had taken in both wars. The resolution also urged solving the Palestinian refugee issue and the internationalization of the city of Jerusalem. In July 1974 the Palestine Liberation Organization (PLO) once again rejected Resolution 242. The resolution would nonetheless form the basis of protracted subsequent efforts to negotiate an Arab-Israeli peace settlement. Meanwhile, all states involved would in future be decidedly more cautious in launching full-scale war. Israel later undertook two brief invasions of Lebanon, but these were relatively small operations. Arab states never again mounted major invasions of Israel, relying instead on diplomacy to regain the territories they had lost. In addition, over the next three decades the focus of the Arab-Israeli question increasingly switched to securing the Palestinian refugees a state of their own.

Primary Source

The Security Council,

1. *Calls upon* all parties to the present fighting to cease all firing and terminate all military activity immediately, no later than 12 hours after the moment of the adoption of this decision, in the positions they now occupy;

2. *Calls upon* all parties concerned to start immediately after the cease-fire the implementation of Security Council Resolution 242 (1967) in all of its parts;

3. *Decides* that, immediately and concurrently with the cease-fire, negotiations start between the parties concerned under appropriate auspices aimed at establishing a just and durable peace in the Middle East.

> **Source:** United Nations Security Council Official Records, S.C. Res. 337, August 15, 1973.

65. Golda Meir, Statement to the Knesset [Excerpt], October 23, 1973

Introduction

On the day after Israel and the Arab states accepted the United Nations (UN) proposal for a cease-fire, Prime Minister Golda Meir addressed the Knesset. She clarified numerous provisions of the agreement, assuring the Knesset that the agreement applied not only to regular armed forces but also to irregular armed groups, that it would end the Arab maritime blockade of Israel, and that Israel's cease-fires with Egypt and Syria were not mutually dependent so that a breach of one cease-fire would not imply that Israel would also resume hostilities with the other nation. Celebrating Israel's achievements in the war, Meir argued that Israel was now in a better strategic defensive or offensive position than it had been when the conflict began. Addressing the thorny question of UN Security Council Resolution 242, which the UN had reaffirmed in its cease-fire resolution, Meir stressed that Israel was not prepared to return to its pre–June 5, 1967, borders, "which make the country a temptation to aggression and which, on various fronts, give decisive advantages to an aggressor." As part of any peace settlement, Israel would require more defensible and secure frontiers. She also stressed that Israel had accepted the cease-fire agreement largely at the urging of its friend and ally, the United States, and that the U.S. government had not put forward any suggestions as to what Israel's post–cease-fire borders should be but had, to the contrary, left those to be negotiated between Israel and its former antagonists. She also warned that if Egypt, which was still making sporadic attacks on Israeli positions, chose to resume fighting, Israel was more than prepared for this. In effect, Meir made no concessions to UN expectations on eventual peace terms and kept all Israeli options open.

Primary Source

[…]

On 22 October the Government of Israel unanimously decided to respond to the approach of the U.S. Government and President Nixon and announce its readiness to agree to a cease-fire according to the resolution of the Security Council following the joint American-Soviet proposal.

According to this proposal, the military forces will remain in the positions they hold at the time when the cease-fire goes into effect.

The implementation of the cease-fire is conditional on reciprocity. Our decision has been brought to the notice of the Foreign Affairs and Security committee, and now to the notice of the Knesset.

As regards the second paragraph of the Security Council resolution, the Government decided to instruct Israel's representative at the United Nations to include in his address to the Security Council a passage clarifying that our agreement to this paragraph is given in the sense in which it was defined by Israel when it decided in August 1970 to respond positively to the United States Government's initiative for a cease-fire, as stated in the United Nations on 4 August, 1970, and by the Prime Minister in the Knesset on the same day. This was also made clear to the U.S. Government. Israel's acceptance of a cease-fire with Egypt is conditional upon Egypt's agreement, but is not conditional upon Syria's agreement to a cease-fire, and vice-versa.

The Government also decided to clarify with the U.S. Government a series of paragraphs intimately connected with the content of the Security Council resolution and the procedure required by it. It is our intention to clarify and ensure, inter alia, that:

The cease-fire shall be binding upon all the regular forces stationed in the territory of a State accepting the cease-fire including the forces of foreign States, such as the armies of Iraq and Jordan in Syria and also forces sent by other Arab States which took part in the hostilities.

The cease-fire shall also be binding upon irregular forces acting against Israel from the area of the States accepting the cease-fire.

The cease-fire shall assure the prevention of a blockade or interference with free navigation, including oil tankers in the Bab-el-Mandeb straits on their way to Eilat.

It shall ensure that the interpretation of the term referring to "negotiations between the parties" is direct negotiations—and, naturally, it must be assured that the procedures, the drawing up of maps and the subject of cease-fire supervision shall be determined by agreement.

A subject of great importance, one dear to our hearts, is the release of prisoners. The Government of Israel has decided to demand an immediate exchange of prisoners. We have discussed this with the Government of the United States, which was one of the initiators of the cease-fire.

[. . .]

I stress again that this subject is one of the principal tests of the cease-fire, and that there will be no relaxation of our demand that the obligations undertaken by the initiators of the cease-fire be indeed carried out.

I will say several things about our military situation on the Syrian and Egyptian fronts before the cease-fire:

On the Syrian Front

The lines we are holding today on the Syrian front are better than those we held on the 6th of October.

Not only do we now hold all the territory which was under our control before, but our situation has been considerably improved by the holding of positions on the Hermon ridge and also on the front line

in the east, which has shifted the previous cease-fire line to a better line supported by a strong flank in the north, on the Hermon ridge.

On the Egyptian Front

The Egyptians did indeed gain a military achievement in crossing the Canal, but in a daring counter-offensive by the Israel Defense Forces, our forces succeeded in regaining control of part of the Eastern Canal line, and to gain control of a large area west of the Canal, an area which opens before us both defensive and offensive possibilities:

(a) This deployment deprives the Egyptian army of its capacity to constitute an offensive threat in the direction of Sinai and Israel, and also prevents them from being able to attack essential installations or areas in our territory.

(b) The forces of the I.D.F. west of the Suez Canal constitute a strong military base for the development of operations initiated by us if required.

In connection with the cease-fire issue, the U.S. Secretary of State, Dr. Henry Kissinger, and his aides called here on their way from Moscow to Washington. The visit was an appropriate opportunity for a thoroughgoing discussion of questions arising from the cease-fire, as well as for an exchange of views, in a friendly spirit, on what was about to happen and what was called for as a result of Israel's response to the U.S. Government's request for agreement to a cease-fire. During this visit, we continued and strengthened the contacts which preceded the Security Council resolution.

In all our contacts with the United States, I learnt that not only does the U.S. have no plan for the borders and other components of peace, but that it is its view that those who offer their "good services" should see to it that the parties themselves—and they alone—should make proposals, plans, for the future.

Furthermore, I must emphasize that, in accordance with authoritative information to hand, the Moscow talks contained nothing more than is contained in the Security Council resolution. I have to inform you that the Syrian Government has so far not responded to the cease-fire resolution. The fighting on that front continues, and the I.D.F. will operate there in accordance with its plans.

As for the Egyptian front—firing against our forces has not yet ceased, and the I.D.F. is obliged to operate as required as long as the firing continues.

At this stage, I will state only that we are examining the conduct of the Egyptians with close military and political attention. Should Egypt persist in belligerent activity, we shall deem ourselves free to take any action and move called for by the situation.

I shall not go into elaborate evaluations of the political activity which preceded the cease-fire. In any event, it was not we who made approaches concerning a cease-fire. As far as the situation on the fronts was concerned, there was no reason for such an approach on our part. It was not we who initiated the timing and clauses of the Security Council's resolution. On the fronts, our forces were not in an inferior battle position. As aforesaid, we deemed it right to respond to the call of the United States and its President, since:

(a) The State of Israel, by its nature, has no wish for war, does not desire loss of life. All Governments of Israel have been convinced that war would not promote peace.

(b) The cease-fire proposal has come when our position is firm on both fronts, when the achievements we hold are of great value and justify agreement to a cease-fire, despite the enemy's achievement east of the Suez Canal.

(c) We responded to the call by the United States and its President out of appreciation and esteem for its positive policy in the Middle East at this time.

Great importance attaches to our response insofar as concerns the continued strengthening of Israel, with particular reference to the continued military and political aid in the War that has been forced upon us....

[...]

On various occasions the Government of Israel has officially defined its attitude towards Security Council Resolution 242. These statements were made from international platforms and at diplomatic meetings, and we have brought them to the knowledge of the Knesset, its Defense and Foreign Affairs Committee and the public at large.

At this time I shall refer to one statement made on 4 August, 1970, to the U.S. Government, to the United Nations and to the Knesset. This statement too, is connected with a cease-fire, and I shall not tire the Knesset by quoting it in full. However, I consider it necessary to quote from my statement in the Knesset on 5 August. This statement was made on the eve of possible talks with the Arab States, and it is still completely valid.

Israel has publicly declared that, by virtue of her right to secure borders, defensible borders, she will not return to the frontiers of 4 June 1967, which make the country a temptation to aggression and which, on various fronts, give decisive advantages to an aggressor. Our position was and still remains that, in the absence of peace, we will continue to maintain the situation as determined at the cease-fire. The cease-fire lines can be replaced only by secure, recognized and agreed boundaries demarcated in a peace treaty.

In accepting the American Government's peace initiative, Israel was not asked to, and did not, undertake any territorial commitments. On the contrary, the Government of Israel received support for its position that not a single Israeli soldier will be withdrawn from the cease-fire lines until a binding contractual peace agreement is reached.

This terrible war that was forced upon us reinforces our awareness of the vital need for defensible borders, for which we shall struggle with all our vigor.

It is worth noting that, since the outbreak of the war on Yom Kippur, the terrorists have also resumed activities from Lebanese territory. Up to this morning, during this period of 17 days, 116 acts of aggression have been perpetrated, 44 civilian settlements on the northern border have been attacked and shelled, and some 20 civilians and 6 soldiers were killed or wounded in these actions. Our people living in the border settlements may be confident that Israel's Defense Forces are fully alert to this situation. Despite the defensive dispositions operative on this front, it has been proved once again that defensive action alone is not sufficient to put an end to acts of terror.

The war in which we are engaged began with a concerted attack on two fronts. The aggressive initiative afforded our enemies preliminary achievements—but, thanks to the spirit and strength of Israel's Defense Army, which is backed by the entire nation, this attack was broken. The aggressors were thrown back. Considerable portions of their forces were destroyed, and the I.D.F. broke through and crossed the cease-fire lines. From holding battles our forces went over to the offensive and gained brilliant achievements.

On both fronts our forces are now holding strong positions beyond the cease-fire lines, unbroken in spirit. The people is united in support of our army.

Israel wants a cease-fire. Israel will observe the cease-fire on a reciprocal basis, and only on that basis. With all her heart Israel wants peace negotiations to start immediately and concurrently with the cease-fire. Israel is capable of evincing the inner strength necessary for the promotion of an honorable peace within secure borders.

We shall be happy if such readiness is also shown by the people and Government of Egypt. However, if the rulers of Egypt propose to renew the war, they shall find Israel prepared, armed and steadfast in spirit....

[...]

Source: Walter Laqueur and Barry Rubin, eds., *The Israel-Arab Reader: A Documentary History of the Middle East Conflict* (New York: Penguin, 2001), 152–157.

66. Richard Nixon, Address to the Nation about Policies to Deal with the Energy Shortages [Excerpt], November 7, 1973

Introduction

In retaliation for U.S. shipments of armaments to Israel during the October 1973 Yom Kippur War, Arab states led by Saudi Arabia cut back on their production of oil and imposed embargos on sales to the United States and other Western nations that had assisted Israel during the conflict. Oil prices quickly quadrupled, fueling already rising inflation and soon contributing to an economic depression that afflicted Europe as well as the United States. As winter approached, fuel oil was in short supply in the United States. In early November, President Richard Nixon addressed the American people, warning that they faced "the most acute shortages of energy since World War II" and that in the coming winter the country would have between 10 percent and 17 percent less oil than it needed. As a short-term measure, he asked all Americans to economize in their use of energy. He also announced a program of government measures to deal with the problem, including the conversion of oil-burning plants and utilities to coal, a reduction in civilian aircraft flights, cutting the consumption of energy by 15 percent in homes and businesses and by 7 percent in federal government offices, accelerating the construction of nuclear power plants, reducing automobile speed limits to 50 miles per hour, and encouraging states, cities, and individuals to introduce other small-scale measures to economize on energy. In addition, he called on Congress to pass a program of specific energy-saving measures, including the introduction of daylight saving time throughout the year, the relaxation of environmental regulations, the introduction of "special energy conservation measures," funding for the faster exploration and development of existing U.S. oil reserves, the introduction of the 50-mile speed limit, and greater governmental authority to regulate transportation to ensure efficient energy use. Warning that Americans were overly reliant on energy and used it too prodigally, Nixon complained that Congress had failed to pass any of his earlier legislative initiatives to conserve and develop energy resources, and he asked that Congress take effective action in this area so that by 1980 the United States would be self-sufficient in energy. Nixon's program was imaginative, ambitious, and largely fruitless. Even though Americans might admit intellectually that they should economize, conserve energy resources, develop both new and existing resources, and reduce American dependence on foreign supplies, the measures involved would have demanded massive and often painful restructuring of the U.S. economic and fiscal status quo, which proved politically impossible for Nixon and his successors as president to introduce.

Primary Source

[...]

I want to talk to you tonight about a serious national problem, a problem we must all face together in the months and years ahead.

As America has grown and prospered in recent years, our energy demands have begun to exceed available supplies. In recent months, we have taken many actions to increase supplies and to reduce consumption. But even with our best efforts, we knew that a period of temporary shortages was inevitable.

Unfortunately, our expectations for this winter have now been sharply altered by the recent conflict in the Middle East. Because of that war, most of the Middle Eastern oil producers have reduced overall production and cut off their shipments of oil to the United States. By the end of this month, more than 2 million barrels a day of oil we expected to import into the United States will no longer be available.

We must, therefore, face up to a very stark fact: We are heading toward the most acute shortages of energy since World War II. Our supply of petroleum this winter will be at least 10 percent short of our anticipated demands, and it could fall short by as much as 17 percent.

Now, even before war broke out in the Middle East, these prospective shortages were the subject of intensive discussions among members of my Administration, leaders of the Congress, Governors, mayors, and other groups. From these discussions has emerged a broad agreement that we, as a nation, must now set upon a new course.

In the short run, this course means that we must use less energy—that means less heat, less electricity, less gasoline. In the long run, it means that we must develop new sources of energy which will give us the capacity to meet our needs without relying on any foreign nation.

The immediate shortage will affect the lives of each and every one of us. In our factories, our cars, our homes, our offices, we will have to use less fuel than we are accustomed to using. Some school and factory schedules may be realigned, and some jet airplane flights will be canceled.

This does not mean that we are going to run out of gasoline or that air travel will stop or that we will freeze in our homes or offices anyplace in America. The fuel crisis need not mean genuine suffering for any American. But it will require some sacrifice by all Americans.

We must be sure that our most vital needs are met first—and that our least important activities are the first to be cut back. And we must be sure that while the fat from our economy is being trimmed, the muscle is not seriously damaged.

To help us carry out that responsibility, I am tonight announcing the following steps:

First, I am directing that industries and utilities which use coal—which is our most abundant resource—be prevented from converting from coal to oil. Efforts will also be made to convert power plants from the use of oil to the use of coal.

Second, we are allocating reduced quantities of fuel for aircraft. Now, this is going to lead to a cutback of more than 10 percent of the number of flights and some rescheduling of arrival and departure times.

Third, there will be reductions of approximately 15 percent in the supply of heating oil for homes and offices and other establishments. To be sure that there is enough oil to go around for the entire winter, all over the country, it will be essential for all of us to live and work in lower temperatures. We must ask everyone to lower the thermostat in your home by at least 6 degrees so that we can achieve a national daytime average of 68 degrees. Incidentally, my doctor tells me that in a temperature of 66 to 68 degrees, you are really more healthy than when it is 75 to 78, if that is any comfort. In offices, factories, and commercial establishments, we must ask that you achieve the equivalent of a 10-degree reduction by either lowering the thermostat or curtailing working hours.

Fourth, I am ordering additional reductions in the consumption of energy by the Federal Government. We have already taken steps to reduce the Government's consumption by 7 percent. The cuts must now go deeper and must be made by every agency and every department in the Government. I am directing that daytime temperatures in Federal offices be reduced immediately to a level of between 65 and 68 degrees, and that means in this room, too, as well as in every other room in the White House. In addition, I am ordering that all vehicles owned by the Federal Government—and there are over a half-million of them—travel no faster than 50 miles per hour except in emergencies. This is a step which I have also asked Governors, mayors, and local officials to take immediately with regard to vehicles under their authority.

Fifth, I am asking the Atomic Energy Commission to speed up the licensing and construction of nuclear plants. We must seek to reduce the time required to bring nuclear plants on line—nuclear plants that can produce power—to bring them on line from 10 years to 6 years, reduce that time lag.

Sixth, I am asking that Governors and mayors reinforce these actions by taking appropriate steps at the State and local level. . . .

Consistent with safety and economic considerations, I am also asking Governors to take steps to reduce highway speed limits to 50 miles per hour. This action alone, if it is adopted on a nationwide basis, could save over 200,000 barrels of oil a day—just reducing the speed limit to 50 miles per hour.

Now, all of these actions will result in substantial savings of energy. More than that, most of these are actions that we can take right now—without further delay.

The key to their success lies, however, not just here in Washington but in every home, in every community across this country. If each of us joins in this effort, joins with the spirit and the determination that have always graced the American character, then half the battle will already be won.

But we should recognize that even these steps, as essential as they are, may not be enough. We must be prepared to take additional steps, and for that purpose, additional authorities must be provided by the Congress.

I have therefore directed my chief adviser for energy policy, Governor Love, and other Administration officials, to work closely with the Congress in developing an emergency energy act.

[. . .]

This proposed legislation would enable the executive branch to meet the energy emergency in several important ways:

First, it would authorize an immediate return to daylight saving time on a year round basis.

Second, it would provide the necessary authority to relax environmental regulations on a temporary, case-by-case basis, thus permitting an appropriate balancing of our environmental interests, which all of us share, with our energy requirements, which, of course, are indispensable.

Third, it would grant authority to impose special energy conservation measures, such as restrictions on the working hours for shopping centers and other commercial establishments.

And fourth, it would approve and fund increased exploration, development, and production from our naval petroleum reserves. Now, these reserves are rich sources of oil. From one of them alone—Elk Hills in California—we could produce more than 160,000 barrels of oil a day within 2 months.

Fifth, it would provide the Federal Government with authority to reduce highway speed limits throughout the Nation.

And finally, it would expand the power of the Government's regulatory agencies to adjust the schedules of planes, ships, and other carriers.

If shortages persist despite all of these actions and despite inevitable increases in the price of energy products, it may then become necessary—may become necessary—to take even stronger measures.

It is only prudent that we be ready to cut the consumption of oil products, such as gasoline, by rationing or by a fair system of taxation, and consequently, I have directed that contingency plans, if this becomes necessary, be prepared for that purpose.

Now, some of you may wonder whether we are turning back the clock to another age. Gas rationing, oil shortages, reduced speed limits—they all sound like a way of life we left behind with Glenn Miller and the war of the forties. Well, in fact, part of our current problem also stems from war—the war in the Middle East. But our deeper energy problems come not from war, but from peace and from abundance. We are running out of energy today because our economy has grown enormously and because in prosperity what were once considered luxuries are now considered necessities.

How many of you can remember when it was very unusual to have a home air-conditioned? And yet, this is very common in almost all parts of the Nation.

As a result, the average American will consume as much energy in the next 7 days as most other people in the world will consume in an entire year. We have only 6 percent of the world's people in America, but we consume over 30 percent of all the energy in the world.

Now, our growing demands have bumped up against the limits of available supply, and until we provide new sources of energy for tomorrow, we must be prepared to tighten our belts today.

Let me turn now to our long-range plans.

[...]

Two years ago, in the first energy message any President has ever sent to the Congress, I called attention to our urgent energy problem. Last April, this year, I reaffirmed to the Congress the magnitude of that problem, and I called for action on seven major legislative initiatives. Again in June, I called for action. I have done so frequently since then.

But thus far, not one major energy bill that I have asked for has been enacted....

Our failure to act now on our long-term energy problems could seriously endanger the capacity of our farms and of our factories to employ Americans at record-breaking rates—nearly 86 million

people are now at work in this country—and to provide the highest standard of living we or any other nation has ever known in history.

It could reduce the capacity of our farmers to provide the food we need. It could jeopardize our entire transportation system. It could seriously weaken the ability of America to continue to give the leadership which only we can provide to keep the peace that we have won at such great cost for thousands of our finest young Americans.

That is why it is time to act now on vital energy legislation that will affect our daily lives, not just this year, but for years to come.

We must have the legislation now which will authorize construction of the Alaska pipeline—legislation which is not burdened with irrelevant and unnecessary provisions.

We must have legislative authority to encourage production of our vast quantities of natural gas, one of the cleanest and best sources of energy.

We must have the legal ability to set reasonable standards for the surface mining of coal.

And we must have the organizational structures to meet and administer our energy programs.

And therefore, tonight, as I did this morning in meeting with the Congressional leaders, I again urge the Congress to give its attention to the initiatives I recommended 6 months ago to meet these needs that I have described.

Finally, I have stressed repeatedly the necessity of increasing our energy research and development efforts. Last June, I announced a 5-year, $10 billion program to develop better ways of using energy and to explore and develop new energy sources. Last month, I announced plans for an immediate acceleration of that program.

We can take heart from the fact that we in the United States have half the world's known coal reserves. We have huge, untapped sources of natural gas. We have the most advanced nuclear technology known to man. We have oil in our continental shelves. We have oil shale out in the western part of the United States, and we have some of the finest technical and scientific minds in the world. In short, we have all the resources we need to meet the great challenge before us. Now we must demonstrate the will to meet that challenge.

[...]

Today the challenge is to regain the strength that we had earlier in this century, the strength of self-sufficiency. Our ability to meet our own energy needs is directly linked to our continued ability to act decisively and independently at home and abroad in the service of peace, not only for America but for all nations in the world.

[...]

Let us unite in committing the resources of this Nation to a major new endeavor, an endeavor that in this Bicentennial Era we can appropriately call "Project Independence."

Let us set as our national goal, in the spirit of Apollo, with the determination of the Manhattan Project, that by the end of this decade we will have developed the potential to meet our own energy needs without depending on any foreign energy sources.

Let us pledge that by 1980, under Project Independence, we shall be able to meet America's energy needs from America's own energy resources.

[...]

Source: Richard Nixon, *Public Papers of the Presidents of the United States: Richard Nixon, 1973* (Washington, DC: U.S. Government Printing Office, 1975), 916–922.

67. Secret Resolutions of the Algiers Summit Conference [Excerpt], December 4, 1973

Introduction

Although the October 1973 Yom Kippur War was at best a qualified success for Arab arms, Arab morale nonetheless received a boost from the fact that Egypt and Syria had inflicted considerable damage on Israel. This was further enhanced by their ability to use the weapon of oil to hold the Western nations at ransom. Meeting in a summit conference at Algiers in early December 1973, the members of the Arab League secretly reaffirmed their determination to regain all the territories Israel had occupied since June 1967, together with complete Arab sovereignty over all Jerusalem. They also pledged to restore the rights of the Palestinian people "according to the decisions of the Palestine Liberation Organization" (PLO), although Jordan, whose King Hussein had waged a bitter civil war during 1970–1971 with the PLO for control of his kingdom, dissented from this. The meeting also affirmed that no Arab state could hold itself aloof from the commitment to the Palestinian cause and pledged military and financial support to Egypt and Syria, as well as the Palestinians, in their efforts to regain their lost territories and eliminate Israel. At least rhetorically, therefore, Arab support for the destruction of Israel remained unwavering.

Primary Source

a. The Current Goals of the Arab Nation

The Conference resolves that the goals of the current phase of the common Arab struggle are:

1. The complete liberation of all the Arab territories conquered during the aggression of June 1967, with no concession or abandonment of any part of them, or detriment to national sovereignty over them.
2. Liberation of the Arab city of Jerusalem, and rejection of any situation which may be harmful to complete Arab sovereignty over the Holy City.
3. Commitment to restoration of the national rights of the Palestinian people, according to the decisions of the Palestine Liberation Organization, as the sole representative of the Palestinian nation. (The Hashemite Kingdom of Jordan expressed reservations.)
4. The Palestine problem is the affair of all the Arabs, and no Arab party can possibly dissociate itself from this commitment, in the light of the resolutions of previous Summit Conferences.

b. Military

In view of continuation of the struggle against the enemy until the goals of our nation are attained, the liberation of the occupied territories and the restoration of the national rights of the Palestinian people, the Conference resolves:

1. Solidarity of all the Arab States with Egypt, Syria and the Palestinian nation, in the common struggle for attainment of the just goals of the Arabs.
2. Provision of all means of military and financial support to both fronts, Egyptian and Syrian, to strengthen their military capacity for embarking on the liberation campaign and standing fast in face of the tremendous amount of supplies and unlimited aid received by the enemy.
3. Support of Palestinian resistance by all possible measures, to ensure its active role in the campaign.

c. Economic

Considering the significance of the economy in the campaign against the enemy, and the need to use every weapon at the disposal of the Arabs, as well as to concentrate all resources to enhance fighting capacity, the Conference resolves:

1. To strengthen economic ties among the Arab States, and empower the Arab Economic Council to set up a plan of operations to that end.
2. To continue the use of oil as a weapon in the campaign, in view of the resolutions of the oil Ministers and the link between the revocation of the ban on oil exports to any country and

the commitment of that country to support the just cause of the Arabs. To establish a committee, subordinate to the oil Ministers, which will follow up the implementation of these resolutions and those of the oil Ministers with regard to the percentage of the cut in oil supply, so as to arrive at coordination between this committee and the committee of Foreign Ministers of the oil-producing countries in respect of the development of the positions of other countries vis-à-vis the Arab cause.

3. To strengthen, as is vital, the steadfast attitude within the occupied territories, and assure it.

4. To make good war-damages of the Arab States, and to heighten the spirit of struggle and the combat capacity of the countries involved in the confrontation.

[...]

Source: Arab League, "Secret Resolutions of the Algiers Summit Conference from Al-Nahar, Beirut, 4 December 1973," Israel Ministry of Foreign Affairs, http://www.mfa.gov.il/MFA.

68. Annex to the Final Declaration of the Copenhagen Summit, December 15, 1973

Introduction

As President Richard Nixon told the American people, if anything the impact of the oil embargo that Arab nations imposed on them after the October 1973 Yom Kippur War affected European nations considerably more severely than the United States. Meeting in Copenhagen, Denmark, in December 1973, the heads of state and government of the nine member countries of the European Community (EC)—Great Britain, France, West Germany, Italy, Denmark, Belgium, the Netherlands, Luxembourg, and Ireland—discussed the international diplomatic and economic situation and the impact on their countries of developments in the Middle East. In an unexpected ploy, the foreign ministers of Algeria, Tunisia, Sudan, and the United Arab Emirates made a surprise visit to the conference and delivered a verbal message on behalf of the other Arab states. The conference's final communiqué, issued by Danish prime minister Anker Jorgensen, called for ever closer cooperation among EC member states so that "Europe should speak with one voice in important world affairs." Turning specifically to the Middle East, the gathering affirmed its support for United Nations (UN) Security Council Resolution 242 "in all its parts taking into account also the legitimate rights of the Palestinians" as the basis for a peace settlement. The European leaders also urged "the conclusion of peace agreements including among other arrangements international guarantees and the establishment of demilitarized zones." Given the critical energy situation facing all European nations, the

communiqué included an annex dealing specifically with that issue. It called for the development of a concerted European energy strategy to ensure adequate supplies for the indefinite future, including the introduction "on a concerted and equitable basis [of] measures to limit energy consumption; the development of existing energy resources; research into new sources of energy; the swift establishment of facilities for the enrichment of uranium and nuclear power; and negotiations with oil-producing countries on comprehensive arrangements for the economic and industrial development of these countries, industrial investments, and stable energy supplies to the member countries at reasonable prices." The conference's focus on energy and the Middle East demonstrated just how crucial to industrialized European nations steady and uninterrupted supplies of oil on a large scale had become.

Primary Source

The Heads of State or Government considered that the situation produced by the energy crisis is a threat to the world economy as a whole, affecting not only developed but also developing countries. A prolonged scarcity of energy resources would have grave effects on production, employment and balances of payment within the Community.

The Heads of State or Government therefore agreed on the necessity for the Community of immediate and effective action along the following lines:

The Council should adopt at its session of December 17–18, 1973, the Community instruments which will enable the Commission to establish by January 15, 1974, comprehensive energy balance sheets covering all relevant aspects of the energy situation in the Community.

The Commission should on this basis proceed to examine all present or foreseeable repercussions of the energy supply situation on production, employment, prices and balances of payments, as well as on the development of monetary reserves.

The Heads of State or Government should ask the Commission to present by January 31, 1974, proposals on which the Council will be invited to decide as quickly as possible and in principle before February 28, 1974, to ensure the orderly functioning of the common market for energy;

In this context the Commission is asked to submit to the Council as quickly as possible for rapid decision proposals aimed at resolving in a concerted manner the problems raised by the developing energy crisis.

For the same reasons they asked the Council to adopt provisions to ensure that all Member States introduce on a concerted and equitable basis measures to limit energy consumption.

With a view to securing the energy supplies of the Community the Council will adopt a comprehensive Community programme of alternative sources of energy. This programme will be designed to promote a diversification of supplies by developing existing resources, accelerating research in new sources of energy and creating new capacities of production, notably a European capacity for enrichment of uranium, seeking the concerted harmonious development of existing projects.

The Heads of State or Government confirmed the importance of entering into negotiations with oil-producing countries on comprehensive arrangements comprising co-operation on a wide scale for the economic and industrial development of these countries, industrial investments, and stable energy supplies to the Member Countries at reasonable prices.

They furthermore considered it useful to study with other oil-consuming countries within the framework of the Organization for Economic Cooperation and Development (OECD), ways of dealing with the common short and long-term energy problems of consumer countries.

The Council should establish at its session of December 17–18, 1973, an Energy Committee of Senior Officials which is responsible for implementing the energy policy measures adopted by the Council.

Source: European Community Information Service, *European Community Background Information: Background Note,* No. 29, December 20, 1973.

69. Communiqué Issued after the Organization of Arab Petroleum Exporting Countries Ministerial Meeting, Kuwait, December 25, 1973

Introduction

Having inflicted major economic difficulties on the United States and European nations by means of their oil embargo, Arab oil ministers were determined to continue their pressure on Israel's international backers. Meeting at Kuwait in late December 1973, oil ministers of the Organization of Arab Petroleum Exporting Countries (OAPEC) discussed what further measures they should take. They had, they stated, initially planned to cut oil supplies in January 1974 by an additional 5 percent, which would have meant an overall 30 percent cut in supplies since October 1973. Instead, they chose to reduce the overall cut to a mere 15 percent that month. The oil ministers' communiqué, issued at the end of the meeting, stated that because Japanese policy had moved in a pro-Arab direction since the embargo was first imposed, no further cuts would be imposed on supplies to Japan. Belgium received similar treatment.

"[C]ertain friendly countries" were promised levels of oil supplies even higher than those they had been receiving in September 1973. Rather complacently, the Arab ministers noted that American public and congressional opinion was becoming less pro-Israeli and more pro-Arab, even though for the time being they still intended to maintain the oil embargo against the United States. They stated their intention of meeting again in February 1974, at which time, they implied, they would reconsider their position on oil exports to various nations. The partial restoration of Arab output may have stemmed in part from a wish to increase oil revenues. The tone of the communiqué also, however, distinctly suggested that the Arab oil ministers were enjoying their power of toying with the various states, favoring those that took a pro-Arab line while punishing those that did not.

Primary Source

Meeting in Kuwait, the Arab Oil Ministers were addressed by His Excellency Sheikh Ahmed Zaki Yamani, Saudi Arabian Minister for Oil and Mining Resources, and His Excellency Belaid Abdesselam, Minister of Industry and Energy of the Algerian Republic. Referring to the results of their visits to certain western capitals, the two Ministers described their impressions and made proposals, taking account of the results and effects of their visits.

The Ministers present considered the real aim of the oil measures they had taken, which was to make international public opinion aware—without however bringing about an economic collapse which might affect one or more of the world's nations—of the injustice done to the Arab nation as a result of the occupation of its territories and the expulsion of an entire Arab people, the Palestinian people.

They again reaffirmed—as stated continuously since 17th October—that the measures taken should in no way affect friendly countries, thus drawing a very clear distinction between those who support the Arabs, those who support the enemy and those who remain neutral.

The Arab Ministers present noted the changes which had occurred in Japanese policy towards the Arab cause as demonstrated in several ways, including the visit by the Japanese Deputy Prime Minister to certain Arab countries. They also took account of Japan's difficult economic situation and decided to accord it special treatment, excluding it completely from the application of the general cut in output in order to protect the Japanese economy and in the hope that the Japanese Government will appreciate this position and persevere in its fair and equitable attitude towards the Arab cause.

The Arab Ministers also considered Belgium's political stand. They decided not to apply the planned cut to its oil supplies and authorised the transit of its supplies through the Netherlands, provided there were full guarantees that all such oil would be delivered to Belgium. Furthermore, they decided to meet the real requirements of certain friendly countries even if such supplies raised their imports above the September 1973 level and provided Arab oil supplied to them was not diverted and did not replace oil from non-Arab sources.

In order to ensure the application of the abovementioned decisions, the Arab Ministers present decided to increase output in their respective countries by 10% as compared with September output, the new cut in output thus being reduced from 25% to 15%.

They also decided not to apply the 5% cut planned for January.

The Arab Ministers present noted with satisfaction the progressive trend emerging in American public opinion. Certain government circles are thus beginning to become aware of Arab problems and expansionist Israeli policy. This has been particularly clear in the objective and neutral positions towards the Arab-Israeli problem adopted by certain members of the American Senate and House of Representatives.

The Arab Oil Ministers hope that the desire of the American Government to help to find a peaceful and fair solution is a positive factor which will allow beneficial results to be achieved for all the nations of the world and for bilateral relations between the American nation and the Arab nations in particular. The embargo will be maintained for the United States and the Netherlands.

The Arab Ministers will meet in Tripoli in the Libyan Arab Republic on 14th February 1974 after the round of visits which the two Ministers representing them are to make, provided circumstances do not make it necessary to convene an earlier meeting.

Source: "Communiqué Issued after the OAPEC Ministerial Meeting (Kuwait, 25 December 1973)," *Western European Union Assembly– General Affairs Committee: A Retrospective View of the Political Year in Europe 1973*, April 1974, 323–324.

70. Final Communiqué of the Washington Conference, February 13, 1974

Introduction

Western leaders continued to seek coordinated policies to address the energy crisis and the economic difficulties it encouraged and intensified. In an effort to devise a common strategy to deal with these, in February 1974 European finance and energy ministers met in Washington, D.C., to review the situation and its implications. The final communiqué they issued called for concerted efforts by all nations, including the oil-producing and oil-consuming coun-

tries, to manage supply and demand and address the inflationary consequences of high oil prices and the impact they were likely to have on international transfers and on the poorer developing nations. As meetings and leaders had previously done, the communiqué urged measures to conserve energy and restrict demand as well as the maximal development of both existing and alternative energy sources. It proposed greater cooperation among governments and such financial institutions as the World Bank and the International Monetary Fund to handle the consequences of the disruptions to the existing balance of payments situation caused by major increases in oil and energy prices. Taking up one of the major grievances of both Arab states and many consumers, they "agreed to examine in detail the role of international oil companies." In a nod to ecological concerns, the finance ministers affirmed their commitment to protecting the "natural environment." As with many such declarations, much of this communiqué remained a dead letter, and throughout the 1970s oil-consuming governments around the world proved largely ineffectual in addressing the damaging economic and political consequences of high oil prices.

Primary Source

Summary Statement

1. Foreign Ministers of Belgium, Canada, Denmark, France, the Federal Republic of Germany, Ireland, Italy, Japan, Luxembourg, the Netherlands, Norway, the United Kingdom, [and] the United States met in Washington from 11 to 13 February 1974. The European Community was represented as such by the President of the Council and the President of the Commission. Finance Ministers, Ministers with responsibility for Energy Affairs, Economic Affairs and Science and Technology Affairs also took part in the meeting. The Secretary-General of the OECD also participated in the meeting. The Ministers examined the international energy situation and its implications and charted a course of actions to meet this challenge which requires constructive and comprehensive solutions. To this end they agreed on specific steps to provide for effective international cooperation. The Ministers affirmed that solutions to the world's energy problem should be sought in consultation with producer countries and other consumers.

Analysis of the Situation

2. They noted that during the past three decades progress in improving productivity and standards of living was greatly facilitated by the ready availability of increasing supplies of energy at fairly stable prices. They recognized that the problem of meeting growing demand existed before the current situation and that the needs of the world economy for increased energy supplies require positive long-term solutions.

3. They concluded that the current energy situation results from an intensification of these underlying factors and from political developments.

4. They reviewed the problems created by the large rise in oil prices and agreed with the serious concern expressed by the International Monetary Fund's Committee of Twenty at its recent Rome meeting over the abrupt and significant changes in prospect for the world balance of payments structure.

5. They agreed that present petroleum prices presented the structure of world trade and finance with an unprecedented situation. They recognized that none of the consuming countries could hope to insulate itself from these developments, or expect to deal with the payments impact of oil prices by the adoption of monetary or trade measures alone. In their view, the present situation, if continued, could lead to a serious deterioration in income and employment, intensify inflationary pressures, and endanger the welfare of nations. They believed that financial measures by themselves will not be able to deal with the strains of the current situation.

6. They expressed their particular concern about the consequences of the situation for the developing countries and recognized the need for efforts by the entire international community to resolve this problem. At current oil prices the additional energy costs for developing countries will cause a serious setback to the prospect for economic development of these countries.

General Conclusions

7. They affirmed that, in the pursuit of national policies, whether in the trade, monetary or energy fields, efforts should be made to harmonize the interests of each country on the one hand and the maintenance of the world economic system on the other. Concerted international cooperation between all the countries concerned including oil producing countries could help to accelerate an improvement in the supply and demand situation, ameliorate the adverse economic consequences of the existing situation and lay the groundwork for a more equitable and stable international energy relationship.

8. They felt that these considerations taken as a whole made it essential that there should be a substantial increase of international cooperation in all fields. Each participant in the Conference stated its firm intention to do its utmost to contribute to such an aim, in close cooperation both with the other consumer countries and with the producer countries.

9. They concurred in the need for a comprehensive action programme to deal with all facets of the world energy situation by cooperative measures. In so doing they will build on the work of the OECD. They recognized that they may wish to invite, as appropriate, other countries to join with them in these efforts. Such an action programme of international cooperation would include, as appropriate, the sharing of means and efforts, while concerting national policies, in such areas as:*

(a) the conservation of energy and restraint of demand;
(b) a system of allocating oil supplies in times of emergency and severe shortages;
(c) the acceleration of development of additional energy sources so as to diversify energy supplies;
(d) the acceleration of energy research and development programmes through international cooperative efforts.

10. With respect to monetary and economic questions, they decided to intensify their cooperation and to give impetus to the work being undertaken in the IMF, the World Bank and the OECD on the economic and monetary consequences of the current energy situation, in particular to deal with balance of payments disequilibria. They agreed that:

(i) In dealing with the balance of payments impact of oil prices, they stressed the importance of avoiding competitive depreciation and the escalation of restrictions on trade and payments or disruptive actions in external borrowing.*

(ii) While financial cooperation can only partially alleviate the problems which have recently arisen for the international economic system, they will intensify work on short-term financial measures and possible longer-term mechanisms to reinforce existing official and market credit facilities.*

(iii) They will pursue domestic economic policies which will reduce as much as possible the difficulties resulting from the current energy cost levels.*

(iv) They will make strenuous efforts to maintain and enlarge the flow of development aid bilaterally and through multilateral institutions, on the basis of international solidarity embracing all countries with appropriate resources.

11. Further, they have agreed to accelerate wherever practicable their own national programmes of new energy sources and technology which will help the overall worldwide supply and demand situation.

12. They agreed to examine in detail the role of international oil companies.

13. They stressed the continued importance of maintaining and improving the natural environment as part of developing energy sources and agreed to make this an important goal of their activity.

14. They further agreed that there was need to develop a cooperative multilateral relationship with producing countries, and other consuming countries that takes into account the long-term interests of all. They are ready to exchange technical information with these countries on the problem of stabilizing energy supplies with regard to quantity and prices.

France does not accept this paragraph.

15. They welcomed the initiatives in the UN to deal with the larger issues of energy and primary products at a worldwide level and in particular for a special session of the UN General Assembly.

Establishment of Follow-on Machinery

16. They agreed to establish a coordinating group headed by senior officials to direct and to coordinate the development of the actions referred to above. The coordinating group shall decide how best to organize its work. It should:*
   (a) Monitor and give focus to the tasks that might be addressed in existing organizations;
   (b) Establish such ad hoc working groups as may be necessary to undertake tasks for which there are presently no suitable bodies;
   (c) Direct preparations of a conference of consumer and producer countries which will be held at the earliest possible opportunity and which, if necessary, will be preceded by a further meeting of consumer countries.

17. They agreed that the preparations for such meetings should involve consultations with developing countries and other consumer and producer countries.*

France does not accept this paragraph.

Source: "Final Communiqué of the Washington Conference," *Bulletin of the European Communities* 2 (February 1974): 19–22.

71. Arab League Summit Conference Communiqué, Rabat, Morocco [Excerpt], October 29, 1974

Introduction

From the late 1960s onward, relations between King Hussein of Jordan and the Palestine Liberation Organization (PLO) were frigid. Jordanian refugee camps housed large numbers of the Palestinian exiles who had fled Israel since 1948, and these camps, with their frustrated and impoverished inhabitants, were among the best recruiting grounds for the PLO. By 1970 the PLO had become so strong in Jordan, which it used as a base for fedayeen guerrilla raids against Israel, attracting retribution unwelcome to the Jordanian rulers, that PLO officials sought to take over the kingdom and overthrow Hussein's government. PLO members refused to recognize the government's authority, and the organization constituted a virtual state within the state. In February 1970 Hussein issued a 10-point statement restricting PLO activities, and fighting broke out between PLO and government forces. In July Hussein began a military campaign against the PLO, surviving several assassination attempts, and in September 1970, later known as Black September,

he declared martial law and launched a full-scale war against the PLO. Syrian forces threatened to intervene but were menaced by Israeli warplanes and eventually withdrew, while the United States dispatched naval forces to the area in a show of support for Hussein. Fighting continued well into mid-1971, as Hussein's troops gradually won control of Jordan. Palestinian militants moved their headquarters to Lebanon. In 1974 the antagonisms dividing Hussein and Palestinian leader Yasser Arafat were still strong. Despite the fact that many of them personally distrusted both Arafat and the PLO, most other Arab leaders sought to reconcile the two. Meeting at Rabat, Morocco, they stated their support for the PLO in its capacity as the organization that spoke for and had defended the interests of the Palestinians and urged Hussein and Arafat, together with the leaders of Egypt and Syria, the major Arab protagonists of the October 1973 Yom Kippur War, all of whom had territorial claims against Israel, to reach an understanding among themselves. One reason for this may have been that Arafat and the PLO were both gaining increasing international recognition as representatives of the Palestinian cause, a status that the leaders of the Arab League did not wish to compromise.

Primary Source

The Seventh Arab Summit Conference after exhaustive and detailed discussions. . . .

And in light of the victories achieved by Palestinian struggle in the confrontation with the Zionist enemy, at the Arab and international levels, at the United Nations, and of the obligation imposed thereby to continue joint Arab action to develop and increase the scope of these victories; and having received the views of all on the above, and having succeeded in cooling the differences between brethren within the framework of consolidating Arab solidarity, the Seventh Arab Summit Conference resolves the following:

1. To affirm the right of the Palestinian people to self-determination and to return to their homeland;
2. To affirm the right of the Palestinian people to establish an independent national authority under the command of the Palestine Liberation Organization, the sole legitimate representative of the Palestinian people in any Palestinian territory that is liberated. This authority, once it is established, shall enjoy the support of the Arab states in all fields and at all levels;
3. To support the Palestine Liberation Organization in the exercise of its responsibility at the national and international levels within the framework of Arab commitment;
4. To call on the Hashemite Kingdom of Jordan, the Syrian Arab Republic, the Arab Republic of Egypt and the Palestine Liberation Organization to devise a formula for the regulation of relations between them in the light of these decisions so as to ensure their implementation;

5. That all the Arab states undertake to defend Palestinian national unity and not to interfere in the internal affairs of Palestinian action.

Source: Library of Congress and Clyde R. Mark, *The Search for Peace in the Middle East: Documents and Statements, 1967–79; Report Prepared for the Subcommittee on Europe and the Middle East of the Committee on Foreign Affairs, U.S. House of Representatives* (Washington, DC: U.S. Government Printing Office, 1979), 273.

72. Yasser Arafat, Speech to the United Nations General Assembly [Excerpt], November 13, 1974

Introduction

One sign of growing international acceptance of the Palestine Liberation Organization (PLO) as the legitimate representative of the Palestinians was an invitation to its leader, Yasser Arafat, to address the United Nations (UN) General Assembly in November 1974. For many of his audience, this was their first opportunity to meet and assess him. Arafat's appearance was dramatic. He wore an empty holster and carried an olive branch, symbols that he came in peace. Using standard Palestinian rhetoric, he gave a lengthy historical exposition of the Palestinian issue, condemning Israel as the product of illegitimate "colonialism" and "Zionism." Palestine, he claimed, had been predominantly Arab in population until the late 19th century. Arafat emphasized similarities among the policies of British businessmen and imperialist Cecil Rhodes in Africa and those of Jewish settlers in Israel, claiming that in the wake of the 1917 Balfour Declaration, tens of thousands of Jews settled in Palestine with the collusion of the imperialist British mandatory power. Rather ironically following tactics that mirrored the habitual Israeli appeals to the lengthy history of anti-Semitic persecutions of international Jewry, Arafat characterized Israel itself as imperialist and racist and as being allied with other like-minded regimes such as white South Africa. In some respects, Arafat's tone was more moderate than usual. Rather than opposing all Jewish settlement in the area, as the PLO normally did, Arafat stated that what Palestinians found objectionable was the Zionist effort to create a Jewish-dominated state in which Palestinians were second-class citizens. On this occasion, he stated that Jews would be welcome to live on free and equal terms in a democratic, secular Palestinian state, and he paid tribute to those Jews who had in the past battled to keep faith and state separate. He highlighted many Israeli acts of oppression against Palestinians and appealed to the Palestinians' history of 25 years of exile during which they had maintained their commitment to regaining their own country. Arafat's appearance at the UN was a symbol not just of his and the PLO's increasing credibility but also of the steady growth of often radical Third World influence in the UN, as former colonies and developing countries aligned themselves—with Soviet encouragement and support—against the Western developed nations, especially the United States. He made a point of thanking his supporters in "the nonaligned countries, the socialist countries, the Islamic countries, the African countries and friendly European countries, as well as all our other friends in Asia, Africa and Latin America." His address to the UN demonstrated that in international affairs Arafat and the PLO had become significant forces that Israel would have to reckon with and could not ignore indefinitely.

Primary Source

[. . .]

Mr. President, I thank you for having invited the PLO to participate in this plenary session of the United Nations General Assembly. I am grateful to all those representatives of States of the United Nations who contributed to the decision to introduce the question of Palestine as a separate item on the agenda of this Assembly. That decision made possible the Assembly's resolution inviting us to address it on the question of Palestine.

This is a very important occasion. The question of Palestine is being re-examined by the United Nations, and we consider that step to be a victory for the world Organization as much as a victory for the cause of our people. It indicates anew that the United Nations of today is not the United Nations of the past, just as today's world is not yesterday's world. Today's United Nations represents 138 nations, a number that more clearly reflects the will of the international community. Thus today's United Nations is more nearly capable of implementing the principles embodied in its Charter and in the Universal Declaration of Human Rights, as well as being more truly empowered to support causes of peace and justice.

Our peoples are now beginning to feel that change. Along with them, the peoples of Asia, Africa and Latin America also feel the change. As a result, the United Nations acquires greater esteem both in our people's view and in the view of other peoples. Our hope is thereby strengthened that the United Nations can contribute actively to the pursuit and triumph of the causes of peace, justice, freedom and independence. Our resolve to build a new world is fortified—a world free of colonialism, imperialism, neo-colonialism and racism in each of its instances, including Zionism.

Our world aspires to peace, justice, equality and freedom. It wishes that oppressed nations, bent under the weight of imperialism, might gain their freedom and their right to self-determination. It hopes to place the relations between nations on a basis of equality, peaceful coexistence, mutual respect for each other's internal affairs, secure national sovereignty, independence and territorial unity on the basis of justice and mutual benefit. This world resolves that the economic ties binding it together should be grounded in justice, parity and mutual interest. It aspires finally to direct its human resources against the scourge of poverty, famine, disease and natural calamity, toward the development of productive scientific and technical capabilities to enhance human wealth—all this in the hope of reducing the disparity between the developing and the developed countries. But all such aspirations cannot be realized in a world that is at present ruled over by tension, injustice, oppression, racial discrimination and exploitation, a world also threatened with unending economic disasters, war and crisis.

Great numbers of peoples, including those of Zimbabwe, Namibia, South Africa and Palestine, among many others, are still victims of oppression and violence. Their areas of the world are gripped by armed struggles provoked by imperialism and racial discrimination, both merely forms of aggression and terror. Those are instances of oppressed peoples compelled by intolerable circumstances into confrontation with such oppression. But wherever that confrontation occurs it is legitimate and just.

It is imperative that the international community should support these peoples in their struggles, in the furtherance of their rightful causes and the attainment of their right to self-determination.

[. . .]

In their efforts to replace an outmoded but still dominant world economic system with a new, more logically rational one, the countries of Asia, Africa and Latin America must nevertheless face implacable attacks on these efforts. These countries have expressed their views at the sixth special session of the General Assembly on raw materials and development. Thus the plundering, the exploitation, the siphoning-off of the wealth of impoverished peoples must be terminated forthwith. There must be no deterring of these peoples' efforts to develop and control their wealth. Furthermore, there is a grave necessity for arriving at fair prices for raw materials from these countries.

[. . .]

The United Nations should therefore bend every effort to achieve a radical alteration of the world economic system, making it possible for developing countries to develop. The United Nations must shoulder the responsibility for fighting inflation, now borne most heavily by the developing countries, especially the oil-producing countries. The United Nations must firmly condemn any threats made against these countries simply because they demand their just rights.

The world-wide armaments race shows no sign of abating. As a consequence, the entire world is threatened with the dispersion of its wealth and the utter waste of its energies. Armed violence is made more likely everywhere. We expect the United Nations to

devote itself single-mindedly to curbing the unlimited acquisition of arms; to preventing even the possibility of nuclear destruction; to reducing the vast sums spent on military technology; to converting expenditure on war into projects for development, for increasing production, and for benefiting common humanity.

And still, the highest tension exists in our part of the world. There the Zionist entity clings tenaciously to occupied Arab territory; Zionism persists in its aggressions against us and our territory. New military preparations are feverishly being made. These anticipate another, fifth war of aggression to be launched against us. Such signs bear the closest possible watching, since there is a grave likelihood that this war would forebode nuclear destruction and cataclysmic annihilation.

The world is in need of tremendous efforts if its aspirations to peace, freedom, justice, equality and development are to be realized, if its struggle is to be victorious over colonialism, imperialism, neo-colonialism and racism in all its forms, including Zionism. Only by such efforts can actual form be given to the aspirations of all peoples, including the aspirations of peoples whose States oppose such efforts. It is this road that leads to the fulfilment of those principles emphasized by the United Nations Charter and the Universal Declaration of Human Rights. Were the status quo simply to be maintained, however, the world would instead be exposed to prolonged armed conflict, in addition to economic, human and natural calamity.

Despite abiding world crises, despite even the gloomy powers of backwardness and disastrous wrong, we live in a time of glorious change. An old world order is crumbling before our eyes, as imperialism, colonialism, neo-colonialism and racism, the chief form of which is Zionism, ineluctably perish. We are privileged to be able to witness a great wave of history bearing peoples forward into a new world that they have created. In that world just causes will triumph. Of that we are confident.

The question of Palestine belongs in this perspective of emergence and struggle. Palestine is crucial amongst those just causes fought for unstintingly by masses laboring under imperialism and aggression. It cannot be, and is not, lost on me today, as I stand here before the General Assembly, that if I have been given the opportunity to address the General Assembly, so too must the opportunity be given to all liberation movements fighting against racism and imperialism. In their names, in the name of every human being struggling for freedom and self-determination, I call upon the General Assembly urgently to give their just causes the same full attention the General Assembly has so rightly given to our cause. Such recognitions once made, there will be a secure foundation thereafter for the preservation of universal peace. For only with such peace will a new world order endure in which peoples can live free of oppression, fear, terror and the suppression of their rights. As I said earlier, this is the true perspective in which to set the question of Palestine. I shall now do so for the General Assembly, keeping firmly in mind both the perspective and the goal of a coming world order.

Even as today we address the General Assembly from what is before all else an international rostrum, we are also expressing our faith in political and diplomatic struggle as complements, as enhancements of our armed struggle. Furthermore, we express our appreciation of the role the United Nations is capable of playing in settling problems of international scope. But this capability, I said a moment ago, became real only once the United Nations had accommodated itself to the living actuality of aspiring peoples, towards which an Organization of so truly international a dimension owes unique obligations.

In addressing the General Assembly today, our people proclaims its faith in the future, unencumbered either by past tragedies or present limitations. If, as we discuss the present, we enlist the past in our service, we do so only to light up our journey into the future alongside other movements of national liberation. If we return now to the historical roots of our cause we do so because present at this very moment in our midst are those who, while they occupy our homes, as their cattle graze in our pastures, and as their hands pluck the fruit of our trees, claim at the same time that we are disembodied spirits, fictions without presence, without traditions or future. We speak of our roots also because until recently some people have regarded—and continued to regard—our problem as merely a problem of refugees. They have portrayed the Middle East question as little more than a border dispute between the Arab States and the Zionist entity. They have imagined that our people claims rights not rightfully its own and fights neither with logic nor valid motive, with a simple wish only to disturb the peace and to terrorize wantonly. For there are amongst you—and here I refer to the United States of America and others like it—those who supply our enemy freely with planes and bombs and with every variety of murderous weapon. They take hostile positions against us, deliberately distorting the true essence of the problem. All this is done not only at our expense, but at the expense of the American people, and of the friendship we continue to hope can be cemented between us and this great people, whose history of struggle for the sake of freedom we honour and salute.

I cannot now forgo this opportunity to appeal from this rostrum directly to the American people, asking it to give its support to our heroic and fighting people. I ask it whole-heartedly to endorse right and justice, to recall George Washington to mind, heroic Washington whose purpose was his nation's freedom and independence, Abraham Lincoln, champion of the destitute and the wretched, and also Woodrow Wilson whose doctrine of Fourteen Points remains subscribed to and venerated by our people. I ask the American people whether the demonstrations of hostility and enmity taking place outside this great hall reflect the true intent of America's will.

What crime, I ask you plainly, has our people committed against the American people? Why do you fight us so? Does such unwarranted belligerence really serve your interests? Does it serve the interests of the American masses? No, definitely not. I can only hope that the American people will remember that their friendship with the whole Arab nation is too great, too abiding and too rewarding for any such demonstrations to harm it.

In any event, as our discussion of the question of Palestine focuses upon historical roots, we do so because we believe that any question now exercising the world's concern must be viewed radically, in the true root sense of that word, if a real solution is ever to be grasped. We propose this radical approach as an antidote to an approach to international issues that obscures historical origins behind ignorance, denial, and a slavish obeisance to the present.

The roots of the Palestinian question reach back into the closing years of the nineteenth century, in other words, to that period we call the era of colonialism and settlement as we know it today. This is precisely the period during which Zionism as a scheme was born; its aim was the conquest of Palestine by European immigrants, just as settlers colonized, and indeed raided, most of Africa. This is the period during which, pouring forth out of the west, colonialism spread into the furthest reaches of Africa, Asia and Latin America, building colonies, everywhere cruelly exploiting, oppressing, plundering the peoples of those three continents. This period persists into the present. Marked evidence of its totally reprehensible presence can be readily perceived in the racism practiced both in South Africa and in Palestine.

Just as colonialism and its demagogues dignified their conquests, their plunder and limitless attacks upon the natives of Africa with appeals to a "civilizing and modernizing" mission, so too did waves of Zionist immigrants disguise their purposes as they conquered Palestine. Just as colonialism as a system and colonialists as its instrument used religion, color, race and language to justify the African's exploitation and his cruel subjugation by terror and discrimination, so too were these methods employed as Palestine was usurped and its people hounded from their national homeland.

Just as colonialism heedlessly used the wretched, the poor, the exploited as mere inert matter with which to build and to carry out settler colonialism, so too were destitute, oppressed European Jews employed on behalf of world imperialism and of the Zionist leaders. European Jews were transformed into the instruments of aggression—they became the elements of settler colonialism intimately allied to racial discrimination.

Zionist theology was utilized against our Palestinian people: the purpose was not only the establishment of Western-style settler colonialism but also the severing of Jews from their various homelands and subsequently their estrangement from their nations. Zionism is an ideology that is imperialist, colonialist, racist; it is profoundly reactionary and discriminatory; it is united with anti-Semitism in its retrograde tenets and is, when all is said and done, another side of the same base coin. For when what is proposed is that adherents of the Jewish faith, regardless of their national residence, should neither owe allegiance to their national residence nor live on equal footing with its other, non-Jewish citizens—when that is proposed we hear anti-Semitism being proposed. When it is proposed that the only solution for the Jewish problem is that Jews must alienate themselves from communities or nations of which they have been a historical part, when it is proposed that Jews solve the Jewish problem by immigrating to and forcibly settling the land of another people—when this occurs, exactly the same position is being advocated as the one urged by anti-Semites against Jews.

Thus, for instance, we can understand the close connection between Cecil Rhodes, who promoted settler colonialism in south-east Africa, and Theodor Herzl, who had settler colonialist designs upon Palestine. Having received a certificate of good settler colonialist conduct from Rhodes, Herzl then turned around and presented this certificate to the British Government, hoping thus to secure a formal resolution supporting Zionist policy. In exchange, the Zionists promised Britain an imperialist base on Palestinian soil so that imperial interests could be safeguarded at one of their chief strategic points.

So the Zionist movement allied itself directly with world colonialism in a common raid on our land. Allow me now to present a selection of historical truths about this alliance.

The Jewish invasion of Palestine began in 1881. Before the first large wave of immigrants started arriving, Palestine had a population of half a million; most of the population was either Muslim or Christian, and only 20,000 were Jewish. Every segment of the population enjoyed the religious tolerance characteristic of our civilization.

Palestine was then a verdant land, inhabited mainly by an Arab people in the course of building its life and dynamically enriching its indigenous culture.

Between 1882 and 1917 the Zionist movement settled approximately 50,000 European Jews in our homeland. To do that it resorted to trickery and deceit in order to implant them in our midst. Its success in getting Britain to issue the Balfour Declaration once again demonstrated the alliance between Zionism and imperialism. Furthermore, by promising to the Zionist movement what was not its to give, Britain showed how oppressive was the rule of imperialism. As it was constituted then, the League of Nations abandoned our Arab people, and Wilson's pledges and promises came to nought. In the guise of a Mandate, British imperialism was cruelly and directly imposed upon us. The Mandate issued by the League of Nations was to enable the Zionist invaders to consolidate their gains in our homeland.

Over a period of 30 years after the Balfour Declaration, the Zionist movement, together with its colonial ally, succeeded in bringing about the immigration of more European Jews and the usurpation of the lands of the Arabs of Palestine. Thus, in 1947 the Jewish population of Palestine was approximately 600,000, owning less than 6 per cent of the fertile lands of Palestine, while the Arab population of Palestine numbered approximately 1,250,000.

As a result of the collusion between the Mandatory Power and the Zionist movement and with the support of some countries, this General Assembly early in its history approved a recommendation to partition our Palestinian homeland. This took place in an atmosphere poisoned with questionable actions and strong pressure. The General Assembly partitioned what it had no right to divide—an indivisible homeland. When we rejected that decision, our position corresponded to that of the natural mother who refused to permit King Solomon to cut her son in two when the unnatural mother claimed the child for herself and agreed to his dismemberment. Furthermore, even though the partition resolution granted the colonialist settlers 54 per cent of the land of Palestine, their dissatisfaction with the decision prompted them to wage a war of terror against the civilian Arab population. They occupied 81 per cent of the total area of Palestine, uprooting a million Arabs. Thus, they occupied 524 Arab towns and villages, of which they destroyed 385, completely obliterating them in the process. Having done so, they built their own settlements and colonies on the ruins of our farms and our groves. The roots of the Palestine question lie here. Its causes do not stem from any conflict between two religions or two nationalisms. Neither is it a border conflict between neighboring States. It is the cause of a people deprived of its homeland, dispersed and uprooted, and living mostly in exile and in refugee camps.

With support from imperialist and colonialist Powers, the Zionist entity managed to get itself accepted as a Member of the United Nations. It further succeeded in getting the Palestine question deleted from the agenda of the United Nations and in deceiving world public opinion by presenting our cause as a problem of refugees in need either of charity from do-gooders, or settlement in a land not theirs.

Not satisfied with all this, the racist entity, founded on the imperialist-colonialist concept, turned itself into a base of imperialism and into an arsenal of weapons. This enabled it to assume its role of subjugating the Arab people and of committing aggression against them, in order to satisfy its ambitions for further expansion on Palestinian and other Arab lands. In addition to the many instances of aggression committed by this entity against the Arab States, it has launched two large-scale wars, in 1956 and 1967, thus endangering world peace and security.

As a result of Zionist aggression in June 1967, the enemy occupied Egyptian Sinai as far as the Suez Canal. The enemy occupied Syria's

Golan Heights, in addition to all Palestinian land west of the Jordan. All these developments have led to the creation in our area of what has come to be known as the "Middle East problem." The situation has been rendered more serious by the enemy's persistence in maintaining its unlawful occupation and in further consolidating it, thus establishing a beachhead for world imperialism's thrust against our Arab nation. All Security Council decisions and appeals to world public opinion for withdrawal from the lands occupied in June 1967 have been ignored. Despite all the peaceful efforts on the international level, the enemy has not been deterred from its expansionist policy. The only alternative open before our Arab nations, chiefly Egypt and Syria, was to expend exhaustive efforts in preparing forcefully to resist that barbarous armed invasion—and this in order to liberate Arab lands and to restore the rights of the Palestinian people, after all other peaceful means had failed.

Under these circumstances, the fourth war broke out in October 1973, bringing home to the Zionist enemy the bankruptcy of its policy of occupation, expansion and its reliance on the concept of military might. Despite all this, the leaders of the Zionist entity are far from having learned any lesson from their experience. They are making preparations for the fifth war, resorting once more to the language of military superiority, aggression, terrorism, subjugation and, finally, always to war in their dealings with the Arabs.

It pains our people greatly to witness the propagation of the myth that its homeland was a desert until it was made to bloom by the toil of foreign settlers, that it was a land without a people, and that the colonialist entity caused no harm to any human being. No: such lies must be exposed from this rostrum, for the world must know that Palestine was the cradle of the most ancient cultures and civilizations. Its Arab people were engaged in farming and building, spreading culture throughout the land for thousands of years, setting an example in the practice of freedom of worship, acting as faithful guardians of the holy places of all religions. As a son of Jerusalem, I treasure for myself and my people beautiful memories and vivid images of the religious brotherhood that was the hallmark of our Holy City before it succumbed to catastrophe. Our people continued to pursue this enlightened policy until the establishment of the State of Israel and their dispersion. This did not deter our people from pursuing their humanitarian role on Palestinian soil. Nor will they permit their land to become a launching pad for aggression or a racist camp predicated on the destruction of civilization, cultures, progress and peace. Our people cannot but maintain the heritage of their ancestors in resisting the invaders, in assuming the privileged task of defending their native land, their Arab nationhood, their culture and civilization, and in safeguarding the cradle of monotheistic religions.

By contrast, we need only mention briefly some Israeli stands: its support of the Secret Army Organization in Algeria, its bolstering of the settler-colonialists in Africa—whether in the Congo, Angola,

Mozambique, Zimbabwe, Tanzania or South Africa—and its backing of South Viet Nam against the Vietnamese revolution. In addition, one can mention Israel's continuing support of imperialists and racists everywhere, its obstructionist stand in the Committee of Twenty-four, its refusal to cast its vote in support of independence for the African States, and its opposition to the demands of many Asian, African and Latin American nations, and several other States in the conferences on raw materials, population, the law of the sea, and food. All these facts offer further proof of the character of the enemy that has usurped our land. They justify the honorable struggle we are waging against it. As we defend a vision of the future, our enemy upholds the myths of the past.

The enemy we face has a long record of hostility even towards the Jews themselves, for there is within the Zionist entity a built-in racism against Oriental Jews. While we were vociferously condemning the massacres of Jews under Nazi rule, Zionist leadership appeared more interested at that time in exploiting them as best it could in order to realize its goal of immigration into Palestine.

If the immigration of Jews to Palestine had had as its objective the goal of enabling them to live side by side with us, enjoying the same rights and assuming the same duties, we would have opened our doors to them, as far as our homeland's capacity for absorption permitted. Such was the case with the thousands of Armenians and Circassians who still live among us in equality as brethren and citizens. But that the goal of this immigration should be to usurp our homeland, disperse our people, and turn us into second-class citizens—this is what no one can conceivably demand that we acquiesce in or submit to. Therefore, since its inception, our evolution has not been motivated by racial or religious factors. Its target has never been the Jew, as a person, but racist Zionism and undisguised aggression. In this sense, ours is also a revolution for the Jew, as a human being, as well. We are struggling so that Jews, Christians and Muslims may live in equality, enjoying the same rights and assuming the same duties, free from racial or religious discrimination.

We do distinguish between Judaism and Zionism. While we maintain our opposition to the colonialist Zionist movement, we respect the Jewish faith. Today, almost one century after the rise of the Zionist movement, we wish to warn of its increasing danger to the Jews of the world, to our Arab people and to world peace and security. For Zionism encourages the Jew to emigrate out of his homeland and grants him an artificially-created nationality. The Zionists proceed with their terrorist activities even though these have proved ineffective. The phenomenon of constant emigration from Israel, which is bound to grow as the bastions of colonialism and racism in the world fall, is an example of the inevitability of the failure of such activities.

We urge the people and Governments of the world to stand firm against Zionist attempts at encouraging world Jewry to emigrate from their countries and to usurp our land. We urge them as well firmly to oppose any discrimination against any human being as to religion, race, or color.

Why should our Arab Palestinian people pay the price of such discrimination in the world? Why should our people be responsible for the problems of Jewish immigration, if such problems exist in the minds of some people? Why do not the supporters of these problems open their own countries, which can absorb and help these immigrants?

Those who call us terrorists wish to prevent world public opinion from discovering the truth about us and from seeing the justice on our faces. They seek to hide the terrorism and tyranny of their acts, and our own posture of self-defense.

The difference between the revolutionary and the terrorist lies in the reason for which each fights. For whoever stands by a just cause and fights for the freedom and liberation of his land from the invaders, the settlers and the colonialists cannot possibly be called terrorist; otherwise the American people in their struggle for liberation from the British colonialists would have been terrorists, the European resistance against the Nazis would be terrorism, the struggle of the Asian, African and Latin American peoples would also be terrorism, and many of you who are in this Assembly hall were considered terrorists. This is actually a just and proper struggle consecrated by the United Nations Charter and by the Universal Declaration of Human Rights. As to those who fight against the just causes, those who wage war to occupy, colonize and oppress other people, those are the terrorists. Those are the people whose actions should be condemned, who should be called war criminals: for the justice of the cause determines the right to struggle.

Zionist terrorism which was waged against the Palestinian people to evict it from its country and usurp its land is registered in your official documents. Thousands of our people were assassinated in their villages and towns; tens of thousands of others were forced at gunpoint to leave their homes and the lands of their fathers. Time and time again our children, women and aged were evicted and had to wander in the deserts and climb mountains without any food or water. No one who in 1948 witnessed the catastrophe that befell the inhabitants of hundreds of villages and towns—in Jerusalem, Jaffa, Lydda, Ramle and Galilee—no one who has been a witness to that catastrophe will ever forget the experience, even though the mass black-out has succeeded in hiding these horrors as it has hidden the traces of 385 Palestinian villages and towns destroyed at the time and erased from the map. The destruction of 19,000 houses during the past seven years, which is equivalent to the complete destruction of 200 more Palestinian villages, and the great number of maimed as a result of the treatment they were subjected to in Israeli prisons cannot be hidden by any black-out.

Their terrorism fed on hatred and this hatred was even directed against the olive tree in my country, which has been a proud sym-

bol and which reminded them of the indigenous inhabitants of the land, a living reminder that the land is Palestinian. Thus they sought to destroy it. How can one describe the statement by Golda Meir which expressed her disquiet about "the Palestinian children born every day"? They see in the Palestinian child, in the Palestinian tree, an enemy that should be exterminated. For tens of years Zionists have been harassing our people's cultural, political, social and artistic leaders, terrorizing them and assassinating them. They have stolen our cultural heritage, our popular folklore and have claimed it as theirs. Their terrorism even reached our sacred places in our beloved and peaceful Jerusalem. They have endeavored to de-Arabize it and make it lose its Muslim and Christian character by evicting its inhabitants and annexing it.

[...]

The small number of Palestinian Arabs who were not uprooted by the Zionists in 1948 are at present refugees in their own homeland. Israeli law treats them as second-class citizens—and even as third-class citizens since Oriental Jews are second-class citizens—and they have been subject to all forms of racial discrimination and terrorism after confiscation of their land and property. They have been victims of bloody massacres such as that of Kfar Kassim; they have been expelled from their villages and denied the right to return, as in the case of the inhabitants of Ikrit and Kfar Birim. For 26 years, our population has been living under martial law and was denied freedom of movement without prior permission from the Israeli military governor, this at a time when an Israeli law was promulgated granting citizenship to any Jew anywhere who wanted to emigrate to our homeland. Moreover, another Israeli law stipulated that Palestinians who were not present in their villages or towns at the time of the occupation were not entitled to Israeli citizenship.

The record of Israeli rulers is replete with acts of terror perpetrated on those of our people who remained under occupation in Sinai and the Golan Heights. The criminal bombardment of the Bahr-al-Bakar School and the Abou Zaabal factory are but two such unforgettable acts of terrorism. The total destruction of the Syrian city of Quneitra is yet another tangible instance of systematic terrorism. If a record of Zionist terrorism in South Lebanon were to be compiled, the enormity of its acts would shock even the most hardened: piracy, bombardments, scorched-earth policy, destruction of hundreds of homes, eviction of civilians and the kidnapping of Lebanese citizens. This clearly constitutes a violation of Lebanese sovereignty and is in preparation for the diversion of the Litani River waters.

Need one remind this Assembly of the numerous resolutions adopted by it condemning Israeli aggressions committed against Arab countries, Israeli violations of human rights and the articles of the Geneva Conventions, as well as the resolutions pertaining to the annexation of the city of Jerusalem and its restoration to its former status?

The only description for these acts is that they are acts of barbarism and terrorism. And yet, the Zionist racists and colonialists have the temerity to describe the just struggle of our people as terror. Could there be a more flagrant distortion of truth than this? . . .

For the past 30 years, our people have had to struggle against British occupation and Zionist invasion, both of which had one intention, namely, the usurpation of our land. Six major revolts and tens of popular uprisings were staged to foil these attempts, so that our homeland might remain ours. Over 30,000 martyrs, the equivalent in comparative terms of 6 million Americans, died in the process.

When the majority of the Palestinian people was uprooted from its homeland in 1948, the Palestinian struggle for self-determination continued under the most difficult conditions. We tried every possible means to continue our political struggle to attain our national rights, but to no avail. Meanwhile, we had to struggle for sheer existence. Even in exile we educated our children. This was all a part of trying to survive.

The Palestinian people produced thousands of physicians, lawyers, teachers and scientists who actively participated in the development of the Arab countries bordering on their usurped homeland. They utilized their income to assist the young and aged amongst their people who remained in the refugee camps. They educated their younger sisters and brothers, supported their parents and cared for their children. All along, the Palestinian dreamt of return. Neither the Palestinian's allegiance to Palestine nor his determination to return waned; nothing could persuade him to relinquish his Palestinian identity or to forsake his homeland. The passage of time did not make him forget, as some hoped he would. When our people lost faith in the international community, which persisted in ignoring its rights, and when it became obvious that the Palestinians would not recuperate one inch of Palestine through exclusively political means, our people had no choice but to resort to armed struggle. Into that struggle it poured its material and human resources. We bravely faced the most vicious acts of Israeli terrorism, which were aimed at diverting our struggle and arresting it.

In the past 10 years of our struggle, thousands of martyrs and twice as many wounded, maimed and imprisoned were offered in sacrifice, all in an effort to resist the imminent threat of liquidation, to regain our right to self-determination and our undisputed right to return to our homeland. With the utmost dignity and the most admirable revolutionary spirit, our Palestinian people has not lost its spirit in Israeli prisons and concentration camps or when faced with all forms of harassment and intimidation. It struggles for sheer existence and it continues to strive to preserve the Arab character of its land. Thus it resists oppression, tyranny and terrorism in their ugliest forms.

It is through our popular armed struggle that our political leadership and our national institutions finally crystallized and a national liberation movement, comprising all the Palestinian factions, organizations and capabilities, materialized in the PLO.

Through our militant Palestine national liberation movement, our people's struggle matured and grew enough to accommodate political and social struggle in addition to armed struggle. The PLO was a major factor in creating a new Palestinian individual, qualified to shape the future of our Palestine, not merely content with mobilizing the Palestinians for the challenges of the present.

The PLO can be proud of having a large number of cultural and educational activities, even while engaged in armed struggle, and at a time when it faced increasingly vicious blows of Zionist terrorism. We established institutes for scientific research, agricultural development and social welfare, as well as centers for the revival of our cultural heritage and the preservation of our folklore. Many Palestinian poets, artists and writers have enriched Arab culture in particular, and world culture generally. Their profoundly humane works have won the admiration of all those familiar with them. In contrast to that, our enemy has been systematically destroying our culture and disseminating racist, imperialist ideologies; in short, everything that impedes progress, justice, democracy and peace.

The PLO has earned its legitimacy because of the sacrifice inherent in its pioneering role, and also because of its dedicated leadership of the struggle. It has also been granted this legitimacy by the Palestinian masses, which in harmony with it have chosen it to lead the struggle according to its directives. The PLO has also gained its legitimacy by representing every faction, union or group as well as every Palestinian talent, either in the National Council or in people's institutions. This legitimacy was further strengthened by the support of the entire Arab nation, and it was consecrated during the last Arab Summit Conference, which reiterated the right of the PLO, in its capacity as the sole representative of the Palestinian people, to establish an independent national State on all liberated Palestinian territory.

[. . .]

The PLO represents the Palestinian people, legitimately and uniquely. Because of this, the PLO expresses the wishes and hopes of its people. Because of this, too, it brings these very wishes and hopes before you, urging you not to shirk the momentous historic responsibility towards our just cause.

For many years now our people has been exposed to the ravages of war, destruction and dispersion. It has paid in the blood of its sons that which cannot ever be compensated. It has borne the burdens of occupation, dispersion, eviction and terror more uninterruptedly than any other people. And yet all this has made our people neither vindictive nor vengeful. Nor has it caused us to resort to the racism of our enemies. Nor have we lost the true method by which friend and foe are distinguished.

For we deplore all those crimes committed against the Jews; we also deplore all the real discrimination suffered by them because of their faith.

I am a rebel and freedom is my cause. I know well that many of you present here today once stood in exactly the same resistance position as I now occupy and from which I must fight. You once had to convert dreams into reality by your struggle. Therefore you must now share my dream. I think this is exactly why I can ask you now to help, as together we bring out our dream into a bright reality, our common dream for a peaceful future in Palestine's sacred land.

[. . .]

In my formal capacity as Chairman of the PLO and leader of the Palestinian revolution I proclaim before you that when we speak of our common hopes for the Palestine of tomorrow we include in our perspective all Jews now living in Palestine who choose to live with us there in peace and without discrimination.

In my formal capacity as Chairman of the PLO and leader of the Palestinian revolution I call upon Jews to turn away one by one from the illusory promises made to them by Zionist ideology and Israeli leadership. They are offering Jews perpetual bloodshed, endless war and continuous thralldom.

We invite them to emerge from their moral isolation into a more open realm of free choice, far from their present leadership's efforts to implant in them a Masada complex.

We offer them the most generous solution, that we might live together in a framework of just peace in our democratic Palestine.

In my formal capacity as Chairman of the PLO I announce here that we do not wish one drop of either Arab or Jewish blood to be shed; neither do we delight in the continuation of killing, which would end once a just peace, based on our people's rights, hopes and aspirations had been finally established.

In my formal capacity as Chairman of the PLO and leader of the Palestinian revolution I appeal to you to accompany our people in its struggle to attain its right to self-determination. This right is consecrated in the United Nations Charter and has been repeatedly confirmed in resolutions adopted by this august body since the drafting of the Charter. I appeal to you, further, to aid our people's return to its homeland from an involuntary exile imposed upon it by force of arms, by tyranny, by oppression, so that we may regain our property, our land, and thereafter live in our national homeland, free and sovereign, enjoying all the privileges of nationhood. Only then can we pour all our resources into the mainstream of human civilization. Only then can Palestinian creativity be concen-

trated on the service of humanity. Only then will our Jerusalem resume its historic role as a peaceful shrine for all religions.

I appeal to you to enable our people to establish national independent sovereignty over its own land.

Today I have come bearing an olive branch and a freedom-fighter's gun. Do not let the olive branch fall from my hand. I repeat: do not let the olive branch fall from my hand.

War flares up in Palestine, and yet it is in Palestine that peace will be born.

Source: United Nations General Assembly Official Records, 29th Sess., *Question of Palestine*, A/PV.2282, November 13, 1974.

73. United Nations General Assembly Resolutions 3236 and 3237, Question of Palestine and Observer Status for the Palestine Liberation Organization, November 22, 1974

Introduction

Yasser Arafat's well-publicized appearance before the United Nations (UN) General Assembly helped to firm up and channel growing support for the Palestinians in that body. Less than 10 days later, the UN General Assembly voted in favor of two resolutions relating to the Palestinians. The first proclaimed the rights of the Palestinians to "self-determination" and "national independence and sovereignty," to return to their homes, and to be involved in the solution of the outstanding issues as "a principal party in the establishment of a just and durable peace in the Middle East." In a somewhat ambiguous statement, whose lack of commas could have been taken to sanction the use of violence, the resolution affirmed that the Palestinian people were entitled to "regain [their] rights by all means in accordance with the purposes and principles of the Charter of the United Nations." All nations and international organizations were asked to support the Palestinians, and the UN secretary general was instructed to make contact with the Palestinians and report to the General Assembly about progress on the implementation of this resolution. Lest there be any doubt as to what the resolutions meant by the "Palestinian people," the accompanying Resolution 3237 invited the Palestine Liberation Organization (PLO) to join the UN with "observer status." Although the PLO could not vote, its representatives were entitled to speak and lobby on all issues. The passage of these resolutions represented a triumph for Arafat and the PLO and marked a major milestone on the road to international acceptance of the organization.

Primary Source

The General Assembly,

Having considered the question of Palestine,

Having heard the statement of the Palestine Liberation Organization, the representative of the Palestinian people,

Having also heard other statements made during the debate,

Deeply concerned that no just solution to the problem of Palestine has yet been achieved and recognizing that the problem of Palestine continues to endanger international peace and security,

Recognizing that the Palestinian people is entitled to self-determination in accordance with the Charter of the United Nations,

Expressing its grave concern that the Palestinian people has been prevented from enjoying its inalienable rights, in particular its right to self-determination,

Guided by the purposes and principles of the Charter,

Recalling its relevant resolutions which affirm the right of the Palestinian people to self-determination,

1. *Reaffirms* the inalienable rights of the Palestinian people in Palestine, including:
    (a) The right to self-determination without external interference;
    (b) The right to national independence and sovereignty;

2. *Reaffirms* also the inalienable right of the Palestinians to return to their homes and property from which they have been displaced and uprooted, and calls for their return;

3. *Emphasizes* that full respect for and the realization of these inalienable rights of the Palestinian people are indispensable for the solution of the question of Palestine;

4. *Recognizes* that the Palestinian people is a principal party in the establishment of a just and lasting peace in the Middle East;

5. *Further recognizes* the right of the Palestinian people to regain its rights by all means in accordance with the purposes and principles of the Charter of the United Nations;

6. *Appeals* to all States and international organizations to extend their support to the Palestinian people in its struggle to restore its rights, in accordance with the Charter;

7. *Requests* the Secretary-General to establish contacts with the Palestine Liberation Organization on all matters concerning the question of Palestine;

8. *Requests* the Secretary-General to report to the General Assembly at its thirtieth session on the implementation of the present resolution;

9. *Decides* to include the item entitled "Question of Palestine" in the provisional agenda of its thirtieth session.

UN General Assembly Resolution 3237
Observer Status for the Palestine Liberation Organization
November 22, 1974
The General Assembly,

Having considered the question of Palestine,

Taking into consideration the universality of the United Nations prescribed in the Charter,

Recalling its resolution 3102 (XXVIII) of 12 December 1973,

Taking into account Economic and Social Council resolutions 1835 (LVI) of 14 May 1974 and 1840 (LVI) of 15 May 1974,

Noting that the Diplomatic Conference on the Reaffirmation and Development of International Humanitarian Law Applicable in Armed Conflicts, the World Population Conference and the World Food Conference have in effect invited the Palestine Liberation Organization to participate in their respective deliberations,

Noting also that the Third United Nations Conference on the Law of the Sea has invited the Palestine Liberation Organization to participate in its deliberations as an observer,

1. *Invites* the Palestine Liberation Organization to participate in the sessions and the work of the General Assembly in the capacity of observer;

2. *Invites* the Palestine Liberation Organization to participate in the sessions and the work of all international conferences convened under the auspices of the General Assembly in the capacity of observer;

3. *Considers* that the Palestine Liberation Organization is entitled to participate as an observer in the sessions and the work of all international conferences convened under the auspices of other organs of the United Nations;

4. *Requests* the Secretary-General to take the necessary steps for the implementation of the present resolution.

Source: United Nations General Assembly Official Records, 29th Sess., *Question of Palestine* and *Observer Status for the Palestine Liberation Organization*, G.A. Res. 3236 and 3237 (XXIX), November 22, 1974.

74. Second Sinai Disengagement Agreement, Egypt and Israel [Excerpt], September 1, 1975

Introduction

Despite Arab states' rhetorical rejection of any dealings with Israel, pragmatic considerations could impel them to open diplomatic negotiations. At the end of hostilities in October 1973, Israeli forces had taken back the Sinai and had advanced deep into Egyptian territory, well beyond the Suez Canal. In January 1974 the Israelis and Egyptians signed a disengagement agreement under whose terms Israeli units withdrew back across the canal, to approximately the 1967 cease-fire line, and in the Sinai a buffer zone held by a United Nations Emergency Force (UNEF) separated Israeli and Egyptian units. In September 1975 a second disengagement agreement widened the buffer zone, and the Israelis withdrew east of the strategically important Gidi and Mitla passes. The agreements were a sign that despite Israel's eventual gains in the Yom Kippur War, the swift Egyptian and Syrian successes at the beginning had greatly dented Israeli military self-confidence, encouraging the Israeli government to seek to reach acceptable territorial arrangements with its neighbors. The Sinai Accords were a precursor to the subsequent Camp David Accords later that decade, when U.S. president Jimmy Carter successfully brokered a formal peace treaty between Egypt and Israel.

Primary Source

A. Egyptian-Israel Accord

The Government of the Arab Republic of Egypt and the Government of Israel have agreed that:

ARTICLE I

The conflict between them and in the Middle East shall not be resolved by military force but by peaceful means.

The agreement concluded by the parties Jan. 18, 1974, within the framework of the Geneva peace conference, constituted a first step towards a just and durable peace according to the provisions of Security Council Resolution 338 of Oct. 22, 1973; and they are determined to reach a final and just peace settlement by means of negotiations called for by Security Council Resolution 338, this agreement being a significant step towards that end.

ARTICLE II

The parties hereby undertake not to resort to the threat or use of force or military blockade against each other.

ARTICLE III

(1) The parties shall continue scrupulously to observe the cease-fire on land, sea and air and to refrain from all military or paramilitary actions against each other.

(2) The parties also confirm that the obligations contained in the annex and, when concluded, the protocol shall be an integral part of this agreement.

ARTICLE IV

A. The military forces of the parties shall be deployed in accordance with the following principles:

(1) All Israeli forces shall be deployed east of the lines designated as lines J and M on the attached map.

(2) All Egyptian forces shall be deployed west of the line designated as line E on the attached map.

(3) The area between the lines designated on the attached map as lines E and F and the area between the lines designated on the attached map as lines J and K shall be limited in armament and forces.

(4) The limitations on armament and forces in the areas described by paragraph (3) above shall be agreed as described in the attached annex.

(5) The zone between the lines designated on the attached map as lines E and J will be a buffer zone. On this zone the United Nations Emergency Force will continue to perform its functions as under the Egyptian-Israeli agreement of Jan. 18, 1974.

(6) In the area south from line E and west from line M, as defined in the attached map, there will be no military forces, as specified in the attached annex.

ARTICLE V

The United Nations Emergency Force is essential and shall continue its functions, and its mandate shall be extended annually.

ARTICLE VI

The parties hereby establish a joint commission for the duration of this agreement. It will function under the aegis of the chief coordinator of the United Nations peace-keeping missions in the Middle East in order to consider any problem arising from this agreement and to assist the United Nations Emergency Force in the execution of its mandate. The joint commission shall function in accordance with procedures established in the protocol.

ARTICLE VII

Nonmilitary cargoes destined for or coming from Israel shall be permitted through the Suez Canal.

ARTICLE VIII

(1) This agreement is regarded by the parties as a significant step toward a just and lasting peace. It is not a final peace agreement.

(2) The parties shall continue their efforts to negotiate a final peace agreement within the framework of the Geneva peace conference in accordance with Security Council Resolution 338.

ARTICLE IX
This agreement shall enter into force upon signature of the protocol and remain in force until superseded by a new agreement.

[...]

C. Annex to the Sinai Agreement

Within five days after the signature of the Egypt-Israel agreement, representatives of the two parties shall meet in the military working group of the Middle East peace conference at Geneva to begin preparation of a detailed protocol for the implementation of the agreement....

[...]

6. Process of Implementation

The detailed implementation and timing of the redeployment of forces, turnover of oil fields and other arrangements called for by the agreement, annex and protocol shall be determined by the working group, which will agree on the stages of this process, including the phased movement of Egyptian troops to line E and Israeli troops to line J. The first phase will be the transfer of the oil fields and installations to Egypt. This process will begin within two weeks from the signature of the protocol with the introduction of the necessary technicians, and it will be completed no later than eight weeks after it begins. The details of the phasing will be worked out in the military working group.

Implementation of the redeployment shall be completed within five months after signature of the protocol.

Source: Walter Laqueur and Barry Rubin, eds., *The Israel-Arab Reader: A Documentary History of the Middle East Conflict* (New York: Penguin, 2001), 194–200.

75. United Nations General Assembly Resolution 3379 (XXX), Elimination of All Forms of Racial Discrimination, November 10, 1975

Introduction

After Israeli forces seized the West Bank of the Jordan and Sinai during the 1967 Six-Day War, resentment against Israel burgeoned dramatically, especially among developing nations in Africa and Asia and the Soviet bloc. The Palestine Liberation Organization (PLO), which represented the Palestinian refugees from the West Bank and elsewhere, could count on substantial international sympathy. By a vote of 72 to 35 with 32 abstentions, in November 1975 the United Nations (UN) General Assembly passed Resolution 3379, which stated that Zionism was a form of racism and racial discrimination. The North Atlantic Treaty Organization (NATO) powers, including the United States, voted en bloc against the resolution, and U.S. ambassador to the UN Daniel Patrick Moynihan publicly stated that the United States "does not acknowledge, it will not abide by, it will never acquiesce in this infamous act." Chaim Herzog, Israeli ambassador to the UN, pointed out that Arabs served in the Israeli government and armed forces, and he characterized the resolution as yet "another manifestation of the bitter anti-Semitic, anti-Jewish hatred which animates Arab society." He further declared, "For us, the Jewish people, this resolution based on hatred, falsehood and arrogance, is devoid of any moral or legal value. For us, the Jewish people, this is no more than a piece of paper and we shall treat it as such." He then tore the document in half. Despite its declared opposition to the resolution, the following month the United States did acquiesce in the seating of PLO representatives as observers in the UN, and one near-perennial quest of U.S. diplomacy would become the search for a settlement acceptable to both Palestinians and Israelis. The passage of this resolution tended to strengthen extreme Zionist politicians in Israel who proclaimed that their country was surrounded by enemies and could not expect justice from the international community. Many felt that it negated the original 1947 UN partition plan under whose auspices Israel had been established. On December 16, 1991, UN General Assembly Resolution 4686 revoked this resolution.

Primary Source

The General Assembly,

Recalling its resolution 1904 (XVIII) of 20 November 1963, proclaiming the United Nations Declaration on the Elimination of All Forms of Racial Discrimination, and in particular its affirmation that "any doctrine of racial differentiation or superiority is scientifically false, morally condemnable, socially unjust and dangerous" and its expression of alarm at "the manifestations of racial discrimination still in evidence in some areas in the world, some of which are imposed by certain Governments by means of legislative, administrative or other measures",

Recalling also that, in its resolution 3151 G (XXVIII) of 14 December 1953, the General Assembly condemned, *inter alia,* the unholy alliance between South African racism and Zionism,

Taking note of the Declaration of Mexico on the Equality of Women and Their Contribution to Development and Peace 1975, proclaimed by the World Conference of the International Women's Year, held at Mexico City from 19 June to 2 July 1975, which promulgated the principle that "international co-operation and peace require the achievement of national liberation and independence, the elimination of colonialism and neo-colonialism, foreign occupation,

Zionism, apartheid and racial discrimination in all its forms, as well as the recognition of the dignity of peoples and their right to self-determination",

Taking note also of resolution 77 (XII) adopted by the Assembly of Heads of State and Government of the Organization of African Unity at its twelfth ordinary session, held at Kampala from 28 July to 1 August1975, which considered "that the racist regime in occupied Palestine and the racist regimes in Zimbabwe and South Africa have a common imperialist origin, forming a whole and having the same racist structure and being organically linked in their policy aimed at repression of the dignity and integrity of the human being",

Taking note also of the Political Declaration and Strategy to Strengthen International Peace and Security and to Intensify Solidarity and Mutual Assistance among Non-Aligned Countries, adopted at the Conference of Ministers for Foreign Affairs of Non-Aligned Countries held at Lima from 25 to 30 August 1975, which most severely condemned Zionism as a threat to world peace and security and called upon all countries to oppose this racist and imperialist ideology,

Determines that Zionism is a form of racism and racial discrimination.

Source: United Nations General Assembly Official Records, 30th Sess., *Elimination of All Forms of Racial Discrimination*, G.A. Res. 3379 (XXX), November 10, 1975.

76. Jimmy Carter, Response to Question on Middle East Peace, Town Meeting, Clinton, Massachusetts, March 16, 1977

Introduction

January 1977 brought a new U.S. presidential administration to power, that of the former Democratic governor of the state of Georgia, Jimmy Carter. A dedicated born-again Christian, Carter was determined to break with traditional Cold War thinking. He intended that on the international scene his administration would emphasize human rights, disarmament, and peaceful development. In Carter's eyes, one of the most salient aspects of this program would be energetic efforts to implement a lasting Middle East peace settlement, one that would enable Arabs and Israelis to live beside each other in relative harmony. Carter warned that failure to achieve this might well lead to a further war in the region, which might easily spread beyond it and involve outside powers, something he wished to avoid. Carter was an acknowledged admirer of Israel, who believed that "one of the finest acts of the world's nations that's ever

occurred was to establish the State of Israel." Speaking in the kind of relatively informal setting he preferred, a town meeting in Massachusetts, two months after he took office, Carter laid out his proposals for ending the Arab-Israeli impasse. They followed fairly closely the prescriptions of United Nations (UN) Security Council Resolution 242. Carter's first prerequisite was that Israel's Arab neighbors recognize Israel's "right to exist … permanently … [and] in peace." He remained noncommittal on whether Israel should withdraw entirely to the 1967 borders, as the Arabs demanded, or whether these should be adjusted, simply saying that this matter was one to be negotiated between the parties involved. The third element that Carter believed any peace settlement must address was the provision of a national homeland for the Palestinian refugees, although he left it unclear whether this would involve the establishment of a separate Palestinian state. Carter offered the services of the United States as a mediator between Israel and its opponents, telling his audience that he hoped that later that year they would all join in talks at the Geneva headquarters of the UN. Pointing out that Japan and the West European nations were far more dependent than the United States on Middle East oil, he implicitly sought assistance from those countries in facilitating a peace settlement. Carter's speech made it very clear that bringing about lasting peace in the Middle East would be one of his administration's top foreign policy priorities.

Primary Source

Q. What do you personally feel must be done to establish a meaningful and a lasting peace in that area of the world? Thank you.

The President. I think all of you know that there has been either war or potential war in the Middle East for the last 29 years, ever since Israel became a nation. I think one of the finest acts of the world of nations that's ever occurred was to establish the State of Israel.

So, the first prerequisite of a lasting peace is the recognition of Israel by her neighbors, Israel's right to exist, Israel's right to exist permanently, Israel's right to exist in peace. This means that over a period of months or years that the borders between Israel and Syria, Israel and Lebanon, Israel and Jordan, Israel and Egypt must be opened up to travel, to tourism, to cultural exchange, to trade, so that no matter who the leaders might be in those countries, the people themselves will have formed a mutual understanding and comprehension and a sense of a common purpose to avoid the repetitious wars and death that have afflicted that region so long. That's the first prerequisite of peace.

The second one is very important and very, very difficult; and that is, the establishment of permanent borders for Israel. The Arab countries say that Israel must withdraw to the pre-1967 border-lines, Israel says that they must adjust those lines to some degree to insure their own security. That is a matter to be negotiated between the Arab countries on the one side and Israel on the other.

But borders are still a matter of great trouble and a matter of great difficulty, and there are strong differences of opinion now.

And the third ultimate requirement for peace is to deal with the Palestinian problem. The Palestinians claim up 'til this moment that Israel has no right to be there, that the land belongs to the Palestinians, and they've never yet given up their publicly professed commitment to destroy Israel. That has to be overcome.

There has to be a homeland provided for the Palestinian refugees who have suffered for many, many years. And the exact way to solve the Palestinian problem is one that first of all addresses itself right now to the Arab countries and then, secondly, to the Arab countries negotiating with Israel.

Those three major elements have got to be solved before a Middle Eastern solution can be prescribed.

I want to emphasize one more time, we offer our good offices. I think it's accurate to say that of all the nations in the world, we are the one that's most trusted, not completely, but most trusted by the Arab countries and also Israel. I guess both sides have some doubt about us. But we'll have to act as kind of a catalyst to bring about their ability to negotiate successfully with one another.

We hope that later on this year, in the latter part of this year, that we might get all of these parties to agree to come together at Geneva, to start talking to one another. They haven't done that yet. And I believe if we can get them to sit down and start talking and negotiating that we have an excellent chance to achieve peace. I can't guarantee that. It's a hope.

I hope that we will all pray that that will come to pass, because what happens in the Middle East in the future might very well cause a major war there which would quickly spread to all the other nations of the world; very possibly it could do that.

Many countries depend completely on oil from the Middle East for their life. We don't. If all oil was cut off to us from the Middle East, we could survive; but Japan imports more than 98 percent of all its energy, and other countries, like in Europe—Germany, Italy, France—are also heavily dependent on oil from the Middle East.

So, this is such a crucial area of the world that I will be devoting a major part of my own time on foreign policy between now and next fall trying to provide for a forum within which they can discuss their problems and, hopefully, let them seek out among themselves some permanent solution.

Source: Library of Congress and Clyde R. Mark, *The Search for Peace in the Middle East: Documents and Statements, 1967–79; Report Prepared for the Subcommittee on Europe and the Middle East of the Committee on Foreign Affairs, U.S. House of Representatives* (Washington, DC: U.S. Government Printing Office, 1979), 311.

77. U.S.-Soviet Joint Communiqué, October 1, 1977

Introduction

Following President Jimmy Carter's appeal for the opening of Arab-Israeli peace negotiations, all states involved were invited to attend talks at Geneva. The cochairs of the Geneva Peace Conference on the Middle East were the two Cold War superpowers, the United States and the Soviet Union, an indication of the desire of both to stabilize the often volatile situation in the Middle East. The United States also hoped that the Soviet Union would be able to pressure its client Syria to accept a peace settlement and cease its efforts to overthrow Israel. In July 1977 the United States and Israel issued a declaration that the objective of these talks would be "an overall peace settlement to be expressed in a peace treaty." Difficulties remained, of which the most crucial was whether the Palestine Liberation Organization (PLO) should be invited to attend and represent the Palestinians, something that Israeli leaders were determined to prevent but that Carter favored, provided the Palestinians were prepared to accept Israel's right to exist. Complicated diplomatic maneuverings ensued, as Israel mobilized its American supporters to pressure the Carter administration to avoid any commitment to a separate Palestinian state. Seeking to keep the process moving, in October 1977 the United States won Soviet support for a joint statement favoring a comprehensive peace settlement. While calling for Israeli withdrawal from "occupied territories," the two powers did not demand that Israel relinquish all such territories, leaving room for some border adjustments. On the vexed Palestinian issue, the two powers promised to "ensur[e] the legitimate rights of the Palestinian people" without specifying whether or not these included the establishment of a Palestinian state. Both pledged to participate in UN efforts to establish demilitarized frontier zones and guarantee the Arab-Israeli borders as defined by the peace conference. The statement had been carefully crafted to fall within the parameters of UN Security Council Resolutions 242 and 338. Even so, the Israeli government, fearful of being forced to deal with the Palestinians or to concede the creation of a Palestinian state in the occupied territories, used it as an excuse to sabotage the Geneva framework. On the same day the statement was issued, the Israeli government attacked the U.S.-Soviet communiqué on the grounds that it demanded that Israel give up all territory acquired since June 1967 and that it failed to mention the two resolutions. Three days later, Israeli foreign minister Moshe Dayan used the threat of appealing to the influential American Jewish community to win from

Carter a public announcement that Israel need not be bound by the U.S.-Soviet framework, even if all other parties accepted it. The entire episode was an indication of the difficulties involved in reaching any comprehensive peace settlement and also helped to convince the Palestinians that they could not count on the United States for assistance against Israel. Given the difficulties involved in even setting a framework for multilateral negotiations, Carter decided that, as things stood, it was more fruitful to turn to brokering bilateral peace agreements between Israel and its Arab opponents.

Primary Source

Having exchanged views regarding the unsafe situation which remains in the Middle East, U.S. Secretary of State Cyrus Vance and Member of the Politbureau of the Central Committee of the CPSU, Minister for Foreign Affairs of the U.S.S.R. A.A. Gromyko have the following statement to make on behalf of their countries, which are cochairmen of the Geneva Peace Conference on the Middle East:

1. Both governments are convinced that vital interests of the peoples of this area, as well as the interests of strengthening peace and international security in general, urgently dictate the necessity of achieving, as soon as possible, a just and lasting settlement of the Arab-Israeli conflict. This settlement should be comprehensive, incorporating all parties concerned and all questions.

The United States and the Soviet Union believe that, within the framework of a comprehensive settlement of the Middle East problem, all specific questions of the settlement should be resolved, including such key issues as withdrawal of Israeli Armed Forces from territories occupied in the 1967 conflict; the resolution of the Palestinian question, including insuring the legitimate rights of the Palestinian people; termination of the state of war and establishment of normal peaceful relations on the basis of mutual recognition of the principles of sovereignty, territorial integrity, and political independence.

The two governments believe that, in addition to such measures for insuring the security of the borders between Israel and the neighboring Arab states as the establishment of demilitarized zones and the agreed stationing in them of U.N. troops or observers, international guarantees of such borders as well as of the observance of the terms of settlement can also be established should the contracting parties so desire. The United States and the Soviet Union are ready to participate in these guarantees, subject to their constitutional processes.

2. The United States and the Soviet Union believe that the only right and effective way for achieving a fundamental solution to all aspects of the Middle East problem in its entirety is negotiations within the framework of the Geneva peace conference, specially convened for these purposes, with participation in its work of the representatives of all the parties involved in the conflict including those of the Palestinian people, and legal and contractual formalization of the decisions reached at the conference.

In their capacity as cochairmen of the Geneva conference, the United States and the U.S.S.R. affirm their intentions, through joint efforts and in their contacts with the parties concerned, to facilitate in every way the resumption of the work of the conference not later than December 1977. The cochairmen note that there still exist several questions of a procedural and organizational nature which remain to be agreed upon by the participants to the conference.

3. Guided by the goal of achieving a just political settlement in the Middle East and of eliminating the explosive situation in this area of the world, the United States and the U.S.S.R. appeal to all the parties in the conflict to understand the necessity for careful consideration of each other's legitimate rights and interests and to demonstrate mutual readiness to act accordingly.

Israel's Response to the US-USSR Joint Declaration on the Middle East
October 1, 1977
1. The Soviet Union's demand that Israel withdraw to the pre-June 1967 borders—a demand which contravenes the true meaning of Security Council Resolution 242—is known to all.

2. Despite the fact that the Governments of the U.S. and Israel agreed on July 7, 1977 that the aim of the negotiations at Geneva should be "an overall peace settlement to be expressed in a peace treaty," the concept of a "peace treaty" is not mentioned at all in the Soviet-American statement.

3. There is no reference at all in this statement to Resolutions 242 and 338, despite the fact that the U.S. Government has repeatedly affirmed heretofore that these resolutions constitute the sole basis for the convening of the Geneva Conference.

4. There can be no doubt that this statement, issued at a time when discussions are proceeding on the reconvening of the Geneva Conference, cannot but still further harden the positions of the Arab states and make the Middle East peace process still more difficult.

5. As the Prime Minister has stated, Israel will continue to aspire to free negotiations with its neighbours with the purpose of signing a peace treaty with them.

Source: Library of Congress and Clyde R. Mark, *The Search for Peace in the Middle East: Documents and Statements, 1967–79; Report Prepared for the Subcommittee on Europe and the Middle East of the Committee on Foreign Affairs, U.S. House of Representatives* (Washington, DC: U.S. Government Printing Office, 1979); and *Jerusalem Post*, October 2, 1977.

78. Anwar Sadat, Speech to the Knesset [Excerpt], November 20, 1977

Introduction

Egyptian president Anwar Sadat initially agreed to participate in the Geneva Conference on the Middle East proposed by President Jimmy Carter. Sadat sought to allay domestic unrest over economic shortages and high prices that brought riots in major Egyptian cities in early 1977 by winning liberal access to U.S. aid programs. He also hoped to bolster his prestige by resolving the status of the Sinai Peninsula so that Egypt regained full control. When negotiations for the Geneva Conference bogged down in stalemate in October 1977, Sadat turned to bilateral negotiations with Israel. In November 1977 he made the spectacular gesture of visiting Jerusalem and delivering a speech to the Israeli Knesset, the first time that an Arab leader had set foot on Israeli soil. Sadat appealed eloquently for peace. He stated that he sought not simply a bilateral peace treaty with Israel but a comprehensive agreement that would resolve the Palestinian refugee problem and end the many years of hostility between Israel and all the Arab states. Perceptively, he stated that while he was prepared on Egypt's behalf to recognize the existence of Israel, the strongest barrier to reaching any settlement was the pervasive suspicion and distrust with which each side in the conflict regarded each other. He warned that peace would depend upon Israeli withdrawal from all the occupied territories, including "Arab Jerusalem," and also on the establishment of a Palestinian state. Sadat's speech was only the opening move in a complicated minuet of negotiations that would take almost a year and whose outcome, despite all his protestations to the contrary, would be a bilateral Egyptian-Israeli peace treaty. His speech was nonetheless an eloquent affirmation of the need for peace in the Middle East.

Primary Source

[…]

Today, I come to you with both feet firmly on the ground, in order that we may build a new life and so that we may establish peace. All of us in this land, the land of God, Moslems, Christians and Jews, worship God and no other god. God's decrees and commandments are: love, honesty, chastity and peace.

I can excuse all those who received my decision to attend your assembly, when I made that decision known to the whole world— I say I can excuse all those who received my decision with astonishment, or rather who were flabbergasted. Some, under the effect of this violent surprise, thought that my decision was nothing more than a verbal maneuver, for home consumption and before world opinion; others described it as a political tactic to conceal my intentions to wage a fresh war.

[…]

I can excuse anyone who was flabbergasted by the decision or who had doubts about the sound intentions behind that declaration. No one could imagine that the President of the largest Arab State, which bears the greatest burden and first responsibility over the question of war or peace in the Middle East region, could take a decision to be prepared to go to enemy territory when we are in a state of war, and we and you are still suffering the effects of four severe wars in a period of 30 years. All this, at the time when the families of the war of October 1973 are still living out the tragedies of losing husbands and sons and the martyrdom of fathers and sisters.

However, as I have already declared, I did not discuss this decision with any of my colleagues and brother heads of the Arab states, not even those of the confrontation states; some of them who got in touch with me after the announcement opposed the decision, because a state of total doubt still existed in everybody's mind, a state of complete lack of confidence between the Arab states, including the Palestinian people, and Israel.

. . . I tell you frankly and with complete sincerity that I took this decision after long thought; and I know quite well that it is a big gamble. But if Almighty God has made it my destiny to assume responsibility for the people of Egypt, and to have a share in the responsibility for the destiny of the entire Arab people, then I think that the first duty dictated by this responsibility is that I must exhaust every possibility in order to stop the Arab people of Egypt, and all the Arab peoples, from enduring the sufferings of other horrendous, destructive wars—only God knows their extent.

After long thought, I was convinced that my responsibility to God and the people imposes on me the obligation to go to the furthest place in the world and, indeed, to come to Jerusalem to speak to the members of the Knesset, the representatives of the people of Israel, about all the facts which I have in my own mind. Afterwards, I shall leave you to decide by yourselves and let Almighty God do whatever he wishes with us after that.

Ladies and gentlemen: There are moments in the life of nations and peoples when those who are known for their wisdom and foresight are required to look beyond the past, with all its complications and remnants, for the sake of a courageous upsurge towards new horizons. These people who, like ourselves, shoulder that responsibility entrusted to us are the first people who must have the courage to take fateful decisions in harmony with the sublimity of the situation.

We must all rise above all forms of fanaticism and self-deception and obsolete theories of superiority. It is important that we should never forget that virtue is God's alone. If I say that I want to protect all the Arab people from the terrors of new, terrifying wars, I declare before you with all sincerity that I have the same feelings and I carry the same responsibility for every human being in the world and, most certainly, for the Israeli people.

A life which is taken away in war is the life of a human being, whether it is an Arab or an Israeli life. The wife who becomes a widow is a human being and has the right to live in a happy family environment whether she is an Arab or an Israeli. The innocent children who lose the care and love of their parents are all our children; they are all our children, whether in the land of the Arabs or in Israel; we have a great responsibility to provide them with a prosperous present and a better future. . . .

I have borne, and shall continue to bear the requirements of a historic responsibility. For this reason some years ago—to be precise on 4th February 1971—I declared that I was ready to sign a peace agreement with Israel. This was the first declaration to come from a responsible Arab since the beginning of the Arab-Israeli conflict.

With all these motives, which are made necessary by the responsibility of leadership, I declared on 16th October 1973 and before the Egyptian People's Assembly that an international conference should be called to determine a lasting and just peace. I was not then in a position to beg for peace or seek a cease-fire. With all these motives, which are made imperative by the duty of history and leadership, we signed the first disengagement agreement and then the second one, on Sinai. Then we tried to knock on open and closed doors to find a specific road towards a lasting and just peace. We have opened our hearts to all the peoples of the world so that they may understand our motives and aims and so that they may really be convinced that we are advocates of justice and seekers of peace.

For all these reasons too, I decided to come to you with an open mind and an open heart and a conscientious will so that we may establish a lasting and just peace.

Destiny has decreed that my visit to you, my visit of peace, should come on the day of the great Islamic feast, the blessed Id al-Adha, the feast of sacrifice and redemption when Ibrahim [Abraham], may peace be upon him, the forefather of both the Arabs and the Jews, our father Ibrahim submitted to God and dedicated himself completely to Him, not through weakness but through colossal spiritual power and through his free choice to sacrifice his son, which arose from his firm, unshakable belief in the sublime ideals which give a deep meaning to life.

Perhaps this coincidence has a new meaning for us all; perhaps it forms a concrete hope for the good signs of security and safety and peace.

Ladies and gentlemen, let us be frank with each other, using straightforward words and clear thoughts which cannot be twisted. Let us be frank with each other today when the whole world, East and West, is following this unique event, this event which could be a turning-point, which could mean a radical change in the history of this part of the world, if not in the whole world. Let us be frank with each other; let us be frank with each other when answering the big question: How can we achieve a just and lasting peace?

First of all, I have come to you bringing with me a clear and frank answer to this major question, so that the people of Israel can hear it; the whole world can hear it; all those whose sincere calls reach me can hear it; and so that the results hoped for by millions of people may materialize from this historic meeting.

Before I make my answer known to you, I want to stress that in this clear and frank answer I rely on a number of facts, facts which no-one can deny. The first fact is that there can be no happiness for some [people] at the expense of the misery of others. The second fact is that I have not spoken and will not speak in two tongues, nor have I used nor shall I use two policies; I deal with everyone with one tongue, one policy and one face. The third fact is that direct confrontation and a straight line are the nearest and most useful methods to achieve the clear aim. The fourth fact is that the call for a just and lasting peace based on the implementation of the UN resolutions has today become the call of all the world, and has become a clear expression of the will of the international community, both at the level of the official capitals—where policy is decided and decisions made—and at the level of world opinion, which influences the policy and decisions.

The fifth fact—and perhaps it is the most obvious one—is that, in its efforts to achieve a just and lasting peace, the Arab nation is not proceeding from a position of weakness or instability; quite the contrary: Its strength and stability are such that its efforts must stem from a genuine desire for peace, from a realization that for the spirit of civilization to survive, for us, you and the whole world to avoid a real disaster, there is no alternative to the establishment of a lasting and just peace that no storms can shake, no doubts can spoil, and no ill-intentions can undermine.

On the basis of these facts—these facts that I wanted to convey to you as I see them—I would like with complete sincerity to warn you about certain thoughts that might cross your minds; the duty to be sincere means that I must state the following:

Firstly, I did not come to you with a view to concluding a separate agreement between Egypt and Israel. This is not provided for in Egypt's policy. The problem does not lie just between Egypt and Israel; moreover, no separate peace between Egypt and Israel—or between any confrontation state and Israel—could secure a lasting and just peace in the region as a whole. Even if a peace agreement was achieved between all the confrontation states and Israel, without a just solution to the Palestinian problem it would never ensure the establishment of the durable, lasting peace the entire world is now trying to achieve.

Secondly, I did not come with a view to securing a partial peace, a peace such that we end the state of war at this stage, and then postpone the whole problem to a second phase. This is not the fundamental solution that will lead us to a lasting peace. Linked to this is the fact that I did not come to you in order that we may agree to a third disengagement of forces either in Sinai alone, or in Sinai, the Golan and the West Bank; this would be merely a postponement of an explosion until a later time. It would also mean that we lacked the courage to face up to peace, we were too weak to shoulder the burden and responsibilities of a lasting and just peace.

I have come to you so that together we can build a lasting and just peace, so that not one more drop of the blood of either side may be shed. For this reason I stated that I was willing to go to the ends of the earth. At this point I shall answer the question: How are we going to achieve permanent and just peace? In my opinion, and I say it from this platform to the whole world, to find an answer is not impossible and neither is it difficult, despite the long years of blood revenge, hatred and rancour, of bringing up generations on terms of complete estrangement and entrenched enmity. The answer is not difficult nor impossible to find, if we follow the path of a straight line with all honesty and faith. You want to live with us in this area of the world, and I say to you with all sincerity that we welcome you among us with security and safety.

This in itself forms a giant turning-point, a decisive landmark of an historic transformation. We used to reject you, and we had our reasons and grievances. Yes, we used to reject meeting you anywhere. Yes, we used to describe you as "so-called Israel". Yes, conferences and international organizations used to bring us together. Our representatives have never and still do not exchange greetings and salaams. Yes, this is what happened, and it still goes on. For any talks, we used to make it conditional that a mediator met each side separately. Yes, this is how the talks on the first disengagement were conducted and this is also how the talks on the second disengagement were held. Our representatives met at the first Geneva conference without exchanging one direct word. Yes, this is what went on. But I say to you today and I say to the whole world that we accept that we should live with you in a lasting and just peace. We do not want to surround you or to be surrounded ourselves with missiles which are ready to destroy, with the missiles of hatred and bitterness.

More than once, I have said that Israel has become a living reality. The world recognized it and the two superpowers shouldered the responsibility of its security and the defence of its existence. And when we want peace both in theory and in practice we welcome you to live amongst us in security and peace, in theory and practice.

There existed between you and us a huge high wall. You tried to build it over a quarter of a century, but it was demolished in 1973. In its ferocity the wall continues the war psychologically. Your wall was a threat with a force capable of destroying the Arab nation from end to end. The wall was based on the view that the Arab peoples had turned into a nation with no defences. Indeed some of you said that even after another 50 years the Arabs would never achieve a position of any strength.

This wall has always threatened, with a long arm capable of reaching any position over any distance. This wall has threatened us with annihilation and extinction if we tried to exercise our legitimate right of liberating the occupied territory.

We must admit together that this wall has fallen, it collapsed in 1973. But there is still another wall, this second wall forms a complex psychological barrier between us and you. It is a barrier of doubt, a barrier of hatred, a barrier of fear of deception, a barrier of illusions about behaviour, actions or decisions, a barrier of cautious and mistaken interpretation of every event or statement. This psychological barrier is the one I have mentioned in official statements, which in my opinion constitutes 70 per cent of the problem.

On my visit to you, I ask you today why we do not extend our hands in sincerity, faith and truth so that we may together destroy this barrier? Why we do not make our intentions the same in truth, faith and sincerity so that we may together eliminate all the doubt, the fear of treachery and ill-intentions, and prove the sincerity of our intentions? Why do we not join together, with the courage of men and the daring of heroes who risk their lives for the sake of a sublime ideal? Why do we not join together with this courage and daring to set up a mammoth edifice of peace, an edifice that builds and does not destroy, that emits to our future generations the light of the human spirit for building, development and the good of man? Why should we leave for these generations the consequences of the bloodletting, the killing of souls, the orphaning of children, the making of widows, the destruction of families and the agony of victims?

Why do we not believe in the wisdom of the Creator, as conveyed in the Proverbs of the wise Solomon: Deceit is in the heart of those who imagine evil, but to the advocates of peace will come joy; better a morsel and peace than a house full of meat with strife. Why don't we repeat together, why don't we sing together from the psalms of David: Hear the voice of my supplications when I cry unto Thee, when I lift up my hands towards Thy holy oracle. Put me not with the wicked and with the evil-doers, who speak of peace to their neighbours, but have evil in their hearts. Treat them according to their actions, according to the wickedness of their deeds. I ask for peace and seek it.

Ladies and gentlemen, the truth is—and it is the truth that I am telling you—that there can be no peace in the true sense of the word, unless this peace is based on justice and not on the occupation of the territory of others. It is not right that you seek for yourselves what you deny to others. In all frankness and in the spirit which prompted me to come to you today, I say to you: you have finally to abandon the dreams of tomorrow and you have also to abandon the belief that force is the best means of dealing with the Arabs. You have to absorb very well the lessons of confrontation between ourselves and you; expansion will be of no avail to you.

To put it clearly, our territory is not a subject of bargaining; it is not a topic for wrangling. To us, the national and nationalist soil occupies the same position which the sacred valley of Tuwa occupies—the valley in which God spoke to Moses, may the peace of God be on him. None of us has the right to accept or to forfeit one inch of it, or to accept the principle of bargaining and wrangling about it. The truth is—and it is the truth that I am telling you—that before us today is a favourable opportunity for peace; it is an opportunity the like of which time will not provide again, if we are really serious in the struggle for peace. It is an opportunity which, if we miss it or waste it, the course of mankind and of history will be on those who plotted against it.

What is peace to Israel? To live in the region, together with her Arab neighbours, in security and safety—this is a logic to which I say: "Yes". For Israel to live within her borders secure from any aggression—this is a logic to which I say: "Yes". For Israel to get all kinds of assurances that ensure for her these two facts—this is a demand to which I say: "Yes".

Furthermore, we declare that we accept all the international assurances which you can imagine and from those whom you approve. We declare that we accept all assurances you want from the two superpowers; or from one of them; or from the big five; or from some of them. I repeat and I declare quite clearly that we accept any guarantees you need because in return we shall take the same guarantees.

The upshot of the matter then is this—when we put the question: What is peace to Israel? The answer would be: That it lives within its borders together with its Arab neighbours in security and safety and within the framework of all that it likes in the way of guarantees which the other side obtains. But how can this be achieved? How can we arrive at this result so that it can take us to a permanent and just peace?

There are facts that must be confronted with all courage and clarity. There is Arab land which Israel has occupied and still occupies by armed force. And we insist that complete withdrawal from this land be undertaken and this includes Arab Jerusalem, Jerusalem to which I have come, as it is considered the city of peace and which has been and will always be the living embodiment of coexistence between believers of the three religions. It is inadmissible for anyone to think of Jerusalem's special position within the context of annexation and expansion. It must be made a free city, open to all the faithful. What is more important is that the city must not be closed to those who have chosen it as a place of residence for several centuries.

Instead of inflaming the feuds of the wars of the crusades we must revive the spirit of Umar Bin al-Khattab and Saladin, that is the spirit of tolerance and respect for rights. The Moslem and Christian houses of worship are not mere places for the performance of religious rites and prayers. They are the true testimonies of our uninterrupted existence in this place, politically, morally and ideologically. Here, nobody must miscalculate the importance and veneration we hold for Jerusalem, we Christians and Moslems.

Let me tell you without hesitation that I have not come to you, under this dome, to beg you to withdraw your forces from the occupied territory. This is because complete withdrawal from the Arab territories occupied after 1967 is a matter that goes without saying, over which we accept no controversy and in respect of which there is no begging to anyone or from anyone. There will be no meaning to talk about a lasting, just peace and there will be no meaning to any step to guarantee our lives together in this part of the world in peace and security, while you occupy an Arab land by armed force. There can never be peace established or built with the occupation of others' land. Yes, this is a self-evident truth, which accepts no controversy or discussion once the intentions are true—once the intentions are true, as is the struggle for the establishment of a lasting, just peace for our generation and for all the generations that will follow us.

As regards the Palestine question, nobody denies that it is the essence of the entire problem. Nobody throughout the entire world accepts today slogans raised here in Israel which disregard the existence of the people of Palestine and even ask where the people of Palestine are. The problem of the Palestinian people, and the legitimate rights of the Palestinian people are now no longer ignored or rejected by anybody; no thinking mind supposes that they could be ignored or rejected; they are facts that meet with the support and recognition of the international community both in the West and the East and in international documents and official declarations. No one could turn a deaf ear to their loud, resounding sound, or turn a blind eye to their historic reality.

Even the USA—your first ally, which is the most committed to the protection of the existence and security of Israel and which has been giving Israel and continues to give it moral, material and military aid—I say even the USA has opted for facing up to the reality and to facts, to recognize that the Palestinian people have legitimate rights, and that the Palestine question is the crux and essence of the conflict, and that so long as this question remains suspended without a solution the conflict will increase, grow more intense and reach new magnitudes.

In all sincerity, I tell you that peace cannot be achieved without the Palestinians, and that it would be a great mistake, the effect of which no one knows, to turn a blind eye to this question or to set it aside.

I shall not recall events of the past, since the issue of the Balfour Declaration 60 years ago. You know the facts quite well. And if you have found it legally and morally justified to set up a national homeland on a land that was not totally yours, you are well placed to show understanding to the insistence of the Palestinian people to set up their own state anew, on their homeland.

When some hardliners and extremists demand that the Palestinians should abandon this higher aim it means, in reality and in actual fact, that this is a demand that they should abandon their identity and every hope they have for the future. I salute some Israeli voices which demanded that the rights of the Palestinian people should be recognized in order to achieve and guarantee peace. Therefore, Ladies and Gentlemen, I say to you that there is no benefit from not recognizing the Palestinian people and their rights to establish their state and to return home. We, the Arabs, have earlier experienced this, over you and the truth of the existence of Israel. The struggle took us from one war to another and from victims to more victims, until we and you have reached today the brink of a terrifying abyss and a frightening disaster if, today, we do not seize together the chance of a permanent and just peace.

You must face the reality courageously, as I have faced it. It is no solution to a problem to run away from it or to be above it. There can never be peace through an attempt to impose fantasy concepts on which the entire world has turned its back and declared its unanimous appeal that right and justice should be respected. There is no need to enter the vicious circle of Palestinian rights. There is no use in creating obstacles, for either they will delay the march of peace or peace itself will be killed.

As I have already told you, there can be no happiness for some at the expense of the misery of others; direct confrontation and straightforwardness are the shortcuts and the surest and most useful ways of reaching a clear objective. Direct confrontation of the Palestine problem and tackling it in one single language with a view to achieving a just and lasting peace lie in the establishment of that state, with all the international reassurances you want. You must have no fear of a young state which needs the assistance of all the states in the world to establish itself.

When the bells of peace ring, there will be no hands to beat the drums of war. Even if such hands existed, they would be stilled. Imagine with me the peace agreement in Geneva, the good news of which we herald to a world thirsty for peace: [Firstly,] a peace agreement based on ending the Israeli occupation of the Arab territory occupied in 1967; [secondly,] the realization of basic rights of the Palestinian people and this people's right to self-determination, including their right to setting up their own state; thirdly, the right of all the countries of the region to live in peace within their secure and guaranteed borders, through agreed measures for the appropriate security of international borders, in addition to the appropriate inter-

national guarantees; fourthly, all the States in the region will undertake to administer relations among themselves in accordance with the principles and aims of the UN Charter, in particular eschewing the use of force and settling differences among them by peaceful means; and fifthly, ending the state of war that exists in the region.

Ladies and gentlemen, peace is not the putting of a signature under written lines. It is a new writing of history. Peace is not a competition in calling for peace so as to defend any greedy designs or to conceal any ambitions. In essence, peace is a mammoth struggle against all greedy designs and ambitions.

The experiences of past and contemporary history perhaps teach us all that missiles, warships and nuclear weapons cannot establish security. On the contrary, they destroy all that was built by security. For the sake of our peoples, for the sake of a civilization made by man, we must protect man in every place from the rule of the force of arms. We must raise high the rule of humanity with the full force of principles and values which hold man high.

If you will permit me to address an appeal from this platform to the people of Israel, I address a genuine sincere word to every man, woman and child in Israel, and tell them:

I bring to you from the people of Egypt who bless this sacred mission for peace, I bring to you the mission of peace, the mission of the Egyptian people who are not fanatics and whose sons, Moslems, Christians and Jews, live in a spirit of amity, love and tolerance. This is the Egypt whose people have entrusted me with carrying the sacred mission to you, the mission of security, hope and peace.

Every man and woman, every child in Israel, encourage your leaders to struggle for peace. Let all efforts be directed towards the building of a mammoth edifice of peace, instead of the building of fortresses and shelters fortified with missiles of destruction. Give to the whole world the picture of the new man in this part of the world so that he may be an example for the man of the age, the man of peace in every position and in every place. Give your children the good tidings that what has passed is the last of wars and the end of agonies, and that what is coming is the new beginning of the new life, the life of love and good, freedom and peace.

Mothers who have lost their sons, widowed wife, son who has lost a brother or a father, all victims of wars, fill the earth and space with the praise of peace. Fill the hearts and breasts with the hopes of peace. Make the song a fact, one that lives and bears fruit. Make hope an article of work and struggle. The will of the peoples is part of the will of God.

[. . .]

I have chosen to depart from all precedents and traditions known to countries at war, despite the fact that the Arab territories are still under occupation. Indeed, my announcement of my readiness to come to Israel was a big surprise which has upset many feelings, astounded many minds and aroused suspicions about what lies behind it. Despite all that, I took my decision in full, open and honest faith and with the full, true expression of the will and intentions of my people. I chose this hard path, which in the eyes of many is the hardest path.

I have chosen to come to you with an open heart and an open mind, to give this great momentum to all the international efforts made to achieve peace. I have chosen to put forward to you, and in your own house, the real facts, free from any scheme or whim, not to maneuver or to win a round, but in order that we may, together, win the most grave round and battle in contemporary history—the battle of a just and lasting peace. It is not just my battle, nor is it just the battle of leaders in Israel; it is truly the battle of all citizens of all our lands, who have the right to live in peace. It is a commitment of conscience and responsibility in the hearts of millions of people.

[...]

Source: "Sadat's Address to the Knesset," *Summary of World Broadcasts: The Middle East and Africa*, 5672, D (1977): 1–8. Courtesy of BBC Monitoring.

79. Menachem Begin, Speech to the Knesset [Excerpt], November 20, 1977

Introduction

When Egyptian president Anwar Sadat visited Israel, his host was Israeli prime minister Menachem Begin, leader of the hard-line Likud Party and a former Jewish terrorist guerrilla leader of the 1940s. At the personal level the two men heartily disliked and distrusted each other, an antagonism that did nothing to facilitate an Egyptian-Israeli accord. Speaking in response to Sadat, Begin hastily riposted on some of the points that Sadat had made. While welcoming Sadat, urging other Arab leaders to emulate the Egyptian president and make overtures to Israel, and expressing his own hopes for peace and for future Arab-Israeli economic cooperation in developing the entire Middle East, Begin expressed serious reservations over Sadat's attacks on the Balfour Declaration and the implication that Jewish settlement in Israel rested on an unjust foundation. Begin also recalled Emir Faisal's 1919 endorsement of the Balfour Declaration and the establishment of a Jewish homeland in Palestine. While rejecting Sadat's stance on Israel's borders, Begin did, however, express his country's willingness to enter into negotiations on the subject with Arab states. Sadat's visit marked the beginning of protracted talks between Egypt and Israel that were designed to resolve at least the outstanding issues separating those two nations.

Primary Source

[...]

I greet and welcome the President of Egypt for coming to our country and on his participating in the Knesset session. The flight time between Cairo and Jerusalem is short, but the distance between Cairo and Jerusalem was until last night almost endless. President Sadat crossed this distance courageously. We, the Jews, know how to appreciate such courage, and we know how to appreciate it in our guest, because it is with courage that we are here and this is how we continue to exist, and we shall continue to exist.

Mr. Speaker, this small nation, the remaining refuge of the Jewish people which returned to its historic homeland, has always wanted peace and, since the dawn of our independence, on 14th May 1948— 5th Iyar Tashah [Hebrew date], in the Declaration of Independence in the founding scroll of our national freedom, David Ben Gurion said: We extend a hand of peace and good-neighborliness to all the neighboring countries and their peoples....

But it is my bounden duty, Mr. Speaker, and not only my right, not to pass over the truth, that our hand outstretched for peace was not grasped and, one day after we had renewed our independence— as was our right, our eternal right, which cannot be disputed—we were attacked on three fronts and we stood almost without arms, the few against many, the weak against the strong, while an attempt was made one day after the Declaration of Independence, to strangle it at birth, to put an end to the last hope of the Jewish people, the yearning renewed after the years of destruction and holocaust.

No, we do not believe in might and we have never based our attitude to the Arab people on might; quite the contrary, force was used against us. Over all the years of this generation we have never stopped being attacked by might, the might of the strong arm stretched out to exterminate our people, to destroy our independence, to deny our rights. We defended ourselves, it is true. We defended our rights, our existence, our honour, our women and children, against these repeated and recurring attempts to crush us through the force of arms and not only on one front. That, too, is true. With the help of Almighty God we overcame the forces of aggression, and we have guaranteed the existence of our nation, not only for this generation, but for the coming generations, too. We do not believe in might; we believe in right, only in right and therefore our aspiration, from the depth of our hearts, has always been, to this very day, for peace.

Mr. President, Mr. President of Egypt, the commanders of all the underground Hebrew fighting organizations are sitting in this democratic house. They had to conduct a campaign of the few against the many, against a huge, a world power. Here are sitting the veteran commanders and captains who had to go forth into battle because it was forced upon them and forward to victory which was unavoidable because they were defending their rights. They belong to different parties, they have different views, but I am sure, Mr. President, that I am expressing the views of everyone with no exceptions, that we have one aspiration in our hearts, one desire in our souls and all of us are united in all these aspirations and desires—to bring peace, peace for our nation, which has not known peace for even one day since we started returning to Zion, and peace for our neighbors, whom we wish all the best, and we believe that if we make peace, real peace, we shall be able to help our neighbors in all walks of life and a new era will open in the Middle East, an era of blossoming and growth, development and expansion of the economy, its growth as it was in the past.

Therefore, permit me, today, to set out the peace programme as we understand it. We want full, real peace, with complete reconciliation between the Jewish and the Arab peoples. . . .

. . . For it is true indeed that we shall have to live in this area, all of us together shall live here, for generations upon generations; the great Arab people in their various states and countries and the Jewish people in their country, Eretz Yisra'el. Therefore we must determine what peace means.

Let us conduct negotiations, Mr. President, as free negotiating partners for a peace treaty and, with the aid of the Lord, we fully believe the day will come when we can sign it with mutual respect, and we shall then know that the era of wars is over, that hands have been extended between friends, that each has shaken the hand of his brother and the future will be shining for all the peoples of this area. The beginning of wisdom in a peace treaty is the abolition of the state of war. I agree, Mr. President, that you did not come here, we did not invite you to our country, in order, as has been said in recent days, to divide the Arab peoples. Somebody quoted an ancient Roman saying: Divide and rule. Israel does not want to rule and therefore does not need to divide. We want peace with all our neighbors, with Egypt, with Jordan, with Syria and with Lebanon. . . .

And there is no need to distinguish between a peace treaty and an abolition of the state of war. Quite the contrary; we are not proposing this nor are we asking for it. The first clause of a peace treaty is cessation of the state of war, for ever. We want to establish normal relations between us, as they exist between all nations, even after wars. We have learned from history, Mr. President, that war is avoidable, peace is unavoidable. Many nations have waged war between each other and sometimes they used the tragic term, a perennial enemy. There are no perennial enemies. And after all the wars the inevitable comes—peace. And so we want to establish, in a peace treaty, diplomatic relations, as is the custom among civilized nations.

Today two flags are flying over Jerusalem—the Egyptian flag and the Israeli flag.

And we saw together, Mr. President, little children waving both the flags. Let us sign a peace treaty and let us establish this situation forever, both in Jerusalem and in Cairo, and I hope the day will come when the Egyptian children wave the Israeli flag and the Egyptian flag just as the children of Israel waved both these flags in Jerusalem.

And you, Mr. President, will have a loyal ambassador in Jerusalem and we shall have an ambassador in Cairo. And even if differences of opinion arise between us, we shall clarify them, like civilized peoples, through our authorized envoys.

We are proposing economic co-operation for the development of our countries.

There are wonderful countries in the Middle East, the Lord created it thus: oases in the desert, but we can make the deserts flourish as well. Let us co-operate in this field, let us develop our countries, let us eliminate poverty, hunger, homelessness. Let us raise our peoples to the level of developed countries, let them call us developing countries no longer.

With all due respect, I am willing to repeat the words of His Majesty, the King of Morocco, who said in public that if peace came about in the Middle East, the combination of Arab genius and Jewish genius together could turn this area into a paradise on earth.

Let us open our countries to free traffic. You come to our country and we shall visit yours. I am ready to announce, Mr. Speaker, this very day, that our country is open to the citizens of Egypt, and I make no conditions. I think it is only proper and just that there should be a joint announcement on this matter. But just as there are Egyptian flags in our streets, and there is an honored delegation from Egypt in our country, in our capital, let the number of visitors increase, our border with you will be open, as will be all [our] other borders.

As I pointed out, we want this in the south, in the north, in the east; so I am renewing my invitation to the President of Syria to follow in your footsteps, Mr. President, and come to us to open negotiations for a peace between Israel and Syria, so that we may sign a peace treaty between us. I am sorry but I must say that there is no justification for the mourning they have declared beyond our northern border. Quite the contrary, such visits, such links, such clarifications can and must be days of joy, days of the raising of spirits of all people. I invite King Husayn to come to us to discuss all the problems which need to be discussed between us. And genuine representatives of the Arabs of Eretz Yisra'el, I invite them to come and hold clarification talks with us about our common future, about guaranteeing the freedom of man, social justice, peace, mutual respect. And if they invite us to come to their capitals, we shall accept their invitations. If they invite us to open negotiations in Damascus, in

Amman or in Beirut, we shall go to those capitals in order to hold negotiations with them there. We do not want to divide; we want real peace with all our neighbors, to be expressed in peace treaties whose contents I have already made clear.

Mr. Speaker, it is my duty today to tell our guest and the peoples watching us and listening to our words about the link between our people and this land. The President [of Egypt] recalled the Balfour Declaration. No, sir, we did not take over any strange land; we returned to our homeland. The link between our people and this land is eternal. It arose in the earliest days of the history of humanity and was never altered. In this country we developed our civilization. We had our prophets here, and their sacred words stand to this day. Here the Kings of Judah and Israel knelt before their God. This is where we became a people; here we established our Kingdom. And when we were expelled from our land, when force was used against us, no matter how far we went from our land, we never forgot it even one day. We prayed for it, we longed for it, we believed in our return to it from the day these words were spoken: When the Lord restores the fortunes of Zion, we shall be like dreamers. Our mouths will be filled with laughter, and our tongues will speak with shouts of joy. These verses apply to all our exiles and all our sufferings, giving us the consolation that the return to Zion would come.

This, our right, was recognized. The Balfour Declaration was included in the mandate laid down by the nations of the world, including the United States of America, and the preface to this recognized international document says: [speaks in English] "Whereas recognition has the Bible given to the historical connection of the Jewish people with Palestine and to the grounds for reconstituting their national home in that country", [ends English] the historic connection between the Jewish people and Palestine or, in Hebrew, Eretz Yisra'el, was given reconfirmation—reconfirmation—as the national homeland in that country, that is, in Eretz Yisra'el.

In 1919 we also won recognition of this right by the spokesman of the Arab people and the agreement of 3rd January 1919, which was signed by Prince Faysal and Hayyim Weizmann. It reads: [speaks in English] Mindful of the racial kinship and ancient bonds existing between the Arabs and the Jewish people and realizing that the surest means of working out the consummation of the national aspirations is the closest possible collaboration in the development of the Arab State and of Palestine. [ends English] And afterwards come all the clauses about co-operation between the Arab State and Eretz Yisra'el. This is our right. The existence—truthful existence.

What happened to us when our homeland was taken from us? I accompanied you this morning, Mr. President, to Yad Vashem. With your own eyes you saw the fate of our people when this homeland was taken from it. It cannot be told. Both of us agreed, Mr. President, that anyone who has not seen with his own eyes everything there is in Yad Vashem cannot understand what happened to this people when it was without a homeland, when its own homeland was taken from it. And both of us read a document dated 30th January 1939, where the word "Vernichtung"—annihilation—appears. If war breaks out, the Jewish race in Europe will be exterminated. Then, too, we were told that we should not pay attention to the racists. The whole world heard. Nobody came to save us. Not during the nine fateful, decisive months after the announcement was made, the like of which had not been seen since the Lord created man and man created the Devil.

And during those six years, too, when millions of our people, among them one and a half million of the little children of Israel who were burnt on all the strange beds, nobody came to save them, not from the East and not from the West. And because of this, we took a solemn oath, this entire generation—the generation of extermination and revival—that we would never again put our people in danger, that we would never again put our women and our children, whom it is our duty to defend—if there is a need for this, even at the cost of our lives—in the Hell of the exterminating fire of an enemy. It is our duty for generations to come to remember that certain things said about our people must be taken with complete seriousness. And we must not, Heaven forbid, for the sake of the future of our people accept any advice whatsoever against taking these things seriously.

President Sadat knows and he knew from us before he came to Jerusalem that we have a different position from his with regard to the permanent borders between us and our neighbors. However, I say to the President of Egypt and to all our neighbors: Do not say, there is not, there will not be negotiations about any particular issue. I propose, with the agreement of the decisive majority of this parliament, that everything be open to negotiation. Anyone who says, with reference to relations between the Arab people, or the Arab peoples around us, and the State of Israel, that there are things which should be omitted from negotiations is taking upon himself a grave responsibility; everything can be negotiated. No side will say the contrary. No side will present prior conditions. We shall conduct the negotiations honorably. If there are differences of opinion between us, this is not unusual. Anyone who has studied the histories of wars and the signing of peace treaties knows that all negotiations over a peace treaty began with differences of opinion between the sides. And in the course of the negotiations they came to an agreement which permitted the signing of peace treaties and agreements. And this is the road we propose to take.

Source: "Begin's Address to the Knesset," *Summary of World Broadcasts: The Middle East and Africa* 5672, D (1977): 8–12. Courtesy of BBC Monitoring.

80. Palestine Six-Point Program, December 4, 1977

Introduction

Sadat's visit to Israel and Egypt's opening of peace negotiations were anathema to the Palestine Liberation Organization (PLO), which adhered to its uncompromising position of refusing to recognize or accept the existence of Israel. Radical Arab leaders vilified Sadat as a traitor to the Arab cause. Meeting in Tripoli, Libya, two weeks later, during the Arab Summit League Conference, the PLO condemned Sadat's visit, affirmed its continuing rejection of United Nations (UN) Security Council Resolutions 242 and 338 and all international negotiations based on these, and announced the formation of a "Steadfastness and Confrontation Front" of the PLO. The more radical Arab states—Libya, Algeria, Iraq, Yemen, and Syria—joined in total opposition to any acceptance of Israel. They also announced a "political boycott" of Egypt. The PLO's adamant opposition to all dealings with Israel perhaps made it easier for Sadat, over the next year, to be satisfied with vague assurances from the Israeli government that it would respect the rights of the Palestinians, with no concrete guarantees as to how this was to be accomplished. The Six-Point Program was also a demonstration of deep divisions within the Arab community between the radical states that accepted this declaration and those more pragmatic governments, such as Egypt and Saudi Arabia, that were prepared to accept Israel's existence as a fait accompli and deal with it on that basis. The following day the Arab League Summit nonetheless endorsed the PLO Six-Point Program and the creation of the "Steadfastness and Confrontation Front." The Arab League also denounced Sadat's visit to Israel as a betrayal of the Palestinian cause, proclaimed its intention of working to frustrate his efforts to negotiate a settlement with Israel, suspended Egypt's membership of the Arab League and all political and diplomatic dealings with Egypt, announced economic sanctions on all Egyptians who did any business with Israel, and called on its member states to emulate its own policies.

Primary Source

In the wake of Sadat's treasonous visit to the Zionist entity, all factions of the Palestinian Resistance Movement have decided to make a practical answer to this step. On this basis, they met and issued the following document:

We, all factions of the PLO, announce the following:

First: We call for the formation of a "Steadfastness and Confrontation Front" composed of Libya, Algeria, Iraq, Democratic Yemen, Syria and the PLO, to oppose all capitulationist solutions planned by imperialism, Zionism and their Arab tools.

Second: We fully condemn any Arab party in the Tripoli Summit which rejects the formation of this Front, and we announce this.

Third: We reaffirm our rejection of Security Council resolutions 242 and 338.

Fourth: We reaffirm our rejection of all international conferences based on these two resolutions, including the Geneva Conference.

Fifth: To strive for the realization of the Palestinian people's rights to return and self-determination within the context of an independent Palestinian national state on any part of Palestinian land, without reconciliation, recognition or negotiations, as an interim aim of the Palestinian Revolution.

Sixth: To apply the measures related to the political boycott of the Sadat regime.

In the name of all the factions, we ratify this unificatory document:

- —The Palestinian National Liberation Movement, Fateh: Abu Ayyad [Salah Khalaf]
- —The Popular Front for the Liberation of Palestine: Dr. George Habbash
- —The Democratic Front for the Liberation of Palestine: Nayef Hawatmeh
- —The P.F.L.P.—General Command: Ahmad Jabril
- —Vanguards of the People's Liberation War, Saiqa: Zuhair Muhsin
- —Arab Liberation Front: Abdul-Rahim Ahmad
- —Palestinian Liberation Front: Talaat Ya'qoub
- —P.L.O.: Hamed Abu-Sitta.

Source: Library of Congress and Clyde R. Mark, *The Search for Peace in the Middle East: Documents and Statements, 1967–79; Report Prepared for the Subcommittee on Europe and the Middle East of the Committee on Foreign Affairs, U.S. House of Representatives* (Washington, DC: U.S. Government Printing Office, 1979), 462.

81. Framework for Peace in the Middle East, September 17, 1978

Introduction

President Jimmy Carter came to office in 1977 determined to seek a lasting Middle East peace settlement, one that would reconcile the warring parties and allow Israel and its neighbors to coexist. In 1977 his administration made protracted but ultimately unavailing efforts to call a peace conference of all parties to the Arab-Israeli conflict in order to reach a comprehensive settlement. Egyptian president Anwar Sadat then made peace overtures to Israel and in November 1977 delivered a highly publicized address to the Israeli Knesset calling for peace. Even so, negotiations between Israel and Egypt for a peace treaty that would end the formal state of war between the two countries, the legacy of four Arab-Israeli conflicts, soon broke down. Israeli demands that Egypt allow Israeli settlers to remain in the Sinai area and grant Israel air bases and oil rights there irritated the Egyptians, while Sadat's stipulations that any agreement include understandings on the Palestinian problem alienated Israeli prime minister Menachem Begin, even though the latter had already in December 1977 promised Arab inhabitants of the Israeli-occupied West Bank and Gaza Strip a large degree of autonomy. After a hiatus of some months, Carter, who had made peace in the Middle East a high priority of his administration's foreign policy objectives, stepped in and invited both Sadat and Begin to attend a summit meeting with Carter in the United States. The Camp David Accords established an agreement under whose terms the two countries could work to secure peace in the Middle East. The Camp David Accords explicitly stated that the framework it laid out was intended as a model not just for the Israel-Egyptian peace agreement but also for similar treaties with Israel's other Arab neighbors. It reaffirmed the principles of United Nations (UN) Security Council Resolutions 242 and 334 and the need to establish secure and recognized borders for all states involved, including Israel. The Camp David Accords envisaged that Israel would grant Palestinian Arabs in the occupied West Bank and Gaza substantial autonomy, arrangements that conceivably might ultimately lead to the establishment of a Palestinian state, and that Israel would withdraw from the Sinai Peninsula, but Egypt would largely demilitarize the area, with a border zone to be controlled by UN forces. The talks, hosted by Carter at the presidential retreat at Camp David, Maryland, are generally considered a high point of his administration. While Carter and his subordinates had a difficult time acting as brokers between two men who personally disliked and distrusted each other, the summit nonetheless marked the first occasion on which top Arab and Israeli leaders were able to meet and negotiate in a relatively civilized atmosphere. Both Egypt and Israel gained substantially, enhancing their military security and receiving lavish economic assistance from the United States. As before, however, other Arab leaders and nations publicly repudiated and condemned these accords and denounced Sadat as a traitor to the broader Arab cause, a demonstration of how deeply entrenched hatred of Israel had become in the Arab world, a major barrier to the negotiation of further such settlements.

Primary Source

Muhammad Anwar al-Sadat, President of the Arab Republic of Egypt, and Menachem Begin, Prime Minister of Israel, met with Jimmy Carter, President of the United States of America, at Camp David from September 5 to September 17, 1978, and have agreed on the following framework for peace in the Middle East. They invite other parties to the Arab-Israel conflict to adhere to it.

Preamble
The search for peace in the Middle East must be guided by the following:

The agreed basis for a peaceful settlement of the conflict between Israel and its neighbors is United Nations Security Council Resolution 242, in all its parts.

After four wars during 30 years, despite intensive human efforts, the Middle East, which is the cradle of civilization and the birthplace of three great religions, does not enjoy the blessings of peace. The people of the Middle East yearn for peace so that the vast human and natural resources of the region can be turned to the pursuits of peace and so that this area can become a model for coexistence and cooperation among nations.

The historic initiative of President Sadat in visiting Jerusalem and the reception accorded to him by the parliament, government and people of Israel, and the reciprocal visit of Prime Minister Begin to Ismailia, the peace proposals made by both leaders, as well as the warm reception of these missions by the peoples of both countries, have created an unprecedented opportunity for peace which must not be lost if this generation and future generations are to be spared the tragedies of war.

The provisions of the Charter of the United Nations and the other accepted norms of international law and legitimacy now provide accepted standards for the conduct of relations among all states.

To achieve a relationship of peace, in the spirit of Article 2 of the United Nations Charter, future negotiations between Israel and any neighbor prepared to negotiate peace and security with it are necessary for the purpose of carrying out all the provisions and principles of Resolutions 242 and 338.

Peace requires respect for the sovereignty, territorial integrity and political independence of every state in the area and their right to live in peace within secure and recognized boundaries free from threats or acts of force. Progress toward that goal can accelerate movement toward a new era of reconciliation in the Middle East marked by cooperation in promoting economic development, in maintaining stability and in assuring security.

Security is enhanced by a relationship of peace and by cooperation between nations which enjoy normal relations. In addition, under the terms of peace treaties, the parties can, on the basis of reciprocity, agree to special security arrangements such as demilitarized zones, limited armaments areas, early warning stations, the presence of international forces, liaison, agreed measures for monitoring and other arrangements that they agree are useful.

Framework
Taking these factors into account, the parties are determined to reach a just, comprehensive, and durable settlement of the Middle East conflict through the conclusion of peace treaties based on Security Council resolutions 242 and 338 in all their parts. Their purpose is

to achieve peace and good neighborly relations. They recognize that for peace to endure, it must involve all those who have been most deeply affected by the conflict. They therefore agree that this framework, as appropriate, is intended by them to constitute a basis for peace not only between Egypt and Israel, but also between Israel and each of its other neighbors which is prepared to negotiate peace with Israel on this basis. With that objective in mind, they have agreed to proceed as follows:

A. West Bank and Gaza

1. Egypt, Israel, Jordan and the representatives of the Palestinian people should participate in negotiations on the resolution of the Palestinian problem in all its aspects. To achieve that objective, negotiations relating to the West Bank and Gaza should proceed in three stages:

   a. Egypt and Israel agree that, in order to ensure a peaceful and orderly transfer of authority, and taking into account the security concerns of all the parties, there should be transitional arrangements for the West Bank and Gaza for a period not exceeding five years. In order to provide full autonomy to the inhabitants, under these arrangements the Israeli military government and its civilian administration will be withdrawn as soon as a self-governing authority has been freely elected by the inhabitants of these areas to replace the existing military government. To negotiate the details of a transitional arrangement, Jordan will be invited to join the negotiations on the basis of this framework. These new arrangements should give due consideration both to the principle of self-government by the inhabitants of these territories and to the legitimate security concerns of the parties involved.

   b. Egypt, Israel, and Jordan will agree on the modalities for establishing elected self-governing authority in the West Bank and Gaza. The delegations of Egypt and Jordan may include Palestinians from the West Bank and Gaza or other Palestinians as mutually agreed. The parties will negotiate an agreement which will define the powers and responsibilities of the self-governing authority to be exercised in the West Bank and Gaza. A withdrawal of Israeli armed forces will take place and there will be a redeployment of the remaining Israeli forces into specified security locations. The agreement will also include arrangements for assuring internal and external security and public order. A strong local police force will be established, which may include Jordanian citizens. In addition, Israeli and Jordanian forces will participate in joint patrols and in the manning of control posts to assure the security of the borders.

   c. When the self-governing authority (administrative council) in the West Bank and Gaza is established and inaugurated, the transitional period of five years will begin. As soon as possible, but not later than the third year after the beginning of the transitional period, negotiations will take place to determine the final status of the West Bank and Gaza and its rela-

tionship with its neighbors and to conclude a peace treaty between Israel and Jordan by the end of the transitional period. These negotiations will be conducted among Egypt, Israel, Jordan and the elected representatives of the inhabitants of the West Bank and Gaza. Two separate but related committees will be convened, one committee, consisting of representatives of the four parties which will negotiate and agree on the final status of the West Bank and Gaza, and its relationship with its neighbors, and the second committee, consisting of representatives of Israel and representatives of Jordan to be joined by the elected representatives of the inhabitants of the West Bank and Gaza, to negotiate the peace treaty between Israel and Jordan, taking into account the agreement reached in the final status of the West Bank and Gaza. The negotiations shall be based on all the provisions and principles of UN Security Council Resolution 242. The negotiations will resolve, among other matters, the location of the boundaries and the nature of the security arrangements. The solution from the negotiations must also recognize the legitimate right of the Palestinian peoples and their just requirements. In this way, the Palestinians will participate in the determination of their own future through:

   i.   The negotiations among Egypt, Israel, Jordan and the representatives of the inhabitants of the West Bank and Gaza to agree on the final status of the West Bank and Gaza and other outstanding issues by the end of the transitional period.

   ii. Submitting their agreements to a vote by the elected representatives of the inhabitants of the West Bank and Gaza.

   iii. Providing for the elected representatives of the inhabitants of the West Bank and Gaza to decide how they shall govern themselves consistent with the provisions of their agreement.

   iv. Participating as stated above in the work of the committee negotiating the peace treaty between Israel and Jordan.

   d. All necessary measures will be taken and provisions made to assure the security of Israel and its neighbors during the transitional period and beyond. To assist in providing such security, a strong local police force will be constituted by the self-governing authority. It will be composed of inhabitants of the West Bank and Gaza. The police will maintain liaison on internal security matters with the designated Israeli, Jordanian, and Egyptian officers.

   e. During the transitional period, representatives of Egypt, Israel, Jordan, and the self-governing authority will constitute a continuing committee to decide by agreement on the modalities of admission of persons displaced from the West Bank and Gaza in 1967, together with necessary measures to prevent disruption and disorder. Other matters of common concern may also be dealt with by this committee.

   f. Egypt and Israel will work with each other and with other interested parties to establish agreed procedures for a prompt, just and permanent implementation of the resolution of the refugee problem.

B. Egypt-Israel

1. Egypt-Israel undertake not to resort to the threat or the use of force to settle disputes. Any disputes shall be settled by peaceful means in accordance with the provisions of Article 33 of the U.N. Charter.

2. In order to achieve peace between them, the parties agree to negotiate in good faith with a goal of concluding within three months from the signing of the Framework a peace treaty between them while inviting the other parties to the conflict to proceed simultaneously to negotiate and conclude similar peace treaties with a view to achieving a comprehensive peace in the area. The Framework for the Conclusion of a Peace Treaty between Egypt and Israel will govern the peace negotiations between them. The parties will agree on the modalities and the timetable for the implementation of their obligations under the treaty.

C. Associated Principles

1. Egypt and Israel state that the principles and provisions described below should apply to peace treaties between Israel and each of its neighbors—Egypt, Jordan, Syria and Lebanon.

2. Signatories shall establish among themselves relationships normal to states at peace with one another. To this end, they should undertake to abide by all the provisions of the U.N. Charter. Steps to be taken in this respect include:

    a. full recognition;

    b. abolishing economic boycotts;

    c. guaranteeing that under their jurisdiction the citizens of the other parties shall enjoy the protection of the due process of law.

3. Signatories should explore possibilities for economic development in the context of final peace treaties, with the objective of contributing to the atmosphere of peace, cooperation and friendship which is their common goal.

4. Claims commissions may be established for the mutual settlement of all financial claims.

5. The United States shall be invited to participate in the talks on matters related to the modalities of the implementation of the agreements and working out the timetable for the carrying out of the obligations of the parties.

6. The United Nations Security Council shall be requested to endorse the peace treaties and ensure that their provisions shall not be violated. The permanent members of the Security Council shall be requested to underwrite the peace treaties and ensure respect for their provisions. They shall be requested to conform their policies and actions with the undertakings contained in this Framework.

For the Government of Israel: Menachem Begin
For the Government of the Arab Republic of Egypt: Muhammed Anwar al-Sadat
Witnessed by Jimmy Carter, President of the United States of America

Framework for the Conclusion of a Peace Treaty between Egypt and Israel

In order to achieve peace between them, Israel and Egypt agree to negotiate in good faith with a goal of concluding within three months of the signing of this framework a peace treaty between them:

It is agreed that:

The site of the negotiations will be under a United Nations flag at a location or locations to be mutually agreed.

All of the principles of U.N. Resolution 242 will apply in this resolution of the dispute between Israel and Egypt.

Unless otherwise mutually agreed, terms of the peace treaty will be implemented between two and three years after the peace treaty is signed.

The following matters are agreed between the parties:

1. the full exercise of Egyptian sovereignty up to the internationally recognized border between Egypt and mandated Palestine;

2. the withdrawal of Israeli armed forces from the Sinai;

3. the use of airfields left by the Israelis near al-Arish, Rafah, Ras en-Naqb, and Sharm el-Sheikh for civilian purposes only, including possible commercial use only by all nations;

4. the right of free passage by ships of Israel through the Gulf of Suez and the Suez Canal on the basis of the Constantinople Convention of 1888 applying to all nations; the Strait of Tiran and Gulf of Aqaba are international waterways to be open to all nations for unimpeded and nonsuspendable freedom of navigation and overflight;

5. the construction of a highway between the Sinai and Jordan near Eilat with guaranteed free and peaceful passage by Egypt and Jordan; and

6. the stationing of military forces listed below.

Stationing of Forces

No more than one division (mechanized or infantry) of Egyptian armed forces will be stationed within an area lying approximately 50 km. (30 miles) east of the Gulf of Suez and the Suez Canal.

Only United Nations forces and civil police equipped with light weapons to perform normal police functions will be stationed within an area lying west of the international border and the Gulf of Aqaba, varying in width from 20 km. (12 miles) to 40 km. (24 miles).

In the area within 3 km. (1.8 miles) east of the international border there will be Israeli limited military forces not to exceed four infantry battalions and United Nations observers.

Border patrol units not to exceed three battalions will supplement the civil police in maintaining order in the area not included above.

The exact demarcation of the above areas will be as decided during the peace negotiations.

Early warning stations may exist to insure compliance with the terms of the agreement.

United Nations forces will be stationed:

1. in part of the area in the Sinai lying within about 20 km. of the Mediterranean Sea and adjacent to the international border, and
2. in the Sharm el-Sheikh area to insure freedom of passage through the Strait of Tiran; and these forces will not be removed unless such removal is approved by the Security Council of the United Nations with a unanimous vote of the five permanent members.

After a peace treaty is signed, and after the interim withdrawal is complete, normal relations will be established between Egypt and Israel, including: full recognition, including diplomatic, economic and cultural relations; termination of economic boycotts and barriers to the free movement of goods and people; and mutual protection of citizens by the due process of law.

Interim Withdrawal

Between three months and nine months after the signing of the peace treaty, all Israeli forces will withdraw east of a line extending from a point east of El-Arish to Ras Muhammad, the exact location of this line to be determined by mutual agreement.

For the Government of the Arab Republic of Egypt: Muhammed Anwar al-Sadat
For the Government of Israel: Menachem Begin
Witnessed by: Jimmy Carter, President of the United States of America

Source: "A Framework for Peace in the Middle East Agreed at Camp David," *Department of State Bulletin* 78(2019) (1978): 7–10.

82. Arab League Summit Conference Final Statement [Excerpt], November 5, 1978

Introduction

The Arab League welcomed the Camp David Accords with predictable hostility. Meeting in Baghdad, the Iraqi capital, in November 1978, the Arab League leaders proclaimed their unwavering support for the Palestinians and their opposition to "the Zionist enemy." Arab solidarity transcended all other causes, they proclaimed, making opposition to Israel and backing the Palestinians vital interests even for those countries that had not lost actual territory to Israel. The Arab states pledged not to interfere in internal Palestinian affairs but instead to give all the assistance they could to the Palestinian cause. Unilateral negotiations with Israel by any state or organization were condemned and were declared illegitimate unless they received endorsement from an Arab summit conference. The conference's final statement specifically denounced the Israeli-Egyptian Camp David Accords as falling "outside the framework of collective Arab responsibility" as defined by successive Arab summit conferences. The communiqué therefore urged Egypt to repudiate the Camp David Accords and refuse to sign any treaty that resulted from them. In an interesting development, however, the conference's final declaration fell short of demanding the complete destruction of Israel, merely stating that any "just peace" must be based on Israeli withdrawal from all the territories occupied after the 1967 war and on recognition of the right of the Palestinian Arabs to "establish their independent state on their national soil." The conference also called on the Arabs to mount large-scale international propaganda efforts to explain the Palestinian cause to the rest of the world.

Primary Source

By the initiative of the Government of the Republic of Iraq and at the invitation of President Ahmad Hasan al-Bakr, the ninth Arab summit conference convened in Baghdad November 2–5, 1978.

In a high spirit of pan-Arab responsibility and joint concern about the unity of the Arab stand, the conference studied confrontation of the dangers and challenges threatening the Arab nation, particularly after the results of the Camp David agreements signed by the Egyptian government and the effects of these agreements on the Arab struggle to face the Zionist aggression against the Arab nation.

Proceeding from the principles in which the Arab nation believes, acting on the unity of Arab destiny and complying with the traditions of joint Arab action, the Arab summit conference has emphasized the following basic principles:

First: The Palestinian question is a fateful Arab issue and is the essence of the conflict with the Zionist enemy. The sons of the Arab nation and all the Arab countries are concerned with it and are obliged to struggle for its sake and to offer all material and moral sacrifices for this cause. The struggle to regain Arab rights in Palestine and in the occupied Arab territory is a general Arab responsibility. All Arabs must share this responsibility, each in accord with his military, economic, political and other abilities.

The conflict with the Zionist enemy exceeds the framework of the conflict of the countries whose territory was occupied in 1967, and it includes the whole Arab nation because of the military, political, economic and cultural danger the Zionist enemy constitutes against the entire Arab nation and its substantial and pan-Arab interests, civilization and destiny. This places on all the countries of the Arab nation the responsibility to share in this conflict with all the resources it possesses.

Second: All the Arab countries must offer all forms of support, backing and facilities to all forms of the struggle of the Palestinian resistance, supporting the PLO in its capacity as the sole legitimate representative of the Palestinian people inside and outside the occupied land, struggling for liberation and restoration of the national rights of its people, including their right to return to their homeland, to determine their future and to establish their independent state on their national soil. The Arab States pledge to preserve Palestinian national unity and not to interfere in the internal affairs of the Palestinian action.

Third: Commitment is reaffirmed to the resolutions of the Arab summit conferences, particularly the sixth and seventh summit conferences of Algiers and Rabat.

Fourth: In light of the above principles it is impermissible for any side to act unilaterally in solving the Palestinian question in particular and the Arab-Zionist conflict in general.

Fifth: No solution shall be accepted unless it is associated with a resolution by an Arab summit conference convened for this purpose.

The conference discussed the two agreements signed by the Egyptian Government at Camp David and considered that they harm the Palestinian people's rights and the rights of the Arab nation in Palestine and the occupied Arab territory. The conference considered that these agreements took place outside the framework of collective Arab responsibility and are opposed to the resolutions of the Arab summit conferences, particularly the resolutions of the Algiers and Rabat summit conferences, the Arab League Charter and the UN resolutions on the Palestinian question. The conference considers that these agreements do not lead to the just peace that the Arab nation desires. Therefore, the conference has decided not to approve of these two agreements and not to deal with their results. The conference has also rejected all the political, economic, legal and other effects resulting from them.

The conference decided to call on the Egyptian Government to go back on these agreements and not to sign any reconciliation treaty with the enemy. The conference hopes that Egypt will return to the fold of joint Arab action, and not act unilaterally in the affairs of the Arab-Zionist conflict. In this respect the conference adopted a number of resolutions to face the new stage and to safeguard the aims and interests of the Arab nation out of faith that with its material and moral resources the Arab nation is capable of confronting the difficult circumstances and all challenges, just as it has always been throughout history, because it is defending right, justice and its national existence.

The conference stressed the need to unify all the Arab efforts in order to remedy the strategic imbalance that has resulted from Egypt's withdrawal from the confrontation arena.

The conference decided that the countries that possess readiness and capability will coordinate participation with effective efforts. The conference also stressed the need to adhere to the regulations of Arab boycott and to tighten application of its provisions.

The conference studied means to develop Arab information media beamed abroad for the benefit of the just Arab issues. The conference decided to hold annual meetings for the Arab summit conferences and decided that the month of November will be the date.

After studying the Arab and international situation, the conference asserts the Arab nation's commitment to a just peace based on the comprehensive Israeli withdrawal from the Arab territories occupied in 1967, including Arab Jerusalem, and the guaranteeing of the inalienable national rights of the Palestinian Arab people including the right to establish their independent state on their national soil.

The conference decided to embark on large scale international activity to explain the just rights of the Palestinian people and the Arab nation. . . .

[. . .]

Source: "Arab League Summit Conference Final Statement," Foreign Broadcast Information Service, *F.B.I.S.-Daily Report Middle East and North Africa,* November 6, 1978.

83. Palestinian National Council Political and Organizational Program [Excerpt], January 15–23, 1979

Introduction

The Palestine Liberation Organization (PLO) denounced the Camp David Accords in terms even more heated than those used by the Arab

League. The Palestinian National Council, meeting in January 1979, reaffirmed the position that the PLO was the only body entitled to speak on behalf of Palestinian Arabs. All Arab states were exhorted to support the PLO and stringently adhere to its policies on Palestinian issues. Whereas the Arab League implicitly accepted United Nations (UN) Security Council 242, the PLO forthrightly rejected it, proclaiming the right of the Palestinian people to return to what had been their homeland, and stated that escalating armed struggle would be essential to achieving this. The Egyptian people were urged to reject the Camp David Accords and rise up against President Anwar Sadat. The PLO was alarmed by the growing number of settlements that Israel had established in the West Bank and East Jerusalem. PLO officials totally rejected the Israeli-backed scheme for granting greater autonomy to the West Bank Arabs, which they perceived primarily as a means whereby Israel sought to dilute PLO influence by working with other more malleable Palestinian Arab leaders and groups. The PLO was also angered by the March 1978 Israeli military intervention in the small, weak neighboring country of Lebanon, where many PLO units had moved after King Hussein expelled them from Jordan, using Lebanese territory as a base to launch attacks against Israel. The Israeli incursion failed to restore order in Lebanon, and for years to come a state of virtual civil war prevailed there, with Israeli-backed Maronite Christian militias fighting the PLO, Syrian forces, and sympathetic Lebanese elements. The PLO statement therefore demanded that other countries respect both Lebanon's "sovereignty" and the special position the PLO enjoyed there. Conclusion of the Camp David Accords further radicalized the PLO's official stance. Condemning U.S. policy in seeking to broker a peace settlement unacceptable to the Palestinians as "aggression," the PLO proclaimed its intention of turning for support to the Soviet Union and other socialist countries. It also expressed its solidarity with other revolutionary national liberation movements, especially black struggles against white rule in South Africa, Zimbabwe, and Namibia. Ironically, the Soviet Union proved itself a somewhat unsatisfactory ally to the PLO. Speaking to the UN in September 1979, Soviet foreign minister Andrei Gromyko expressed great sympathy for the "legitimate rights of the Arab people including the right to create their own state," warned that the separate Egyptian-Israeli peace treaty had "resolve[d] nothing," and called upon all states present to realize "how vast is the tragedy of the Arab peoples of Palestine." Even so, Gromyko endorsed UN Security Council Resolution 242 and broke with the PLO when he warned that a lasting Middle East peace settlement would require not only "that Israel should end its occupation of all the Arab lands it seized in 1967" but also "that the right of all states in the Middle East, including Israel, to independent existence under conditions of peace be effectively guaranteed."

Primary Source

The US settlement of the Arab-Zionist conflict embodied in the Camp David agreements poses grave threats to the cause of Palestine and of Arab national liberation. That settlement condones the Zionist enemy's continued usurpation of the national soil of Palestine, and abrogates the inalienable right of the Palestinian Arab people to their homeland, Palestine, as well as their right to return to it and their right to self-determination and to the exercise of their national independence on their soil. It dissipates other Arab territories and overrides the PLO, the leader of our people's national struggle and their sole legitimate representative and spokesman expressing their will.

In addition, these agreements violate Palestinian, Arab and international legitimacy and pave the way for tighter imperialist and Zionist control over our Arab region and Africa, employing the Egyptian regime, in the context of its alliance with imperialism and Zionism, as a tool for the repression of the Arab and African national liberation movements.

Motivated by our awareness of the gravity of this new conspiracy and its implications and by our national responsibilities in the PLO, which represents our Palestinian Arab people with all their national groups and forces, we are obliged to reject this new conspiratorial scheme, to confront it and to defend our people and their inalienable national rights to their homeland, Palestine, as well as to safeguard our Palestinian revolution.

The courageous position adopted by our Palestinian masses inside and outside the occupied homeland and by the masses of our Arab nation through their rejection of the Camp David agreements and their open determination to confront this new conspiracy against our people and their inalienable national rights and our Arab nation strengthens our resolve to resist this conspiracy and our faith in defeating it.

At the same time, we shoulder a great responsibility which can be carried out only by adopting a united national and popular stand, within the framework of the PLO.

In response to the will of our people and to the challenges that we face, and motivated by our faith in national unity within the PLO as the sole means to achieve victory; basing ourselves upon the Palestine National Charter, the resolutions of the Palestine National Councils and the Tripoli document which established unity among the various organizations of the Palestinian revolution; believing in the right of our people to establish a democratic state on the whole of national soil and in order to confront this critical and dangerous stage in the struggle of our people, we, the representatives of all organizations of the Revolution and Palestinian national forces, declare the following:

In the Palestinian Sphere

1. [That we] adhere to the inalienable national rights of our people to their homeland, Palestine, and to their right to return and to

self-determination on their soil without foreign interference, and to their right to establish their independent state on their soil unconditionally.

2. [That we shall] defend the PLO and adhere to it as the sole legitimate representative of our people, as leader of their national struggle and as their spokesman in all Arab and international forums; resist all attempts to harm, override or circumvent the PLO, or to create alternatives or partners to it as regards representation of our Palestinian people; adhere to the resolutions of the Arab summits of Algiers and Rabat and to UN resolutions—especially resolutions 3236 and 3237—which affirm our inalienable national rights as well as Arab and international recognition of the PLO as the sole legitimate representative of the Palestinian people.

3. [That we] resolve firmly to continue and escalate the armed struggle and use all other forms of political and mass struggle, especially inside the occupied homeland which is the principal arena of conflict with the Zionist enemy, in order to achieve the inalienable and non-negotiable national rights of the Palestinian Arab people.

4. [That we] affirm that the problem of Palestine is the crux and the basis of the Arab-Zionist conflict, and [we] reject all resolutions, agreements and settlements that do not recognize or that impinge upon the inalienable rights of our people to their homeland, Palestine, including their right to return, to self-determination and to the establishment of their independent national state. This applies in particular to Security Council resolution 242.

5. [That we] reject and resist the self-rule scheme in the occupied homeland, which entrenches Zionist settler colonization of our occupied land and denies the rights of our Palestinian people.

6. [That we] affirm the unity of our Palestinian Arab people inside and outside the occupied homeland, and their sole representation through the PLO; [we shall] resist all attempts and schemes that seek to divide our people or to circumvent the PLO; [and] work to support the struggle of our people in the occupied territories and to fortify their unity and their steadfastness.

7. [That we shall] consolidate the framework of the Palestinian National Front inside Palestine since it is an integral part of the PLO, and [shall] furnish it with all means of political and financial aid so that it can mobilize our masses inside to face the Zionist occupation, its schemes and its projects which are inimical to our people and to their inalienable national rights.

8. [That we] cling to Palestine as the historic homeland of the Palestinian people for which there can be no substitute; [and] resist all schemes for resettlement or for an "alternative homeland", which the imperialist and Zionist enemy is proposing in order to liquidate the Palestinian cause and Palestinian national struggle, and to circumvent our right to return.

In the Arab Sphere

1. [That we] emphasize that the task of confronting the Camp David agreements, their annexes and their consequences, with the fateful dangers they pose to the cause of Arab struggle, is the responsibility of all the Arab masses and their national and progressive forces, [and] that the Arab Front for Steadfastness and Confrontation, with Syria and the PLO as its central link, is the primary base from which to confront the US-Zionist conspiratorial settlement.

2. [That we must] work to fortify and strengthen the Arab Front for Steadfastness and Confrontation and to expand its scope on the basis of resistance to imperialist and Zionist settlement schemes; adhere to the objective of liberating the occupied Palestinian and Arab territories and to the inalienable national rights of the Palestinian people, and not dissipate or infringe upon these rights; [and we must] furnish all possible mass and financial support to the Arab Front for Steadfastness and Confrontation, especially to the PLO and the Syrian Arab region.

3. The PLO calls upon all national and progressive parties, movements and forces in the Arab homeland to support the Arab Front for Steadfastness and Confrontation and to furnish it with all possible mass and financial aid. It further calls upon them to unite and to struggle on the basis of resistance to the imperialist and Zionist schemes for settlement.

4.
   a) The PLO asserts its firm commitment to the unity, Arab character and independence of Lebanon, its respect for Lebanese sovereignty and its adherence to the Cairo Agreement and its sequels which regulate relations between the PLO and Lebanon's legitimate authority.
   b) The PLO highly values the role that has been and is being played by the Lebanese people and their national, progressive and patriotic forces in support of and in defence of the struggle of the Palestinian people. In expressing its pride in the solidarity between our Palestinian people and the people of Lebanon and their national, progressive and patriotic forces in defence of Lebanese territory and of the Palestinian revolution against Zionist aggression, its schemes and its local agents, the PLO emphasizes the importance of continuing and strengthening this solidarity.

5.
   a) The PLO affirms the special character of the relationship linking the two fraternal peoples, Palestinian and Jordanian, and its concern that the solidarity between these two fraternal peoples should continue.

b) The PLO declares its adherence to the resolutions of the Arab summits of Algiers and Rabat which affirm that the PLO is the sole legitimate representative of the Palestinian people and that our people have a right to establish their national and independent state. The PLO considers that the commitment of the Jordanian regime to these resolutions, its rejection of the Camp David agreements and their aftermath as well as its refusal to be involved in them and its role in enabling the PLO to exercise its responsibility for militant and mass struggle against the Zionist enemy, constitute the basis that governs relations between the PLO and the Jordanian regime.

6. The PLO affirms its right to exercise its responsibility for struggle on the Arab and national levels, and across any Arab territory, in order to liberate the occupied Palestinian territories.

7. The PLO declares that its policies toward and its relations with any Arab regime are determined by the policy of that regime as regards adherence to the resolutions of the summits of Algiers and Rabat and to the rejection of and the opposition to the Camp David agreements with their annexes and their consequences.

8. The PLO calls upon all Arab and national forces and all national and friendly regimes to support and aid the Egyptian people and their national movement to enable them to confront the Sadat conspiracy and to foil the Camp David agreement and its effect upon the Egyptian people, their Arabism and their history of struggle against Zionism and imperialism.

In the International Sphere

1. The role played by the US against our Palestinian people and their national struggle and against the Arab national liberation movement and its objectives of liberation and independence, whether this is manifested in its support of the Zionist entity or through its agents in the Arab region, constitutes a naked aggression against our people and their national cause. The PLO, by acting in solidarity with all groups in the Arab national liberation struggle and their national and progressive forces and regimes, declares its determination to resist the policy, objectives and actions of the US in the region.

2. The PLO affirms the importance of alliance with the socialist countries, and first and foremost with the Soviet Union, since this alliance is a national necessity in the context of confronting American-Zionist conspiracies against the Palestine cause, the Arab national liberation movement and their achievements.

3. The PLO affirms the importance of consolidating its cooperation with the non-aligned, Islamic, African and friendly states which support the PLO and its struggle to achieve the national rights of the Palestinian people to return to their homeland, to self-determination and to establish their independent national state.

4. The PLO, as a national liberation movement, expresses its solidarity with national liberation movements throughout the world, especially with Zimbabwe, Namibia and South Africa, and its determination to consolidate relations of struggle with them since the fight against imperialism, Zionism and racism is a joint cause for all forces of liberation and progress in the world.

5. The PLO declares its firm adherence to the achievements won by Palestinian struggle in the international sphere, such as the wide international recognition accorded to the PLO and to the inalienable right of the Palestinian Arab people to their homeland, Palestine, their right to return, to self-determination and to the establishment of their independent national state on their national soil. These are the achievements embodied in UN resolutions adopted since 1974 and up to the present, especially resolutions 3236 and 3237. It underlines the right of the PLO to participate in all meetings and conferences that discuss the Palestine question on these bases and considers that any discussion or agreement that takes place in its absence about matters related to the Palestine question are totally invalid.

[...]

Source: "Political and Organizational Programme . . . Palestine National Council," *Wafa*, Palestine News Agency, January 18, 1979.

84. Israel-Egypt Peace Treaty, March 26, 1979

Introduction

In the face of fierce Arab League and Palestine Liberation Organization (PLO) opposition, the Camp David Peace Treaty, also known as the Egyptian-Israeli Peace Treaty, was signed in 1979 as an outcome of the 1978 Camp David Summit Conference that brought leaders from Israel and Egypt to U.S. president Jimmy Carter's Camp David retreat. During the 13-day conference, a framework for peace between Israel and Egypt was negotiated and formally agreed upon. The treaty ended the state of war between Egypt and Israel and established a fixed boundary between the two, setting aside the status of the Gaza Strip—home to numerous Palestine refugees—for future resolution. The two states also opened full diplomatic relations, exchanging ambassadors. In accordance with the treaty, the following year Israel returned most of the Sinai Peninsula to Egypt, a process completed in 1982. The treaty contained no references to Israel's earlier suggestions that Palestinian Arabs in the Gaza Strip and the West Bank would be granted a substantial degree of autonomy, although talks on the issue began in May 1979, with

Egyptian president Anwar Sadat urging the Israeli government to allow Palestinians in the occupied territories political freedoms far more extensive than those that Israeli officials were prepared to accord them. Western leaders and commentators greeted the treaty with enormous enthusiasm. Even relatively hard-line Israeli leaders, such as former prime minister Golda Meir, welcomed it, stating that it would ensure that their grandchildren could live in peace. Carter and others hoped that the peace treaty would prove a preliminary step to the subsequent negotiation of similar agreements between Israel and other Arab states, breaking the logjam blocking the conclusion of lasting Middle East peace settlements. In practice, fellow Arab states boycotted Egypt for making peace with Israel. In October 1981, moreover, Muslim extremist gunmen who resented the peace treaty assassinated Sadat, chief Egyptian architect of the Camp David Accords, while he was watching a military parade in Cairo, a discouraging omen for any Arab leader who might be tempted to emulate Sadat's efforts for peace.

Primary Source

PREAMBLE

The Government of the Arab Republic of Egypt and the Government of the State of Israel;

Convinced of the urgent necessity of the establishment of a just, comprehensive and lasting peace in the Middle East in accordance with Security Council Resolution 242 and Resolution 338;

Reaffirming their adherence to the 'Framework for Peace in the Middle East Agreed at Camp David,' dated September 17, 1978. . . .

Agree to the following provisions:

ARTICLE I

1. The state of war between the Parties will be terminated and peace will be established between them upon the exchange of instruments of ratification of this Treaty.

2. Israel will withdraw all its armed forces and civilians from the Sinai behind the international boundary between Egypt and mandated Palestine . . . and Egypt will resume the exercise of its full sovereignty over the Sinai.

3. Upon completion of the interim withdrawal . . . the Parties will establish normal and friendly relations. . . .

ARTICLE II

The permanent boundary between Egypt and Israel is the recognized international boundary between Egypt and the former mandated territory of Palestine . . . without prejudice to the issue of the Gaza Strip. . . .

ARTICLE IV

1. In order to provide maximum security for both Parties on the basis of reciprocity, agreed security arrangements will be established including limited force zones in Egyptian and Israeli territory, and United Nations forces and observers . . . and other security arrangements the Parties may agree upon. . . .

ARTICLE V

1. Ships of Israel, and cargoes destined for or coming from Israel, shall enjoy the right of free passage through the Suez Canal and its approaches through the Gulf of Suez and the Mediterranean Sea. . . . Israeli nationals, vessels and cargoes, as well as persons, vessels and cargoes destined for or coming from Israel, shall be accorded non-discriminatory treatment in all matters connected with usage of the canal.

2. The Parties consider the Strait of Tiran and the Gulf of Aqaba to be international waterways open to all nations for unimpeded and nonsuspendable freedom of navigation and overflight. The Parties will respect each other's right to navigation and overflight for access to either country through the Strait of Tiran and the Gulf of Aqaba.

[Annex I describes the details of Israeli withdrawal from the Sinai Peninsula over a three-year period. It also establishes several zones in the Sinai and surrounding territory in Egypt and Israel and the restricted distribution of military forces in these areas, including the distribution of United Nations forces.]

[Annex II is a map of the Sinai Peninsula and the agreed upon boundary between Egypt and Israel.]

[Annex III sets the terms for the normalization of relations between Egypt and Israel in regard to diplomacy, economics and trade, culture, the freedom of movement of the citizens of each nation, transportation and communication, human rights, and territorial waters.]

Source: "Treaty of Peace between the Arab Republic of Egypt and the State of Israel," *Department of State Bulletin* 79(2026) (1979): 3–14.

85. Hafez al-Assad, Condemnation of the Camp David Accords, March 8, 1980

Introduction

Political rivalries divided the Arab states. Within the Arab world Syria, which had lost the Golan Heights to Israel in 1967 and failed to regain them in 1973, sought to enhance its position at the expense of Egypt. Syrian President Hafez al-Assad, who seized power in 1970, headed a radical leftist-oriented Baath Party government that looked to the Soviet Union for military aid and economic support. He was less extreme than the Palestine Liberation Organization (PLO) in that he was prepared to accept a settlement along the lines of

United Nations (UN) Security Council Resolution 242 guaranteeing Israel's right to exist in return for withdrawal from the occupied territories. Unlike President Anwar Sadat of Egypt, however, al-Assad did not seek a separate U.S.-brokered peace with Israel, preferring the earlier format of a comprehensive international conference co-sponsored by the Soviet Union as well as the United States. Assailing Egypt's action in signing a bilateral peace treaty with Israel, in the spring of 1980 al-Assad condemned the Camp David settlement as one that left Israel in control of the occupied territories, where it was expanding Jewish settlements. He also complained that the U.S. government was too timid to restrain Israeli actions in the West Bank, the Gaza Strip, and Lebanon and identified itself completely with Israeli interests. Al-Assad therefore affirmed Syria's loyalty to the Soviet Union, pledging that he would resist all efforts to divide his country from its Soviet patron. The only real solution to the Middle East conflict, in his opinion, would be through the establishment of a genuinely independent Palestinian state. Al-Assad's statement was undoubtedly tailored to bolster Syria's position as a leader of the more radical Arab states and organizations. In the interests of attaining this status, he was prepared to defer efforts to persuade Israel to restore the Golan Heights to Syria.

Primary Source

To us, to the whole world and as outlined in the UN resolutions, peace means Israel's complete withdrawal from the occupied Arab territories and the acknowledgement of the Palestinians' inalienable rights, including their right to determine their own destiny and set up their independent state. Peace under the Camp David accords means Israel's false withdrawal from Sinai—and it has not yet withdrawn—so that eventually it would be in a position to take all Egypt.

To us, peace means that Arab flags should fly over the liberated territories. Under the Camp David accords, peace means that the Israeli flag should be hoisted in an official ceremony in Cairo, while Israel is still occupying Egyptian, Syrian and Palestinian territory and is still adamantly denying Palestinian rights.

To us, peace means we should exercise our free will. Under the Camp David accords, peace means that the al-Sadat regime should keep Egypt's doors wide open to a Zionist economic, cultural and psychological invasion. It also means that Israel should continue to expand settlements.

To us, peace means a step further toward Arab unity. Under the Camp David accords, peace means Egypt should disengage from the Arab nation and move closer to usurper and aggressor Israel.

We do not make any distinction between one Arab territory and another, while the Camp David partners insist on making a distinction between Egyptian territory and other Arab territories.

The whole world calls for the establishment of a Palestinian state, while al-Sadat and his two allies talk about autonomy. The whole world knows, and the Israeli opposition leaders confirm, that the autonomy farce is a figment of Begin's imagination which he presented during his visit to Ismailia. On the other hand, al-Sadat presents autonomy as the distillation of his genius and most ideal solution.

Israel stresses daily that it will not withdraw from the West Bank and Gaza at any time in the future, and al-Sadat does not stop speaking about great hopes for the success of the autonomy farce. Despite their meager means, our heroic people in the occupied territory are resisting and waging a mighty struggle against the plot. But al-Sadat is using every material and psychological pressure on these people to force them to surrender to the plot.

The world condemns Israel's policy and aggression and supports the just Arab cause. But al-Sadat considers his close friend Begin as the messenger of peace, and his own Arab nation as the enemy of peace. Al-Sadat makes peace with the Israeli leaders and slanders the Arab nation, to which he has turned his back, forgetting that Egypt is part of this nation.

As for the third party, or the full partner as they like to call it, or the honest broker as it likes to call itself, it is determined not to annoy the Israeli leaders even in words. It is not prepared to draw a line between U.S. and Israeli interests in this region. To the United States, therefore, Israeli interests must come first, before anything else.

The Palestine question is the central issue of our struggle and the substance of our cause. We consider the PLO the sole legitimate representative of the Palestinian people. We will continue to support and strengthen the Palestinian revolution against all potential dangers. Syria and the Palestinian revolution are in one trench, something which must be understood by both friend and foe.

I frankly and truly say that the Soviet Union is the real friend of all peoples fighting for their freedom and independence. In my opinion, the imperialists have discovered from experience that they cannot weaken this friendship. But this does not mean that they will stop their attempts to destroy this friendship if they can. We know that we need the assistance of this big friend in our current battle. We must not miscalculate. This is a big battle. Israel is backed by the United States with large quantities of sophisticated weapons. Therefore, how can we possibly shut our eyes to a maneuver aimed at dragging us into a conflict with this big friend and closing the door through which we obtain assistance in the fiercest confrontation that we and all Arabs have in this age?

Source: Walter Laqueur and Barry Rubin, eds., *The Israel-Arab Reader: A Documentary History of the Middle East Conflict* (New York: Penguin, 2001), 231–232.

86. European Council, Venice Declaration [Excerpt], June 12–13, 1980

Introduction

The fall of Mohammad Reza Shah Pahlavi of Iran in 1979 and his replacement by a radical Islamic regime, headed by Ayatollah Ruhollah Khomeini, drastically reduced oil sales to Western powers, leading to oil shortages and massive price increases that greatly intensified existing economic difficulties. These developments led to renewed European interest in reaching a permanent settlement of the Arab-Israeli dispute, something that the European powers hoped would remove at least one source of conflict in the volatile Middle East. They also recognized that U.S. president Jimmy Carter had expended all his political capital in negotiating the Israeli-Egyptian Camp David agreements, and given the political influence of the pro-Israeli lobby in the United States, no further progress on an Arab-Israeli peace settlement could be expected until after the November 1980 U.S. presidential election was over. Meeting at Venice in June 1980, the nine member states of the European Community (EC) issued a declaration giving their position on a potential settlement. Like most such proposals, it was based on the principles stated in United Nations (UN) Security Council Resolutions 242 and 338, namely, "the right to existence and to security of all the states in the region, including Israel, and justice for all the peoples, which implies the recognition of the legitimate rights of the Palestinian people." The European nations also made it clear that they would not recognize any unilateral Israeli attempts to change the status of Jerusalem and called upon Israel to withdraw from the occupied territories and cease establishing Jewish settlements in those areas. With decided optimism, which the signatories themselves almost certainly knew to be misplaced, they also called on all parties involved, implicitly including the Palestinians and other nonstate armed groups as well as all government militaries, to renounce the use of force. The EC member states announced their intention of opening exploratory consultations with all parties involved to try to determine the most fruitful route for opening a new peace initiative.

Primary Source

The Heads of State and Government and the Ministers for Foreign Affairs held a comprehensive exchange of views on all aspects of the present situation in the Middle East, including the state of negotiations resulting from the agreements signed between Egypt and Israel in March 1979. They agreed that growing tensions affecting this region constitute a serious danger and render a comprehensive solution to the Israeli-Arab conflict more necessary and pressing than ever.

The nine member states of the European Community consider that the traditional ties and common interests which link Europe to the Middle East oblige them to play a special role and now require them to work in a more concrete way towards peace.

[…]

… [T]he time has come to promote the recognition and implementation of the two principles universally accepted by the international community: the right to existence and to security of all States in the region, including Israel, and justice for all the peoples, which implies the recognition of the legitimate rights of the Palestinian people.

All of the countries in the area are entitled to live in peace within secure, recognized and guaranteed borders. The necessary guarantees for a peace settlement should be provided by the United Nations by a decision of the Security Council and, if necessary, on the basis of other mutually agreed procedures. The Nine declare that they are prepared to participate within the framework of a comprehensive settlement in a system of concrete and binding international guarantees, including [guarantees] on the ground.

A just solution must finally be found to the Palestinian problem, which is not simply one of refugees. The Palestinian people, which is conscious of existing as such, must be placed in a position, by an appropriate process defined within the framework of the comprehensive peace settlement, to exercise fully its right to self-determination.

The achievement of these objectives requires the involvement and support of all the parties concerned in the peace settlement which the Nine are endeavoring to promote in keeping with the principles formulated in the declaration referred to above. These principles are binding on all the parties concerned, and thus on the Palestinian people, and on the PLO, which will have to be associated with the negotiations.

The Nine recognize the special importance of the role played by the question of Jerusalem for all the parties concerned. The Nine stress that they will not accept any unilateral initiative designed to change the status of Jerusalem and that any agreement on the city's status should guarantee freedom of access for everyone to the Holy Places.

The Nine stress the need for Israel to put an end to the territorial occupation which it has maintained since the conflict of 1967, as it has done for part of Sinai. They are deeply convinced that the Israeli settlements constitute a serious obstacle to the peace process in the Middle East. The Nine consider that these settlements, as well as modifications in population and property in the occupied Arab territories, are illegal under international law.

Concerned as they are to put an end to violence, the Nine consider that only the renunciation of force or the threatened use of force by all the parties can create a climate of confidence in the area, and constitute a basic element for a comprehensive settlement of the conflict in the Middle East.

[...]

Source: European Council, "Declaration Adopted at Meeting of the European Council," Venice, Italy, June 13, 1980.

87. Basic Law: Jerusalem, Capital of Israel, July 30, 1980

Introduction

Since June 1967 Israel had controlled all of Jerusalem, including the city's predominantly eastern quarter. Israel treated Jerusalem as its capital, and most major government institutions and ministries were situated there. Even so, the United Nations (UN) and the international community had repeatedly stated that under the 1947 Palestine partition agreement Jerusalem was an international city whose status was yet to be determined. Since 1950 Israel had treated West Jerusalem as its capital. Arab states regarded East Jerusalem as a central portion of the occupied territories whose return they so frequently demanded. In the summer of 1980, however, the Israeli Knesset, which was itself sited in Jerusalem, passed a law proclaiming that "Jerusalem, whole and united, is the capital of Israel." The law did not define the precise boundaries of Jerusalem, nor did it use the loaded word "sovereignty." It was probably not coincidental that this action was taken in the middle of a U.S. presidential campaign, when neither Republican nor Democratic politicians would wish to alienate American Jewish voters. The nonbinding UN Security Council Resolution 478, passed in response to the law in August 1980, stated that the Israeli move was "null and void and must be rescinded forthwith" and called on those nations—12 Latin American states plus the Netherlands—that still had embassies in what had been West Jerusalem to move them elsewhere. Saudi Arabia, Iraq, Kuwait, and Libya soon announced that they would impose oil embargoes on any country that kept its embassy in Jerusalem, prompting a mass exodus of foreign diplomats to Tel Aviv and other Israeli cities. Palestinians continued to claim East Jerusalem, arguing that it should serve as the capital of the Palestinian state that they wished to establish. In 1995 the U.S. Congress passed the Jerusalem Embassy Act, mandating the transfer of the U.S. embassy to Jerusalem, but the U.S. State Department repeatedly deferred construction of the new facility.

Primary Source

1. Jerusalem, complete and united, is the capital of Israel.

2. Jerusalem is the seat of the President of the State, the Knesset, the Government and the Supreme Court.

3. The Holy Places shall be protected from desecration and any other violation and from anything likely to violate the freedom of access of the members of the different religions to the places sacred to them or their feelings towards those places.

4. (a) The Government shall provide for the development and prosperity of Jerusalem and the well-being of its inhabitants by allocating special funds, including a special annual grant to the Municipality of Jerusalem (Capital City Grant) [subject to] the approval of the Finance Committee of the Knesset.

   (b) Jerusalem shall be given special priority in the activities of the authorities of the State so as to further its development in economic and other matters.

   (c) The Government shall set up a special body or special bodies for the implementation of this provision.

MENAHEM BEGIN
Prime Minister

YITZCHAK NAVON
President of the State

Source: "Basic Law—Jerusalem—Capital of Israel, 30 July 1980," Israel Ministry of Foreign Affairs, http://www.mfa.gov.il/MFA.

88. Israeli Government: Fundamental Policy Guidelines, August 5, 1981

Introduction

The Republican administration of U.S. president Ronald Reagan, which took office in January 1981, was far more pro-Israeli in its emphasis than the preceding administration of President Jimmy Carter had been. In early 1979 a ferociously anti-American fundamentalist Islamic regime headed by the Muslim cleric Ayatollah Ruhollah Khomeini came to power in Iran, replacing Mohammad Reza Shah Pahlavi under whose rule Iran had been a pillar of U.S. strategy in the Middle East. What Reagan perceived as growing Soviet assertiveness around the world, including the December 1979 invasion of Afghanistan, also alarmed the president and his advisers. Given that many Arab states, such as Libya and Syria, had radical governments at odds with the United States, their choice of potential regional allies in the Middle East seemed rather limited, and Israel assumed new salience as a strategic asset. Reagan was, moreover, a born-again Christian and was sympathetic to calls by conservative American Christian groups to give greater support to the State of Israel, whose existence they believed had been foreseen by Old Testament prophecies, and to acquiesce in new Jewish settlements in the occupied territories. Under these circumstances, in August 1981 an emboldened Israeli government headed by conservative Likud Party leader Menachem Begin announced new policy guidelines on peace and the Palestinian issue. While pledging its adherence to and pride in the Camp David Accords and the treaty with Egypt and its determination to maintain peace and seek a lasting settlement, the Begin government was far more assertive than in the past. The new guidelines specifically stated that while Israel would seek to give the Palestinian Arabs in the occupied territories greater autonomy, "under no conditions [would] a Palestinian state emerge" there. The areas of "Judea, Samaria [the West Bank] and the Gaza Strip" were all specifically defined as falling under Israeli sovereignty and forming part of "western 'Yeretz Israel.'" Israel further proclaimed its right to expand Jewish settlement in these regions and also in the formerly Syrian Golan Heights, which Israel proclaimed itself unwilling to abandon except on its own terms. This uncompromisingly hard-line position marked a great departure from the far more conciliatory past Israeli endorsements of United Nations (UN) Security Resolutions 242 and 334, signaling a new willingness by the Israeli government to confront and ignore international censure.

Primary Source

The right of the Jewish people to the land of Israel is an eternal right that cannot be called into question, and which is intertwined with the right of security and peace.

The Government will continue to place its aspirations for peace at the head of its concerns, and no effort will be spared in order to further peace. The peace treaty between Israel and Egypt is a historic turning point in Israel's status in the Middle East.

The Government will continue to use all means to prevent war.

The Government will diligently observe the Camp David agreements.

The Government will work for the renewal of negotiations on the implementation of the agreement on full autonomy for the Arab residents of Judea, Samaria and the Gaza Strip.

The autonomy agreed upon at Camp David means neither sovereignty nor self-determination. The autonomy agreements set down at Camp David are guarantees that under no conditions will a Palestinian state emerge in the territory of western "Eretz Yisrael."

At the end of the transition period set down in the Camp David agreements, Israel will raise its claim, and act to realize its right of sovereignty over Judea, Samaria and the Gaza Strip.

Settlement in the land of Israel is a right and an integral part of the nation's security. The Government will continue to honor the principle that Jewish settlement will not cause the eviction of any person from his land, his village or his city.

Equality of rights for all residents will continue to exist in the land of Israel, with no distinctions [on the basis] of religion, race, nationality, sex, or ethnic community.

Israel will not descend from the Golan Heights, nor will it remove any settlement established there. It is the Government that will decide on the appropriate timing for the imposition of Israeli law, jurisdiction and administration on the Golan Heights.

> **Source:** "Israeli Government: Fundamental Policy Guidelines (August 5, 1981)," in Walter Laqueur and Barry Rubin, *The Israel-Arab Reader: A Documentary History of the Middle East Conflict* (New York: Penguin, 2001), 233–234.

89. Fahd Plan [Excerpt], August 7, 1981

Introduction

Arab governments deeply resented what they perceived as growing Israeli aggression, expansionism, and intransigence under Prime Minister Menachem Begin. Speaking two days after Israel announced its new policy guidelines, Crown Prince Fahd of relatively conservative Saudi Arabia reiterated Arab adherence to the principles of United Nations (UN) Resolution 242. Besides calling for Israeli withdrawal from the occupied territories and the establishment of an independent Palestinian state with Jerusalem as its capital, he also proposed the dismantling of post-1967 Israeli settlements in these areas, a demand that would become increasingly central to future peace plans. Fahd reaffirmed the right of the Palestinians to return to their former homes in Israel or to receive compensation. The West Bank and the Gaza Strip, he stated, should be under UN administration for a brief transitional period of no more than a few months before reverting to independent Palestinian rule. Fahd's proposals demonstrated that the quest for an independent Palestinian state, not simply a homeland, had now become part of mainstream Arab peace policy, while the continuing and rapid expansion of Israeli settlements in the occupied territory was increasingly fraught and contentious. The Palestinian question was, Fahd stated, "the basic figure in the Middle Eastern equation." In addition, he undiplomatically assailed what he characterized as the "unlimited support" that the United States gave to Israel and demanded an "end to Israeli arrogance, whose ugliest facet is embodied in Begin's government." He forthrightly stated that if the United States ceased its unthinking endorsement of Israel's policies, this would "automatically" put a stop to Israel's arrogance. This decidedly frank pronouncement by Fahd was an index of the frustration that by 1981 even nonradical Arab states such as Saudi Arabia, a conservative monarchy that enjoyed close relations with the United States, were experiencing over what they perceived as the boundless U.S. support Israel was receiving. Rather than being a serious peace plan, Fahd's proposals were meant to serve as a wake-up call to the United States that Arab patience was by no means unlimited. They were also intended to deflect charges among radical Arab militants that Saudi Arabian leaders lacked the courage to stand up to their U.S. ally and break ranks with U.S. policies. Predictably, Israel immediately denounced these proposals.

Primary Source

There are a number of principles which may be taken as guidelines toward a just settlement; they are principles which the United Nations has taken and reiterated many times in the last few years. They are:

First, that Israel should withdraw from all Arab territory occupied in 1967, including Arab Jerusalem.

Second, that Israeli settlements built on Arab land after 1967 should be dismantled.

Third, a guarantee of freedom of worship for all religions in the holy places.

Fourth, an affirmation of the right of the Palestinian people to return to their homes and to compensate those who do not wish to return.

Fifth, that the West Bank and the Gaza Strip should have a transitional period, under the auspices of the United Nations, for a period not exceeding several months.

Sixth, that an independent Palestinian state should be set up with Jerusalem as its capital.

Seventh, that all states in the region should be able to live in peace.

Eighth, that the United Nations or member states of the United Nations should guarantee to execute these principles.

[...]

I wish to reaffirm that the principles of a just comprehensive solution have become familiar and do not require great effort:

1. An end to unlimited American support for Israel.
2. An end to Israeli arrogance, whose ugliest facet is embodied in Begin's government. This condition will be automatically fulfilled if the first condition is fulfilled.
3. A recognition that, as Yasir Arafat says, the Palestinian figure is the basic figure in the Middle Eastern equation.

Source: Walter Laqueur and Barry Rubin, eds., *The Israel-Arab Reader: A Documentary History of the Middle East Conflict* (New York: Penguin, 2001), 234–235.

90. U.S.-Israel Memorandum of Understanding on Strategic Cooperation [Excerpt], November 30, 1981

Introduction

Undeterred by Arab resentment of what was perceived as unstinted U.S. support for Israel, in November 1981 the administration of U.S. president Ronald Reagan signed a memorandum of understanding with Israel. Reagan and his advisers were motivated in large part by what they perceived as a rising Soviet military threat around the world and their desire to find suitable allies to counter this. The two nations proclaimed their intention "to enhance cooperation to deter all threats from the Soviet Union in the region." They promised to provide each other with military assistance when necessary. The specifics of their intended collaboration were left rather vague, but they included "joint military exercises" in the area of the eastern Mediterranean and "joint readiness activities." The agreement specifically noted that it was "not directed at any State or group of States within the region" but instead was intended only to deal with the Soviet threat. Soviet ties to the Palestine Liberation Organization (PLO) and several of the neighboring Arab regimes, however, undoubtedly meant that the understanding could be stretched to cover action against the latter. One of the major areas of cooperation was likely to be strategic intelligence gathering. The agreement confirmed Israel's Arab neighbors in their conviction that under Reagan the United States had identified Israel's security interests with its own and was unlikely to act to restrain either moves by its partner against themselves or Israeli efforts to annex the occupied territories. In public speeches delivered during the following months, both Defense Minister Ariel Sharon and Foreign Minister Yitzhak Shamir emphasized that besides opposition to radical Arab regimes and the PLO, one of Israel's major strategic priorities must be the effort to counter a growing threat of Soviet expansion in the Middle East and Africa. They argued that not only was Soviet assistance a major factor in facilitating PLO and Arab threats to Israel, but this was only part of a broader Soviet strategy in the region that constituted a danger to the entire free world. Given the Reagan administration's fiercely anticommunist preoccupations, Israel found that playing the Soviet card was a decidedly rewarding strategic posture.

Primary Source
PREAMBLE

This Memorandum of Understanding reaffirms the common bonds of friendship between the United States and Israel and builds on the mutual security relationship that exists between the two nations. The Parties recognize the need to enhance Strategic Cooperation to deter all threats from the Soviet Union to the region. Noting the long-standing and fruitful cooperation for mutual security that has developed between the two countries, the Parties have decided to establish a framework for continued consultation and cooperation to enhance their national security by deterring such threats to the whole region.

The Parties have reached the following agreements in order to achieve the above aims.

ARTICLE I

United States–Israeli Strategic Cooperation, as set forth in this Memorandum, is designed against the threat to peace and security of the region caused by the Soviet Union or Soviet-controlled forces from outside the region introduced into the region. It has the following broad purposes:

   a. To enable the Parties to act cooperatively and in a timely manner to deal with the above mentioned threat.
   b. To provide each other with military assistance for operations of their forces in the area that may be required to cope with this threat.
   c. The Strategic Cooperation between the Parties is not directed at any State or group of States within the region. It is intended solely for defensive purposes against the above mentioned threat.

ARTICLE II

1. The fields in which Strategic Cooperation will be carried out to prevent the above mentioned threat from endangering the security of the region include:
   a. Military cooperation between the Parties, as may be agreed by the Parties.
   b. Joint military exercises, including naval and air exercises in the Eastern Mediterranean Sea, as agreed upon by the Parties.
   c. Cooperation for the establishment and maintenance of joint readiness activities, as agreed upon by the Parties.
   d. Other areas within the basic scope and purpose of this agreement, as may be jointly agreed.

2. Details of activities within these fields of cooperation shall be worked out by the Parties in accordance with the provisions of Article III below. The cooperation will include, as appropriate, planning, preparations, and exercises.

[. . .]

ARTICLE VI

The Parties share the understanding that nothing in this Memorandum is intended to or shall in any way prejudice the rights and obligations which devolve or may devolve upon either government under the Charter of the United Nations or under International Law. The Parties reaffirm their faith in the purposes and principles of the Charter of the United Nations and their aspiration to live in peace with all countries in the region.

For the Government of the United States
Caspar W. Weinberger
Secretary of Defense

For the Government of Israel
Ariel Sharon
Minister of Defense

> **Source:** U.S. Department of State, "Memorandum of Understanding between the Government of the United States and the Government of Israel on Strategic Cooperation, November 30, 1981, *International Legal Materials* 20: 1420.

91. Golan Heights Law, December 14, 1981

Introduction

By late 1981, the Israeli government contemplated incorporating the Golan Heights, seized from Syria in 1967, within Israel's boundaries. In December the Knesset passed legislation placing the Golan Heights under Israeli law, jurisdiction, and administration. The move seemed merely a preliminary step to outright Israeli annexation of the Golan Heights. To Arab leaders, the measure was yet another inflammatory indication that Israel had abandoned any intention of pursuing the peace process as laid down in United Nations (UN) Security Council Resolution 242 and planned to rely entirely on military strength to cement its hold on the occupied territories.

Primary Source

1. The Law, jurisdiction and administration of the state shall apply to the Golan Heights, as described in the Appendix.

2. This Law shall become valid on the day of its passage in the Knesset.

3. The Minister of the Interior shall be charged with the implementation of this Law, and he is entitled, in consultation with the Minister of Justice, to enact regulations for its implementation and to formulate in regulations transitional provisions concerning the continued application of regulations, orders, administrative orders, rights and duties which were in force on the Golan Heights prior to the application of this Law.

> **Source:** "Golan Heights Law, December 14, 1981," Israel Ministry of Foreign Affairs, http://www.israel-mfa.gov.il/MFA.

92. Menachem Begin, Address at the National Defense College [Excerpt], August 8, 1982

Introduction

After King Hussein of Jordan expelled the Palestine Liberation Organization (PLO) during 1970–1971, the small country of Lebanon, immediately to the north of Israel, became a new haven for PLO guerrillas and officials, who used it as a base from which to mount attacks on Israel. Lebanon's eastern neighbor, Syria, also supported radical Shiite groups within the country whose members were hostile to Israel but also fierce rivals of the PLO. Israel sought to assist Lebanon's Maronite Christian forces and the associated Phalange militias, headed by the politician Bashir Gemayel, against both PLO and Syrian-backed forces, and the Israeli military launched numerous raids on Palestinian positions in Lebanon. By 1981 Lebanon was in a state of civil war. In June 1981 U.S. special envoy Philip Habib negotiated a cease-fire between Israel and the PLO, a development that alarmed many Israeli politicians, including Prime Minister Menachem Begin. Even though Habib had held separate talks with Israel and the PLO and the two sides had never dealt with each other directly, Israeli hard-liners feared that this arrangement amounted to implicit Israeli recognition of the PLO. After winning reelection in August 1981, Begin and his defense minister, Ariel Sharon, moved to take decisive action to eliminate the PLO, which was still continuing raids against Israel from Jordanian territory and arguing that the cease-fire applied only to Lebanon. One unspoken objective was to destroy the PLO leadership in the hope that this would preclude any future Israeli negotiations with the organization. Opposition from moderates in the Israeli cabinet meant that not until June 1982 did Israeli forces invade Lebanon, advancing 25 miles to the north and attacking Beirut, Lebanon's capital, that was also a PLO stronghold. From mid-June until August 12, Israeli leaders, seeking to force a complete PLO withdrawal from Lebanon, besieged and bombed Beirut, resulting in heavy loss of civilian life. On August 12, Habib announced that he had negotiated a cease-fire under whose terms PLO forces and leaders would leave Lebanon for other Arab states by September 1. Speaking at the National Defense College on August 8, Begin justified Israel's policies toward Lebanon on the grounds that while PLO attacks on Israel had not threatened his own country's very survival, the Israeli invasion of Lebanon had finally halted PLO and Syrian terrorist assaults on Israeli civilians. He claimed that now that the PLO menace had been removed, no Arab state possessed the ability to attack Israel, thus finally opening the road to the negotiation of lasting peace agreements.

Primary Source

[. . .]

Let us turn from the international example to ourselves. Operation Peace for Galilee is not a military operation resulting from the lack of an alternative. The terrorists did not threaten the existence of the State of Israel; they "only" threatened the lives of Israel's citizens and members of the Jewish people. There are those who find fault with the second part of that sentence. If there was no danger to the existence of the state, why did you go to war?

I will explain why. We had three wars which we fought without alternative. The first was the War of Independence, which began on November 30, 1947, and lasted until January 1949. It is worthwhile remembering these dates, because there are also those who try to deceive concerning the nine weeks which have already passed since the beginning of Operation Peace for Galilee. This was a war without alternative, after the Arab armies invaded Eretz Israel. If not for our ability, none of us would have remained alive.

What happened in that war, which we went off to fight with no alternative?

Six thousand of our fighters were killed. We were then 650,000 Jews in Eretz Israel, and the number of fallen amounted to about 1 percent of the Jewish population. In proportion to our population today, about 1 percent would mean 30,000 killed and about 90,000 wounded. Could we live with such losses? Let us imagine 30,000 soldiers killed, the best of our youth, those who say, "Follow me!"

We carried on our lives then by a miracle, with a clear recognition of life's imperative: to win, to establish a state, a government, a parliament, a democracy, an army—a force to defend Israel and the entire Jewish people.

The second war of no alternative was the Yom Kippur War and the War of Attrition that preceded it. What was the situation on that Yom Kippur day [October 6, 1973]? We had 177 tanks deployed on the Golan Heights against 1,400 Soviet Syrian tanks; and fewer than 500 of our soldiers manned positions along the Suez Canal against five divisions sent to the front by the Egyptians.

[. . .]

Our total casualties in that war of no alternative were 2,297 killed, 6,067 wounded. Together with the War of Attrition—which was also a war of no alternative—2,659 killed, 7,251 wounded. The terrible total: almost 10,000 casualties.

Our other wars were not without an alternative. In November 1956 we had a choice. The reason for going to war then was the need to destroy the fedayeen, who did not represent a danger to the existence of the state.

However, the political leadership of the time thought it was necessary to do this. As one who served in the parliamentary opposition, I was summoned to David Ben-Gurion before the cabinet received information of the plan, and he found it necessary to give my colleagues and myself these details: We are going to meet the enemy before it absorbs the Soviet weapons which began to flow to it from Czechoslovakia in 1955.

I said: "We shall stand together, with no reservations. This is a holy war." And indeed, we stood together until the withdrawal, without a peace treaty and without the demilitarization of Sinai.

Thus we went off to the Sinai Campaign. At that time we conquered most of the Sinai Peninsula and reached Sharm el-Sheikh. Actually, we accepted and submitted to an American dictate, mainly regarding the Gaza Strip (which David Ben-Gurion called "the liberated portion of the homeland"). John Foster Dulles, the then secretary of state, promised Ben-Gurion that an Egyptian army would not return to Gaza.

The Egyptian army did enter Gaza. David Ben-Gurion sent Mrs. Meir to Washington to ask Foster Dulles: "What happened? Where are the promises?" And he replied: "Would you resume the war for this?"

After 1957, Israel had to wait 10 full years for its flag to fly again over that liberated portion of the homeland.

In June 1967 we again had a choice. The Egyptian army concentrations in the Sinai approaches do not prove that Nasser was really about to attack us. We must be honest with ourselves. We decided to attack him.

This was a war of self-defence in the noblest sense of the term. The government of national unity then established decided unanimously: We will take the initiative and attack the enemy, drive him back, and thus assure the security of Israel and the future of the nation.

We did not do this for lack of an alternative. We could have gone on waiting. We could have sent the army home. Who knows if there would have been an attack against us? There is no proof of it. There are several arguments to the contrary. While it is indeed true that the closing of the Straits of Tiran was an act of aggression, a *casus belli,* there is always room for a great deal of consideration as to whether it is necessary to make a *casus* into a *bellum.*

And so there were three wars with no alternative—the War of Independence, the War of Attrition and the Yom Kippur War—and it is our misfortune that our wars have been so. If in the two other wars, the wars of choice—the Sinai Campaign and the Six Day War—we had losses like those in the no alternative wars, we would have been left today with few of our best youth, without the strength to withstand the Arab world.

As for Operation Peace for Galilee, it does not really belong to the category of wars of no alternative. We could have gone on seeing our civilians injured in Metulla or Kiryat Shmona or Nahariya. We could have gone on counting those killed by explosive charges left in a Jerusalem supermarket, or a Petah Tikva bus stop.

All the orders to carry out these acts of murder and sabotage came from Beirut. Should we have reconciled ourselves to the ceaseless killing of civilians, even after the agreement ending hostilities reached last summer, which the terrorists interpreted as an agreement permitting them to strike at us from every side, besides southern Lebanon? They tried to infiltrate gangs of murderers via Syria and Jordan, and by a miracle we captured them. We might also not have captured them. There was a gang of four terrorists which infiltrated from Jordan, whose members admitted they had been about to commandeer a bus (and we remember the bus on the coastal road).

[. . .]

There are slanderers who say that a full year of quiet has passed between us and the terrorists. Nonsense. There was not even one month of quiet. The newspapers and communications media, including *The New York Times* and *The Washington Post,* did not publish even one line about our capturing the gang of murderers that crossed the Jordan in order to commandeer a bus and murder its passengers.

True, such actions were not a threat to the existence of the state. But they did threaten the lives of civilians, whose number we cannot estimate, day after day, week after week, month after month.

During the past nine weeks, we have in effect destroyed the combat potential of 20,000 terrorists. We hold 9,000 in a prison camp. Between 2,000 and 3,000 were killed and between 7,000 and 9,000 have been captured and cut off in Beirut. They have decided to leave there only because they have no possibility of remaining there. They will leave soon. We made a second condition: after the exit of most of the terrorists, an integrated multi-national force will enter. But if the minority refuse to leave, you—the U.S., Italy and France—must promise us in writing that you, together with the Lebanese army, will force them, the terrorists, to leave Beirut and Lebanon. They have the possibility of forcing 2,000–2,500 terrorists who will remain after the majority leaves.

And one more condition: if you aren't willing to force them, then, please, leave Beirut and Lebanon, and the I.D.F. will solve the problem.

This is what I wrote the Secretary of State today, and I want you and all the citizens of Israel and the U.S. to know it.

The problem will be solved. We can already now look beyond the fighting. It will end, as we hope, shortly. And then, as I believe, recognize and logically assume, we will have a protracted period of peace. There is no other country around us that is capable of attacking us.

We have destroyed the best tanks and planes the Syrians had. We have destroyed 24 of their ground-to-air missile batteries. After everything that happened, Syria did not go to war against us, not in Lebanon and not in the Golan Heights.

Jordan cannot attack us. We have learned that Jordan is sending telegrams to the Americans, warning that Israel is about to invade across the Jordan and capture Amman.

For our part, we will not initiate any attack against any Arab country. We have proved that we do not want wars. We made many painful sacrifices for a peace treaty with Egypt. That treaty stood the test of the fighting in Lebanon; in other words, it stood the test.

The demilitarized zone of 150 kilometres in Sinai exists and no Egyptian soldier has been placed there. From the experience of the 1930s, I have to say that if ever the other side violated the agreement about the demilitarized zone, Israel would be obliged to introduce, without delay, a force stronger than that violating the international commitment: not in order to wage war, but to achieve one of two results: restoration of the previous situation, i.e., resumed demilitarization, and the removal of both armies from the demilitarized zone; or attainment of strategic depth, in case the other side has taken the first step towards a war of aggression, as happened in Europe only three years after the abrogation of the demilitarized zone in the Rhineland.

Because the other Arab countries are completely incapable of attacking the State of Israel, there is reason to expect that we are facing a historic period of peace. It is obviously impossible to set a date.

It may well be that "The land shall be still for 40 years." Perhaps less, perhaps more. But from the facts before us, it is clear that, with the end of the fighting in Lebanon, we have ahead of us many years of establishing peace treaties and peaceful relations with the various Arab countries.

The conclusion—both on the basis of the relations between states and on the basis of our national experience—is that there is no divine mandate to go to war only if there is no alternative. There is no moral imperative that a nation must, or is entitled to, fight only when its back is to the sea, or to the abyss. Such a war may avert tragedy, if not a Holocaust, for any nation; but it causes it terrible loss of life.

Quite the opposite. A free, sovereign nation, which hates war and loves peace, and which is concerned about its security, must create the conditions under which war, if there is a need for it, will not be for lack of alternative. The conditions much be such—and their creation depends upon man's reason and his actions—that the price of victory will be few casualties, not many.

Source: "Address by Prime Minister Begin at the National Defense College, 8 August 1982," Israel Ministry of Foreign Affairs, http://www.israel-mfa.gov.il/MFA.

93. Ronald Reagan, Address to the Nation on U.S. Policy for Peace in the Middle East [Excerpt], September 1, 1982

Introduction

Immediately after U.S. special envoy Philip Habib brokered a cease-fire agreement between Israeli and Palestine Liberation Organization (PLO) forces that involved the PLO's departure from Lebanon, U.S. troops arrived in Beirut as part of a United Nations (UN) peacekeeping mission entrusted with overseeing the agreement's implementation. Once the PLO personnel had left, U.S. president Ronald Reagan proposed a new Arab-Israeli peace plan. George Shultz, who had just become U.S. secretary of state, had already publicly informed the U.S. Congress of his commitment to revitalizing the Camp David framework by reaching arrangements with Israel that would give Palestinians in the West Bank and Gaza "full autonomy." Shultz had also stated that peace talks would have to include representatives of the Palestinians and other Arab states and that the United States needed to improve its relations with the latter. He argued that a solid peace settlement was the only true guarantee of Israel's security, to which the United States and the Reagan administration were deeply committed. U.S. and Israeli officials were at one in seeking to avoid direct negotiations with the PLO and hoped that the PLO's expulsion from Lebanon would clear the way to deal with more moderate Palestinian elements. In eloquent language, Reagan called for "a fresh start" on peace negotiations in which Arab states and Israel would build on the Camp David foundations and the United States would act as mediator. He called for full autonomy for the Palestinians of the West Bank and Gaza, with local government authorities to be elected by the Palestinians, but on behalf of the United States he explicitly opposed both the establishment of an independent Palestinian state in those areas and their annexation or permanent control by Israel. Reagan did envisage that the West Bank and Gaza would have close ties with the kingdom of Jordan. He also demanded a freeze on further Israeli settlements in the occupied territories. Jerusalem, Reagan stated, should remain undivided, its ultimate status to be decided through subsequent negotiations. Once again, he affirmed the U.S. commitment to UN Security Council Resolution 242 guaranteeing Arab recognition of Israel's existence in return for Israeli withdrawal from most if not all of the occupied territories. Seeking to reassure Israel, Reagan uncompromisingly warned that "America's commitment to the security of Israel is ironclad."

Primary Source

My fellow Americans:

Today has been a day that should make us proud. It marked the end of the successful evacuation of the PLO from Beirut, Lebanon. This peaceful step could never have been taken without the good offices of the United States and especially the truly heroic work of a great American diplomat, Ambassador Philip Habib.

Thanks to his efforts, I am happy to announce that the U.S. Marine contingent helping to supervise the evacuation has accomplished its mission. Our young men should be out of Lebanon within two weeks. They, too, have served the cause of peace with distinction, and we can all be very proud of them.

[. . .]

The evacuation of the PLO from Beirut is now complete, and we can now help the Lebanese to rebuild their war-torn country. We owe it to ourselves, and to posterity, to move quickly to build upon this achievement. A stable and revived Lebanon is essential to all our hopes for peace in the region. The people of Lebanon deserve the best efforts of the international community to turn the nightmares of the past several years into a new dawn of hope. But the opportunities for peace in the Middle East do not begin and end in Lebanon. As we help Lebanon rebuild, we must also move to resolve the root causes of conflict between Arabs and Israelis.

The war in Lebanon has demonstrated many things, but two consequences are key to the peace process. First, the military losses of the PLO have not diminished the yearning of the Palestinian people for a just solution of their claims; and, second, while Israel's military successes in Lebanon have demonstrated that its armed forces are second to none in the region, they alone cannot bring just and lasting peace to Israel and her neighbors.

The question now is how to reconcile Israel's legitimate security concerns with the legitimate rights of the Palestinians. And that answer can only come at the negotiating table. Each party must recognize that the outcome must be acceptable to all and that true peace will require compromises by all.

So, tonight I am calling for a fresh start. This is the moment for all those directly concerned to get involved—or lend their support— to a workable basis for peace. The Camp David agreement remains the foundation of our policy. Its language provides all parties with the leeway they need for successful negotiations.

I call on Israel to make clear that the security for which she yearns can only be achieved through genuine peace, a peace requiring magnanimity, vision, and courage.

I call on the Palestinian people to recognize that their own political aspirations are inextricably bound to recognition of Israel's right to a secure future.

And I call on the Arab States to accept the reality of Israel—and the reality that peace and justice are to be gained only through hard, fair, direct negotiation.

In making these calls upon others, I recognize that the United States has a special responsibility. No other nation is in a position to deal with the key parties to the conflict on the basis of trust and reliability.

The time has come for a new realism on the part of all the peoples of the Middle East. The State of Israel is an accomplished fact; it deserves unchallenged legitimacy within the community of nations. But Israel's legitimacy has thus far been recognized by too few countries and has been denied by every Arab State except Egypt. Israel exists; it has a right to exist in peace behind secure and defensible borders; and it has a right to demand of its neighbors that they recognize those facts.

I have personally followed and supported Israel's heroic struggle for survival, ever since the founding of the State of Israel thirty-four years ago. In the pre-1967 borders Israel was barely ten miles wide at its narrowest point. The bulk of Israel's population lived within artillery range of hostile Arab armies. I am not about to ask Israel to live that way again.

The war in Lebanon has demonstrated another reality in the region. The departure of the Palestinians from Beirut dramatizes more than ever the homelessness of the Palestinian people. Palestinians feel strongly that their cause is more than a question of refugees. I agree. The Camp David agreement recognized that fact when it spoke of the legitimate rights of the Palestinian people and their just requirements.

For peace to endure it must involve all those who have been most deeply affected by the conflict. Only through broader participation in the peace process, most immediately by Jordan and by the Palestinians, will Israel be able to rest confident in the knowledge that its security and integrity will be respected by its neighbors. Only through the process of negotiation can all the nations of the Middle East achieve a secure peace.

These, then, are our general goals. What are the specific new American positions, and why are we taking them? In the Camp David talks thus far, both Israel and Egypt have felt free to express openly their views as to what the outcome should be. Understandably their views have differed on many points. The United States has thus far sought to play the role of mediator. We have avoided public comment on the key issues. We have always recognized and continue to recognize that only the voluntary agreement of those parties most directly involved in the conflict can provide an enduring solution. But it has become evident to me that some clearer sense of America's position on the key issues is necessary to encourage wider support for the peace process.

First, as outlined in the Camp David accords, there must be a period of time during which the Palestinian inhabitants of the West Bank and Gaza will have full autonomy over their own affairs. Due consideration must be given to the principle of self-government by the inhabitants of the territories and to the legitimate security concerns of the parties involved. The purpose of the five-year period of transition which would begin after free elections for a self-governing Palestinian authority is to prove to the Palestinians that they can run their own affairs and that such Palestinian autonomy poses no threat to Israel's security.

The United States will not support the use of any additional land for the purpose of settlements during the transitional period. Indeed, the immediate adoption of a settlement freeze by Israel, more than any other action, could create the confidence needed for wider participation in these talks. Further settlement activity is in no way necessary for the security of Israel and only diminishes the confidence of the Arabs that a final outcome can be freely and fairly negotiated.

I want to make the American position well understood. The purpose of this transitional period is the peaceful and orderly transfer of authority from Israel to the Palestinian inhabitants of the West Bank and Gaza. At the same time, such a transfer must not interfere with Israel's security requirements.

Beyond the transition period, as we look to the future of the West Bank and Gaza, it is clear to me that peace cannot be achieved by the formation of an independent Palestinian state in those territories, nor is it achievable on the basis of Israeli sovereignty or permanent control over the West Bank and Gaza. So, the United States will not support the establishment of an independent Palestinian state in the West Bank and Gaza, and we will not support annexation or permanent control by Israel.

There is, however, another way to peace. The final status of these lands must, of course, be reached through the give and take of negotiations. But it is the firm view of the United States that self-government by the Palestinians of the West Bank and Gaza in association with Jordan offers the best chance for a durable, just, and lasting peace. We base our approach squarely on the principle that the Arab-Israeli conflict should be resolved through negotiations involving an exchange of territory for peace.

This exchange is enshrined in United Nations Security Council Resolution 242, which is, in turn, incorporated in all its parts in the Camp David agreements. U.N. Resolution 242 remains wholly valid as the foundation stone of America's Middle East peace effort. It is the United States position that, in return for peace, the withdrawal provision of Resolution 242 applies to all fronts, including the West Bank and Gaza. When the border is negotiated between Jordan and Israel, our view on the extent to which Israel should be asked to give up territory will be heavily affected by the extent of true peace and normalization, and the security arrangements offered in return.

Finally, we remain convinced that Jerusalem must remain undivided, but its final status should be decided through negotiation.

In the course of the negotiations to come, the United States will support positions that seem to us fair and reasonable compromises and likely to promote a sound agreement. We will also put forward our own detailed proposals when we believe they can be helpful. And, make no mistake, the United States will oppose any proposal from any party and at any point in the negotiating process that threatens the security of Israel. America's commitment to the security of Israel is ironclad, and, I might add, so is mine.

During the past few days, our Ambassadors in Israel, Egypt, Jordan, and Saudi Arabia have presented to their host governments the proposals, in full detail, that I have outlined here today. Now I am convinced that these proposals can bring justice, bring security, and bring durability to an Arab-Israeli peace. The United States will stand by these principles with total dedication. They are fully consistent with Israel's security requirements and the aspirations of the Palestinians.

We will work hard to broaden participation at the peace table as envisaged by the Camp David accords. And I fervently hope that the Palestinians and Jordan, with the support of their Arab colleagues, will accept this opportunity.

[...]

Source: Ronald Reagan, *Public Papers of the Presidents of the United States: Ronald Reagan, 1982,* Vol. 2 (Washington, DC: U.S. Government Printing Office, 1983), 1093–1097.

94. Israeli Cabinet Resolution on the Reagan Plan, September 2, 1982

Introduction

Ronald Reagan's explicit efforts to reassure Israeli leaders that his peace proposals in no way diluted the U.S. commitment to Israel's security were unavailing in persuading them to support the Reagan

Plan. The following day, the Israeli cabinet issued a communiqué detailing Israeli objections to the plan. Formally, Israel based most of its objections to Reagan's proposals on the fact that they were inconsistent with, or at least not mentioned in, the Camp David Accords. Israel took issue with Reagan's suggestions on the future status of Jerusalem; full autonomy for the Palestinians of the West Bank and Gaza, especially their responsibility for internal security, which Israeli officials argued would inevitably bring a resurgence of terrorist activities by the Palestine Liberation Organization (PLO); his denial of Israel's sovereignty over the West Bank and Gaza; and his support for the development of close "economic, commercial, and cultural ties between the West Bank, Gaza, and Jordan." Israeli officials also warned that despite Reagan's explicit pronouncement that the United States would not endorse the creation of an independent Palestinian state, there could be no guarantee that this would not be the end result. Seeking to appeal to Reagan's Cold War and anti-Soviet sensibilities, they warned that an autonomous Palestinian territorial entity within Israel would be likely to become a haven for PLO leaders, who would in turn acquire advanced weaponry from the Soviet Union. Ultimately, Israel warned, the Palestinians would ally themselves with other hostile Arab states and "launch an onslaught against Israel to destroy her." While stating its willingness to resume its Camp David Accord negotiations with Egypt and the United States on Palestinian autonomy, Israel therefore refused to enter into any negotiations based on the Reagan Plan, which was effectively dead at birth. Their near-instantaneous and far from tactful rejection of Reagan's proposals was an indication of just how self-confident Israeli leaders felt when dealing with their country's greatest patron and ally.

Primary Source

The positions conveyed to the Prime Minister of Israel on behalf of the President of the United States consist of partial quotations from the Camp David agreements, or are nowhere mentioned in that agreement or contradict it entirely.

The following are the major positions of the Government of the United States:

1. Jerusalem
"Participation by the Palestinian inhabitants of East Jerusalem in the election for the West Bank-Gaza authority."

No mention whatsoever is made in the Camp David agreement of such a voting right. The single meaning of such a vote is the repartition of Jerusalem into two authorities, the one—of the State of Israel, and the other—of the Administrative Council of the autonomy. Jerusalem is nowhere mentioned in the Camp David agreement. With respect to the capital of Israel, letters were forwarded and attached to that agreement. In his letter to the President of the United States, Mr. Jimmy Carter, the Prime Minister of Israel, Mr. Menachem Begin, stated that "Jerusalem is one city, indivisible, the capital of the State of Israel." Thus shall it remain for all generations to come.

2. Security
"Progressive Palestinian responsibility for internal security based on capability and performance."

In the Camp David agreement it is stated: "A withdrawal of Israeli armed forces will take place and there will be a redeployment of the remaining Israeli forces into specified security locations. The agreement will also include arrangements for assuring internal and external order and security and public order."

It is, therefore, clear that in the Camp David agreement no distinction is made between internal security and external security. There can be no doubt that were internal security not to be the responsibility of Israel, the terrorist organization called P.L.O.—even after its defeat by the I.D.F. in Lebanon—would act to perpetrate constant bloodshed, shedding the blood of Jews and Arabs alike. For the citizens of Israel this is a question of life and death.

3. "A Real Settlement Freeze"
In the Camp David agreement no mention whatsoever is made of such a freeze. At Camp David the Prime Minister agreed that new settlements could not be established (though population would be added to existing ones) during the period of the negotiations for the signing of the peace treaty between Egypt and Israel (three months being explicitly stated). This commitment was carried out in full. That three month period terminated on December 17, 1978. Since then many settlements have been established in Judea, Samaria and the Gaza District, without evicting a single person from his land, village or town. Such settlement is a Jewish inalienable right and an integral part of our national security. Therefore, there shall be no settlement freeze. We shall continue to establish them in accordance with our natural right. President Reagan announced at the time that the "settlements are not illegal." A double negative makes a positive meaning that the settlements are legal. We shall act, therefore, in accordance with our natural right and the law, and we shall not deviate from the principle that these vital settlements will not lead to any evictions.

4. The Definition of Full Autonomy
"The definition of full autonomy as giving the Palestinian inhabitants real authority over themselves, the land and its resources, subject to fair safeguards on water." Such a definition is nowhere mentioned in the Camp David agreement, which states: "In order to provide full autonomy to the *inhabitants* (our emphasis), etc." In the lengthy discussion at Camp David, it was made absolutely clear that the autonomy applies not to the *territory* but to the *inhabitants*.

5. Ties with Jordan
"Economic, commercial and cultural ties between the West Bank, Gaza and Jordan." In all the clauses of the Camp David agreement there is no reference whatsoever to such ties.

6. Israeli Sovereignty

There is nothing in the Camp David agreement that precludes the application of Israeli sovereignty over Judea, Samaria and the Gaza District following the transitional period which begins with the establishment and inauguration of the self-government authority (Administrative Council). This was also stated by an official spokesman of the government of the United States.

7. Palestinian State

The Government of the United States commits itself not to support establishment of a Palestinian state in Judea, Samaria and the Gaza District. Regrettably, the visible reality proves this to be an illusion. Were the American plan to be implemented, there would be nothing to prevent King Hussein from inviting his new-found friend, Yasser Arafat, to come to Nablus and hand the rule over to him. Thus would come into being a Palestinian state which would conclude a pact with Soviet Russia and arm itself with every kind of modern weaponry. If the P.L.O. could do this in Lebanon, establishing a state-within-a-state, how much more so will the terrorists do so ruling over Judea, Samaria and the Gaza District. Then a joint front would be established of that "Palestinian State" with Jordan and Iraq behind her, Saudi Arabia to the south and Syria to the north. All these countries, together with other Arab states, would, after a while, launch an onslaught against Israel to destroy her. It is inconceivable that Israel will ever agree to such an "arrangement" whose consequences are inevitable.

Since the positions of the Government of the United States seriously deviate from the Camp David agreements, contradict it, and could create a serious danger to Israel, its security and its future, the Government of Israel has resolved that on the basis of these positions it will not enter into any negotiations with any party.

The Government of Israel is ready to renew the autonomy negotiations forthwith with the governments of the United States and Egypt, signatories to the Camp David agreements, and with other states and elements invited at Camp David to participate in the negotiations, with a view to reaching agreement on the establishment of full autonomy for the Arab inhabitants of Judea, Samaria and the Gaza District, in total conformity with the Camp David Accords.

Source: "Cabinet Resolution on the Reagan Plan, 2 September 1982," Israel Ministry of Foreign Affairs, http://www.mfa.gov.il/MFA.

95. Saddam Hussein, Statement on Israel's Right to a Secure State, January 2, 1983

Introduction

By the 1980s, several Arab leaders were willing to publicly endorse the concept of recognition of Israel. President Saddam Hussein of Iraq, then engaged in a lengthy war with Iran in which he was receiving substantial U.S. support, was among them. Hussein, heading a largely secular government dominated by the socialist Baath Party, was by no means a dedicated Muslim. Interviewed by Democratic congressman Stephen Solarz in 1983, Hussein stated "that the simultaneous existence of an independent Palestinian State acceptable to the Palestinians and the existence of a secure state for the Israelis are both necessary." His greatest concern over such an arrangement was apparently not the status of Israel but rather his opposition to any potential union of the West Bank and Gaza with the kingdom of Jordan. This would, he claimed, be "unacceptable" to Iraq and other Arab states. Hussein argued that were the Palestinian territories to join Jordan, other Arab states would regard this as threatening "their entire existence" and exposing them to manipulation and menace from "an international conspiracy" or any "big power." His underlying objection may well have been that a merger of Jordan with the West Bank and Gaza would have enhanced Jordan both territorially and in terms of its international visibility, prestige, and allies, boosting that kingdom's ability to withstand pressure from Iraq.

Primary Source

[Question:] Mr. President, I do appreciate your frank answers. I would like to ask you the second question and I would like you to give, with all sincerity, your viewpoint: should Israel agree to return to the pre-1967 borders, but only within an objective framework, giving Jordan the primary responsibility for administrating the West Bank and Gaza Strip [? Does] this represent an acceptable solution to the problem? Would it be sufficient for Israel to withdraw to the 1967 lines and to accept the establishment of a Palestinian State in the West Bank and Gaza Strip as a way to solve the conflict?

[Answer:] I do not believe that forcing the Palestinians, under the current circumstances, to accept a constitutional formula with any Arab State is a sound action. However, I believe that the simultaneous existence of an independent Palestinian State acceptable to the Palestinians and the existence of a secure state for the Israelis are both necessary.

I believe that you will be committing a grave mistake, unacceptable of course to the Arabs and Iraq, if you think that Jordan is suitable as a Palestinian State. In other words, the state of Palestine would be on the east bank of the Jordan, as some Israeli officials have remarked. The Arabs would feel that their entire existence was threatened and that the political map of their national entity could be threatened any time by an international conspiracy or by the desire of this or that big power.

Source: "Saddam Hussein Interview with Stephen Solarz, January 2, 1983," Foreign Broadcast Information Service, *F.B.I.S.-Daily Report Middle East and North Africa,* January 4, 1983.

96. Kahan Commission Report [Excerpt], February 8, 1983

Introduction

United Nations (UN) and Israeli forces were both present in Lebanon after Palestinian forces left on September 1, 1982. Two weeks later, several hundred civilians were massacred in Beirut. Even though peace had supposedly been restored, the situation was still confused, with local militias violently vying for power. Seeking to assure its continued influence in Lebanon, in presidential elections held there in August 1982 Israel backed the Maronite Christian Phalange militia leader Bashir Gemayel, who was successful. On September 14 Gemayel was assassinated. Two days earlier, Israeli defense minister Ariel Sharon and Chief of Staff Rafael Eitan had already negotiated a deal with Gemayel under which Phalangist forces would be permitted to enter Palestinian refugee camps at Sabra and Shatila, on the outskirts of Beirut, purportedly to clean out up to 2,000 Palestinian fighting men who had allegedly taken refuge there. After Gemayel's death, Sharon and Eitan paid a visit of condolence to his family and then, leaving the Israeli cabinet ignorant of their intentions, went ahead with this plan. Violating the terms of the truce that U.S. negotiator Philip Habib had arranged some weeks before, on September 16 Israeli troops entered West Beirut and then arranged the transportation of around 200 Phalangist militiamen to the area outside the two camps. Entering the camps at 6:00 p.m., the Phalangists sought vengeance for Gemayel's death and began a massacre that continued until early September 19. Over these three days, Eitan and high-ranking Israeli officers ignored reports that atrocities were in progress and civilians were being murdered. The Maronites left the camps on September 19, leaving hundreds—estimates ranged from 460 to 2,000—of dead refugees behind them, the majority of whom were women and children, with none apparently belonging to any Palestine Liberation Organization (PLO) unit. Reports of the massacres quickly appeared in the Israeli and international press, creating a wave of revulsion and disgust against Israel and sparking major protests and demonstrations within Israel itself. These events prompted the Israeli government to establish a commission of inquiry chaired by Yitzhak Kahan, president of the Supreme Court. The commission held 60 sessions, some open but many closed, and interviewed 58 witnesses. The Israeli military initially claimed to have been unaware of these events and to have played no role in them, but the commission's report showed that this was untrue. Sharon, Eitan, and Deputy Prime Minister David Levy had not only facilitated the movement of Phalange forces into the camps but had also anticipated that major bloodshed would ensue. The report therefore held them morally responsible for the events that followed. Despite the Israeli government's decision to investigate these events, the implication of senior Israeli officials in the massacres served to discredit the country on the international stage. When the commission's report appeared Sharon was forced to resign as defense minister, although he would later stage a polit-

ical comeback. In the wake of the massacres, U.S. troops returned to Beirut as part of the international peacekeeping force.

Primary Source

[...]

Before we discuss the essence of the problem of the indirect responsibility of Israel, or of those who operated at its behest, we perceive it to be necessary to deal with objections that have been voiced on various occasions, according to which if Israel's direct responsibility for the atrocities is negated—i.e., if it is determined that the blood of those killed was not shed by I.D.F. soldiers and I.D.F. forces, or that others operating at the behest of the state were not parties to the atrocities—then there is no place for further discussion of the problem of indirect responsibility. The argument is that no responsibility should be laid on Israel for deeds perpetrated outside of its borders by members of the Christian community against Palestinians in that same country, or against Muslims located within the area of the camps. A certain echo of this approach may be found in statements made in the cabinet meeting of 19.9.82, and in statements released to the public by various sources.

We cannot accept this position. If it indeed becomes clear that those who decided on the entry of the Phalangists into the camps should have foreseen—from the information at their disposal and from things which were common knowledge—that there was danger of a massacre, and no steps were taken which might have prevented this danger or at least greatly reduced the possibility that deeds of this type might be done, then those who made the decisions and those who implemented them are indirectly responsible for what ultimately occurred, even if they did not intend this to happen and merely disregarded the anticipated danger. A similar indirect responsibility also falls on those who knew of the decision; it was their duty, by virtue of their position and their office, to warn of the danger, and they did not fulfill this duty. It is also not possible to absolve of such indirect responsibility those persons who, when they received the first reports of what was happening in the camps, did not rush to prevent the continuation of the Phalangists' actions and did not do everything within their power to stop them....

[...]

We would like to note here that we will not enter at all into the question of indirect responsibility of other elements besides the State of Israel. One might argue that such indirect responsibility falls, inter alia, on the Lebanese army, or on the Lebanese government to whose orders this army was subject, since despite Major General Drori's urgings in his talks with the heads of the Lebanese army, they did not grant Israel's request to enter the camps before the Phalangists or instead of the Phalangists, until 19.9.82. It should also be noted that in meetings with U.S. representatives during the critical days, Israel's spokesmen repeatedly requested that the U.S. use its influence to get the Lebanese Army to fulfill the function of maintaining public peace and order in West Beirut, but it does not seem that these requests had any result. One might also make charges concerning the hasty evacuation of the multi-national force by the countries whose troops were in place until after the evacuation of the terrorists. . . .

[. . .]

As has already been said above, the decision to enter West Beirut was adopted in conversations held between the Prime Minister and the Defense Minister on the night between 14–15 September 1982. No claim may be made that this decision was adopted by these two alone without convening a cabinet session. On that same night, an extraordinary emergency situation was created which justified immediate and concerted action to prevent a situation which appeared undesirable and even dangerous from Israel's perspective. There is great sense in the supposition that had I.D.F. troops not entered West Beirut, a situation of total chaos and battles between various combat forces would have developed, and the number of victims among the civilian population would have been far greater than it ultimately was. The Israeli military force was the only real force nearby which could take control over West Beirut so as to maintain the peace and prevent a resumption of hostile actions between various militias and communities. The Lebanese army could have performed a function in the refugee camps, but it did not then have the power to enforce order in all of West Beirut. Under these circumstances it could be assumed that were I.D.F. forces not to enter West Beirut, various atrocities would be perpetrated there in the absence of any real authority; and it may be that world public opinion might then have placed responsibility on Israel for having refrained from action.

[. . .]

The demand made in Israel to have the Phalangists take part in the fighting was a general and understandable one; and political, and to some extent military, reasons existed for such participation. The general question of relations with the Phalangists and cooperation with them is a saliently political one, regarding which there may be legitimate differences of opinion and outlook. We do not find it justified to assert that the decision on this participation was unwarranted or that it should not have been made.

It is a different question whether the decision to have the Phalangists enter the camps was justified in the circumstances that were created. . . .

[. . .]

In our view, everyone who had anything to do with events in Lebanon should have felt apprehension about a massacre in the camps, if armed Phalangist forces were to be moved into them without the

I.D.F. exercising concrete and effective supervision and scrutiny of them. All those concerned were well aware that combat morality among the various combatant groups in Lebanon differs from the norm in the I.D.F., that the combatants in Lebanon belittle the value of human life far beyond what is necessary and accepted in wars between civilized peoples, and that various atrocities against the non-combatant population had been widespread in Lebanon since 1975. It was well known that the Phalangists harbor deep enmity for the Palestinians, viewing them as the source of all the troubles that afflicted Lebanon during the years of the civil war. . . .

[. . .]

The decision on the entry of the Phalangists into the refugee camps was taken on Wednesday (15.9.82) in the morning. The Prime Minister was not then informed of the decision. The Prime Minister heard about the decision, together with all the other ministers, in the course of a report made by the Chief of Staff at the Cabinet session on Thursday (16.9.82) when the Phalangists were already in the camps. Thereafter, no report was made to the Prime Minister regarding the excesses of the Phalangists in the camps, and the Prime Minister learned about the events in the camps from a BBC broadcast on Saturday (18.9.82) afternoon. . . .

[. . .]

Recommendations and Closing Remarks
Recommendations

With regard to the following recommendations concerning a group of men who hold senior positions in the Government and the Israel Defense Forces, we have taken into account [the fact] that each one of these men has to his credit [the performance of] many public or military services rendered with sacrifice and devotion on behalf of the State of Israel. If nevertheless we have reached the conclusion that it is incumbent upon us to recommend certain measures against some of these men, it is out of the recognition that the gravity of the matter and its implications for the underpinnings of public morality in the State of Israel call for such measures.

The Prime Minister, The Foreign Minister, and the Head of the Mossad

We have heretofore established the facts and conclusions with regard to the responsibility of the Prime Minister, the Foreign Minister, and the head of the Mossad. In view of what we have determined with regard to the extent of the responsibility of each of them, we are of the opinion that it is sufficient to determine responsibility and there is no need for any further recommendations.

[. . .]

The Minister of Defense, Mr. Ariel Sharon

We have found, as has been detailed in this report, that the Minister of Defense bears personal responsibility. In our opinion, it is fitting that the Minister of Defense draw the appropriate personal conclusions arising out of the defects revealed with regard to the manner in which he discharged the duties of his office—and if necessary, that the Prime Minister consider whether he should exercise his authority under Section 21-A(a) of the Basic Law: the Government, according to which "the Prime Minister may, after informing the Cabinet of his intention to do so, remove a minister from office."

The Chief of Staff, Lt.-Gen. Rafael Eitan

We have arrived at grave conclusions with regard to the acts and omissions of the Chief of Staff, Lt-Gen. Rafael Eitan. The Chief of Staff is about to complete his term of service in April, 1983. Taking into account the fact that an extension of his term is not under consideration, there is no [practical] significance to a recommendation with regard to his continuing in office as Chief of Staff, and therefore we have resolved that it is sufficient to determine responsibility without making any further recommendation.

[...]

Closing Remarks

In the witnesses' testimony and in various documents, stress is laid on the difference between the usual battle ethics of the I.D.F. and the battle ethics of the bloody clashes and combat actions among the various ethnic groups, militias, and fighting forces in Lebanon. The difference is considerable. In the war the I.D.F. waged in Lebanon, many civilians were injured and much loss of life was caused, despite the effort the I.D.F. and its soldiers made not to harm civilians. On more than one occasion, this effort caused I.D.F. troops additional casualties. During the months of the war, I.D.F. soldiers witnessed many sights of killing, destruction, and ruin. From their reactions (about which we have heard) to acts of brutality against civilians, it would appear that despite the terrible sights and experiences of the war and despite the soldier's obligation to behave as a fighter with a certain degree of callousness, I.D.F. soldiers did not lose their sensitivity to atrocities that were perpetrated on non-combatants either out of cruelty or to give vent to vengeful feelings. It is regrettable that the reaction by I.D.F. soldiers to such deeds was not always forceful enough to bring a halt to the despicable acts. It seems to us that the I.D.F. should continue to foster the [consciousness of] basic moral obligations which must be kept even in war conditions, without prejudicing the I.D.F.'s combat ability. The circumstances of combat require the combatants to be tough—which means to give priority to sticking to the objective and being willing to make sacrifices—in order to attain the objectives assigned to them, even under the most difficult conditions. But the end never justifies the means, and basic ethical and human values must be maintained in the use of arms.

Among the responses to the commission from the public, there were those who expressed dissatisfaction with the holding of an inquiry on a subject not directly related to Israel's responsibility.

The argument was advanced that in previous instances of massacre in Lebanon, when the lives of many more people were taken than those of the victims who fell in Sabra and Shatila, world opinion was not shocked and no inquiry commissions were established. We cannot justify this approach to the issue of holding an inquiry, and not only for the formal reason that it was not we who decided to hold the inquiry, but rather the Israeli Government resolved thereon. The main purpose of the inquiry was to bring to light all the important facts relating to the perpetration of the atrocities; it therefore has importance from the perspective of Israel's moral fortitude and its functioning as a democratic state that scrupulously maintains the fundamental principles of the civilized world.

We do not deceive ourselves that the results of this inquiry will convince or satisfy those who have prejudices or selective consciences, but this inquiry was not intended for such people. We have striven and have spared no effort to arrive at the truth, and we hope that all persons of good will who will examine the issue without prejudice will be convinced that the inquiry was conducted without any bias.

[...]

Source: "Report of the Commission of Inquiry into the Events at the Refugee Camps in Beirut, 8 February 1983," Israel Ministry of Foreign Affairs, http://www.mfa.gov.il/MFA.

97. Palestinian National Council Political Resolutions [Excerpt], February 22, 1983

Introduction

Forced to move out of Lebanon, the Palestine Liberation Organization (PLO) reestablished itself in Tunisia. Although North African Arab regimes, especially the radical governments of Algeria and Libya, remained sympathetic, the distance of the new PLO base made renewed attacks there by the organization considerably more difficult. Rhetorically, the PLO remained defiant, holding a meeting of the Palestinian National Council in Algiers in February 1983 that celebrated the organization's heroic struggles in Beirut and affirmed its intention of carrying on the armed struggle by all means possible. Once again, the PLO rejected the Camp David Accords and the Reagan Plan, condemned U.S. support for Israel, and proclaimed "the right of the Palestinian people . . . to establish an independent state under the leadership of the PLO." All Arab states were exhorted to support the PLO and implement the resolutions of successive Arab summit conferences on the subject of Palestine. Jordan in particular was urged to develop close relations with the Palestinians and accept the PLO as their only legitimate representative, since many peace plans envisaged an ultimate confederation linking Jordan and any Palestinian state. The PLO appealed to Iran and Iraq to end the war that had broken out between the two in 1980, a conflict that divided and weakened the Muslim world. The PLO intended to launch enhanced international propaganda efforts to put forward the Palestinian case. However, at this juncture the PLO, despite its enthusiastic verbal support for violent means of struggle, did not openly advocate the destruction of Israel, and outside observers commented that even the PLO was moving in the direction of accommodation with Israel. Indeed, seeking to strengthen its ties with the Soviet Union, the PLO resolutions praised peace proposals put forward by Soviet president Leonid Brezhnev in 1980 that called for an independent Palestinian state, even though Brezhnev was on record then and again in September 1982 as favoring Arab recognition of Israel in return for Israeli withdrawal from the occupied territories. Aligning itself with international radicalism and revolutionary struggles, especially those in South Africa and Namibia, the PLO expressed its intention of deepening its relations with "the socialist countries, primarily the Soviet Union, and various international progressive and liberation forces opposed to racism, colonialism, Zionism and imperialism." The United States and American imperialism were, by contrast, characterized as "standing at the head of the camp hostile to our just cause and the causes of struggling peoples." Long on bombastic rhetoric and revolutionary fervor, the PLO declaration was nonetheless unable to hide the fact that the Israeli military campaign against the organization had greatly curtailed its influence and options. Disillusionment with Yasser Arafat's leadership and his growing willingness to endorse compromise proposals put forward by other Arab leaders soon persuaded members of the Fatah group within the PLO to stage a revolt against him and also encouraged the emergence of other more extreme Palestinian groups.

Primary Source

1. Palestinian National Unity:

The battle of steadfastness of heroism in Lebanon and Beirut epitomizes Palestinian national unity in its best form. The PNC affirms continued adherence to independent Palestinian decision making, its protection, and the resisting of all pressures from whatever source to detract from this independence.

Palestinian Armed Struggle:

The PNC affirms the need to develop and escalate the armed struggle against the Zionist enemy. It affirms the right of the Palestine revolution forces to carry out military action against the Zionist enemy from all Arab Fronts.

[. . .]

2. The Occupied Homeland:

The PNC salutes our steadfast masses in the occupied territory in the face of the occupation, colonization, and uprooting. It also

salutes their comprehensive national unity and their complete rallying around the PLO, the sole legitimate representative of the Palestinian people, both internally and externally. The PNC condemns and denounces all the suspect Israeli and American attempts to strike at Palestinian national unanimity and calls on the masses of our people to resist them.

[. . .]

The National Council salutes the steadfastness of its people inside the areas occupied in 1948 and is proud of their struggle and stand, in the face of racist Zionism, to assert their national identity, it being an indivisible part of the Palestinian people. The council asserts the need to provide all the means of backing for them so as to consolidate their unity and that of their national forces.

Our Dispersed People:

The PNC asserts the need to mobilize the resources of our people wherever they reside outside our occupied land and to consolidate their rallying around the PLO as the sole legitimate representative of our people. It recommends to the Executive Committee to work to preserve the social and economic interests of Palestinians and to defend their gained rights and their basic liberties and security.

Contacts with Jewish Forces:

Affirming resolution 14 of the political declaration issued by the PNC at its thirteenth session held on December 3, 1977, the PNC calls on the Executive Committee to study movement within this framework in line with the interest of the cause of Palestine and the Palestinian national interest.

On the Arab Level:

Deepening cohesion between the Palestinian revolution and the Arab national liberation movement throughout the Arab homeland so as to effectively stand up to the imperialist and Zionist plots and liquidation plans, particularly the Camp David accords and the Reagan plan, and also ending the Zionist occupation of the occupied Arab land, relations between the PLO and the Arab states shall be based on the following:

A. Commitment to the cause of the Arab struggle, first and foremost the cause of and struggle for Palestine.
B. Adherence to the rights of the Palestinian people, including their right to return, self-determination, and the establishment of their own independent state under the leadership of the PLO—rights that were confirmed by the resolutions of the Arab summit conferences.
C. Adherence to the question of sole representation and national unity and respect for national and independent Palestinian decision making.

D. Rejection of all schemes aimed at harming the right of the PLO to be the sole representative of the Palestinian people through any formula such as assigning powers, acting on its behalf, or sharing its right to representation.

The Arab Peace Plan:

The PNC considers the Fez summit resolutions as the minimum for political moves by the Arab states, moves which must complement military action with all its requirements for adjusting the balance of forces in favor of the struggle and Palestinian and Arab rights. The council, in understanding these resolutions, affirms it is not in conflict with the commitment to the political program and the resolutions of the National Council.

Jordan:

Emphasizing the special and distinctive relations linking the Jordanian and Palestinian peoples and the need for action to develop them in harmony with the national interest of the two peoples and the Arab nation, and in order to realize the rights [as] the sole legitimate representative of the Palestinian people, both inside and outside the occupied land, the PNC deems that future relations with Jordan should be founded on the basis of a confederation between two independent states.

Lebanon:

1. Deepening relations with the Lebanese people and their National Forces and extending support and backing to them in their valiant struggle to resist the Zionist occupation and its instruments.

2. At the forefront of the current missions of the Palestinian revolution will be participation with the Lebanese masses and their National and democratic forces in the fight against and the ending of Zionist occupation.

Relations with Syria:

Relations with sister Syria are based on the resolutions of successive PNC sessions which confirm the importance of the strategic relationship between the PLO and Syria in the service of the nationalist and pan-Arab interests of struggle and in order to confront the imperialist and the Zionist enemy, in light of the PLO's and Syria's constituting the vanguard in the face of the common danger.

The Steadfastness and Confrontation Front:

The PNC entrusts the PLO Executive Committee to have talks with the sides of the pan-Arab Steadfastness and Confrontation Front to discuss how it should be revived anew on sound, clear, and effective foundations, working from the premise that the front was not at the level of the tasks requested of it during the Zionist invasion of Lebanon.

Egypt:

The PNC confirms its rejection of the Camp David accords and the autonomy and civil administrations plans linked to them. The council calls on the Executive Committee to develop PLO relations with Egyptian nationalist, democratic, and popular forces struggling against moves to normalize relations with the Zionist enemy in all their forms.

The Iran-Iraq War:

The PNC holds in esteem the efforts of the PLO executive committee to end the Iran-Iraq war through the committees of the non-aligned countries and the Islamic countries. The council calls on the executive committee to continue its efforts to join the war, after Iraq declares the withdrawal of its forces from Iranian territories in response to the call of the Palestinian revolution, to mobilize all forces in the battle for the liberation of Palestine.

On the International Front:

The Brezhnev Plan:

The PNC expresses its esteem and support for the proposals contained in the plan of President Brezhnev published on September 16, 1980 and which affirm the inalienable national rights of our Palestinian people, including those of return, self-determination and the establishment of an independent Palestinian State under the leadership of the PLO, the sole legitimate representative of the Palestinian people. The council also expresses its esteem for the stand of the socialist bloc countries on the just cause of our people as affirmed by the Prague declaration on the Middle East situation, published on January 3, 1983.

The Reagan Plan:

The Reagan Plan, in style and content, does not respect the established national rights of the Palestinian people since it denies the right of return and self-determination and the setting up of the independent Palestinian state and also the PLO—the sole legitimate representative of the Palestinian people—and since it contradicts international legality. Therefore, the PNC rejects the considering of the plan as a sound basis for the just and lasting solution of the cause of the Palestine and the Arab-Zionist conflict.

Source: "Political Statement Issued by the Palestinian National Council," *Al-Fajr,* English version, March 4 1983.

98. Ronald Reagan, Address to the Nation on Events in Lebanon and Grenada [Excerpt], October 27, 1983

Introduction

On October 23, 1983, suicide bombers drove trucks loaded with explosives into the barracks of peacekeeping forces of U.S. marines and French troops stationed in Beirut, the capital of Lebanon. These troops had been deployed there since late 1982 as part of an international peacekeeping force that was trying to maintain order in Beirut after Israeli forces intent on driving out the Palestine Liberation Organization (PLO) had invaded, triggering a complicated civil war among various Lebanese political factions. The bombing killed 241 American servicemen, 58 French paratroopers, and some civilians. The episode was one of the first suicide bombings in the Middle East. Addressing the nation four days later, U.S. president Ronald Reagan affirmed his country's commitment to maintaining order in the Middle East, particularly in Lebanon, and claimed that the attacks were themselves evidence that the marines were succeeding in their mission of restoring stability and normal conditions in Beirut. In practice, nonetheless, shortly afterward the U.S. government, reluctant to face the prospect of further major casualties in such episodes, proclaimed that the marines had accomplished their mission and withdrew them from Lebanon, a decision that hawks later criticized as proving that terrorist tactics were effective. In the same address, Reagan also highlighted the U.S. invasion of the Caribbean island of Grenada, an operation launched two days earlier to overthrow a Marxist government that had murdered socialist prime minister Maurice Bishop and seized power the previous week. Cuban troops and construction workers were present on the island building an airport that it was feared would be used for military purposes, and 1,000 American students were believed to be in danger. In conjunction with forces from seven other Caribbean countries, 5,000 U.S. marines invaded the island and, after some heavy fighting, subdued the Grenadian ground and air forces and the Cuban contingents. They also found a cache of heavy weapons sufficient to arm 10,000 troops. Nineteen American soldiers died and 119 were wounded, while Grenadian casualties were 45 dead and 337 wounded. By mid-December 1983 most resistance had ended except for some rebels who fled to the hills, and U.S. forces were withdrawn. Parliamentary elections held in 1984 returned the noncommunist New National Party to power. The two near-simultaneous episodes encapsulated the degree to which Reagan's bold rhetoric belied his pragmatic caution in international affairs. Like most American presidents and military men in the aftermath of the Vietnam War, he preferred to keep U.S. military interventions brief and limited and to pick conflicts in which victory would be relatively quick and easy.

Primary Source

[. . .]

Some two months ago we were shocked by the brutal massacre of 269 men, women, and children, more than sixty of them Americans, in the shooting down of a Korean airliner. Now, in these past several days, violence has erupted again, in Lebanon and Grenada.

In Lebanon, we have some 1,600 marines, part of a multinational force that is trying to help the people of Lebanon restore order and stability to that troubled land. Our marines are assigned to the south of the city of Beirut, near the only airport operating in Lebanon. Just a mile or so to the north is the Italian contingent and not far from them, the French and a company of British soldiers.

This past Sunday, at 22 minutes after 6 Beirut time, with dawn just breaking, a truck, looking like a lot of other vehicles in the city, approached the airport on a busy, main road. There was nothing in its appearance to suggest it was any different than the trucks or cars that were normally seen on and around the airport. But this one was different. At the wheel was a young man on a suicide mission.

The truck carried some 2,000 pounds of explosives, but there was no way our marine guards could know this. Their first warning that something was wrong came when the truck crashed through a series of barriers, including a chain-link fence and barbed wire entanglements. The guards opened fire, but it was too late. The truck smashed through the doors of the headquarters building in which our marines were sleeping and instantly exploded. The four-story concrete building collapsed in a pile of rubble.

More than 200 of the sleeping men were killed in that one hideous, insane attack. Many others suffered injury and are hospitalized here or in Europe.

This was not the end of the horror. At almost the same instant, another vehicle on a suicide and murder mission crashed into the headquarters of the French peacekeeping force, an eight-story building, destroying it and killing more than 50 French soldiers.

Prior to this day of horror, there had been several tragedies for our men in the multinational force. Attacks by snipers and mortar fire had taken their toll.

I called bereaved parents and/or widows of the victims to express on behalf of all of us our sorrow and sympathy. Sometimes there were questions. And now many of you are asking: Why should our young men be dying in Lebanon? Why is Lebanon important to us?

Well, it is true, Lebanon is a small country, more than five-and-a-half thousand miles from our shores on the edge of what we call the Middle East. But every President who has occupied this office in recent years has recognized that peace in the Middle East is of vital concern to our nation and, indeed, to our allies in Western Europe and Japan. We've been concerned because the Middle East is a powderkeg; four times in the last thirty years, the Arabs and Israelis have gone to war. And each time, the world has teetered near the edge of catastrophe.

The area is key to the economic and political life of the West. Its strategic importance, its energy resources, the Suez Canal, and the well-being of the nearly 200 million people living there—all are vital to us and to world peace. If that key should fall into the hands of a power or powers hostile to the free world, there would be a direct threat to the United States and to our allies.

We have another reason to be involved. Since 1948 our Nation has recognized and accepted a moral obligation to assure the continued existence of Israel as a nation. Israel shares our democratic values and is a formidable force an invader of the Middle East would have to reckon with.

For several years, Lebanon has been torn by internal strife. Once a prosperous, peaceful nation, its government had become ineffective in controlling the militias that warred on each other. Sixteen months ago, we were watching on our TV screens the shelling and bombing of Beirut which was being used as a fortress by PLO bands. Hundreds and hundreds of civilians were being killed and wounded in the daily battles.

Syria, which makes no secret of its claim that Lebanon should be a part of a Greater Syria, was occupying a large part of Lebanon. Today, Syria has become a home for 7,000 Soviet advisers and technicians who man a massive amount of Soviet weaponry, including SS-21 ground-to-ground missiles capable of reaching vital areas of Israel.

A little over a year ago, hoping to build on the Camp David accords, which had led to peace between Israel and Egypt, I proposed a peace plan for the Middle East to end the wars between the Arab States and Israel. It was based on U.N. resolutions 242 and 338 and called for a fair and just solution to the Palestinian problem, as well as a fair and just settlement of issues between the Arab States and Israel.

Before the necessary negotiations could begin, it was essential to get all foreign forces out of Lebanon and to end the fighting there. So, why are we there? Well, the answer is straightforward: to help bring peace to Lebanon and stability to the vital Middle East. To that end, the multinational force was created to help stabilize the situation in Lebanon until a government could be established and a Lebanese army mobilized to restore Lebanese sovereignty over its own soil as the foreign forces withdrew. Israel agreed to withdraw as did Syria, but Syria then reneged on its promise. Over 10,000 Palestinians who had been bringing ruin down on Beirut, however, did leave the country.

Lebanon has formed a government under the leadership of President Gemayel, and that government, with our assistance and training, has set up its own army. In only a year's time, that army has been rebuilt. It's a good army, composed of Lebanese of all factions.

A few weeks ago, the Israeli army pulled back to the Awali River in southern Lebanon. Despite fierce resistance by Syrian-backed forces, the Lebanese army was able to hold the line and maintain the defensive perimeter around Beirut.

In the year that our marines have been there, Lebanon has made important steps toward stability and order. The physical presence of the marines lends support to both the Lebanese Government and its army. It allows the hard work of diplomacy to go forward. Indeed, without the peacekeepers from the U.S., France, Italy, and Britain, the efforts to find a peaceful solution in Lebanon would collapse.

As to that narrower question—what exactly is the operational mission of the marines—the answer is, to secure a piece of Beirut, to keep order in their sector, and to prevent the area from becoming a battlefield. Our marines are not just sitting in an airport. Part of their task is to guard that airport. Because of their presence, the airport has remained operational. In addition, they patrol the surrounding area. This is their part—a limited, but essential part—in the larger effort that I've described.

If our marines must be there, I am asked, why cannot we make them safer? Who committed this latest atrocity against them and why?

Well, we will do everything we can to ensure that our men are as safe as possible. We ordered the battleship *New Jersey* to join our naval forces offshore. Without even firing them, the threat of its sixteen-inch guns silenced those who once fired down on our marines from the hills, and they are a good part of the reason we suddenly had a cease-fire. We're doing our best to make our forces less vulnerable to those who want to snipe at them or send in future suicide missions.

Secretary Shultz called me today from Europe, where he was meeting with the Foreign Ministers of our allies in the multinational force. They remain committed to our task. And plans were made to share information as to how we can improve security for all our men.

We have strong circumstantial evidence that the attack on the marines was directed by terrorists who used the same method to destroy our Embassy in Beirut. Those who directed this atrocity must be dealt justice, and they will be. The obvious purpose behind the sniping and, now, this attack was to weaken American will and force the withdrawal of U.S. and French forces from Lebanon. The clear intent of the terrorists was to eliminate our support of the Lebanese Government and to destroy the ability of the Lebanese people to determine their own destiny.

To answer those who ask if we are serving any purpose in being there, let me answer a question with a question. Would the terrorists have launched their suicide attacks against the multinational force if it were not doing its job? The multinational force was attacked precisely because it is doing the job it was sent to do in Beirut. It is accomplishing its mission.

Now then, where do we go from here? What can we do now to help Lebanon gain greater stability so that our marines can come home? Well, I believe we can take three steps now that will make a difference.

First, we will accelerate the search for peace and stability in that region. Little attention has been paid to the fact that we have had special envoys there working, literally, around the clock to bring the warring factions together. This coming Monday in Geneva, President Gemayel of Lebanon will sit down with other factions from his country to see if national reconciliation can be achieved. He has our firm support. . . .

Second, we will work even more closely with our allies in providing support for the Government of Lebanon and for the rebuilding of a national consensus.

Third, we will ensure that the multinational peace-keeping forces, our marines, are given the greatest possible protection. . . .

Beyond our progress in Lebanon, let us remember that our main goal and purpose is to achieve a broader peace in all of the Middle East. The factions and bitterness that we see in Lebanon are just a microcosm of the difficulties that are spread across much of that region. A peace initiative for the entire Middle East, consistent with the Camp David accords and U.N. resolutions 242 and 338, still offers the best hope for bringing peace to the region.

Let me ask those who say we should get out of Lebanon: If we were to leave Lebanon now, what message would that send to those who foment instability and terrorism? If America were to walk away from Lebanon, what chance would there be for a negotiated settlement, producing a unified democratic Lebanon?

If we turned our backs on Lebanon now, what would be the future of Israel? At stake is the fate of only the second Arab country to negotiate a major agreement with Israel. That is another accomplishment of this past year, the May 17th accord signed by Lebanon and Israel.

If terrorism and intimidation succeed, it will be a devastating blow to the peace process and to Israel's search for genuine security. It will not just be Lebanon sentenced to a future of chaos. Can the United States, or the free world, for that matter, stand by and see the Middle East incorporated into the Soviet bloc? What of Western Europe and Japan's dependence on Middle East oil for the energy to fuel their industries? The Middle East is, as I have said, vital to our national security and economic well-being.

Brave young men have been taken from us. Many others have been grievously wounded. Are we to tell them their sacrifice was wasted? They gave their lives in defense of our national security every bit as much as any man who ever died fighting in a war. We must not strip every ounce of meaning and purpose from their courageous sacrifice.

We are a nation with global responsibilities. We are not somewhere else in the world protecting someone else's interests; we are there protecting our own.

[. . .]

Let us meet our responsibilities. For longer than any of us can remember, the people of the Middle East have lived from war to war with no prospect for any other future. That dreadful cycle must be broken. Why are we there? Well, a Lebanese mother told one of our Ambassadors that her little girl had only attended school two of the last eight years. Now, because of our presence there, she said her daughter could live a normal life.

With patience and firmness, we can help bring peace to that strife-torn region—and make our own lives more secure. Our role is to help the Lebanese put their country together, not to do it for them.

[. . .]

Source: Ronald Reagan, *Public Papers of the Presidents of the United States: Ronald Reagan, 1983,* Vol. 2 (Washington, DC: U.S. Government Printing Office, 1985), 1517–1522.

99. Larry Speakes, Statement on the *Achille Lauro* Hijacking [Excerpt], October 10, 1985

Introduction

Within the Palestine Liberation Organization (PLO), extremists weakened Yasser Arafat's authority as leader. On October 8, 1985, PLO operatives hijacked the *Achille Lauro,* a passenger liner cruising the Mediterranean. They were apparently seeking to retaliate for an Israeli bombing raid one week earlier on the PLO's headquarters in Tunis. The Israeli raid was an operation ostensibly launched as revenge for a Palestinian assassination unit's murder of three Israelis on the island of Cyprus but was probably intended primarily as an attempt to kill Arafat, removing him and the PLO as a factor in ongoing peace negotiations spearheaded by Jordan. The United States endorsed the Israeli raid and thus angered PLO members, 4 of whom decided to seize the cruise ship, take the passengers and crew hostage, and direct the vessel to Israel, where they could disembark and undertake some violent action in revenge for the Israeli attacks. Surprised by a crew member, the 4 gunmen acted prematurely, took over the ship, and then demanded the release of 50 Palestinian prisoners who were in Israeli custody. The gunmen held the vessel for several days, during which they shot and killed one wheelchair-bound American Jewish passenger, Leon Klinghoffer, and dumped his body overboard. The hijackers acted without Arafat's knowledge or authorization, and when he learned of their actions he condemned the operation and ordered them to surrender. After several days of negotiations, they agreed to abandon the liner under a safe conduct and boarded an Egyptian commercial aircraft bound for Tunisia. The U.S. government was not prepared to allow the hijackers to escape unscathed, and U.S. military jets intercepted the airplane and forced it to land at Sigonella airbase in Italy, where the Italians arrested the hijackers. The hijackers were later tried in Italy and received lengthy prison sentences. Over U.S. protests, the Italian government released the plane's other passengers, who included Palestinian operative Abu Abbas, widely believed to have planned the attack. Larry Speakes, U.S. president Ronald Reagan's press spokesman, issued a statement celebrating the capture of the hijackers, praising the cooperation that the United States had received from the Egyptian government, and stating that the United States would never "tolerate terrorism in any form." The episode added ammunition for the opposition that the U.S. and Israeli governments had already expressed to any direct dealings with Arafat and the PLO in peace efforts, since it proved either that the PLO had not abandoned the use of terrorist tactics or that Arafat no longer possessed the authority to control his followers and was therefore an unreliable negotiating partner who could not deliver the PLO behind any agreement that might be concluded.

Primary Source

At the President's direction, U.S. military forces intercepted an aircraft over international airspace that was transporting the *Achille Lauro* terrorists. The aircraft was diverted to the airbase at Sigonella, Italy. In cooperation with the Government of Italy, the terrorists were then taken into Italian custody for appropriate legal proceedings. Earlier today, upon learning that the terrorists would be flown from Egypt to their freedom, the President directed that U.S. forces intercept the aircraft and escort it to a location where the terrorists could be apprehended by those with appropriate jurisdiction. U.S. F-14 aircraft, flying from the carrier *Saratoga*, detected the aircraft in international airspace and intercepted it. They instructed it to follow them and escorted it to the military airbase at Sigonella, Italy. This operation was conducted without firing a shot. The aircraft landed with Italian consent and was surrounded by American and Italian troops. The terrorists aboard were taken into custody by Italian authorities. The Egyptian aircraft, with its crew and other personnel on board, is returning to Egypt.

We have been assured by the Government of Italy that the terrorists will be subject to full due process of law. For our part, we intend to pursue prompt extradition to the United States of those involved in the crime. This action affirms our determination to see that terrorists are apprehended, prosecuted, and punished. This episode also reflects our close cooperation with an exemplary ally and close friend—Italy—in combating international terrorism. The American Government and people are grateful to Prime Minister Craxi, his Government, and the Italian people for their help. . . .

[. . .]

The decision on ending the hijacking was an independent one by the Government of Egypt. When we were consulted, we advised strongly against any arrangements which would permit the terrorists to escape justice. Since the time the terrorists were taken off the ship, we have continued intensive contacts with the Government of Egypt to pursue that point. The United States wants to emphasize the fundamental and durable interests that the United States and Egypt share, interests which transcend this difficult incident. These have been trying times for both our governments. We will do all we can to ensure that the basic U.S.-Egyptian relationship—in which both our countries have taken so much pride for so long—remains unaffected.

In closing, the President wants to emphasize once again that the international scourge of terrorism can only be stamped out if each member of the community of civilized nations meets its responsibility squarely—passing up no opportunity to apprehend, prosecute, and punish terrorists wherever they may be found. We cannot tolerate terrorism in any form. We will continue to take every appropriate measure available to us to deal with these dastardly deeds. There can be no asylum for terrorism or terrorists.

[. . .]

Source: Ronald Reagan, *Public Papers of the Presidents of the United States: Ronald Reagan, 1985*, Vol. 2 (Washington, DC: U.S. Government Printing Office, 1988), 1230–1231.

100. Yasser Arafat, Declaration on Terrorism [Excerpt], November 7, 1985

Introduction

In the wake of the *Achille Lauro* episode, which had the potential to derail ongoing Jordanian–Palestine Liberation Army (PLO) efforts to open a dialogue on permanent peace with Israel, PLO chairman Yasser Arafat stated publicly the PLO's opposition to the use "of all forms of terrorism" and to operations outside the territory of "Palestine." His declaration did not mean that Israel would be immune to attack, since Arafat carefully reserved the Palestinians' right "to resist the Israeli occupation of its land by all available means." He warned, however, that "terrorist operations" elsewhere were counterproductive, since these would merely "hurt the cause of the Palestinian people." Arafat's stance marked another milestone in his gradual embrace of more moderate and accommodating positions, the product, perhaps, of his desire, after decades of struggle, to win back a genuine territorial base for the Palestinians.

Primary Source

The Palestinian people has and continues to struggle to liberate its occupied land, to exercise its right to self-determination, and to establish a state as a necessary condition for achieving a just and lasting peace in the region in which all peoples would coexist, free from acts of terrorism or subjugation.

Despite the political and military changes which the region has witnessed, especially in the last few years, beginning with the Israeli aggression against the PLO in Beirut, Lebanon in 1982 and the Israeli raid on Tunis against the PLO headquarters in 1985, the Palestinian people has continued to struggle and to cling to peace in pursuit of preparing the climate in the region and internationally for a just and peaceful solution. . . .

[. . .]

As an impetus to the efforts which have been exerted to convene an international peace conference, the PLO announces its criticism and condemnation of all acts of terrorism, whether they be those in which states become involved or those committed by individuals or groups against the innocent and defenseless, wherever they may be.

The PLO reaffirms its declaration issued in 1974 which condemned all operations outside [Palestine] and all forms of terrorism. And it restates the adherence of all its groups and institutions to that declaration. Beginning today, the PLO will take all measures to deter violators.

In view of the fact that this adherence cannot be achieved unilaterally, it is up to the international community to force Israel to stop all of its acts of terrorism both inside and outside [Palestine].

In this context, the PLO stresses its insistence upon the right of the Palestinian people to resist the Israeli occupation of its land by all available means, with the goal of achieving withdrawal from its land. For the right to resist foreign occupation is a legitimate right, not abrogated by the UN Charter, which calls for disavowing the use of force or threatening to use it to settle conflicts, and which considers the resort to force a violation of its principles and goals. The right of the Palestinian people to resist the occupation in the occupied ter-

ritories has been stressed in numerous UN resolutions and in the rules of the Geneva Convention.

Events underline the certainty that terrorist operations committed outside [Palestine] hurt the cause of the Palestinian people and distort its legitimate struggle for freedom. From another perspective, these events deepen our conviction that terminating the occupation and putting limits on its policies is the one way to achieve peace and security in the region. The PLO implores all peace-loving powers in all parts of the world to stand beside it as it takes this step to participate in ridding the world of the phenomenon of terrorism and in freeing the individual from fear and protecting him from danger. For in the end, our goal is achieving a just, comprehensive, and lasting peace which will safeguard the affirmation of the enduring national rights of the Palestinian people in order to establish a safe society everywhere.

Source: "Cairo Declaration on the PLO and Terrorism as Read by PLO Chairman Yasir Arafat, Cairo, 7 November 1985," *Journal of Palestine Studies* 15(58) (1986): 214–216. Reprinted with permission.

101. Program of Hezbollah [Excerpt], February 16, 1986

Introduction

As the Palestine Liberation Organization (PLO) moved, however tentatively, in the direction of accommodation with Israel, more radical anti-Israeli groups emerged within the Arab world, their fervor fueled by the growing strength of Islamic fundamentalism. In 1979 a theocratic government headed by the Shia Muslim cleric Ayatollah Ruhollah Khomeini seized power in Iran. Deeply resentful of 25 years of past U.S. support for the deposed Mohammad Reza Shah Pahlavi of Iran, the new Iranian government assailed the United States as the "great Satan." Among the groups competing for power within Lebanon were at least two Shiite factions that received support from Iran and also from Syria, Lebanon's dominant neighbor. Hezbollah was the more extreme of the two. Unlike the largely secular PLO, Hezbollah members prided themselves on their strict adherence to Islamic principles, which, they claimed, demanded that they wage jihad, or holy war, against Israel and also against Phalangist forces in Lebanon. The Hezbollah platform, inspired by the group's mentor, Sheikh Muhammad Hussein Fadlallah, was first published in February 1985 in Beirut. Hezbollah sought to expel all U.S., Western, and Israeli forces from Lebanon and also rejected the United Nations (UN) peacekeeping force. In addition, Hezbollah sought the complete destruction of Israel. Thanks in part to the armaments and other support it received from both Iran and Syria, Hezbollah quickly became a formidable player in Lebanon's convoluted, violent, and faction-ridden politics, making that country as hazardous for Israel as when the PLO held sway there. In southern

Lebanon, which bordered Israel to the north, the organization established mosques, school, and social welfare organizations funded by Iran. Hezbollah forces soon came to number around 4,000, their equipment including more than 11,000 rockets, heavy mortars, and antitank weapons. They used Lebanon as a base from which to attack Israel, lobbing missiles over the border and also crossing over for brief raids and guerrilla attacks. Hezbollah's activities provoked a brief Israeli military intervention in 1996 and a full-scale invasion in July 2006. The organization's emergence meant that Arab and Islamic opposition to Israel was becoming increasingly multipolar and that the PLO now had more radical rivals.

Primary Source

Our Identity

We are often asked: Who are we, the Hizballah, and what is our identity? We are the sons of the *umma* (Muslim community)—the party of God (Hizb Allah) the vanguard of which was made victorious by God in Iran. There the vanguard succeeded to lay down the bases of a Muslim state which plays a central role in the world. We obey the orders of one leader, wise and just, that of our tutor and *faqih* (jurist) who fulfills all the necessary conditions: Ruhollah Musawi Khomeini. God save him!

By virtue of the above, we do not constitute an organized and closed party in Lebanon, nor are we a tight political cadre. We are an *umma* linked to the Muslims of the whole world by the solid doctrinal and religious connection of Islam, whose message God wanted to be fulfilled by the Seal of the Prophets, i.e., Muhammad. This is why whatever touches or strikes the Muslims in Afghanistan, Iraq, the Philippines and elsewhere reverberates throughout the whole Muslim *umma* of which we are an integral part. Our behavior is dictated to us by legal principles laid down by the light of an overall political conception defined by the leading jurist (*wilayat al-faqih*).

As for our culture, it is based on the Holy Koran, the Sunna and the legal rulings of the *faqih* who is our source of imitation (*marja' al-taqlid*). Our culture is crystal clear. It is not complicated and is accessible to all.

No one can imagine the importance of our military potential as our military apparatus is not separate from our overall social fabric. Each of us is a fighting soldier. And when it becomes necessary to carry out the Holy War, each of us takes up his assignment in the fight in accordance with the injunctions of the Law, and that in the framework of the mission carried out under the tutelage of the Commanding Jurist.

Our Fight

The US has tried, through its local agents, to persuade the people that those who crushed their arrogance in Lebanon and frustrated their conspiracy against the oppressed (*mustad'afin*) were nothing but a bunch of fanatic terrorists whose sole aim is to dynamite bars and destroy slot machines. Such suggestions cannot and will not mislead our *umma,* for the whole world knows that whoever wishes to oppose the US, that arrogant superpower, cannot indulge in marginal acts which may make it deviate from its major objective. We combat abomination and we shall tear out its very roots, its primary roots, which are the US. All attempts made to drive us into marginal actions will fail, especially as our determination to fight the US is solid.

We declare openly and loudly that we are an *umma* which fears God only and is by no means ready to tolerate injustice, aggression and humiliation. America, its Atlantic Pact allies, and the Zionist entity in the holy land of Palestine, attacked us and continue to do so without respite. Their aim is to make us eat dust continually. This is why we are, more and more, in a state of permanent alert in order to repel aggression and defend our religion, our existence, our dignity. They invaded our country, destroyed our villages, slit the throats of our children, violated our sanctuaries and appointed masters over our people who committed the worst massacres against our *umma*. They do not cease to give support to these allies of Israel, and do not enable us to decide our future according to our own wishes.

[. . .]

Our people could not bear any more treachery. It decided to oppose infidelity—be it French, American or Israeli—by striking at their headquarters and launching a veritable war of resistance against the Occupation forces. Finally, the enemy had to decide to retreat by stages.

Our Objectives

Let us put it truthfully: the sons of Hizballah know who are their major enemies in the Middle East—the Phalanges, Israel, France and the US. The sons of our *umma* are now in a state of growing confrontation with them, and will remain so until the realization of the following three objectives:

(a) to expel the Americans, the French and their allies definitely from Lebanon, putting an end to any colonialist entity on our land;
(b) to submit the Phalanges to a just power and bring them all to justice for the crimes they have perpetrated against Muslims and Christians;
(c) to permit all the sons of our people to determine their future and to choose in all the liberty the form of government they desire. We call upon all of them to pick the option of Islamic government which, alone, is capable of guaranteeing justice and liberty for all. Only an Islamic regime can stop any further tentative attempts of imperialistic infiltration into our country.

These are Lebanon's objectives; those are its enemies. As for our friends, they are all the world's oppressed peoples. Our friends are also those who combat our enemies and who defend us from their evil. Towards these friends, individuals as well as organizations, we turn and say:

Friends, wherever you are in Lebanon . . . we are in agreement with you on the great and necessary objectives: destroying American hegemony in our land; putting an end to the burdensome Israeli Occupation; beating back all the Phalangists' attempts to monopolize power and administration.

Even though we have, friends, quite different viewpoints as to the means of the struggle, on the levels upon which it must be carried out, we should surmount these tiny divergencies and consolidate cooperation between us in view of the grand design.

We are an *umma* which adheres to the message of Islam. We want all the oppressed to be able to study the divine message in order to bring justice, peace and tranquillity to the world. This is why we don't want to impose Islam upon anybody, as much as we [don't want] that others impose upon us their convictions and their political systems. We don't want Islam to reign in Lebanon by force as is the case with the Maronites today. This is the minimum that we can accept in order to be able to accede by legal means to realize our ambitions, to save Lebanon from its dependence upon East and West, to put an end to foreign occupation and to adopt a regime freely wanted by the people of Lebanon.

This is our perception of the present state of affairs. This is the Lebanon we envision. In the light of our conceptions, our opposition to the present system is the function of two factors: (1) the present regime is the product of an arrogance so unjust that no reform or modification can remedy it. It should be changed radically, and (2) World Imperialism which is hostile to Islam.

We consider that all opposition in Lebanon voiced in the name of reform can only profit, ultimately, the present system. All such opposition which operates within the framework of the conservation and safeguarding of the present constitution without demanding changes at the level of the very foundation of the regime is, hence, an opposition of pure formality which cannot satisfy the interests of the oppressed masses. . . .

[. . .]

To the Christians

If you, Christians, cannot tolerate that Muslims share with you certain domains of government, Allah has also made it intolerable for Muslims to participate in an unjust regime, unjust for you and for us, in a regime which is not predicated upon the prescriptions (*ahkam*) of religion and upon the basis of the Law (the Shari'a) as laid down by Muhammad, the Seal of the Prophets. If you search for justice, who is more just than Allah? It is He who sent down from the sky the message of Islam through his successive prophets in order that they judge the people and give everyone his rights. If you were deceived and misled into believing that we anticipate vengeance against you—your fears are unjustified. For those of you who are peaceful, continue to live in our midst without anybody even thinking to trouble you.

We don't wish you evil. We call upon you to embrace Islam so that you can be happy in this world and the next. If you refuse to adhere to Islam, maintain your ties with the Muslims and don't take part in any activity against them. Free yourselves from the consequences of hateful confessionalism. Banish from your hearts all fanaticism and parochialism. Open your hearts to our Call (*da'wa*) which we address to you. Open yourselves up to Islam where you'll find salvation and happiness upon earth and in the hereafter. We extend this invitation also to all the oppressed among the non-Muslims. As for those who belong to Islam only formally, we exhort them to adhere to Islam in religious practice and to renounce all fanaticisms which are rejected by our religion.

World Scene

We reject both the USSR and the US, both Capitalism and Communism, for both are incapable of laying the foundations for a just society.

With special vehemence we reject UNIFIL as they were sent by world arrogance to occupy areas evacuated by Israel and serve for the latter as a buffer zone. They should be treated much like the Zionists. . . .

[. . .]

The Necessity for the Destruction of Israel

We see in Israel the vanguard of the United States in our Islamic world. It is the hated enemy that must be fought until the hated ones get what they deserve. This enemy is the greatest danger to our future generations and to the destiny of our lands, particularly as it glorifies the ideas of settlement and expansion, initiated in Palestine, and yearning outward to the extension of the Great Israel, from the Euphrates to the Nile.

Our primary assumption in our fight against Israel states that the Zionist entity is aggressive from its inception, and built on lands wrested from their owners, at the expense of the rights of the Muslim people. Therefore our struggle will end only when this entity is obliterated. We recognize no treaty with it, no cease fire, and no peace agreements, whether separate or consolidated.

We vigorously condemn all plans for negotiation with Israel, and regard all negotiators as enemies, for the reason that such negotiation is nothing but the recognition of the legitimacy of the Zionist occupation of Palestine. Therefore we oppose and reject the Camp David Agreements, the proposals of King Fahd, the Fez and Reagan plan, Brezhnev's and the French-Egyptian proposals, and all other programs that include the recognition (even the implied recognition) of the Zionist entity.

Source: "The Hizballah Program," *Jerusalem Quarterly* 48 (Fall 1988): 111–116.

102. Mikhail Gorbachev, Speech on Relations with Israel [Excerpt], April 24, 1987

Introduction

For several decades from the early 1950s onward, Soviet policy in the Middle East tilted in favor of the Arabs and Palestinians. For many years, Soviet leaders had nonetheless aligned themselves with those who favored the United Nations (UN) Security Council Resolution 242 blueprint for peace under whose terms all states in the region would recognize and accept each other's boundaries in return for Israeli withdrawal from most of the occupied territories. The Soviet Union generally provided aid and assistance to radical leftist-oriented governments in the Middle East but nonetheless would have welcomed the greater stability that a lasting Arab-Israeli peace settlement would bring to this volatile region, an area where any crisis had the potential to burgeon into a major confrontation involving the superpowers. Hosting a dinner for visiting Syrian president Hafez al-Assad in 1987, Soviet general secretary Mikhail Gorbachev welcomed new preparations for an international conference on the Middle East, intended to result in comprehensive peace accords, as "the only road out of the impasse." Gorbachev suggested that the UN Security Council's permanent members, including the Soviet Union and the United States, should take the initiative in facilitating preparatory work for this conference. Fearing that Israeli leaders might seek to sabotage this peace move as they had many others, he urged Israel to show goodwill toward the Arabs. Gorbachev nonetheless unequivocally stated that the Soviet Union "recognize[d] without any reservations—to the same extent as with all other countries—the right of Israel to a secure and peaceful existence."

Primary Source

[. . .]

We express solidarity with the Arabs who refuse to recognize the occupation of their lands. We categorically condemn the discrim-

ination against the Palestinian people denied the right to self-determination and the right of a homeland. In the future, like in the past, we will oppose any separate deals, as they are only holding back and thwarting the search for a genuine settlement.

Israeli leaders are stubbornly clinging to a policy which has no prospects. They are trying to build the security of their country by intimidating its neighbors and are using all means, even state terror, for that purpose. This is a faulty and short-sighted policy, the more so since it is directed against almost 200 million Arabs.

There is another, correct and reliable, way for ensuring a secure future for the state of Israel. It is a just peace and, in the final analysis, good neighborly relations with the Arabs.

Much has been said lately about relations between the Soviet Union and Israel, and a lot of lies have been spread, too. Let me put it straight: The absence of such relations cannot be considered normal. But they were severed by Israel in the first place. It happened as a result of the aggression against the Arab countries.

We recognize without any reservations—to the same extent as with all other states—the right of Israel to a peaceful and secure existence. At the same time, like in the past, the Soviet Union is categorically opposed to Tel Aviv's policy of strength and annexations. It should be plain—changes in relations with Israel are conceivable only in the mainstream of the process of settlement in the Middle East. This issue cannot be taken out of such a context. This interrelationship has been created by the course of events, by Israel's policy.

We are confident that preparations for an international conference on the Middle East involving all the sides concerned should be a focal point for collective efforts to bring about a settlement.

This idea, as you know, has no easy fate—it was not accepted at once. But the past years have demonstrated that it is the only road out of the impasse. Today it would not be an exaggeration to say that a substantial part of the international community of nations favors such a conference. Even the United States and Israel cannot maintain an openly negative stand.

The time has come to start careful and painstaking preparatory work. The permanent members of the Security Council could take the initiative in that matter. The Soviet Union, let me reaffirm, is prepared for honest and constructive efforts on a collective bilateral basis.

[. . .]

Source: Mikhail Gorbachev, Speech, April 24, 1987, Foreign Broadcast Information Service, *F.B.I.S.-Daily Report Soviet Union,* April 28, 1987.

103. Communiqué of the Intifada, January 8, 1988

Introduction

By the mid-1980s, the frustration of Palestinians in the occupied territories was growing as faith in the perennially stalemated peace process declined, Israeli settlements expanded, and the prospect of any kind of Palestinian state was perpetually receding. Egypt had renounced its outstanding claims to the occupied Gaza Strip and Jordan was wearying of advocating its own rights in the occupied West Bank. Most Arab leaders had by this time toned down their rhetoric in support of the Palestinians and had some kind of dealings, whether official or not, with Israel. Palestinians in the occupied territories had high birthrates and only limited access to land for either housing or agriculture, and unemployment was rising. Many still lived in camps. In the absence of elections they lacked a political voice and also resented repressive Israeli tactics designed to crush dissent, including sporadic killings of leading agitators, mass detentions, the demolition of houses, and deportations. Muslim clerical leaders also urged opposition to Israel. Although the Palestine Liberation Organization (PLO) quickly claimed credit for the First Intifada, its origins were apparently spontaneous. It was sparked by rioting that broke out near the Jabalya camp in Gaza, home to 60,000 refugees, when 4 Palestinians were killed in a traffic accident in early December 1987. Israeli troops shot dead an 18-year-old Palestinian man who was throwing stones, and the situation snowballed. Riots broke out in camps across the occupied territories, particularly among teenage youths who threw stones and sometimes grenades or Molotov cocktails, to which Israeli forces often responded with bullets. On December 22, 1987, the United Nations (UN) Security Council condemned Israel for violating the Geneva Conventions by shooting numerous protesters dead. The intifada continued until the Oslo Accords were signed in 1993, by which time 1,162 Palestinians, including 241 children, and 160 Israelis had died. Casualties were highest in the first year, with 332 Palestinian and 12 Israeli deaths by the end of 1988. The intifada, especially the large number of fatalities among young people under age 16, refocused foreign attention on the Palestinians and put the issue of their future firmly back on the international agenda, encouraging what would become the Oslo peace process. The plight of the Palestinians increasingly became an embarrassment to Israel. European countries began to give extensive financial support to the Palestinians and their institutions. Criticism of Israel's humanitarian record became intense, both internationally and among many Israelis. The communiqués clandestinely distributed among the Palestinians conveyed the sense of excitement, purpose, and solidarity that emerged among the Palestinian community in the intifada's early days, reenergizing people who had almost lost faith in themselves and, eventually, revitalizing long-stalled peace negotiations.

Primary Source

In the name of God, the merciful, the compassionate.

Our people's glorious uprising continues. We affirm the need to express solidarity with our people wherever they are. We continue to be loyal to the pure blood of our martyrs and to our detained brothers. We also reiterate our rejection of the occupation and its policy of repression, represented in the policy of deportation, mass arrests, curfews, and the demolition of houses.

We reaffirm the need to achieve further cohesion with our revolution and our heroic masses. We also stress our abidance by the call of the PLO, the Palestinian people's legitimate and sole representative, and the need to pursue the bountiful offerings and the heroic uprising. For all these reasons, we address the following call:

All sectors of our heroic people in every location should abide by the call for a general and comprehensive strike until Wednesday evening, 13 January 1988. The strike covers all public and private trade utilities, the Palestinian workers and public transportation. Abidance by the comprehensive strike must be complete. The slogan of the strike will be: Down with occupation; long live Palestine as a free and Arab country.

Brother workers, your abidance by the strike by not going to work and to plants is real support for the glorious uprising, a sanctioning of the pure blood of our martyrs, a support for the call to liberate our prisoners, and an act that will help keep our brother deportees in their homeland.

Brother businessmen and grocers, you must fully abide by the call for a comprehensive strike during the period of the strike. Your abidance by previous strikes is one of the most splendid images of solidarity and sacrifice for the sake of rendering our heroic people's stand a success.

We will do our best to protect the interests of our honest businessmen against measures the Zionist occupation force may resort to against you. We warn against the consequences of becoming involved with some of the occupation authorities' henchmen who will seek to make you open your businesses. We promise you that we will punish such traitor businessmen in the not too distant future. Let us proceed united to forge victory.

Brother owners of taxi companies, we will not forget your honorable and splendid stand of supporting and implementing the comprehensive strike on the day of Palestinian steadfastness. We pin our hopes on you to support and make the comprehensive strike a success. We warn some bus companies against the consequences of not abiding by the call for the strike, as this will make them liable to revolutionary punishment.

Brother doctors and pharmacists, you must be on emergency status to offer assistance to those of our kinfolk who are ill. The brother pharmacists must carry out their duties normally. The brother doctors must place the doctor badge in a way that can be clearly identified.

General warning: We would like to warn people that walking in the streets will not be safe in view of the measures that will be taken to make the comprehensive strike a success. We warn that viscous material will be poured on main and secondary streets and everywhere, in addition to the roadblocks and the strike groups that will be deployed throughout the occupied homeland.

Circular: The struggler and brother members of the popular committees and the men of the uprising who are deployed in all the working locations should work to support and assist our people within the available means, particularly the needy families of our people. The strike groups and the popular uprising groups must completely abide by the working program, which is in their possession. Let us proceed united and loudly chant: Down with occupation; long live Palestine as a free and Arab country.

Source: Zachary Lockman and Joel Beinin, eds., *Intifada: The Palestinian Uprising against Israeli Occupation* (Boston: South End Press, 1989), 328–329.

104. West Bank–Gaza Leaders, Fourteen Points, January 14, 1988

Introduction

Little more than a month after the First Intifada began, Palestine Liberation Organization (PLO) leaders in the occupied territories decided to capitalize on their new international visibility to improve their own standing and to pressure the Israeli government to open serious peace negotiations designed to establish a Palestinian state. They implied that without this the uprising would continue indefinitely, tying down Israeli forces and tarnishing Israel's image, a constant source of friction and instability. Besides demanding that Israeli forces observe the Geneva conventions, release all prisoners arrested during the uprising, cease expulsions of agitators, and withdraw Israeli armed forces from the occupied territories, the statement called for an end to new Israeli settlements in the occupied territories and the termination of various political and economic restrictions and discriminatory practices to which Israel subjected Palestinian inhabitants of the occupied territories. In addition, the statement urged that the PLO be allowed to operate freely in the occupied territories and that Palestinians living there be allowed to serve on its governing body, the Palestinian National Council. After several years of deliberately stalemating peace negotiations, U.S. officials responded quickly to a situation that appeared to be spiraling out of control. In March 1988, U.S. secretary of state George

Shultz announced that with U.S. participation, Israeli and Jordanian-Palestinian delegations were about to open negotiations, intended to be completed in one year, to establish first a transitional and then a final settlement of the Palestinian issue. The process would be based on United Nations (UN) Security Council Resolutions 242 and 334. Other Arab states were also invited to begin bilateral peace talks with Israel, likewise based on these resolutions, under the broad general auspices of a special UN conference for establishing peace. Growing unrest in the unoccupied territories had finally broken the negotiating logjam.

Primary Source

During the past few weeks the Occupied Territories have witnessed a popular uprising against Israel's occupation and its oppressive measures. This uprising has so far resulted in the martyrdom of tens of our people, the wounding of hundreds more, and the imprisonment of thousands of unarmed civilians.

This uprising has come to further affirm our people's unbreakable commitment to its national aspirations. These aspirations include our people's firm national rights of self-determination and of the establishment of an independent state on our national soil under the leadership of the PLO, as our sole legitimate representative. The uprising also comes as further proof of our indefatigable spirit and our rejection of the sense of despair which has begun to creep [in]to the minds of some Arab leaders who claim that the uprising is the result of despair.

The conclusion to be drawn from this uprising is that the present state of affairs in the Palestinian Occupied Territories is unnatural and that Israeli occupation cannot continue forever. Real peace cannot be achieved except through the recognition of Palestinian national rights, including the right of self-determination and the establishment of an independent Palestinian State on Palestinian national soil. Should these rights not be recognized, then the continuation of Israeli occupation will lead to further violence and bloodshed, and the further deepening of hatred. The opportunity for peace will also move farther away.

The only way to extricate ourselves from this scenario is through the convening of an international conference with the participation of all concerned parties including the PLO, the sole legitimate representative of the Palestinian people, as an equal partner, as well as the five permanent members of the Security Council, under the supervision of the two superpowers.

On this basis we call upon the Israeli authorities to comply with the following list of demands as a means to prepare the atmosphere for the convening of the suggested international peace conference, which conference will ensure a just and lasting settlement of the Palestinian problem in all its aspects, bringing about the realization of the inalienable national rights of the Palestinian people, peace and stability for the peoples of the region, and an end to violence and bloodshed:

1. To abide by the 4th Geneva Convention and all other international agreements pertaining to the protection of civilians, their properties and rights under a state of military occupation; to declare the Emergency Regulations of the British Mandate null and void, and to stop applying the iron fist policy;

2. The immediate compliance with Security Council Resolutions 605 and 607, which call upon Israel to abide by the Geneva Convention of 1949 and the Declaration of Human Rights; and which further call for the achievement of a just and lasting settlement of the Arab-Israeli conflict;

3. The release of all prisoners who were arrested during the recent uprising, and foremost among them our children. Also the rescinding of all proceedings and indictments against them;

4. The cancellation of the policy of expulsion, allowing all exiled Palestinians, including the four sent yesterday into exile, to return to their homes and families; also the release of all administrative detainees and the cancellation of the hundreds of house arrest orders. In this connection, special mention must be made of the several hundreds of applications for family reunions, which we call upon the authorities to accept forthwith;

5. The immediate lifting of the siege of all Palestinian refugee camps in the West Bank and Gaza, and the withdrawal of the Israeli army from all population centres;

6. Carrying out a formal inquiry into the behaviour of the soldiers and settlers in the West Bank and Gaza, as well as inside jails and detention camps, and taking due punitive measures against all those convicted of having caused death or bodily harm to unarmed civilians;

7. A cessation of all settlement activity and land confiscation and the release of lands already confiscated, especially in the Gaza Strip, and an end to the harassments and provocations of the Arab population by settlers in the West Bank and Gaza as well as in the Old City of Jerusalem. In particular, the curtailment of the provocative activities in the old city of Jerusalem by Sharon and the ultra-religious settlers of Shuvu Banim and Ateret Cohanim;

8. Refraining from any act which might impinge on the Muslim and Christian holy sites or which might introduce changes to the status quo in the city of Jerusalem;

9. The cancellation of the VAT and all other Israeli taxes which are imposed on Palestinian residents in Jerusalem, the rest of the West Bank, and in Gaza; and the putting to an end of the harassments caused to Palestinian business and tradesmen;

10. The cancellation of all restrictions on political freedoms, including the restrictions on meetings and conventions; also making provisions for free municipal elections under the supervision of a neutral authority;

11. The immediate release of monies deducted from the wages of labourers from the Occupied Territories who worked and still work inside the green line, which amount to several hundreds of millions of dollars. These accumulated deductions, with interest, must be returned to their rightful owners through the agency of the nationalist institutions headed by the worker's unions;

12. The removal of all restrictions on building permits and licences for industrial projects and artesian wells as well as agricultural development programs in the Occupied Territories, and the rescinding of all measures taken to deprive the Occupied Territories of their water resources;

13. The termination of the policy of discrimination being practised against industrial and agricultural produce from the Occupied Territories either by removing the restrictions on the transfer of goods to within the green line, or by placing comparable trade restrictions on the transfer of Israeli goods into the Occupied Territories.

14. The removal of the restrictions on political contacts between inhabitants of the Occupied Territories and the PLO, in such a way as to allow for the participation of Palestinians from the Occupied Territories in the proceedings of the Palestinian National Council, in order to ensure a direct input into the decision-making processes of the Palestinian Nation by the Palestinians under occupation.

Source: Walter Laqueur and Barry Rubin, eds., *The Israel-Arab Reader: A Documentary History of the Middle East Conflict* (New York: Penguin, 2001), 317–319.

105. King Hussein of Jordan, Address to the Nation [Excerpt], July 31, 1988

Introduction

As unrest in the occupied territories intensified and the Palestinians there increasingly asserted both their independent identity and the right of the Palestine Liberation Organization (PLO) to represent them, King Hussein of Jordan decided to renounce all Jordanian claims to the West Bank. In a public statement, he described his hopes that an "independent Palestinian state will be established on the occupied Palestinian land after its liberation." He pledged to continue to support the Palestinians and their position economically and in diplomatic terms. His new position reflected his pragmatic recognition that any Jordanian attempt to retain the West Bank was likely to face fierce PLO opposition, which would in turn destabilize his own kingdom. It was perhaps not entirely coincidental that in this pronouncement Jordan's monarch also declared that "stable and productive societies, are those where orderliness and discipline prevail . . . bind[ing] all members of a community in a solid, harmonious structure." Maintaining these characteristics in his own kingdom had become a higher priority for Hussein than the problematic acquisition of additional contested territory.

Primary Source

[. . .]

. . . I would like to address your hearts and minds in all parts of our beloved Jordanian land. This is all the more important at this juncture, when we have initiated—after seeking God's help and after thorough and extensive study—a series of measures to enhance Palestinian national orientation and highlight Palestinian identity; our goal is the benefit of the Palestinian cause and the Arab Palestinian people.

Our decision, as you know, comes after 38 years of the unity of the two banks, and fourteen years after the Rabat Summit resolution designating the Palestine Liberation Organization (PLO) as the sole legitimate representative of the Palestinian people. It also comes six years after the Fez Summit resolution that agreed unanimously on the establishment of an independent Palestinian state in the occupied West Bank and the Gaza Strip as one of the bases and results of the peaceful settlement.

We are certain that our decision to initiate these measures does not come as a surprise to you. Many among you have anticipated it, and some of you have been calling for it for some time. As for its contents, it has been a topic of discussion and consideration for everyone since the Rabat Summit.

Nevertheless, some may wonder: Why now? Why today and not after the Rabat or Fez summits, for instance?

To answer this question, we need to recall certain facts that preceded the Rabat resolution. We also need to recall considerations that led to the debate over the slogan-objective which the PLO raised and worked to gain Arab and international support for. Namely, the establishment of an independent Palestinian state. This meant, in addition to the PLO's ambition to embody the Palestinian identity on Palestinian national soil, the separation of the West Bank from the Hashemite Kingdom of Jordan.

I reviewed the facts preceding the Rabat resolution, as you recall, before the Arab leaders in the Algiers Extraordinary Summit last June. It may be important to recall that one of the main facts I emphasized was the text of the unity resolution of the two banks of April 1950. This resolution affirms the preservation of all Arab rights in Palestine and the defense of such rights by all legitimate means without prejudicing the final settlement of the just cause of the Palestinian people—within the scope of the people's aspirations and of Arab cooperation and international justice.

Among these facts, there was our 1972 proposal regarding our concept of alternatives, on which the relationship between Jordan on the one hand and the West Bank and Gaza on the other, may be based after their liberation. Among these alternatives was the establishment of a relationship of brotherhood and cooperation between the Hashemite Kingdom of Jordan and the independent Palestinian state in case the Palestinian people opt for that. Simply, this means that we declared our clear-cut position regarding our adherence to the Palestinian people's right to self-determination on their national soil, including their right to establish their own independent state, more than two years before the Rabat Summit resolution. This will be our position until the Palestinian people achieve their complete national goals, God willing.

The relationship of the West Bank with the Hashemite Kingdom of Jordan in light of the PLO's call for the establishment of an independent Palestinian state, can be confined to two considerations: First, the principle[d] consideration pertaining to the issue of Arab unity as a pan-Arab aim, which Arab peoples aspire to and want to achieve. Second, the political consideration pertaining to the extent of the Palestinian struggles from the continuation of the legal relationship to the Kingdom's two banks. Our answer to the question, "why now?", also derives from these two factors, and the background of the clear and constant Jordanian position on the Palestinian cause, as already outlined.

Regarding the principled consideration, Arab unity between any two or more countries is an option of any Arab people. This is what we believe. Accordingly, we responded to the wish of the Palestinian people's representatives for unity with Jordan in 1950. From this premise, we respect the wish of the PLO, the sole and legitimate representative of the Palestinian people, to secede from us as an independent Palestinian state. . . .

[. . .]

Lately, it has transpired that there is a general Palestinian and Arab orientation which believes in the need to highlight the Palestinian identity in full in all efforts and activities that are related to the Palestine question and its developments. It has also become clear that there is a general conviction that maintaining the legal and administrative links with the West Bank, and the ensuing Jordanian interaction with our Palestinian brothers under occupation through Jordanian institutions in the occupied territories, contradicts this orientation. It is also viewed that these links hamper the Palestinian struggle to gain international support for the Palestinian cause of a people struggling against foreign occupation.

In view of this line of thought, which is certainly inspired by genuine Palestinian will, and Arab determination to support the Palestinian cause, it becomes our duty to be part of this direction, and to respond to its requirements. After all, we are a part of our nation, supportive of its causes, foremost among which is the Palestinian cause. Since there is a general conviction that the struggle to liberate the occupied Palestinian land could be enhanced by dismantling the legal and administrative links between the two banks, we have to fulfill our duty, and do what is required of us.

At the Rabat Summit of 1974 we responded to the Arab leaders' appeal to us to continue our interaction with the Occupied West Bank through Jordanian institutions, to support the steadfastness of our brothers there. Today we respond to the wish of the Palestine Liberation Organization, the sole legitimate representative of the Palestinian People, and to the Arab orientation to affirm the Palestinian identity in all its aspects. We pray to God that this step be a substantive addition to the intensifying Palestinian struggle for freedom and independence.

Brother Citizens,

These are the reasons, the considerations, and the convictions that led us to respond favorably to the wish of the PLO, and to the general Arab direction consistent with it. We cannot continue in this state of suspension, which can neither serve Jordan nor the Palestinian cause. We had to leave the labyrinth of fears and doubts, towards clearer horizons where mutual trust, understanding, and cooperation can prevail, to the benefit of the Palestinian cause and Arab unity. This unity will remain a goal which all the Arab peoples cherish and seek to realize.

At the same time, it has to be understood in all clarity, and without any ambiguity or equivocation, that our measures regarding the West Bank concern only the occupied Palestinian land and its people. They naturally do not relate in any way to the Jordanian citizens of Palestinian origin in the Hashemite Kingdom of Jordan. They all have the full rights of citizenship and all its obligations, the same as any other citizen irrespective of his origin. They are an integral part of the Jordanian state to which they belong, on whose soil they live, and in whose life and various activities they participate. Jordan is not Palestine and the independent Palestinian state will be established on the occupied Palestinian territory after its liberation, God willing. There the Palestinian identity will be embodied, and there the Palestinian struggle shall come to fruition, as confirmed by the glorious uprising of the Palestinian people under occupation.

If national unity in any country is dear and precious, it is for us in Jordan more than that. It is the basis of our stability and the cause of our development and prosperity, as well as the foundation of our national security and the source of our faith in the future. It is also a living embodiment of the principles of the Great Arab Revolt which we inherited and whose banner we are proudly carrying. It is also a living example of constructive plurality and a sound nucleus of wider Arab unity.

Based on that, safeguarding national unity is a sacred duty that will not be compromised. Any attempt to undermine it, under any pretext, would only help the enemy carry out his policy of expansion at the expense of Palestine and Jordan alike. Consequently, true nationalism lies in bolstering and fortifying national unity. Moreover, the responsibility to safeguard it falls on every one of you, leaving no place in our midst for sedition or treachery. With God's help, we shall be as always, a united cohesive family, whose members are joined by bonds of brotherhood, affection, awareness, and common national objectives.

It is most important to remember, as we emphasize the importance of safeguarding national unity, that stable and productive societies, are those where orderliness and discipline prevail. Discipline is the solid fabric that binds all members of a community in a solid, harmonious structure, blocking all avenues before the enemies, and opening horizons of hope for future generations.

The constructive plurality which Jordan has lived since its foundation, and through which it has witnessed progress and prosperity in all aspects of life, emanates not only from our faith in the sanctity of national unity, but also in the importance of Jordan's pan-Arab role. Jordan presents itself as the living example of the merger of various Arab groups on its soil, within the framework of good citizenship, and one Jordanian people. This paradigm that we live on our soil gives us faith in the inevitability of attaining Arab unity, God willing.

[. . .]

To dispel any doubts that may arise out of our measures, we assure you that these measures do not mean the abandonment of our national duty, either towards the Arab-Israeli conflict, or towards the Palestinian cause. Nor do they mean relinquishing our faith in Arab unity. As I have stated, these steps were taken only in response to the wish of the Palestine Liberation Organization, the sole legitimate representative of the Palestinian people, and the prevailing Arab conviction that such measures will contribute to the struggle of the Palestinian people and their glorious uprising. Jordan will continue its support for the steadfastness of the Palestinian people, and their courageous uprising in the occupied Palestinian land, within its capabilities. . . .

[. . .]

In addition, Jordan will not give up its commitment to take part in the peace process. We have contributed to the peace process until it reached the stage of a consensus to convene an international peace conference on the Middle East. The purpose of the conference would be to achieve a just and comprehensive peace settlement to the Arab-Israeli conflict, and the settlement of the Palestinian problem in all its aspects. We have defined our position in this regard, as everybody knows, through the six principles which we have already made public.

[...]

106. Hamas Charter, Defining the Hamas Movement [Excerpt], August 18, 1988

Introduction

As the Palestine Liberation Organization (PLO) moved closer to opening genuine negotiations with Israel and accepting, however grudgingly, the right to existence of its longtime enemy, more militant Islamic-influenced elements among the Palestinians and other Arabs dissented, establishing the Islamic Resistance Movement, usually known as Hamas. The organization evolved from the Islamic Mujama group, established in 1973 in Gaza with Israeli encouragement as a Muslim welfare group that was itself an off-shoot of the Muslim Brotherhood, a Palestinian organization established in 1946 to encourage the development of a religious outlook within Palestinian society. The fundamentalist Muslim resurgence of the 1980s, fueled by the establishment of an Islamic government in Iran in 1979, encouraged the Mujama to take a harder line in asserting strict Islamic principles and tenets among the Gazan population. In February 1988 soon after the First Intifada began, the Mujama established Hamas so that its members could join in the uprising. A political wing conducted propaganda; an intelligence section handled internal policing, killing or punishing collaborators with Israel; and the military wing—later merged with the intelligence branch—undertook violent action against Israel, including the kidnapping and killing of Israeli soldiers. PLO and Hamas representatives were often at odds, and Hamas gradually became an influential faction within the PLO, soon rivaling Arafat's original Fatah organization. The lengthy Hamas charter, promulgated in August 1988, took a far more uncompromising line than Arafat was now embracing. Hamas claimed that all of Palestine, including Israeli territory, was a sacred Islamic trust, none of which could or should be abandoned. Islamic Sharia, or religious law, ought to prevail throughout Palestine. Hamas opposed all peace negotiations, stating: "Initiatives, and so-called peaceful solutions and international conferences, contradict the Islamic Resistance Movement's ideological position." Jihad, or holy war, was the only solution to the Palestinian question. The struggle against Israel could not end until Israel had been totally destroyed. Hamas embraced violence and terror as the only methods that could accomplish the return of all Palestine to the Palestinians and Islamic rule. The emergence of Hamas as a significant factor in Palestinian politics, given the organization's strong religious orientation and its belief that compromise or negotiations with Israel amounted to sacrilege, greatly complicated subsequent efforts for peace. Hamas would not be content with establishing a Palestinian state in the occupied territories but instead also sought to regain all the lands considered part of Israel. Hamas's emphasis on providing welfare services to ordinary Palestinians along with its unsubtle message and staunch religious orientation soon won it considerable popularity among the Arab masses, while its programs received substantial financial support from other Arab governments.

Primary Source

The ideological tenets
Article 1

The path of the Islamic Resistance Movement is the path of Islam, from which it draws its principles, concepts, terms and worldview with regard to life and man. It turns to [Islam] when religious rulings are required and asks [Islam] for inspiration to guide its steps.

The relationship between the Islamic Resistance Movement and the Muslim Brotherhood
Article 2

The Islamic Resistance Movement is the branch of the Muslim Brotherhood in Palestine. The Muslim Brotherhood is a global organization and the largest Islamic movement in modern times. It excels in profound understanding and has an exact, fully comprehensive perception of all Islamic concepts in all areas of life: understanding and thought, politics and economics, education and social affairs, law and government, spreading Islam and teaching, art and the media, by that which is hidden and by martyrdom and in the other areas of life.

Structure and composition [of the organization]
Article 3

The basic structure of the Islamic Resistance Movement is founded on Muslims who have put their faith in Allah and worship him as is fit [as it is written in the Qur'an], "I created the jinns and humans only for the purpose that they worship me." They have recognized their duties towards themselves, their families and their homeland. They have feared Allah in all these matters and flown the banner of jihad in the faces of tyrants to expel them from the land, and to clean pollution from the faithful, [and to remove] their malice and evil. . . .

Article 4

The Islamic Resistance Movement welcomes every Muslim who adopts its worldview and its way of thinking, who adheres to its path, keeps its secrets, wishes to join its ranks to fulfill the duty [*sic*], and Allah will grant him his reward.

Article 5

The dimension of time for the Islamic Resistance Movement is the adoption of Islam as a way of life. Time continues from the day the Islamic mission was born and the first generation of the faithful who trod the path of righteousness. Allah is its purpose, the messenger [the prophet Muhammad] is its exemplary figure and the Qur'an is its constitution. The dimension of space is every place Muslims are found who have adopted Islam as their way of life, in every corner of the globe. Thus Hamas strikes root in the depths of the ground and spreads to encompass the sky.

"For see to what Allah has likened a good word: to a beautiful tree whose roots are firmly planted and whose branches reach the sky, and whose fruit is always given at the right time, with the permission of its master. Allah gave [such] parables to men so that they might heed" ([Surah 14] Ibrahim [Verses] 24–25).

Uniqueness and Independence
Article 6

The Islamic Resistance Movement is uniquely Palestinian. It has faith in Allah and adopts Islam as its way of life. It acts to fly the banner of Allah over all of Palestine, because people of all religions can live in the shadow of Islam in tranquility and security for their lives, property and rights. However, in the absence of Islam a conflict develops so that injustice, corruption grow, more conflicts are created, and [eventually] war breaks out.

How great is the Muslim poet Muhammad Iqbal who wrote:

"When faith is lost there is no safety and no life for anyone who does not revive religion. He who is content with life without religion has made obliteration of the self his life's companion."

The universality of the Islamic Resistance Movement
Article 7

Muslims who adopt the path of the Islamic Resistance Movement and act to support it, to adopt its positions and to strengthen its holy war are spread over the face of the earth, making the movement universal. The movement is qualified for that because of the clarity of its worldview, its noble purpose and the exalted quality of its goals.

That is how the movement should be considered, how its value should be judged and how its role should be recognized. Whoever denies its right, refrains from supporting it or whose vision is impaired and who works unceasingly to blur its role, is like someone contesting fate [as determined by Allah], and who closes his eyes to the facts, either intentionally or unintentionally. When he opens his eyes, he will realize that events have passed him by. Then he will become exhausted in his [useless] effort to justify his previous position, unable to sustain it any longer [compared to someone who] preceded him [and joined the movement and] has preference [over him].

[As written:] The injustice inflicted by one's close relatives is more painful to the soul than a sharp, powerful blow from the sharpest sword. [As it is written in the Qur'an]: "We brought to you [Muhammad] from on high the [holy] book [i.e., scripture] with the truth, confirming the scripture[s] that came before it and with final authority over them. Therefore, judge between them according to everything Allah brought down [to you], and do not follow their whims which deviate from the truth which has been revealed to you. Each of you was given a law and a path. If [Allah] had so willed, he would have made you one community of believers, but he also desired to test you with what he has given to you. Therefore, aspire among yourselves to be first in good deeds, for you will all return to Allah, and then he will clarify for you all the matters you did not agree upon" ([Surah 5] Al-Ma'idah [Verse] 48).

The Islamic Resistance Movement is [also] one link in the chain of holy war in its confrontation with the Zionist invasion. [The movement] has had a strong connection with and is linked to the holy martyr Izzedine al-Qassam and his jihad warrior brethren [mujahideen] from among the Muslim Brotherhood since 1936. From there it is closely related and connected to the next link [namely] the holy war of the Palestinians, and to the efforts and holy war of the Muslim Brotherhood in the war of 1948 and the jihad operations of the Muslim Brotherhood in 1968 and afterwards.

Actually, the links are distant from one another [in time], and the obstacles placed before the jihad warriors by the followers of Zionism stopped the jihad from continuing. Nevertheless the Islamic Resistance Movement aspires to bring the promise of Allah to pass, no matter how long it takes. As the prophet [Muhammad], may the prayer of Allah and his blessing of peace be upon him, said: "The time [Judgment Day] will not come until Muslims fight the Jews and kill them and until the Jew hides behind the rocks and trees, and [then] the rocks and trees will say: 'Oh Muslim, oh servant of Allah, there is a Jew hiding [behind me], come and kill him', except for the gharqad [salt-bush tree], so it is the tree of the Jews" ([Hadith] recorded in [the reliable collections of] Al-Bukhari and Muslim).

The Islamic Resistance Movement's motto
Article 8

Allah is its purpose, the messenger [the prophet Muhammad] is its exemplary figure and the Qur'an is its constitution, jihad is its path and death for the sake of Allah is the most exalted wish.

Goals
Causes and targets
Article 9

The Islamic Resistance Movement was born in an era in which Islam was absent from daily life. As a result, balances were upset, concepts were confused, values altered and evil people took power. Injustice and darkness prevailed, cowards behaved like tigers, homelands were taken by force and people were driven out and wandered purposelessly all over the earth. The Country of Truth disappeared and was replaced by the Country of Falsehood, [consequently] nothing was left in its rightful place. That is the state of affairs when Islam vanishes from the scene, everything changes, and those are the causes.

As to the goals [of the Islamic Resistance Movement], they are: a war to the death against falsehood, conquering it and stamping it out so that truth may prevail, homelands may be returned [to their rightful owners] and the call of the muezzin may be heard from the turrets of the mosques, announcing the [re]institution of an Islamic state, so that Muslims might return and everything return to its rightful place, with the help of Allah, [as it is written in the Qur'an:] "If Allah did not urge people not to lay hands upon one another, the land would [certainly] be in disarray, but Allah bestows his grace on all human beings" ([Surah 2] Al-Baqarah [Verse] 251).

Article 10

The Islamic Resistance Movement, while making its way forward, with all its might [offers] support to anyone oppressed and protects anyone who feels he was unjustly treated. It does not spare any effort to institute justice and wipe out falsehood, in word and deed, both in this place and in every place it reaches and wherever it can have influence.

Strategy and means
The strategy of the Islamic Resistance Movement
Palestine is Islamic Waqf [Religious Endowment] land
Article 11

The Islamic Resistance Movement believes that the land of Palestine is a religious Islamic endowment for all Muslims until Resurrection Day. It is forbidden to relinquish it or any part of it or give it up or any part of it. It does not belong to any Arab country, or to all the Arab countries, or to any king or president, or kings or presidents, or to any organization or organizations, whether they are Palestinian or Arab, because Palestine is sacred Islamic endowment land and belongs to Muslims until Resurrection Day. Its legal status is in accordance with Islamic law. It is subject to the same law to which are subject all the territories conquered by Muslims by force, for at the time of the conquest [the Muslim conquerors] consecrated it as a Muslim religious endowment for all Muslim generations until Resurrection Day.

It happened thus: after the commanders of the Islamic armies conquered Al-Sham and Iraq, they sent the Muslim Caliph, Omar bin al-Khattab, [messages] in which they consulted with him about [the fate of] the conquered land—whether to divide it among the soldiers or to leave it to its owners [or act in some other way]. After consultations and deliberations between the Muslim Caliph, Omar bin al-Khattab, and the companions of Allah's messenger, may

Allah's prayer and blessing of peace be upon him, the decision was made whereby the land would remain in the hands of its [original] owners, who would be able to enjoy it and its fruits. With regard to [the right] of possession of the land and of the land itself, [it was decided that] it would be sacred to Muslims forever until Resurrection Day, but its owners would have the right to enjoy [only] its fruits. That endowment exists as long as the sky and earth exist. Therefore any act performed in opposition to Muslim law with regard to Palestine is null and void, [as it is written in the Qur'an:] "For this is indeed certain truth, and therefore praise the name of your exalted lord" ([Surah 56] Al Waqi'ah [Verse] 95).

The homeland and particular nationalism from the Islamic Resistance Movement's point of view
Article 12

From the point of view of the Islamic Resistance Movement, particular nationalism is part of the religious faith. There is nothing more serious or profound which reflects that type of nationalism than the fact that the enemy has trampled on Muslim soil. In such a situation, launching a holy war [against] him and confronting him become the personal duty of every Muslim man and woman: the woman goes out to fight [the enemy] without her husband's permission, and [even] the slave [is obliged to go out to fight the enemy] without the permission of his master. There is nothing like it in any other political system and that is an indisputable fact. If all the various national particularist [movements] are linked to [and characterized] by physical, human or regional factors, then the Islamic Resistance Movement is also characterized by all of the above. Moreover, and most important, it is [also] characterized by divine motives which breathe life and soul into it, since it is strongly linked to the source of the spirit and [to him who] gives [it] life. It [i.e., Hamas] waves the divine banner in the sky of the homeland, strongly joining together heaven and earth, [as the widely known Muslim Arab saying states:] "When Moses came and threw down his rod, it was the end of magic and magicians. True guidance has become distinct from error; therefore, whoever rejects false gods and believes in Allah has grasped the firmest hand-hold, one that will never break, for Allah is all-hearing and all-knowing" ([Surah 2] Al-Baqarah [Verse] 256).

Peaceful solutions, diplomatic initiatives and international conferences
Article 13

Initiatives, the so-called peaceful solutions and international conferences to find a solution to the Palestinian problem, contradict the Islamic Resistance Movement's ideological position. Giving up any part whatsoever of [the land of] Palestine is like ignoring a part of [the Muslim] faith. Accordingly, the particular nationalism of the Islamic Resistance Movement is [also] part of its faith. For the sake of hoisting the banner of Allah over their homeland they fight, [and it is written in the Qur'an that] "Allah always prevails [in the end], although most people do not realize that" ([Surah 12] Yusuf [Verse] 20).

Sometimes the call is heard for an international conference to discuss a solution for the [Palestinian] problem. There are those who agree [to that proposal] and those who reject it for one reason or another. They demand the fulfillment of a certain condition or conditions in return for their agreement to hold a conference and to participate in it. The Islamic Resistance Movement is very familiar with both sides of the conferences and their [negative] positions regarding Muslim interests in the past and present. Therefore, the Movement does not consider such frameworks capable of meeting the demands [of the Palestinians] or of restoring their rights or of bringing justice to the oppressed. Thus such conferences are but one of the means used by the infidels to prevail over Muslim land, and when have the infidels treated the faithful justly?

"The Jews will never be pleased with you, nor will the Christians, until you have followed their religion. Say therefore, Allah's guidance is the only true guidance. But if you were to follow their desires after the knowledge that has come to you, then you would find no one to protect or guard you from Allah" ([Surah 2] Al-Baqarah [Verse] 120).

There is no solution to the Palestinian problem except jihad. As for international initiatives, suggestions and conferences, they are an empty waste of time and complete nonsense. . . .

The three spheres
Article 14

The problem of the liberation of Palestine has three spheres: the Palestinian, the pan-Arab and the Islamic. Each has a role to play in the struggle against the Zionists and [also has] duties. Neglecting one of the spheres is a terrible mistake and shameful ignorance, for Palestine is Islamic land. In it is the first of the two directions [to which] worshippers at prayer [turn], and the third [most holy place] after the first two. It is also the destination of the night ride of the prophet of Allah, may Allah's prayer and blessing of peace be upon him. "Praised be he who took his servant on a night ride from the sacred mosque to the farthest mosque whose precincts we blessed, to show him some of our signs. He alone is the all-hearing, the all-seeing" ([Surah 17] Al-Israa' [Verse] 1).

That being the case, the liberation [of Palestine] is the personal duty of every Muslim, wherever he may be. [Only] on that basis can [a solution for] the [Palestinian] problem be considered, and every Muslim must fully understand that. On the day the [Palestinian] problem is treated on that basis, when all the capabilities of the three spheres are mobilized, the current situation will change and the day of liberation will be nearer. "The fear of you [believers] in their [the Jews'] hearts is greater than their fear of Allah, because they are a people devoid of understanding" ([Surah 59] Al-Hashr [Verse] 13).

The jihad for the sake of liberating Palestine is a personal duty
Article 15

The day enemies steal part of Muslim land, jihad [becomes] the personal duty of every Muslim. With regard to the usurpation of Palestine by the Jews, it is a must to fly the banner of jihad. That means the propagation of Islamic awareness among the masses—locally [in Palestine], the Arab world and the Muslim world. The spirit of jihad must be disseminated within the [Islamic] nation, the enemies must be engaged in battle and [every Muslim must] join the ranks of the jihad warriors [mujahideen].

It is therefore necessary that religious scholars ['ulamaa], educators, media personalities, the educated public and especially the younger generation and the leaders of the Islamic movement take part in [this] campaign to create awareness [i.e., indoctrination]. In addition, fundamental changes must be made in the school curricula to free them from the influences of the intellectual [Western] invasion they have been subjected to by Orientalists and missionaries. That invasion took the region by surprise after Salah al-Din al-Ayoubi [Saladin] defeated the Crusader armies. The Crusaders then realized that the Muslims could not be conquered unless the way had [first] been prepared by an ideological invasion to muddle the [Muslims'] thoughts, distort their heritage and defame their ideals, and [only] then could a military invasion take place. [All] that happened in preparation for the [Western] imperialist invasion, when [General] Allenby announced on his entrance to Jerusalem: "Finally the Crusades are over," and General Gouraud stood on Salah al-Din's grave and said: "Salah al-Din, we have returned." Imperialism reinforced the intellectual invasion and deepened its roots, and it still [does so]. All that paved the way for the loss of Palestine.

Therefore, what must be done is to instill in the minds of all the Muslim generations that the problem of Palestine is religious, and on that basis it must be dealt with. After all, there are holy sites in Palestine which are sacred to Islam: Al-Aqsa mosque is there, and it has an indissoluble tie to the holy mosque in Mecca as long as the heaven and earth endure, because of the night ride of the prophet of Allah, may Allah's prayer and a blessing of peace be upon him, and his ascension to heaven from there. "Being stationed on the frontier for the sake of Allah [for only] one day is better than this world and everything in it. Likewise, a portion of paradise as small as [the place] which is taken by a [horseman's] whip belonging to any of you [i.e., the jihad warriors] is better than all this world and everything in it." The incursion to the ranks of the enemy and the tactical withdrawal in preparation for another attack [as part of jihad] by any Muslim are better than this world and what is in it (as recounted in [the collection of hadiths of] Al-Bukhari, Muslim, al-Tirmidhi and Ibn Majah). "By the life of him in whose hands rests Muhammad's, I wish I could participate in an invasion for the sake of Allah and be killed in it, and after that to fight and then to die, and after to fight and then to die" (as is told [in the collection of hadiths of] Al-Bukhari and Muslim).

Educating the next generations
Article 16

The coming generations raised in our region must receive an Islamic education based on carrying out the commandments of [the Islamic] religion and a conscious study of the book of Allah [the Qur'an] and of the Muslim tradition and of the prophet [Muhammad]. In addition, we must teach them from reliable sources of Islamic history and heritage under the instruction of specialists and scholars, and prepare curricula which will create the correct outlook in the thoughts and beliefs of the Muslim [student]. At the same time it is necessary to make an attentive study of the enemy and his material and human resources, while recognizing his weak spots and sources of power and the general forces supporting and standing by him. [Likewise] it is necessary to be familiar with events as they happen, to be up-to-date and to study their analyses and interpretations. It is also necessary to plan for the present and the future and to examine everything that happens so that the Muslim jihad warrior will live his life aware of his purpose, aim, path and what takes place around him, [as it is written in the Qur'an:] "My son, something whose weight is but the weight of a mustard seed even if it is within a rock or in the sky or in the depths of the earth, Allah will find [and bring] it [to light]. Allah is most kind and knows everything inside out. My small son, say the prayer and command what is right and forbid that which is wrong and bear everything that happens to you steadfastly. That is a sign of treating things with firmness. Do not treat people with contempt or behave arrogantly in public. Allah does not like any person behaving with arrogance" ([Surah 31] Al-Luqman [Verses] 16–18).

The role of the Muslim woman
Article 17

The role of the Muslim woman in the battle for liberation is no less important than that of the man, for she is the maker of men. She has a supremely important role in guiding the coming generations and educating them. Indeed, enemies have long since understood the importance of her role. Their view toward her is that if they can guide her and raise her as they please, devoid of Islam, then they will win the battle [against us]. Therefore you discover that they devote a great deal of continuous effort to their attempts using the media, movies and curricula [which they wield] through their proxies within the Zionist organizations, the latter assuming all sorts of names and forms, such as The Organization of Freemasons, Rotary clubs, espionage groups and others, all of which are nothing more than dens of sabotage and saboteurs.

[...]

On the day Islam [will be in a position to] direct life, it will eradicate the organizations hostile to humanity and to Islam.

Article 18

The woman in the home of a jihad warrior and a jihad warrior family, whether she is a mother or a sister, fills the most important role of taking care of the home, raising the children according to the moral ideas and values derived from Islam and educating her children to follow the precepts of [the Islamic] religion in preparation for the role in the jihad that awaits them. Therefore, much attention must be paid to the schools and curricula of the Muslim girl's education so that she may grow up and be a proper mother, aware of her role in the battle [for the] liberation [of Palestine].

She must also have enough perception and awareness to conduct household affairs. Being economical and avoiding waste in the family's expenses are part of the necessary requirements for surviving in the difficult conditions prevailing. Thus she must always be aware [that] the money available [to her] is like blood which must run through the veins solely for the purpose of continuing the life of young and old alike, [as it is written in the Qur'an:] "Muslim men and women who are faithful and devout, true, brave, modest, give charity, fast, are chaste and often call upon Allah—for them Allah has prepared mercy and a great reward" ([Surah 33] Al-Ahzab [Verse] 35).

The function of Islamic art in the battle for liberation
Article 19

Art has its own rules and standards, by which it is possible to determine whether it is Islamic or jahili [pagan]. The issues of Islamic liberation need Islamic art which will uplift the spirit without making one aspect of a person more prominent than the other; on the contrary, it must raise all aspects of the individual in a balanced, harmonious fashion.

Indeed, the human being is a unique and wonderful creature, [made from] a handful of clay [combined with] a spiritual soul [of Allah]. Accordingly, Islamic art relates to humans based on that basis, while jahili art relates only to the body, and gives predominance to the aspect of clay.

Therefore, if books, articles, publications, sermons, treatises, folk songs, poetry, [patriotic] songs, plays, etc., contain the characteristics of Islamic art, they are among the elements needed for ideological recruitment. They are also the refreshing nourishment necessary to continue the journey and provide rest for the soul, for the way is long and the suffering great and the souls become weary. That is, Islamic art renews activity, sets [things] in motion, and awakens within the soul sublime meaning and sound behavior. There is nothing that can repair the soul if it is in retreat except the change from one state to another. These are all very serious things and not to be taken lightly, for the jihad warrior nation knows no jest.

Mutual guarantees and [Muslim] solidarity
Article 20

Muslim society is [characterized by] solidarity. Indeed, the messenger [the prophet Muhammad], may Allah's prayer and his blessing of peace be upon him, said [in the hadith]: "Blessed are the sons of the al-Ash'ariyyun tribe. When they were required to make an effort either in an area where they had settled or during [a long] journey, they would collect everything they had and divide it equally." That is the Islamic spirit that must prevail in Muslim society. A society facing a cruel enemy who behaves like a Nazi that does not distinguish between man and woman, young and old, must wrap itself in such an Islamic spirit. For our enemy relies on collective punishment. It deprives people [i.e., the Palestinians] of their homes and possessions. It hunts them down in exile and wherever they gather. [The Zionist enemy] relies on breaking bones, shooting women, children and old people, with or without a reason. He opened detention camps to throw into them many thousands of people [i.e., Palestinians], [who live there] in subhuman conditions. In addition, he destroys homes, turns children into orphans and unjustly convicts thousands of young people so that they may spend the best years of their lives in the dark pits of their jails.

The Jews' Nazism includes [brutal behavior towards Palestinian] women and children and terrifies the entire [population]. They battle against [the Palestinians'] making a living, extort their money and trample their honor. In their behavior [towards these people] they are as bad as the worst war criminals. [Their] deportation [of people] from their homeland is in fact a form of murder. Therefore, to cope with such acts, solidarity must prevail and [these people] must face the enemy as one body. Accordingly, if one member of the body complains [of an injury which has led to the development of a high fever] then the other members identify with it by watching over it all night long and partaking of the fever [to ease the member's suffering].

Article 21

Mutual social responsibility includes providing material or moral aid to anyone in need or participation in carrying out part of one's duties. [Therefore] members of the Islamic Resistance Movement must relate to the interests of the masses as though they were their own personal interests, and must spare no effort to realize and preserve them. They must prevent manipulations regarding everything that negatively influences the future of the [next] generations and [everything that] might harm their society. In fact, the masses are [members] of [the Islamic Resistance Movement] and [work] on their behalf, and the strength [of the Islamic Resistance Movement] stems from [the masses'] strength and [the Islamic Resistance Movement's] future is [the masses'] future. The members of the Islamic Resistance Movement must therefore take part in [the Palestinians'] joys and sorrows, espouse the demands of the masses and everything which promotes [the movement's] interest and [the Palestinian masses'] interests [at the same time]. The day such a spirit prevails, brotherhood will become more profound and there will be cooperation and mutual compassion, unity will become stronger and the ranks will stand closer together in the face of enemies.

The forces which support the enemy
Article 22

[Our] enemies planned their deeds well for a long time [and managed] to achieve whatever they have, employing the factors influencing the course of events. Therefore, they acted to pile up huge amounts of influential material resources, which they utilized to fulfill their dream. Thus [the Jews], by means of their money, have taken over the international communications media: the news agencies, newspapers, publishing houses, broadcasting stations, etc. [Not only that,] they used their money to incite revolutions in various places all over the world for their own interests and to reap the fruits thereof. They were behind the French Revolution, the Communist Revolution and most of the revolutions we have heard about [that happened here and there]. They used their money to found secret organizations and scattered them all over the globe to destroy other societies and realize the interests of Zionism. [Such organizations] include the Freemasons, the Rotary clubs, the Lions, The Sons of the Covenant [i.e., B'nai Brith] and others. They are all destructive espionage organizations which, by means of money, succeeded in taking over the imperialist countries and encouraged them to take over many other countries to be able to completely exploit their resources and spread corruption.

[Their involvement in] local and world wars can be spoken of without fear of embarrassment. In fact, they were behind the First World War, through which they achieved the abolishment of the Islamic Caliphate, made a profit and took over many of the sources of wealth. They [also] got the Balfour Declaration and established the League of the United [sic] Nations to enable them to rule the world. They were also behind the Second World War, in which they made immense profits by buying and selling military equipment, and also prepared the ground for the founding of their [own] state. They ordered the establishment of the United Nations and the Security Council [sic] which replaced the League of the United [sic] Nations, to be able to use it to rule the world. No war takes place anywhere in the world without [the Jews] behind the scenes having a hand in it [as it is written in the Qur'an:] "Whenever they fan the flames of war, Allah will extinguish them. They strive [to fill] the land with corruption, and Allah does not like the corrupt" ([Surah 5] Al-Ma'ida [Verse] 64).

In fact, the forces of imperialism in the capitalist west and Communist east support the [Zionist] enemy as stoutly as possible with both material and manpower. They alternate with one another [in giving support]. On the day Islam appears [in all its might] all the infidels will join forces to confront it for [all] the infidels are one community, [as it is written in the Qur'an:] "Oh ye who believe, do not become close to those who are not of your own faith, for they will not spare any effort to corrupt you. They are happy with your misfortune and hatred [for you] burns in their mouths, but what they hide in their hearts is worse. We have made that clear to you with signs, if only you [could] understand" ([Surah 3] Aal-'Imran

[Verse] 118). It is not a matter of chance that the verse ends with the words, "if only you [could] understand."

The other Islamic movements
Article 23
The Islamic Resistance Movement respects and has great estimation for the other Islamic movements. Even if it disagrees with them regarding a particular position or view, it agrees with them regarding [other] positions and views. It considers those movements, as long as they demonstrate good intentions and faithfulness to Allah, as acting within the realm—gate(s)—of ijtihad [Islamic law], and as long as they operate within the general Islamic sphere....

[...]

Article 24
The Islamic Resistance Movement forbids the libeling and defaming of individuals or groups. A true believer does not defame or curse. In addition, a distinction must be made between [defamation] and taking a stand or having an opinion or behaving in a certain way. The Islamic Resistance Movement has the right to identify a mistake and to warn [people] of it while striving to clarify the truth and adopting it in relation to any specific issue about which an objective attitude is taken [by Hamas]. Wisdom is what the true believer is searching for, and he should therefore embrace it wherever he finds it, [as it is written in the Qur'an:] "Allah does not like bad words to be spoken in public unless because someone has been treated unjustly. Allah is all-hearing and all-knowing. Whether you do good openly or whether you hide it or whether you show forgiveness for evil, surely Allah is most forgiving" ([Surah 4] Al-Nisaa' [Verses] 148–149).

The national movements in the Palestinian arena
Article 25
The Islamic Resistance Movement behaves toward them with mutual respect, appreciates their circumstances and the factors surrounding and influencing them, and supports them as long as they are not loyal to the Communist east or the Christian [Crusader] west. The Islamic Resistance Movement assures anyone who immerses himself in or identifies with it that it is a jihadist and moral movement and aware in its world view and its dealings with others. It loathes opportunism and wants only good for people, be they individuals or groups. It does not strive for material gains or a good reputation or the profits that arise from that—[as it is written in the Qur'an:] "Muster against them [the enemy] all the force you can" ([Surah 8] Al-Aufal [Verse] 60),—and in order to perform your duty so that Allah might be pleased with you. [The Islamic Resistance Movement] has no aspiration beyond that.

It reassures all the national trends [i.e., groups] operating within the Palestinian arena for the liberation of Palestine that it lends support and aid to them and will never behave otherwise in word or in deed in the present and future. [The Islamic Resistance Movement] brings people together and does not separate them, protects and does not cast aside, unites and does not divide, values every good word and genuine effort and commendable endeavor. It closes the door in the face of petty disagreements and does not heed rumors and biased words; it is fully aware of the right to self defense. Anything that opposes or contradicts these positions is a libel fabricated by the enemy or by his lackeys to spread confusion, divide the ranks and create destruction through marginal issues, [as it is written in the Qur'an:] "Oh ye true believers, when a sinful person comes to you with information, investigate what he says carefully lest people be harmed inadvertently, and you regret what you have done" ([Surah 49] Al-Hujurat [Verse] 6).

Article 26
The Islamic Resistance Movement treats other Palestinian national movements positively if they are loyal to neither east nor west. However, that does not prevent it from discussing new developments locally and internationally regarding the Palestinian issue in an effective manner which reveals the degree of [their] agreement or disagreement with national interests and based on [its] Islamic worldview.

The Palestine Liberation Organization
Article 27
The Palestine Liberation Organization is closest to the Islamic Resistance Movement and it is [considered] father, brother, relative [and] friend. Can any Muslim shun his father or brother or relative or friend? After all, our homeland is one, our catastrophe one, our fate one and we have a common enemy.

The circumstances under which the organization [the Palestine Liberation Organization] was founded and the atmosphere of ideological confusion prevailing in the Arab world following the intellectual invasion that the Arab world was subjected to, and is still influenced by, since its defeat at the hands of the Crusaders, Orientalism, Christian missionary activity and imperialism, made the Palestine Liberation Organization adopt the ideology of a secular state and that is how we see it. However, a secular ideology is diametrically opposed to a religious ideology, and eventually positions, modes of behavior and the decision-making process are all based on ideology.

Therefore, despite our esteem for the Palestine Liberation Organization and what it is capable of developing into, and without belittling its role in the Arab-Israeli conflict, we cannot exchange the Islamic nature of Palestine in the present or future for the adoption of secular ideas. That is because the Islamic nature of Palestine is part of our faith and whoever does not take his faith seriously is defeated, [as it is written in the Qur'an:] "Who would despise the religion of Abraham except for the one who has made a fool of himself?" ([Surah 2] Al-Baqarah [Verse] 130).

Hence the day on which the Palestine Liberation Organization adopts Islam as its way of life we will be its soldiers and the fuel of its fire which will burn the enemy. However, until then—and we pray to Allah that it happens soon—the Islamic Resistance Movement will treat the Palestine Liberation Organization as a son treats his father, brother treats brother, relative treats relative. One suffers for the other when he is pricked by a thorn, supports him in his confrontation with his enemies and wishes he may go along the true path and [act with] wisdom.

Your brother [is also] your [guardian and supporting] brother. One who has no brother is like someone who hastens into battle without a weapon [to guard and support him]. Remember, a [person's] cousin serves as his [second] wing [which guards and supports] him, hence can the falcon fly with only one wing?

Arab and Islamic states and governments
Article 28

The Christian [Crusader] conquest is evil, it does not stop at anything, it makes use of every despicable and vicious means to achieve its ends. In its infiltration and espionage operations it relies heavily on the secret organizations it gave birth to, such as the Freemasons, Rotary and Lions Clubs, and similar espionage groups. All those organizations, both covert and overt, act for the good of and are directed by Zionism. They aim to collapse society, undermine values, destroy the security of life and property, [and] create [moral degeneration] and the annihilation of Islam. They are behind trafficking in drugs and alcohol, to make it easier for them to take over [the world] and to expand [and gain more territory].

Therefore, the Arab states bordering Israel are required to open their borders to the jihad warriors belonging to the Arab/Muslim nations, so that they may fulfill their role and join their efforts to those of the Muslim brethren in Palestine.

With regard to the other Arab/Muslim nations, they are required to facilitate the passage of the jihad warriors through their territory, which is the very least they can do.

Nor do we forget to remind every Muslim that when the Jews conquered the holy [site] in Jerusalem in 1967 and stood on the threshold of the blessed Al-Aqsa mosque they cheered: Muhammad died and left [only] daughters.

Thus Israel with its Judaism and Jews challenges Islam and Muslims. And the cowards shall know no sleep.

National and religious groups, institutions, educated people and the Arab/Muslim world
Article 29

The Islamic Resistance Movement expects these groups to stand by it and support it at various levels, to adopt its positions, support

its activities and movements and act to gain support for it, so that Muslim peoples will give it their support, backing and a strategic depth on all levels: human, material, information, time and place. [That should be done] by organizing conferences, publishing committed pamphlets and creating mass awareness [through indoctrination] with regard to the Palestinian issue and what [dangers] it faces, what is plotted against it, and by recruiting Muslims through ideology, education and culture. Thus they [the Muslim peoples] will play a part in the decisive battle for liberation [just] as they contributed to the defeat of the Crusaders and the rout of the Tatars and rescued human civilization. That [victory of the Muslim peoples] is not difficult for Allah [to achieve], [as it is written in the Qur'an:] "Allah wrote, for I will most certainly overcome, I and my messengers. Allah is strong and powerful" ([Surah 58] Al-Mujadalah [Verse] 21).

Article 30

Writers and the educated, media people, preachers in mosques, educators and the other sectors of the Arab/Muslim world: they are all called upon to play their roles, to fulfill their duties in view of the vicious invasion of Zionism and its infiltration into most of the countries [of the world] and its material and media control, and with all its ramifications in most countries of the world.

Indeed, jihad is not limited to bearing arms and fighting the enemy face to face. A good word, a good article, an effective book, support and aid—if the intentions are pure—so that Allah's banner becomes supreme, all constitute the essence of jihad for the sake of Allah. . . .

Followers of other religions
The Islamic Resistance Movement is a humane movement
Article 31

The Islamic Resistance Movement is a humane movement which respects human rights. It is committed to the tolerance of Islam toward the followers of other religions. It is not hostile to them except insofar as they are hostile to it or to whoever stands in its way to make it fail or frustrate its efforts.

Those who believe in the three [monotheistic] religions, Islam, Christianity and Judaism, can live side by side under the aegis of Islam in security and safety, for only under the aegis of Islam can there be complete security. In fact, ancient and recent history are the best proof of that. Therefore, the followers of other religions are called upon to stop fighting Islam in regard to sovereignty over this region. On the day that they become rulers, they will rule only by killing, torture and expulsion. That is because they are incapable of dealing with each other, let alone with the followers of other religions. Both the past and the present are full of examples proving that, [as it is written in the Qur'an regarding the Jews:] "They do not ever go out as one man to fight you, except from within fortified strongholds or from behind high walls. There is much hostility among them. They seem to you to be united, but their hearts are divided because they are a people which are devoid of understanding" ([Surah 59] Al-Hashr [Verse] 14).

Islam provides rights to anyone who is eligible to have them, and prevents the rights of others from being infringed upon. [As opposed to that,] the Nazi Zionists' harsh measures taken against our people will not prolong the duration of their invasion. Indeed, the regime of injustice will last but one hour, while the regime of truth [will last] until the hour of resurrection [i.e., Judgment Day]. [As it is written in the Qur'an:] "Allah does not forbid you to respect and be just with those who do not fight you because of your faith and do not drive you out of your homes. Allah loves those who are just" ([Surah 60] Al-Mumtahinah [Verse] 8).

The attempt to isolate the Palestinian people
Article 32
World Zionism and the forces of imperialism are trying in a subtle way and with carefully studied planning, to remove the Arab states, one by one, from the sphere of the conflict with Zionism, thereby eventually isolating the Palestinian people.

The aforementioned forces have already removed Egypt to a large extent, through the treacherous Camp David accords [September 1978]. They are now trying to draw other [Arab] states into [signing] similar agreements, so that they may also be outside the conflict.

Therefore the Islamic Resistance Movement calls upon the Arab and Muslim peoples to act in all seriousness and with all diligence to frustrate that monstrous plan [or plot] and to alert the masses to the danger [inherent in] leaving the sphere of confrontation with Zionism: today it is Palestine and tomorrow part of another country [qutr], or other countries [aqtar]. The Zionist plan has no limit; after Palestine [the Zionists] aspire to expand to the Nile and the Euphrates. Once they have devoured the region they arrive at, they will aspire to spread further and [then] on and on. Their plan [or plot appears] in The Protocols of the Elders of Zion and their present [behavior] is [the best] proof of what we are saying. Therefore, leaving the conflict with the Zionists is [an act of] high treason and a curse which rests upon whoever [does so]. [As it is written in the Qur'an:] "Whoever retreats [while fighting the infidels] before them on that day—unless he does so to return and fight again, or to join the other warriors—will have Allah's wrath visited upon him and hell will be his abode. What a wretched fate!" ([Surah 8] Al-Anfal [Verse] 16).

Therefore, all forces and resources must be pulled together to confront this vicious Nazi Mongol invasion, lest homelands be lost, residents expelled, corruption spread all over the earth and all religious values destroyed. Therefore every man must know that he will bear responsibility before Allah, [as it is written in the Qur'an:] "Whoever does a good deed, although it may be as small as a grain,

will realize his [reward in the afterworld], and whoever does an evil deed, although it may be as small as a grain, will realize his [reward in the afterworld]" ([Surah 99] Al-Zalzalah [Verses] 7–8).

Regarding the scope of conflict with world Zionism, the Islamic Resistance Movement sees itself as the spearhead or a step on the road [to victory]. It joins its efforts to the efforts of those who are active in the Palestinian arena and expects that additional steps will be taken at the level of the Arab/Muslim world. It is [best] prepared for the next stage [of the conflict] with the Jews, the war mongers, [as it is written in the Qur'an:] "We have sown enmity and hatred among them until Resurrection Day. Whenever they kindle the fire of war, Allah will extinguish it. They seek to fill the land with corruption, but Allah does not love those who corrupt" ([Surah 5] Al-Ma'idah [Verse] 64).

Article 33
The Islamic Resistance Movement starts off from these general views, which are coordinated and compatible with the laws of nature. [In addition,] it sails upon the river of divine destiny [toward] confrontation with the enemy and the waging of a holy war against him to protect Muslim persons, civilization and holy places, foremost among them the blessed Al-Aqsa mosque. [All that is said and all that is done] to urge on the Arab and Muslim peoples, their governments and popular and official groups, to fear Allah in their outlook on and their dealing with the Islamic Resistance Movement. They should also, as Allah so wishes, support and back it and give it aid again and again until Allah's supreme rule has been established. [In that way,] the ranks will close and the jihad warriors will join together. Then the masses will set out and come from all over the Muslim world, answering the [Muslim religious] call of duty, again and again making the call to jihad heard, the call that will rend the heavens, and its voice will echo until liberation has been achieved. Thus the invaders will be defeated and the victory of Allah will come to pass, [as it is written in the Qur'an:] "Allah will provide aid for all those who come to his aid, for Allah is strong and mighty" ([Surah 22] Al-Hajj [Verse] 40).

Historical proof throughout history [sic] regarding the confrontation with the aggressors
Article 34
Palestine is the heart of the globe, the place where the continents meet, the place that has attracted greedy [aggressors] since the dawn of history. The prophet, may Allah's prayer and blessing of peace be upon him, mentions in his noble hadith in which he addressed his revered companion, Mu'adh bin Jabel: "Mu'adh, Allah will enable you to conquer Al-Sham after my death, from El-'Arish to the Euphrates, its men, women and handmaidens will be [permanently] stationed at the frontier until Judgment Day. Whoever among them chooses [to dwell permanently in] one of the shores of Al-Sham or Jerusalem, will be in a [permanent] state of jihad until Resurrection Day."

Indeed, many times a greedy [aggressor] coveted Palestine and took it by surprise with columns [of soldiers] to satisfy their greed. Thus the huge armies of the Crusaders invaded it in the name of their faith and flew the banner of the Cross over it. They succeeded in defeating the Muslims for quite a while, and the Muslims only succeeded in reconquering it after they gathered together under the banner of their [own] religion. Then they joined forces and cried [the Muslim battle cry] Allahu Akbar, and set out to fight for almost two decades as jihad warriors under the command of Salah al-Din al-Ayyoubi, and were manifestly victorious. The Crusaders were defeated and Palestine was liberated, [as it is written in the Qur'an:] "Tell the infidels, you will be defeated and brought together in hell. How terrible [will] the resting place [there be]" ([Surah 3] Aal-'Imran [Verse] 12).

That is the only way to liberate [Palestine]. There is no doubt as to the true proof of history. It is one of the laws of the universe and one of the rules of existence. Only iron can break iron, and [the infidels'] false and faked faith can be overcome only by the true Islamic faith. Religious faith can only be confronted by religious faith. Eventually, justice will prevail, since justice is [always] triumphant, [as it is written in the Qur'an:] "We have already given our word to our servants the messengers, that they are those who will indeed be triumphant and that our battalions are the ones that will prevail" ([Surah 37] Al-Saffat [Verses] 171–173).

Article 35

The Islamic Resistance Movement has given to the defeat of the Crusaders at the hands of Salah al-Din al-Ayyoubi and the wresting of Palestine from their hands very deep thought, as it has done to the overthrow of the Mongols at 'Ayn Jalout when their force was broken by Qutuz and Al-Zahir Baybars, who thus rescued the Arab [*sic*] world from the Mongol invasion which destroyed every vestige of human culture. [The Islamic Resistance Movement] takes those things seriously and draws inspiration and learns lessons from [all of] them. To be sure, the current Zionist invasion was preceded by Crusader invasions from the west and Mongol invasions from the east. As the Muslims withstood those invasions and made plans to confront them and [eventually] defeated them, thus it has the capability to face the Zionist invasion and to defeat it [as well]. That is not difficult for Allah, if intentions are pure and resolve is honest, and if the Muslims learn the lessons of the past, shed the influences of intellectual invasion and follow the practice of their ancestors.

The Islamic Resistance Movement consists of soldiers for the Cause

Article 36

While making its way forward, the Islamic Resistance Movement again emphasizes to all the [Palestinian] people, and to all Arab and Islamic peoples, that it is not seeking glory for itself, material gain or social status. It is not directed against any one of our people since

it does not wish to compete with any one of them or try to take his place, nothing of the kind. Moreover, it will not in any way oppose any Muslim or those non-Muslims who wish it well, here [in Palestine] or any other place. It will only serve as a support for any group or organization active against the Zionist enemy and its lackeys.

The Islamic Resistance Movement regards Islam as its way of life. Islam is its faith [and the ideology] which it professes. Whoever regards Islam as the way of life, either here or elsewhere, be it an organization, group, state or any other body, the Islamic Resistance Movement will serve as its soldiers and nothing else. We ask Allah to guide us and to guide [others] through us [along the straight path] and judge us and our people with the truth, [as it is written in the Qur'an:] "Our sovereign, judge between us and our people with the truth, for you are the best of judges" ([Surah 7] Al-A'raf [Verse] 89).

Our final prayer [is]: Praise be to Allah, lord of the universe.

> **Source:** "The Hamas Charter (1988)," Intelligence & Terrorism Information Center, http://www.terrorism-info.org.il.

107. Palestinian National Council, Political Resolution and Declaration of Independence [Excerpt], November 15, 1988

Introduction

Meeting in Algiers in November 1988, almost one year into the First Intifada, the Palestinian National Council (PNC) formally declared the existence of an independent Palestinian state, its capital in Jerusalem. The Declaration of Independence gave a historical exposition of the struggles of the Palestinian people to regain their country and then invoked the resolutions of the successive Arab Summit Conferences and the United Nations (UN) in justification of its own legitimacy. The declaration was carefully vague as to which occupied territories constituted Palestine. A political resolution passed at the same meeting by the PNC made it clear, however, that these constituted the lands occupied by Israel since 1967 and urged the UN to call a conference that would make a peace settlement based on the principles of UN Security Council Resolutions 242 and 338. Israel would withdraw from those territories occupied since 1967, and these would form the new Palestinian state. The international community and the United States were asked to pressure Israel to take part in genuine negotiations for a final peace settlement on these lines. The PNC also expressed strong support for the intifada, urging Arab nations to provide it with all the assistance they could in this. The Political Revolution and the Declaration of Independence were striking demonstrations of just how dramatically the intifada had reinvigorated the previously flagging Palestinian cause.

Primary Source

[...]

The primary features of our great people's intifada were obvious from its inception and have become clearer in the 12 months since then during which it has continued unabated. It is a total popular revolution that embodies the consensus of an entire nation—women and men, old and young, in the camps, the villages and the cities—on the rejection of the occupation and on the determination to struggle until the occupation is defeated and terminated.

The glorious intifada has demonstrated our people's deeply rooted national unity and their full adherence to the Palestine Liberation Organization, the sole legitimate representative of our people, all our people, wherever they congregate—in our homeland or outside it. This was manifested by the participation of the Palestinian masses—their unions, their vocational organizations, their students, their workers, their farmers, their women, their merchants, their landlords, their artisans, their academics—in the intifada through its Unified National Command, the Popular Committees that were formed in the urban neighborhoods, the villages and the camps.

This, our people's revolutionary furnace and their blessed intifada, along with the cumulative impact of our innovative and continuous revolution inside and outside our homeland, have destroyed the illusion our people's enemies have harbored that they can turn the occupation of the Palestinian land into a permanent fait accompli and consign the Palestinian issue to oblivion. For our generations have been weaned on the goals and principles of the Palestinian revolution and have lived all its battles since its birth in 1965—including its heroic resistance to the Zionist invasion of 1982 and the steadfastness of the revolution's camps as they endured the siege of death and starvation in Lebanon. Those generations—the children of the revolution and of the Palestine Liberation Organization—rose to demonstrate the dynamism and continuity of the revolution, detonating the land under the feet of its occupiers and proving that our people's reserves of resistance are inexhaustible and their faith is too deep to uproot.

[...]

In all this, our people relied on the sustenance of the masses and forces of our Arab nation, which have stood by us and backed us, as demonstrated by the wide popular Arab support for the intifada and by the consensus and resolutions that emerged at the Arab summit in Algiers—all of which goes to confirm that our people do not stand alone as they face the fascist, racist assault, and this precludes any possibility of the Israeli aggressors isolating our people and cutting them off from the support of their Arab nation.

In addition to this Arab solidarity, our people's revolution and their blessed intifada have attracted widespread worldwide solidarity, as seen in the increased understanding of the Palestinian people's issue, the growing support of our just struggle by the peoples and states of the world, and the corresponding condemnation of Israeli occupation and the crimes it is committing, which has helped to expose Israel and increase its isolation and the isolation of its supporters.

Security Council Resolutions 605, 607 and 608 and the resolutions of the General Assembly against the deportation of the Palestinians from their land and against the repression and terrorism with which Israel is lashing the Palestinian people in the occupied Palestinian territories—these are strong manifestations of the growing support of international opinion, public and official, for our people and their representative, the Palestine Liberation Organization, and of mounting international rejection of Israeli occupation with all the fascist, racist practices it entails.

The UN General Assembly's resolution of 3.11.1988, which was adopted in the session dedicated to the intifada, is another sign of the stand the peoples and states of the world in their majority are taking against the occupation and with the just struggle of the Palestinian people and their firm right to liberation and independence. The crimes of the occupation and its savage, inhuman practices have exposed the Zionist lie about the democracy of the Zionist entity that has managed to deceive the world for 40 years, revealing Israel in its true light—a fascist, racist, colonialist state built on the usurpation of the Palestinian land and the annihilation of the Palestinian people, a state that threatens and undertakes attacks and expansion into the neighboring Arab lands.

It has thus been demonstrated that the occupation cannot continue to reap the fruits of its actions at the expense of the Palestinian people's rights without paying a price—either on the ground or in terms of international public opinion.

In addition to the rejection of the occupation and the condemnation of its repressive measures by the democratic and progressive Israeli forces, Jewish groups all over the world are no longer able to continue their defense of Israel or maintain their silence about its crimes against the Palestinian people. Many voices have risen among those groups to demand an end to these crimes and call for Israel's withdrawal from the Occupied Territories in order to allow the Palestinian people to exercise their right to self-determination.

The fruits that our people's revolution and their blessed intifada have borne on the local, Arab and international levels have established the soundness and realism of the Palestine Liberation Organization's national program, a program aimed at the termination of the occupation and the achievement of our people's right to repatriation, self-determination and independent statehood. Those results have also confirmed that the struggle of our people is the decisive factor in the effort to snatch our national rights from the jaws of the occupation. It is the authority of our people, as represented in the Popular Committees, that controls the situation as we challenge the authority of the occupation's crumbling agencies.

The international community is now more prepared than ever before to strive for a political settlement of the Middle East crisis and its root cause, the Palestinian issue. The Israeli occupation authorities, and the American administration that stands behind them, cannot continue to ignore the international will, which is now unanimous on the necessity of holding an international peace conference on the Middle East and enabling the Palestinian people to gain their national rights, foremost among which is their right to self-determination and national independence on their own soil.

In the light of this, and toward the reinforcement of the steadfastness and blessed intifada of our people, and in accordance with the will of our masses in and outside our homeland, and in fidelity to those of our people who have been martyred, wounded or taken captive, the Palestinian National Council resolves:

First: On the escalation and continuity of the intifada

A. To provide all the means and capabilities needed to escalate our people's intifada in various ways and on various levels to guarantee its continuation and intensification.

B. To support the popular institutions and organizations in the occupied Palestinian territories.

C. To bolster and develop the Popular Committees and other specialized popular and trade union bodies, including the attack groups and the popular army, with a view to expanding their role and increasing their effectiveness.

D. To consolidate the national unity that emerged and developed during the intifada.

E. To intensify efforts on the international level for the release of the detainees, the repatriation of the deportees and the termination of the organized, official acts of repression and terrorism against our children, our women, our men, and our institutions.

F. To call on the United Nations to place the occupied Palestinian land under international supervision for the protection of our people and the termination of the Israeli occupation.

G. To call on the Palestinian people outside our homeland to intensify and increase their support, and to expand the family assistance program.

H. To call on the Arab nation, its people, forces, institutions and governments, to increase their political, material and informational support of the intifada.

I. To call on all free and honorable people worldwide to stand by our people, our revolution, our intifada against the Israeli occupation, the repression, and the organized, fascist official terrorism to which the occupation forces and the armed fanatic settlers are subjecting our people, our universities,

our institutions, our national economy, and our Islamic and Christian holy places.

Second: In the political field

Proceeding from the above, the Palestine National Council, being responsible to the Palestinian people, their national rights and their desire for peace as expressed in the Declaration of Independence issued on November 15, 1988; and in response to the humanitarian quest for international entente, nuclear disarmament and the settlement of regional conflicts by peaceful means, affirms the determination of the Palestine Liberation Organization to arrive at a political settlement of the Arab-Israeli conflict and its core, the Palestinian issue, in the framework of the UN charter, the principles and rules of international legitimacy, the edicts of international law, the resolutions of the United Nations, the latest of which are Security Council Resolutions 605, 607 and 608, and the resolutions of the Arab Summits, in a manner that ensures the Palestinian Arab people's right to repatriation, self-determination and the establishment of their independent state on their national soil, and that institutes arrangements for the security and peace of all states in the region.

Toward the achievement of this, the Palestine National Council affirms:

1. The necessity of convening an effective international conference on the issue of the Middle East and its core, the Palestinian issue, under the auspices of the United Nations and with the participation of the permanent members of the Security Council and all parties to the conflict in the region, including, on an equal footing, the Palestine Liberation Organization, the sole legitimate representative of the Palestinian people; on the understanding that the international conference will be held on the basis of Security Council Resolutions 242 and 338 and the safeguarding of the legitimate national rights of the Palestinian people, foremost among which is the right to self-determination, in accordance with the principles and provisions of the UN charter as they pertain to the right of people to self-determination and the inadmissibility of the acquisition of others' territory by force or military conquest, and in accordance with the UN resolutions relating to the Palestinian issue.

2. The withdrawal of Israel from all the Palestinian and Arab territories it occupied in 1967, including Arab Jerusalem.

3. The annulment of all expropriation and annexation measures and the removal of the settlements established by Israel in the Palestinian and Arab territories since 1967.

4. Endeavoring to place the occupied Palestinian territories, including Arab Jerusalem, under the supervision of the United Nations for a limited period, to protect our people, to create an atmosphere conducive to the success of the proceedings

of the international conference toward the attainment of a comprehensive political settlement and the achievement of peace and security for all on the basis of mutual consent, and to enable the Palestinian state to exercise its effective authority in these territories.

5. The settlement of the issue of the Palestinian refugees in accordance with the pertinent United Nations resolutions.

6. Guaranteeing the freedom of worship and the right to engage in religious rites for all faiths in the holy places in Palestine.

7. The Security Council shall draw up and guarantee arrangements for the security of all states concerned and for peace between them, including the Palestinian state.

The Palestine National Council confirms its past resolutions that the relationship between the fraternal Jordanian and Palestinian peoples is a privileged one and that the future relationship between the states of Jordan and Palestine will be built on confederated foundations, on the basis of the two fraternal peoples' free and voluntary choice, in consolidation of the historic ties that bind them and the vital interests they hold in common.

The National Council also renews its commitment to the United Nations resolutions that affirm the right of peoples to resist foreign occupation, imperialism and racial discrimination, and their right to fight for their independence; and it once more announces its rejection of terrorism in all its forms, including state terrorism, emphasizing its commitment to the resolutions it adopted in the past on this subject, and to the resolutions of the Arab Summit in Algiers in 1988, and to UN Resolutions 42/159 of 1967 and 61/40 of 1985, and to what was stated in this regard in the Cairo Declaration of 7.11.1985.

Third: In the Arab and international fields

The Palestine National Council emphasizes the importance of the unity of Lebanon in its territory, its people and its institutions, and stands firmly against the attempts to partition the land and disintegrate the fraternal people of Lebanon. It further emphasizes the importance of the joint Arab effort to participate in a settlement of the Lebanese crisis that helps crystallize and implement solutions that preserve Lebanese unity. The Council also stresses the importance of consecrating the right of the Palestinians in Lebanon to engage in political and informational activity and to enjoy security and protection; and of working against all the forms of conspiracy and aggression that target them and their right to work and live; and of the need to secure the conditions that assure them the ability to defend themselves and provide them with security and protection.

The Palestine National Council affirms its solidarity with the Lebanese nationalist Islamic forces in their struggle against the Israeli occupation and its agents in the Lebanese south; expresses its pride in the allied struggle of the Lebanese and Palestinian peoples against the aggression and toward the termination of the Israeli occupation of parts of the south; and underscores the importance of bolstering this kinship between our people and the fraternal, combative people of Lebanon.

And on this occasion, the Council addresses a reverent salute to the long suffering people of our camps in Lebanon and its south, who are enduring the aggression, massacres, murder, starvation, destruction, air raids, bombardments and sieges perpetrated against the Palestinian camps and Lebanese villages by the Israeli army, air force and navy, aided and abetted by hireling forces in the region; and it rejects the resettlement conspiracy, for the Palestinians' homeland is Palestine.

The Council emphasizes the importance of the Iraq-Iran cease-fire resolution toward the establishment of a permanent peace between the two countries and in the Gulf region; and calls for an intensification of the efforts being exerted to ensure the success of the negotiations toward the establishment of peace on stable and firm foundations; affirming, on this occasion, the pride of the Palestinian Arab people and the Arab nation as a whole in the steadfastness and triumphs of fraternal Iraq as it defended the eastern gate of the Arab nation.

The National Council also expresses its deep pride in the stand taken by the peoples of the Arab nation in support of our Palestinian Arab people and of the Palestine Liberation Organization and of our people's intifada in the occupied homeland; and emphasizes the importance of fortifying the bonds of combat among the forces, parties and organizations of the Arab national liberation movement, in defense of the right of the Arab nation and its peoples to liberation, progress, democracy and unity. The Council calls for the adoption of all measures needed to reinforce the unity of struggle among all members of the Arab national liberation movement.

[...]

The National Council expresses deep pain at the continued detention of hundreds of combatants from among our people in a number of Arab countries, strongly condemns their continued detention, and calls upon those countries to put an end to these abnormal conditions and release those fighters to play their role in the struggle.

In conclusion, the Palestine National Council affirms its complete confidence that the justice of the Palestinian cause and of the demands for which the Palestinian people are struggling will continue to draw increasing support from honorable and free people around the world; and also affirms its complete confidence in victory on the road to Jerusalem, the capital of our independent Palestinian state.

THE FOLLOWING IS THE PROCLAMATION OF THE CONSTITUTION OF THE PROVISIONAL GOVERNMENT OF THE STATE OF PALESTINE.

The Palestine National Council decides in its extraordinary 19th session, the session of intifada:

1) The constitution, as soon as possible, of a provisional government for the State of Palestine in conformity with the circumstances and the course of events.
2) The Central Council and the Executive Committee of the Palestine Liberation Organization are in charge of fixing the date for the constitution of the provisional government. The Executive Committee is in charge of this constitution, which will be submitted to the Central Council to be entrusted. The Central Council will adopt the provisional character of the government until the recovery by the Palestinian people of its full sovereignty on the Palestinian land.
3) The provisional government will be composed of the Palestinian leaders, personalities and competences within the occupied motherland and outside on the basis of political variety and in such way as to achieve national unity.
4) The provisional government will establish its program on the basis of the Independence document, the political program of the Palestine Liberation Organization and the decisions of the National Councils.
5) The Palestine National Council invests the Palestine Liberation Organization with the prerogatives and responsibilities of the provisional government until the constitution of the government.

DECLARATION OF INDEPENDENCE

In the name of God, the compassionate, the merciful,

It was in Palestine, cradle of humanity's three monotheistic faiths, that the Palestinian Arab people was born, and it was there that it grew and developed, its unbroken, uninterrupted organic relationship with its land and its history molding its human and national being.

With epic steadfastness, the Palestinian people forged their national identity, rising in their tenacious defense of it to miraculous heights. The magic of this ancient land and its location at the crossroads of powers and civilizations aroused ambitions and cravings, inviting invasions that led to the denial of political independence to its people. But the people's perpetual adherence to the land gave the land its identity and breathed the spirit of the homeland into the people.

Grafted with a succession of civilizations and cultures, inspired by their temporal and spiritual heritage, the Palestinian Arab people continued, across the ages, to develop their persona in a total union between Land and Man, and, walking in the footsteps that the prophets left on this blessed land, raised prayers of thanks to the Creator from every minaret and hymns of mercy and peace from every church and temple.

From generation to generation, the Palestinian Arab people never ceased their valiant defense of their homeland, embodying in their successive revolutions their will for national independence.

And when the contemporary world drafted its new order of values, the balance of local and international forces denied the Palestinian Arab people a share of the general weal, once more demonstrating that justice alone does not turn the wheel of history.

The painful inequity poured salt on the Palestinian wound. The people that had been denied independence and whose homeland had become the victim of a new breed of occupation became the target of attempts to propagate the lie that "Palestine is a land without a people". This historical fraud notwithstanding, the international community, in Article 22 of the covenant of the League of Nations of 1919, and in the Lausanne Treaty of 1923, had recognized that the Palestinian Arab people, like the other Arab peoples that had broken away from the Ottoman Empire, was a free and independent people.

Despite the historical injustice done to the Palestinian Arab people by their dispersion and deprivation of the right of self-determination after the United Nations General Assembly Resolution 181 of 1947, which partitioned Palestine into two states, Arab and Jewish, that resolution still provides the legal basis for the right of the Palestinian Arab people to national sovereignty and independence.

The occupation of the Palestinian land and of Arab territory by the Israeli forces, and the uprooting and expulsion of the majority of the Palestinians from their homes by organized terrorism, and the subjection of the Palestinians who remained to occupation, persecution and the destruction of all semblances of national life, constitute a flagrant violation of all legal principles, and of the charter of the United Nations, and of those United Nations resolutions that recognize the national rights of the Palestinian people, including their rights to repatriation, self-determination, and independence and sovereignty on their national soil.

In the heart of our homeland, along its frontiers, and in their exiles near and far, the Palestinian Arab people never lost their deep faith in their right to return and their right to independence. The occupation, the massacres, the dispersion failed to loosen the Palestinian's grip on his national consciousness. He pressed his epic struggle and, through that struggle, continued to crystallize his national identity. And the national Palestinian will formed its own political framework: the Palestine Liberation Organization, the sole legitimate representative of the Palestinian people, recognized as such by the international community as represented by the United Nations and its institutions and by the other international and regional organizations. Armed with a belief in its people's inalienable rights, and with Arab national identity, and with international legitimacy, the Palestine Liberation Organization led the battles of its great people, a people fused into a solid national unity by the massacres and sieges to which it was subjected in its homeland and outside it. The epic of the Palestinian resistance entered the Arab and international records as one of the most distinguished national liberation movements of this era.

The titanic popular intifada waxing in the occupied land and the legendary steadfastness displayed in the camps of the homeland and the diaspora have raised human awareness of the Palestinian reality and the national rights of the Palestinians to the level of mature comprehension, bringing the curtain down on the phase of rampant deception and sedentary consciences, and besieging the official Israeli mentality that had grown addicted to reliance on myth and terrorism in its denial of the existence of the Palestinians.

The rise of the intifada and the cumulative fruit of the revolution in all its aspects have brought the Palestinian saga to another historic juncture where the Palestinian Arab people must once more claim their rights and affirm their determination to exercise them on their Palestinian soil.

By virtue of the Palestinian Arab people's natural, historic and legal right to their homeland Palestine, and of the sacrifices of their successive generations in defense of the liberty and independence of their homeland;

Pursuant to the resolutions of the Arab Summit conferences;

By the authority of the international legitimacy, as embodied in the resolutions of the United Nations since 1947;

In implementation of the Palestinian Arab people's rights to self-determination, political independence, and sovereignty on their soil;

The National Council proclaims, in the name of God and the Palestinian Arab people, the establishment of the State of Palestine on our Palestinian land, with the Holy City of Jerusalem as its capital.

The State of Palestine is the state of Palestinians wherever they may be. In it they shall develop their national and cultural identity and enjoy full equality in rights.

Their religious and political beliefs and their human dignity shall be safeguarded under a democratic parliamentary system of government built on the freedom of opinion; and on the freedom to form parties; and on the protection of the rights of the minority by the majority and respect of the decisions of the majority by the minority; and on social justice and equal rights, free of ethnic, religious, racial or sexual discrimination; and on a constitution that guarantees the rule of law and the independence of the judiciary; and on the basis of total allegiance to the centuries-old spiritual and civilizational Palestinian heritage of religious tolerance and coexistence.

The State of Palestine is an Arab state, an integral part of the Arab nation and that nation's heritage, its civilization and its aspiration to attain its goals of liberation, development, democracy and unity. Affirming its commitment to the charter of the League of Arab States and its insistence on the reinforcement of joint Arab action, the State of Palestine calls on the people of its nation to assist in the completion of its birth by mobilizing their resources and augmenting their efforts to end the Israeli occupation.

The State of Palestine declares its commitment to the principles and objectives of the United Nations, and to the Universal Declaration of Human Rights, and to the principles and policy of non-alignment.

The State of Palestine, declaring itself a peace-loving state committed to the principles of peaceful coexistence, shall strive with all states and peoples to attain a permanent peace built on justice and respect of rights, in which humanity's constructive talents can prosper, and creative competition can flourish, and fear of tomorrow can be abolished, for tomorrow brings nothing but security for the just and those who regain their sense of justice.

As it struggles to establish peace in the land of love and peace, the State of Palestine exhorts the United Nations to take upon itself a special responsibility for the Palestinian Arab people and their homeland, and exhorts the peace-loving, freedom-cherishing peoples and states of the world to help it attain its objectives and put an end to the tragedy its people are suffering by providing them with security and endeavoring to end the Israeli occupation of the Palestinian territories.

The State of Palestine declares its belief in the settlement of international and regional disputes by peaceful means in accordance with the charter and resolutions of the United Nations; and its rejection of threats of force or violence or terrorism and the use of these against its territorial integrity and political independence or the territorial integrity of any other state, without prejudice to its natural right to defend its territory and independence.

On this glorious day, the 15th of November 1988, as we stand on the threshold of a new age, we bow in awe and reverence before the souls of our martyrs and the martyrs of the Arab nation, whose untainted blood fueled the flame of this dawn, who died so that their homeland can live. And we bask in the brilliant glow of the blessed intifada, and of the epic steadfastness of our people in their camps and their diaspora and their exiles, and of the standard-bearers of our freedoms; our children, our youth and our aged; those of our people who, wounded or taken captive, continue to man their posts on the holy soil of every village and city; and the brave Palestinian women, guardian of our life and posterity, keeper of our eternal flame.

To the innocent souls of our martyrs, to the masses of our Palestinian Arab people and our Arab nation, and to all the world's free and honorable people we make this pledge: that we shall continue our struggle to roll back the occupation and entrench our sovereignty and independence.

We call upon our great people to rally around their Palestinian flag, to take pride in it and defend it, so that it will remain forever the symbol of our liberty and dignity in a homeland that will forever remain the free homeland of a free people.

Source: "Palestinian National Council Political Statement and Declaration of Independence," Israel Ministry of Foreign Affairs, http://www.israel-mfa.gov.il/MFA.

108. Yasser Arafat, Speech to the United Nations General Assembly [Excerpt], December 13, 1988

Introduction

In December 1988 after the United States had declined to issue him a visa to go to New York, Palestine Liberation Organization (PLO) chairman Yasser Arafat addressed the United Nations (UN) in its Geneva headquarters. In an emotional speech, he recounted the history of past Arab-Israeli negotiations on a peace settlement, emphasizing—and sometimes exaggerating—the Palestinian commitment to peace initiatives. He also reminded the assembly that when the UN sponsored the creation of Israel in 1947, it had also mandated the establishment of a separate Palestinian state. By this time, U.S. president Ronald Reagan's initiative earlier that year to move quickly to establish a Palestinian state had bogged down, and Arafat called upon the UN to restart the peace process. On behalf of the Palestinian National Council, Arafat specifically accepted UN Security Council Resolutions 242 and 338 and called upon the UN to convene an international conference based upon these resolutions. The situation in the Palestinian territories had, he argued, become intolerable, and the UN must step in, since the United States could not be trusted to be an evenhanded honest broker in any peace negotiations but instead would favor Israel over the Palestinians. Arafat also stated that the Palestinians were willing to allow temporary UN administration and supervision of the occupied territories as well as "Arab Jerusalem" as a stage on the way to an independent Palestinian state. Indeed, he hoped that the UN would assume such a role in the near future and that Israeli forces would withdraw from the occupied territories and be replaced by UN units. The other conditions of a peace settlement were Israeli withdrawal from the territories occupied since 1967, the removal of all Israeli settlements established there since 1967, the rescinding of all post-1967 Israeli annexations, and, first and foremost, the establishment of a Palestinian state. Arafat also publicly renounced the

use of "terrorist" tactics, although even as he did so he saluted the efforts of those Palestinians and others in the assembly who had been accused of terrorism while fighting for "liberation" from "colonialism." At a press conference two days later, Arafat used rather less flowery and more straightforward language to reaffirm the PLO's acceptance of Resolutions 242 and 338 and its renunciation of terrorism, both of which represented major concessions and broke with its previous positions.

Primary Source

Mr. ARAFAT

[...]

Our Palestinian people will never forget the stand that this august Assembly and those friendly States have taken on the side of right and justice in defence of the very values and principles for the preservation of which the United Nations came into being. That stand will for ever be a source of faith and assurance to every people that suffers injustice, oppression and occupation, and like our Palestinian people, struggles for freedom, dignity and survival.

To all the States, forces, international organizations and world figures that have backed our people and supported their national rights, particularly our friends in the Soviet Union, the People's Republic of China, the socialist countries, the non-aligned States, the Islamic States, the African States, the Asian States, the Latin American States, and all other friendly States, I extend our sincerest thanks. I also thank the States of Western Europe and Japan for their latest stands towards our people and invite them to take further steps to work out their resolutions in a positive way in order to pave the way for peace and a just settlement in our region, the Middle East.

I reiterate our solidarity with and support for the liberation movements in Namibia and South Africa in their struggle, and our support for the African front-line States against the aggression of the South African regime.

I seize this opportunity to express my gratitude to those friendly States which have taken the initiative in supporting us, in endorsing our Palestine National Council resolutions and in recognizing the State of Palestine.

[...]

Fourteen years ago, on 13 November 1974, I received a gracious invitation from you to brief this august Assembly on the cause of our Palestinian people. As I stand here among you now, after all those eventful years, I see that new peoples have taken their places in your midst, thereby crowning their victories in their battles for freedom and independence. To the representatives of those peoples, I extend the warm congratulations of our own people and declare that I return to you with a stronger voice, a more resolute determination and greater confidence to reiterate my conviction that our struggle will bear fruit and that the State of Palestine, which we proclaimed at our Palestine National Council, will take its place among you to join hands with you in consolidating the Charter of this Organization and the universal Declaration of Human Rights by putting an end to the tragedies besetting humanity and upholding the principles of right, justice, peace and freedom for all.

[…]

I bring you greetings from those sons of our heroic people, from our men and our women, from the masses of the blessed intifadah, which is now entering its second year with great momentum and painstaking organization, using a civilized, democratic approach to weather and confront occupation, oppression, injustice and the barbaric crimes committed daily by the Israeli occupiers.

I bring you greetings from our young men and women in the gaols and collective detention camps of occupation, greetings from the children of stones who are challenging an occupation force armed with warplanes, armour and weapons, thus reviving the image of Palestinian David confronting the heavily armed Israeli Goliath.

At the conclusion of my address in our first encounter, I, as Chairman of the Palestine Liberation Organization and leader of the Palestinian Revolution, reaffirmed that we had no wish to see a single drop of Jewish or Arab blood shed, that we had no wish for the fighting to continue for one more minute. I appealed to you then to spare us all those ordeals and agonies and speed up the laying of the foundations of a just peace based on securing the rights, hopes and aspirations of our people and the equal rights of all peoples.

I said then that I was calling upon you to stand by the struggle of our people to exercise their right to self-determination and enable our people to return from the compulsory exile into which they were forced at gunpoint. I asked you to help put an end to the injustice dished out to successive generations of our people over several decades, so that they may live as free and sovereign people on their native soil and in their homes, and enjoy all their national and human rights.

The last thing I said from this rostrum was that war breaks out from Palestine and peace starts in Palestine.

The dream we had then was the establishment of a democratic State of Palestine wherein Moslems, Christians and Jews would live as equals who enjoy the same rights and have the same obligations in a unified integrated community just like any other people in this contemporary world of ours.

Our amazement was great indeed at the interpretation that Israeli officialdom chose to put on that Palestinian dream whose fountainhead was none other than the teachings of the monotheistic religions that illuminated the Palestine sky and the cultural and humanistic values that call for coexistence in a free democratic society. The interpretation was that the dream was an evil design to destroy and obliterate their identity.

We had to draw the inescapable conclusion from that response. We had to take cognizance of the chasm between reality and the dream. We set out, in the Palestine Liberation Organization, to look for alternative realistic and achievable formulas capable of resolving the issue on the basis of possible rather than absolute justice while securing the rights of our people to freedom, sovereignty and independence; ensuring peace, security and stability for all; and sparing Palestine and the Middle East wars and battles that have been going on for 40 years.

Were we not the ones who took the initiative of relying on the Charter and resolutions of the United Nations, the Declaration of Human Rights and international legitimacy as the basis for the settlement of the Arab-Israeli conflict?

Did we not welcome the Vance-Gromyko communiqué of 1977 as a move that could form the basis of a proposed solution to this conflict?

Did we not agree to participate in the Geneva Conference on the basis of the American-Egyptian statement of 1977 in order to promote the prospects of a settlement and peace in our region?

Did we not endorse the Fez Arab peace plan in 1982 and later the call for an international peace conference under the auspices of the United Nations in conformity with its resolutions?

Did we not support the Brezhnev plan for peace in the Middle East?

Did we not welcome and support the Venice Declaration by the European Community on the basis of a just peace in the area?

Did we not welcome and support the joint initiative of Presidents Gorbachev and Mitterrand on a preparatory committee for the international conference?

Did we not welcome scores of political statements and initiatives by African, Islamic, non-aligned, socialist, European States and groups of States which aimed at finding a settlement based on the principles of international legitimacy that would safeguard peace and end the conflict?

And what was Israel's posture in relation to all this? When we put this question, we must keep in mind that not a single one of those initiatives, plans or communiqués lacked political balance or overlooked the claims and interests of any of the parties to the Arab-Israeli conflict.

Israel's posture in relation to all this has been to escalate further its settler expansionist schemes, to fan the flames of conflict with more destruction, devastation and bloodshed and the expansion of the fronts of confrontation to include Lebanon, which was invaded by the armies of occupation in 1982. That invasion involved the slaughtering and massacring of the Lebanese and Palestinian peoples, including the Sabra and Shatila horrors. Up to the present, Israel has continued to occupy part of South Lebanon. Lebanon continues to face daily raids and air, sea and land attacks on its cities and villages and on our camps in the South.

It is painful and distressing that the American Government alone should continue to back and support those Israeli aggressive and expansionist schemes and support Israel's continued occupation of Palestinian and Arab territories, its ongoing crimes and its pursuance of the iron-fist policy against our women and children.

It is equally painful and distressing that the American Government should persist in refusing to recognize the right of 6 million Palestinians to self-determination, a right which is sacred to the American people and other peoples on this planet.

Should I remind them of the position of President Wilson, author of the two universal principles of international relations, namely, the inadmissibility of the acquisition of territory by force and the right of peoples to self-determination? When the Palestinian people were consulted by the King-Crane commission in 1919, they chose the United States as the Mandatory Power. Circumstances having prevented that, the Mandate was given to Britain. My question to the American people is: Is it fair that the Palestinian people should be deprived of what President Wilson prescribed?

Successive American Administrations have been aware that the only birth certificate upon which the State of Israel was established has been General Assembly Resolution 181 (II) of 29 November 1947, endorsed at the time by the United States and the Soviet Union. It provides for the establishment of two States in Palestine, one Palestinian Arab and the other Jewish.

How then can the American Government justify a position whereby it acknowledges and recognizes the half of that resolution that pertains to Israel and rejects the half pertaining to the Palestinian State? How does the United States Government explain its lack of commitment to the implementation of a resolution it has endorsed on more than one occasion in the Assembly, namely General Assembly Resolution 194 (III), which provides for the right of the Palestinians to return to the homes and properties from which they were evicted and calls for compensating those who may not wish to exercise that right?

The United States Government knows that neither the United States nor anyone else has the right of fragmenting international legitimacy and the provisions of international law.

The unremitting struggle of our people for their rights has been going on for several decades now. In waging that struggle, our people have offered hundreds of thousands of martyrs and wounded and endured all kinds of tragic suffering. This, however, has not weakened our people's resolve. Rather, it has strengthened their determination to hold on to their Palestinian homeland and their national identity.

The leaders of Israel, in their excitement, deluded themselves into believing that, after our exit from Beirut, the sea was going to swallow the Palestine Liberation Organization. Little did they expect the march into exile to turn into a procession of return to the homeland, to the real arena of the conflict, to occupied Palestine. The valiant popular intifadah erupted within our occupied land, the intifadah that has come to stay until the achievement of our goals of freedom and national independence.

[. . .]

The world-wide embrace of our just cause, pressing for the realization of peace based on justice, clearly demonstrates that the world has come to realize, unequivocally, who the executioner is and who the victim is, who the aggressor is and who the victim is, who the fighter for freedom and peace is and who the terrorist is.

The day-to-day practices of the occupation army and the gangs of fanatic armed settlers against our people, our children and our women, have unmasked the ugly face of Israeli occupation and exposed its true aggressive nature.

This growing world-wide awareness has reached Jewish groups within Israel itself and without. Their eyes have been opened to the reality of the problem and the essence of the conflict, particularly since they have witnessed the inhuman, day-to-day Israeli practices that undermine the tolerant spirit of Judaism itself.

It has become difficult, nay, near impossible, for a Jew to reject racial persecution and uphold freedoms and human rights while remaining silent about Israel's crimes against Palestinian human rights, the Palestinian people and the Palestinian homeland, particularly the ugly day-to-day practices of the occupiers and the gangs of armed settlers.

We distinguish between the Jewish citizen whom the Israeli ruling circles have continuously sought to disinform and mislead and the practices of the leaders of Israel.

We even realize that within and outside Israel there are courageous and honourable Jewish people who do not condone the Israeli Government's policy of repression, massacre, expansion, settlement and expulsion and who recognize that our people have equal rights to life, freedom and independence. On behalf of the

Palestinian people, I thank them all for their courageous and honourable stance.

Our people do not want a right that is not theirs or that is not vested in them under international legitimacy and international law. They do not seek freedom at the expense of anyone else's, nor do they want a destiny which negates that of another people. Our people refuse to feel superior to, and refuse to be less than, any other people. Our people want equality with all other peoples to have the same rights and the same obligations. I call upon all the peoples of the world, especially those who experienced Nazi occupation and [who have] considered it their duty to put paid to the practice of oppression and injustice by one people against another and help all those who fall victim to terrorism, fascism and nazism. I call upon all those peoples to face up today to the responsibilities put upon them by history towards our long-suffering people, who only want a place for their children under the sun, in their homeland—a place where they can live as free people in a free land, like all other children in the world.

[…]

No one here would dispute the fact that the Palestine problem is the paramount problem of our contemporary world. It is the oldest on the United Nations agenda. It is the most intricate and complex. Of all the regional issues, it is the issue that poses the most serious threat to international peace and security. Hence, it has a priority among the issues which command the attention of the two super-Powers and, indeed, all the countries of the world. Therefore, it is necessary to make the required effort to define a course for its resolution on a basis of justice. This, in itself, would be the greatest guarantee of peace in the Middle East.

We in the Palestine Liberation Organization—in our capacity as the leadership responsible for the people of Palestine and their destiny; in all faithfulness to the struggle of our people and respect for the sacrifices of our martyrs; in our desire to contribute to the prevailing climate of coexistence and detente, and our awareness of the importance of participating in the peaceful political efforts to find a political solution that would put an end to the tragedies of war and fighting and pave the way to peaceful coexistence under international law—summoned our Palestine National Council to an extraordinary session in Algiers from 12 to 15 November 1988 with the purpose of defining and clarifying our position as a main party to the Arab-Israeli conflict, a party without whose participation and agreement that conflict cannot be resolved.

I am pleased to inform the Assembly, with great pride, that our Palestine National Council, through a totally free exercise of democracy, has again demonstrated its ability to shoulder its national responsibilities and has adopted serious, constructive and responsible resolutions which pave the way for us to reinforce and highlight our desire to find and contribute to a peaceful settlement that would secure the national and political rights of our people and ensure peace and security for all.

The first and decisive resolution of our Palestine National Council was the proclamation of the establishment of the State of Palestine, with the Holy City of Jerusalem, Al-Quds al-Sharif, as its capital. The State of Palestine was declared by virtue of the Palestinian Arab people's natural, historic and legal right to its homeland, Palestine, and of the sacrifices of its successive generations in defence of the liberty and independence of their homeland; pursuant to the resolutions of the Arab summit conferences; by the authority of international legitimacy, as embodied in the resolutions of the United Nations since 1947; and in exercise by the Palestinian Arab people of their right to self-determination, political independence and sovereignty over their soil, and in conformity with your successive resolutions.

It is important, while repeating this historic proclamation before the international community, now that it has become one of the official United Nations documents, to reaffirm that this is an irreversible decision and that we will not relent until it succeeds in casting off the occupation, enabling our Palestinian people to exercise their sovereignty in their State, the State of Palestine of the Palestinians, wherever they may be, so that they may develop their national and cultural identity and enjoy full equality in rights. Their religious and political beliefs and their human dignity shall be safeguarded under a democratic parliamentary system of government built on the freedom of opinion, the freedom to form political parties and where the rights of the minority will be protected by the majority and the decisions of the majority will be respected by the minority. That democratic system will be based on the precepts of social justice and equal rights, freedom from ethnic, religious, racial or sexual discrimination, under a constitution that will guarantee the rule of law and the independence of the judiciary, in full allegiance to the centuries-old spiritual and cultural Palestinian heritage of religious tolerance and coexistence.

The State of Palestine is an Arab state; its people are an integral part of the Arab nation and of that nation's heritage, its civilization and its aspiration after the goals of social progress, unity and liberation. The State of Palestine is committed to the Charter of the League of Arab States, the Charter of the United Nations, the Universal Declaration of Human Rights and the principles of non-alignment.

It is a peace-loving State committed to the principles of peaceful coexistence, and it shall work with all States and peoples to attain a permanent peace built on justice and respect of rights.

It is a State that believes in the settlement of international and regional disputes by peaceful means in accordance with the Charter and resolutions of the United Nations. It rejects the use of and the threat to use, force, violence or terrorism against its territorial integrity and political independence and, equally, against the territorial integrity of any other State, without prejudice to its natural right to defend its territory and independence.

It is a State that believes that the future can only bring security to those who are just or have returned to justice. This is the State of Palestine which we have proclaimed and which we shall endeavour to embody so that it can take its place among the States of the world and share in and creatively contribute to the shaping of a free world in which justice and peace would prevail.

Our State, God willing, will have its provisional Government at the earliest possible opportunity. The Palestine National Council has mandated the PLO Executive Committee to assume the functions of that government in the interim.

In order to give the aforementioned decision a concrete form, our Palestine National Council adopted a series of resolutions. I would like to highlight the most salient of those resolutions, which underline our determination to earnestly pursue the path of an equitable peace settlement and to exert the maximum effort to ensure its success.

Our PNC stressed the need to convene an international conference on the subject of the Middle East and its essence, the question of Palestine, under the auspices of the United Nations and with the participation of the permanent members of the Security Council and all the parties to the conflict in the region, including the Palestine Liberation Organization, the sole, legitimate representative of the Palestinian people, on an equal footing, with the provision that the international conference should be convened on the basis of Security Council resolutions 242 (1967) and 338 (1973) and should guarantee the legitimate national and political rights of the Palestinian people, first and foremost among which is their right to self-determination.

Our PNC also reasserted the need for Israel's withdrawal from all the Palestinian and Arab territories it had occupied since 1967, including Arab Jerusalem; the establishment of the Palestinian State; and the cancellation of all measures of attachment and annexation and removal of the settlements established by Israel in the Palestinian and Arab territories since 1967, as called for in the Arab summit resolutions of Fez and Algiers.

Our PNC also reaffirmed the necessity of seeking to place the occupied Palestinian territories, including Arab Jerusalem, under United Nations supervision for a limited period, in order to protect our people and to provide an atmosphere conducive to a successful outcome for the international conference, the attainment of a comprehensive political settlement and the establishment of security and peace for all peoples and States in the Middle East, through mutual acceptance, and in order to enable the State of Palestine to exercise its effective authority over those territories, as called for by the resolutions of the Arab summits.

Our PNC called also for the solution of the Palestine refugee problem in accordance with United Nations resolutions on the subject. It also stressed that freedom of worship and the practice of religious rites for all faiths should be assured at the holy places in Palestine. The PNC also confirmed its previous resolution with regard to the privileged and special relationship between the fraternal peoples of Jordan and Palestine and that the future relationship between the Hashemite Kingdom of Jordan and the State of Palestine would be established on the basis of a confederacy and of free and voluntary choice by the two fraternal peoples in corroboration of the historical ties and vital common interests which linked them.

The PNC reaffirmed the need for the Security Council's establishment and assurance of arrangements for security and peace among all the States in the region.

It is important for me here to point out that these resolutions reflect clearly, both in content and wording, our firm belief in peace and freedom and our total awareness and deep appreciation of the climate of international detente and the eagerness of the international community to reach balanced solutions that address the requirements and fundamental interests of the parties to the conflict. Those resolutions also attest to the earnestness of the Palestinian people's position on the question of peace: that they are committed to peace and believe that it should be secured and guaranteed by the Security Council under the aegis of the United Nations.

The resolutions constitute a firm, unambiguous rebuttal to all arguments, prejudices, stands and pretexts used by some States to cast doubt on the position and policy of the Palestine Liberation Organization.

While our people, through their intifadah and their representatives in the PNC, were voting for peace and, thereby, confirming their positive responsiveness to the prevailing mood of detente in international relations and the growing tendency to settle world conflicts by peaceful means, the Israeli Government went on fanning the flames of aggression, expansionism and religious bigotry, thereby announcing its insistence on opting for belligerence and the denial of our people's right.

The Palestinian side, for its part, has formulated clear and responsible political positions, in consonance with the will of the international community, in order to help convene the International Peace Conference and ensure the success of its proceedings. This gratifying and courageous international backing, as expressed in the recognition of the State of Palestine, is but further proof of the soundness of our course and the credibility of our resolutions, which are fully in harmony with the international will for peace.

While we greatly appreciate the free United States voices that have explained and supported our position and resolutions, we note that the United States Administration remains uncommitted to even-handedness in its dealings with the parties to the conflict. It continues to demand from us alone the acceptance of positions which cannot be determined prior to negotiation and dialogue within the framework of the International Conference.

I would point out here that the recognition of the equality and the mutual rights of both parties to the dispute is the only way to answer the many questions being posed, regardless of their source. If policies as practised on the ground are any reflection of the policy-makers' intentions, then it is the Palestinian side that has more cause to worry and demand reassurances about its fate and its future, facing as it does a State of Israel that is bristling with the latest in arms, including nuclear weapons.

Our Palestine National Council has reaffirmed its commitment to the United Nations resolutions that uphold the right of peoples to resist foreign occupation, colonialism and racial discrimination, and their right to struggle for independence. It has also reaffirmed its rejection of terrorism in all its forms, including State terrorism, emphasizing its commitment to its past resolutions in this regard, to the resolution of the Arab summit in Algiers in 1988, to General Assembly resolutions 42/159 of 1987 and 40/61 of 1985, and to what was stated on this subject in the relevant Cairo Declaration of 7 November 1985.

This is a position that is clear enough and completely unambiguous. And yet, as chairman of the Palestine Liberation Organization, I hereby declare once more: I condemn terrorism in all its forms, and at the same time salute those sitting before me in this Hall who, in the days when they fought to free their countries from the yoke of colonialism, were accused of terrorism by their oppressors and who today are the faithful leaders of their peoples, stalwart champions of the values of justice and freedom.

[...]

The situation in our Palestinian homeland can abide no further abeyance. Here are our people and our children in the vanguard of the march, carrying the torch of liberty, and giving their lives daily in order to end the occupation and lay the foundations of peace in their free, independent homeland and in the region as a whole.

For this reason, the Palestine National Council adopted its resolutions from a standpoint of realism, taking into account the circumstances of the Palestinians and the Israelis and the need to foster a spirit of tolerance between them.

[...]

Therefore, in my capacity as Chairman of the PLO Executive Committee, which at present shoulders the functions of the provisional government of the State of Palestine, I present the following Palestinian peace initiative:

First, that a serious effort be made to convene, under the supervision of the Secretary-General of the United Nations, the preparatory committee of the International Peace Conference on the Middle East—in accordance with the initiative of President Gorbachev and President Mitterrand, which President Mitterrand presented to the Assembly towards the end of last September and which was supported by many States, in order to pave the way for the convening of the International Conference, which commands universal support, with the exception of the Government of Israel;

Secondly, on the basis of our belief in international legitimacy and the vital role of the United Nations, that actions be undertaken to place our occupied Palestinian land under temporary United Nations supervision, and that international forces be deployed there to protect our people and at the same time supervise the withdrawal of the Israeli forces from our country;

Thirdly, that the PLO will work for the achievement of a comprehensive settlement among the parties concerned in the Arab-Israeli conflict, including the State of Palestine, Israel and the other neighbouring States, within the framework of the International Peace Conference on the Middle East, on the basis of Security Council resolutions 242 (1967) and 338 (1974), so as to guarantee equality and the balance of interests, especially our people's rights to freedom and national independence, and respect for the right of all the parties to the conflict to exist in peace and security.

If those principles are endorsed at the International Conference, we shall have come a long way towards a just solution, and that will make it possible to reach agreement on all security and peace arrangements.

[...]

If we offer the olive branch of peace, it is because that branch sprouts in our hearts from the tree of our homeland, the tree of freedom.

I have come to you in the name of my people, offering my hand so that we can make real peace, peace based on justice. On that basis I ask the leaders of Israel to come here, under the sponsorship of the United Nations, so that together we can forge that peace. I say to them, as I say to you, that our people, who seek dignity, freedom and peace for themselves and security for their State, want the same thing for all the States and parties involved in the Arab-Israeli conflict.

Here, I would address myself specifically to the Israeli people in all their parties and forces, and especially to the forces among them which advocate democracy and peace. I say to them: Come, cast away fear and intimidation. Let us make peace. Leave behind the spectre of the wars that have raged continuously over the past 40 years. Set aside all threats of wars to come, whose fuel could only be the bodies of our children and yours. Come, let us make peace. Let us make the peace of the bold, of the courageous, far from the arrogance of power and the weapons of destruction, far from occupation and oppression and humiliation and murder and torture.

[...]

Source: United Nations General Assembly Official Records, 43rd Sess., A/43/PV.78, January 3, 1989.

109. Yitzhak Shamir, Israel's Peace Initiative, May 14, 1989

Introduction

Once the Palestine Liberation Organization (PLO) and its chairman, Yasser Arafat, had announced their readiness to negotiate with Israel on the basis of United Nations (UN) Security Council Resolutions 242 and 338, thereby accepting Israel's right to exist, pressure on Israel to respond intensified. U.S. officials began quiet informal conversations with PLO representatives. Top officials in the new presidential administration that took office in January 1989, including President George H. W. Bush and Secretary of State James A. Baker III, were eager to make real progress on a Middle East peace settlement, and influential members of the American Jewish community were also eager to move toward peace. This meant that Israeli prime minister Yitzhak Shamir, who headed a relatively conservative National Unity government that took power in early 1988, needed to respond in some way to Palestinian overtures. In May 1989 Shamir put forward a plan for "free and democratic elections" in the occupied territories as part of a two-stage initiative of negotiations over the next five years to resolve their status. This would, he stated, be "based on Resolutions 242 and 338 upon which the Camp David Accords are founded." Palestinian residents of the occupied areas would obtain greater autonomy in the "affairs of daily life," while Israel continued to handle security matters, foreign affairs, and all issues relating to Israeli settlers in the occupied territories. As "basic guidelines," however, Shamir reiterated Israel's adamant opposition to negotiations with the PLO and its opposition to "the establishment of an additional Palestinian state" in the Gaza Strip and the West Bank. Both the Palestinians and the PLO rejected Shamir's proposals, and leaders in Gaza and the West Bank refused to work with him on them. In any case, the prime minister's scheme was as much a delaying effort to gain time

and appease critics of Israeli intransigence as it was a serious peace plan.

Primary Source

GENERAL:

1. This document presents the principles of a political initiative of the Government of Israel which deals with the continuation of the peace process; the termination of the state of war with the Arab states; a solution for the Arabs of Judea, Samaria and the Gaza district; peace with Jordan; and a resolution of the problem of the residents of the refugee camps in Judea, Samaria and the Gaza district.

2. The document includes:
    a. The principles upon which the initiative is based.
    b. Details of the processes for its implementation.
    c. Reference to the subject of the elections under consideration. Further details relating to the elections as well as other subjects of the initiative will be dealt with separately.

BASIC PREMISES:

3. The initiative is founded upon the assumption that there is a national consensus for it on the basis of the basic guidelines of the Government of Israel, including the following points:
    a. Israel yearns for peace and the continuation of the political process by means of direct negotiations based on the principles of the Camp David Accords.
    b. Israel opposes the establishment of an additional Palestinian state in the Gaza district and in the area between Israel and Jordan.
    c. Israel will not conduct negotiations with the PLO.
    d. There will be no change in the status of Judea, Samaria and Gaza other than in accordance with the basic guidelines of the Government.

SUBJECTS TO BE DEALT WITH IN THE PEACE PROCESS:

4.
    a. Israel views as important that the peace between Israel and Egypt, based on the Camp David Accords, will serve as a cornerstone for enlarging the circle of peace in the region, and calls for a common endeavor for the strengthening of the peace and its extension, through continued consultation.
    b. Israel calls for the establishment of peaceful relations between it and those Arab states which still maintain a state of war with it for the purpose of promoting a comprehensive settlement for the Arab-Israel conflict, including recognition, direct negotiations, ending the boycott, diplomatic relations, cessation of hostile activity in international institutions or forums and regional and bilateral cooperation.

c. Israel calls for an international endeavour to resolve the problem of the residents of the Arab refugee camps in Judea, Samaria and the Gaza district in order to improve their living conditions and to rehabilitate them. Israel is prepared to be a partner in this endeavour.

d. In order to advance the political negotiation process leading to peace, Israel proposes free and democratic elections among the Palestinian Arab inhabitants of Judea, Samaria and the Gaza district in an atmosphere devoid of violence, threats and terror.

In these elections a representation will be chosen to conduct negotiations for a transitional period of self-rule. This period will constitute a test for co-existence and cooperation. At a later stage, negotiations will be conducted for a permanent solution during which all the proposed options for an agreed settlement will be examined, and peace between Israel and Jordan will be achieved.

e. All the above-mentioned steps should be dealt with simultaneously.

f. The details of what has been mentioned in (d) above will be given below.

THE PRINCIPLES CONSTITUTING THE INITIATIVE:

STAGES:

5. The initiative is based on two stages:
   a. Stage A—A transitional period for an interim agreement.
   b. Stage B—Permanent Solution.

6. The interlock between the stages is a timetable on which the Plan is built: the peace process delineated by the initiative is based on Resolutions 242 and 338 upon which the Camp David Accords are founded.

TIMETABLE:

7. The transitional period will continue for 5 years.

8. As soon as possible, but not later than the third year after the beginning of the transitional period, negotiations for achieving a permanent solution will begin.

PARTIES PARTICIPATING IN THE NEGOTIATIONS IN BOTH STAGES:

9. The parties participating in the negotiations for the First Stage (the interim agreement) shall include Israel and the elected representation of the Palestinian Arab inhabitants of Judea, Samaria and the Gaza district. Jordan and Egypt will be invited to participate in these negotiations if they so desire.

10. The parties participating in the negotiations for the Second Stage (Permanent Solution) shall include Israel and the elected representation of the Palestinian Arab inhabitants of Judea, Samaria and the Gaza district, as well as Jordan; furthermore, Egypt may participate in these negotiations. In negotiations between Israel and Jordan, in which the elected representation of the Palestinian Arab inhabitants of Judea, Samaria and the Gaza district will participate, the peace treaty between Israel and Jordan will be concluded.

SUBSTANCE OF TRANSITIONAL PERIOD:

11. During the transitional period the Palestinian Arab inhabitants of Judea, Samaria and the Gaza district will be accorded self-rule by means of which they will, themselves, conduct their affairs of daily life. Israel will continue to be responsible for security, foreign affairs and all matters concerning Israeli citizens in Judea, Samaria and the Gaza district. Topics involving the implementation of the plan for self-rule will be considered and decided within the framework of the negotiations for an interim agreement.

SUBSTANCE OF PERMANENT SOLUTION:

12. In the negotiations for a permanent solution every party shall be entitled to present for discussion all the subjects it may wish to raise.

13. The aim of the negotiations should be:
   a. The achievement of a permanent solution acceptable to the negotiating parties.
   b. The arrangements for peace and borders between Israel and Jordan.

DETAILS OF THE PROCESS FOR THE IMPLEMENTATION OF THE INITIATIVE:

14. First and foremost dialogue and basic agreement by the Palestinian Arab inhabitants of Judea, Samaria and the Gaza district, as well as Egypt and Jordan if they wish to take part, as above-mentioned, in the negotiations, on the principles constituting the initiative.

15.

a. Immediately afterwards will follow the stage of preparations and implementation of the election process in which a representation of the Palestinian Arab inhabitants of Judea, Samaria and Gaza will be elected. This representation:
   i) Shall be a partner to the conduct of negotiations for the transitional period (interim agreement).
   ii) Shall constitute the self-governing authority in the course of the transitional period.

iii) Shall be the central Palestinian component, subject to agreement after three years, in the negotiations for the permanent solution.

b. In the period of the preparation and implementation there shall be a calming of the violence in Judea, Samaria and the Gaza district.

16. As to the substance of the elections, it is recommended that a proposal of regional elections be adopted, the details of which shall be determined in further discussions.

17. Every Palestinian Arab residing in Judea, Samaria, and the Gaza district, who shall be elected by the inhabitants to represent them—after having submitted his candidacy in accordance with the detailed document which shall determine the subject of the elections—may be a legitimate participant in the conduct of negotiations with Israel.

18. The elections shall be free, democratic and secret.

19. Immediately after the election of the Palestinian representation, negotiations shall be conducted with it on an interim agreement for a transitional period which shall continue for 5 years, as mentioned above. In these negotiations the parties shall determine all the subjects relating to the substance to the self-rule and the arrangements necessary for its implementation.

20. As soon as possible, but not later than the third year after the establishment of the self-rule, negotiations for a permanent solution shall begin. During the whole period of these negotiations until the signing of the agreement for a permanent solution, the self-rule shall continue in effect as determined in the negotiations for an interim agreement.

Source: Yitzhak Shamir, "Israel's Peace Initiative, May 14, 1989," Israel Ministry of Foreign Affairs, http://www.mfa.gov.il/MFA.

110. European Council, Declaration on the Middle East (The Madrid Declaration), June 27, 1989

Introduction

The ongoing First Intifada and the 1988 conversion of the Palestine Liberation Organization (PLO) to embracing United Nations (UN) Security Council Resolution 242 and Israel's right to exist made European nations particularly eager to encourage the Middle East peace process. This contributed to growing international pressure on Israel to moderate its stance of no negotiations with the PLO. Meeting at Madrid, Spain, in June 1989, leaders of the 12 member states of the European Community (EC) endorsed the call for a

UN-sponsored peace conference as a venue for direct negotiations between Israeli and Arab representatives, including the PLO. The declaration also praised the U.S. government for opening a dialogue with PLO officials and the stance of the PLO itself and the Arab League in endorsing talks based on Resolutions 242 and 338. While expressing its strong support for Israel's right "to live within secure, recognized and guaranteed frontiers," the EC also advocated "recognition of the legitimate rights of the Palestinian people, including their right to self-determination with all that this implies." European leaders urged Israel to end repressive measures against the intifada. They welcomed Israeli prime minister Yitzhak Shamir's proposal of elections in the occupied territories, provided that these were genuinely free and were held "in the context of a process towards a comprehensive, just, and lasting settlement of the conflict." No solution compatible with Resolutions 242 and 338 should be excluded from consideration. The EC also urged the Arab states, many of which still had no diplomatic relations with Israel, to recognize that country and establish "peace and cooperation" with it.

Primary Source

The European Council has examined the situation in the Middle East conflict in the light of recent events and of contacts undertaken over several months by the Presidency and the Troika (the incumbent Presidency, its immediate predecessor and successor) with the parties concerned, and it has drawn the following conclusions:

1. The policy of the Twelve on the Middle East conflict is defined in the Venice Declaration of June 13, 1980 and other subsequent declarations. It consists in upholding the right to security of all States in the region, including Israel, that is to say, to live within secure, recognized and guaranteed frontiers, and in upholding justice for all the peoples of the region, which includes recognition of the legitimate rights of the Palestinian people, including their right to self-determination with all that this implies.

The Twelve consider that these objectives should be achieved by peaceful means in the framework of an international peace conference under the auspices of the United Nations, as the appropriate forum for the direct negotiations between the parties concerned, with a view to a comprehensive, just, and lasting settlement.

The European Council is also of the view that the Palestinian Liberation Organization (PLO) should participate in this process. It expresses its support for every effort by the permanent members of the Security Council of the United Nations to bring the parties closer together, create a climate of confidence between them, and facilitate in this way the convening of the international peace conference.

2. The Community and its Member States have demonstrated their readiness to participate actively in the search for a negotiated

solution to the conflict, and to cooperate fully in the economic and social development of the peoples of the region.

The European Council expressed its satisfaction regarding the policy of contacts with all the parties undertaken by the Presidency and the Troika, and has decided to pursue it.

3. The European Council welcomes the support given by the Extraordinary Summit Meeting of the Arab League, held in Casablanca, to the decisions of the Palestinian National Council in Algiers, involving acceptance of Security Council Resolutions 242 and 338, which resulted in the recognition of Israel's right to exist, as well as the renunciation of terrorism.

It also welcomes the efforts undertaken by the United States in their contacts with the parties directly concerned and particularly the dialogue entered into with the PLO.

Advantage should be taken of these favorable circumstances to engender a spirit of tolerance and peace with a view to entering resolutely on the path of negotiations.

4. The European Council deplores the continuing deterioration of the situation in the Occupied Territories and the constant increase in the number of dead and wounded and the suffering of the population.

It appeals urgently to the Israeli authorities to put an end to repressive measures, to implement Resolutions 605, 607 and 608 of the Security Council and to respect the provisions of the Geneva Convention on the Protection of Civilian Populations in Times of War. They appeal in particular for the reopening of educational facilities in the West Bank.

5. On the basis of the positions of principle of the Twelve, the European Council welcomes the proposal for elections in the Occupied Territories as a contribution to the peace process, provided that:
—the elections are set in the context of a process towards a comprehensive, just, and lasting settlement of the conflict.
—the elections take place in the Occupied Territories including East Jerusalem, under adequate guarantees of freedom.
—no solution is excluded and the final negotiation takes place on the basis of Resolutions 242 and 338 of the Security Council of the United Nations, based on the principle of "land for peace".

6. The European Council launches a solemn appeal to the parties concerned to seize the opportunity to achieve peace. Respect by each of the parties for the legitimate rights of the other should facilitate the normalizing of relations between all the countries of the region. The European Council calls upon the Arab countries to establish normal relations of peace and cooperation with Israel and asks that country in turn to recognize the right of the Palestinian people to exercise self-determination.

Source: European Council, "Declaration on the Middle East," *European Community News* 21(89) (June 28, 1989): 16–17.

111. Hosni Mubarak, Ten-Point Plan, September 4, 1989

Introduction

Although the Palestine Liberation Organization (PLO) originally rejected Prime Minister Yitzhak Shamir's call for elections in the occupied territories, Arab leaders and the United States saw these as a potentially beneficial step forward. By 1989 President Hosni Mubarak of Egypt was working closely with U.S. secretary of state James A. Baker III on efforts to facilitate and encourage the peace process. In September 1989 Mubarak put forward what he considered would be suitable conditions for elections among the Palestinians in the occupied territories. The Israeli government was expected to make a prior statement endorsing these principles, and the U.S. government was asked to guarantee these conditions. Mubarak demanded that all Palestinians, including inhabitants of East Jerusalem and those under "administrative detention"—that is, those held only on suspicion of being disruptive elements—be entitled to vote and run for office; that campaigning be free and unhindered; that elections be conducted under international supervision; and that the Israeli government pledge itself to accept their outcome. Israeli forces were to withdraw from the West Bank and Gaza during the election period, and on election day Israeli nonresidents would be banned from entering these areas. The Israeli government must make a commitment that these elections would be only the starting point of efforts to reach a peace settlement on the principles of United Nations (UN) Security Council Resolutions 242 and 338. Israel must also halt all further settlements in the occupied territory. Lengthy but inconclusive bargaining ensued over this election program, but not until 1996, after the 1993 Oslo Accords had established the autonomous Palestinian Authority, were elections held in the occupied territories.

Primary Source

1. The necessity for participation of all citizens of the West Bank and Gaza (including the residents of East Jerusalem) in the elections both in the voting and in the right to stand as a candidate for any person who has not been convicted by a court of committing a crime. This allows for the participation of those under administrative detention.

2. Freedom to campaign before and during the elections.

3. Acceptance of international supervision of the election process.

4. Prior commitment of the government of Israel that it will accept the results of the elections.

5. Commitment of the government of Israel that the elections will be part of the efforts which will lead not only to an interim phase, but also to a final settlement and that all efforts from beginning to end will be based on the principles of solution according to the U.S. conception, namely resolutions 242 and 338, territory for peace, insuring the security of all the states of the region including Israel, and Palestinian political rights.

6. Withdrawal of the Israeli army during the election process at least one kilometer outside the perimeters of the polling stations.

7. Prohibition of Israelis from entering the West Bank and Gaza on election day with permission to enter only for those who work there and the residents of the settlements.

8. The preparatory period for the elections should not exceed two months. These preparations shall be undertaken by a joint Israeli-Palestinian committee. (The U.S. and Egypt may assist in forming this committee.)

9. Guarantee by the U.S. of all the above points together with a prior declaration to that effect on the part of the government of Israel.

10. A halt to settlement.

Source: Walter Laqueur and Barry Rubin, eds., *The Israel-Arab Reader: A Documentary History of the Middle East Conflict* (New York: Penguin, 2001), 362–363.

112. James A. Baker, Five-Point Peace Plan, October 10, 1989

Introduction

During 1989, U.S. government officials became increasingly irritated by the stubborn Israeli refusal to include Palestinians in any peace negotiations. With President Hosni Mubarak's energetic support and involvement, Egypt was at this time playing a key role in talks with Israel on the peace process. Although they constantly liaised quietly with Palestinian and Palestine Liberation Organization (PLO) representatives, Egyptian officials nonetheless found it difficult and cumbersome to try to speak for the Palestinians. Eventually, in October 1989, U.S. secretary of state James A. Baker III publicly endorsed a proposal that Israeli and Palestinian delegations should meet in Cairo, Egypt's capital, to begin direct talks on the Israeli proposal to hold Palestinian elections in the occupied territories. The U.S. government offered to serve as a facilitator for this encounter and proposed that the Egyptian and Israeli foreign ministers meet with Baker within two weeks to iron out any remaining details. In ongoing talks with U.S. officials, PLO leader Yasser Arafat, seeking enhanced Palestinian input in the peace talks, had endorsed this proposal, which marked a departure from his earlier insistence that

the PLO be recognized as the only legitimate representative of Palestinians in the occupied territories. Baker's proposal intentionally left room for the Palestinian delegation to include not just Palestinians from the occupied territories but also from elsewhere, including disputed East Jerusalem and other countries. With its most important sponsor clearly determined on this, pressure was steadily growing for Israel to deal directly with the Palestinians, a move that Israeli leaders feared might ultimately force them to recognize and work with the PLO.

Primary Source

1. The United States understands that because Egypt and Israel have been working hard on the peace process, there is agreement that an Israeli delegation should conduct a dialogue with a Palestinian delegation in Cairo.

2. The United States understands that Egypt cannot substitute itself for the Palestinians and Egypt will consult with Palestinians on all aspects of that dialogue. Egypt will also consult with Israel and the United States.

3. The United States understands that Israel will attend the dialogue only after a satisfactory list of Palestinians has been worked out.

4. The United States understands that the Government of Israel will come to the dialogue on the basis of the Israeli Government's May 14 initiative. The United States further understands that Palestinians will come to the dialogue prepared to discuss elections and the negotiating process in accordance with Israel's initiative. The United States understands, therefore, that Palestinians would be free to raise issues that relate to their opinions on how to make elections and the negotiating process succeed.

5. In order to facilitate this process, the United States proposes that the Foreign Ministers of Israel, Egypt, and the United States meet in Washington within two weeks.

Source: Walter Laqueur and Barry Rubin, eds., *The Israel-Arab Reader: A Documentary History of the Middle East Conflict* (New York: Penguin, 2001), 367–368.

113. Israel's Assumptions with Regard to the Baker Peace Plan, November 5, 1989

Introduction

Israeli prime minister Yitzhak Shamir was less than responsive to U.S. secretary of state James A. Baker's efforts to persuade Israel to negotiate directly with Palestinian representatives over projected Palestinian elections in the occupied territories. The Israeli government took several weeks to reply and then stated that it would talk only with Palestinian residents of the occupied territories. The Israeli statement specifically excluded negotiations with the Palestine Liberation Organization (PLO) and also, by implication, meant that Palestinians living in disputed East Jerusalem as well as those who resided in other countries would not be eligible to participate. Moreover, to make such assurances doubly sure, Israel would have to approve the membership of the Palestinian delegation in advance. Israel also demanded that the talks be limited strictly to the issue of elections, that the United States agree in advance to support Israel's position on the membership of delegations to these talks, and that Israel only be committed to attend one such meeting whose "results will determine if the talks will continue." The intransigent Israeli response to Baker's proposal, after PLO leader Yasser Arafat had made substantial concessions on direct PLO involvement in these talks, undermined Arafat's credibility within his own organization. Radical critics argued that he had gained nothing by abandoning the principle that the PLO was the only body that could represent the Palestinians.

Primary Source

a. The dialogue will begin after the composition of a list of Palestinian Arabs, residents of Judea, Samaria and Gaza, acceptable to Israel.

b. Israel will not negotiate with the PLO.

c. The substantive issues of the dialogue will be the election process in the territories, in a manner consistent with the outline included in the peace initiative of the Government of Israel.

d. The U.S. will publicly support the above Israeli positions and will stand by Israel in the event that another party to the dialogue deviates from what has been agreed upon.

e. The U.S. and Egypt will declare their support for the principles of the Camp David Accords, which are the foundation of the Israeli peace initiative, including the stages of negotiations and their substance.

f. The first meeting will take place in Cairo. The next step will be considered according to the results of the first meeting.

> **Source:** "Cabinet Decision on the Five-Point Plan of Secretary Baker, 5 November 1989," Israel Ministry of Foreign Affairs, http://mfa.gov.il/MFA.

114. Saddam Hussein, Speech to the Arab Cooperation Council [Excerpt], February 1990

Introduction

By early 1990, Israeli intransigence on direct negotiations with Palestinians, the ineffectiveness of the continuing First Intifada in forcing genuine concessions from Israel, and a major Israeli program to settle new immigrants, including thousands of Soviet Jews, in the occupied territories had left leaders of the Palestine Liberation Organization (PLO) increasingly frustrated. One PLO faction, the Rejection Front, favored withdrawing from all negotiations. PLO chairman Yasser Arafat, who had previously worked closely with the conciliatory Egyptian president Hosni Mubarak as the latter endeavored to persuade Israel to talk with the Palestinians and grant the inhabitants of the West Bank and Gaza greater autonomy, began to turn to more confrontational allies. After eight years of expensive and inconclusive war with Iran, Iraqi president Saddam Hussein sought to enhance his own country's standing within the Arab and Muslim worlds. Championing the PLO against Israel was one means of accomplishing this. When Hussein addressed the Arab Cooperation Council in February 1990, he assailed the continuing support that the United States was according Israel, especially U.S. acquiescence in the settlement of a major wave of Soviet Jewish immigrants in the occupied territories and growing U.S. arms sales to Israel that enabled the latter to build up massive stockpiles of weaponry. Warning that some time during the next five years Israel, fearing that time was not on its side, might launch another military campaign to gain additional land, Hussein urged all the Arab states to develop "a joint regional policy" and stand together against Israel. They should, he contended, reinforce their assistance and encouragement of the intifada. Hussein warned that with the end of the Cold War, the Arab nations could no longer expect serious assistance from the Soviet Union against Israel and therefore must be prepared to fight their own battles and if necessary stand up to "undisciplined and irresponsible behavior" on the part of the now unrivaled United States. He fiercely criticized recent statements by the U.S. government that it intended to maintain a substantial naval presence in the Persian Gulf, warning that "if the Gulf people, along with all the Arabs, are not careful, the Arab Gulf will be governed by the U.S. will." He feared that such a hegemonic position would enable the United States to dominate and supervise international commerce in oil. The United States would welcome continued discord in the Middle East, whether between Israel and its neighbors or Iran and Iraq, because this would give its forces further excuses to remain there. Hussein urged all Arab states to unite together to resist not just Israel but also domination by the United States and to deploy their control over international oil supplies to put pressure on both the United States and other Western countries. Within a few months, his own desire to dominate the Middle East led him to annex the emirate of Kuwait, a move that brought down on him the full wrath of U.S. military power. His support for the Palestinians would soon prove a double-edged sword, as Arafat was forced to choose between standing fast behind his Arab patron or retaining the good graces of U.S. president George H. W. Bush.

Primary Source

[...]

The Arabs possess an extraordinary ability to accelerate the creation of an international balance because, in addition to the known traditional elements including the known strategic elements involving the region's geography and their influence, there is an additional element: the possession of an energy source unparalleled in the world. All the major influential powers are affected by this, be it the United States, Japan, or Europe, or even the Soviet Union. Consequently, when Arab influence, by virtue of this extra element, reaches this point, then we can speed up the creation of a balance that at least does not make Arab interests vulnerable.

[...]

The Arabs should not only settle their differences, but also organize their course of action by adopting positive steps. The more their course is organized through positive action, the more their influence will be....

[...]

What draws attention in the Americans' behavior is the quick appearance of the spirit of unilateralism although the international imbalance is not old. An example of this is encouraging Jewish emigration, particularly Soviet Jewish immigration to the occupied territory, although the declared U.S. position is that it works for peace and that it is in touch with Egypt and the Palestinians on the basis that it wants to establish peace. Would someone who wants to achieve peace act this way? It is a superpower and it has become the first-ranking superpower, while the USSR, as a superpower, is undergoing a series of changes. In addition to this, we have taken note of U.S. statements on the Gulf and the assertions that the Israelis can use weapons stored in Israel. None of these signs is good.

In case of danger, there are always early signs. Israel always takes international changes and their effect into consideration. Israel has never lost an opportunity to take advantage of the atmosphere of change. Since the establishment of Israel—and even before it was established when it opened contacts with the Ottoman Empire and until the Balfour Declaration—the Jews who believe in the establishment of the State of Israel have always exploited opportunities. We must expect Israel to exploit the opportunity resulting from the current changes in the world.

Israel now is facing a clear question; that is, in light of its present situation time is not on its side. Tension in relations among the Arabs

has begun to ease; the Arabs want to understand, resolve their problems, and cooperate among themselves. There is a real desire to know about the changes in the world and their effect on their situation; they want to know what they should do to become effective in the world. Arab scientific cadres are being formed and our intrinsic military capabilities are growing. The Israelis say that the news of Arab capabilities has surprised them.

Therefore, all this makes the Israelis realize that time is against them in terms of topography and politics, as well as other factors. Let us not rule out that some Israeli strategists will say that time is against us in this situation. If we can change this situation and change the military geography, time might be on our side.

Therefore, we should be alert over the next five years because when Israel wants to embark on military aggression it will take new land; it might launch a new attack to come out of its deadlock. Who will oppose them internationally?

The answer is no one, even if no one offered direct support to encourage it to launch aggression, no one will stand against Israeli aggression, as happened in the wars of 1967 and 1973 because the United States has remained alone in the arena of the big powers, and the U.S. policy is the policy we are now experiencing. Will the Soviet Union be capable of confronting the aggression if it takes place, or will it be Europe that confronts the aggression? All this makes us wonder what then is the situation?

The most influential stand *vis-à-vis* such a situation should come from within ourselves and our capabilities. There is no better way than this to remove the minefields that mar Arab relations. The second best way under these circumstances is also to push ahead joint action as expeditiously as possible. Faced with the quick developments, we should have a joint policy as Arabs on the regional level.

All these elements limit the Israeli ability to make inroads during the mentioned five-year period not only in the Arab land but also in terms of influencing the Arabs in the technological, political and military fields with its own efforts or with the help of Jewish influence in the world. If the Arabs take all these elements into consideration, they will find themselves in an excellent position and will prevent the wave from destroying their barriers....

It is not enough to show Arab solidarity with the *intifada* in a traditional manner that may become ineffective if it remains unchanged. It is necessary to overhaul the means and formulas of attention and support. At the top of the list is extending real financial support to the militant Palestinian people and enhancing organized and meaningful political action in the international arena.... The *intifada* and its actions represent an Arab army corps that is carrying out the task of weakening the Zionists in the occupied territories by using stones. We must provide the *intifada* with its needs out of pan-Arab principles and regional security considerations. Let us then provide it with what an army corps needs in supplies and ammunition. Then, and only then, will we ensure the strength of the *intifada.*

What weakens the enemy most is psychological exhaustion. Israel used to say that its soldier was invincible and some of us even believed it. Now, and due to the *intifada,* that soldier looks weak and undisciplined. He no longer wears his beret or helmet and does not rise to salute his officers when they pass by. This, and other things, show that he lacks discipline. It is well known that the soldier's strength lies in his discipline.

The *intifada* of the young people and valiant women has shown us the true, pathetic state of the Israeli soldier. They have told us: Here you see the Israeli soldier—a man whom we can defeat if we exhaust him. If we, the little ones and women, have destroyed the Israeli soldiers' morale, then Arabs, united and with greater power, are able to defeat the enemy and regain their rights.

Now we see certain new factors emerging on the ground that affect the residents of the West Bank and Gaza. Immigration to Israel has made some of them leave their lands and go to Jordan. Last year, Mr. President, 55,000 young Palestinians left the West Bank and Gaza and came to Jordan. This should make us think about maintaining, through resistance, what is left of Arab rights on the land until such time as we can use more effective methods to regain more than what we can regain now. We know that 80 percent of Israelis live on the Mediterranean coast and do not care about the *intifada.* As for us, we are affected by the *intifada.* The Israeli people have become used to the fact that there are children throwing stones, and the one who is really affected is the Israeli soldier who returns to his hometown at the weekend. What I mean, Mr. President, is that without real, constant, and strong support for the *intifada,* it may become ineffective in the future. Immigration itself and the absorption of thousands of new immigrants into Palestinian territory—whether in Israel or in the occupied territories—aim to end the Arab presence in Palestinian territory.

Palestine was usurped through deliberate planning, and it can only be restored through deliberate planning backed by determination to achieve justice. The struggler sons of Palestine have proved to be an example of determination and readiness for sacrifice. The loss of Palestine was not essentially due to the Zionists' faith in the Zionist cause, but due to the Arabs' abandonment of the Arab cause. It was also not essentially due to Zionist strength, but to Arab weakness. Now that the Arabs have realized—through different factors and reasons, including their triumph over their enemies and the enemies of God on the eastern front and the heroic stand of the people of the deadly stones—that they are capable of taking action, then Palestine will return. Light will chase out darkness and the banners of justice shall fly over holy Jerusalem, God willing.

[. . .]

Among the most important developments since the international conflict in World War II has been the fact that some countries which used to enjoy broad international influence, such as France and Britain, have declined, while the influence and impact of two countries expanded until they became the two superpowers among the countries of the world—I mean the United States and the Soviet Union. Of course, with these results, two axes have developed: the Western axis under the leadership of the United States, with its known capitalist approach and its imperialist policy; or the East bloc under the leadership of the Soviet Union and its communist philosophy.

Among the results of World War II: The Zionist state has become a reality, and the original owners of the land, the Palestinians, have become refugees. While the imperialist Western world helped the expansionist scheme and aggression of the Zionist entity in 1967, the communist bloc sided with the Arabs in the concept of balance of interests in the context of the global competition between the two blocs, and sought to secure footholds for the East bloc against the Western interests in the Arab homeland. The East bloc, led by the USSR, supported the Arabs' basic rights, including their rights in the Arab-Zionist conflict. The global policy continued on the basis of the existence of two poles that were balanced in term of force. They are the two superpowers, the United States and the USSR.

And suddenly, the situation changed in a dramatic way. The USSR turned to tackle its domestic problems after relinquishing the process of continuous conflict and its slogans. The USSR shifted from the balanced position with the United States in a practical manner, although it has not acknowledged this officially so far. The USSR went to nurse the wounds that were inflicted on it as a result of the principles and the mistaken policy it followed for such a long time, and as a result of the wave of change it embarked on, which began to depart from the charted course. It has become clear to everyone that the United States has emerged in a superior position in international politics. This superiority will be demonstrated in the U.S. readiness to play such a role more than in the predicted guarantees for its continuation.

We believe that the world can fill the vacuum resulting from the recent changes and find a new balance in the global arena by developing new perspectives and reducing or adding to this or that force. The forces that laid the ground for filling the vacuum and for the emergence of the two superpowers, the U.S. and the USSR, after World War II at the expense of France, Britain, and Germany can develop new forces, which we expect will be in Europe and Japan. America will lose its power just as quickly as it gained it by frightening Europe, Japan, and other countries through the continuous hinting at the danger of the USSR and communism. The United States will lose its power as the fierce competition for gaining the upper hand between the two superpowers and their allies recedes.

However, we believe that the U.S. will continue to depart from the restrictions that govern the rest of [the] world throughout the next five years until new forces of balance are formed. Moreover, the undisciplined and irresponsible behavior will engender hostility and grudges if it embarks on rejected stupidities.

Given the relative erosion of the role of the Soviet Union as the key champion of the Arabs in the context of the Arab-Zionist conflict and globally, and given that the influence of the Zionist lobby on U.S. policies is as powerful as ever, the Arabs must take into account that there is a real possibility that Israel might embark on new stupidities within the five-year span I have mentioned. This might take place as a result of direct or tacit U.S. encouragement. . . . Recent American utterances and behavior as far as pan-Arab security and Palestinian Arab rights to their homeland are concerned inevitably cause alarm and warrant Arab vigilance, or are supposed to evoke such a reaction on our part. One may cite recurrent statements by U.S. officials about their intention to keep their fleets in the Gulf for an unlimited period of time, and their support for an unprecedented exodus of Soviet Jews to Palestinian territory, neither of which would have been possible solely under the cover of the human rights slogan had not the Americans put pressure on the Soviets, exploiting the latter's special circumstances so as to incorporate the issue into their bilateral agreements with the Soviets. Add to that the increasing support for the Zionist entity's strategic arms stockpiles and giving it license to deploy them when necessary, the judgment on when to use them being left up to Israel. This is above and beyond U.S. assistance to Israel in other areas.

We all remember, as does the whole world, the circumstances under which the United States deployed and bolstered its fleets in the Gulf. Most important of these circumstances: The war that was raging between Iraq and Iran; Iranian aggression had extended to other Arabian Gulf countries, most notably the sisterly state of Kuwait. At the time, beyond the conflicting views regarding the presence of foreign fleets in Arab territorial waters and foreign bases on their territory and their repercussions for pan-Arab security, that excessive deployment was somehow comprehensible. But now, and against the background of the recent world developments and the cessation of hostilities between Iraq and Iran, and with Kuwait no longer being the target of Iranian aggression, the Arabian Gulf states, including Iraq, and even the entire Arabs would have liked the Americans to state their intention to withdraw their fleets.

Had they said that under the same circumstances and causes they would have returned to the Gulf, it might have been understandable also. But U.S. officials are making such statements as if to show that their immediate and longer-term presence in Gulf waters and, maybe, on some of its territory, is not bound to a time frame. These suspect policies give Arabs reason to feel suspicious of U.S. policies and intentions as to whether it is officially and actually interested in a termination of the Iraq-Iran war and thus contributing to much needed regional stability.

The other side is the immigration of Soviet Jews to the occupied Palestinian land. How can we explain the Americans' support and backing for Jewish immigration to the occupied Arab territories, except that the United States does not want peace as it claims and declares? If it really and actually wants peace, the United States would not have encouraged Israel and the aggressive trends in it to adopt such policies, which enhance Israel's capability to commit aggression and carry out expansion.

We the Arabs, proceeding from a long-standing friendship with the Soviet Union, did not expect that the Soviets would give in to this U.S. pressure in such a way that it would lead to these grave consequences for the Arabs and their pan-Arab security. As we tackle these challenges, it would be just as compromising to the destiny and cause of the Arabs to feel fear as it would be to be lax in our evaluating and working out a reaction to them. Therefore, there is no place among the ranks of good Arabs for the fainthearted who would argue that as a superpower, the United States will be the decisive factor, and others have no choice but to submit. . . . It is only natural that the Arabs take a realistic approach to the new posture and power of the United States that has led the Soviet Union to abandon its erstwhile position of influence. However, America must respect the Arabs and respect their rights, and should not interfere in their internal affairs under any cover. The United States must not forget that the Arab nation is a great nation that taught humanity things it had been ignorant of. Otherwise, there is no room for unilateral friendship or unilateral respect, and there will be no consideration for the interests and rights of any party unless it is capable of understanding and respecting the Arabs' rights, interests, dignity, options, and pan-Arab security. Against the backdrop of the vital issues related to the substance of national Arab security, the question arises as to what we the Arabs have to do.

One of certain indisputable things, brothers, is that the correct description for a certain situation is not necessarily the correct solution to that situation, but an inevitable introduction leading to the correct solution. Therefore, in all cases, a solution does not merely consist of defining which issues are rejected, both concerning our behavior or the behavior and thinking of others who harm our pan-Arab security and national and pan-Arab interests. Another thing over which there is no room for dispute is that the policy of the age is not set by concerned foreign parties on any basis other than policies and strategies whose expected final result is to serve the interest of their countries.

Zionism realized these facts and concentrated its international effort here and there in accordance with an accurate perception and longer-lasting knowledge than that of the Arabs. The Zionists were progressive initiators in fields where they would disrupt the calculations and influences of the Arabs. In accordance with this basis, and not only on the basis of developing public opinion, Zionism directed its special concentration on the United States of America to involve it in its strategy, after realizing that the future of its goals and joint action with the Europeans would come up against special obstacles. The United States accepted the concept of joining interests and action with Zionism out of its concept of its own interests, after the United States had taken over the role of the European colonialists following World War II.

Despite all the harm the United States inflicted upon the Arabs due to its alliance with Zionism, there remained the fear of communism, the Soviet Union, and the Arab friends and allies of the Soviet Union in the region, in addition to other factors. This continued to prevent the Arabs from taking influential stands towards U.S. policy, with minor exceptions. Their stands became restricted to a mere ineffective rejection or an ineffective silence and acceptance. The United States began not to take Arab stances seriously. The United States may have the famous red lines beyond which it does not tread concerning the interests of other nations that deal peacefully with it, but its policy so far has no red lines warning the concerned sides in the United States not to tread beyond them where Arab interests are concerned.

Realizing Arab solidarity on the basis of pan-Arab interests, correctly defining Arab interests, clearly and accurately defining everything that threatens their security and stability, and proceeding from this basis of capability, frankness, and solidarity with the United States, or other countries in general, prevents these countries from exceeding the proper bounds with the Arab nation and thus becoming a threat.

This might be a realistic basis for the establishment of Arab relations with the United States and other states, based on the principles I have mentioned. These are mutual respect, noninterference in internal affairs, and respect for the requirements of pan-Arab security and common interests on a legitimate and agreed-upon basis.

Brothers, Zionism and its entity, Israel, have been used to embark upon areas and affairs to which the Arabs do not pay attention. The Arabs have also been used on occasion to rise all together to counter the Zionists' political, informational, or any other offensive for which Zionism has prepared all requirements through effective work over a long period of time. The Arabs would launch a counteroffensive without being fully prepared and soon their rising would dwindle and vanish. Therefore, the Arab reaction is often verbal or ineffective even if part of it takes the form of real action. . . .

[. . .]

It has been proven that Arabs are capable of being influential when they make a decision and set their minds to it for actual application

purposes. We have much evidence of how effective they can be; for example, the joint Iraqi-Saudi resolution of 6 August, 1980, and the warning the two countries issued together that embassies must not be moved to Jerusalem, one of whose direct results in less than a month—the duration of the warning—was not only that the concerned countries did not transfer their embassies to Jerusalem, but also that embassies that had already long been transferred to the city returned to Tel Aviv.

The reason the United States stays in the Gulf is that the Gulf has become the most important spot in the region and perhaps the whole world due to developments in international policy, the oil market, and increasing demands from the United States, Europe, Japan, Eastern Europe, and perhaps the Soviet Union, for this product. The country that will have the greatest influence in the region through the Arab Gulf and its oil will maintain its superiority as a superpower without an equal to compete with it. This means that if the Gulf people, along with all Arabs, are not careful, the Arab Gulf region will be governed by the U.S. will. If the Arabs are not alerted and the weakness persists, the situation could develop to the extent desired by the United States; that is, it would fix the amount of oil and gas produced in each country and sold to this or that country in the world. Prices would also be fixed in line with a special perspective, benefitting U.S. interests and ignoring the interests of others.

[. . .]

Brothers, the weakness of a big body lies in its bulkiness. All strong men have their Achilles' heel. Therefore, irrespective of our known stand on terror and terrorists, we saw that the United States as a superpower departed Lebanon immediately when some Marines were killed, the very men who are considered to be the most prominent symbol of its arrogance. The whole U.S. Administration would have been called into question had the forces that conquered Panama continued to be engaged by the Panamanian Armed Forces. The United States has been defeated in some combat arenas for all the forces it possesses, and it has displayed signs of fatigue, frustration, and hesitation when committing aggression on other peoples' rights and acting from motives of arrogance and hegemony. This is a natural outcome for those who commit aggression on other peoples' rights. Israel, once dubbed the invincible country, has been defeated by some of the Arabs. The resistance put up by Palestinian and Lebanese militia against Israeli invasion forces in 1982 and before that the heroic Egyptian crossing of the Suez Canal in 1973 have had a more telling psychological and actual impact than all Arab threats. Further, the threat to use Arab oil in 1973 during the October war proved more effective than all political attempts to protest or to beg at the gates of American decisionmaking centers. The stones in occupied Palestine now turn into a virtual and potentially fatal bullet if additional requirements are made available. It is the best proof of what is possible and indeed gives us cause to hold our heads high.

Just as Israel controls interests to put pressure on the U.S. Administration, hundreds of billions invested by the Arabs in the United States and the West may be similarly deployed. Indeed, for instance, some of these investments may be diverted to the USSR and East European countries. It may prove even more profitable than investment in the West, which has grown saturated with its national resources. Such a course of action may yield inestimable benefits for the Arabs and their national causes.

Our purported weakness does not lie in our ideological and hereditary characteristics. Contemporary experience has shown our nation to be distinguished and excellent, just as our nation's history over the centuries has shown this to be the case. Our purported weakness lies in a lack of mutual trust among ourselves, our failure to concentrate on the components of our strength, and our failure to focus on our weaknesses with a view to righting them. Let our motto be: All of us are strong as long as we are united, and all of us are weak as long as we are divided. Then we will see how all of us will reach safe shores, God willing, so we can take off together on the road of stability and prosperity, heartening our people and ourselves. We will also see how Satan will grow weaker wherever he may be and the evil will depart our homeland and our nation. . . .

[. . .]

Source: "Saddam Hussein, Inaugural Speech, February 1990," Foreign Broadcast Information Service, *F.B.I.S.-Daily Report Near East and South Asia*, February 27, 1990.

115. George H. W. Bush, Statement on Jewish Settlements in the West Bank and East Jerusalem, March 3, 1990

Introduction

Israeli hard-liners sought to undermine the possibility of a Palestinian state in the occupied territories and East Jerusalem by encouraging extensive Jewish settlement in those areas. The government of Likud prime minister Yitzhak Shamir ignored private requests by the U.S. government that such settlements cease and if anything only intensified its efforts. In early 1990 a major influx of Jews from the former Soviet Union began to arrive in Israel, and many of them promptly moved to the occupied territories. Eventually, U.S. president George H. W. Bush lost patience with his Israeli ally's intransigence. Speaking at a press conference in California, he forthrightly stated that the United States did not "believe there should be new settlements in the West Bank or in East Jerusalem." Shamir's defiant response was a public declaration that Israel fully intended to settle as many Soviet Jews as possible in East Jerusalem. With U.S. encouragement, Shimon Peres, leader of the Israeli Labor Party, dissented from Shamir's policies on peace negotiations and settle-

ments. When Shamir fired Peres as finance minister, the Labor Party withdrew from the governing coalition and won a vote of no confidence against Shamir in the Knesset. The Shamir government fell, but Peres himself could not put together a government. Meanwhile, discontent was rising among the Palestinians. In late May 1990 the Palestine Liberation Front, an extreme Palestine Liberation Organization (PLO) faction headed by Abu Abbas, attempted a seaborne terrorist infiltration into Israel with the intention of mounting major attacks on civilian targets. To protest this act, on June 20 Bush temporarily suspended the U.S.-PLO dialogue until the PLO was willing to renounce terrorist activities. His announcement of this measure did, however, state that the United States remained committed to furthering the peace process, and PLO participation in this enterprise was essential. In June 1990 Shamir returned to power, heading an even less conciliatory Likud-dominated government. The settlement program accelerated, and in late June 1990 Shamir repudiated the peace plan that he himself had proposed in May 1989, effectively stalling all further negotiations toward Palestinian autonomy or elections. U.S. pressure had, if anything, proved counterproductive.

Primary Source

My position is that the foreign policy of the United States says we do not believe there should be new settlements in the West Bank or in East Jerusalem. And I will conduct that policy as if it's firm, which it is, and I will be shaped in whatever decisions we make to see whether people can comply with that policy. And that's our strongly held view, and we think it's constructive to peace—the peace process, too—if Israel will follow that view. And so there's divisions in Israel on this question, incidentally. Parties are divided on it. But this is the position of the United States and I'm not going to change that position.

Source: "Excerpts of President Bush's Remarks at News Conference at End of Talks," *New York Times*, March 4, 1990. Copyright © 1990 by The New York Times Co. Reprinted with permission.

116. Yasser Arafat on the Gulf Crisis, December 13, 1990

Introduction

Arab-Israeli peace talks remained effectively suspended from June 1990 until the end of the Persian Gulf War in March 1991. In August 1990 Iraqi president Saddam Hussein's army annexed the oil-rich emirate of Kuwait, an ally of the United States, and at the end of February 1991 a U.S.-led military coalition forcibly reversed this. Throughout those months, the Gulf Crisis dominated international affairs. Hussein sought to win support from the Arab world by linking his annexation of Kuwait, in defiance of the United States, with his vocal opposition to Israel. During the Gulf Crisis Hussein threatened to attack Israel, seeking to redefine the conflict as a jihad, or holy war, against Israel, and after hostilities began he launched several Scud missiles against Israel. Emphasizing their joint opposition to Hussein, embattled Israel turned to the United States for protection and offered military assistance and facilities against the common enemy. During the previous year Hussein, seeking to enhance his status and influence within the Arab world, had been increasingly vocal in his opposition to Israel and the United States and his support for the Palestinian cause, which led Palestine Liberation Organization (PLO) chairman Yasser Arafat to forge an alliance with the Iraqi president. During the Gulf Crisis Arafat and the PLO therefore sided with Hussein, a somewhat impolitic choice given the central role that the United States was likely to play in any resumed peace process. Ironically, most other Arab leaders, fearful that they might easily become Hussein's targets, backed the United States. In a decidedly rambling interview published in a Croatian newspaper in December 1990, an apparently depressed Arafat sought to justify his position. He highlighted the growing U.S. military presence in the Persian Gulf well before Hussein's invasion as evidence of its unjustified ambitions. Arafat apparently hoped that war against Iraq might still be avoided. He complained that the recent United Nations (UN) Security Council resolution on Iraq that the United States had obtained was "some kind of declaration of war." Arafat feared that such a conflict would "leave behind nothing but catastrophe" and asked why the Arab states could not have been left to mediate the Iraqi-Kuwaiti dispute among themselves, without U.S. intervention. Arafat's interview gave the impression of a man who, watching two of his past partners coming ever closer to outright hostilities, believed that the Palestinian cause was foundering and had almost totally lost his bearings.

Primary Source

Do not forget that I was continually warning about the constant possibility of an escalation in this region. Most specifically, last April I pointed out two possible explosive points: On the one hand this involved increased U.S.-Israeli threats to Iraq and the Palestinians in southern Lebanon, and on the other the mass settlement of Jews into our occupied Palestine—a problem that I was constantly pointing out and to which I was trying to attract the world's attention because it involved a move with unpredictable consequences. I also said that the Arab summit in Baghdad in March this year should be a summit to straighten things out. Anyway, I will give you the letter the Americans sent us at that time through the Arab League. This is the dangerous letter that no one has wanted to talk about. I will give you a copy: go ahead and publish it if you wish. In this letter they openly announce that they will increase their presence in the Gulf and warned the Arabs that they will not tolerate any resistance to their presence. When I spoke about this on 17 May, two lines concerning the U.S. intentions were already apparent among the Arabs. One line approved of their presence and the other did not.

Another issue was the question of Israel and its expansion. The letter itself was a classic ultimatum. They issued a metal coin—here,

I will give you one—with a sketch on it of the map of Israel as they see it. This Israel contains half of Iraq, half of Syria, the whole of Lebanon, Jordan, the whole of Palestine, a part of Saudi Arabia, and a good part of Sinai. They have not forsaken this dream. When I left Beirut in 1982, I said that the storm that had overtaken that city would not stop. The storm at that point had one center, one "eye" as we would say: Palestine. Today that storm has two eyes—one in the Gulf and the other in Palestine. . . .

A few days ago, when I was with Saddam Husayn, it seemed to me that the chances of peace were great. What the Americans have prepared through the Security Council, however . . . this is some kind of declaration of war. This is an ultimatum. Really, there is the danger of the Middle East's exploding, not only in the Gulf but on all sides. If Israel is in this war—and it certainly will be—we will fight against it as well as against the Americans. They must know that not one single Arab soldier—neither Egyptian, nor Syrian, nor Saudi—will agree to be in the same trench as Israeli soldiers. This is the reality.

There is no doubt about it. No matter what the outcome of the war, the Arab order as a whole will collapse. . . .

We are the greatest losers even now. Our people in Kuwait were the richest. The total losses of the Palestinian colony in Kuwait amounted to $8.5 billion. Our people had almost $3 billion in the banks there alone. Look what happened. The U.S.-European committee discussed, and to a considerable extent has already paid, compensation to the whole world for the money lost in Kuwait, but the Palestinians did not receive anything. What is this meant to be? A punishment for the Palestinians? Where are the principles here? Are they not ashamed of this? Or do they really only want to ignite a new explosion? Viewed in the long term, perhaps there is cause for optimism. In the shorter term, the situation is exceptionally difficult. It seems that we have definitely come closer to a war which will leave behind nothing but catastrophe. Both Asia and Europe will feel the repercussions. In order for people to come to their senses, it is necessary for a lot of effort to be made throughout the world. But there is no sense. Look at the Security Council—what is its duty? To foment war or to seek peaceful solutions? I cannot accept this. As regards the solution, it is very strange that, for example, it is being demanded of the Palestinians that they talk with the Israelis while they are occupying the Palestinians' country, but at the same time we are not being allowed to ask that Arabs look for a solution among themselves for the new problem in the Gulf. So one can have negotiations among enemies but not among Arabs. What do they want? That I reject one occupation but accept another, or something like this? I cannot accept a foreign presence in this region. I know that they are literally punishing the Palestinians because of this, but I will not sell my opinion for any sum of money. I could easily say that I support the Saudis or the Americans. You know, however, that I have fought for principles, and I will not betray them.

Source: Walter Laqueur and Barry Rubin, eds., *The Israel-Arab Reader: A Documentary History of the Middle East Conflict* (New York: Penguin, 2001), 378–380.

117. Syrian-Lebanese Cooperation Agreement [Excerpt], May 20, 1991

Introduction

After United Nations (UN) forces withdrew from Lebanon in 1983 following the death of several American and French troops in their Beirut barracks, Syrian influence increased. Civil war raged as Christian Maronite Phalange and Druze Al-Amal militias contended for power with rival Muslim military groupings, including the fiercely anti-Israeli Hezbollah. Car bombings, assassinations, kidnappings, and violence were standard features of political life. Syrian armed forces held much of eastern Lebanon, and Israeli forces controlled large parts of southern Lebanon, treating it as a security zone. Under pressure from Saudi Arabia and Syria, which sought to stabilize the situation, in October 1989 the Lebanese National Assembly held a meeting in Taif, Saudi Arabia, and drew up the National Reconciliation Accord, also known as the Taif Accords. Under its terms, Muslims and Christians would share political power and cabinet positions, militias were to be disbanded, and Syrian forces would be deployed within Lebanon under a military cooperation agreement. Israeli forces were to be pressured to end their occupation and leave, as mandated by UN Security Council Resolution 425. The Syrian and Lebanese governments would cooperate in enforcing these accords and implementing political reforms, and Syrian military forces would remain in Lebanon indefinitely. The Taif Accords were never fully implemented: Lebanon's Christian prime minister Michael Aoun rejected them, Syrian-backed Druze militia leaders thought them overly favorable to Muslims, and the Lebanese Army failed to disarm the various militias. Syrian forces did, however, defeat government and militia forces that supported Aoun, after which Lebanon and Syria signed a one-sided military cooperation agreement legitimizing the presence of Syrian troops in Lebanon. Despite growing popular resentment of Lebanon's political subordination to its larger Syrian neighbor, from then on Syria functioned virtually as Lebanon's overlord, a dominance enforced when necessary by assassinations of overly independent political or military figures. More often than not, the United States, Israel, and Lebanon's Arab neighbors effectively acquiesced in this situation.

Primary Source

The Syrian Arab Republic and the Lebanese Republic,

On the basis of the distinctive fraternal ties that link them and that draw their strength from their roots of kinship, history, common affiliation, joint destiny and shared interests,

In the belief that the attainment of the fullest cooperation and coordination will serve their interests and provide means of ensuring their development and progress and of safeguarding their regional and national security, that it will promote their prosperity and stability and will enable them to cope with all regional and international developments, and that it will meet the aspirations of the peoples of the two countries in compliance with the Lebanese National Charter approved by the National Assembly on 5 November 1989,

Have agreed as follows:

Article 1

The two States shall endeavour to achieve the highest degree of cooperation and coordination in the political, economic, security, cultural, scientific and other fields for the benefit of both fraternal countries within the framework of their individual sovereignty and independence and so as to enable the two countries to use their political, economic and security potential to provide for their prosperity and stability, protect their regional and national security and broaden and strengthen their joint interests in confirmation of their fraternal relations and as a pledge of their common destiny.

Article 2

The two States shall endeavour to achieve cooperation and coordination between them in the fields of the economy, agriculture, industry, commerce, transport and communications and customs, to set up joint projects and to coordinate development plans.

Article 3

The interdependence of the security of the two countries shall require that Lebanon shall not, under any circumstances, be made a source of threat to the security of Syria, or Syria to the security of Lebanon. Accordingly, Lebanon shall not afford passage or provide a base for any force, State or organization seeking to infringe upon its security or the security of Syria, and Syria, desiring to ensure the security, independence and unity of Lebanon and harmony among its citizens, shall not permit any action which threatens the security, independence or sovereignty of Lebanon.

Article 4

After the institution of political reforms in constitutional form in accordance with the provisions of the Lebanese National Charter and on the expiry of the time-limits prescribed in the Charter, the Syrian and Lebanese Governments shall decide on the redeployment of Syrian forces in the region of the Bekaa and the entry to the Western Bekaa at Dahr el Baidar as far as the line Hammana-Mdairej-Ain Dara and, in case of need, at other points to be determined through the agency of a joint Syrian-Lebanese military commission, and agreement shall be reached between the two Governments concerning the determination of the size of the Syrian forces, the duration of their presence in the above-mentioned areas and the relationship between these forces and the authorities of the Lebanese State in the places where they are present.

Article 5

The inter-Arab and international foreign policy of the two States shall be based on the following principles:

1. Syria and Lebanon, as Arab countries, are bound by the pact of the League of Arab States, by the Joint Defence and Economic Cooperation Treaty between the States of the Arab League and by all agreements ratified within the framework of the League. They are also Members of the United Nations and are bound by its Charter and are members of the Non-Aligned Movement;
2. The common destiny and common interests of the two countries;
3. Each of them shall support the other in matters pertaining to its security and national interests in accordance with the provisions of the present Treaty.

Accordingly, the Governments of the two countries shall endeavour to coordinate their inter-Arab and international policies, to achieve the fullest cooperation in inter-Arab and international institutions and organizations and to coordinate their positions on the various regional and international issues.

[...]

Source: "Treaty of Brotherhood, Cooperation and Coordination between the Syrian Arab Republic and the Lebanese Republic, May 22, 1991," *United Nations Treaty Series,* Vol. 1675, I-28932.

118. Palestinian National Council, Political Communiqué [Excerpt], September 28, 1991

Introduction

In return for their support during the 1990–1991 Gulf Crisis and the Persian Gulf War, Arab states, including Syria, Saudi Arabia, and Egypt as well as Jordan, which had sought to remain a neutral intermediary, urged the United States to sponsor a conference, in collaboration with the Soviet Union, to resolve outstanding Arab-Israeli disputes. Syria hoped to regain the Israeli-occupied Golan Heights and took a joint stand with Egypt, Jordan, and the Saudis in agreeing to end the Arab economic boycott of Israel if the Israelis stopped building new settlements in the occupied territories. As a groundswell mounted in favor of new talks, the Palestinian National Council (PNC) on behalf of the Palestinian Liberation Organization (PLO) jumped on the bandwagon and issued a communiqué urging the resumption of the stalled peace initiative to establish an independent Palestinian state in the occupied territories in exchange for Arab acceptance of Israel. The communiqué also demanded that Israel cease building further settlements in the West Bank, Gaza, and East Jerusalem. The PLO welcomed the efforts of U.S. president

George H. W. Bush and Soviet leader Mikhail Gorbachev in convening an international peace conference to this end to be held in Madrid, Spain. PLO chairman Yasser Arafat's outspoken support for Iraq during the Gulf Crisis had made him an uncomfortably controversial figure, so he was not named among the communiqué's authors although it praised his past endeavors for peace.

Primary Source

In the name of God, the merciful, the compassionate. From the date of its beginning in 1965, the Palestinian revolution has embarked on a long, bitter, and strenuous struggle during which our people have made huge sacrifices. This beginning came after years of excluding the Palestinian question and considering it a refugee question.

The long years of struggle in all forms, under the PLO leadership, the sole legitimate representative of our people, have again posed the question of Palestine to the international community on the grounds that it is the national cause of a people entitled to liberation, self-determination, and independence.

The question of Palestine occupied a central position in the Arab-Israel conflict. Peace, security, and stability in the Middle East cannot be secure unless this conflict is resolved.

Then came the blessed *intifada,* with its popular and democratic depth as a creative continuation of the Palestinian national struggle. It has constituted a distinct phase which has left its imprint on the whole world and reverberated around it. It has consolidated international recognition of our people's rights and of the PLO, which has always and immediately put such international support and polarization to use.

Thus, our National Council convened its 19th session and launched the Palestinian peace initiative, and the historic birth of the state of Palestine was proclaimed on 15 November 1988.

The world had welcomed our peace initiative through the resolutions of the UN General Assembly in its 43rd session, which was held in Geneva. Also, most countries recognized the state of Palestine and established diplomatic and political relations with it.

Despite the international welcome with which the Palestinian initiative and the historic speech by the president of the state of Palestine, brother Yasir' Arafat, who demonstrated to the whole world our wish for a just peace, was met—thus for the first time the United States announced the opening of an official dialogue with the PLO—the Israeli policy of stubbornness and pressure led to the failure of all initiatives and peaceful efforts, bringing them down a dead-end street.

Afterwards, there came regional and international developments, most prominent of which was the Gulf war and the changes that occurred in the socialist bloc. This resulted in a substantial change in the balance of power. Thus, the cold war came to an end, and the features of a new age in international relations began to develop, especially in the field of U.S.-Soviet relations and cooperation between the two nations to resolve regional conflicts and problems peacefully.

The PLO has closely monitored the course of events in the world and their effect on the Palestinian question and the Arab-Israeli conflict. If the Palestinian people have had their homeland usurped as a result of the prejudices of the old world order, it is impermissible, according to any logic, that they be denied these rights in a phase witnessing the emergence of the new world order that raises slogans of democracy, human rights, and the sanctity of peoples' right to self-determination.

The current situation requires us to deal with it in the spirit of political responsibility and national realism and to examine the new regional and international developments. This situation also requires us to learn the lessons and experience from the popular *intifada* that has turned the aim of Palestinian independence into a feasible program.

In harmony with the Palestinian initiative proposed in 1989 and with international and Arab legitimacy, the PLO has dealt positively and effectively with international and peaceful ideas, proposals, and initiatives that relied on international legality. The PLO also welcomed the positive elements mentioned in the declaration of U.S. President George Bush and the positions of the EEC, the Soviet Union, the Nonaligned Movement states, and other international quarters.

The PLO, which had welcomed the current peaceful efforts and initiatives and dealt with them positively, including the call launched by Presidents Bush and Gorbachev for convening a peace conference related to settling the conflict in the Middle East, believes that the success of the efforts aimed at holding the peace conference requires the continuation of work with the other sides so as to achieve the following foundations:

1. The peace conference should rely on international legitimacy and its resolutions, including UN Security Council Resolutions 242 and 338, and should undertake to implement them. These resolutions secure a full Israeli withdrawal from Arab and Palestinian occupied territories, including sacred Jerusalem; the realization of the land-for-peace exchange principle; and the national and political rights of the Palestinian people.
2. It must be stressed that Jerusalem is an indivisible part of occupied Palestinian territory and that what applies to the rest of the occupied territories applies to it, as stipulated by the resolutions of the Security Council and the United Nations.
3. Halting settlement in the occupied territories, including holy Jerusalem, is an indispensable necessity to start the peace

process, and international guarantees must be provided to achieve that.
4. The PLO, as the legitimate and sole representative of the Palestinian people, has the right to form the Palestinian delegation from within and outside the homeland, including Jerusalem, and to define the formula of their participation in the peace process on an equitable basis and in a way that stresses its authority.
5. Arab positions should be coordinated to ensure the realization of a comprehensive settlement, excluding unilateral solutions, in accordance with the resolutions of Arab summits.
6. The connection between the stages of the settlement toward reaching a comprehensive settlement should be ensured according to the resolutions of international legitimacy.

The PLO, which starts from these bases and premises on the peace efforts, aims to accomplish the following:

1. The right to self-determination must be secured for our Palestinian people in a way that guarantees the right to freedom and national independence.
2. There must be a full Israeli withdrawal from all Palestinian and Arab lands occupied in 1967, including Holy Jerusalem.
3. The problem of Palestinian refugees driven out of their homeland by force and against their will must be resolved, in accordance with UN resolutions, especially Resolution 194, issued by the UN General Assembly.
4. Any provisional arrangements must include the right of our people to sovereignty of land, water, natural resources, and all political and economic affairs.
5. International protection for the Palestinian people, in preparation for the exercise of the right to self-determination, must be provided.
6. Full guarantees must be provided for an effort to remove the existing settlements by declaring them illegal, in accordance with the resolutions of international law, including UN Security Council Resolution No. 465.

The National Council charges the Executive Committee to continue current efforts to provide the best conditions for guaranteeing the success of the peace process in accordance with the resolution of the Palestine National Council [PNC]. However, the committee will submit the results to the Central Council to make a final decision in light of the supreme national interest of our people.

The PLO, which in the previous phase made all possible efforts to propel the peace process, hopes that the other parties, especially the United States and the USSR, will also make efforts to help ease the obstacle placed by Israel before this ongoing political process and to leave the door open for a return to the UN Security Council so as to implement the resolutions of international legitimacy.

Working toward the achievement of our national objectives in the next phase and toward facing up to obstacles marring our struggle requires the consolidation and entrenchment of national unity in various fields. It requires developing the contribution of all national forces, bodies, and personalities inside and outside the occupied homeland—along with the political leadership of the PLO—to all issues related to our people's future and the ongoing political process, and to finding the appropriate formula for achieving this purpose.

In this respect, the PNC calls for increasing the activities and role of the PLO Central Council in monitoring and implementing the resolutions of the National Council as a way of consolidating democracy and its practice The council considers promoting the *intifada* and consolidating its popular and democratic character and the participation of our entire people in backing and supporting it to be the real guarantee for securing the political and national objectives in the next phase of our national struggle.

In this respect, the Council addresses its struggle greetings to the masses of the brave *intifada* and stresses the consolidation of the role and prestige of the Unified National Command of the *Intifada,* the development of its struggle wings, the continuation of the formation of cadres, and the setting up of supreme sectorial councils.

The Council reaffirms that the protection and support of the *intifada* and the provision of all requirements for its development are at the forefront of Palestinian national action.

The Council extends greetings to our heroic prisoners in the detention centers of Zionist occupation and to our brave wounded who are watching over the path of the *intifada,* which was built by our pure martyrs.

The National Council extends its struggle greetings to the masses of our steadfast people in Galilee, the Triangle, Negev, and the coast, and reaffirms its appreciation of their struggle in defense of their rights against the policies of persecution and segregation and their active support for the brave *intifada.*

The council also affirms that guaranteeing the realization of the objectives of our people and Arab nation, through the peace process, in order to secure a full Israeli withdrawal from Arab and Palestinian lands, and to guarantee the right of return, the self-determination to our people, and the setting up of a Palestinian state with Holy Jerusalem as its capital, require the restoration of inter-Arab solidarity in order to protect the Arab future in light of current international and regional changes.

In this respect, the council invites the five Arab states concerned in the peace process to achieve the highest levels of political and diplomatic coordination between them, in order to face up to the requirements of the coming stage and to reinforce the Arab nego-

tiating position, so as to guarantee the realization of a comprehensive solution at all levels and prevent any separate solutions at the expense of the national rights of our people and the rights of our Arab nation.

[...]

The PNC urges the international community to deal with the issue of Jewish colonizing emigration in a way that ensures that Israel does not use it to serve its objectives of expansion, colonization, and depriving our people of the right to decide their destiny in the territory of their homeland. The Council believes that the continuation of this emigration, in accordance with Israeli plans to intensify settlement in our occupied land, constitutes a direct obstacle, a danger threatening the future of peace in the region, and a violation of the Palestinian people's rights and international conventions.

The PNC draws attention to the attempts and endeavors currently under way in some international circles to repeal the UN General Assembly's resolution on Zionism as a form of racism. The Council urges the Executive Committee to work with the friendly and fraternal states to face up to these attempts and to abort them.

[...]

Source: Walter Laqueur and Barry Rubin, eds., *The Israel-Arab Reader: A Documentary History of the Middle East Conflict* (New York: Penguin, 2001), 380–384.

119. U.S. Letter of Assurances to the Palestinians, October 18, 1991

Introduction

The U.S. government responded positively to the autumn of 1991 Palestinian call for renewed peace negotiations with Israel under U.S. and Soviet auspices. The U.S. government welcomed the Palestinian approach and reaffirmed its own commitment to a comprehensive settlement based on United Nations (UN) Security Council Resolutions 242 and 338. The coming conference would take place with the good offices of the United States, the Soviet Union, and the European Community (EC), with UN observers present, and would include both multilateral and bilateral negotiations. The Palestinians were invited to take part in all multilateral negotiations and all negotiations on refugees. The U.S. government clearly proclaimed: "The United States is determined to achieve a comprehensive settlement of the Arab-Israeli conflict and will do its utmost to ensure that the process moves forward along both tracks toward this end." U.S. officials also emphasized their commitment to "serious negotiations" and warned that they would "also seek to avoid prolongation and stalling by any party." The Palestinians were invited to send a joint Jordanian-Palestinian delegation whose members could include Palestinians not just from the occupied territories but also from East Jerusalem, whose status was still under dispute, as well as Palestinians based in other countries. So long as they were prepared to accept the UN Security Council resolutions, the right of Israel to exist, and the two-track negotiating process, delegates with ties to the Palestine Liberation Organization (PLO) were not excluded. It was hoped that talks on transitional arrangements for the occupied territories would be completed within one year and would establish an interim system of government there that would last for five years, during which negotiations on the permanent status of these areas would take place. The tone was forceful, and President George H. W. Bush's administration was now clearly determined to try to resolve this long-standing and thorny foreign policy question.

Primary Source

The Palestinian decision to attend a peace conference to launch direct negotiations with Israel represents an important step in the search for a comprehensive, just and lasting peace in the region. The United States has long believed that Palestinian participation is critical to the success of our efforts.

In the context of the process on which we are embarking, we want to respond to your request for certain assurances related to this process. These assurances constitute U.S. understandings and intentions concerning the conference and ensuing negotiations.

These assurances are consistent with United States policy and do not undermine or contradict United Nations Security Council Resolutions 242 and 338. Moreover, there will be no assurances provided to one party that are not known to all the others. By this we can foster a sense of confidence and minimize chances for misunderstandings.

As President Bush stated in his March 6, 1991, address to Congress, the United States continues to believe firmly that a comprehensive peace must be grounded in United Nations Security Council Resolutions 242 and 338 and the principle of territory for peace. Such an outcome must also provide for security and recognition for all states in the region, including Israel, and for legitimate political rights of the Palestinian people. Anything else, the President noted, would fail the twin tests of fairness and security.

The process we are trying to create offers Palestinians a way to achieve these objectives. The United States believes that there should be an end to the Israeli occupation which can occur only through genuine and meaningful negotiations. The United States also believes that this process should create a new relationship of mutuality where Palestinians and Israelis can respect one another's security, identity and political rights. We believe Palestinians should gain control over political, economic and other decisions that affect their lives and fate.

Direct bilateral negotiations will begin four days after the opening of the conference; those parties who wish to attend multilateral negotiations will convene two weeks after the opening of the conference to organize those negotiations. In this regard, the United States will support Palestinian involvement in any bilateral or multilateral negotiations on refugees and in all multilateral negotiations. The conference and the negotiations that follow will be based on UN Security Council Resolutions 242 and 338. The process will proceed along two tracks through direct negotiations between Israel and Arab states and Israel and Palestinians. The United States is determined to achieve a comprehensive settlement of the Arab-Israeli conflict and will do its utmost to ensure that the process moves forward along both tracks toward this end.

In pursuit of a comprehensive settlement, all the negotiations should proceed as quickly as possible toward agreement. For its part, the United States will work for serious negotiations and will also seek to avoid prolongation and stalling by any party.

The conference will be co-sponsored by the United States and the Soviet Union. The European Community will be a participant in the conference alongside the United States and the Soviet Union and be represented by its Presidency. The conference can reconvene only with the consent of all the parties.

With regard to the role of the United Nations, the UN secretary-general will send a representative to the conference as an observer. The co-sponsors will keep the secretary-general apprised of the progress of the negotiations. Agreements reached between the parties will be registered with the UN Secretariat and reported to the Security Council, and the parties will seek the council's endorsement of such agreements. Since it is in the interest of all parties for this process to succeed, while this process is actively ongoing, the United States will not support a competing or parallel process in the United Nations Security Council.

The United States does not seek to determine who speaks for Palestinians in this process. We are seeking to launch a political negotiating process that directly involves Palestinians and offers a pathway for achieving the legitimate political rights of the Palestinian people and for participation in the determination of their future. We believe that a joint Jordanian-Palestinian delegation offers the most promising pathway toward this end.

Only Palestinians can choose their delegation members, which are not subject to veto from anyone. The United States understands that members of the delegation will be Palestinians from the territories who agree to negotiations on two tracks, in phases, and who are willing to live in peace with Israel. No party can be forced to sit with anyone it does not want to sit with.

Palestinians will be free to announce their component of the joint delegation and to make a statement during the opening of the conference. They may also raise any issue pertaining to the substance of the negotiations during the negotiations.

The United States understands how much importance Palestinians attach to the question of east Jerusalem. Thus, we want to assure you that nothing Palestinians do in choosing their delegation members in this phase of the process will affect their claim to east Jerusalem, or be prejudicial or precedential to the outcome of negotiations. It remains the firm position of the United States that Jerusalem must never again be a divided city and that its final status should be decided by negotiations. Thus, we do not recognize Israel's annexation of east Jerusalem or the extension of its municipal boundaries, and we encourage all sides to avoid unilateral acts that would exacerbate local tensions or make negotiations more difficult or preempt their final outcome. It is also the United States position that a Palestinian resident in Jordan with ties to a prominent Jerusalem family would be eligible to join the Jordanian side of the delegation.

Furthermore, it is also the United States position that Palestinians of east Jerusalem should be able to participate by voting in the elections for an interim self-governing authority. The United States further believes that Palestinians from east Jerusalem and Palestinians outside the occupied territories who meet the three criteria should be able to participate in the negotiations on final status. And, the United States supports the right of Palestinians to bring any issue, including east Jerusalem, to the table.

Because the issues at stake are so complex and the emotions so deep, the United States has long maintained that a transitional period is required to break down the walls of suspicion and mistrust and lay the basis for sustainable negotiations on the final status of the occupied territories. The purpose of negotiations on transitional arrangements is to effect the peaceful and orderly transfer of authority from Israel to Palestinians. Palestinians need to achieve rapid control over political, economic, and other decisions that affect their lives and to adjust to a new situation in which Palestinians exercise authority in the West Bank and Gaza. For its part, the United States will strive from the outset and encourage all parties to adopt steps that can create an environment of confidence and mutual trust, including respect for human rights.

As you are aware with respect to negotiations between Israelis and Palestinians, negotiations will be conducted in phases, beginning with talks on interim self-government arrangements. These talks will be conducted with the objective of reaching agreement within one year. Once agreed, the interim self-government arrangements will last for a period of five years. Beginning the third year of the period of interim self-government arrangements, negotiations will take place on permanent status. It is the aim of the United States that permanent status negotiations will be concluded by the end of the transitional period.

It has long been our position that only direct negotiations based on UN Security Council Resolutions 242 and 338 can produce a real peace. No one can dictate the outcome in advance. The United States understands that Palestinians must be free, in opening statements at the conference and in the negotiations that follow, to raise any issue of importance to them. Thus, Palestinians are free to argue for whatever outcome they believe best meets their requirements. The United States will accept any outcome agreed by the parties. In this regard and consistent with longstanding U.S. policies, confederation is not excluded as a possible outcome of negotiations on final status.

The United States has long believed that no party should take unilateral actions that seek to predetermine issues that can only be resolved through negotiations. In this regard the United States has opposed and will continue to oppose settlement activity in the territories occupied in 1967, which remains an obstacle to peace.

The United States will act as an honest broker in trying to resolve the Arab-Israeli conflict. It is our intention, together with the Soviet Union, to play the role of a driving force in this process to help the parties move forward toward a comprehensive peace. Any party will have access to the co-sponsors at any time. The United States is prepared to participate in all stages of the negotiations, with the consent of the parties to each negotiation.

These are the assurances that the United States is providing concerning the implementation of the initiative we have discussed. We are persuaded that we have a real opportunity to accomplish something very important in the peace process. And we are prepared to work hard together with you in the period ahead to build on the progress we have made. There will be difficult challenges for all parties. But with the Palestinians' continued commitment and creativity, we have a real chance of moving to a peace conference and to negotiations and then on toward the broader peace that we all seek.

Source: "Letter of Assurances from the US to the Palestinians—18 October 1991," Israel Ministry of Foreign Affairs, http://www.mfa.gov.il/MFA.

120. Yitzhak Shamir and Haydar Abd al-Shafi, Madrid Peace Conference [Excerpt], October 31, 1991

Introduction

The Madrid talks began at the end of October 1991 and lasted until the summer of 1993, during which time nine rounds of negotiations took place. Separate Israeli teams negotiated bilaterally with Arab delegations from Syria, Egypt, Lebanon, and Jordan and the Palestinians, whose diplomatic merger with the Jordanians proved merely an arrangement of convenience. For diplomatic reasons Palestine Liberation Organization (PLO) chairman Yasser Arafat, so prominently identified with the cause of President Saddam Hussein of Iraq during the recent Gulf Crisis, did not attend as a member of the Palestinian delegation. This was the first occasion on which Israelis and Palestinians had negotiated directly. The great powers also held concurrent negotiations on such regional issues as arms control, trade, water supplies and rights, environmental issues, and maritime policies. Israeli prime minister Yitzhak Shamir and Haydar abd al-Shafi, leader of the Palestinian delegation, opened the conference by making eloquent appeals for peace. Shamir begged Arab leaders and peoples to "renounce the jihad against Israel" and urged "rejectionist" elements within the PLO to "condemn declarations that call for Israel's annihilation." He also begged the Palestinians to end the First Intifada in which so many young Arabs were dying. Al-Shafi proclaimed the Palestinians' unalterable determination to regain their homeland and made a direct appeal to the Israeli people for peace. He brought up the foremost Palestinian grievances: Israel's continuing harsh repression of the intifada and its headlong drive to build ever more settlements in the occupied territories. He also, however, made the by now almost ritual necessary restatement of the Palestinian commitment to United Nations (UN) Security Council Resolutions 242 and 338 and the recognition of Israel's right to exist within secure borders. In practice, some of this rhetoric was mere window dressing largely designed for international public consumption. Shamir later admitted that his major objective in attending the Madrid talks was to drag them out for as long as he could while Israel mounted a drive to establish as many new Jewish settlements as possible in the occupied territories.

Primary Source

Israeli prime minister Yitzhak Shamir:

We pray that this meeting will mark the beginning of a new chapter in the history of the Middle East; that it will signal the end of hostility, violence, terror, and war; that it will bring dialogue, accommodation, coexistence, and above all, peace.

Ladies and gentlemen, to appreciate the meaning of peace for the people of Israel, one has to view today's Jewish sovereignty in the Land of Israel against the background of our history. Jews have been persecuted throughout the ages in almost every continent. Some countries barely tolerated us; others oppressed, tortured, slaughtered, and exiled us. This century saw the Nazi regime set out to exterminate us. The Shoah—the Holocaust, the catastrophic genocide of unprecedented proportions which destroyed a third of our people—became possible because no one defended us. Being homeless, we were also defenseless. But it was not the Holocaust which made the world community recognize our rightful claim to the Land of Israel. In fact, the rebirth of the State of Israel so soon after the Holocaust has made the world forget that our claim is immemorial. We are the only people who have lived in the Land of Israel without interruption for nearly 4,000 years. We are the only people, except

for a short Crusader kingdom, who have had an independent sovereignty in this land. We are the only people for whom Jerusalem has been a capital. We are the only people whose sacred places are only in the Land of Israel. No nation has expressed its bond with its land with as much intensity and consistency as we have. For millennia, our people repeated at every occasion the cry of the psalmist: If I forget thee, Jerusalem, may my right hand lose its cunning. For millennia, we have encouraged each other with the greeting: Next year in Jerusalem. For millennia, our prayers, literature, and folklore have expressed powerful longing to return to our land. Only Eretz Yisra'el, the Land of Israel, is our true homeland.

Any other country, no matter how hospitable, is still a diaspora, a temporary station on the way home. To others, it was not an attractive land; no one wanted it. Mark Twain described it only 100 years ago as a desolate country which sits in sackcloth and ashes—a silent, mournful expanse which not even imagination can grace with the pomp of life.

The Zionist movement gave political expression to our claim to the Land of Israel, and in 1922, the League of Nations recognized the justice of this claim. They understood the compelling historic imperative of establishing a Jewish homeland in the Land of Israel. The United Nations organization reaffirmed this recognition after World War II.

Regrettably, the Arab leaders, whose friendship we wanted most, opposed a Jewish state in the region. With a few distinguished exceptions, they claimed that the Land of Israel is part of the Arab domain that stretches from the Atlantic to the Persian Gulf. In defiance of international will and legality, the Arab regimes attempted to overrun and destroy the Jewish state even before it was born. The Arab spokesmen at the United Nations declared that the establishment of a Jewish state would cause a bloodbath which would make the slaughters of Genghis Khan pale into insignificance. In its declaration of independence on May 15, 1948, Israel stretched out its hand in peace to its Arab neighbors, calling for an end to war and bloodshed. In response, seven Arab states invaded Israel. The UN resolution that partitioned the country was thus violated and effectively annulled.

The United Nations did not create Israel. The Jewish state came into being because the tiny Jewish community in what was Mandatory Palestine rebelled against foreign imperialist rule. We did not conquer a foreign land; we repulsed the Arab onslaught, prevented Israel's annihilation, declared its independence, and established a viable state and government institutions within a very short time.

After their attack on Israel failed, the Arab regimes continued their fight against Israel with boycott, blockade, terrorism, and outright war. Soon after the establishment of Israel, they turned against the Jewish communities in Arab countries. A wave of oppression, expropriation, and expulsion caused a mass exodus of some 800,000 Jews from lands they had inhabited from before the rise of the Islam. Most of the Jewish refugees, stripped of their considerable possessions, came to Israel. They were welcomed by the Jewish state, they were given shelter and support, and they were integrated into Israeli society, together with half a million survivors of the European Holocaust.

The Arab regimes' rejection of Israel's existence in the Middle East and the continuous war they have waged against it are part of history. There have been attempts to rewrite this history, which depicts the Arabs as victims and Israel as the aggressor. Like attempts to deny the Holocaust, they will fail. With the demise of totalitarian regimes in most of the world, this perversion of history will disappear.

In their war against Israel's existence, the Arab governments took advantage of the cold war. They enlisted the military, economic, and political support of the communist world against Israel, and they turned a local regional conflict into an international powder keg. This caused the Middle East to be flooded with arms, which fueled wars and turned the area into a dangerous battleground and a testing arena for sophisticated weapons. At the UN, the Arab states mustered the support of other Muslim countries and the Soviet bloc. Together, they had an automatic majority for countless resolutions that perverted history, paraded fiction as fact, and made a travesty of the UN and its charter.

Arab hostility to Israel has also brought tragic human suffering to the Arab people. Tens of thousands have been killed and wounded; hundreds of thousands of Arabs who lived in Mandatory Palestine were encouraged by their own leaders to flee from their homes. Their suffering is a blot on humanity. No decent person—least of all a Jew of this era—can be oblivious to this suffering. Several hundreds of thousands of Palestinian Arabs live in slums known as refugee camps in Gaza, Judaea, and Samaria. Attempts by Israel to rehabilitate and house them have been defeated by Arab objections. Nor has their fate been any better in Arab states. Unlike the Jewish refugees who came to Israel from Arab countries, most Arab refugees were neither welcomed nor integrated by their hosts. Only the Kingdom of Jordan awarded them citizenship. Their plight has been used as a political weapon against Israel. The Arabs who have chosen to remain in Israel—Christian and Muslim—have become full-fledged citizens, enjoying equal rights and representation in the legislature, in the judiciary, and in all walks of life.

We, who over the centuries were denied access to our holy places, respect the religion of all faiths in our country. Our law guarantees freedom of worship and protects the holy places of every religion.

Distinguished co-chairmen, ladies, and gentlemen, I stand before you today in yet another quest for peace—not only on behalf of the State of Israel, but in the name of the entire Jewish people that has maintained an unbreakable bond with the Land of Israel for almost 4,000 years. Our pursuit of accommodation and peace has been relentless. For us, the ingathering of Jews into their ancient homeland, their integration into our society, and the creation of the necessary infrastructure are at the very top of our national agenda.

A nation that faces such a gigantic challenge would most naturally desire peace with all its neighbors. Since the beginning of Zionism, we formulated innumerable peace proposals and plans. All of them were rejected. The first crack in the wall of hostility occurred in 1977, when the late President Anwar al-Sadat of Egypt decided to break the taboo and come to Jerusalem. His gesture was reciprocated with enthusiasm by the people and Government of Israel, headed by Menahem Begin. This development led to the Camp David accords and a treaty of peace between Egypt and Israel. Four years later, in May 1983, an agreement was signed with the lawful government of Lebanon. Unfortunately, this agreement was not fulfilled because of outside intervention. But a precedent was set, and we look forward to courageous steps, similar to those of Anwar al-Sadat. Regrettably, not one Arab leader has seen fit to come forward and respond to our call for peace.

Today's gathering is a result of a sustained American effort based on our own peace plan of May 1989, which in turn was founded on the Camp David accords. According to the American initiative, the purpose of this meeting is to launch direct peace negotiations between Israel and each of its neighbors and multilateral negotiations on regional issues among all the countries of the region. We have always believed that only direct bilateral talks can bring peace. We have agreed to precede such talks with this ceremonial conference, but we hope that Arab consent to direct bilateral talks indicates an understanding that there is no other way to peace. In the Middle East, this has special meaning, because such talks imply mutual acceptance, and the root cause of the conflict is the Arab refusal to recognize the legitimacy of the State of Israel.

The multilateral talks that would accompany the bilateral negotiations are a vital component in the process. In these talks, the essential ingredients of coexistence and regional cooperation will be discussed. There cannot be genuine peace in our region unless these regional issues are addressed and resolved.

We believe the goal of the bilateral negotiations is to sign peace treaties between Israel and its neighbors and to reach an agreement on interim self-government arrangements with the Palestinian Arabs. But nothing can be achieved without goodwill. I appeal to the Arab leaders—those who are here and those who have not yet joined the process: Show us and the world that you accept Israel's existence. Demonstrate your readiness to accept Israel as a permanent entity in the region. Let the people in our region hear you speak in the language of reconciliation, coexistence, and peace with Israel.

In Israel, there is an almost total consensus for the need for peace. We only differ on the best ways to achieve it. In most Arab countries, the opposite seems to be true. The only differences are over the ways to push Israel into a defenseless position and, ultimately, to destruction. We would like to see in your countries an end to poisonous preachings against Israel. We would like to see an indication of the kind of hunger for peace which characterizes Israeli society.

We appeal to you to renounce the jihad against Israel; we appeal to you to denounce the PLO Covenant which calls for Israel's destruction; we appeal to you to condemn declarations that call for Israel's annihilation, like the one issued by the rejectionist conference in Tehran last week; we appeal to you to let Jews who wish to leave your countries go. And we address a call to the Palestinian Arabs: Renounce violence and terrorism. Use the universities in the administered territories, whose existence was made possible only by Israel, for learning and development, not agitation and violence. Stop exposing your children to danger by sending them to throw bombs and stones at soldiers and civilians.

[...]

Ladies and gentlemen, we come to this process with an open heart, sincere intentions, and great expectations. We are committed to negotiating without interruption, until an agreement is reached. There will be problems, obstacles, crises, and conflicting claims, but it is better to talk than to shed blood. Wars have not solved anything in our region; they have only caused misery, suffering, bereavement, and hatred.

We know our partners to the negotiations will make territorial demands on Israel but, as an examination of the conflict's long history makes clear, its nature is not territorial. It raged well before Israel acquired Judaea, Samaria, Gaza, and the Golan in a defensive war. There was no hint at recognition of Israel before the war in 1967, when the territories in question were not under Israel's control.

We are a nation of 4 million. The Arab nations from the Atlantic to the Gulf number 170 million. We control only 28,000 square km. The Arabs possess a land mass of 14 million square km. The issue is not territory, but our existence. It will be regrettable if the talks focus primarily and exclusively on territory. It is the quickest way to an impasse.

What we need, first and foremost, is the building of confidence, the removal of the danger of confrontation, and the development of relations in as many spheres as possible. The issues are complex, and the negotiations will be lengthy and difficult. We submit that the best venue for the talks is in our region, in close proximity to the decisionmakers, not in a foreign land. We invite our partners to this process to come to Israel for the first round of talks. On our part, we are ready to go to Jordan, to Lebanon, and to Syria for the same purpose. There is no better way to make peace than to talk in each other's home. Avoiding such talks is a denial of the purpose of the negotiations. I would welcome a positive answer from the representatives of these states here and now. We must learn to live together. We must learn to live without war, without hatred.

[...]

We are convinced that human nature prefers peace to war and belligerence. We, who have had to fight seven wars and sacrifice many thousands of lives, glorify neither death nor war. The Jewish faith exalts peace, even to the extent that it considers it a synonym for the Creator himself. We yearn for peace; we pray for peace.

We believe the blessing of peace can turn the Middle East into a paradise, a center of cultural, scientific, medical, technological creativity. We can foresee a period of great economic progress that would put an end to misery, hunger, and illiteracy. It could put the Middle East, the cradle of civilization, on the road to a new era. Such a goal merits our devotion and dedication for as long as it is necessary, until, in the words of the prophet Isaiah, we shall be able to turn swords into plowshares and bring the blessings of peace to all the peoples of our region.

[...]

Palestine Delegation Leader Haydar Abd al-Shafi
[...]

We, the people of Palestine, stand before you in the fullness of our pain, our pride, and our anticipation, for we long harbored a yearning for peace and a dream of justice and freedom. For too long, the Palestinian people have gone unheeded, silenced and denied. Our identity negated by political expediency; our right for struggle against injustice maligned; and our present existence subdued by the past tragedy of another people. For the greater part of this century we have been victimized by the myth of a land without a people and described with impunity as the invisible Palestinians. Before such willful blindness, we refused to disappear or to accept a distorted identity. Our *intifada* is a testimony to our perseverance and resilience waged in a just struggle to regain our rights. It is time for us to narrate our own story, to stand witness as advocates of truth which has long lain buried in the consciousness and conscience of the world. We do not stand before you as supplicants, but rather as the torchbearers who know that, in our world of today, ignorance can never be an excuse. We seek neither an admission of guilt after the fact, nor vengeance for past inequities, but rather an act of will that would make a just peace a reality.

We speak out, ladies and gentlemen, from the full conviction of the rightness of our cause, the verity of our history, and the depth of our commitment. Therein lies the strength of the Palestinian people today, for we have scaled walls of fear and reticence, and we wish to speak out with the courage and integrity that our narrative and history deserve. The cosponsors have invited us here today to present our case and to reach out to the other with whom we have had to face a mutually exclusive reality on the land of Palestine. But even in the invitation to this peace conference, our narrative was distorted and our truth only partially acknowledged.

The Palestinian people are one, fused by centuries of history in Palestine, bound together by a collective memory of shared sorrows and joys, and sharing a unity of purpose and vision. Our songs and ballads are full of tales and children's stories, the dialect of our jokes, the image of our poems, that hint of melancholy which colors even our happiest moments, are as important to us as the blood ties which link our families and clans. Yet, an invitation to discuss peace, the peace we all desire and need, comes to only a portion of our people. It ignores our national, historical, and organic unity. We come here wrenched from our sisters and brothers in exile to stand before you as the Palestinians under occupation, although we maintain that each of us represents the rights and interests of the whole.

We have been denied the right to publicly acknowledge our loyalty to our leadership and system of government. But allegiance and loyalty cannot be censored or severed. Our acknowledged leadership is more than [the] justly democratically chosen leadership of all the Palestinian people. It is the symbol of our national unity and identity, the guardian of our past, the protector of our present, and the hope of our future. Our people have chosen to entrust it with their history and the preservation of our precious legacy. This leadership has been clearly and unequivocally recognized by the community of nations, with only a few exceptions who had chosen for so many years shadow over substance. Regardless of the nature and conditions of our oppression, whether the disposition and dispersion of exile or the brutality and repression of the occupation, the Palestinian people cannot be torn asunder. They remain united—a nation wherever they are, or are forced to be.

And Jerusalem, ladies and gentlemen, that city which is not only the soul of Palestine, but the cradle of three world religions, is tangible even in its claimed absence from our midst at this stage. It is apparent, through artificial exclusion from this conference, that this is a denial of its right to seek peace and redemption. For it, too, has suffered from war and occupation. Jerusalem, the city of peace, has been barred from a peace conference and deprived of its calling. Palestinian Jerusalem, the capital of our homeland and future state, defines Palestinian existence, past, present, and future, but itself has been denied a voice and an identity. Jerusalem defies exclusive possessiveness or bondage. Israel's annexation of Arab Jerusalem remains both clearly illegal in the eyes of the world community, and an affront to the peace that this city deserves.

We come to you from a tortured land and a proud, though captive people, having been asked to negotiate with our occupiers, but leaving behind the children of the *intifada* and a people under occupation and under curfew who enjoined us not to surrender or forget. As we speak, thousands of our brothers and sisters are languishing in Israeli prisons and detention camps, most detained without evidence, charge, or trial, many cruelly mistreated and tortured in interrogation, guilty only of seeking freedom or daring to defy the occupation. We speak in their name and we say: Set them free. As we speak, the tens of thousands who have been wounded or permanently disabled are in pain. Let peace heal their wounds. As we speak, the eyes of thousands of Palestinian refugees, deportees, and displaced persons since 1967, are haunting us, for exile is a cruel fate. Bring them home. They have the right to return. As we speak, the silence of demolished homes echoes through the halls and in our minds. We must rebuild our homes in our free state.

And what do we tell the loved ones of those killed by army bullets? How do we answer the questions and the fear in our children's eyes? For one out of three Palestinian children under occupation has been killed, injured, or detained in the past four years. How can we explain to our children that they are denied education or schools are so often closed by the army fate? [sentence as heard] Or why their life is in danger for raising a flag in a land where even children are killed or jailed? What requiem can be sung for trees uprooted by army bulldozers? And most of all, who can explain to those whose lands are confiscated and clear waters stolen, a message of peace? Remove the barbed wire. Restore the land and its life-giving water. The settlements must stop now. Peace cannot be waged while Palestinian land is [being] confiscated in myriad ways and the status of the occupied territories is being decided each day by Israeli bulldozers and barbed wire. This is not simply a position. It is an irrefutable reality. Territory for peace is a travesty when territory for illegal settlement is official Israeli policy and practice. The settlements must stop now.

In the name of the Palestinian people, we wish to directly address the Israeli people with whom we have had a prolonged exchange of pain: Let us share hope, instead. We are willing to live side by side on the land and the promise of the future. Sharing, however, requires two partners, willing to share as equals. Mutuality and reciprocity must replace domination and hostility for genuine reconciliation and coexistence under international legality. Your security and ours are mutually dependent, as entwined as the fears and nightmares of our children. We have seen some of you at your best and at your worst. For the occupier can hide no secrets from the occupied, and we are witness to the toll that occupation has exacted from you and yours.

We have seen you agonize over the transformation of your sons and daughters into instruments of a blind and violent occupation. And we are sure that at no time did you envisage such a role for the children whom you thought would forge your future. We have seen you look back in deepest sorrow at the tragedy of your past, and look on in horror at the disfigurement of the victim-turned-oppressor. Not for this have you nurtured your hopes, dreams, and your offspring. This is why we have responded with solemn appreciation to those of you who came to offer consolation to our bereaved, to give support to those whose homes were being demolished, and to extend encouragement and counsel to those detained behind barbed wire and iron bars. And we have marched together, often choking together in the nondiscriminatory tear gas or crying out in pain as the clubs descended on both Palestinian and Israeli alike, for pain knows no national boundaries, and no one can claim a monopoly on suffering. We once formed a human chain around Jerusalem, joining hands and calling for peace. Let us today form a moral chain around Madrid and continue that noble effort for peace and a promise of freedom for our sons and daughters. Break through the barriers of mistrust and manipulated fears. Let us look forward in magnanimity and in hope.

To our Arab brothers and sisters, most of whom are represented here in this historic occasion, we express our loyalty and gratitude for their lifelong support and solidarity. We are here together seeking a just and lasting peace, whose cornerstone is freedom for Palestine, justice for the Palestinians, and an end to the occupation of all Palestinian and Arab lands. Only then can we really enjoy together the fruits of peace, prosperity, security, and human dignity and freedom.

[. . .]

To the co-sponsors and participants in this occasion of awe and challenge, we pledge our commitment to the principle of justice, peace, and reconciliation based on international legitimacy and uniform standards. We shall persist in our quest for peace to place before you the substance and determination of our people, often victimized but never defeated. We shall pursue our people's right to self-determination, to the exhilaration of freedom, and to the warmth of the sun as a nation among equals.

[. . .]

We, the Palestinian people, made the imaginative leap in the Palestine National Council of November 1988, during which the Palestine Liberation Organization launched its peace initiative based on Security Council Resolutions 242 and 338, and declared Palestinian independence based on Resolution 181 of the United Nations, which gave birth to two states in 1948, Israel and Palestine. In December 1988, a historic speech before the United Nations in Geneva led directly to the launching of the Palestinian-American dialogue. Ever since then, our people has responded positively to every serious peace initiative and has done its utmost to ensure the success of this process. Israel, on the other hand, has placed many ob-

stacles and barriers in the path of peace to negate the very validity of the process. Its illegal and frenzied settlement activity is the most glaring evidence of its rejectionism, the latest settlement being erected just two days ago. These historic decisions of the Palestine National Council wrench the course of history from inevitable confrontation and conflict towards peace and mutual recognition. With our own hands, and in an act of sheer will, we have molded the shape of the future of our people. Our parliament has articulated the message of the people, with the courage to say yes to the challenge of history, just as it provided the reference in its resolutions last month in Algiers and in the Central Council meeting this month in Tunis, to go forward to this historic conference. We cannot be made to bear the brunt of other people's "no". We must have reciprocity. We must have peace.

Ladies and Gentlemen: In the Middle East, there is no superfluous people outside time and place, but rather a state sorely missed by time and place—the state of Palestine. It must be born on the land of Palestine to redeem the injustice of the destruction of its historical reality and to free the people of Palestine from the shackles of their victimization.

Our homeland has never ceased to exist in our minds and hearts, but it has to exist as a state on all the territories occupied by Israel in the war of 1967, with Arab Jerusalem as its capital, in the context of that city's special status and its non-exclusive character.

This state, in a condition of emergence, has already been a subject of anticipation for too long. It should take place today rather than tomorrow. However, we are willing to accept the proposal for a transitional stage provided interim arrangements are not transformed into permanent status. The time frame must be condensed to respond to the dispossessed Palestinians' urgent need for sanctuary and to the occupied Palestinians' right to gain relief from oppression and to win recognition of their authentic will.

During this phase, international protection for our people is most urgently needed, and the de jure application of the Fourth Geneva Convention is a necessary condition. The phases must not prejudice the outcome. Rather, they require an internal momentum and motivation to lead sequentially to sovereignty. Bilateral negotiations on the withdrawal of Israeli forces, the dissolution of Israeli administration, and the transfer of authority to the Palestinian people cannot proceed under coercion or threat in the current asymmetry of power. Israel must demonstrate its willingness to negotiate in good faith by immediately halting all settlement activity and land confiscation while implementing meaningful confidence-building measures.

Without genuine progress, tangible constructive changes and just agreements during the bilateral talks, multilateral negotiations will be meaningless. Regional stability, security, and development are

1420 121. Yitzhak Rabin, Inaugural Speech

the logical outcome of an equitable and just solution to the Palestinian question, which remains the key to the resolution of wider conflicts and concerns.

In its confrontation of wills between the legitimacy of the people and the illegality of the occupation, the *intifada*'s message has been consistent: to embody the Palestinian state and to build its institutions and infrastructure. We seek recognition for this creative impulse which nurtures within it the potential nascent state.

[...]

The *intifada* is our drive towards nation-building and social transformation. We are here today with the support of our people, who have given itself the right to hope and to make a stand for peace. We must recognize as well that some of our people harbor serious doubts and skepticism about this process. Within our democratic, social, and political structures, we have evolved a respect for pluralism and diversity and we shall guard the opposition's right to differ within the parameters of mutual respect and national unity.

The process launched here must lead us to the light at the end of the tunnel. And this light is the promise of a new Palestine—free, democratic, and respectful of human rights and the integrity of nature.

Self-determination, ladies and gentlemen, can neither be granted nor withheld at the will of the political self-interest of others. For it is enshrined in all international charters and humanitarian law. We claim this right; we firmly assert it here before you and in the eyes of the rest of the world. For it is a sacred and inviolable right which we shall relentlessly pursue and exercise with dedication and self-confidence and pride.

Let us end the Palestinian-Israeli fatal proximity in this unnatural condition of occupation, which has already claimed too many lives. No dream of expansion or glory can justify the taking of a single life. Set us free to reengage as neighbors and as equals on our holy land.

[...]

Source: Walter Laqueur and Barry Rubin, eds., *The Israel-Arab Reader: A Documentary History of the Middle East Conflict* (New York: Penguin, 2001), 388–400.

121. Yitzhak Rabin, Inaugural Speech, July 13, 1992

Introduction

Almost nine months after the Madrid Peace talks began, Labor politician Yitzhak Rabin won Israel's July 1992 elections and became prime minister. In terms of his willingness to deal with the Pales-

tinians and make genuine concessions in the interests of peace, Rabin was far less of a hawk than his predecessor, the Likud politician Yitzhak Shamir. In his inaugural speech before the Knesset (Israeli Parliament), Rabin proclaimed his readiness to "launch vigorous steps to bring about the termination of the Arab-Israeli conflict" and assure permanent peace for Israel. He was prepared to credit the willingness of both Arab states and the Palestinians to accept Israel's existence as a precondition of peace. In his first official utterance as prime minister, he therefore invited the Jordanian-Palestinian delegation to visit Israel to discuss the implementation of Palestinian autonomy in the West Bank. Although Rabin still made substantial concessions to Israeli hard-liners, refusing to end new Israeli settlements in East Jerusalem and the Golan Heights, he did curtail settlements in the West Bank and Gaza and in December 1992 obtained legislation from the Knesset permitting direct negotiations with the Palestine Liberation Organization (PLO). Like several other participants in the peace process, including PLO chairman Yasser Arafat and King Hussein of Jordan, Rabin had to take account of his political constituency, which included elements deeply suspicious of any other moves toward accommodation. His accession to power nonetheless marked a break with the far more obstructionist attitude that had dominated Israeli policy under Shamir.

Primary Source

... This government is determined to embrace every possible effort, pave every road, and do every possible and impossible thing for the sake of national and personal security, for the sake of peace and of preventing war, for the sake of eliminating unemployment, for the sake of *aliyah* and its absorption, for the sake of economic growth, to enhance the foundations of democracy and the rule of law; and for the sake of ensuring equality for all citizens, while upholding human rights.

We will change the national order of priorities. We know well that the road we are about to tread will be fraught with obstacles; crises will erupt, and there will be disappointment, tears, and pain. After all this is over, however, once we come to the end of this road, we will have acquired a strong country, a good country, a country in which we all share in the big efforts and are proud to be its citizens. As the poet Rahel put it: *Will a concerted, stubborn, and persistent effort of a thousand arms not move mountains?* The answer lies with us and is up to us.

.... In the last decade of the 20th century, the atlases and the history and geography books no longer depict reality. Walls of hatred have crumbled, borders have been erased, superpowers have collapsed, ideologies have broken down, countries have been born and passed away, and the gates have opened to immigration to Israel. It is our duty, both to ourselves and to our children, to see the new world as it is today, to examine the risks and explore the chances, and to do everything so that the State of Israel becomes part of the changing world. We are no longer an isolated nation, and it is no longer true that the entire world is against us. We must rid ourselves of the feeling of isolation that has afflicted us for almost 50 years. We must join the campaign of peace, reconciliation, and international cooperation that is currently engulfing the entire globe, lest we miss the train and be left alone at the station.

This is why the new government made its main goal to promote the attainment of peace for Israel and to launch vigorous steps to bring about the termination of the Arab-Israeli conflict. We will do this on the basis of recognition by the Arab countries and the Palestinians of Israel as a sovereign state and of its right to live in peace and security. We sincerely believe that this is possible, imperative, and will come to be. As the poet Saul Tchernichowsky wrote: *Believe I in the future. Though it may be far off, the day will yet come when peace shall be spoken and nation will bless nation.* I would like to believe that this day is not far off.

The government will propose to the Arab countries and to the Palestinians to pursue the peace negotiations based on the format consolidated at the Madrid conference. As a first step on the way to the permanent solution, we will discuss the implementation of autonomy in Judea, Samaria, and the Gaza district. It is not our intention to waste valuable time. The first directive the government will issue to the negotiating teams will be to accelerate the talks and to conduct intensive deliberations between the sides.

Within a short period of time, we will reopen the talks to dampen the flame of hatred between the Palestinians and the State of Israel. As a first step, and in order to demonstrate our integrity and goodwill, I wish to invite the Palestinian-Jordanian delegation for an informal meeting here in Jerusalem, to hear them and to let them hear us, in order to create the proper atmosphere for a good partnership.

From this podium I want to send a message to you, the Palestinians in the territories: We have been destined to live together on the same piece of land in the same country. Our life proceeds alongside yours, with you, and against you. You have failed in the wars against us. A hundred years of bloody terror on your part only inflicted suffering, pain, and bereavement upon you. You have lost thousands of your sons and daughters, and you have constantly lost ground. For over 44 years you have been deluding yourselves, your leaders have been leading you by the nose with falsehoods and lies. They missed all the opportunities, they rejected all our proposed solutions, and they led you from one disaster to another. You, the Palestinians in the territories, living in miserable exile in Gaza and Khan Yunus and in the refugee camps in Nabulus and Hebron, you who have never in your lives known even one day of freedom and happiness: You had better listen to us, if only this time. We are offering you the most fair and realistic offer we can put forth today: autonomy, self-rule, with its advantages and limitations. You will not get all that you want. We, too, may not get everything we want. Once and for all, take your fate into your own hands. Do not once again miss the opportunity

which may never recur. Take our proposal seriously, give it the seriousness it deserves to spare yourselves yet more suffering and bereavement. Enough of tears and blood!

Today the new government proposes to the Palestinians in the territories to give peace a chance and to stop all violent and terrorist activities during the autonomy negotiations. We know very well that the Palestinians are not of one mind and that some of them think differently, but the people have been suffering for years.

To the troublemakers in the territories we propose to drop the stones and the knives and await the outcome of the talks which may engender peace in the Middle East. If the Palestinians accept this proposal, we will pursue the talks. Nevertheless, we will deal with the territories as if there were no negotiations going on between us. Instead of stretching out a friendly hand, we will enforce all the measures to prevent terror and violence. The choice is in the hands of the Palestinians in the territories.

We have lost our best sons and daughters in the struggle over this land and in the wars against the Arab armies. My longtime comrades in the IDF [Israel Defense Forces] and I, as a former military man who fought in Israel's wars, carry their memory in our hearts with great love. We share the grief of the families whose nights are sleepless and for whom all days of the year are one long memorial day, because only those who have lost their best friends can understand the feeling. Our heart also goes out to the disabled whose bodies are marked with the scars of war and terror. Even at this festive time, we do not forget the Israeli MIA's and POW's. We will continue to wage every possible effort to bring them back home. Our thoughts today, as always, are with their families.

Members of the Knesset, we will continue to fight for our right to live here in peace and tranquility. No knife, stone, firebomb, or mine will stop us. The government being presented here today sees itself responsible for the security of each and every Israeli citizen, Jew and Arab alike, in the State of Israel, in Judaea, Samaria, and the Gaza Strip. We will strike hard and relentlessly at the terrorists and their henchmen. There will be no compromises in the war against terror. The IDF and the other security forces will prove to the bloodthirsty men that our lives are not expendable. We will take action to reduce hostile activities as much as possible and safeguard the personal safety of the inhabitants of Israel and the inhabitants of the territories while meticulously upholding the law and individual freedoms.

Members of the Knesset, on your behalf, too, allow me to seize this occasion to convey our gratitude to the soldiers and commanders of the IDF, to the secret warriors of the Shin Bet, to the men of the Border Police and the Israel Police for the nights spent in pursuit and lying in ambush, for the days spent on guard and on the alert. On behalf of all of us, I shake your hand.

Members of the Knesset, the plan for Palestinian self-rule in Judaea, Samaria, and Gaza—the autonomy—included in the Camp David accords involves a five-year interim arrangement. No later than three years after its establishment, discussions will begin on the permanent solution. By definition, the very fact that this issue is being discussed arouses concern among those of us who chose to settle in Judaea, Samaria, and the Gaza district. I hereby inform you that the government, by means of the IDF and the other security forces, will be responsible for the security and welfare of the residents in Judaea, Samaria, and the Gaza Strip. At the same time, the government will avoid moves and acts that would disturb the proper conduct of the peace negotiations. We would like to emphasize that the government will continue to strengthen and build up Jewish settlement along the confrontation lines, due to their security importance, and in metropolitan Jerusalem.

This government, just like all its predecessors, believes there are no differences of opinion within this House concerning the eternalness of Jerusalem as the capital of Israel. Jerusalem, whole and united, has been and will remain the capital of the Israeli people under Israeli sovereignty, the place every Jew yearns and dreams of. The government is resolute in its position that Jerusalem is not a negotiable issue. The coming years, too, will witness the expansion of construction in metropolitan Jerusalem. Every Jew, both religious and secular, vows: If I forget thee, O Jerusalem, let my right hand wither! This vow unites all of us and certainly applies to me, being a native of Jerusalem.

The government will uphold the freedom of worship of members of all other faiths in Jerusalem. It will meticulously maintain free access to the holy sites of all faiths and sects and will make a normal and comfortable life possible for all those visiting and living in it.

Members of the Knesset, the winds of peace that have been blowing recently from Moscow to Washington, from Berlin to Beijing; the voluntary elimination of weapons of mass destruction; and the abrogation of military pacts have decreased the risks of war in the Middle East as well. Nevertheless, this region—made up of Syria, Jordan, Iraq, and Lebanon—is still rife with dangers, which is why we will not make even the slightest concession on issues of security. As far as we are concerned, security comes even before peace.

Several countries in our region have recently stepped up their efforts to develop and export nuclear weapons. According to reports, Iraq was very close to possessing nuclear arms. Fortunately, the Iraqi nuclear capability was exposed in time and, according to various testimonies, it was affected and damaged in and after the Gulf war. The possibility that nuclear weapons may make their appearance in the Middle East in the next few years is a negative and very serious development from Israel's point of view. Already in its initial steps, the government—possibly with the cooperation of other countries—will give its attention to the foiling of every possibility that any of Israel's enemies should get a hold on nuclear weapons. For a long time, Israel has been ready for the danger of the existence of nuclear weapons. Nevertheless, this reality requires us to give additional thought to the urgent need to terminate the Arab-Israeli conflict and to attain peace with our neighbors.

Members of the House, from this moment on, the term "peace process" is no longer relevant. Starting today we will not talk of a process, but of making peace. In making peace, we would like to employ the good services of Egypt, whose late leader Anwar al-Sadat mustered the courage and had the wisdom to award his people and us the first peace treaty. The government will seek other ways to improve neighborly relations and to enhance the ties with Egypt and its president, Husni Mubarak.

I call on the leaders of the Arab countries to follow in the footsteps of Egypt and its presidents, to make the move that will bring peace to us and them. I invite the king of Jordan and the Syrian and Lebanese presidents to come here to this podium, here in Israel's Knesset in Jerusalem, and talk peace. I am willing to travel today, tomorrow, to Amman, Damascus, Beirut on behalf of peace, because there is no greater triumph than the triumph of peace. In wars, there are victors and vanquished. In peace, all are victors.

In making peace, we will also be joined by the United States, whose friendship and special closeness we sincerely appreciate and hold dear. We will spare no effort to tighten and improve the special relations we have with the only superpower in the world. Although we will receive its advice, the decisions will be ours only—of Israel as a sovereign and independent state.

Source: Walter Laqueur and Barry Rubin, eds., *The Israel-Arab Reader: A Documentary History of the Middle East Conflict* (New York: Penguin, 2001), 403–407.

122. Letters between Yasser Arafat and Yitzhak Rabin, September 9, 1993

Introduction

Like many before them, the protracted 1991–1993 Madrid talks on a Middle East peace settlement bogged down inconclusively as violence and terror escalated in the occupied territories. Particularly in Gaza but also in the West Bank, Arabs attacked Israeli settlers and soldiers and themselves took heavy casualties at the hands of Israeli troops, while Hezbollah Islamic militants launched rocket attacks on Israeli territory from Lebanon. Israeli prime minister Yitzhak Rabin feared the growing strength within the Palestinian and Arab camp of more extreme, often Islamic elements dedicated to Israel's destruction and also found the violence destabilizing. Palestine Liberation Organization (PLO) leader Yasser Arafat's failure, despite concessions, to win a peace accord, improve the conditions of the Palestinians, or even halt the continuing new Israeli settlements in the occupied territories left him vulnerable to attack from more radical rivals who opposed his accommodationist approach. From December 1992 to August 1993, Israel's deputy foreign minister Yossi Beilin and PLO treasurer Ahmad Quarai held talks in Oslo, Norway, outside the Madrid framework. Israel's foreign minister, Shimon Peres, was kept fully informed of the progress of negotiations, but Rabin showed little interest. In the United States the new administration headed by Democratic president Bill Clinton knew in general terms of the talks but did not receive reports on their contents or progress. Perhaps because of their low-key character, the Oslo negotiations produced an accord establishing Palestinian autonomy in Gaza and the West Bank district of Jericho and setting out a timetable for the future establishment of Palestinian self-rule throughout Gaza and the entire West Bank. This was preceded by an exchange of letters between Arafat and Rabin committing the PLO to recognize Israel's "right . . . to exist in peace and security," accepting UN Security Council Resolutions 242 and 338, renouncing the use of violence to achieve a settlement of the issues dividing Israel and the Palestinians, and pledging to amend the PLO Charter to this effect. Rabin, in return, promised on Israel's behalf "to recognize the PLO as the representative of the Palestinian people and commence negotiations with the PLO within the Middle East peace process." In a letter to the Norwegian foreign minister, who had brokered the Oslo talks, Arafat also called on Palestinians in the occupied territories to renounce violence and work with the Israelis in efforts to reach a peaceful and productive settlement there. Israeli critics subsequently complained that not all PLO members endorsed or recognized Arafat's commitments, while PLO dissenters assailed the Israeli prime minister's failure to promise the Palestinians of the occupied territories an independent state. This was nonetheless the first occasion on which Israel's government had shown itself prepared to deal directly with the PLO.

Primary Source

Letter from Yasser Arafat to Yitzhak Rabin
September 9, 1993
Yitzhak Rabin
Prime Minister of Israel

Mr. Prime Minister,

The signing of the Declaration of Principles marks a new era in the history of the Middle East. In firm conviction thereof, I would like to confirm the following PLO commitments:

The PLO recognizes the right of the State of Israel to exist in peace and security.

The PLO accepts United Nations Security Council Resolutions 242 and 338.

The PLO commits itself to the Middle East peace process, and to a peaceful resolution of the conflict between the two sides and declares that all outstanding issues relating to permanent status will be resolved through negotiations.

The PLO considers that the signing of the Declaration of Principles constitutes a historic event, inaugurating a new epoch of peaceful coexistence, free from violence and all other acts which endanger peace and stability. Accordingly, the PLO renounces the use of terrorism and other acts of violence and will assume responsibility over all PLO elements and personnel in order to assure their compliance, prevent violations, and discipline violators.

In view of the promise of a new era and the signing of the Declaration of Principles and based on Palestinian acceptance of Security Council Resolutions 242 and 338, the PLO affirms that those articles of the Palestinian Covenant which deny Israel's right to exist, and the provisions of the Covenant which are inconsistent with the commitments of this letter are now inoperative and no longer valid. Consequently, the PLO undertakes to submit to the Palestinian National Council for formal approval the necessary changes in regard to the Palestinian Covenant.

Sincerely,

Yasser Arafat
Chairman
The Palestine Liberation Organization

Letter from Yitzhak Rabin to Yasser Arafat
September 9, 1993
Yasser Arafat
Chairman
The Palestinian Liberation Organization

Mr. Chairman,

In response to your letter of September 9, 1993, I wish to confirm to you that, in light of the PLO commitments included in your letter, the Government of Israel has decided to recognize the PLO as the representative of the Palestinian people and commence negotiations with the PLO within the Middle East peace process.

Yitzhak Rabin
Prime Minister of Israel

Source: "Israel-PLO Recognition—Exchange of Letters between PM Rabin and Chairman Arafat, September 9, 1993," Israel Ministry of Foreign Affairs, http://www.israel-mfa.gov.il/MFA.

123. Oslo Declaration of Principles [Excerpt], September 13, 1993

Introduction

Four days after Palestine Liberation Organization (PLO) chairman Yasser Arafat and Israeli prime minister Yitzhak Rabin exchanged letters formally recognizing the status of both Israel and the PLO, they signed the Oslo Declaration on the future of the occupied territories of Gaza and the West Bank. The new accords called for the establishment of a "Palestinian Interim Self-Government Authority" in these areas for a transitional period not to exceed five years, after which their status would be determined by a permanent settlement based on the principles of United Nations (UN) Security Council Resolutions 242 and 338. Palestinians in the occupied territories would be able to govern themselves through a council and an authority, for which they would be able to vote, and that would have jurisdiction over "education and culture, health, social welfare, direct taxation, and tourism." Palestinian police would maintain order in the area. Israel would be responsible for defense and also for the "overall security of Israelis for the purpose of safeguarding their internal security and public order." Israeli forces would initially withdraw from the Gaza Strip and the Jericho area and eventually from the entire West Bank. The Israeli settlements and settlers, however, would still fall under Israel's jurisdiction and protection. Israel and the Palestinian areas would cooperate extensively in the industrial, economic, financial, commercial, training, and educational fields in developing water resources, electricity, energy, and tourism and on environmental issues. Future negotiations, to be completed within five years, would reach agreement on outstanding "issues, including: Jerusalem, refugees, settlements, security arrangements, borders, relations and cooperation with other neighbors, and other issues of common interest." U.S. president Bill Clinton, who flew to Oslo to attend the signing of these accords and was photographed with one arm around Arafat and the other around Rabin, hailed the accords as "the dawn of a new era" and a "new beginning." The Oslo Accords nonetheless left many salient issues open or ambivalent. It was never clear whether the ultimate objective of the "final status" agreement to be negotiated in the future would be an independent Palestinian state. The fate of the Israeli settlements in these areas was yet to be determined, and Israel still reserved to itself jurisdiction over and protection of Israeli settlers in the occupied territories, a provision that could easily justify the continuing presence of Israeli troops there. All these questions left ample room for bitter disagreement. As occurred so often, the devil would be in such details.

Primary Source

The Government of the State of Israel and the P.L.O. team (in the Jordanian-Palestinian delegation to the Middle East Peace Conference) (the "Palestinian Delegation"), representing the Palestinian people, agree that it is time to put an end to decades of confrontation and conflict, recognize their mutual legitimate and political rights, and strive to live in peaceful coexistence and mutual dignity and security and achieve a just, lasting and comprehensive peace settlement and historic reconciliation through the agreed political process. Accordingly, the two sides agree to the following principles:

ARTICLE I
AIM OF THE NEGOTIATIONS
The aim of the Israeli-Palestinian negotiations within the current Middle East peace process is, among other things, to establish a Palestinian Interim Self-Government Authority, the elected Council (the "Council"), for the Palestinian people in the West Bank and the Gaza Strip, for a transitional period not exceeding five years, leading to a permanent settlement based on Security Council Resolutions 242 and 338.

It is understood that the interim arrangements are an integral part of the whole peace process and that the negotiations on the permanent status will lead to the implementation of Security Council Resolutions 242 and 338.

ARTICLE II
FRAMEWORK FOR THE INTERIM PERIOD
The agreed framework for the interim period is set forth in this Declaration of Principles.

ARTICLE III
ELECTIONS
In order that the Palestinian people in the West Bank and Gaza Strip may govern themselves according to democratic principles, direct, free and general political elections will be held for the Council under agreed supervision and international observation, while the Palestinian police will ensure public order.

An agreement will be concluded on the exact mode and conditions of the elections in accordance with the protocol attached as Annex I, with the goal of holding the elections not later than nine months after the entry into force of this Declaration of Principles.

These elections will constitute a significant interim preparatory step toward the realization of the legitimate rights of the Palestinian people and their just requirements.

ARTICLE IV
JURISDICTION
Jurisdiction of the Council will cover West Bank and Gaza Strip territory, except for issues that will be negotiated in the permanent status negotiations. The two sides view the West Bank and the Gaza Strip as a single territorial unit, whose integrity will be preserved during the interim period.

ARTICLE V
TRANSITIONAL PERIOD AND PERMANENT STATUS NEGOTIATIONS

The five-year transitional period will begin upon the withdrawal from the Gaza Strip and Jericho area.

Permanent status negotiations will commence as soon as possible, but not later than the beginning of the third year of the interim period, between the Government of Israel and the Palestinian people representatives.

It is understood that these negotiations shall cover remaining issues, including: Jerusalem, refugees, settlements, security arrangements, borders, relations and cooperation with other neighbors, and other issues of common interest.

The two parties agree that the outcome of the permanent status negotiations should not be prejudiced or preempted by agreements reached for the interim period.

ARTICLE VI
PREPARATORY TRANSFER OF POWERS AND RESPONSIBILITIES

Upon the entry into force of this Declaration of Principles and the withdrawal from the Gaza Strip and the Jericho area, a transfer of authority from the Israeli military government and its Civil Administration to the authorised Palestinians for this task, as detailed herein, will commence. This transfer of authority will be of a preparatory nature until the inauguration of the Council.

Immediately after the entry into force of this Declaration of Principles and the withdrawal from the Gaza Strip and Jericho area, with the view to promoting economic development in the West Bank and Gaza Strip, authority will be transferred to the Palestinians on the following spheres: education and culture, health, social welfare, direct taxation, and tourism. The Palestinian side will commence in building the Palestinian police force, as agreed upon. Pending the inauguration of the Council, the two parties may negotiate the transfer of additional powers and responsibilities, as agreed upon.

ARTICLE VII
INTERIM AGREEMENT

The Israeli and Palestinian delegations will negotiate an agreement on the interim period (the "Interim Agreement").

The Interim Agreement shall specify, among other things, the structure of the Council, the number of its members, and the transfer of powers and responsibilities from the Israeli military government and its Civil Administration to the Council. The Interim Agreement shall also specify the Council's executive authority, legislative author-

ity in accordance with Article IX below, and the independent Palestinian judicial organs.

The Interim Agreement shall include arrangements, to be implemented upon the inauguration of the Council, for the assumption by the Council of all of the powers and responsibilities transferred previously in accordance with Article VI above.

In order to enable the Council to promote economic growth, upon its inauguration, the Council will establish, among other things, a Palestinian Electricity Authority, a Gaza Sea Port Authority, a Palestinian Development Bank, a Palestinian Export Promotion Board, a Palestinian Environmental Authority, a Palestinian Land Authority and a Palestinian Water Administration Authority, and any other Authorities agreed upon, in accordance with the Interim Agreement that will specify their powers and responsibilities.

After the inauguration of the Council, the Civil Administration will be dissolved, and the Israeli military government will be withdrawn.

ARTICLE VIII
PUBLIC ORDER AND SECURITY

In order to guarantee public order and internal security for the Palestinians of the West Bank and the Gaza Strip, the Council will establish a strong police force, while Israel will continue to carry the responsibility for defending against external threats, as well as the responsibility for overall security of Israelis for the purpose of safeguarding their internal security and public order.

ARTICLE IX
LAWS AND MILITARY ORDERS

The Council will be empowered to legislate, in accordance with the Interim Agreement, within all authorities transferred to it.

Both parties will review jointly laws and military orders presently in force in remaining spheres.

ARTICLE X
JOINT ISRAELI-PALESTINIAN LIAISON COMMITTEE

In order to provide for a smooth implementation of this Declaration of Principles and any subsequent agreements pertaining to the interim period, upon the entry into force of this Declaration of Principles, a Joint Israeli-Palestinian Liaison Committee will be established in order to deal with issues requiring coordination, other issues of common interest, and disputes.

ARTICLE XI
ISRAELI-PALESTINIAN COOPERATION IN ECONOMIC FIELDS

Recognizing the mutual benefit of cooperation in promoting the development of the West Bank, the Gaza Strip and Israel, upon the entry into force of this Declaration of Principles, an Israeli-Palestinian Economic Cooperation Committee will be established in order to develop and implement in a cooperative manner the programs identified in the protocols attached as Annex III and Annex IV.

ARTICLE XII
LIAISON AND COOPERATION WITH JORDAN AND EGYPT

The two parties will invite the Governments of Jordan and Egypt to participate in establishing further liaison and cooperation arrangements between the Government of Israel and the Palestinian representatives, on the one hand, and the Governments of Jordan and Egypt, on the other hand, to promote cooperation between them. These arrangements will include the constitution of a Continuing Committee that will decide by agreement on the modalities of admission of persons displaced from the West Bank and Gaza Strip in 1967, together with necessary measures to prevent disruption and disorder. Other matters of common concern will be dealt with by this Committee.

ARTICLE XIII
REDEPLOYMENT OF ISRAELI FORCES

After the entry into force of this Declaration of Principles, and not later than the eve of elections for the Council, a redeployment of Israeli military forces in the West Bank and the Gaza Strip will take place, in addition to withdrawal of Israeli forces carried out in accordance with Article XIV.

In redeploying its military forces, Israel will be guided by the principle that its military forces should be redeployed outside populated areas.

Further redeployments to specified locations will be gradually implemented commensurate with the assumption of responsibility for public order and internal security by the Palestinian police force pursuant to Article VIII above.

ARTICLE XIV
ISRAELI WITHDRAWAL FROM THE GAZA STRIP AND JERICHO AREA

Israel will withdraw from the Gaza Strip and Jericho area, as detailed in the protocol attached as Annex II.

ARTICLE XV
RESOLUTION OF DISPUTES

Disputes arising out of the application or interpretation of this Declaration of Principles or any subsequent agreements pertaining to the interim period, shall be resolved by negotiations through the Joint Liaison Committee to be established pursuant to Article X above.

Disputes which cannot be settled by negotiations may be resolved by a mechanism of conciliation to be agreed upon by the parties.

The parties may agree to submit to arbitration disputes relating to the interim period, which cannot be settled through conciliation. To this end, upon the agreement of both parties, the parties will establish an Arbitration Committee.

ARTICLE XVI
ISRAELI-PALESTINIAN COOPERATION CONCERNING REGIONAL PROGRAMS

Both parties view the multilateral working groups as an appropriate instrument for promoting a "Marshall Plan", the regional programs and other programs, including special programs for the West Bank and Gaza Strip, as indicated in the protocol attached as Annex IV.

[. . .]

ANNEX I
PROTOCOL ON THE MODE AND CONDITIONS OF ELECTIONS

Palestinians of Jerusalem who live there will have the right to participate in the election process, according to an agreement between the two sides.

In addition, the election agreement should cover, among other things, the following issues:

the system of elections;
the mode of the agreed supervision and international observation and their personal composition; and
rules and regulations regarding election campaign, including agreed arrangements for the organizing of mass media, and the possibility of licensing a broadcasting and TV station.

The future status of displaced Palestinians who were registered on 4th June 1967 will not be prejudiced because they are unable to participate in the election process due to practical reasons.

ANNEX II
PROTOCOL ON WITHDRAWAL OF ISRAELI FORCES FROM THE GAZA STRIP AND JERICHO AREA

The two sides will conclude and sign within two months from the date of entry into force of this Declaration of Principles, an agreement on the withdrawal of Israeli military forces from the Gaza Strip and Jericho area. This agreement will include comprehensive arrangements to apply in the Gaza Strip and the Jericho area subsequent to the Israeli withdrawal.

Israel will implement an accelerated and scheduled withdrawal of Israeli military forces from the Gaza Strip and Jericho area, beginning immediately with the signing of the agreement on the Gaza Strip and Jericho area and to be completed within a period not exceeding four months after the signing of this agreement.

The above agreement will include, among other things:

Arrangements for a smooth and peaceful transfer of authority from the Israeli military government and its Civil Administration to the Palestinian representatives.

Structure, powers and responsibilities of the Palestinian authority in these areas, except: external security, settlements, Israelis, foreign relations, and other mutually agreed matters.

Arrangements for the assumption of internal security and public order by the Palestinian police force consisting of police officers recruited locally and from abroad holding Jordanian passports and Palestinian documents issued by Egypt. Those who will participate in the Palestinian police force coming from abroad should be trained as police and police officers.

A temporary international or foreign presence, as agreed upon.

Establishment of a joint Palestinian-Israeli Coordination and Cooperation Committee for mutual security purposes.

An economic development and stabilization program, including the establishment of an Emergency Fund, to encourage foreign investment, and financial and economic support. Both sides will coordinate and cooperate jointly and unilaterally with regional and international parties to support these aims.

Arrangements for a safe passage for persons and transportation between the Gaza Strip and Jericho area.

The above agreement will include arrangements for coordination between both parties regarding passages:

Gaza—Egypt; and
Jericho—Jordan.

The offices responsible for carrying out the powers and responsibilities of the Palestinian authority under this Annex II and Article VI of the Declaration of Principles will be located in the Gaza Strip and in the Jericho area pending the inauguration of the Council.

Other than these agreed arrangements, the status of the Gaza Strip and Jericho area will continue to be an integral part of the West Bank and Gaza Strip, and will not be changed in the interim period.

[...]

The two sides will encourage the multilateral working groups, and will coordinate towards their success. The two parties will encourage intersessional activities, as well as pre-feasibility and feasibility studies, within the various multilateral working groups.

[...]

Annex II
It is understood that, subsequent to the Israeli withdrawal, Israel will continue to be responsible for external security, and for internal security and public order of settlements and Israelis. Israeli military forces and civilians may continue to use roads freely within the Gaza Strip and the Jericho area.

[...]

Source: "Declaration of Principles on Interim Self-Government Arrangements, September 13, 1993," U.S. Department of State, http://www.state.gov/p/nea/rls/22602.htm.

124. West Bank–Gaza Palestinian Leaders, Memorandum to Chairman Yasser Arafat, November 1993

Introduction

Implementation of the Oslo Accords soon proved problematic. Arab leaders, such as Syria's President Hafez al-Assad, complained that the new agreements had ignored and circumvented the lengthy Madrid peace process, making all those efforts redundant. Palestinian critics, including exiles driven out in 1948, charged that the Palestine Liberation Organization (PLO) had betrayed its constituents, assailing the negotiators' failure to insist on independent Palestinian statehood, obtain assurances on the future of East Jerusalem, or win 1948 refugees the right of return. The creation of a Palestinian "entity" that might well remain under Israeli sovereignty was not, in their eyes, sufficient to justify the concessions that the PLO had made to Israel. Palestinian leaders in the West Bank and Gaza also had complaints and reservations. Yasser Arafat's habit of appointing PLO officials previously based in Tunis to high, well-paid positions in the occupied territories, with which they were unfamiliar, caused considerable resentment. While applauding the accord as "a decisive political event" that had some "positive" features, local leaders charged that as they proceeded to the implementation of the agreements, the PLO "political leadership is practicing its role in a manner that is closer to improvisation and without prior preparation." They also assailed poor communication and lack of consultation between PLO leaders and the rank and file. Gaza and West Bank Palestinian leaders therefore demanded the establishment of specialized working groups to implement the provisions of the Oslo Accords, the formulation of an integrated negotiating plan for the future, and an improved dialogue between PLO leaders and their constituents in the occupied territories. While relatively respectful in tone, these representatives of the Palestinians clearly had serious reservations as to the competence and openness of the PLO leadership.

Primary Source

Mr. President of Palestine and Chairman of the PLO Executive Committee; Members of the PLO Executive Committee:

Greetings from Palestine:

Since the signing of the Declaration of Principles and the mutual recognition agreement between the PLO and the Israeli Government, the Palestinian people, together with their national forces, have been facing a new situation that has imposed new challenges. This is because the Declaration of Principles is an event that separates a militant stage, which aimed at underscoring Palestinian presence on the political map of the region and the world, from another militant stage that moves toward a greater and more advanced achievement; namely, the setting up of an independent Palestinian state on the land of Palestine by Palestinian hands.

Your Excellency the President: We assume that our Palestinian people, together with their national forces, have studied the agreement in terms of preambles, texts, and prospects as the various national institutions did in order to endorse it constitutionally through the PLO Executive Committee and the PLO Central Council. However, the agreement has produced an opposition that has different principles and objectives. And this is natural in an arena which pioneered the entrenching of democratic dialogue and relations among its forces as the only way to govern national life in the various fields.

The signatories to this memorandum believe that the Palestinian-Israeli agreement is a decisive political event which should be dealt with in a positive and responsible way in order to develop what is positive in it and besiege what is negative.

In light of all this, we declare:

First, our total affiliation with our people's potentials to build our new entity on the ground;

Second, our commitment to the PLO and its legitimate institutions as the sole representative of the Palestinian people and the national framework to which there is no alternative in order to organize and lead the national potentials toward achieving all the national legitimate objectives of the Palestinian people.

Proceeding from this, and in order to benefit from our democratic right of taking the initiative to propose ideas and procedures which are important and vital in this qualitative stage of our national struggle, we reiterate the following:

First: We are not satisfied with the political leadership's method of work in this stage, either in terms of running the difficult and delicate negotiations with the Israeli side or in terms of the preparations to embark on the stage of national construction in the interim period. It is obvious to everybody that the political leadership is practicing its role in a manner that is close to improvisation and without prior preparation for the necessary practical steps toward embodying the national interests through a planned implementation of our obligations to what was signed.

Second: The political leadership has not made sufficient effort to invigorate the required national dialogue whether on the level of the national forces, which adopted the agreement as an opportunity that would provide serious possibilities to proceed toward our national objectives, or on the level of the principled opposition to the agreement. Our national traditions require that we expeditiously launch such dialogue and work seriously to render it a success. The objective is to create a reasonable level of national harmony that will entrench Palestinian national security and create a healthy atmosphere for further mobilization toward the new tasks of the Palestinian people.

Third: The political leadership failed to present the agreement in an objective way to the Palestinian people so that this people would be aware of the prospects and potentials of their present and future moves. Consequently, this increased the confusion, ambiguity, and concern, particularly when the Palestinian people receive various and contradictory interpretations, not only on the level of the PLO and Israel, but also within the PLO itself.

Fourth: If we return to the statements and comments of the majority who voted, during the recent meeting of the PLO Central Council, in favor of the Declaration of Principles agreement, we will find that their support was on condition that the leadership performance will develop, Palestinian potentials will be mobilized, Palestinian skills and expertise will be exploited in the best way possible, and that the peace process will be dealt with as a militant process, not an administrative or bureaucratic one. As many of the PLO Central Council members said, whether the result of the Declaration of Principles agreement will be good or bad for the Palestinian people, and whether it will pave the way for national independence and an independent state, or whether it will consecrate the occupation, this result will be basically decided through the materialization of the previous conditions.

While we present these general remarks as a first step, we ask the political leadership to shoulder its responsibilities in dealing with the negative aspects in a manner that guarantees a balanced, viable, and responsible performance during the next stage.

Based on this, we present the following urgent demands:

1. The political leadership should set up specialized councils in all fields of political action, whether on the level of building the new entity or on the level of organizing moves in the Arab and international arenas.

2. The political leadership should appeal to all specialists in various sectors to join these councils and their working groups, whether through planning or implementation. In order to regulate this great process, a department should be set up in the PLO assigned with following up this issue and working out the appropriate action frame-works.

3. Adopting the principle of professional and political efficiency in forming the working groups, establishments, negotiating committees, and other bodies, and abandoning the fractional mentality and appeasement at the expense of efficiency.

4. Working out an integrated negotiating plan that is based on the Declaration of Principles and that ensures integration and harmony of the working groups and the various negotiating teams.

5. Forming a mini-leadership team to lead the entire negotiating process, supervise and follow it up, and coordinate between the various committees and groups.

6. Forming the Palestinian Development and Reconstruction Council according to certain specifications that ensure sound performance, planning, follow up and monitoring, and the credibility of our people with the donor countries and in order to develop the infrastructure of our national economy. Any delay in the formation of this council will waste more time and weaken the credibility of the Palestinians with the international parties that assist our people.

7. Completing the work of the Legal Committee assigned with drafting the bylaw of the Palestinian national authority (the constitutional document) in a manner that emphasizes its democratic nature and commitment to all principles contained in the Palestinian Declaration of Principles. This constitutional document should then be presented for broad deliberations by the Palestinian people as soon as possible.

8. The political leadership should immediately form a higher leadership authority that will start a national dialogue and work for the continuation and success of this dialogue. The political leadership should benefit from its previous mistakes in this respect, since the committees that used to be formed did not work with sufficient seriousness.

9. Setting up a higher planning, consulting, and guidance authority of experts that operates alongside the Executive Committee and assists it in carrying out its major tasks in this stage.

While making such a proposal, we are not undermining the role and jurisdiction of the first executive authority. We present these proposals because we know how this authority has been adversely affected by the resignation of some of its members and the possibility that others may resign or freeze their membership. . . .

The signatories: Dr. Haydar 'Abd al-Shafi, Bashir al-Barghuthi, Ibrahim Abu 'Ayyash, Dr. Anis Fawzi al-Qasim, Tawfiq Abu Bakr, Dr. Taysir 'Aruri, Samih 'Abd al-Fattah, known as Abu Hisham, Lawyer 'Ali al Safarini, Faysal Hurani, Lawyer Muhammad 'Ayyash

Milham, Nabil Amr, the Reverend Ibrahim 'Ayyad, Dr. Mundhir Salah, Dr. 'Izz aI-Din al Manasirah, and Ghazi aI-Sa'di.

Source: Walter Laqueur and Barry Rubin, eds., *The Israel-Arab Reader: A Documentary History of the Middle East Conflict* (New York: Penguin, 2001), 436–439.

125. The Washington Declaration, Israel–Jordan–United States, July 25, 1994

Introduction

Since at least the early 1990s King Hussein, monarch of the Hashemite Kingdom of Jordan bordering Israel and home to many Palestinians, was eager to reach a firm understanding and peace treaty with his neighbor. Peace would enable Hussein, who ruled over a youthful and poor population, to concentrate on the economic development that he believed was essential to maintaining stability in his country. With the exception of Egypt, Arab states had pledged themselves not to make formal peace treaties with Israel until a satisfactory settlement of the Palestinian issue had been reached. In 1992 Jordanian and Israeli diplomats had formulated a draft peace treaty, one they hoped would become effective if a comprehensive Arab-Israeli settlement emerged from the ongoing Madrid talks. The signing of the Oslo Accords in October 1993 gave a green light to these efforts. Between then and July 1994, U.S. president Bill Clinton brokered an agreement, announced in Washington, D.C., whereby Israel and Jordan would restore normal relations, recognizing each other's frontiers, ending the formal state of war dividing them, opening their borders to each other, establishing direct links between their telephone systems and electricity grids as well as direct air flights, and agreeing to cooperate in promoting bilateral and regional economic development and fighting crime. Jordan was also promised a permanent "special role . . . in Moslem holy shrines in Jerusalem." In eloquent speeches, both Hussein and Israeli prime minister Yitzhak Rabin expressed their countries' intentions of putting the past decades of bitter hostility and war behind them and moving forward to an era of peace and constructive collaboration.

Primary Source

A. After generations of hostility, blood and tears and in the wake of years of pain and wars, His Majesty King Hussein and Prime Minister Yitzhak Rabin are determined to bring an end to bloodshed and sorrow. It is in this spirit that His Majesty King Hussein of the Hashemite Kingdom of Jordan and Prime Minister and Minister of Defense, Mr. Yitzhak Rabin of Israel, met in Washington today at the invitation of President William J. Clinton of the United States of America. This initiative of President William J. Clinton constitutes an historic landmark in the United States' untiring efforts in promoting peace and stability in the Middle East. The personal involvement of the President has made it possible to realise agreement on the content of this historic declaration. The signing of this declaration bears testimony to the President's vision and devotion to the cause of peace.

B. In their meeting, His Majesty King Hussein and Prime Minister Yitzhak Rabin have jointly reaffirmed the five underlying principles of their understanding on an Agreed Common Agenda designed to reach the goal of a just, lasting and comprehensive peace between the Arab States and the Palestinians, with Israel.

1. Jordan and Israel aim at the achievement of just, lasting and comprehensive peace between Israel and its neighbours and at the conclusion of a Treaty of Peace between both countries.
2. The two countries will vigorously continue their negotiations to arrive at a state of peace, based on Security Council Resolutions 242 and 338 in all their aspects, and founded on freedom, equality and justice.
3. Israel respects the present special role of the Hashemite Kingdom of Jordan in Muslim holy shrines in Jerusalem. When negotiations on the permanent status will take place, Israel will give high priority to the Jordanian historic role in these shrines. In addition the two sides have agreed to act together to promote interfaith relations among the three monotheistic religions.
4. The two countries recognise their right and obligation to live in peace with each other as well as with all states within secure and recognised boundaries. The two states affirmed their respect for and acknowledgment of the sovereignty, territorial integrity and political independence of every state in the area.
5. The two countries desire to develop good neighbourly relations of cooperation between them to ensure lasting security and to avoid threats and the use of force between them.

C. The long conflict between the two states is now coming to an end. In this spirit the state of belligerency between Jordan and Israel has been terminated.

D. Following this declaration and in keeping with the Agreed Common Agenda, both countries will refrain from actions or activities by either side that may adversely affect the security of the other or may prejudice the final outcome of negotiations. Neither side will threaten the other by use of force, weapons, or any other means, against each other and both sides will thwart threats to security resulting from all kinds of terrorism.

E. His Majesty King Hussein and Prime Minister Yitzhak Rabin took note of the progress made in the bilateral negotiations within the Jordan-Israel track last week on the steps decided to implement the sub-agendas on borders, territorial matters, security, water, energy, environment and the Jordan Rift Valley.

In this framework, mindful of items of the Agreed Common Agenda (borders and territorial matters) they noted that the boundary sub-commission has reached agreement in July 1994 in fulfillment of part of the role entrusted to it in the sub-agenda. They also noted that the sub-commission for water, environment and energy agreed to mutually recognise, as the role of their negotiations, the rightful allocations of the two sides in Jordan River and Yarmouk River waters and to fully respect and comply with the negotiated rightful allocations, in accordance with agreed acceptable principles with mutually acceptable quality. Similarly, His Majesty King Hussein and Prime Minister Yitzhak Rabin expressed their deep satisfaction and pride in the work of the trilateral commission in its meeting held in Jordan on Wednesday, July 20th 1994, hosted by the Jordanian Prime Minister, Dr. Abdessalam al-Majali, and attended by Secretary of State Warren Christopher and Foreign Minister Shimon Peres. They voiced their pleasure at the association and commitment of the United States in this endeavour.

F. His Majesty King Hussein and Prime Minister Yitzhak Rabin believe that steps must be taken both to overcome psychological barriers and to break with the legacy of war. By working with optimism towards the dividends of peace for all the people in the region, Jordan and Israel are determined to shoulder their responsibilities towards the human dimension of peace making. They recognise imbalances and disparities are a root cause of extremism which thrives on poverty and unemployment and the degradation of human dignity. In this spirit His Majesty King Hussein and Prime Minister Yitzhak Rabin have today approved a series of steps to symbolise the new era which is now at hand:

1. Direct telephone links will be opened between Jordan and Israel.
2. The electricity grids of Jordan and Israel will be linked as part of a regional concept.
3. Two new border crossings will be opened between Jordan and Israel—one at the southern tip of Aqaba-Eilat and the other at a mutually agreed point in the north.
4. In principle free access will be given to third country tourists traveling between Jordan and Israel.
5. Negotiations will be accelerated on opening an international air corridor between both countries.
6. The police forces of Jordan and Israel will cooperate in combating crime with emphasis on smuggling and particularly drug smuggling. The United States will be invited to participate in this joint endeavour.
7. Negotiations on economic matters will continue in order to prepare for future bilateral cooperation including the abolition of all economic boycotts.

All these steps are being implemented within the framework of regional infrastructural development plans and in conjunction with the Jordan-Israel bilaterals on boundaries, security, water and related issues and without prejudice to the final outcome of the negotiations on the items included in the Agreed Common Agenda between Jordan and Israel.

G. His Majesty King Hussein and Prime Minister Yitzhak Rabin have agreed to meet periodically or whenever they feel necessary to review the progress of the negotiations and express their firm intention to shepherd and direct the process in its entirety.

H. In conclusion, His Majesty King Hussein and Prime Minister Yitzhak Rabin wish to express once again their profound thanks and appreciation to President William J. Clinton and his Administration for their untiring efforts in furthering the cause of peace, justice and prosperity for all the peoples of the region. They wish to thank the President personally for his warm welcome and hospitality. In recognition of their appreciation to the President, His Majesty King Hussein and Prime Minister Yitzhak Rabin have asked President William J. Clinton to sign this document as a witness and as a host to their meeting.

His Majesty King Hussein

Prime Minister Yitzhak Rabin

President William J. Clinton

> **Source:** "The Washington Declaration," U.S. Embassy, Israel, U.S. Department of State, http://telaviv.usembassy.gov/publish/peace/washdecl.htm.

126. Agreement on Preparatory Transfer of Powers and Responsibilities [Excerpt], August 29, 1994

Introduction

In March 1994, six months after the Oslo Accords had been signed, the Palestine Liberation Organization (PLO) and the government of Israel reached agreement on the withdrawal of Israeli forces from the Gaza Strip and the Jericho area of the West Bank and on the transfer of numerous governmental functions to the new Palestinian Authority (PA). It was expected that this understanding, signed in Cairo, Egypt, would soon be superseded by an interim agreement covering the entire West Bank. Responsibility for law and order within these areas was to be transferred to the Palestinian Police. The jurisdiction of the PA did not, however, include "foreign relations, internal security and public order of Settlements and the Military Installation Area and Israelis, and external security," and it had no powers over Israelis. These responsibilities were reserved for Israel, whose "military government" would continue to exercise these powers. Israel was also empowered to decide whether legislation passed by the PA exceeded its jurisdiction. As a goodwill gesture, Israel agreed to free 5,000 Palestinian detainees within five weeks of signing the Cairo Agreement. The arrangements laid down by the agreement, especially the fact that Israel reserved for itself all authority over Israeli citizens, settlers, and settlements in these areas and ultimate responsibility for "internal security," left ominous scope for military friction between the new PA and Israeli forces and settlers. Hamas extremists among the Palestinians were already targeting and killing Israeli settlers. In the previous week, a militant settler had killed 29 Arabs at a mosque in Hebron, provoking antisettler riots in which another 25 Palestinians were killed, events of which the parties to the Cairo Agreement were highly conscious. Speaking at the signing ceremony, Israeli prime minister Yitzhak Rabin expressed his determination to guarantee the security of all Israelis and his hope that the murder of an Israeli soldier two weeks earlier would be Israel's last fatality in more than a century of Arab-Israeli confrontations in the territory. Arafat warned that continuing the policy of settling yet more Israelis in the occupied territories would provoke still further violence, and he condemned measures banning Palestinians from "holy Jerusalem." Despite the hopes for peace that both Rabin and Arafat still expressed, as the efforts to resolve the Israeli-Palestinian conflict continued, many more Arabs and Israelis would die.

Primary Source

The Government of the State of Israel and the Palestine Liberation Organization (hereinafter "the PLO"), the representative of the Palestinian people;

PREAMBLE
WITHIN the framework of the Middle East peace process initiated at Madrid in October 1991;

REAFFIRMING their determination to live in peaceful coexistence, mutual dignity and security, while recognizing their mutual legitimate and political rights;

REAFFIRMING their desire to achieve a just, lasting and comprehensive peace settlement through the agreed political process;

REAFFIRMING their adherence to the mutual recognition and commitments expressed in the letters dated September 9, 1993, signed by and exchanged between the Prime Minister of Israel and the Chairman of the PLO;

REAFFIRMING their understanding that the interim self-government arrangements, including the preparatory arrangements to apply in the West Bank contained in this Agreement, are an integral part of the whole peace process and that the negotiations on the permanent status will lead to the implementation of Security Council Resolutions 242 and 338;

FOLLOWING the Agreement on the Gaza Strip and the Jericho Area as signed at Cairo on May 4, 1994 (hereinafter "the Gaza-Jericho Agreement");

DESIROUS of putting into effect the Declaration of Principles on Interim Self-Government Arrangements as signed at Washington, D.C. on September 13, 1993 (hereinafter "the Declaration of Principles"), and in particular Article VI regarding preparatory transfer of powers and responsibilities and the Agreed Minutes thereto;

HEREBY AGREE to the following arrangements regarding the preparatory transfer of powers and responsibilities in the West Bank:

[…]

ARTICLE II
PREPARATORY TRANSFER OF POWERS AND RESPONSIBILITIES

Israel shall transfer and the Palestinian Authority shall assume powers and responsibilities from the Israeli military government and its Civil Administration in the West Bank in the following spheres: education and culture, health, social welfare, tourism, direct taxation and Value Added Tax on local production (hereinafter "VAT"), as specified in this Agreement (hereinafter "the Spheres").

For the purposes of this Agreement, the Palestinian Authority shall constitute the authorized Palestinians referred to in Article VI of the Declaration of Principles.

The Parties will explore the possible expansion of the transfer of powers and responsibilities to additional spheres.

ARTICLE III
SCOPE OF THE TRANSFERRED POWERS AND RESPONSIBILITIES
[…]

In accordance with the Declaration of Principles, the jurisdiction of the Palestinian Authority with regard to the powers and responsibilities transferred by this Agreement will not apply to Jerusalem, settlements, military locations and, unless otherwise provided in this Agreement, Israelis.

The transfer of powers and responsibilities under this Agreement does not include powers and responsibilities in the sphere of foreign relations, except as indicated in Article VI(2)(b) of the Gaza-Jericho Agreement.

ARTICLE IV
MODALITIES OF TRANSFER

The transfer of powers and responsibilities in the sphere of education and culture pursuant to this Agreement will be implemented on August 29, 1994. The transfer of powers and responsibilities in the remaining Spheres will be implemented in accordance with Article XI below.

The transfer of powers and responsibilities shall be coordinated through the Civil Affairs Coordination and Cooperation Committee referred to in Article X below and shall be implemented in accordance with the arrangements set out in this Agreement in a smooth, peaceful and orderly manner.

Upon the signing of this Agreement, the Israeli side shall provide the Palestinian side with, or enable free access to, all information that is necessary for an effective and smooth transfer.

On the date of the transfer of powers and responsibilities, Israel shall also transfer all movable and immovable property which exclusively serves the offices of the Civil Administration in the Spheres, including premises, whether government-owned or rented, equipment, registers, files and computer programs. The treatment of property which serves the offices transferred to the Palestinian Authority as well as offices which are not so transferred will be as mutually agreed between the two sides, such as on the basis of sharing or exchange.

The coordination of the transfer of powers and responsibilities pursuant to this Article shall also include a joint review of the Civil Administration contracts the duration of which extends beyond the date of the transfer with a view to deciding which contracts will remain in force and which will be terminated.

ARTICLE V
ADMINISTRATION OF THE TRANSFERRED OFFICES

The Palestinian Authority shall be fully responsible for the proper functioning of the offices included in the Spheres and for the management of their personnel in all aspects, including employment and placement of employees, payment of their salaries and pensions and ensuring other employee rights.

The Palestinian Authority will continue to employ Palestinian Civil Administration employees currently employed in the offices included in each Sphere and shall maintain their rights.

The main office of each of the Spheres will be situated in the Jericho Area or in the Gaza Strip. The Palestinian Authority will operate the existing subordinate offices in the West Bank. The two sides may agree on the establishment of additional subordinate offices in the West Bank, if necessary, in such locations as mutually agreed.

The Palestinian Authority has the right to coordinate its activities in each of the Spheres with other Spheres in which it is empowered.

ARTICLE VI
RELATIONS BETWEEN THE TWO SIDES
With regard to each Sphere, the Palestinian Authority shall coordinate with the Civil Administration on issues relating to other spheres in which the Palestinian Authority is not empowered.

The military government and its Civil Administration shall assist and support the Palestinian Authority in promoting the effective exercise of its powers and responsibilities. In addition, the military government and its Civil Administration shall, in exercising their own powers and responsibilities, take into account the interests of the Palestinian Authority and do their utmost to remove obstacles to the effective exercise of powers and responsibilities by the Palestinian Authority.

The Palestinian Authority shall prevent any activities with a military orientation within each of the Spheres and will do its utmost to maintain decorum and discipline and to avoid disruption in the institutions under its responsibility.

The Palestinian Authority will notify the military government and its Civil Administration and will coordinate with them regarding any planned public large-scale events and mass gatherings within the Spheres.

Nothing in this Agreement shall affect the continued authority of the military government and its Civil Administration to exercise their powers and responsibilities with regard to security and public order, as well as with regard to other spheres not transferred.

ARTICLE VII
LEGISLATIVE POWERS OF THE PALESTINIAN AUTHORITY
The Palestinian Authority may promulgate secondary legislation regarding the powers and responsibilities transferred to it. Such legislation includes amendments and changes to the existing laws, regulations and military orders specified in Appendix A to each Annex.

Legislation promulgated by the Palestinian Authority shall be consistent with the provisions of this Agreement.

Legislation promulgated by the Palestinian Authority shall be communicated to Israel which may, within a period of thirty (30) days, notify the Palestinian Authority that it opposes such legislation for any of the following reasons:

it exceeds the powers and responsibilities transferred to the Palestinian Authority;
it is inconsistent with the provisions of this Agreement; or
it otherwise affects legislation or powers and responsibilities which were not transferred to the Palestinian Authority.

Where Israel opposes proposed legislation, it shall specify the reason for the opposition.

If Israel has no reservations concerning the proposed legislation, it shall accordingly notify the Palestinian Authority at the earliest opportunity. If at the end of the thirty-day period Israel has not communicated any opposition concerning the proposed legislation, such legislation shall enter into force.

The Palestinian Authority may, in the event of opposition to the proposed draft legislation, submit a new draft or request a review by the Legislation Subcommittee established under the Gaza-Jericho Agreement.

The Legislation Subcommittee shall attempt to reach a decision on the merits of the matter within thirty days. If the Legislation Subcommittee is unable to reach a decision within this period, the Palestinian Authority shall be entitled to refer the matter to the Joint Liaison Committee. The Joint Liaison Committee shall consider the matter immediately and will attempt to settle it within thirty days.

Where, upon communicating to Israel proposed legislation consisting of detailed technical regulations, the Palestinian Authority states that such regulations fulfill the requirements of paragraph 3 above and requests a speedy review, Israel shall immediately respond to such a request.

Legislation regarding the West Bank shall be published as a separate part of any publication of legislation regarding the Gaza Strip and the Jericho Area issued by the Palestinian Authority.

ARTICLE VIII
LAW ENFORCEMENT
The Palestinian Authority may bring disciplinary proceedings concerning persons it employs in the West Bank before disciplinary tribunals operating in the Gaza Strip or the Jericho Area.

The Palestinian Authority may, within each of the Spheres, authorize employees to act as civilian inspectors to monitor compliance with laws and regulations in that Sphere, within the powers and responsibilities transferred to the Palestinian Authority. Such inspectors shall operate in each Sphere separately and shall not be organized into a central unit. These inspectors shall not wear uniforms or carry arms, and shall not in any other way have the nature of a police force. They shall be required to carry the identification documentation referred to in paragraph 3 below. The number of employees to be authorized as civilian inspectors shall be agreed upon by both sides. The names of these employees shall be notified to Israel and, where these employees enjoy privileges pursuant to subparagraph 3 below, shall be agreed upon by both sides.

The Palestinian Authority shall issue the civilian inspectors in the West Bank with identification documentation specifying the office in which they are employed. Such documentation shall be used for identification and will not grant privileges, except those agreed in the Civil Affairs Coordination and Cooperation Committee referred to in Article X below, or immunities. This committee shall determine the format of the identification documentation.

Except as specifically provided in this Agreement, all powers and responsibilities regarding law enforcement, including investigation, judicial proceedings and imprisonment, will continue to be under the responsibility of the existing authorities in the West Bank.

[...]

ARTICLE XII
MUTUAL CONTRIBUTION TO PEACE AND
RECONCILIATION
With regard to each of the Spheres, Israel and the Palestinian Authority will ensure that their respective systems contribute to the peace between the Israeli and Palestinian peoples and to peace in the entire region, and will refrain from the introduction of any motifs that could adversely affect the process of reconciliation.

ARTICLE XIII
FINAL CLAUSES
This Agreement shall enter into force on the date of its signing.

The arrangements established by this Agreement are preparatory measures and shall remain in force until and to the extent superseded by the Interim Agreement or by any other agreement between the Parties.

Nothing in this Agreement shall prejudice or preempt the outcome of the negotiations on the Interim Agreement or on the permanent status to be conducted pursuant to the Declaration of Principles. Neither Party shall be deemed, by virtue of having entered into this Agreement, to have renounced or waived any of its existing rights, claims or positions.

The two Parties view the West Bank and the Gaza Strip as a single territorial unit, the integrity of which will be preserved during the interim period.

The Gaza Strip and the Jericho Area shall continue to be an integral part of the West Bank and the Gaza Strip. The status of the West Bank shall not be changed for the period of this Agreement. Nothing in this Agreement shall be considered to change this status.

[...]

Source: "Agreement on Preparatory Transfer of Powers and Responsibilities," U.S. Department of State, http://www.state.gov/p/nea/rls/22676.htm.

127. Treaty of Peace between the State of Israel and the Hashemite Kingdom of Jordan [Excerpt], October 26, 1994

Introduction

The announcement of the new Jordanian-Israeli accord was followed three months later by the formal signing of the peace treaty between the two states. With minor adjustments, the two states agreed to accept the existing border between themselves as their permanent frontier. They not only agreed on peace but also agreed not to participate in or encourage any hostile acts against each other, including terrorist actions, and to refuse to allow third parties or governments to use their territory to launch attacks against the other. In addition, neither would allow groups or individuals within their own countries to incite or plan violent action against the other. Such active security cooperation went well beyond a simple declaration of peace. Israel and Jordan pledged themselves to further efforts to seek stable and lasting peace and disarmament throughout the Middle East and to work together to resolve outstanding refugee problems. In what may have been an effort to divide Jordan and the Palestinians by winning Jordan's apparent acquiescence in Israeli control of that city, Israel promised to respect Jordan's "present special role . . . in Moslem holy shrines in Jerusalem" and to accord this a high priority in negotiations over the ultimate status of Jerusalem. Israel promised Jordan reliable access to supplies of water. Both declared that they considered the strategic Strait of Tiran and Gulf of Aqaba as "international waterways" open to all and that navigation of them could not be suspended. The two countries agreed to cooperate in economic development; commerce; finance; education; cultural and scientific exchanges; the development of transportation, roads, energy, and electrical power; and efforts to combat crime and the trade in narcotics. They also agreed to launch a major program to develop the Jordan Rift Valley. From Israel's perspective, the treaty was a demonstration to other Arab states of the substantial tangible benefits they might derive from normalizing relations with Israel.

Primary Source
PREAMBLE
The Government of the State of Israel and the Government of the Hashemite Kingdom of Jordan:
Bearing in mind the Washington Declaration, signed by them on 25th July, 1994, and which they are both committed to honor;
Aiming at the achievement of a just, lasting and comprehensive peace in the Middle East based on Security Council resolutions 242 and 338 in all their aspects;

Bearing in mind the importance of maintaining and strengthening peace based on freedom, equality, justice and respect for fundamental human rights, thereby overcoming psychological barriers and promoting human dignity;

Reaffirming their faith in the purposes and principles of the Charter of the United Nations and recognizing their right and obligation to live in peace with each other as well as with all states, within secure and recognized boundaries;

Desiring to develop friendly relations and co-operation between them in accordance with the principles of international law governing international relations in time of peace;

Desiring as well to ensure lasting security for both their States and in particular to avoid threats and the use of force between them;

Bearing in mind that in their Washington Declaration of 25th July, 1994, they declared the termination of the state of belligerency between them;

Deciding to establish peace between them in accordance with this Treaty of Peace;

Have agreed as follows:

ARTICLE 1—ESTABLISHMENT OF PEACE

Peace is hereby established between the State of Israel and the Hashemite Kingdom of Jordan (the "Parties") effective from the exchange of the instruments of ratification of this Treaty.

ARTICLE 2—GENERAL PRINCIPLES

The Parties will apply between them the provisions of the Charter of the United Nations and the principles of international law governing relations among states in times of peace. In particular:

1. They recognize and will respect each other's sovereignty, territorial integrity and political independence.
2. They recognize and will respect each other's right to live in peace within secure and recognized boundaries.
3. They will develop good neighborly relations of cooperation between them to ensure lasting security, will refrain from the threat or use of force against each other and will settle all disputes between them by peaceful means.
4. They respect and recognize the sovereignty, territorial integrity and political independence of every state in the region.
5. They respect and recognize the pivotal role of human development and dignity in regional and bilateral relationships.
6. They further believe that within their control, involuntary movements of persons in such a way as to adversely prejudice the security of either Party should not be permitted.

ARTICLE 3—INTERNATIONAL BOUNDARY

1. The international boundary between Israel and Jordan is delimited with reference to the boundary definition under the Mandate as is shown in Annex I (a), on the mapping materials attached thereto and co-ordinates specified therein.
2. The boundary, as set out in Annex I (a), is the permanent, secure and recognized international boundary between Israel and Jordan, without prejudice to the status of any territories that came under Israeli military government control in 1967.
3. The parties recognize the international boundary, as well as each other's territory, territorial waters and airspace, as inviolable, and will respect and comply with them.

[. . .]

ARTICLE 4—SECURITY

1. a. Both Parties, acknowledging that mutual understanding and co-operation in security-related matters will form a significant part of their relations and will further enhance the security of the region, take upon themselves to base their security relations on mutual trust, advancement of joint interests and co-operation, and to aim towards a regional framework of partnership in peace.

   b. Towards that goal the Parties recognize the achievements of the European Community and European Union in the development of the Conference on Security and Co-operation in Europe (CSCE) and commit themselves to the creation, in the Middle East, of a CSCME (Conference on Security and Co-operation in the Middle East).

   This commitment entails the adoption of regional models of security successfully implemented in the post–World War era (along the lines of the Helsinki process) culminating in a regional zone of security and stability.

2. The obligations referred to in this Article are without prejudice to the inherent right of self-defense in accordance with the United Nations Charter.

3. The Parties undertake, in accordance with the provisions of this Article, the following:

   a. to refrain from the threat or use of force or weapons, conventional, non-conventional or of any other kind, against each other, or of other actions or activities that adversely affect the security of the other Party;

   b. to refrain from organizing, instigating, inciting, assisting or participating in acts or threats of belligerency, hostility, subversion or violence against the other Party;

   c. to take necessary and effective measures to ensure that acts or threats of belligerency, hostility, subversion or violence against the other Party do not originate from, and are not committed within, through or over their territory (hereinafter the term "territory" includes the airspace and territorial waters).

4. Consistent with the era of peace and with the efforts to build regional security and to avoid and prevent aggression and violence, the Parties further agree to refrain from the following:

   a. joining or in any way assisting, promoting or co-operating with any coalition, organisation or alliance with a military or security character with a third party, the objectives or activities of which include launching aggression or other acts of military hostility against the other Party, in contravention of the provisions of the present Treaty;

   b. allowing the entry, stationing and operating on their territory, or through it, of military forces, personnel or materiel of a third party, in circumstances which may adversely prejudice the security of the other Party.

5. Both Parties will take necessary and effective measures, and will co-operate in combating terrorism of all kinds. The Parties undertake:

   a. to take necessary and effective measures to prevent acts of terrorism, subversion or violence from being carried out from their territory or through it and to take necessary and effective measures to combat such activities and all their perpetrators;

   b. without prejudice to the basic rights of freedom of expression and association, to take necessary and effective measures to prevent the entry, presence and co-operation in their territory of any group or organisation, and their infrastructure, which threatens the security of the other Party by the use of or incitement to the use of, violent means;

   c. to co-operate in preventing and combating cross-boundary infiltrations.

6. Any question as to the implementation of this Article will be dealt with through a mechanism of consultations which will include a liaison system, verification, supervision, and where necessary, other mechanisms, and higher level consultation. The details of the mechanism of consultations will be contained in an agreement to be concluded by the Parties within 3 months of the exchange of the instruments of ratification of this Treaty.

7. The Parties undertake to work as a matter of priority, and as soon as possible in the context of the Multilateral Working Group on Arms Control and Regional Security, and jointly, towards the following:

   a. the creation in the Middle East of a region free from hostile alliances and coalitions;

   b. the creation of a Middle East free from weapons of mass destruction, both conventional and non-conventional, in the context of a comprehensive, lasting and stable peace, characterized by the renunciation of the use of force, reconciliation and goodwill.

ARTICLE 5—DIPLOMATIC AND OTHER BILATERAL RELATIONS

1. The Parties agree to establish full diplomatic and consular relations and to exchange resident ambassadors within one month of the exchange of the instruments of ratification of this Treaty.

2. The Parties agree that the normal relationship between them will further include economic and cultural relations.

ARTICLE 6—WATER

With the view to achieving a comprehensive and lasting settlement of all the water problems between them:

1. The Parties agree mutually to recognize the rightful allocations of both of them in Jordan River and Yarmouk River waters and Araba/Arava ground water in accordance with the agreed acceptable principles, quantities and quality as set out in Annex II, which shall be fully respected and complied with.

2. The Parties, recognizing the necessity to find a practical, just and agreed solution to their water problems and with the view that the subject of water can form the basis for the advancement of co-operation between them, jointly undertake to ensure that the management and development of their water resources do not, in any way, harm the water resources of the other Party.

3. The Parties recognize that their water resources are not sufficient to meet their needs. More water should be supplied for their use through various methods, including projects of regional and international co-operation.

4. In light of paragraph 3 of this Article, with the understanding that co-operation in water-related subjects would be to the benefit of both Parties, and will help alleviate their water shortages, and that water issues along their entire boundary must be dealt with in their totality, including the possibility of trans-boundary water transfers, the Parties agree to search for ways to alleviate water shortage and to co-operate in the following fields:

   a. development of existing and new water resources, increasing the water availability including co-operation on a regional basis as appropriate, and minimising wastage of water resources through the chain of their uses;

   b. prevention of contamination of water resources;

   c. mutual assistance in the alleviation of water shortages;

   d. transfer of information and joint research and development in water-related subjects, and review of the potentials for enhancement of water resources development and use.

[...]

ARTICLE 7—ECONOMIC RELATIONS

1. Viewing economic development and prosperity as pillars of peace, security and harmonious relations between states, peoples and individual human beings, the Parties, taking note of understandings reached between them, affirm their mutual desire to promote economic co-operation between them, as well as within the framework of wider regional economic co-operation.

2. In order to accomplish this goal, the Parties agree to the following:

a. to remove all discriminatory barriers to normal economic relations, to terminate economic boycotts directed at each other, and to co-operate in terminating boycotts against either Party by third parties;

b. recognizing that the principle of free and unimpeded flow of goods and services should guide their relations, the Parties will enter into negotiations with a view to concluding agreements on economic co-operation, including trade and the establishment of a free trade area, investment, banking, industrial co-operation and labour, for the purpose of promoting beneficial economic relations, based on principles to be agreed upon, as well as on human development considerations on a regional basis. These negotiations will be concluded no later than 6 months from the exchange of the instruments of ratification of this Treaty;

c. to co-operate bilaterally, as well as in multilateral forums, towards the promotion of their respective economies and of their neighborly economic relations with other regional parties.

ARTICLE 8—REFUGEES AND DISPLACED PERSONS

1. Recognizing the massive human problems caused to both Parties by the conflict in the Middle East, as well as the contribution made by them towards the alleviation of human suffering, the Parties will seek to further alleviate those problems arising on a bilateral level.

2. Recognizing that the above human problems caused by the conflict in the Middle East cannot be fully resolved on the bilateral level, the Parties will seek to resolve them in appropriate forums, in accordance with international law, including the following:

a. in the case of displaced persons, in a quadripartite committee together with Egypt and the Palestinians;

b. in the case of refugees,

(i) in the framework of the Multilateral Working Group on Refugees.

(ii) in negotiations, in a framework to be agreed, bilateral or otherwise, in conjunction with and at the same time as the permanent status negotiations pertaining to the territories referred to in Article 3 of this Treaty;

c. through the implementation of agreed United Nations programs and other agreed international economic programs concerning refugees and displaced persons, including assistance to their settlement.

ARTICLE 9—PLACES OF HISTORICAL AND RELIGIOUS SIGNIFICANCE

1. Each party will provide freedom of access to places of religious and historical significance.

2. In this regard, in accordance with the Washington Declaration, Israel respects the present special role of the Hashemite

Kingdom of Jordan in Muslim holy shrines in Jerusalem. When negotiations on the permanent status will take place, Israel will give high priority to the Jordanian historic role in these shrines.

3. The Parties will act together to promote interfaith relations among the three monotheistic religions, with the aim of working towards religious understanding, moral commitment, freedom of religious worship, and tolerance and peace.

ARTICLE 10—CULTURAL AND SCIENTIFIC EXCHANGES

The Parties, wishing to remove biases developed through periods of conflict, recognize the desirability of cultural and scientific exchanges in all fields, and agree to establish normal cultural relations between them. Thus, they shall, as soon as possible and not later than 9 months from the exchange of the instruments of ratification of this Treaty, conclude the negotiations on cultural and scientific agreements.

ARTICLE 11—MUTUAL UNDERSTANDING AND GOOD NEIGHBORLY RELATIONS

1. The Parties will seek to foster mutual understanding and tolerance based on shared historic values, and accordingly undertake:

a. to abstain from hostile or discriminatory propaganda against each other, and to take all possible legal and administrative measures to prevent the dissemination of such propaganda by any organization or individual present in the territory of either Party;

b. as soon as possible, and not later than 3 months from the exchange of the instruments of ratification of this Treaty, to repeal all adverse or discriminatory references and expressions of hostility in their respective legislation;

c. to refrain in all government publications from any such references or expressions;

d. to ensure mutual enjoyment by each other's citizens of due process of law within their respective legal systems and before their courts.

2. Paragraph 1 (a) of this Article is without prejudice to the right to freedom of expression as contained in the International Covenant on Civil and Political Rights.

3. A joint committee shall be formed to examine incidents where one Party claims there has been a violation of this Article.

[...]

ARTICLE 19—ENERGY

1. The Parties will co-operate in the development of energy resources, including the development of energy-related projects such as the utilisation of solar energy.

2. The Parties, having concluded their negotiations on the interconnecting of their electric grids in the Eilat-Aqaba area, will implement the interconnecting upon the signature of

this Treaty. The Parties view this step as a part of a wider binational and regional concept. They agree to continue their negotiations as soon as possible to widen the scope of their interconnected grids.

3. The Parties will conclude the relevant agreements in the field of energy within 6 months from the date of exchange of the instruments of ratification of this Treaty.

ARTICLE 20—RIFT VALLEY DEVELOPMENT

The Parties attach great importance to the integrated development of the Jordan Rift Valley area, including joint projects in the economic, environmental, energy-related and tourism fields. Taking note of the Terms of Reference developed in the framework of the Trilateral Israel-Jordan-US Economic Committee towards the Jordan Rift Valley Development Master Plan, they will vigorously continue their efforts towards the completion of planning and towards implementation.

[...]

Source: "Treaty of Peace between The State of Israel and the Hashemite Kingdom of Jordan," United States Embassy, Israel, http://telaviv.usembassy.gov/publish/peace/ijpeace.htm.

128. Israeli-Palestinian Interim Agreement on the West Bank and Gaza Strip [Excerpt], September 28, 1995

Introduction

The original timetable for the signature of the interim accords on the West Bank and the Gaza Strip envisaged under the Oslo Accords was delayed. Israeli settlement activity there continued unabated, while Palestinians from the Hamas faction of the Palestine Liberation Organization (PLO) launched violent operations against soldiers and civilians there, including suicide bombings, car bombings, and kidnappings. Between April 1994 and January 1995, 65 Israelis were killed and more than 200 were wounded, while Israeli troops in suppressing violent demonstrations killed many more Palestinians. Israel temporarily suspended peace talks in October 1994 after Hamas kidnapped an Israeli soldier and demanded that Israel release 200 Arab prisoners to obtain his return. PLO chairman Yasser Arafat tried to crack down on Palestinian violence, causing many Palestinians to reject his leadership. Suicide bombings of Israeli military checkpoints by the Islamic Jihad group in January 1995 led to another Israeli suspension of negotiations. Secret talks nonetheless continued between Arafat and Israeli officials, even though Arab extremists and hard-line Israelis sought to derail these. In September 1995 Israel and the PLO finally signed the Oslo

Interim Agreement, also known as Oslo II. The interim agreement mandated elections for the Palestinian Interim Self-Governing Authority to be held no later than January 1996, after which negotiations on the permanent status of the occupied territories, including the West Bank and the Gaza Strip, would begin. Until then, the status of these areas was to be left unchanged, a provision that meant that the Palestinians could not proclaim an independent state there. In the West Bank, the Palestinian Authority (PA) would expand its jurisdiction to cover most of that area's territory following a schedule whereby Israeli forces would during an eighteen-month period stage a staggered three-stage withdrawal from various areas. Zone A, the least sensitive and comprising major population centers, would come under immediate Palestinian control; Zone B, largely small town and rural settlements, would soon shift to Zone A; while portions of Zone C, which included the most sensitive areas, would finally be returned. Once again, unspecified exceptions and exemptions were made for Jerusalem, Israeli settlements, border areas, and military installations, whose ultimate disposition was left to the permanent status negotiations. Arafat claimed that the agreement placed 80 percent of the West Bank under Palestinian control, whereas Israeli prime minister Yitzhak Rabin claimed that 70 percent would remain in Israeli hands. The Israeli government swiftly constructed roads to link all the settlements to each other and to Israel proper, and these further divided the Palestinian-controlled areas from each other. Palestinians who wished to move around the West Bank were forced to pass through a time-consuming network of Israeli military roadblocks, checkpoints, and inspections that were established for security reasons. These barriers restricted freedom of trade and employment among Palestinian population centers and also impeded those Palestinians who had jobs within Israel. Arafat and the United States nonetheless hailed the interim agreements as a step that revitalized the stalled peace process. Meanwhile, conservative Israeli politicians and religious leaders launched furious attacks on them and their architects, Prime Minister Yitzhak Shamir and Foreign Minister Shimon Peres. Ultraorthodox Jews, extremist settlers, and Likud politicians proclaimed the existence of a "greater Israel" and claimed that the abandonment of any West Bank territory should be regarded as treasonous. The Knesset approved the agreements by a narrow 61–59 majority.

Primary Source

The Government of the State of Israel and the Palestine Liberation Organization (hereinafter "the PLO"), the representative of the Palestinian people;

PREAMBLE

WITHIN the framework of the Middle East peace process initiated at Madrid in October 1991;

REAFFIRMING their determination to put an end to decades of confrontation and to live in peaceful coexistence, mutual dignity and security, while recognizing their mutual legitimate and political rights;

REAFFIRMING their desire to achieve a just, lasting and comprehensive peace settlement and historic reconciliation through the agreed political process;

RECOGNIZING that the peace process and the new era that it has created, as well as the new relationship established between the two Parties as described above, are irreversible, and the determination of the two Parties to maintain, sustain and continue the peace process;

RECOGNIZING that the aim of the Israeli-Palestinian negotiations within the current Middle East peace process is, among other things, to establish a Palestinian Interim Self-Government Authority, i.e. the elected Council (hereinafter "the Council" or "the Palestinian Council"), and the elected Ra'ees of the Executive Authority, for the Palestinian people in the West Bank and the Gaza Strip, for a transitional period not exceeding five years from the date of signing the Agreement on the Gaza Strip and the Jericho Area (hereinafter "the Gaza-Jericho Agreement") on May 4, 1994, leading to a permanent settlement based on Security Council Resolutions 242 and 338;

REAFFIRMING their understanding that the interim self-government arrangements contained in this Agreement are an integral part of the whole peace process, that the negotiations on the permanent status, that will start as soon as possible but not later than May 4, 1996, will lead to the implementation of Security Council Resolutions 242 and 338, and that the Interim Agreement shall settle all the issues of the interim period and that no such issues will be deferred to the agenda of the permanent status negotiations;

REAFFIRMING their adherence to the mutual recognition and commitments expressed in the letters dated September 9, 1993, signed by and exchanged between the Prime Minister of Israel and the Chairman of the PLO;

DESIROUS of putting into effect the Declaration of Principles on Interim Self-Government Arrangements signed at Washington, D.C. on September 13, 1993, and the Agreed Minutes thereto (hereinafter "the DOP") and in particular Article III and Annex I concerning the holding of direct, free and general political elections for the Council and the Ra'ees of the Executive Authority in order that the Palestinian people in the West Bank, Jerusalem and the Gaza Strip may democratically elect accountable representatives;

RECOGNIZING that these elections will constitute a significant interim preparatory step toward the realization of the legitimate rights of the Palestinian people and their just requirements and will provide a democratic basis for the establishment of Palestinian institutions;

REAFFIRMING their mutual commitment to act, in accordance with this Agreement, immediately, efficiently and effectively against acts or threats of terrorism, violence or incitement, whether committed by Palestinians or Israelis;

FOLLOWING the Gaza-Jericho Agreement; the Agreement on Preparatory Transfer of Powers and Responsibilities signed at Erez on August 29, 1994 (hereinafter "the Preparatory Transfer Agreement"); and the Protocol on Further Transfer of Powers and Responsibilities signed at Cairo on August 27, 1995 (hereinafter "the Further Transfer Protocol"); which three agreements will be superseded by this Agreement;

HEREBY AGREE as follows:

CHAPTER I—THE COUNCIL
ARTICLE I
Transfer of Authority

1. Israel shall transfer powers and responsibilities as specified in this Agreement from the Israeli military government and its Civil Administration to the Council in accordance with this Agreement. Israel shall continue to exercise powers and responsibilities not so transferred.

2. Pending the inauguration of the Council, the powers and responsibilities transferred to the Council shall be exercised by the Palestinian Authority established in accordance with the Gaza-Jericho Agreement, which shall also have all the rights, liabilities and obligations to be assumed by the Council in this regard. Accordingly, the term "Council" throughout this Agreement shall, pending the inauguration of the Council, be construed as meaning the Palestinian Authority.

3. The transfer of powers and responsibilities to the police force established by the Palestinian Council in accordance with Article XIV below (hereinafter "the Palestinian Police") shall be accomplished in a phased manner, as detailed in this Agreement and in the Protocol concerning Redeployment and Security Arrangements attached as Annex I to this Agreement (hereinafter "Annex I").

4. As regards the transfer and assumption of authority in civil spheres, powers and responsibilities shall be transferred and assumed as set out in the Protocol Concerning Civil Affairs attached as Annex III to this Agreement (hereinafter "Annex III").

5. After the inauguration of the Council, the Civil Administration in the West Bank will be dissolved, and the Israeli military government shall be withdrawn. The withdrawal of the military government shall not prevent it from exercising the powers and responsibilities not transferred to the Council.

6. A Joint Civil Affairs Coordination and Cooperation Committee (hereinafter "the CAC"), Joint Regional Civil Affairs Subcommittees, one for the Gaza Strip and the other for the West Bank, and District Civil Liaison Offices in the West Bank shall be established in order to provide for coordination and cooperation in civil affairs between the Council and Israel, as detailed in Annex III.

7. The offices of the Council, and the offices of its Ra'ees and its Executive Authority and other committees, shall be located in areas under Palestinian territorial jurisdiction in the West Bank and the Gaza Strip.

ARTICLE II
Elections

1. In order that the Palestinian people of the West Bank and the Gaza Strip may govern themselves according to democratic principles, direct, free and general political elections will be held for the Council and the Ra'ees of the Executive Authority of the Council in accordance with the provisions set out in the Protocol concerning Elections attached as Annex II to this Agreement (hereinafter "Annex II").

2. These elections will constitute a significant interim preparatory step towards the realization of the legitimate rights of the Palestinian people and their just requirements and will provide a democratic basis for the establishment of Palestinian institutions.

3. Palestinians of Jerusalem who live there may participate in the election process in accordance with the provisions contained in this Article and in Article VI of Annex II (Election Arrangements concerning Jerusalem).

4. The elections shall be called by the Chairman of the Palestinian Authority immediately following the signing of this Agreement to take place at the earliest practicable date following the redeployment of Israeli forces in accordance with Annex I, and consistent with the requirements of the election timetable as provided in Annex II, the Election Law and the Election Regulations, as defined in Article I of Annex II.

ARTICLE III
Structure of the Palestinian Council

1. The Palestinian Council and the Ra'ees of the Executive Authority of the Council constitute the Palestinian Interim Self-Government Authority, which will be elected by the Palestinian people of the West Bank, Jerusalem and the Gaza Strip for the transitional period agreed in Article I of the DOP.

2. The Council shall possess both legislative power and executive power, in accordance with Articles VII and IX of the DOP. The Council shall carry out and be responsible for all the legislative and executive powers and responsibilities transferred to it under this Agreement. The exercise of legislative powers shall be in accordance with Article XVIII of this Agreement (Legislative Powers of the Council).

3. The Council and the Ra'ees of the Executive Authority of the Council shall be directly and simultaneously elected by the Palestinian people of the West Bank, Jerusalem and the Gaza Strip, in accordance with the provisions of this Agreement and the Election Law and Regulations, which shall not be contrary to the provisions of this Agreement.

4. The Council and the Ra'ees of the Executive Authority of the Council shall be elected for a transitional period not exceeding five years from the signing of the Gaza-Jericho Agreement on May 4, 1994.

5. Immediately upon its inauguration, the Council will elect from among its members a Speaker. The Speaker will preside over the meetings of the Council, administer the Council and its committees, decide on the agenda of each meeting, and lay before the Council proposals for voting and declare their results.

6. The jurisdiction of the Council shall be as determined in Article XVII of this Agreement (Jurisdiction).

7. The organization, structure and functioning of the Council shall be in accordance with this Agreement and the Basic Law for the Palestinian Interim Self-government Authority, which Law shall be adopted by the Council. The Basic Law and any regulations made under it shall not be contrary to the provisions of this Agreement.

8. The Council shall be responsible under its executive powers for the offices, services and departments transferred to it and may establish, within its jurisdiction, ministries and subordinate bodies, as necessary for the fulfillment of its responsibilities.

9. The Speaker will present for the Council's approval proposed internal procedures that will regulate, among other things, the decision-making processes of the Council.

ARTICLE IV
Size of the Council

The Palestinian Council shall be composed of 82 representatives and the Ra'ees of the Executive Authority, who will be directly and simultaneously elected by the Palestinian people of the West Bank, Jerusalem and the Gaza Strip.

[...]

ARTICLE IX
Powers and Responsibilities of the Council

1. Subject to the provisions of this Agreement, the Council will, within its jurisdiction, have legislative powers as set out in Article XVIII of this Agreement, as well as executive powers.

2. The executive power of the Palestinian Council shall extend to all matters within its jurisdiction under this Agreement or any future agreement that may be reached between the two Parties during the interim period. It shall include the power to formulate and conduct Palestinian policies and to supervise their implementation, to issue any rule or regulation under powers given in approved legislation and administrative decisions necessary for the realization of Palestinian self-government, the power to employ staff, sue and be sued and conclude contracts, and the power to keep and administer registers and records of the population, and issue certificates, licenses and documents.

3. The Palestinian Council's executive decisions and acts shall be consistent with the provisions of this Agreement.

4. The Palestinian Council may adopt all necessary measures in order to enforce the law and any of its decisions, and bring proceedings before the Palestinian courts and tribunals.

5. a. In accordance with the DOP, the Council will not have powers and responsibilities in the sphere of foreign relations, which sphere includes the establishment abroad of embassies, consulates or other types of foreign missions and posts or permitting their establishment in the West Bank or the Gaza Strip, the appointment of or admission of diplomatic and consular staff, and the exercise of diplomatic functions.

   b. Notwithstanding the provisions of this paragraph, the PLO may conduct negotiations and sign agreements with states or international organizations for the benefit of the Council in the following cases only:

   (1) economic agreements, as specifically provided in Annex V of this Agreement;

   (2) agreements with donor countries for the purpose of implementing arrangements for the provision of assistance to the Council;

   (3) agreements for the purpose of implementing the regional development plans detailed in Annex IV of the DOP or in agreements entered into in the framework of the multilateral negotiations; and

   (4) cultural, scientific and educational agreements. Dealings between the Council and representatives of foreign states and international organizations, as well as the establishment in the West Bank and the Gaza Strip of representative offices other than those described in sub-paragraph 5.a above, for the purpose of implementing the agreements referred to in subparagraph 5.b above, shall not be considered foreign relations.

6. Subject to the provisions of this Agreement, the Council shall, within its jurisdiction, have an independent judicial system composed of independent Palestinian courts and tribunals.

CHAPTER 2—REDEPLOYMENT AND SECURITY ARRANGEMENTS
ARTICLE X
Redeployment of Israeli Military Forces

1. The first phase of the Israeli military forces redeployment will cover populated areas in the West Bank—cities, towns, villages, refugee camps and hamlets—as set out in Annex I, and will be completed prior to the eve of the Palestinian elections, i.e., 22 days before the day of the elections.

2. Further redeployments of Israeli military forces to specified military locations will commence after the inauguration of the Council and will be gradually implemented commensurate with the assumption of responsibility for public order and internal security by the Palestinian Police, to be completed within 18 months from the date of the inauguration of the Council as detailed in Articles XI (Land) and XIII (Security) below and in Annex I.

3. The Palestinian Police shall be deployed and shall assume responsibility for public order and internal security for Palestinians in a phased manner in accordance with XIII (Security) below and Annex I.

4. Israel shall continue to carry the responsibility for external security, as well as the responsibility for overall security of Israelis for the purpose of safeguarding their internal security and public order.

5. For the purpose of this Agreement, "Israeli military forces" includes Israel Police and other Israeli security forces.

ARTICLE XI
Land

1. The two sides view the West Bank and the Gaza Strip as a single territorial unit, the integrity and status of which will be preserved during the interim period.

2. The two sides agree that West Bank and Gaza Strip territory, except for issues that will be negotiated in the permanent status negotiations, will come under the jurisdiction of the Palestinian Council in a phased manner, to be completed within 18 months from the date of the inauguration of the Council, as specified below:

   a. Land in populated areas (Areas A and B), including government and Al Waqf land, will come under the jurisdiction of the Council during the first phase of redeployment.

   b. All civil powers and responsibilities, including planning and zoning, in Areas A and B, set out in Annex III, will be transferred to and assumed by the Council during the first phase of redeployment.

   c. In Area C, during the first phase of redeployment Israel will transfer to the Council civil powers and responsibilities not relating to territory, as set out in Annex III.

d. The further redeployments of Israeli military forces to specified military locations will be gradually implemented in accordance with the DOP in three phases, each to take place after an interval of six months, after the inauguration of the Council, to be completed within 18 months from the date of the inauguration of the Council.

e. During the further redeployment phases to be completed within 18 months from the date of the inauguration of the Council, powers and responsibilities relating to territory will be transferred gradually to Palestinian jurisdiction that will cover West Bank and Gaza Strip territory, except for the issues that will be negotiated in the permanent status negotiations.

f. The specified military locations referred to in Article X, paragraph 2 above will be determined in the further redeployment phases, within the specified time-frame ending not later than 18 months from the date of the inauguration of the Council, and will be negotiated in the permanent status negotiations.

3. For the purpose of this Agreement and until the completion of the first phase of the further redeployments:

a. "Area A" means the populated areas delineated by a red line and shaded in brown on attached map No. 1;

b. "Area B" means the populated areas delineated by a red line and shaded in yellow on attached map No. 1, and the built-up area of the hamlets listed in Appendix 6 to Annex I; and

c. "Area C" means areas of the West Bank outside Areas A and B, which, except for the issues that will be negotiated in the permanent status negotiations, will be gradually transferred to Palestinian jurisdiction in accordance with this Agreement.

ARTICLE XII
Arrangements for Security and Public Order

1. In order to guarantee public order and internal security for the Palestinians of the West Bank and the Gaza Strip, the Council shall establish a strong police force as set out in Article XIV below. Israel shall continue to carry the responsibility for defense against external threats, including the responsibility for protecting the Egyptian and Jordanian borders, and for defense against external threats from the sea and from the air, as well as the responsibility for overall security of Israelis and Settlements, for the purpose of safeguarding their internal security and public order, and will have all the powers to take the steps necessary to meet this responsibility.

2. Agreed security arrangements and coordination mechanisms are specified in Annex I.

3. A Joint Coordination and Cooperation Committee for Mutual Security Purposes (hereinafter "the JSC"), as well as Joint Regional Security Committees (hereinafter "RSCs") and Joint District Coordination Offices (hereinafter "DCOs"), are hereby established as provided for in Annex I.

4. The security arrangements provided for in this Agreement and in Annex I may be reviewed at the request of either Party and may be amended by mutual agreement of the Parties. Specific review arrangements are included in Annex I.

5. For the purpose of this Agreement, "the Settlements" means, in the West Bank the settlements in Area C; and in the Gaza Strip—the Gush Katif and Erez settlement areas, as well as the other settlements in the Gaza Strip, as shown on attached map No. 2.

ARTICLE XIII
Security

1. The Council will, upon completion of the redeployment of Israeli military forces in each district, as set out in Appendix 1 to Annex I, assume the powers and responsibilities for internal security and public order in Area A in that district.

2. a. There will be a complete redeployment of Israeli military forces from Area B. Israel will transfer to the Council and the Council will assume responsibility for public order for Palestinians. Israel shall have the overriding responsibility for security for the purpose of protecting Israelis and confronting the threat of terrorism.

b. In Area B the Palestinian Police shall assume the responsibility for public order for Palestinians and shall be deployed in order to accommodate the Palestinian needs and requirements in the following manner:

(1) The Palestinian Police shall establish 25 police stations and posts in towns, villages, and other places listed in Appendix 2 to Annex I and as delineated on map No. 3. The West Bank RSC may agree on the establishment of additional police stations and posts, if required.

(2) The Palestinian Police shall be responsible for handling public order incidents in which only Palestinians are involved.

(3) The Palestinian Police shall operate freely in populated places where police stations and posts are located, as set out in paragraph b(1) above.

(4) While the movement of uniformed Palestinian policemen in Area B outside places where there is a Palestinian police station or post will be carried out after coordination and confirmation through the relevant DCO, three months after the completion of redeployment from Area B, the DCOs may decide that movement of Palestinian policemen from the police stations in Area B to Palestinian towns and villages in Area B on roads that are used only by Palestinian traffic will take place after notifying the DCO.

(5) The coordination of such planned movement prior to confirmation through the relevant DCO shall include a scheduled plan, including the number of policemen, as well as the type and number of weapons and vehicles intended to take part. It shall also include details of arrangements for ensuring continued coordination through appropriate communication links, the exact schedule of movement to the area of the planned operation, including the destination and routes thereto, its proposed duration and the schedule for returning to the police station or post.

    The Israeli side of the DCO will provide the Palestinian side with its response, following a request for movement of policemen in accordance with this paragraph, in normal or routine cases within one day and in emergency cases no later than 2 hours.

(6) The Palestinian Police and the Israeli military forces will conduct joint security activities on the main roads as set out in Annex I.

(7) The Palestinian Police will notify the West Bank RSC of the names of the policemen, number plates of police vehicles and serial numbers of weapons, with respect to each police station and post in Area B.

(8) Further redeployments from Area C and transfer of internal security responsibility to the Palestinian Police in Areas B and C will be carried out in three phases, each to take place after an interval of six months, to be completed 18 months after the inauguration of the Council, except for the issues of permanent status negotiations and of Israel's overall responsibility for Israelis and borders.

(9) The procedures detailed in this paragraph will be reviewed within six months of the completion of the first phase of redeployment.

ARTICLE XIV
The Palestinian Police

1. The Council shall establish a strong police force. The duties, functions, structure, deployment and composition of the Palestinian Police, together with provisions regarding its equipment and operation, as well as rules of conduct, are set out in Annex I.

2. The Palestinian police force established under the Gaza-Jericho Agreement will be fully integrated into the Palestinian Police and will be subject to the provisions of this Agreement.

3. Except for the Palestinian Police and the Israeli military forces, no other armed forces shall be established or operate in the West Bank and the Gaza Strip.

4. Except for the arms, ammunition and equipment of the Palestinian Police described in Annex I, and those of the Israeli military forces, no organization, group or individual in the West Bank and the Gaza Strip shall manufacture, sell, acquire, possess, import or otherwise introduce into the West Bank or the Gaza Strip any firearms, ammunition, weapons, explosives, gunpowder or any related equipment, unless otherwise provided for in Annex I.

ARTICLE XV
Prevention of Hostile Acts

1. Both sides shall take all measures necessary in order to prevent acts of terrorism, crime and hostilities directed against each other, against individuals falling under the other's authority and against their property and shall take legal measures against offenders.

2. Specific provisions for the implementation of this Article are set out in Annex I.

ARTICLE XVI
Confidence Building Measures

With a view to fostering a positive and supportive public atmosphere to accompany the implementation of this Agreement, to establish a solid basis of mutual trust and good faith, and in order to facilitate the anticipated cooperation and new relations between the two peoples, both Parties agree to carry out confidence building measures as detailed herewith:

1. Israel will release or turn over to the Palestinian side, Palestinian detainees and prisoners, residents of the West Bank and the Gaza Strip. The first stage of release of these prisoners and detainees will take place on the signing of this Agreement and the second stage will take place prior to the date of the elections. There will be a third stage of release of detainees and prisoners. Detainees and prisoners will be released from among categories detailed in Annex VII (Release of Palestinian Prisoners and Detainees). Those released will be free to return to their homes in the West Bank and the Gaza Strip.

2. Palestinians who have maintained contact with the Israeli authorities will not be subjected to acts of harassment, violence, retribution or prosecution. Appropriate ongoing measures will be taken, in coordination with Israel, in order to ensure their protection.

3. Palestinians from abroad whose entry into the West Bank and the Gaza Strip is approved pursuant to this Agreement, and to whom the provisions of this Article are applicable, will not be prosecuted for offenses committed prior to September 13, 1993.

CHAPTER 3—LEGAL AFFAIRS
[...]

ARTICLE XIX
Human Rights and the Rule of Law

Israel and the Council shall exercise their powers and responsibilities pursuant to this Agreement with due regard to internationally-accepted norms and principles of human rights and the rule of law.

[...]

CHAPTER 4—COOPERATION
ARTICLE XXII
Relations between Israel and the Council

1. Israel and the Council shall seek to foster mutual understanding and tolerance and shall accordingly abstain from incitement, including hostile propaganda, against each other and, without derogating from the principle of freedom of expression, shall take legal measures to prevent such incitement by any organizations, groups or individuals within their jurisdiction.

2. Israel and the Council will ensure that their respective educational systems contribute to the peace between the Israeli and Palestinian peoples and to peace in the entire region, and will refrain from the introduction of any motifs that could adversely affect the process of reconciliation.

3. Without derogating from the other provisions of this Agreement, Israel and the Council shall cooperate in combating criminal activity which may affect both sides, including offenses related to trafficking in illegal drugs and psychotropic substances, smuggling, and offenses against property, including offenses related to vehicles.

ARTICLE XXIII
Cooperation with Regard to Transfer of Powers and Responsibilities

In order to ensure a smooth, peaceful and orderly transfer of powers and responsibilities, the two sides will cooperate with regard to the transfer of security powers and responsibilities in accordance with the provisions of Annex I, and the transfer of civil powers and responsibilities in accordance with the provisions of Annex III.

[...]

ARTICLE XXV
Cooperation Programs

1. The Parties agree to establish a mechanism to develop programs of cooperation between them. Details of such cooperation are set out in Annex VI.

[...]

ARTICLE XXVII
Liaison and Cooperation with Jordan and Egypt

1. Pursuant to Article XII of the DOP, the two Parties have invited the Governments of Jordan and Egypt to participate in establishing further liaison and cooperation arrangements between the Government of Israel and the Palestinian representatives on the one hand, and the Governments of Jordan and Egypt on the other hand, to promote cooperation between them. As part of these arrangements a Continuing Committee has been constituted and has commenced its deliberations.

2. The Continuing Committee shall decide by agreement on the modalities of admission of persons displaced from the West Bank and the Gaza Strip in 1967, together with necessary measures to prevent disruption and disorder.

3. The Continuing Committee shall also deal with other matters of common concern.

ARTICLE XXVIII
Missing Persons

1. Israel and the Council shall cooperate by providing each other with all necessary assistance in the conduct of searches for missing persons and bodies of persons which have not been recovered, as well as by providing information about missing persons.

2. The PLO undertakes to cooperate with Israel and to assist it in its efforts to locate and to return to Israel Israeli soldiers who are missing in action and the bodies of soldiers which have not been recovered.

CHAPTER 5—MISCELLANEOUS PROVISIONS
[...]

ARTICLE XXXI
Final Clauses

1. This Agreement shall enter into force on the date of its signing.

2. The Gaza-Jericho Agreement, except for Article XX (Confidence-Building Measures), the Preparatory Transfer Agreement and the Further Transfer Protocol will be superseded by this Agreement.

3. The Council, upon its inauguration, shall replace the Palestinian Authority and shall assume all the undertakings and obligations of the Palestinian Authority under the Gaza-Jericho Agreement, the Preparatory Transfer Agreement, and the Further Transfer Protocol.

4. The two sides shall pass all necessary legislation to implement this Agreement.

5. Permanent status negotiations will commence as soon as possible, but not later than May 4, 1996, between the Parties. It is understood that these negotiations shall cover remaining issues, including: Jerusalem, refugees, settlements, security arrangements, borders, relations and cooperation with other neighbors, and other issues of common interest.

6. Nothing in this Agreement shall prejudice or preempt the outcome of the negotiations on the permanent status to be conducted

pursuant to the DOP. Neither Party shall be deemed, by virtue of having entered into this Agreement, to have renounced or waived any of its existing rights, claims or positions.

7. Neither side shall initiate or take any step that will change the status of the West Bank and the Gaza Strip pending the outcome of the permanent status negotiations.

8. The two Parties view the West Bank and the Gaza Strip as a single territorial unit, the integrity and status of which will be preserved during the interim period.

9. The PLO undertakes that, within two months of the date of the inauguration of the Council, the Palestinian National Council will convene and formally approve the necessary changes in regard to the Palestinian Covenant, as undertaken in the letters signed by the Chairman of the PLO and addressed to the Prime Minister of Israel, dated September 9, 1993 and May 4, 1994.

10. Pursuant to Annex I, Article IX of this Agreement, Israel confirms that the permanent checkpoints on the roads leading to and from the Jericho Area (except those related to the access road leading from Mousa Alami to the Allenby Bridge) will be removed upon the completion of the first phase of redeployment.

11. Prisoners who, pursuant to the Gaza-Jericho Agreement, were turned over to the Palestinian Authority on the condition that they remain in the Jericho Area for the remainder of their sentence, will be free to return to their homes in the West Bank and the Gaza Strip upon the completion of the first phase of redeployment.

[...]

Source: "Israeli-Palestinian Interim Agreement on the West Bank and the Gaza Strip," U.S. Department of State, http://www.state.gov/p/nea/rls/22678.htm.

129. Yitzhak Rabin's Last Speech, Peace Rally, Kings of Israel Square, Tel Aviv, November 4, 1995

Introduction

Even though the 1995 Oslo Interim Agreements permitted Israeli forces to maintain effective control of much of the West Bank and the Gaza Strip and the Israeli government continued to expand new settlements in the West Bank and East Jerusalem, they were anathema to many conservative Israeli politicians, extremist settlers, and ultraorthodox Jews. The issue polarized the Israeli population. In the fall of 1995, right-wing Israelis held massive demonstrations against the interim agreements and any Israeli withdrawals from West Bank territories. Moderate Israelis likewise organized huge rallies in favor of peace, and Prime Minister Yitzhak Rabin agreed to appear at a peace demonstration in Tel Aviv, scheduled for November 4, 1995. Rabin, who one year earlier had shared the Nobel Peace Prize with Israel's foreign minister, Shimon Peres, and Palestine Liberation Organization (PLO) chairman Yasser Arafat, again spoke eloquently in favor of the peace process as the only way of ensuring Israel's long-term survival. Recalling his own 27 years in the military, Rabin argued that while fighting was sometimes necessary and inevitable, whenever it was feasible peace was the better course. He also assailed those ultraorthodox and right-wing Israeli critics of the interim agreements who were advocating the use of violence against their architects, himself included, warning that such behavior was "undermining the very foundations of Israeli democracy." Ironically, during the rally he was assassinated by Yigal Amir, an orthodox and deeply anti-Arab Jewish student of theology and a former Israeli soldier who believed that Rabin's policies were endangering Israel and therefore justified his death as a threat to state security. The assassination, revealing as it did the depths of political divisions, extremism, and hatred within the country, shocked Israel and the international community. For supporters of the peace process, Rabin became a posthumous icon and martyr, the earlier ambiguities and reservations of his policies forgotten.

Primary Source

Allow me to say, I am also moved. I want to thank each and every one of you who stood up here against violence and for peace. This government, which I have the privilege to lead, together with my friend Shimon Peres, decided to give peace a chance. A peace that will solve most of the problems of the State of Israel. I was a military man for twenty-seven years. I fought as long as there were no prospects for peace. Today I believe that there are prospects for peace, great prospects. We must take advantage of it for the sake of those standing here, and for the sake of those who do not stand here. And they are many among our people.

I have always believed that the majority of the people want peace, are prepared to take risks for peace. And you here, by showing up at this rally, prove it, along with the many who did not make it here, that the people truly want peace and oppose violence. Violence is undermining the very foundations of Israeli democracy. It must be condemned, denounced, and isolated. This is not the way of the State of Israel. Controversies may arise in a democracy, but the decision must be reached through democratic elections, just as it happened in 1992, when we were given the mandate to do what we are doing, and to continue to do it.

I want to thank from here the President of Egypt, the King of Jordan, and the King of Morocco, whose representatives are present here, conveying their partnership with us on the march toward peace. But above all—the people of Israel, who have proven, in the three years this government has been in office, that peace is attainable, a peace that will provide an opportunity for a progressive society and economy. Peace exists first and foremost in our prayers, but not only in prayers. Peace is what the Jewish People aspire to, a true aspiration.

Peace entails difficulties, even pain. Israel knows no path devoid of pain. But the path of peace is preferable to the path of war. I say this to you as one who was a military man and minister of defense, and who saw the pain of the families of IDF soldiers. It is for their sake, and for the sake of our children and grandchildren, that I want this government to exert every effort, exhaust every opportunity, to promote and to reach a comprehensive peace.

This rally must send a message to the Israeli public, to the Jewish community throughout the world, to many, many in the Arab world and in the entire world, that the people of Israel want peace, support peace, and for that, I thank you very much.

Source: U.S. Congress, "Anniversary of the Death of Israeli Prime Minister Yitzak Rabin," *Congressional Record*, November 19, 2003, H11628, http://www.congress.gov/cgi-bin/query/z?r108: H19NO3–0068:.

130. Israel-Lebanon Cease-Fire Understanding, April 26, 1996

Introduction

The fact that Arab groups hostile to Israel frequently used Lebanon as a base from which to launch their attacks was a recurrent irritant in Israel's relations with Lebanon and on several occasions provoked Israeli military hostilities intended to eradicate the threat. Extremist Shiite groups, notably Hezbollah (the Party of Allah), who were backed by Iran and Syria, two nations that often sought to undermine the Israeli-Palestinian peace process, looked on Lebanon as a convenient safe haven within easy range of Israel. In 1995 and 1996 Hezbollah and other guerrilla groups, including the Islamic Suicide Squads and Hamas, intensified their terrorist attacks against Israeli civilians, moves that eventually contributed to the defeat of the Labor Party in the May 1996 Israeli elections and the discrediting of its peace faction, headed by Prime Minister Shimon Peres. In the spring of 1996 repeated Hezbollah rocket attacks on civilians and property in northern Israel from bases in Lebanon provoked the Israeli government to mount a large-scale bombardment of southern Lebanon, a move christened Operation GRAPES OF WRATH. The episode resulted in numerous Lebanese casualties, and many refugees left their homes and fled into northern Lebanon. U.S. secretary of state Warren Christopher successfully negotiated an understanding among Israel, Lebanon, the Hezbollah and its backer, the Syrian government, that supposedly ended both the Hezbollah attacks and the Israeli reprisals. In practice, both sides disagreed on the interpretation of the agreement and periodically resumed their military operations against the other but at a somewhat lower level. Ten years later, in July 2006, the use of Lebanon by Hezbollah forces resulted in an outright Israeli invasion of Lebanon, in some ways a reprisal of the 1983 Israeli-Lebanese conflict.

Primary Source

Following is the text of the "understanding" reached on Friday, April 26, 1996, for the cease-fire in Lebanon:

The United States understands that after discussions with the governments of Israel and Lebanon, and in consultation with Syria, Lebanon and Israel will ensure the following:

1. Armed groups in Lebanon will not carry out attacks by Katyusha rockets or by any kind of weapon into Israel.
2. Israel and those cooperating with it will not fire any kind of weapon at civilians or civilian targets in Lebanon.
3. Beyond this, the two parties commit to ensuring that under no circumstances will civilians be the target of attack and that civilian populated areas and industrial and electrical installations will not be used as launching grounds for attacks.
4. Without violating this understanding, nothing herein shall preclude any party from exercising the right of self-defense.

A Monitoring Group is established consisting of the United States, France, Syria, Lebanon and Israel. Its task will be to monitor the application of the understanding stated above. Complaints will be submitted to the Monitoring Group.

In the event of a claimed violation of the understanding, the party submitting the complaint will do so within 24 hours. Procedures for dealing with the complaints will be set by the Monitoring Group.

The United States will also organize a Consultative Group, to consist of France, the European Union, Russia and other interested parties, for the purpose of assisting in the reconstruction needs of Lebanon.

It is recognized that the understanding to bring the current crisis between Lebanon and Israel to an end cannot substitute for a permanent solution. The United States understands the importance of achieving a comprehensive peace in the region.

Toward this end, the United States proposes the resumption of negotiations between Syria and Israel and between Lebanon and Israel at a time to be agreed upon, with the objective of reaching comprehensive peace.

The United States understands that it is desirable that these negotiations be conducted in a climate of stability and tranquility.

This understanding will be announced simultaneously at 1800 hours, April 26, 1996, in all countries concerned.

The time set for implementation is 0400 hours, April 27, 1996.

Following is the text of a letter written by U.S. Secretary of State Warren Christopher to Prime Minister Peres on 30 April 1996:

Dear Mr. Prime Minister:

With regard to the right of self-defense referred to in the Understanding dated April 26, 1996, the United States understands that if Hizballah or any other group in Lebanon acts inconsistently with the principles of the Understanding or launches attacks on Israeli forces in Lebanon, whether that attack has taken the form of firing, ambushes, suicide attacks, roadside explosives, or any other type of attack, Israel retains the right in response to take appropriate self-defense measures against the armed groups responsible for the attack.

With regard to the prohibitions on the use of certain areas as launching grounds for attacks, the United States understands that the prohibition refers not only to the firing of weapons, but also to the use of these areas by armed groups as bases from which to carry out attacks.

Source: U.S. Department of State, "Israel-Lebanon Ceasefire Understanding," United States Embassy Israel, http://telaviv.usembassy.gov/publish/peace/documents/ceasefire_understanding.html.

131. Hebron Accords, "Note for the Record," January 15, 1997

Introduction

In May 1996, Likud Party leader Benjamin Netanyahu, a staunch opponent of the Oslo Accords, became Israeli prime minister, heading a coalition government in which the right-wing orthodox religious parties were also included. Netanyahu openly proclaimed his opposition to the U.S. peace proposals put forward by President Bill Clinton. Netanyahu asserted his views by subjecting Palestinian leaders to petty humiliations and announcing the resumption of new Israeli settlements in the occupied territories and East Jerusalem. In September 1996, however, major Palestinian riots erupted when Israeli archaeologists opened a second entrance in East Jerusalem to the Hasmonean Tunnel, a symbolically significant site on the Dome of the Rock. Palestinian security forces waged pitched battles with Israeli troops, and for the first time since 1967 Israeli

tanks and helicopters were deployed in the West Bank. In the aftermath of these internationally embarrassing events, Israel and the Palestine Liberation Organization (PLO) reached agreement on an outstanding issue: the administration of the city of Hebron, a sacred site for both Jews and Muslims, where 450 militant Jews lived among 200,000 Arabs. The Hebron Accords divided the city into two, the larger (H-1) part under the Palestinian Authority (PA), and the smaller (H-2) portion, shared by 450 Jews and 20,000 Arabs, supposedly under Palestinian Authority (PA) control although an Israeli military presence remained to protect the Jewish residents and maintain public order. The city remained divided, with checkpoints and barbed wire preventing easy transit among the Palestinian-controlled areas, while Jewish settlers used special access routes and bypass roads guarded by Israeli security personnel. The Jewish residents felt free to taunt their Arab neighbors and even call for their expulsion or death. Many Arabs deeply resented the Hebron Accords, which they felt encapsulated Israeli plans for the Palestinians, who would always be relegated to an inferior position in the occupied territories. Urged by the United States and with the inducement of U.S. funding to restore the main Arab thoroughfare and market in Hebron, PLO leader Yasser Arafat nonetheless welcomed the Hebron Accords. This was mainly because in an appendix to the accords Netanyahu committed Israel to revitalizing the peace process, scheduling three further redeployments of Israeli forces and the resumption within two months of negotiations on the permanent status of the occupied territories. In return, the PLO pledged to complete its promised revisions of the Palestinian National Charter on the renunciation of terrorism and the acceptance of United Nations (UN) Security Council Resolutions 232 and 338 and to take active measures against Palestinian terrorists and propaganda hostile to Israel and the peace process. U.S. secretary of state Warren Christopher followed up the Hebron Accords with a letter to Netanyahu urging further progress in implementation of the interim agreement, especially the speedy implementation of the three promised redeployments of Israeli forces in the West Bank. Christopher told Netanyahu that in conversations with Arafat he had already stressed that the PA should "make every effort to ensure public order and internal security within the West Bank and Gaza Strip." Christopher assured Netanyahu that "the United States' commitment to Israel's security is ironclad and constitutes the fundamental cornerstone of our special relationship." Christopher also stressed that Israel was "entitled to secure and defensible borders" and that ensuring these was central to the peace process. Yet, however diplomatic the language, Netanyahu was clearly under pressure from the Clinton administration to move forward with the program envisaged in the interim agreements.

Primary Source

The two leaders agreed that the Oslo peace process must move forward to succeed. Both parties to the Interim Agreement have concerns and obligations. Accordingly, the two leaders reaffirmed their commitment to implement the Interim Agreement on the basis of reciprocity and, in this context, conveyed the following undertakings to each other:

ISRAELI RESPONSIBILITIES

The Israeli side reaffirms its commitments to the following measures and principles in accordance with the Interim Agreement:

Issues for Implementation

1. Further Redeployment Phases

The first phase of further redeployments will be carried out during the first week of March.

2. Prisoner Release Issues

Prisoner release issues will be dealt with in accordance with the Interim Agreement's provisions and procedures, including Annex VII.

Issues for Negotiation

3. Outstanding Interim Agreement Issues

Negotiations on the following outstanding issues from the Interim Agreement will be immediately resumed. Negotiations on these issues will be conducted in parallel:

   a. Safe Passage
   b. Gaza Airport
   c. Gaza port
   d. Passages
   e. Economic, financial, civilian and security issues
   f. People-to-people

4. Permanent Status Negotiations

Permanent status negotiations will be resumed within two months after implementation of the Hebron Protocol.

PALESTINIAN RESPONSIBILITIES

The Palestinian side reaffirms its commitments to the following measures and principles in accordance with the Interim Agreement:

1. Complete the process of revising the Palestinian National Charter
2. Fighting terror and preventing violence
   a. Strengthening security cooperation
   b. Preventing incitement and hostile propaganda, as specified in Article XXII of the Interim Agreement
   c. Combat systematically and effectively terrorist organizations and infrastructure
   d. Apprehension, prosecution and punishment of terrorists

   e. Requests for transfer of suspects and defendants will be acted upon in accordance with Article II(7)(f) of Annex IV to the Interim Agreement
   f. Confiscation of illegal firearms
3. Size of Palestinian Police will be pursuant to the Interim Agreement.
4. Exercise of Palestinian governmental activity, and location of Palestinian governmental offices, will be as specified in the Interim Agreement.

The aforementioned commitments will be dealt with immediately and in parallel.

Other Issues

Either party is free to raise other issues not specified above related to implementation of the Interim Agreement and obligations of both sides arising from the Interim Agreement.

Prepared by Ambassador Dennis Ross at the request of Prime Minister Benjamin Netanyahu and Ra'ees Yasser Arafat

> **Source:** "Note for the Record," U.S. Embassy, Israel, http://israel.usembassy.gov/publish/peace/note_record.htm.

132. Wye River Memorandum [Excerpt], October 23, 1998

Introduction

Determined to reinvigorate the Israeli-Palestinian peace process, in the fall of 1998 U.S. president Bill Clinton's administration pressured the reluctant but beleaguered Israeli prime minister Benjamin Netanyahu to follow up on the statements in the appendices to the Hebron Accords with a definite timetable for the three promised Israeli troop redeployments. Israeli and Palestinian representatives met at Wye Plantation, Maryland, and spent nine days in fraught and tense negotiations. Clinton attended portions of the meeting and the final ceremony. King Hussein of Jordan, undergoing treatment for the cancer of which he died early in 1999, also made a poignant appearance at the signing ceremony in which he begged those present to think of their children's future, saying: "There has been enough destruction. Enough death. Enough waste." The Palestinian Authority (PA) and Israel eventually concluded an agreement setting a timetable for further troop redeployments, most of which were never implemented. The Palestinians promised to take active measures to prevent and punish terrorism and violence directed at Israel and its forces and to cooperate closely with Israeli military and security forces. They also promised to amend the Palestinian National Charter by removing those clauses that sought Israel's destruction and endorsed the use of terrorism and violence. Israel promised to release 750 Palestinian prisoners, although in practice these included numerous hardened criminals, an action that merely helped to stoke simmering Palestinian hostility. Israel also permitted the Palestinians to open an airport in Gaza and to open talks on establishing a corridor to allow safe passage from Gaza to the West Bank, ending the separation of the constituent occupied areas under the PA. The agreement promised to begin negotiations as to the permanent status of the occupied territories almost immediately and complete them as originally scheduled by the following May, a timetable that all present knew was unlikely to be feasible. In addition, both sides stated that they would not "initiate or take any step that will change the status of the West Bank and the Gaza Strip," a provision the continuing Israeli commitment to new settlements constantly breached. Although it represented a paper triumph for U.S. optimism over Israeli intransigence, the prospects for the agreement's genuine implementation were poor.

Primary Source

I. Further Redeployments

A. Phase One and Two Further Redeployments

1. Pursuant to the Interim Agreement and subsequent agreements, the Israeli side's implementation of the first and second F.R.D. will consist of the transfer to the Palestinian side of 13% from Area C as follows:

1% to Area (A) 12% to Area (B)

The Palestinian side has informed that it will allocate an area/areas amounting to 3% from the above Area (B) to be designated as Green Areas and/or Nature Reserves. The Palestinian side has further informed that they will act according to the established scientific standards, and that therefore there will be no changes in the status of these areas, without prejudice to the rights of the existing inhabitants in these areas including Bedouins; while these standards do not allow new construction in these areas, existing roads and buildings may be maintained.

The Israeli side will retain in these Green Areas/Nature Reserves the overriding security responsibility for the purpose of protecting Israelis and confronting the threat of terrorism. Activities and movements of the Palestinian Police forces may be carried out after coordination and confirmation; the Israeli side will respond to such requests expeditiously.

2. As part of the foregoing implementation of the first and second F.R.D., 14.2% from Area (B) will become Area (A).

B. Third Phase of Further Redeployments

With regard to the terms of the Interim Agreement and of Secretary Christopher's letters to the two sides of January 17, 1997 relating to the further redeployment process, there will be a committee to address this question. The United States will be briefed regularly.

II. Security

In the provisions on security arrangements of the Interim Agreement, the Palestinian side agreed to take all measures necessary in order to prevent acts of terrorism, crime and hostilities directed against the Israeli side, against individuals falling under the Israeli side's authority and against their property, just as the Israeli side agreed to take all measures necessary in order to prevent acts of terrorism, crime and hostilities directed against the Palestinian side, against individuals falling under the Palestinian side's authority and against their property. The two sides also agreed to take legal measures against offenders within their jurisdiction and to prevent incitement against each other by any organizations, groups or individuals within their jurisdiction.

Both sides recognize that it is in their vital interests to combat terrorism and fight violence in accordance with Annex I of the Interim Agreement and the Note for the Record. They also recognize that the struggle against terror and violence must be comprehensive in that it deals with terrorists, the terror support structure, and the environment conducive to the support of terror. It must be continuous and constant over a long term, in that there can be no pauses in the work against terrorists and their structure. It must be cooperative in that no effort can be fully effective without Israeli-Palestinian cooperation and the continuous exchange of information, concepts, and actions.

Pursuant to the prior agreements, the Palestinian side's implementation of its responsibilities for security, security cooperation, and other issues will be as detailed below during the time periods specified in the attached time line:

A. Security Actions

1. Outlawing and Combating Terrorist Organizations

   (a) The Palestinian side will make known its policy of zero tolerance for terror and violence against both sides.

   (b) A work plan developed by the Palestinian side will be shared with the U.S. and thereafter implementation will begin immediately to ensure the systematic and effective combat of terrorist organizations and their infrastructure.

   (c) In addition to the bilateral Israeli-Palestinian security cooperation, a U.S.-Palestinian committee will meet biweekly to review the steps being taken to eliminate terrorist cells and the support structure that plans, finances, supplies and abets terror. In these meetings, the Palestinian side will inform the U.S. fully of the actions it has taken to outlaw all organizations (or wings of organizations, as appropriate) of a military, terrorist or violent character and their support structure and to prevent them from operating in areas under its jurisdiction.

   (d) The Palestinian side will apprehend the specific individuals suspected of perpetrating acts of violence and terror for the purpose of further investigation, and prosecution and punishment of all persons involved in acts of violence and terror.

(e) A U.S.-Palestinian committee will meet to review and evaluate information pertinent to the decisions on prosecution, punishment or other legal measures which affect the status of individuals suspected of abetting or perpetrating acts of violence and terror.

2. Prohibiting Illegal Weapons

(a) The Palestinian side will ensure an effective legal framework is in place to criminalize, in conformity with the prior agreements, any importation, manufacturing or unlicensed sale, acquisition or possession of firearms, ammunition or weapons in areas under Palestinian jurisdiction.

(b) In addition, the Palestinian side will establish and vigorously and continuously implement a systematic program for the collection and appropriate handling of all such illegal items in accordance with the prior agreements. The U.S. has agreed to assist in carrying out this program.

(c) A U.S.-Palestinian-Israeli committee will be established to assist and enhance cooperation in preventing the smuggling or other unauthorized introduction of weapons or explosive materials into areas under Palestinian jurisdiction.

3. Prevention Incitement

(a) Drawing on relevant international practice and pursuant to Article XXII (1) of the Interim Agreement and the Note for the Record, the Palestinian side will issue a decree prohibiting all forms of incitement to violence or terror, and establishing mechanisms for acting systematically against all expressions or threats of violence or terror. This decree will be comparable to the existing Israeli legislation which deals with the same subject.

(b) A U.S.-Palestinian-Israeli committee will meet on a regular basis to monitor cases of possible incitement to violence or terror and to make recommendations and reports on how to prevent such incitement. The Israeli, Palestinian and U.S. sides will each appoint a media specialist, a law enforcement representative, an educational specialist and a current or former elected official to the committee.

B. Security Cooperation

The two sides agree that their security cooperation will be based on a spirit of partnership and will include, among other things, the following steps:

1. Bilateral Cooperation
   There will be full bilateral security cooperation between the two sides which will be continuous, intensive and comprehensive.

2. Forensic Cooperation
   There will be an exchange of forensic expertise, training, and other assistance.

3. Trilateral Committee
   In addition to the bilateral Israeli-Palestinian security cooperation, a high-ranking U.S.-Palestinian-Israeli committee will meet as required and not less than biweekly to assess current threats, deal with any impediments to effective security cooperation and coordination and address the steps being taken to combat terror and terrorist organizations. The committee will also serve as a forum to address the issue of external support for terror. In these meetings, the Palestinian side will fully inform the members of the committee of the results of its investigations concerning terrorist suspects already in custody and the participants will exchange additional relevant information. The committee will report regularly to the leaders of the two sides on the status of cooperation, the results of the meetings and its recommendations.

C. Other Issues

(a) The Palestinian side will provide a list of its policemen to the Israeli side in conformity with the prior agreements.

(b) Should the Palestinian side request technical assistance, the U.S. has indicated its willingness to help meet those needs in cooperation with other donors.

(c) The Monitoring and Steering Committee will, as part of its functions, monitor the implementation of this provision and brief the U.S.

2. PLO Charter

The Executive Committee of the Palestine Liberation Organization and the Palestinian Central Council will reaffirm the letter of 22 January 1998 from PLO Chairman Yasir Arafat to President Clinton concerning the nullification of the Palestinian National Charter provisions that are inconsistent with the letters exchanged between the PLO and the Government of Israel on 9–10 September 1993. PLO Chairman Arafat, the Speaker of the Palestine National Council, and the Speaker of the Palestinian Council will invite the members of the PNC, as well as the members of the Central Council, the Council, and the Palestinian Heads of Ministries to a meeting to be addressed by President Clinton to reaffirm their support for the peace process and the aforementioned decisions of the Executive Committee and the Central Council.

[. . .]

IV. Permanent Status Negotiations

The two sides will immediately resume permanent status negotiations on an accelerated basis and will make a determined effort to achieve the mutual goal of reaching an agreement by May 4, 1999. The negotiations will be continuous and without interruption. The United States has expressed its willingness to facilitate these negotiations.

V. Unilateral Actions

Recognizing the necessity to create a positive environment for the negotiations, neither side shall initiate or take any step that will change the status of the West Bank and the Gaza Strip in accordance with the Interim Agreement.

Source: "Wye River Memorandum," U.S. Department of State, http://www.state.gov/www/regions/nea/981023_interim_agmt.html.

133. U.S. Letters of Assurance to Israel, October 1998

Introduction

Israel's acquiescence, under hard-line Likud Party prime minister Benjamin Netanyahu, in the October 1998 Wye River Accords was largely due to U.S. pressure. In a series of letters dispatched during the 10 days after the accords were signed, Edward S. Walker Jr., the U.S. ambassador to Israel, seeking to encourage implementation of these agreements and writing on behalf of the administration of President Bill Clinton, offered additional clarifications and guarantees to Israel. Walker reaffirmed the significance that the United States placed on launching further negotiations to "resolve permanent status issues" between Israel and the Palestinians and also reiterated his country's "ironclad" commitment to Israel's security. He stressed that only Israel could "determine its own security needs" and "satisfactory" solutions to these. He also pledged that the Palestinian Authority (PA) would place Palestinians accused of violence against Israelis under genuine arrest rather than holding them briefly and then, in a "revolving door" policy, quickly releasing them. Walker stated that the United States firmly opposed any unilateral Palestinian declaration of an independent national state and that in the near future President Clinton intended to ensure that the Palestine Liberation Organization (PLO) nullified those clauses of its charter that endorsed the use of terrorist tactics against Israel and called for Israel's annihilation or destruction. The series of letters was evidence of just how reluctant Netanyahu had been to accept the Wye River Accords and how little faith the Israeli government placed in them. In the Knesset, Netanyahu's Likud Party rebelled against ratifying the accords, although they passed due to support from the rival Labor Party. Netanyahu still tried to evade implementing the Wye River agreement, and at the end of the year he suspended the scheduled troop redeployments. He called elections for May 1999, which he then lost to Labor politician and former Israeli Army chief of staff Ehud Barak, a candidate who celebrated Israel's military strength and believed that a Palestinian state of some kind was inevitable.

Primary Source

Embassy of the United States of America
Tel Aviv
October 31, 1998

Mr. Dani Naveh
Cabinet Secretary
Office of the Prime Minister
Jerusalem

Dear Dani:

I wanted to confirm our policy on the issues of Permanent Status Negotiations and Prisoner Releases. In this regard, the statements issued publicly by the State Department are accurate and represent our policies.

With regard to Permanent Status Negotiations, the statement said: "the U.S. is highly sensitive to the vital importance of the permanent status issues to Israel's future. We recognize that the security of the State of Israel and the Israeli public is at stake, and the U.S. commitment to Israel's security remains ironclad."

"We appreciate that if the U.S. is invited by both parties to participate in the permanent status talks, which are to be conducted between Israel and the Palestinians on a bilateral basis, we will do so for the purpose of facilitating the negotiations."

"Only Israel can determine its own security needs and decide what solutions will be satisfactory."

"We also understand that any decision to convene or seek to convene a summit to resolve permanent status issues will need the agreement of both parties."

As for the issue of prisoner releases and the question of a "revolving door", the statement said: "we have had discussions with the Palestinians and they have given us a firm commitment that there will be no 'revolving door'."

These public statements by the State Department represent our policies. We will not change them and they will remain our policies in the future.

Sincerely,

Edward S. Walker Jr.
Ambassador

Embassy of the United States of America
Tel Aviv
October 29, 1998

Mr. Dani Naveh
Cabinet Secretary
Office of the Prime Minister
Jerusalem

Dear Dani:

I wanted to confirm our policy on the issue of the 3rd phase of further redeployment. In this regard, the statement issued publicly by the State Department on October 27, 1998, is accurate and represents our policy.

Regarding the third further redeployment, the statement said: "during the discussions leading to this agreement, the U.S. made clear to both parties that it will not adopt any position or express any view about the size or the content of the third phase of Israel's further redeployment, which is an Israeli responsibility to implement rather than negotiate."

"Under the terms of the memorandum, an Israeli-Palestinian committee is being established. Nonetheless we urge the parties not to be distracted from the urgent task of negotiating permanent status arrangements, which are at the heart of the matter and which will determine the future of the area."

"Our own efforts have been and will continue to be dedicated to that vital task."

This public statement by the State Department represents our policy. We will not change it and it will remain our policy in the future.

Sincerely,

Edward S. Walker, Jr.
Ambassador

Embassy of the United States of America
Tel Aviv
October 29, 1998

Mr. Dani Naveh
Cabinet Secretary
Office of the Prime Minister
Jerusalem

Dear Dani:

I wanted to confirm our policy on the issues of unilateral actions and the Charter of the PLO. In this regard, the statements issued publicly by the State Department on October 27, 1998, are accurate and represent our policies.

With regard to unilateral declarations or other unilateral actions, the statement said: "as regards to the possibility of a unilateral declaration of statehood or other unilateral actions by either party outside the negotiating process that prejudge or predetermine the outcome of those negotiations, the U.S. opposes and will oppose any such unilateral actions."

"Indeed, the U.S. has maintained for many years that an acceptable solution to the Israeli-Palestinian conflict can only be found through negotiations, not through unilateral actions. And as we look to the future, that will remain our policy."

"For the present, we are doing all we can to promote permanent status negotiations on an accelerated basis. And we are stressing that those who believe that they can declare unilateral positions or take unilateral acts, when the interim period ends, are courting disaster."

With regard to the PNC, the statement said: "the Wye River Agreement specifies that the members of the PNC (as well as the members of the PLO Central Council, the Palestinian Council and the Heads of Palestinian Ministries) will be invited to a meeting which President Clinton will attend."

"The purpose of this meeting of the PNC and other PLO organizations is to reaffirm Chairman Arafat's January 22 letter to President Clinton nullifying each of the Charter's provisions that are inconsistent with the PLO's commitments to renounce terror, and to recognize and live in peace with Israel."

"This process of reaffirmation will make clear, once and for all, that the provisions of the PLO Charter that call for the destruction of Israel are null and void."

These public statements by the State Department represent our policies. We will not change them and they will remain our policies in the future.

Sincerely,

Edward S. Walker, Jr.
Ambassador

U.S. State Department
Washington, D.C.
October 30, 1998

Mr. Dani Naveh
Cabinet Secretary
Government of Israel

Dear Mr. Naveh:

I wanted to provide further clarification of the understanding of the United States regarding one of the issues addressed in the "Wye River Memorandum."

With respect to the Palestinian side's provision of its list of policemen to Israel (II(C)(1)(a)), the U.S. has been assured that it will receive all appropriate information concerning current and former policemen as part of our assistance program. It is also our understanding that it was agreed by the two sides that the total number of Palestinian policemen would not exceed 30,000.

Sincerely,

Dennis B. Ross
Special Middle East Coordinator

United States Department of State
Washington, D.C. 20520
October 23, 1998

Mr. Dani Naveh
Israeli-Palestinian Monitoring
and Steering Committee

Dear Dani:

With regard to the current or former U.S. elected official to be appointed to the trilateral incitement committee referred to in "The Wye River Memorandum", we intend to consult with the Israeli Government to confirm that the appointment would be mutually satisfactory.

Sincerely,

Dennis B. Ross
Special Middle East Coordinator

Source: "The Wye River Memorandum—US Letters of Assurance to Israel, 29 Oct 1998," Israel Ministry of Foreign Affairs, http://www.mfa.gov.il/MFA.

134. Bill Clinton, Remarks to the Palestinian National Council and Other Palestinian Organizations in Gaza City [Excerpt], December 14, 1998

Introduction

By the late 1990s U.S. president Bill Clinton, determined to win himself a place in history and redeem his public image, which had been badly tarnished by a tawdry sex scandal in which he barely escaped impeachment by the U.S. House of Representatives, was personally committed to making every effort to bring about a permanent settlement of the Israeli-Palestinian conflict. Under the October 1998 Wye River Accords, Clinton promised to attend the next meeting of the Palestinian National Council, which was expected to revise those provisions of the Palestinian National Charter that called for the destruction of Israel and endorsed the use of violence and terrorist tactics in pursuit of this objective. Less than two months later, in December 1998, Clinton honored this pledge. Attending their meeting in Gaza, he urged the assembled Palestinians to focus on how great, despite all the shortcomings and the restrictions and frustrations they faced, was the progress they had made toward their goals over the previous 10 years. He praised Palestine Liberation Organization (PLO) chairman Yasser Arafat's perseverance in his quest for peace and pledged substantial additional U.S. economic aid to the Palestinian Authority. He urged Palestinians to cease preaching hatred and war and to ensure that the next generation of young children would be able to pursue fruitful and productive lives in peace. While anticipating further breakdowns on the road to a final settlement between the Palestinians and Israel, Clinton called on both sides to show "courage," understanding, and tolerance toward each other and to continue to work toward this and ensure a lasting peace for their descendants. Clinton paid tribute to the teachings of all three faiths, Islam, Christianity, and Judaism. His speech, which contained few specifics, was intended to uplift and inspire, not to provide a concrete program. The very presence of the American president and his wife at this gathering, however, gave an enormous boost to the Palestinians' status and morale.

Primary Source

I am profoundly honored to be the first American President to address the Palestinian people in a city governed by Palestinians.

I have listened carefully to all that has been said. I have watched carefully the reactions of all of you to what has been said. I know that the Palestinian people stand at a crossroads: behind you a history of dispossession and dispersal, before you the opportunity to shape a new Palestinian future on your own land.

I know the way is often difficult and frustrating, but you have come to this point through a commitment to peace and negotiations. You reaffirmed that commitment today. I believe it is the only way to fulfill the aspirations of your people. And I am profoundly grateful to have had the opportunity to work with Chairman Arafat for the cause of peace, to come here as a friend of peace and a friend of your future, and to witness you raising your hands, standing up tall, standing up not only against what you believe is wrong but for what you believe is right in the future.

I was sitting here thinking that this moment would have been inconceivable a decade ago: no Palestinian Authority; no elections in Gaza and the West Bank; no relations between the United States and Palestinians; no Israeli troop redeployments from the West Bank and Gaza; no Palestinians in charge in Gaza, Ramallah, Bethlehem, Hebron, Tulkarem, Jenin, Nablus, Jericho, and so many other places; there was no Gaza International Airport.

Today I had the privilege of cutting the ribbon on the international airport. Hillary and I, along with Chairman and Mrs. Arafat, celebrated a place that will become a magnet for planes from throughout the Middle East and beyond, bringing you a future in which Palestinians can travel directly to the far corners of the world; a future in which it is easier and cheaper to bring materials, technology, and expertise in and out of Gaza; a future in which tourists and traders can flock here, to this beautiful place on the Mediterranean; a future, in short, in which the Palestinian people are connected to the world.

[...]

I want the people of Israel to know that for many Palestinians, 5 years after Oslo, the benefits of this process remain remote; that for too many Palestinians lives are hard, jobs are scarce, prospects are uncertain, and personal grief is great. I know that tremendous pain remains as a result of losses suffered from violence, the separation of families, the restrictions on the movement of people and goods. I understand your concerns about settlement activity, land confiscation, and home demolitions. I understand your concerns and theirs about unilateral statements that could prejudge the outcome of final status negotiations. I understand, in short, that there's still a good deal of misunderstanding 5 years after the beginning of this remarkable process.

It takes time to change things and still more time for change to benefit everyone. It takes determination and courage to make peace and sometimes even more to persevere for peace. But slowly but surely, the peace agreements are turning into concrete progress: the transfer of territories, the Gaza industrial estate, and the airport. These changes will make a difference in many Palestinian lives.

I thank you—I thank you, Mr. Chairman, for your leadership for peace and your perseverance, for enduring all the criticism from all sides, for being willing to change course, and for being strong enough to stay with what is right. You have done a remarkable thing for your people.

America is determined to do what we can to bring tangible benefits of peace. I am proud that the roads we traveled on to get here were paved, in part, with our assistance, as were hundreds of miles of roads that knit together towns and villages throughout the West Bank and Gaza.

Two weeks ago in Washington, we joined with other nations to pledge hundreds of millions of dollars toward your development, including health care and clean water, education for your children, [and] rule of law projects that nurture democracy. Today I am pleased to announce we will also fund the training of Palestinian health care providers and airport administrators, [and] increase our support to Palestinian refugees. And next year I will ask the Congress

for another several hundred million dollars to support the development of the Palestinian people.

But make no mistake about it, all this was made possible because of what you did, because 5 years ago you made a choice for peace, and because through all the tough times since, when in your own mind you had a hundred good reasons to walk away, you didn't. Because you still harbor the wisdom that led to the Oslo accords, that led to the signing in Washington in September of '93, you still can raise your hand and stand and lift your voice for peace.

Mr. Chairman, you said some profound words today in embracing the idea that Israelis and Palestinians can live in peace as neighbors. Again I say, you have led the way, and we would not be here without you.

I say to all of you, I can come here and work; I can bring you to America, and we can work; but in the end, this is up to you—you and the Israelis—for you have to live with the consequences of what you do. I can help because I believe it is my job to do so; I believe it is my duty to do so; because America has Palestinian-Americans, Jewish-Americans, other Arab-Americans who desperately want us to be helpful. But in the end, you have to decide what the understanding will be, and you have to decide whether we can get beyond the present moment where there is still, for all the progress we have made, so much mistrust. And the people who are listening to us today in Israel, they have to make the same decisions.

Peace must mean many things: legitimate rights for Palestinians—[applause] thank you—legitimate rights for Palestinians, real security for Israel. But it must begin with something even more basic: mutual recognition, seeing people who are different, with whom there have been profound differences, as people.

I've had two profoundly emotional experiences in the last less than 24 hours. I was with Chairman Arafat, and four little children came to see me whose fathers are in Israeli prisons. Last night, I met some little children whose fathers had been killed in conflict with Palestinians, at the dinner that Prime Minister Netanyahu had for me. Those children brought tears to my eyes. We have to find a way for both sets of children to get their lives back and to go forward.

Palestinians must recognize the right of Israel and its people to live safe and secure lives today, tomorrow, and forever. Israel must recognize the right of Palestinians to aspire to live free today, tomorrow, and forever.

And I ask you to remember these experiences I had with these two groups of children. If I had met them in reverse order, I would not have known which ones were Israeli and which Palestinian. If they had all been lined up in a row and I had seen their tears, I could not tell whose father was dead and whose father was in prison or what the story of their lives were, making up the grief that they bore. We must acknowledge that neither side has a monopoly on pain or virtue.

At the end of America's Civil War, in my home State, a man was elected Governor who had fought with President Lincoln's forces, even though most of the people in my home State fought with the secessionist forces. And he made his inaugural speech after 4 years of unbelievable bloodshed in America, in which he had been on the winning side but in the minority in our home. And everyone wondered what kind of leader he would be. His first sentence was, "We have all done wrong." I say that because I think the beginning of mutual respect, after so much pain, is to recognize not only the positive characteristics of people on both sides but the fact that there has been a lot—a lot—of hurt and harm.

The fulfillment of one side's aspirations must not come at the expense of the other. We must believe that everyone can win in the new Middle East. It does not hurt Israelis to hear Palestinians peacefully and pridefully asserting their identity, as we saw today. That is not a bad thing. And it does not hurt Palestinians to acknowledge the profound desire of Israelis to live without fear. It is in this spirit that I ask you to consider where we go from here.

I thank you for your rejection fully, finally, and forever of the passages in the Palestinian Charter calling for the destruction of Israel, for they were the ideological underpinnings of a struggle renounced at Oslo. By revoking them once and for all, you have sent, I say again, a powerful message not to the Government but to the people of Israel. You will touch people on the street there. You will reach their hearts there.

I know how profoundly important this is to Israelis. I have been there four times as President. I have spent a lot of time with people other than the political leaders, Israeli schoolchildren who heard about you only as someone who thought they should be driven into the sea. They did not know what their parents or grandparents did that you thought was so bad; they were just children, too. Is it surprising that all this has led to the hardening of hearts on both sides, that they refused to acknowledge your existence as a people and that led to a terrible reaction by you?

By turning this page on the past, you are taking the lead in writing a new story for the future. And you have issued a challenge to the Government and the leaders of Israel to walk down that path with you. I thank you for doing that. The children of all the Middle East thank you.

But declaring a change of heart still won't be enough. Let's be realistic here. First of all, there are real differences. And secondly, a lot of water has flowed under the bridge, as we used to say at home. An American poet has written, "Too long a sacrifice can make a stone of the heart." Palestinians and Israelis in their pasts both share a

history of oppression and dispossession; both have felt their hearts turn to stone for living too long in fear and seeing loved ones die too young. You are two great people of strong talent and soaring ambition, sharing such a small piece of sacred land.

The time has come to sanctify your holy ground with genuine forgiveness and reconciliation. Every influential Palestinian, from teacher to journalist, from politician to community leader, must make this a mission to banish from the minds of children glorifying suicide bombers, to end the practice of speaking peace in one place and preaching hatred in another, to teach schoolchildren the value of peace and the waste of war, to break the cycle of violence. Our great American prophet Martin Luther King once said, "The old law of an eye for an eye leaves everybody blind."

I believe you have gained more in 5 years of peace than in 45 years of war. I believe that what we are doing today, working together for security, will lead to further gains and changes in the heart. I believe that our work against terrorism, if you stand strong, will be rewarded, for that must become a fact of the past. It must never be a part of your future.

Let me say this as clearly as I can: No matter how sharp a grievance or how deep a hurt, there is no justification for killing innocents.

Mr. Chairman, you said at the White House that no Israeli mother should have to worry if her son or daughter is late coming home. Your words touched many people. You said much the same thing today. We must invest those words with the weight of reality in the minds of every person in Israel and every Palestinian.

I feel this all the more strongly because the act of a few can falsify the image of the many. How many times have we seen it? How many times has it happened to us? We both know it is profoundly wrong to equate Palestinians, in particular, and Islam, in general, with terrorism or to see a fundamental conflict between Islam and the West. For the vast majority of the more than one billion Muslims in the world, tolerance is an article of faith and terrorism a travesty of faith.

I know that in my own country, where Islam is one of the fastest growing religions, we share the same devotion to family and hard work and community. When it comes to relations between the United States and Palestinians, we have come far to overcome our misperceptions of each other. Americans have come to appreciate the strength of your identity and the depth of your aspirations. And we have learned to listen to your grievances as well.

I hope you have begun to see America as your friend. I have tried to speak plainly to you about the need to reach out to the people of Israel, to understand the pain of their children, to understand the history of their fear and mistrust, their yearning, gnawing desire for security, because that is the only way friends can speak and the only way we can move forward.

I took the same liberty yesterday in Israel. I talked there about the need to see one's own mistakes, not just those of others; to recognize the steps others have taken for peace, not just one's own; to break out of the politics of absolutes; to treat one's neighbors with respect and dignity. I talked about the profound courage of both peoples and their leaders which must continue in order for a secure, just, and lasting peace to occur: the courage of Israelis to continue turning over territory for peace and security; the courage of Palestinians to take action against all those who resort to and support violence and terrorism; the courage of Israelis to guarantee safe passage between the West Bank and Gaza and allow for greater trade and development; the courage of Palestinians to confiscate illegal weapons of war and terror; the courage of Israelis to curtail closures and curfews that remain a daily hardship; the courage of Palestinians to resolve all differences at the negotiating table; the courage of both peoples to abandon the rhetoric of hate that still poisons public discourse and limits the vision of your children; and the courage to move ahead to final status negotiations together, without either side taking unilateral steps or making unilateral statements that could prejudice the outcome, whether governing refugee settlements, borders, Jerusalem, or any other issues encompassed by the Oslo accord.

Now, it will take good faith, mutual respect, and compromise to forge a final agreement. I think there will be more breakdowns, frankly, but I think there will be more breakthroughs, as well. There will be more challenges to peace from its enemies. And so I ask you today never to lose sight of how far you have come. With Chairman Arafat's leadership, already you have accomplished what many said was impossible. The seemingly intractable problems of the past can clearly find practical solutions in the future. But it requires a consistent commitment and a genuine willingness to change heart.

[...]

In Biblical times, Jews and Arabs lived side by side. They contributed to the flowering of Alexandria. During the Golden Age of Spain, Jews, Muslims, and Christians came together in an era of remarkable tolerance and learning. A third of the population laid down its tools on Friday, a third on Saturday, a third on Sunday. They were scholars and scientists, poets, musicians, merchants, and statesmen setting an example of peaceful coexistence that we can make a model for the future. There is no guarantee of success or failure today, but the challenge of this generation of Palestinians is to wage an historic and heroic struggle for peace.

[...]

Chairman Arafat said he and Mrs. Arafat are taking Hillary and Chelsea and me—we're going to Bethlehem tomorrow. For a Chris-

tian family to light the Christmas tree in Bethlehem is a great honor. It is an interesting thing to contemplate that in this small place, the home of Islam, Judaism, and Christianity, the embodiment of my faith was born a Jew and is still recognized by Muslims as a prophet. He said a lot of very interesting things, but in the end, He was known as the Prince of Peace. And we celebrate at Christmastime the birth of the Prince of Peace. One reason He is known as the Prince of Peace is He knew something about what it takes to make peace. And one of the wisest things He ever said was, "We will be judged by the same standard by which we judge, but mercy triumphs over judgment."

In this Christmas season, in this Hanukkah season, on the edge of Ramadan, this is a time for mercy and vision and looking at all of our children together. You have reaffirmed the fact that you now intend to share this piece of land, without war, with your neighbors, forever. They have heard you. They have heard you.

Now, you and they must now determine what kind of peace you will have. Will it be grudging and mean-spirited and confining, or will it be generous and open? Will you begin to judge each other in the way you would like to be judged? Will you begin to see each other's children in the way you see your own? Will they feel your pain, and will you understand theirs?

Surely to goodness, after 5 years of this peace process and decades of suffering and after you have come here today and done what you have done, we can say, "Enough of this gnashing of teeth. Let us join hands and proudly go forward together."

[...]

Source: William J. Clinton, *Public Papers of the Presidents of the United States: William J. Clinton, 1998,* Vol. 2 (Washington, DC: U.S. Government Printing Office, 2000), 2175–2179.

135. Basic Guidelines of the Government of Israel [Excerpt], July 6, 1999
Introduction

The same month that Ehud Barak became prime minister, the Israeli government issued new guidelines for the peace process designed "to bring an end to the cycle of blood-shed in our region." "Making peace," this document stated, required a firm military foundation and must be "grounded in the strength of the IDF [Israel Defense Forces] and on the overall strength of Israel, on the deterrent capabilities of the State," and on the desire by all parties concerned for "stability and economic development." The guidelines promised "an all-out war against terrorist organizations." Israel proposed to "accelerate the negotiations with the Palestinians" and to seek a "permanent settlement" with them, one that would have to be approved by a popular referendum. Barak pledged that his government would implement its existing agreements with the Palestinians but would insist that the Palestinians also honor their own commitments. Israel intended to open peace negotiations with Syria on the basis of United Nations (UN) Security Council Resolutions 242 and 338, to sign a peace treaty with Lebanon, and to withdraw its forces from Lebanese territory, although it would take measures to protect inhabitants of northern Israel from attack by hostile groups based in Lebanon. Jordan, Egypt, and the Palestinian Authority (PA) were all embraced as Israeli partners in peace that would cooperate in the economic, cultural, and commercial fields. The Israeli government would work closely with the United States in the peace process and would also make every effort to "intensify" the two countries' "special relationship" and enhance their "strategic cooperation." Jerusalem would remain Israel's capital, "united and complete under the sovereignty of Israel." While promising to support and safeguard the interests of existing Jewish settlers in the occupied territories, the Israeli government would not authorize any new communities until the status of those already established had been decided. The new guidelines contained some provisions, notably those on Jerusalem and existing settlements in the occupied territories, that Arab states and the Palestinians were likely to find extremely unpalatable. They were, however, a reasonably clear and straightforward statement of precisely what peace terms Israel would find acceptable and as such could serve as a genuine basis for opening negotiations. By the end of the year, in December 1999, Barak had gone some way in implementing these proposals by reopening Israel's long-stalled peace negotiations with Syria, although no treaty resulted from this. While Barak did not authorize any new Jewish settlements in the occupied territories and dismantled some—though not all—of those deemed to have been established illegally, to alleviate rightist discontent he did permit rapid construction of new housing in existing settlements. With assistance from a UN peacekeeping force, by June 2000 the withdrawal of Israeli forces from southern Lebanon had also been completed.

Primary Source

General

1.1 The main objectives of the Government are: national and personal security by way of a determined struggle against terrorism; an end to the Arab-Israeli conflict by achieving genuine peace; the prevention of war and bloodshed; the war on unemployment and the cultivation of stable, employment-creating growth; the reduction of social gaps; the promotion of immigration and immigrant absorption through integration and partnership; the creation of living conditions and an environment that offer a sense of purpose and hope, and promote immigration to Israel; the fortification of democracy, the rule of law, Jewish heritage and human rights, with respect for the courts; the promise of equal opportunity for all; the making [of] education its top priority, ensuring an education for

the young generation from kindergarten through university; and the struggle against violence and traffic accidents.

1.2 The Government of Israel will act to bring an end to the Arab-Israeli conflict through peaceful means, and by standing firm on Israel's national security, integrity and development. The Government will strive to establish peace based on mutual respect, ensuring the security and other vital interests of the State and offering personal security for all its citizens.

[...]

The Peace, Security and Foreign Relations of Israel

2.1 The Government views peace as a basic value of life in Israel, whose sources draw on the vision of the Prophets, as expressed in the Declaration of Independence and in the continued yearning of the Israeli people for peace and security. The Government believes that it is possible to bring an end to the cycle of bloodshed in our region. Making peace is grounded in the strength of the IDF and on the overall strength of Israel, on the deterrent capabilities of the State, and on the desire for stability in the Middle East—that will allow resources to be directed toward economic and social development.

2.2 Peace is a component in the national security conception and the foreign relations of Israel. The arrangements and peace treaties to which Israel will be a partner will be grounded in the preservation of the security and national interests of Israel, resting on the broad support of the people in Israel.

2.3 The Government will cultivate the strength of the IDF as the defensive and deterrent force of Israel.

2.4 The Government will conduct an all-out war against terrorist organizations and the initiators and perpetrators of terrorism, and guarantee the personal security of all residents of Israel.

2.5 As part of its policy to bring about and establish peace in the Middle East, the Government will act toward the development of mechanisms for political, economic, scientific and cultural cooperation between peoples of the region.

2.6 The Government will act to accelerate the negotiations with the Palestinians, based on the existing process, with a view toward ending the conflict with a permanent settlement that guarantees the security and vital interests of Israel. The permanent settlement with the Palestinians will be submitted for approval in a referendum.

2.7 The Government will honor and implement the agreements which Israel has signed with the Palestinians, while, at the same time, insisting that the Palestinian Authority also honor and implement these agreements.

2.8 The Government will resume the negotiations with Syria with a view toward concluding a peace treaty therewith—full peace that bolsters the security of Israel, grounded in UN Security Council Resolutions 242 and 338 and on the existence of a normal relationship between two neighboring states, living side by side in peace. The peace treaty with Syria will be submitted for approval in a referendum.

2.9 The Government will act toward bringing the IDF out of Lebanon, while guaranteeing the welfare and security of residents of the north, and aspiring to conclude a peace treaty with Lebanon.

2.10 The Government views Egypt, Jordan and the Palestinian Authority as important partners in the effort to establish peace in our region, and will conduct an on-going political dialogue with each of them. The Government will also work to advance understanding and friendship, as well as the development of the economy, commerce and tourism between the Israeli people and the Egyptian, Jordanian and Palestinian peoples.

2.11 The Government will conduct an on-going dialogue with the United States with regard to its positions on the permanent settlement. The dialogue will also relate to American political, economic and defense assistance to Israel. The Government will work to intensify the special friendship between the United States and Israel, and to continue and cultivate the strategic cooperation with the United States.

2.12 The Government will work to strengthen and enhance ties with the European Union and its member states. The Government will also act to strengthen ties with Russia, the Commonwealth of Independent States and China, as well as with the entire international community.

2.13 The Government will do everything in its power to bring about the release of Israeli prisoners of war and missing soldiers, and to bring them back to Israel.

Jerusalem
3.1 Greater Jerusalem, the eternal capital of Israel, will remain united and complete under the sovereignty of Israel.

3.2 Members of all religions will be guaranteed free access to the holy places, and freedom of worship.

3.3 The Government will work toward the development and prosperity of Jerusalem, and for continued construction therein—for the welfare of all its residents.

Settlement
4.1 The Government views all forms of settlement as a valued social and national enterprise, and will work to improve its ability to contend with the difficulties and challenges it faces.

4.2 Until the status of the Jewish communities in Judea, Samaria and Gaza is determined, within the framework of the permanent settlement, no new communities will be built and no existing communities will be detrimentally affected.

4.3 The Government will work to ensure the security of the Jewish residents in Judea, Samaria and Gaza, and to provide regular Government and municipal services—equal to those offered to residents of all other communities in Israel. The Government will offer a response to the on-going development needs of existing communities. Socio-economic standards will be equally applied to all communities everywhere.

[...]

Source: "Basic Guidelines of the Government of Israel, 6 July 1999," Israel Ministry of Foreign Affairs, http://www.mfa.gov.il/MFA.

136. Ehud Barak, Speech on the Presentation of the Government to the Knesset [Excerpt], July 6, 1999

Introduction

In July 1999 General Ehud Barak, a Labor Party politician and former Israel Army chief of staff and a tough pragmatist, replaced the hard-line Likud leader Benjamin Netanyahu as Israel's prime minister. During his election campaign Barak had argued that Israel's security depended upon a solid peace settlement, keeping his options open by not pledging himself to any particular terms but expressing considerable sympathy for Palestinian economic difficulties. In his first speech to the Knesset, Israel's parliamentary assembly, Barak took up this theme. He stated that Israel faced a historic opportunity to assure itself "long-term security and peace." Such a comprehensive peace settlement must, he stated, rest on agreements with Egypt, Jordan, Syria, Lebanon, and the Palestinians. Barak urged all parties to put the past behind them and cease disputing its rights and wrongs. He expressed his eagerness to end "violence and suffering" and to work with Palestine Liberation Organization (PLO) chairman Yasser Arafat for "a fair and agreed settlement for coexistence." To Syria, Barak offered peace negotiations based on United Nations (UN) Security Council Resolutions 242 and 338. Jordan and Egypt, which had already signed treaties with Israel, were promised that Israel would observe these, as the Netanyahu government had not done the previous year when it failed to supply drought-stricken Jordan with the water supplies guaranteed under its peace treaty with Israel. Barak also pledged to remove Israeli security forces from Lebanon within one year, although he intended to leave Israeli Defense Force (IDF) personnel along the Israeli-Lebanese border. Barak, no sentimentalist but a man who believed that military strength was the ultimate assurance of Israel's position, also promised to maintain and improve the quality, training, and equipment of Israel's armed forces. His assumption of power marked the ascendancy of a new tough and realistic Israeli movement toward a lasting peace settlement with its Arab neighbors.

Primary Source

[. . .]

Now it is our duty to complete the mission, and establish a comprehensive peace in the Middle East which has known so much war. It is our duty to ourselves and our children to take decisive measures to strengthen Israel by ending the Arab-Israeli conflict. This government is determined to make every effort, pursue every path and do everything necessary for Israel's security, the achievement of peace and the prevention of war.

We have an historic obligation to take advantage of the "window of opportunity" which has opened before us in order to bring long-term security and peace to Israel. We know that comprehensive and stable peace can be established only if it rests, simultaneously, on four pillars: Egypt, Jordan, and Syria and Lebanon, in some sense as a single bloc, and of course the Palestinians. As long as peace is not grounded on all these four pillars, it will remain incomplete and unstable. The Arab countries must know that only a strong and self-confident Israel can bring peace.

Here, today, I call upon all the leaders of the region to extend their hands to meet our outstretched hand, and toward a "peace of the brave," in a region which has known so much war, blood and suffering. To our neighbors the Palestinians, I wish to say: the bitter conflict between us has brought great suffering to both our peoples. Now, there is no reason to settle accounts over historical mistakes. Perhaps things could have been otherwise, but we cannot change the past; we can only make the future better. I am not only cognizant of the sufferings of my people, but I also recognize the sufferings of the Palestinian people. My ambition and desire is to bring an end to violence and suffering, and to work with the elected Palestinian leadership, under Chairman Yasser Arafat, in partnership and respect, in order to jointly arrive at a fair and agreed settlement for co-existence in freedom, prosperity and good neighborliness in this beloved land where the two peoples will always live.

To Syrian President Hafez Assad, I say that the new Israeli government is determined, as soon as possible, to advance the negotiations for the achievement of a full, bilateral treaty of peace and security, on the basis of Security Council Resolutions 242 and 338.

We have been tough and bitter adversaries on the battlefield. The time has come to establish a secure and courageous peace which will ensure the futures of our peoples, our children and our grandchildren.

It is my intention to bring an end to the IDF presence in Lebanon within one year, to deploy the IDF, through agreement, along the border, and to bring our boys home while also taking the necessary measures to guarantee the welfare and security of residents along the northern border, as well as the future of the Lebanese security and civilian assistance personnel who have worked alongside us, over all these years, for the sake of the residents of the region.

I wish to take advantage of this opportunity to praise the residents of Kiryat Shmona and communities along the confrontation line for their firm stand in the face of the Katyushas. From here, on behalf of us all, I offer my support to them. Their determination and the strength of the IDF are what will enable us to create the new situation.

Mr. Speaker, distinguished Knesset,

These two missions—arriving at a permanent settlement with the Palestinians, and achieving peace with Syria and Lebanon—are, in my eyes, equally vital and urgent. One neither outranks the other, nor has priority over it.

The Government's objective will be to act, at the same time, to bring peace closer on all fronts, but without compromising on Israel's security needs and most vital interests—first and foremost among them, a united Jerusalem, the eternal capital of Israel, under our sovereignty. We will not be deterred by the difficulties.

I know very well that difficult negotiations, replete with crises and ups-and-downs, await us before we reach our desired goal.

I can only promise that, if the other side displays the same degree of determination and good will to reach an agreement as on our side, no force in the world will prevent us from achieving peace here.

In this context, I attach the greatest importance to the support of our partners to peace treaties: Egypt and Jordan. I believe that President Hosni Mubarak and King Abdullah can play a vital role in creating the dynamics and an atmosphere of trust so needed for progress toward peace. They can also advance education for peace among the children of Egypt and Jordan, the Palestinians and, in the future, also of Syria and Lebanon—education for peace, which is a condition for any long-term, stable peace. I am convinced that King Hassan of Morocco can also contribute to this, as can other countries who already, in the past, opened channels of communication with Israel, cooperating with the peace process in various spheres. My aspiration will be to firmly resume these contacts in order to create a favorable regional atmosphere that can assist the negotiations.

It goes without saying that the assistance of the United States is a fundamental condition for any progress toward resolving the conflict in the region. The friendship of America, under the leadership of President Clinton, its generosity and the intensity of its support for the peace process in the Middle East constitute a vital component in the chance to achieve our goal. I will soon leave for the United States, at the invitation of President Clinton, a loyal friend of Israel, in order to discuss the gamut of issues facing us, first and foremost, the renewal of the peace process on all tracks, and the fortification of the strength and security of Israel.

[...]

Source: Ehud Barak, "Speech by Prime Minister Barak on the Presentation of the Government to the Knesset, Jerusalem, July 6, 1999," Israel Ministry of Foreign Affairs, http://www.mfa.gov.il/MFA.

137. The Clinton Bridging Proposals [Excerpt], December 23, 2000

Introduction

In his last weeks as U.S. president, Bill Clinton made one final effort to revitalize the stalled peace process. On December 20, 2000, Israeli foreign minister Shlomo Ben-Ami and Palestinian Authority (PA) representative Saeb Erekat both visited the White House, where they met and held discussions with Clinton and Secretary of State Madeleine Albright. The two sides failed to reach agreement, impelling Clinton on December 23 to put forward proposals that he claimed summarized the differences separating each side and suggested means of resolving each issue. Although the proposals were never formally published, they were leaked to the press and published in the Israeli newspaper *Ha'aretz* a few days later. Clinton suggested that more than 90 percent of the West Bank be left in Palestinian hands and that the Israelis swap some of their own territory for those portions of the West Bank they intended to retain. He also raised the possibility that each side lease some territory from the other. Israel had stated its opposition to the creation of a Palestinian army. Clinton advocated the introduction of an international peacekeeping force that would supervise the implementation of the agreements, with Israeli forces also present in Palestinian territory for an initial three years. With the approval of the international force, Israeli military units would be able to enter Palestinian territory in case of an "[i]mminent and demonstrable threat to Israel's national security of a military nature that requires the activation of a national state emergency." In the case of Jerusalem, he suggested that Arab areas and Muslim holy places should come under Palestinian sovereignty and that Jewish ones should come under Israeli sovereignty. Palestinian refugees would have the right to return to the Palestinian state but could only return to Israel if the Israeli government agreed to admit them.

Primary Source

Territory:

Based on what I heard, I believe that the solution should be in the mid-90 percents, between 94–96 percent of the West Bank territory of the Palestinian State. The land annexed by Israel should be compensated by a land swap of 1–3 percent in addition to territorial arrangements such as a permanent safe passage. The parties also should consider the swap of leased land to meet their respective needs. . . . The Parties should develop a map consistent with the following criteria:

— 80 percent of settlers in blocks;
— Contiguity;
— Minimize the annexed areas;
— Minimize the number of Palestinians affected.

Security:

The key lies in an international presence that can only be withdrawn by mutual consent. This presence will also monitor the implementation of the agreement between both sides.

[...]

My best judgment is that the Israeli presence would remain in fixed locations in the Jordan Valley under the authority of the international force for another 36 months. This period could be reduced in the event of favorable regional developments that diminish the threat to Israel.

On early warning stations, Israel should maintain three facilities in the West Bank with a Palestinian liaison presence. The stations will be subject to review every 10 years with any changes in the status to be mutually agreed.

Regarding emergency developments, I understand that you will still have to develop a map of the relevant areas and routes. I propose the following definition: imminent and demonstrable threat to Israel's national security of a military nature that requires the activation of a national state emergency. Of course, the international forces will need to be notified of any such determination.

On airspace, I suggest that the state of Palestine will have sovereignty over its airspace but that the two sides should work out special arrangements for Israeli training and operational needs.

I understand that the Israeli position is that Palestine should be defined as a "demilitarized state" while the Palestinian side proposes "a state with limited arms." As a compromise, I suggest calling it a "non-militarized state." This will be consistent with the fact that in addition to a strong Palestinian security force, Palestine will have an international force for border security and deterrent purposes.

[...]

Jerusalem:

The general principle is that Arab areas are Palestinian and Jewish ones are Israeli. This would apply to the Old City as well. I urge the two sides to work on maps to create maximum contiguity for both sides.

Regarding the Haram/Temple Mount, I believe that the gaps are not related to practical administration but to symbolic issues of sovereignty and to finding a way to accord respect to the religious beliefs of both sides.

I know you have been discussing a number of formulations. . . . I add to these two additional formulations guaranteeing Palestinian effective control over the Haram while respecting the conviction of the Jewish People. Regarding either one of those two formulations will be international monitoring to provide mutual confidence.

Palestinian sovereignty over the Haram and Israeli sovereignty over a) the Western Wall and the space sacred to Judaism of which it is a part or b) the Western Wall and the Holy of Holies of which it is a part. There will be a firm commitment by both not to excavate beneath the Haram or behind the Wall.

Palestinian sovereignty over the Haram and Israeli sovereignty over the Western Wall and shared functional sovereignty over the issue of excavation under the Haram and behind the Wall such that mutual consent would be required before any excavation can take place.

Refugees:
I sense that the differences are more relating to formulations and less to what will happen on a practical level. I believe that Israel is prepared to acknowledge the moral and material suffering caused to the Palestinian people as a result of the 1948 war and the need to assist the international community in addressing the problem. . . .

The fundamental gap is on how to handle the concept of the right of return. I know the history of the issue and how hard it will be for the Palestinian leadership to appear to be abandoning the principle.

The Israeli side could not accept any reference to a right of return that would imply a right to immigrate to Israel in defiance of Israel's sovereign policies and admission or that would threaten the Jewish character of the state.

Any solution must address both needs. The solution will have to be consistent with the two-state approach—the state of Palestine as the homeland of the Palestinian people and the state of Israel as the homeland of the Jewish people.

Under the two-state solution, the guiding principle should be that the Palestinian state should be the focal point for the Palestinians who choose to return to the area without ruling out that Israel will accept some of these refugees.

I believe that we need to adopt a formulation on the right of return that will make clear that there is no specific right of return to Israel itself but that does not negate the aspiration of the Palestinian people to return to the area.

I propose two alternatives:

1. Both sides recognize the right of Palestinian refugees to return to Historic Palestine. Or
2. Both sides recognize the right of Palestinian refugees to return to their homeland.

The agreement will define the implementation of this general right in a way that is consistent with the two-state solution. It would list the five possible homes for the refugees:

1. The State of Palestine
2. Areas in Israel being transferred to Palestine in the land swap
3. Rehabilitation in host country
4. Resettlement in third country
5. Admission to Israel

In listing these options, the agreement will make clear that the return to the West Bank, Gaza Strip and area acquired in the land swap would be [a] right to all Palestinian refugees, while rehabilitation in host countries, resettlement in third countries and absorption into Israel will depend upon the policies of those countries.

Israel could indicate in the agreement that it intends to establish a policy so that some [of] the refugees would be absorbed into Israel consistent with Israeli sovereign decision.

I believe that priority should be given to the refugee population in Lebanon.

The parties would agree that this implements Resolution 194.

The End of Conflict:
I propose that the agreement clearly mark the end of the conflict and its implementation put an end to all claims. This could be implemented through a UN Security Council Resolution that notes that resolutions 242 and 338 have been implemented and through the release of Palestinian prisoners.

Source: Walter Laqueur and Barry Rubin, eds., *The Israel-Arab Reader: A Documentary History of the Middle East Conflict* (New York: Penguin, 2001), 562–564.

138. Palestinian Negotiating Team, Remarks and Questions regarding the Clinton Plan [Excerpt], January 2, 2001

Introduction

After summaries of U.S. president Bill Clinton's December 2000 bridging proposals appeared in the international press, the Palestinian negotiating team quickly issued a statement explaining its own position and, more specifically, why the Palestinians found these suggestions unsatisfactory. Their fundamental objections were that Clinton's plan would divide the Palestinian state into three separate and largely unconnected territories, while Palestinian Jerusalem would consist of "unconnected islands" joined neither to each other nor to the rest of Palestine, a patchwork that the Palestinians considered unworkable. They charged that the territorial provisions for Israeli settlers were far too generous, especially given that the settlements, in their view, constituted only 2 percent of all West Bank lands. The Palestinians called instead for the resettlement in Israel of the 60,000 West Bank settlers. The Palestinian delegation also found unacceptable the provisions denying Palestinian refugees the right to return to their former homes in Israeli territory. In addition, the Palestinians were unwilling to give Israel any special military or security rights within Palestinian territory, arguing that the presence of an international force would more than suffice to handle any emergency that might arise. Clinton's proposals, the Palestinians argued, were too vague and general when the situation called for extremely specific commitments that Israel could not subsequently modulate to its own advantage. Reiterating longtime complaints that the United States always favored Israel, the Palestinians charged that overall "the United States proposal seems to respond to Israeli demands while neglecting the basic Palestinian need: a viable state." At this juncture, efforts by a lame-duck U.S. president to find a compromise solution were clearly doomed to failure.

Primary Source

[...]

We wish to explain why the latest United States proposals, taken together and as presented without clarification, fail to satisfy the condition required for a permanent peace. As it stands now, the United States proposal would:

1) divide a Palestinian state into three separate cantons connected and divided by Jewish-only and Arab-only roads and jeopardize the Palestinian state's viability;

2) divide Palestinian Jerusalem into a number of unconnected islands separate from each other and from the rest of Palestine;

3) force Palestinians to surrender the right of return of Palestinian refugees. It also fails to provide workable security arrangements between Palestine and Israel, and to address a number of other issues of importance to the Palestinian

people. The United States proposal seems to respond to Israeli demands while neglecting the basic Palestinian need: a viable state.

The United States proposals were couched in general terms that in some instances lack clarity and detail. A permanent status agreement, in our view, is not merely a document that declares general political principles. It is, rather, a comprehensive instrument that spells out the details, modalities, and timetables of ending the Palestinian-Israeli conflict. For such an agreement to be effective, it must be backed by clear, effective international implementation guarantees. We believe that a general, vague agreement at this advanced stage of the peace process will be counterproductive. This conviction has resulted from our past experiences with vague agreements and from Israel's history of noncompliance with signed agreements. The permanent status agreement must be a truly final agreement rather than an agreement to negotiate.

The United States side presented proposals regarding four primary issues: territory, Jerusalem, refugees, and security.

On the issue of territory, the United States proposed that Israel annex 4 to 6 percent of the West Bank; that the annexation be compensated through a "land swap" of 1 to 3 percent; and that the Parties also consider a swap of leased land. The United States recommended that the final map be drawn in a manner that would place 80 percent of Israeli settlers in annexed settlement blocs, but that would nevertheless promote territorial contiguity, minimize annexed areas and minimize the number of Palestinians affected.

This proposal poses a number of serious problems. As the proposal is not accompanied by a map, and because the total area from which the percentages are calculated is not defined, it is difficult to imagine how the percentages presented can be reconciled with the goal of Palestinian contiguity. This is especially worrisome in light of the fact that the Israeli side continues to insist, and the United States has never questioned, that Jerusalem, as defined by Israel, the "no-man's land," and the Dead Sea are not part of the total area from which the percentages are calculated. Moreover, the United States proposal calls for the "swap of leased land." It is not entirely clear if Palestinian interests are served by such a swap since the Palestinian side has no territorial needs in Israel, except for a corridor linking the West Bank and the Gaza Strip, which will be covered in a land swap. This proposal, taken together with the map presented by the Israeli side in the most recent round of negotiations in Washington, provides Israel with control over large swaths of land, rendering the Palestinian state unviable and lacking direct access to international borders.

Without a map clarifying the above ambiguities, the United States proposal does nothing to foreclose a return by Israel to its proposals at Camp David which leaves 10 percent of the West Bank under

Israeli sovereignty, and an additional 10 percent under Israeli control pursuant to ill-defined security arrangements. It is important to bear in mind that all of the settlements in the West Bank currently occupy approximately 2 percent of the West Bank.

In this context, the Palestinian side rejects the use of "settlement blocs" as a guiding principle as recommended by the United States proposal. The use of this criterion subordinates Palestinian interests in the contiguity of their state and control over their natural resources to Israeli interests regarding the contiguity of settlements, recognized as illegal by the international community. It also contradicts the United States proposal's criteria concerning minimizing annexed areas and the number of Palestinians affected. In addition, the Palestinian side needs to know exactly which settlements Israel intends to annex.

Ultimately, it is impossible to agree to a proposal that punishes Palestinians while rewarding Israel's illegal settlement policies. A proposal involving annexation of 4 to 6 percent (not to mention 10 percent) of the land would inevitably damage vital Palestinian interests. Under such a proposal, a number of Palestinian villages will be annexed to Israel, adding to the already great number of displaced Palestinians.

Moreover, as the attached map demonstrates, a large quantity of unsettled land in key development areas such as Jerusalem and Bethlehem will also be annexed by Israel, destroying the territorial contiguity of the State of Palestine. In addition to compromising Palestinians' freedom of movement within their own state, this would also have serious ramifications for the state's development potential. In addition, any such large-scale annexation will inevitably prejudice Palestinian water rights.

As for the "land swap," the United States proposal does not identify which areas within Israel are to compensate for the annexed land. The Palestinian side continues to insist that any annexed land must be compensated with land of equal size and value. No argument has been presented as to why this should not be the case. However, the United States proposal explicitly rejects the principle that compensation of land must be of equal size and remains silent on the issue of the location and quality of the compensated land. All previous Israeli and United States proposals concerning compensated land have referred to land near the Gaza Strip in exchange for valuable real estate in the West Bank. In addition to being desert areas the lands being offered near the Gaza Strip are currently being used by Israel to dump toxic waste. Obviously, we cannot accept trading prime agricultural and development land for toxic waste dumps.

[. . .]

Jerusalem
On the issue of Jerusalem, President Clinton articulated a general principle that "Arab areas are Palestinian and Jewish areas are

Israeli," but urged the two sides to work on maps to create maximum contiguity for both. Two alternative formulations were presented addressing each State's sovereignty over and rights to the Haram al-Sharif ("Haram") and the "Western Wall" ("Wall"). Both formulations provide for Palestinian sovereignty over the Haram and Israeli sovereignty over the Wall, restricting the Parties from excavating beneath the Haram or behind the Wall.

The United States formulations on the Haram are problematic. First, the proposal appears to recognize Israeli sovereignty under the Haram by implying that it has a right, which it voluntarily relinquishes, to excavate behind the Western Wall (i.e., the area under the Haram). Moreover, the "Western Wall" extends to areas beyond the Wailing Wall, including the tunnel opened in 1996 by Israel's former Prime Minister Benjamin Netanyahu which caused widespread confrontations.

The territorial aspects of the United States proposals concerning Jerusalem also raise very serious concerns and call for further clarification. As the attached map shows, as a result of Israel's internationally condemned settlement policy in occupied East Jerusalem, the United States formulation "that Arab areas are Palestinian and Jewish ones are Israeli" will be impossible to reconcile with the concept of "maximum contiguity for both," presented in the proposal. Rather, the formulation will inevitably result in Palestinian islands within the city separated from one another. Israel, however, will be able to maintain contiguity.

Therefore, the proposal in actually calling for "maximum contiguity for both" translates in practice into "maximum contiguity for Israel."

Israel's continued demand for sovereignty over a number of geographically undefined "religious sites" in Jerusalem, and its refusal to present maps clearly showing its territorial demands in Jerusalem only compounds the Palestinian concerns. Any formulation that will be acceptable by the Palestinian side must guarantee the contiguity of Palestinian areas within the city as well as the contiguity of Jerusalem with the rest of Palestine.

A key element of the Palestinian position on Jerusalem is its status as an Open City with free access for all. This status is imperative not only to ensure access to and worship in all holy sites for all those who hold the city sacred, but also to guarantee free movement through the State of Palestine. Unfortunately, the United States proposal makes no reference to this essential concept.

Palestinian Refugees
On the issue of Palestinian refugees, driven from their homes as a result of the establishment of the State of Israel, the United States proposed that both sides recognize the right of Palestinian refugees to return either to "historic Palestine" or to "their homeland," but added that the agreement should make clear that there is no

specific right of return to what is now Israel. Instead, it proposed five possible final homes for the refugees: (1) the State of Palestine; (2) areas in Israel transferred to Palestine in the "land swap"; (3) rehabilitation in the host countries; (4) resettlement in third countries; and (5) admission to Israel. All refugees would have the right to "return" to the State of Palestine; however, rehabilitation in host countries, resettlement in third countries, and admission to Israel all would depend on the policies of those individual countries.

The United States proposal reflects a wholesale adoption of the Israeli position that the implementation of the right of return be subject entirely to Israel's discretion. It is important to recall that Resolution 194, long regarded as the basis for a just settlement of the refugee problem, calls for the return of Palestinian refugees to "their homes," wherever located, not to their "homeland" or to "historic Palestine."

The essence of the right of return is choice: Palestinians should be given the option to choose where they wish to settle, including return to the homes from which they were driven. There is no historical precedent for a people abandoning their fundamental right to return to their homes whether they were forced to leave or fled in fear. We will not be the first people to do so. Recognition of the right to return and the provision of choice to refugees is a prerequisite for the closure of the conflict.

The Palestinians are prepared to think flexibly and creatively about the mechanisms for implementing the right of return. In many discussions with Israel, mechanisms for implementing this right in such a way so as to end the refugee status and refugee problem, as well as to otherwise accommodate Israeli concerns, have been identified and elaborated in some detail. The United States proposal fails to make reference to any of these advances and refers back to earlier Israeli negotiating positions.

In addition, the United States proposal fails to provide any assurance that refugee rights to restitution and compensation will be fulfilled.

Security
On the issue of security, the United States proposed that there be an international presence to guarantee the implementation of the agreement. The United States proposal suggests that the Israeli withdrawal should be carried out over a three-year period, with international forces phased in on a gradual basis. Then, at the end of this period, an Israeli military presence would be allowed to remain in the Jordan Valley for another three years under the authority of the international force.

The United States also proposed that Israel be permitted to maintain three early warning stations for at least ten years and that it be given the right to deploy its forces in Palestinian territory during

"a national state of emergency." In addition, the United States has suggested that Palestine be defined as a "nonmilitarized State," and, while acknowledging Palestinian sovereignty over its own airspace, it has proposed that the two sides develop special arrangements for Israeli training and operational needs.

Although the United States proposals place less burdens on Palestinian sovereignty than earlier Israeli proposals, they nevertheless raise a number of concerns. There is no reason why Israel would require three years to withdraw from the West Bank and Gaza Strip. In view of the fact that Israel resettled more than one million immigrants from the former Soviet Union in a few years, one year is more than enough time to resettle less than 60,000 Israeli settlers. It is moreover unclear from the United States proposal that the withdrawal period relates to both soldiers and settlers, both of whom are considered part of the occupation forces in the Palestinian Territories. A protracted withdrawal process could jeopardize the peaceful implementation of the agreement and would create a continued source of friction.

There are other Palestinian concerns. Israel has yet to make a persuasive case regarding why it would require either a standing force in the Jordan Valley or emergency deployment rights—much less both. This is especially the case given that international forces will be present in these areas. Furthermore, Israel requires no more than one early warning station in the West Bank to satisfy its strategic needs. The maintenance of stations at current locations near Ramallah and Nablus and in East Jerusalem will seriously inhibit Palestinian development. Moreover, the United States proposal would give Israel sole discretion for determining how long these stations will be operational.

The United States proposal's suggestion that special arrangements be made for Israeli training and operational needs in Palestinian airspace is also extremely problematic. Without specific clarification, this might be used to defend a right for Israel to use Palestinian airspace for military training exercises with all the accompanying dangers to the Palestinian civilian population and the environment while sparing Israeli citizens from any similar infringement. Palestinians remain committed to working out regional agreements concerning aviation in line with commonly accepted international regulations. Any arrangement to the contrary would infringe on Palestinian sovereignty and harm relations with neighboring countries.

Other Issues
The United States proposal remains silent on a number of issues that are essential for the establishment of a lasting and comprehensive peace. By focusing solely on the four issues above, the United States proposal not only neglects matters relating to ending the conflict, but also disregards ways to ensure that the future relations between the two peoples will be mutually beneficial. Specifically,

the proposal does not address water, compensation for damages resulting from over thirty years of occupation, the environment, future economic relations, and other state-to-state issues.

End of Conflict

While we are totally committed to ending the Palestinian-Israeli conflict, we believe that this can only be achieved once the issues that have caused and perpetrated the conflict are resolved in full. This in turn can only be achieved by a comprehensive agreement that provides detailed modalities for the resolution of the issues at the core of the conflict. It must be remembered that in reaching a settlement between Israel and, respectively, Egypt and Jordan, the end of conflict came only after the final, detailed peace treaty.

Even putting aside the requirements of international law and justice, the United States proposals—unless clarified to take into account the above concerns—do not even allow for a pragmatic resolution of the conflict. If no such solutions are reached in practice, we believe that any formalistic pronouncement of the end of conflict would be meaningless.

Conclusion

We would like, once again, to emphasize that we remain committed to a peaceful resolution of the Palestinian-Israeli conflict in accordance with UN Security Council Resolutions 242 and 338 and international law. In view of the tremendous human cost caused by each delay in negotiations, we recognize the need to resolve this conflict as soon as possible. We cannot, however, accept a proposal that secures neither the establishment of a viable Palestinian state nor the right of Palestinian refugees to return to their homes.

Source: Walter Laqueur and Barry Rubin, eds., *The Israel-Arab Reader: A Documentary History of the Middle East Conflict* (New York: Penguin, 2001), 567–573.

139. United Nations Report on Human Rights in Occupied Territories [Excerpt], March 16, 2001

Introduction

In late September 2000, a new wave of violence erupted in the occupied territories, provoked in the first instance by an ill-judged visit by Israeli opposition politician and former defense minister Ariel Sharon to the Muslim al-Aqsa Mosque on the Temple Mount in Jerusalem. Ever since his implication in the 1982 massacre of hundreds of Palestinians in Beirut, Sharon had been a controversial figure, much hated by Arabs. Within a day, his visit on September 28 triggered large-scale riots in Arab Jerusalem that quickly spread to the occupied territories under the jurisdiction of the Palestinian Authority (PA). Israeli forces responded drastically, and in the first

six days of what became the Second (al-Aqsa) Intifada, which lasted four years, killed 61 Palestinians, and injured another 2,567. During the Yom Kippur (Day of Atonement) holiday, groups of Israelis attacked Arabs with stones, and communal violence quickly escalated. On October 12 a Palestinian mob seized from police custody and beat to death 2 Israeli reservists whom Palestinian authorities had arrested after they entered the town of Ramallah in the West Bank, murders that were filmed by a foreign camera crew and broadcast on television. On October 19 the United Nations (UN) set up a commission to investigate the human rights situation in Israel. In February 2001 the three commissioners, Professor Richard Falk of Princeton University, Professor John Dugard of Leiden University, and Dr. Kamal Hosain, former prime minister of Bangladesh, visited Israel and the occupied territories. The report they submitted the following March painted a grim picture of mutual Palestinian and Israeli incomprehension of each other's positions and perspectives. "Each side," they stated, "has felt justified in taking the action that has accompanied recent moves, although each side gives its own self-serving interpretation of its legal, moral and political character." The report was highly critical of the human rights situation in the occupied territories and especially of what the commissioners considered the "disproportionate" use of force by Israeli security personnel to repress the riots, tactics that the commissioners charged amounted to the "comprehensive denial of human rights and the continuing pattern of behaviour violative of international humanitarian law." The commissioners highlighted the greatly disproportionate ratio of Palestinian to Israeli casualties, charging that Israeli soldiers frequently responded with bullets to groups of young people armed largely with stones. Hostile Israeli critics charged that the commission was biased against Israel and had failed to interview Israeli officials, but the publication of its report was nonetheless a harsh indictment of the conduct of Israeli security personnel and did much to damage Israel's international image.

Primary Source

[. . .]

III. CLARIFYING THE CONTEXT: ILLUSION AND REALITY

16. It was evident in all phases of our inquiry into the patterns of violations of human rights and international humanitarian law during the second intifada that an appreciation of the behaviour of the parties involved depended on having an understanding of the surrounding context. Each side has felt justified in taking the action that has accompanied recent moves, although each side gives its own self-serving interpretation of its legal, moral and political character. It is important to comprehend these differences in the process of seeking an objective assessment of the various allegations of violative conduct. It is just as important to avoid equating adversary positions as equally persuasive. In the setting of the Israeli-Palestinian relationship it is of pervasive significance that

the Palestinian people are struggling to realize their right of self-determination, which by virtue of international law and morality provides the foundation for the exercise of other rights. Of comparable significance is the appreciation of the extent to which Israel's continued occupation of Palestinian territories has remained the most formidable obstacle to Palestinian self-determination.

17. The Commission came away from this inquiry with two overriding assessments that are at once discouraging and illuminating.

18. The first involves perceptions, and focuses on the extent to which the two sides perceive the central reality of their respective positions from diametrically opposed constructions of the meaning of recent events. In essence, the Government of Israel and most Israelis conceive of the breakdown of the Oslo process as creating for them a severe and novel security crisis. Most Israelis view the second intifada as an indication that Palestinians are unwilling to resolve their conflict by peaceful means, having rejected what is regarded as a generous offer by the Government of Israel at the Camp David II and Taba stages of the Final Status negotiations. The nature of this crisis is such that, according to this dominant Israeli perspective, the encounter with the Palestinians has moved from a relationship between an occupying Power and an occupied people to one between conflicting parties in a state of belligerency or war, implying a virtual absence of legal and moral constraints, at least on the Israeli side, provided only that a self-serving argument of military necessity is set forth.

19. In the starkest possible contrast, the Palestinian Authority and most Palestinians perceive the current phase of their relationship with Israel as brought about by a combination of the distortions associated with the implementation of the Oslo principles, the failure to implement a series of authoritative United Nations resolutions, most particularly Security Council resolutions 242 (1968) and 338 (1973), and grave breaches by Israel of the Fourth Geneva Convention. These aspects of the situation are further seen as responsible for the full harshness of Israeli occupation as it affects adversely the daily lives of the Palestinians. Such circumstances are regarded as profoundly aggravated by the continued expansion of Israeli settlements throughout the period of the Oslo process and by the IDF role in their protection. The combination of these elements is regarded by most Palestinians as the proximate cause of the escalating spiral of violence set off by the provocative events at Harem al-Sharif/Temple Mount on 28 September 2000. In this regard, the second intifada is viewed as a spontaneous series of moderate and proportional responses to an occupation that has been maintained and perpetuated in defiance of the authority of the United Nations since it was established in 1967. From this perspective, the Palestinians contend that they continue to seek a negotiated end to the conflict to attain a peaceful settlement that is fair to both sides and upholds the security of both peoples on the basis of mutuality.

20. Our second closely related conclusion is associated with the somewhat disguised link between the modality of Israeli occupation as a result of changes brought about by the Oslo process and the subsequent intifada, with its escalating spiral of violence. It is of critical importance to appreciate the interaction between the redeployment of the IDF since 1994 and the implementation of the Oslo Accords. In effect, the IDF withdrew by stages from most of the areas on the West Bank and Gaza inhabited by the bulk of the Palestinian population, and yet sustained, and even intensified, its control over the borders between the Palestinian territories and Israel and among the various districts internal to the OPT. Even more significantly, owing to the retention of the settlements situated throughout the Palestinian territories, as the accompanying map makes clear (annex IV), the West Bank and Gaza were divided into "A", "B", and "C" areas, with the Palestinian Authority exercising full administrative control over A, while Israel exercises security control over B and retains exclusive control over C. In effect, a series of internal boundaries were established by agreements implementing the Oslo Accords, so as to enable Israel to provide protection to the settlements while withdrawing from areas densely populated by Palestinians. The effect of such a redistricting of the Palestinian territories was to produce a situation of extreme fragmentation, making travel very burdensome for Palestinians who went, for work or otherwise, from one part of the territories to another: checkpoints were maintained where detailed searches were carried out that resulted in long waits and frequent humiliation, greatly burdening Palestinian rights of movement even under normal circumstances. In the course of the second intifada, this already difficult situation has been severely aggravated by frequent closures and blockades that have prevented the movement of goods and persons across both internal and external borders. Most Palestinians described the situation of recent months as living under "a state of siege".

21. Such a pattern of control and security can only be understood in relation to the settlements and their need for safe access to and from Israel. The main IDF function in the occupied Palestinian territories is to guard the settlements and the access and bypass roads. The relationship is such that the settlers are given unconditional priority whenever their presence impinges upon that of the Palestinian indigenous population. For instance, all Palestinian traffic is stopped while a single settler vehicle passes on an access road, causing long delays and much resentment. While travelling, particularly in Gaza, the Commission had its own direct experience of this situation. When a violent incident occurs, Israeli closures further inhibit travel, often preventing or greatly detaining even emergency traffic, such as ambulances. The Commission verified several accounts of deaths due to an inability of Palestinians to receive timely medical attention. Israel has invested heavily in an elaborate system of bypass roads in the West Bank designed to provide most settlements and the IDF with the means to travel to and from Israel, and between settlements, without passing through Palestinian-controlled areas. Palestinians view these roads with alarm, both because of their

substantial and symbolic encroachment upon the heart of a future Palestinian State and, more so, because the magnitude of the investment and effort involved in such a development seems to impart an Israeli view that most of the settlements on the West Bank will never be removed. This situation contrasts with Gaza, where access roads cut through Palestinian territory and have not been specially constructed. In this regard, the settlement structure in Gaza seems removable by negotiations on final status in a manner that at present does not appear likely in relation to the West Bank.

22. Part of the perceptual gap is associated with the effects and nature of the violence. Israelis appear to connect most of their casualties with the stone-throwing demonstrations, interspersed at times with Palestinian gunfire. The Palestinians associate casualties on their side mainly with what they view as Israeli/IDF overreaction to these demonstrations. It was the clear judgement of the Commission that Palestinian casualties were indeed mainly associated with these direct encounters, but that, to the best of our knowledge, the IDF, operating behind fortifications with superior weaponry, endured not a single serious casualty as a result of Palestinian demonstrations and, further, their soldiers seemed to be in no life-threatening danger during the course of these events. It was the definite view of the Commission that the majority of Israeli casualties resulted from incidents on settlement roads and at relatively isolated checkpoints at the interface between A, B, and C areas, that is, as a consequence of the settlements, and irritations resulting indirectly therefrom. In this regard, account must be taken of settler violence against Palestinian civilians in areas adjoining settlements, and of IDF complicity in such violence. A pervasive feature of the tensions associated with the second intifada is the clear affinity between the IDF and Jewish settlement communities, and the equally evident hostility between these communities and the surrounding Palestinian population.

23. The language associated with the second intifada is also relevant to an assessment of human rights violations and violations of international humanitarian law. Both sides tend to view the violence of the other side as comprising "terrorism". The Israelis view attacks by Palestinians, especially beyond "the Green Line" (pre-1967 Israel), as terrorism even if directed against official targets such as IDF soldiers or government officials. Palestinians regard the IDF tactics involving shooting unarmed civilian demonstrators (especially children) or relying on tanks and helicopters against demonstrators, in retaliation for shots fired from refugee camps, and assassinations of targeted individuals as State terrorism. The legal status of these patterns of violence is difficult to establish authoritatively. Part of the current complexity relates to the Israeli contention that a condition of armed conflict has replaced that of belligerent occupancy as a result of IDF withdrawals from A zones, and the transfer of governing authority in those areas to the PA. Another part of the complexity arises from the Palestinians' contention that they enjoy a right of resistance to an illegal occupation.

24. There is another fundamental discrepancy of perception. Israel believes that its security measures, including border and road closures, represent reasonable, even restrained, measures of response to Palestinian unrest and opposition. To the extent that Israel relies on the superiority of its weaponry or inflicts most of the casualties, such behaviour is rationalized as necessary to demoralize a numerically superior enemy, nipping its resistance in the bud. Such lines of explanation were set forth by Israeli witnesses to explain and justify even the use of live ammunition by the IDF against unarmed Palestinian demonstrators during the opening days of the second intifada. During these crucial days there was no evidence of Palestinian gunfire.

25. The Palestinians view this link between Palestinian acts of resistance and Israeli responses from an entirely different angle of interpretation. To Palestinians, the Israeli use of force from day one of the second intifada, and indeed before Ariel Sharon's visit on 28 September to the Al Aqsa mosque, was intended to crush any Palestinian impulse to oppose openly the continued Israeli domination and occupation of the West Bank and Gaza. For most Palestinians, the closures of roads and borders, destruction of homes and property, and accompanying measures of curfews and restrictions are regarded as clear expressions of an Israeli policy of inflicting collective punishment upon all Palestinian inhabitants. Palestinians also rejected the view that the Palestinian Authority, and its police, had the capacity to prevent hostile demonstrations or to ensure the absence of violent incidents involving targets within Israel. When Israel responded to such events by punishing the territories as a whole it was viewed by Palestinians as vindictive, unjust and illegal because such a response lacked any discernible connection to either the perpetrator or to prospects for deterrence of future violence.

26. Closely related to such perceptions are differences of viewpoint as to the nature of the second intifada. Israelis tended to contrast the first with [the] second intifadas. The first intifada was seen in retrospect by Israelis as having been a largely spontaneous, bottom-up and non-violent expression of opposition to Israeli occupation. It was, in such circumstances, not reasonable to hold the Palestinian leadership responsible for the disorder. According to Israelis, the second intifada was instigated from above so as to mount a timely challenge to the Israeli leadership at a delicate moment in the peace negotiations. It was a calculated plan to improve upon an exceedingly weak Palestinian bargaining position and it also represented a serious failure by the Palestinian Authority to carry out its obligations under the Interim Agreements flowing from Oslo to maintain security for Israel in areas subject to its authority.

27. The Palestinians see the second intifada from an entirely different perspective, essentially from the outlook of an occupied people. They regard the demonstrations as spontaneous eruptions of pent-up hostile sentiment arising from years of frustration, disappointment and humiliation. Palestinians interpret the Israeli responses

as consistent with the basic structure of the occupation of their territories, as one-sided, lacking in empathy for the Palestinian civilian population, and designed to punish and crush any signs of resistance.

28. From this perspective, the Palestinians see the greater reliance by Israel on heavy weapons and deadly fire in the second intifada, as compared to the first, as seeking to discourage Palestinians from either raising the level of their resistance or resisting altogether. This reliance on the tactics of war is also perceived as providing Israel with a pretext for avoiding the restraints associated with the exercise of police responsibilities or relating to the application of standards of human rights.

29. In addition to these basic structural issues, it is of great importance to appreciate the added vulnerability of Palestinian refugees who comprise about 50 per cent of the population in the Palestinian territories and whose number is increasing at a rate of more than 3 per cent per annum. While the Israelis tend to perceive Palestinians resident in the territories as a single reality, without according any special attention to the refugees, the Palestinians are far more conscious of the acute suffering that Israeli security measures have brought to the refugee communities during this second intifada.

30. These refugees have been particularly victimized during the second intifada, often being trapped within their crowded confines by closure and curfew measures, which has made it impossible for many refugees to keep their jobs. Unemployment is high, savings almost non-existent, with great suffering resulting. Also, for historical reasons, the Palestinian refugees, alone among refugee communities in the world, fall outside the protective regime of the Office of the United Nations High Commissioner for Refugees (UNHCR). UNRWA provides relief and humanitarian aid, but is not constitutionally or politically empowered to provide needed protection, a conclusion supported for us by discussions with leading United Nations officials and NGO experts.

31. A further fundamental question of human rights relates to the extreme differences between the parties on matters pertaining to the core dispute, the wider refugee issue and its relationship to a successful peace process. The Israeli consensus regards the assertion of any serious demand to implement a Palestinian right of return in relation to Palestinians expelled from 530 villages in 1948 as a decisive complication in the search for "peace". The Palestinian approach is more varied and tentative. Some Palestinians do insist that the right of return be fully implemented in accordance with international law, which accords priority to repatriation to the extent desired. More frequently, Palestinians seem more flexible on this matter, seeking mainly a symbolic acknowledgement by Israel of the hardships associated with the expulsions, some provision for compensation and some possibilities for Palestinian family unification. This Palestinian view suggests that if there is Israeli good will

on other outstanding issues, such as Jerusalem and the settlements, then controversy over the right of return can be addressed in a manner that takes account of practical realities that have developed in the course of the more than 50 years since the critical events.

32. Overall, the Government of Israel and Israeli public opinion tend to regard all Israeli uses of force as reasonable measures of security, given the altered connection between the two societies as a result of the IDF redeployment associated with the Oslo process. Such security measures need to be stringent and intrusive so as to afford protection to the settlements, and to settler movement to and from Israel. Israeli security is a catch-all justification for all policies directed coercively at the people of Palestine. Such a major premise enables the Israeli outlook to view any Palestinian recourse to force as tantamount to "terrorism". The perceptual gap is greatest on this issue of violence and its interpretation, as Palestinians view their acts of opposition as reasonable responses to an illegal occupation of their homeland, treating their violence as produced by consistent Israeli overreaction to non-violent resistance. Additionally, Palestinians universally reject Israel's wider security rationale and view restrictions on movement, closures, property destruction, political assassinations, sniper shootings and the like as punitive and vindictive practices inconsistent with their fundamental human rights, as well as with the minimum restraints embodied in international humanitarian law.

33. There is one comprehensive observation bearing on the perception of United Nations authority by the two sides. Israelis tend to view the United Nations and most of the international community as completely unsympathetic to their quest for security, as well as biased in favour of Palestinian claims and grievances. On their side, the Palestinians feel disillusioned about the effectiveness of United Nations support and abandoned in their hour of need for elemental protection. Palestinians refer to the myriad United Nations resolutions supporting their cause, but never implemented. In this sense, both sides are currently suspicious about the role of the United Nations, its outlook, capacity and commitment.

34. Three conclusions follow from this consideration of Israeli-Palestinian perceptual gaps:

(a) The importance of encouraging better contact between persons of good will on both sides so that communication between the parties is more open and takes greater account of the views of the other side. This observation applies particularly to journalists, currently by and large confined within their respective societies, who tend to provide readers with partisan accounts of the interaction of Israelis and Palestinians that are uncritical of their respective official positions and to employ language that reinforces "enemy" stereotypes of "the other";

(b) The challenge to the organs of the United Nations to rehabilitate their reputation in relation to both Israel and the

Palestinian Authority, and the two populations, by seeking to achieve objectivity in apportioning legal and political responsibility, in calling for certain conduct in the name of international law, and in fashioning proposals for peace and reconciliation. As important, or more so, is the need to take steps to ensure that United Nations directives, whether in the form of resolutions or otherwise, are implemented to the extent possible, and that non-compliance is addressed by follow-up action;

(c) An appreciation that a commitment to objectivity does not imply a posture of "neutrality" with respect to addressing the merits of controversies concerning alleged violations of human rights and international humanitarian law. Judgements can and must be made. It is useful to recall in this connection the statement of the Israeli Minister for Foreign Affairs, Shlomo Ben-Ami, on 28 November 2000 in the course of a Cabinet discussion, opposing the release of supposed Palestinian transgressors during the early stages of the second intifada: "Accusations made by a well-established society about how a people it is oppressing is breaking the rules to attain its rights do not have much credence" (article by Akiva Elder in *Ha'aretz*, 28 November 2000). Such a perspective underlies the entire undertaking of our report. We have attempted to the extent possible to reflect the facts and law fairly and accurately in relation to both sides, but we have evaluated the relative weight of facts and contending arguments about their legal significance. This process alone enables us to draw firm conclusions about the existence of violations of international legal standards of human rights and of international humanitarian law.

[…]

X. CONCLUSIONS AND RECOMMENDATIONS

104. The commission of inquiry has been deeply mindful of its responsibility to exercise every care to be objective and impartial in gathering information and evaluating the evidence upon which it would base its conclusions and recommendations with the aim of calling attention to violations of human rights and international humanitarian law since 29 September 2000, and encouraging future compliance with international obligations to the extent possible.

105. In making its recommendations, the Commission from the outset emphasizes the need to understand the context and circumstances in which violations of human rights and breaches of international humanitarian law have occurred and the situation which has given rise to an ascending spiral of violence since the end of September 2000, resulting in a serious deterioration of the human rights situation.

106. The historical context is one of conflict and successive wars (over 50 years), prolonged occupation (over 30 years) and a pro-

tracted peace process (over 7 years). The peoples affected continue to suffer from a legacy of distrust, humiliation and frustration, only occasionally relieved by glimmerings of hope, which has all but disappeared of late.

107. The most worrying aspect of the recent escalation of violence leading to the loss of lives, disabling injuries caused to thousands, and the destruction of property and livelihoods is that the hopes and expectations created by the peace process are for the moment being smothered by mutual perceptions ascribing the worst of motives to each other, thus generating intense distrust and negative and destructive emotions.

108. It is important to emphasize that both the Palestinian people and the people of Israel have a yearning for peace and security, and that a precondition for achieving a just and durable peace is for every effort to be made on all sides to ease tensions, calm passions and promote a culture of peace. This could be helped if the process through which negotiations for peace are pursued is transparent, so that both Palestinian and Israeli public opinion can be built up in support of the process and of its eventual outcome. In this way, the mutual confidence upon which a durable peace must rest could be nurtured.

109. The Commission was encouraged by the extent to which its own assessments of the main issues addressed in the report substantially coincided with the most trustworthy third party views, including those of diplomatic representatives of the European Union and senior international civil servants with years of experience in the region. Thus, an informed and impartial consensus reinforces the conclusions and recommendations set forth here.

110. It is with an understanding of the tragic history of the peoples involved, and its psychological legacy, that our recommendations, aimed at discouraging the persistence of recent violations of human rights, are set out in three parts. The first part seeks to address the root causes that need to be resolutely addressed and resolved. The second part lists safeguards and procedures that need to be observed while negotiations aimed at a comprehensive, just and durable peace are pursued in good faith. The third part presents a series of measures which can be taken immediately to deter further violence and to end the destruction of lives, property and livelihoods. The fourth part is more ambitious, recommending steps for establishing a climate conducive to the emergence over time of a just and durable peace for the peoples of Israel and Palestine.

1. Conditions for a just and durable peace

111. A comprehensive, just and durable peace is to be sought through negotiations in good faith that would end the occupation and establish a dispensation that meets the legitimate expectations of the Palestinian people concerning the realization of their right to

self-determination and the genuine security concerns of the people of Israel.

112. While noting that it is the Israeli position that occupation has in effect ended in much of the occupied territories following the agreements reached leading to the establishment of the Palestinian Authority, as well as the fact that the ultimate disposition of the settlements in those territories is a matter for negotiation between the parties, it needs to be recognized that, from the Palestinian perspective, so long as the settlements remain as a substantial presence in the occupied territories, and Israeli military forces are deployed to protect those settlements, no meaningful end to occupation can be said to have taken place.

2. Human rights and humanitarian law imperatives

113. The framework for a final peaceful settlement and the process through which it is pursued should be guided at all stages by respect for human rights and humanitarian law and the full application of international human rights standards set out in the Universal Declaration of Human Rights and in applicable human rights instruments, in particular those relating to women, children and refugees.

114. An adequate and effective international presence needs to be established to monitor and regularly report on compliance by all parties with human rights and humanitarian law standards in order to ensure full protection of the human rights of the people of the occupied territories. Such an international mechanism should be established immediately and constituted in such a manner as to reflect a sense of urgency about protecting the human rights of the Palestinian people.

115. Protection needs to be accorded to the people of the occupied territories in strict compliance with the 1949 Geneva Convention Relative to the Protection of Civilians in Time of War (Fourth Geneva Convention). The High Contracting Parties, individually and collectively, need urgently to take appropriate and effective action to respond to an emergency situation calling for measures to alleviate the daily suffering of the Palestinian people flowing from the severe breaches of the Fourth Geneva Convention. Article One of the Convention places a duty on the High Contracting Parties "to respect and ensure respect" of the provisions of the Convention "in all circumstances". The Commission recalls that the Conference of the High Contracting Parties to the Fourth Geneva Convention, convened in Geneva on 15 July 1999, in its concluding statement reaffirmed the applicability of the Fourth Geneva Convention to the occupied Palestinian territory, including East Jerusalem, and reiterated the need for full respect for the provisions of the Convention in that Territory, and further recorded the following decision:

Taking into consideration the improved atmosphere in the Middle East as a whole, the Conference was adjourned on the understand-

ing that it will convene again in the light of consultations on the development of the humanitarian situation in the field.

In view of the serious deterioration of the humanitarian situation in the Territory, the Commission recommends that the High Contracting Parties should act with urgency to reconvene the Conference. Such a Conference should establish an effective international mechanism for taking the urgent measures needed.

3. Urgent measures for the protection of human rights

116. It seems incontestable that the Israeli Security Forces (i.e. the IDF and the Israeli Police Force) have used excessive and disproportionate force from the outset of the second intifada, whether their conduct is measured by the standards of international humanitarian law applicable to armed conflict, the codes of conduct applicable to policing in situations not amounting to armed conflict or by the open-fire regulations binding upon members of the Israeli Security Forces. In these circumstances there is an urgent need for the Israeli Security Forces to ensure that, even in life-threatening situations, great care is taken not to inflict injury on civilians not directly involved in hostile activities and not to cause disproportionate harm and injury. In non-life-threatening situations, particularly demonstrations, the security forces should comply fully with the policing codes of 1979 and 1990, as well as their own open-fire regulations. Every effort should be made by the Government of Israel to ensure that its security forces observe these rules, that such rules are made effectively known to members of the security forces, that the rules are not arbitrarily and summarily altered and that it is made clear to the security forces that violations will result in meaningful disciplinary action being taken against them.

117. The Israeli Security Forces should not resort to the use of rubber-coated bullets and live ammunition, except as a last resort. Even in life-threatening situations minimum force should be used against civilians. The Israeli Security Forces should be amply equipped and trained in non-lethal means of response, particularly for dealing with violent demonstrations. Every effort should be made to use well-established methods of crowd control.

118. The use of force by the IDF in the exercise of its role of providing security to settlers is also subject to international humanitarian law standards, including the Fourth Geneva Convention, and cannot be used for pre-emptive shooting of unarmed civilians in areas near settlements or on access and bypass roads leading to settlements or for the destruction of Palestinian property, including the demolition of homes, the cutting down of trees and the destruction of farms, and appropriate instructions to that effect should be issued to all concerned.

119. Targeted shooting of individuals by the IDF or by settlers or by sharpshooters of either side amounts to extrajudicial execution, which is a gross violation of the right to life, constitutes a breach

of international humanitarian law and would attract international criminal responsibility. Instructions should be urgently issued and disseminated by all the concerned authorities immediately to end such targeted killing.

120. Complaints regarding the use of lethal force or the excessive use of force which has caused death or serious injury should be investigated and persons found responsible should be held accountable and should not enjoy impunity.

121. Immediate and effective measures need to be taken to end closures, curfews and other restrictions on the movement of people and goods in the occupied territories so that the right to livelihood and normal economic activities are restored, as also the right of access to education and health.

122. Immediate and effective measures need to be taken to prevent the destruction of property in the occupied territories, including the demolition of houses, the cutting down of fruit and other trees, and the destruction of farms and standing crops by the use of bull-dozers and other means.

123. Prohibitions and restrictions derogating from the rights of the Palestinian people, including economic and social rights, imposed by invoking security considerations must be specifically justified and are in all cases subject to compliance with international humanitarian law standards.

124. All concerned authorities must refrain from measures that amount to collective punishment. This would include withholding transfer to the Palestinian Authority of taxes and duties collected by the Government of Israel, the imposition of restrictions on movement, or violent acts of reprisal by either side.

125. Instructions need to be issued immediately by all concerned authorities to security forces strictly to refrain from using force against or impeding the provision of medical relief and treatment by those working for the Red Cross, the Red Crescent and Magen David Adom, and in hospitals, and to ensure protection to ambulances and hospitals. These instructions should require all concerned to ensure unimpeded access for the sick, the injured and pregnant women to hospitals.

126. Compensation should be provided to victims of unlawful use of force where this has caused death, disablement, destruction of property or economic loss.

127. All impediments to the flow of humanitarian assistance, now even more urgently needed, should be removed as a matter of urgency and every effort should be made to facilitate the work of the United Nations and other bodies involved in providing humanitarian assistance and medical relief.

128. The life and safety of children and their access to education and health care should be especially protected. Special instructions should be urgently issued prohibiting shooting at unarmed children and pointing out that such acts would engage international and national criminal responsibility. Every care should be taken to ensure that children are not involved in situations where they expose themselves to risk of becoming victims of acts of violence.

129. Steps should be taken to apply article 1D of the 1951 Convention relating to the Status of Refugees to ensure that a regime of protection under the authority of the United Nations High Commissioner for Refugees is extended to Palestinian refugees, especially those currently residing in West Bank and Gaza camps. These refugees have been particularly victimized during the second intifada, are not now protected by the application of the UNRWA framework and urgently require international protection on a priority basis.

130. A mutually acceptable comprehensive settlement must deal equitably with the issue of Palestinian refugees and their rightful claims, including those refugees living outside of the Palestinian Territories. Such arrangements should be negotiated in a manner that is sensitive to legitimate Israeli concerns.

131. All restrictions on access to places of worship and all holy sites should be removed and access to them by all faiths should be respected.

4. Transforming the climate of hostility

132. The Euro-Mediterranean Agreement between the European Communities and their Member States and the State of Israel declares in article 2 that their relationship is to be based on respect for human rights and democratic principles which guide their internal and international policy; this could provide the basis for an initiative by the former to play a more pro-active role in promoting acceptance and implementation of these recommendations and in supporting the holding of consultations and dialogue at all levels between the Palestinian people and the Israeli people.

133. To improve prospects for durable peace, especially given the fundamental gaps in perception that currently separate the two sides, it is strongly recommended that the Commission on Human Rights take concrete steps to facilitate dialogue between representative Israelis and Palestinians at all levels of social interaction, formally and informally. In this regard, the Commission on Human Rights is urged to convene a consultation between leaders of Israeli and Palestinian civil society on a people-to-people basis in Geneva at the earliest possible time. In a similar spirit, to engage Europe more directly in the realities of the crisis the Commission on Human Rights is urged to convene a round table of representatives of European civil society and government to discuss steps that can be taken to alleviate the suffering of the Palestinian people and to ensure

greater respect on both sides for human rights standards and for international humanitarian law.

134. In view of the comprehensive denial of human rights and the continuing pattern of behaviour violative of international humanitarian law, this Commission recommends to the Commission on Human Rights that it establish a high profile periodic monitoring and reporting undertaking to consider the degree to which the recommendations of this report to the parties are being implemented.

[...]

> **Source:** United Nations Economic and Social Council, Commission on Human Rights, 57th Session, Item 8 of the provisional agenda, E/CN.4/2001/121, March 16, 2001, http://domino.un.org.

140. The Mitchell Report [Excerpt], April 30, 2001

Introduction

Like the United Nations (UN), the U.S. government responded quickly to the eruption of violent Palestinian-Israeli hostilities in late September 2000 that quickly developed into the Second (al-Aqsa) Intifada. In October 2000 U.S. president Bill Clinton, fearful that the spread of riots and killings throughout the Palestinian territories might derail the peace process, called a summit meeting of the principals in the hope of defusing the growing crisis. In mid-October Egyptian president Hosni Mubarak hosted a meeting at Sharm al-Sheikh in his country with Israeli prime minister Ehud Barak, Palestinian Authority (PA) president Yasser Arafat, and Clinton. Israel agreed to lift some of the restrictions imposed on the Palestinians, and Barak and Arafat each consented to resume their bilateral security cooperation. Both sought to check the escalation of violence and pledged to try to institute measures to this end. The Palestinians also insisted—over Israeli opposition—that a fact-finding commission be established to investigate the reasons for the outbreak of violence and make recommendations intended to address the situation. The body established was chaired by George Mitchell, former majority leader of the U.S. Senate. Its members comprised Suleyman Demirel, ninth president of the Republic of Turkey; Norwegian foreign minister Thorbjoern Jagland; former U.S. senator Warren B. Rudman; and Javier Solana, European Union (EU) high representative for the Common Foreign and Security Policy. Although less harshly critical of Israel's human rights record and more sympathetic to the Israeli position, the findings and recommendations of the Mitchell Report, completed at the end of April 2001 and published in May, largely resembled those of the UN human rights commission that subjected the new intifada to similar scrutiny. Both reports depicted the near total failure of Israelis and Palestinians to understand each other's positions, growing Pales-

tinian frustration over the lack of progress in the peace process, and disproportionate use of force by Israeli security personnel in response to far less well-equipped and often youthful Palestinian protestors. The Mitchell Report urged action on the part of both Israeli and Palestinian authorities to resume talks, rebuild trust, and defuse the growing conflict, measures to discourage violence on both sides and encourage the building of confidence, bilateral cooperation on security issues, and a halt to all new settlement building. Israel's response to the Mitchell Report was far more conciliatory than its reaction to the near contemporaneous findings of the admittedly more hostile UN Commission on Human Rights. Seeking to mollify public opinion in the United States, on May 30 Barak announced to the Knesset that the Israeli government accepted the Mitchell Report in full. Israel declared a unilateral cease-fire and a partial freeze on settlements, while the PA likewise, though often unavailingly, deplored violence and terrorist acts. The UN also endorsed the recommendations of the Mitchell Report. Ultimately, however, the Mitchell Report failed to halt the spiral of violence, and for several more years the intifada continued and intensified, with young Palestinian suicide bombers carrying the struggle to the civilian population of Israel.

Primary Source

SUMMARY OF RECOMMENDATIONS

The Government of Israel (GOI) and the Palestinian Authority (PA) must act swiftly and decisively to halt the violence. Their immediate objectives then should be to rebuild confidence and resume negotiations. During this mission our aim has been to fulfil the mandate agreed at Sharm el-Sheikh. We value the support given our work by the participants at the summit, and we commend the parties for their cooperation. Our principal recommendation is that they recommit themselves to the Sharm el-Sheikh spirit and that they implement the decisions made there in 1999 and 2000. We believe that the summit participants will support bold action by the parties to achieve these objectives.

The restoration of trust is essential, and the parties should take affirmative steps to this end. Given the high level of hostility and mistrust, the timing and sequence of these steps are obviously crucial. This can be decided only by the parties. We urge them to begin the process of decision immediately.

Accordingly, we recommend that steps be taken to:

END THE VIOLENCE

The GOI and the PA should reaffirm their commitment to existing agreements and undertakings and should immediately implement an unconditional cessation of violence.

The GOI and PA should immediately resume security cooperation.

REBUILD CONFIDENCE

The PA and GOI should work together to establish a meaningful "cooling off period" and implement additional confidence building measures, some of which were detailed in the October 2000 Sharm el-Sheikh Statement and some of which were offered by the U.S. on January 7, 2001 in Cairo (see Recommendations section for further description).

- The PA and GOI should resume their efforts to identify, condemn and discourage incitement in all its forms.
- The PA should make clear through concrete action to Palestinians and Israelis alike that terrorism is reprehensible and unacceptable, and that the PA will make a 100 percent effort to prevent terrorist operations and to punish perpetrators. This effort should include immediate steps to apprehend and incarcerate terrorists operating within the PA's jurisdiction.
- The GOI should freeze all settlement activity, including the "natural growth" of existing settlements.
- The GOI should ensure that the IDF adopt and enforce policies and procedures encouraging non-lethal responses to unarmed demonstrators, with a view to minimizing casualties and friction between the two communities.
- The PA should prevent gunmen from using Palestinian populated areas to fire upon Israeli populated areas and IDF positions. This tactic places civilians on both sides at unnecessary risk.
- The GOI should lift closures, transfer to the PA all tax revenues owed, and permit Palestinians who had been employed in Israel to return to their jobs; and should ensure that security forces and settlers refrain from the destruction of homes and roads, as well as trees and other agricultural property in Palestinian areas. We acknowledge the GOI's position that actions of this nature have been taken for security reasons. Nevertheless, the economic effects will persist for years.
- The PA should renew cooperation with Israeli security agencies to ensure, to the maximum extent possible, that Palestinian workers employed within Israel are fully vetted and free of connections to organizations and individuals engaged in terrorism.
- The PA and GOI should consider a joint undertaking to preserve and protect holy places sacred to the traditions of Jews, Muslims, and Christians.
- The GOI and PA should jointly endorse and support the work of Palestinian and Israeli non-governmental organizations involved in cross-community initiatives linking the two peoples.

RESUME NEGOTIATIONS

In the spirit of the Sharm el-Sheikh agreements and understandings of 1999 and 2000, we recommend that the parties meet to reaffirm their commitment to signed agreements and mutual understandings, and take corresponding action. This should be the basis for resuming full and meaningful negotiations.

INTRODUCTION

On October 17, 2000, at the conclusion of the Middle East Peace Summit at Sharm el-Sheikh, Egypt, the President of the United States spoke on behalf of the participants (the Government of Israel, the Palestinian Authority, the Governments of Egypt, Jordan, and the United States, the United Nations, and the European Union).

Among other things, the President stated that: The United States will develop with the Israelis and Palestinians, as well as in consultation with the United Nations Secretary General, a committee of fact-finding on the events of the past several weeks and how to prevent their recurrence. The committee's report will be shared by the U.S. President with the U.N. Secretary General and the parties prior to publication. A final report shall be submitted under the auspices of the U.S. President for publication.

On November 7, 2000, following consultations with the other participants, the President asked us to serve on what has come to be known as the Sharm el-Sheikh Fact-Finding Committee. In a letter to us on December 6, 2000, the President stated that: The purpose of the Summit, and of the agreement that ensued, was to end the violence, to prevent its recurrence, and to find a path back to the peace process. In its actions and mode of operation, therefore, the Committee should be guided by these overriding goals. . . . [T]he Committee should strive to steer clear of any step that will intensify mutual blame and finger-pointing between the parties. As I noted in my previous letter, "the Committee should not become a divisive force or a focal point for blame and recrimination but rather should serve to forestall violence and confrontation and provide lessons for the future." This should not be a tribunal whose purpose is to determine the guilt or innocence of individuals or of the parties; rather, it should be a fact-finding committee whose purpose is to determine what happened and how to avoid it recurring in the future.

After our first meeting, held before we visited the region, we urged an end to all violence. Our meetings and our observations during our subsequent visits to the region have intensified our convictions in this regard. Whatever the source, violence will not solve the problems of the region. It will only make them worse. Death and destruction will not bring peace, but will deepen the hatred and harden the resolve on both sides. There is only one way to peace, justice, and security in the Middle East, and that is through negotiation.

Despite their long history and close proximity, some Israelis and Palestinians seem not to fully appreciate each other's problems and concerns. Some Israelis appear not to comprehend the humiliation and frustration that Palestinians must endure every day as a result of living with the continuing effects of occupation, sustained by the presence of Israeli military forces and settlements in their midst, or the determination of the Palestinians to achieve independence and genuine self-determination. Some Palestinians appear not to comprehend the extent to which terrorism creates fear among the Israeli people and undermines their belief in the possibility of co-existence, or the determination of the GOI to do whatever is necessary to protect its people. Fear, hate, anger, and frustration have risen on both sides.

The greatest danger of all is that the culture of peace, nurtured over the previous decade, is being shattered. In its place there is a growing sense of futility and despair, and a growing resort to violence. Political leaders on both sides must act and speak decisively to reverse these dangerous trends; they must rekindle the desire and the drive for peace. That will be difficult. But it can be done and it must be done, for the alternative is unacceptable and should be unthinkable. Two proud peoples share a land and a destiny. Their competing claims and religious differences have led to a grinding, demoralizing, dehumanizing conflict. They can continue in conflict or they can negotiate to find a way to live side-by-side in peace. There is a record of achievement. In 1991 the first peace conference with Israelis and Palestinians took place in Madrid to achieve peace based on UN Security Council Resolutions 242 and 338. In 1993, the Palestine Liberation Organization (PLO) and Israel met in Oslo for the first face-to-face negotiations; they led to mutual recognition and the Declaration of Principles (signed by the parties in Washington, D.C. on September 13, 1993), which provided a road map to reach the destination agreed in Madrid. Since then, important steps have been taken in Cairo, in Washington, and elsewhere. Last year the parties came very close to a permanent settlement. So much has been achieved. So much is at risk. If the parties are to succeed in completing their journey to their common destination, agreed commitments must be implemented, international law respected, and human rights protected. We encourage them to return to negotiations, however difficult. It is the only path to peace, justice and security.

[. . .]

WHY DID IT HAPPEN?

The roots of the current violence extend much deeper than an inconclusive summit conference. Both sides have made clear a profound disillusionment with the behavior of the other in failing to meet the expectations arising from the peace process launched in Madrid in 1991 and then in Oslo in 1993. Each side has accused the other of violating specific undertakings and undermining the spirit of their commitment to resolving their political differences peacefully.

Divergent Expectations: We are struck by the divergent expectations expressed by the parties relating to the implementation of the Oslo process. Results achieved from this process were unthinkable

less than 10 years ago. During the latest round of negotiations, the parties were closer to a permanent settlement than ever before.

Nonetheless, Palestinians and Israelis alike told us that the premise on which the Oslo process is based—that tackling the hard "permanent status" issues be deferred to the end of the process—has gradually come under serious pressure. The step-by-step process agreed to by the parties was based on the assumption that each step in the negotiating process would lead to enhanced trust and confidence. To achieve this, each party would have to implement agreed-upon commitments and abstain from actions that would be seen by the other as attempts to abuse the process in order to predetermine the shape of the final outcome. If this requirement is not met, the Oslo road map cannot successfully lead to its agreed destination.

Today, each side blames the other for having ignored this fundamental aspect, resulting in a crisis in confidence. This problem became even more pressing with the opening of permanent status talks. The GOI has placed primacy on moving toward a Permanent Status Agreement in a nonviolent atmosphere, consistent with commitments contained in the agreements between the parties. "Even if slower than was initially envisaged, there has, since the start of the peace process in Madrid in 1991, been steady progress towards the goal of a Permanent Status Agreement without the resort to violence on a scale that has characterized recent weeks." The "goal" is the Permanent Status Agreement, the terms of which must be negotiated by the parties. The PLO view is that delays in the process have been the result of an Israeli attempt to prolong and solidify the occupation. Palestinians "believed that the Oslo process would yield an end to Israeli occupation in five years," the timeframe for the transitional period specified in the Declaration of Principles. Instead there have been, in the PLO's view, repeated Israeli delays culminating in the Camp David summit, where "Israel proposed to annex about 11.2% of the West Bank (excluding Jerusalem) . . ." and offered unacceptable proposals concerning Jerusalem, security and refugees. "In sum, Israel's proposals at Camp David provided for Israel's annexation of the best Palestinian lands, the perpetuation of Israeli control over East Jerusalem, a continued Israeli military presence on Palestinian territory, Israeli control over Palestinian natural resources, airspace and borders, and the return of fewer than 1% of refugees to their homes."

Both sides see the lack of full compliance with agreements reached since the opening of the peace process as evidence of a lack of good faith. This conclusion led to an erosion of trust even before the permanent status negotiations began.

Divergent Perspectives: During the last seven months, these views have hardened into divergent realities. Each side views the other as having acted in bad faith; as having turned the optimism of Oslo into the suffering and grief of victims and their loved ones. In their statements and actions, each side demonstrates a perspective that fails to recognize any truth in the perspective of the other.

The Palestinian Perspective: For the Palestinian side, "Madrid" and "Oslo" heralded the prospect of a State, and guaranteed an end to the occupation and a resolution of outstanding matters within an agreed time frame. Palestinians are genuinely angry at the continued growth of settlements and at their daily experiences of humiliation and disruption as a result of Israel's presence in the Palestinian territories. Palestinians see settlers and settlements in their midst not only as violating the spirit of the Oslo process, but also as an application of force in the form of Israel's overwhelming military superiority, which sustains and protects the settlements. The Interim Agreement provides that "the two parties view the West Bank and Gaza as a single territorial unit, the integrity and status of which will be preserved during the interim period." Coupled with this, the Interim Agreement's prohibition on taking steps which may prejudice permanent status negotiations denies Israel the right to continue its illegal expansionist settlement policy. In addition to the Interim Agreement, customary international law, including the Fourth Geneva Convention, prohibits Israel (as an occupying power) from establishing settlements in occupied territory pending an end to the conflict. The PLO alleges that Israeli political leaders "have made no secret of the fact that the Israeli interpretation of Oslo was designed to segregate the Palestinians in non-contiguous enclaves, surrounded by Israeli military-controlled borders, with settlements and settlement roads violating the territories' integrity."

According to the PLO, "In the seven years since the [Declaration of Principles], the settler population in the West Bank, excluding East Jerusalem and the Gaza Strip, has doubled to 200,000, and the settler population in East Jerusalem has risen to 170,000. Israel has constructed approximately 30 new settlements, and expanded a number of existing ones to house these new settlers." The PLO also claims that the GOI has failed to comply with other commitments such as the further withdrawal from the West Bank and the release of Palestinian prisoners. In addition, Palestinians expressed frustration with the impasse over refugees and the deteriorating economic circumstances in the West Bank and Gaza Strip.

The Israeli Perspective: From the GOI perspective, the expansion of settlement activity and the taking of measures to facilitate the convenience and safety of settlers do not prejudice the outcome of permanent status negotiations. Israel understands that the Palestinian side objects to the settlements in the West Bank and the Gaza Strip. Without prejudice to the formal status of the settlements, Israel accepts that the settlements are an outstanding issue on which there will have to be agreement as part of any permanent status resolution between the sides. This point was acknowledged and agreed upon in the Declaration of Principles of 13 September 1993 as well as other agreements between the two sides. There has in fact been

a good deal of discussion on the question of settlements between the two sides in the various negotiations toward a permanent status agreement. Indeed, Israelis point out that at the Camp David summit and during subsequent talks the GOI offered to make significant concessions with respect to settlements in the context of an overall agreement. Security, however, is the key GOI concern. The GOI maintains that the PLO has breached its solemn commitments by continuing the use of violence in the pursuit of political objectives. "Israel's principal concern in the peace process has been security. This issue is of overriding importance. . . . [S]ecurity is not something on which Israel will bargain or compromise. The failure of the Palestinian side to comply with both the letter and spirit of the security provisions in the various agreements has long been a source of disturbance in Israel."

According to the GOI, the Palestinian failure takes several forms: institutionalized anti-Israel anti-Jewish incitement; the release from detention of terrorists; the failure to control illegal weapons; and the actual conduct of violent operations, ranging from the insertion of riflemen into demonstrations to terrorist attacks on Israeli civilians. The GOI maintains that the PLO has explicitly violated its renunciation of terrorism and other acts of violence, thereby significantly eroding trust between the parties. The GOI perceives "a thread, implied but nonetheless clear, that runs throughout the Palestinian submissions. It is that Palestinian violence against Israel and Israelis is somehow explicable, understandable, legitimate."

[...]

RESUME NEGOTIATIONS

Israeli leaders do not wish to be perceived as "rewarding violence." Palestinian leaders do not wish to be perceived as "rewarding occupation." We appreciate the political constraints on leaders of both sides. Nevertheless, if the cycle of violence is to be broken and the search for peace resumed, there needs to be a new bilateral relationship incorporating both security cooperation and negotiations. We cannot prescribe to the parties how best to pursue their political objectives. Yet the construction of a new bilateral relationship solidifying and transcending an agreed cessation of violence requires intelligent risk-taking. It requires, in the first instance, that each party again be willing to regard the other as a partner. Partnership, in turn, requires at this juncture something more than was agreed in the Declaration of Principles and in subsequent agreements. Instead of declaring the peace process to be "dead," the parties should determine how they will conclude their common journey along their agreed "road map," a journey which began in Madrid and continued in spite of problems—until very recently.

To define a starting point is for the parties to decide. Both parties have stated that they remain committed to their mutual agreements and undertakings. It is time to explore further implementation. The parties should declare their intention to meet on this basis, in order to resume full and meaningful negotiations, in the spirit of their undertakings at Sharm el-Sheikh in 1999 and 2000. Neither side will be able to achieve its principal objectives unilaterally or without political risk. We know how hard it is for leaders to act—especially if the action can be characterized by political opponents as a concession —without getting something in return. The PA must—as it has at previous critical junctures—take steps to reassure Israel on security matters. The GOI must—as it has in the past—take steps to reassure the PA on political matters. Israelis and Palestinians should avoid, in their own actions and attitudes, giving extremists, common criminals and revenge seekers the final say in defining their joint future. This will not be easy if deadly incidents occur in spite of effective cooperation.

Notwithstanding the daunting difficulties, the very foundation of the trust required to re-establish a functioning partnership consists of each side making such strategic reassurances to the other.

RECOMMENDATIONS

The GOI and the PA must act swiftly and decisively to halt the violence. Their immediate objectives then should be to rebuild confidence and resume negotiations. What we are asking is not easy. Palestinians and Israelis—not just their leaders, but two publics at large—have lost confidence in one another. We are asking political leaders to do, for the sake of their people, the politically difficult: to lead without knowing how many will follow. During this mission our aim has been to fulfil the mandate agreed at Sharm el-Sheikh. We value the support given our work by the participants at the summit, and we commend the parties for their cooperation. Our principal recommendation is that they recommit themselves to the Sharm el-Sheikh spirit, and that they implement the decisions made there in 1999 and 2000. We believe that the summit participants will support bold action by the parties to achieve these objectives.

END THE VIOLENCE

- The GOI and the PA should reaffirm their commitment to existing agreements and undertakings and should immediately implement an unconditional cessation of violence.
- Anything less than a complete effort by both parties to end the violence will render the effort itself ineffective, and will likely be interpreted by the other side as evidence of hostile intent.
- The GOI and PA should immediately resume security cooperation.
- Effective bilateral cooperation aimed at preventing violence will encourage the resumption of negotiations. We are particularly concerned that, absent effective, transparent security cooperation, terrorism and other acts of violence will continue and may be seen as officially sanctioned whether they are or not. The parties should consider widening the scope of security cooperation to reflect the priorities of both communities and to seek acceptance for these efforts from those communities.
- We acknowledge the PA's position that security cooperation presents a political difficulty absent a suitable political context, i.e., the relaxation of stringent Israeli security measures combined with ongoing, fruitful negotiations. We also acknowledge the PA's fear that, with security cooperation in hand, the GOI may not be disposed to deal forthrightly with Palestinian political concerns. We believe that security cooperation cannot long be sustained if meaningful negotiations are unreasonably deferred, if security measures "on the ground" are seen as hostile, or if steps are taken that are perceived as provocative or as prejudicing the outcome of negotiations.

REBUILD CONFIDENCE

- The PA and GOI should work together to establish a meaningful "cooling off period" and implement additional confidence building measures, some of which were proposed in the October 2000 Sharm el-Sheikh Statement and some of which were offered by the U.S. on January 7, 2001 in Cairo.
- The PA and GOI should resume their efforts to identify, condemn and discourage incitement in all its forms.
- The PA should make clear through concrete action to Palestinians and Israelis alike that terrorism is reprehensible and unacceptable, and that the PA will make a 100 percent effort to prevent terrorist operations and to punish perpetrators. This effort should include immediate steps to apprehend and incarcerate terrorists operating within the PA's jurisdiction.
- The GOI should freeze all settlement activity, including the "natural growth" of existing settlements. The kind of security cooperation desired by the GOI cannot for long co-exist with settlement activity described very recently by the European Union as causing "great concern" and by the U.S. as "provocative."
- The GOI should give careful consideration to whether settlements which are focal points for substantial friction are valuable bargaining chips for future negotiations or provocations likely to preclude the onset of productive talks.
- The GOI may wish to make it clear to the PA that a future peace would pose no threat to the territorial contiguity of a Palestinian State to be established in the West Bank and the Gaza Strip.
- The IDF should consider withdrawing to positions held before September 28, 2000 which will reduce the number of friction points and the potential for violent confrontations.
- The GOI should ensure that the IDF adopt and enforce policies and procedures encouraging non-lethal responses to unarmed demonstrators, with a view to minimizing casualties and friction between the two communities.

The IDF should:

- Re-institute, as a matter of course, military police investigations into Palestinian deaths resulting from IDF actions in the Palestinian territories in incidents not involving terrorism. The IDF should abandon the blanket characterization of the current uprising as "an armed conflict short of war," which fails to discriminate between terrorism and protest.
- Adopt tactics of crowd-control that minimize the potential for deaths and casualties, including the withdrawal of metal-cored rubber rounds from general use.
- Ensure that experienced, seasoned personnel are present for duty at all times at known friction points. Ensure that the stated values and standard operating procedures of the IDF effectively instill the duty of caring for Palestinians in the West Bank and Gaza Strip as well as Israelis living there, consistent with The Ethical Code of The IDF.
- The GOI should lift closures, transfer to the PA all tax revenues owed, and permit Palestinians who had been employed in Israel to return to their jobs; and should ensure that security forces and settlers refrain from the destruction of homes and roads, as well as trees and other agricultural property in Palestinian areas. We acknowledge the GOI's position that actions of this nature have been taken for security reasons. Nevertheless, their economic effects will persist for years.
- The PA should renew cooperation with Israeli security agencies to ensure, to the maximum extent possible, that Palestinian workers employed within Israel are fully vetted and free of connections to organizations and individuals engaged in terrorism.
- The PA should prevent gunmen from using Palestinian populated areas to fire upon Israeli populated areas and IDF positions. This tactic places civilians on both sides at unnecessary risk.
- The GOI and IDF should adopt and enforce policies and procedures designed to ensure that the response to any gunfire emanating from Palestinian populated areas minimizes the danger to the lives and property of Palestinian civilians, bearing in mind that it is probably the objective of gunmen to elicit an excessive IDF response.
- The GOI should take all necessary steps to prevent acts of violence by settlers.
- The parties should abide by the provisions of the Wye River Agreement prohibiting illegal weapons.
- The PA should take all necessary steps to establish a clear and unchallenged chain of command for armed personnel operating under its authority.
- The PA should institute and enforce effective standards of conduct and accountability, both within the uniformed ranks and between the police and the civilian political leadership to which it reports.

- The PA and GOI should consider a joint undertaking to preserve and protect holy places sacred to the traditions of Muslims, Jews, and Christians. An initiative of this nature might help to reverse a disturbing trend: the increasing use of religious themes to encourage and justify violence.
- The GOI and PA should jointly endorse and support the work of Palestinian and Israeli non-governmental organizations (NGOs) involved in cross-community initiatives linking the two peoples. It is important that these activities, including the provision of humanitarian aid to Palestinian villages by Israeli NGOs, receive the full backing of both parties.

RESUME NEGOTIATIONS

We reiterate our belief that a 100 percent effort to stop the violence, an immediate resumption of security cooperation and an exchange of confidence building measures are all important for the resumption of negotiations. Yet none of these steps will long be sustained absent a return to serious negotiations.

It is not within our mandate to prescribe the venue, the basis or the agenda of negotiations. However, in order to provide an effective political context for practical cooperation between the parties, negotiations must not be unreasonably deferred and they must, in our view, manifest a spirit of compromise, reconciliation and partnership, notwithstanding the events of the past seven months.

In the spirit of the Sharm el-Sheikh agreements and understandings of 1999 and 2000, we recommend that the parties meet to reaffirm their commitment to signed agreements and mutual understandings, and take corresponding action. This should be the basis for resuming full and meaningful negotiations. The parties are at a crossroads. If they do not return to the negotiating table, they face the prospect of fighting it out for years on end, with many of their citizens leaving for distant shores to live their lives and raise their children. We pray they make the right choice. That means stopping the violence now. Israelis and Palestinians have to live, work, and prosper together. History and geography have destined them to be neighbors. That cannot be changed. Only when their actions are guided by this awareness will they be able to develop the vision and reality of peace and shared prosperity.

[...]

Source: "Sharm El-Sheikh Fact-Finding Committee Report," U.S. Department of State, http://www.state.gov/p/nea/rls/rpt/3060.htm.

141. Tenet Plan, June 13, 2001

Introduction

The Mitchell Report was only the first of several efforts by prominent U.S. officials and politicians to end the continuing violence and destruction the Second (al-Aqsa) Intifada inflicted on the Palestinian occupied territories and Israel. In June 2001 after the Mitchell Report's recommendations had proved unavailing, U.S. Central Intelligence Agency (CIA) director George Tenet put forward a plan for a comprehensive cease-fire and the end to all violent activities. The Tenet proposals envisaged the resumption of Palestinian and Israeli cooperation on security issues in which U.S. security officials would also be closely involved. Both sides were to take drastic action to restrain and discourage violence by their own people. Israel would not attack any Palestinian Authority (PA) facilities, including prisons and its security and police headquarters, while the PA would make every effort to arrest and incarcerate terrorists, and PA officials would cease giving them any assistance. Israel, on its side, would act against any Israeli citizens who were inciting violence against Palestinians and would cease responding with undue violence to crowds and demonstrations, employing only "nonlethal measures" against such opponents. Israeli and Palestinian forces would cooperate in developing methods to deal with and defuse security incidents, and each would make every effort to prevent riots occurring in the first place, preferably by establishing buffer zones, and to keep any demonstrations under control. Both would also "make a concerted effort to locate and confiscate illegal weapons." Once there had been a one-week period free of violent incidents, internal roads linking Palestinian areas would be reopened, Israeli security checkpoints would be reduced to a minimum, and the suspended negotiations on the redeployment of Israeli forces could be resumed. This plan supposedly went into effect on June 13, 2001, but the required week of peace and quiet never occurred. In March 2002 Israeli prime minister Ariel Sharon said that he would be prepared to resume the suspended talks without demanding one nonviolent week. In the interim, however, Israeli security forces had invaded previously Palestinian areas, and the Palestinians refused to begin negotiations until Israel withdrew them.

Primary Source

Palestinian-Israel Security Implementation Work Plan
The security organizations of the Government of Israel (GOI) and of the Palestinian Authority (PA) reaffirm their commitment to the security agreements forged at Sharm al-Sheikh in October 2000 embedded in the Mitchell Report of April 2001.

The operational premise of the workplan is that the two sides are committed to a mutual, comprehensive cease-fire, applying to all violent activities, in accordance with the public declaration of both leaders. In addition, the joint security committee referenced in this workplan will resolve issues that may arise during the implementation of this workplan.

The security organizations of the GOI and PA agree to initiate the following specific, concrete, and realistic security steps immediately to re-establish security cooperation and the situation on the ground as they existed prior to 28 September.

1. The GOI and the PA will immediately resume security cooperation.

A senior-level meeting of Israeli, Palestinian, and US security officials will be held immediately and will reconvene at least once a week, with mandatory participation by designated senior officials.

Israeli-Palestinian DCOs will be reinvigorated. They will carry out their daily activities, to the maximum extent possible, according to the standards established prior to 28 September 2000. As soon as the security situation permits, barriers to effective cooperation, which include the erection of walls between the Israeli and Palestinian sides, will be eliminated and joint Israeli-Palestinian patrols will be reinitiated.

US-supplied video conferencing systems will be provided to senior-level Israeli and Palestinian officials to facilitate frequent dialogue and security cooperation.

2. Both sides will take immediate measures to enforce strict adherence to the declared cease-fire and to stabilize the security environment.

Specific procedures will be developed by the senior-level security committee to ensure the secure movement of GOI and PA security personnel traveling in areas outside their respective control, in accordance with existing agreements.

Israel will not conduct attacks of any kind against the Palestinian Authority Ra'is facilities; the headquarters of Palestinian security, intelligence, and police organizations; or prisons in the West Bank and Gaza.

The PA will move immediately to apprehend, question, and incarcerate terrorists in the West Bank and Gaza and will provide the security committee the names of those arrested as soon as they are apprehended, as well as a readout of actions taken.

Israel will release all Palestinians arrested in security sweeps who have no association with terrorist activities.

In keeping with its unilateral cease-fire declaration, the PA will stop any Palestinian security officials from inciting, aiding, abetting, or conducting attacks against Israeli targets, including settlers.

In keeping with Israel's unilateral cease-fire declaration, Israeli forces will not conduct "proactive" security operations in areas under the control of the PA or attack against innocent civilian targets.

The GOI will re-institute military police investigations into Palestinian deaths resulting from IDF actions in the West Bank and Gaza in incidents not involving terrorism.

3. Palestinian and Israeli security officials will use the security committee to provide each other, as well as designated US officials, terrorist threat information, including information on known or suspected terrorist operations in—or moving to—areas under the other's control.

Legitimate terrorist and threat information will be acted upon immediately, with follow-up actions and results reported to the security committee.

The PA will undertake pre-emptive operations against terrorists, terrorist safehouses, arms depots, and mortar factories. The PA will provide regular progress reports on these actions to the security committee.

Israeli authorities will take action against Israeli citizens inciting, carrying out, or planning to carry out violence against Palestinians, with progress reports on these activities provided to the security committee.

4. The PA and GOI will move aggressively to prevent individuals and groups from using areas under their respective control to carry out acts of violence. In addition, both sides will take steps to ensure that areas under their control will not be used to launch attacks against the other side nor be used as refuge after attacks are staged.

The security committee will identify key flash points, and each side will inform the other of the names of senior security personnel responsible for each flash point.

Joint Standard Operating Procedures (SOPs) will be developed for each flash point. These SOPs will address how the two sides handle and respond to security incidents; the mechanisms for emergency contact; and the procedures to deescalate security crises.

Palestinian and Israeli security officials will identify and agree to the practical measures needed to enforce "no demonstration zones" and "buffer zones" around flash points to reduce opportunities for confrontation. Both sides will adopt all necessary measures to prevent riots and to control demonstrations, particularly in flash point areas.

Palestinian and Israeli security officials will make a concerted effort to locate and confiscate illegal weapons, including mortars, rockets, and explosives, in areas under their respective control. In addition, intensive efforts will be made to prevent smuggling and illegal production of weapons. Each side will inform the security committee of the status and success of these efforts.

The Israeli Defense Forces (IDF) will adopt additional non-lethal measures to deal with Palestinian crowds and demonstrators, and more generally, seek to minimize the danger to lives and property of Palestinian civilians in responding to violence.

5. The GOI and the PA, through the auspices of the senior-level security committee, will forge, within one week of the commencement of security committee meetings and resumption of security cooperation, an agreed-upon schedule to implement the complete redeployment of IDF forces to positions held before 28 September 2000.

Demonstrable on-the-ground redeployment will be initiated within the first 48 hours of this one-week period and will continue while the schedule is being forged.

6. Within one week of the commencement of security committee meetings and resumption of security cooperation, a specific timeline will be developed for the lifting of internal closures as well as for the reopening of internal roads, the Allenby Bridge, Gaza Airport, Port of Gaza, and border crossings. Security checkpoints will be minimized according to legitimate security requirements and following consultation between the two sides.

Demonstrable on-the-ground actions on the lifting of the closures will be initiated within the first 48 hours of this one-week period and will continue while the timeline is being developed.

The parties pledge that even if untoward events occur, security cooperation will continue through the joint security committee.

> **Source:** "Palestinian-Israeli Security Implementation Work Plan (Tenet Ceasefire Plan)," United Nations Information System on the Question of Palestine, http://domino.un.org/UNISPAL.NSF/frontpage5!OpenPage.

142. United Nations Security Council Resolution 1397, March 12, 2002

Introduction

Despite numerous international calls for an end to the brutal violence in the Palestinian territories and Israel, the situation continued to escalate, and efforts to impose a cease-fire all proved abortive. So too did the recommendations of a United Nations (UN) investigative commission and the U.S.-backed Mitchell Commission, both of which published extensive reports on the Palestinian situation in the spring of 2001. U.S. Central Intelligence Agency (CIA) director George Tenet and Crown Prince Abdullah of Saudi Arabia likewise put forward plans to resolve the spiraling internal hostilities, while special envoys from the United States, the Russian Federation, the European Union (EU), and the UN all sought to negotiate a cease-fire. At the time they were advanced, all these initiatives proved equally unavailing. In February 2002, Israeli troops pursuing gunmen invaded the Balata refugee camp in Nablus in the West Bank, home to 20,000 Palestinian refugees, killing 13 and wounding more than 60 Palestinians, many of them young children. This was only the first of repeated Israeli raids on Balata and represented an escalation of Israeli tactics. In response, the UN Security Council passed a resolution demanding the "immediate cessation of all acts of violence" in Israel and the Palestine territories and urged all parties to respect the safety of civilians and observe international humanitarian standards of conduct. The Security Council called on both sides to work to implement the Mitchell Report recommendations and the Tenet Plan and reaffirmed its support for the establishment of an independent Palestinian state, which would live in harmony with Israel as its neighbor.

Primary Source

The Security Council,

Recalling all its previous relevant resolutions, in particular resolutions 242 (1967) and 338 (1973),

Affirming a vision of a region where two States, Israel and Palestine, live side by side within secure and recognized borders,

Expressing its grave concern at the continuation of the tragic and violent events that have taken place since September 2000, especially the recent attacks and the increased number of casualties,

Stressing the need for all concerned to ensure the safety of civilians,

Stressing also the need to respect the universally accepted norms of international humanitarian law,

Welcoming and encouraging the diplomatic efforts of special envoys from the United States of America, the Russian Federation, the European Union and the United Nations Special Coordinator and others, to bring about a comprehensive, just and lasting peace in the Middle East,

Welcoming the contribution of Saudi Crown Prince Abdullah,

1. *Demands* immediate cessation of all acts of violence, including all acts of terror, provocation, incitement and destruction;

2. *Calls upon* the Israeli and Palestinian sides and their leaders to cooperate in the implementation of the Tenet work plan and Mitchell Report recommendations with the aim of resuming negotiations on a political settlement;

3. *Expresses* support for the efforts of the Secretary-General and others to assist the parties to halt the violence and to resume the peace process;

4. *Decides* to remain seized of the matter.

Source: United Nations Security Council Official Records, 02-28359 (E), S.C. Res. 1397, March 12, 2002, http://daccessdds.un.org/.

143. United Nations Security Council Resolution 1402, March 30, 2002

Introduction

Far from moderating under U.S. pressure, in late 2001 and early 2002 anti-Israeli Palestinian violence and harsh Israeli repression both intensified. From June 2001 onward Palestinian suicide bombers organized by the extremist Hamas organization, most of them in their teens or early 20s, repeatedly entered Israel and detonated bombs worn under their clothing. In June 2001 a suicide bomber killed 21 Israelis, mostly young high school students, at a Tel Aviv dance club. Attacks reached their peak in April 2002 when more than 130 Israelis, mostly civilians, died in such incidents, with 30 Israelis killed during a Passover dinner at the Park Hotel in Netanya. At the beginning of March 2002, the Israel Defense Forces (IDF) launched Operation DEFENSIVE SHIELD, in the course of which they reoccupied Palestinian areas and camps in Jenin, Ramallah, and Bethlehem that they believed to be hotbeds of terrorist activities orchestrated by the guerilla organization al-Aqsa Martyrs Brigades. From March through the first week of May 2002, according to United Nations (UN) estimates, 497 Palestinians were killed and another 1,447 were wounded as Palestinians and Israeli forces waged pitched battles in which 27 Israeli soldiers died. Alarmed by the ever escalating levels of violence, in March 2002 Norway drafted a resolution, passed by the UN Security Council, calling for an immediate "meaningful ceasefire" and end to all violence and demanding that Israeli forces withdraw from Palestinian cities. All parties were urged to cooperate with UN and other special envoys in ending the conflict. As so often occurred, all parties involved ignored the resolution. The follow-up UN Security Council Resolution 1403, passed on April 4, 2002, expressed concern that Resolutions 1397 and 1402, both passed the previous month, had not yet been implemented.

Primary Source

The Security Council,

Reaffirming its resolutions 242 (1967) of 22 November 1967, 338 (1973) of 22 October 1973, 1397 (2002) of 12 March 2002 and the Madrid principles,

Expressing its grave concern at the further deterioration of the situation, including the recent suicide bombings in Israel and the military attack against the headquarters of the president of the Palestinian Authority,

1. *Calls upon* both parties to move immediately to a meaningful cease-fire; calls for the withdrawal of Israeli troops from Palestinian cities, including Ramallah; and calls upon the parties to cooperate fully with Special Envoy Zinni, and others, to implement the Tenet security work plan as a first step towards implementation of the Mitchell Committee recommendations, with the aim of resuming negotiations on a political settlement;

2. *Reiterates* its demand in resolution 1397 (2002) of 12 March 2002 for an immediate cessation of all acts of violence, including all acts of terror, provocation, incitement and destruction;

3. *Expresses* support for the efforts of the Secretary-General and the special envoys to the Middle East to assist the parties to halt the violence and to resume the peace process;

4. *Decides* to remain seized of the matter.

> **Source:** United Nations Security Council Official Records, 02-31053 (E), S.C. Res. 1402, March 30, 2002, http://daccessdds.un.org.

144. George W. Bush, Remarks on the Middle East [Excerpt], June 24, 2002

Introduction

By the spring of 2002, the continuously deteriorating and ever more violent situation in Israel and the Palestinian territories, as the Second (al-Aqsa) Intifada continued and Israeli policy grew ever more repressive in defiance of all efforts for peace, seriously concerned the administration of Republican president George W. Bush. In late March 2002 Israel launched a massive operation known as DEFENSIVE SHIELD, and by May Israeli forces had retaken all of the occupied territories. In a highly publicized standoff, for more than a month, from April 2 to May 10, armed Fatah gunmen and Israel Defense Forces (IDF) soldiers confronted each other at the Church of the Nativity in Bethlehem, one of the holiest Christian sites, during which Israel snipers killed 7 people and wounded another 40 inside the church. Eventually, 13 of the Palestinian militants inside were deported to Europe, ending the stalemate. On April 4, 2002, Bush announced his intention of sending Secretary of State Colin Powell to try to negotiate a cease-fire. Bush called on all Arab governments and people to cease supporting terrorist activities and organizations but also urged the Israeli government to end settlement activity in the occupied territories and treat ordinary Palestinians with dignity and respect, easing restrictions on their movements. He specifically called on Iran to cease supporting terrorism with arms supplies and demanded that Syria withdraw its assistance to the militantly anti-Israeli radical Palestinian groups Hamas and Hezbollah. In late June, after Powell's return, Bush announced new U.S. policies toward the Palestinian-Israeli conflict. Convinced by Israeli intelligence evidence that Chairman Yasser Arafat and the Palestinian Authority (PA) he headed were financing Palestinian terrorist activities, specifically those of the al-Aqsa Martyrs Brigades, one of the main organizers of suicide bombings against Israel, Bush demanded that the Palestinians in the occupied territories hold elections by the end of the year for new leaders "not compromised by terror" and establish a new constitution giving their elected legislature real authority. Bush expected those new leaders to mount a major campaign to eliminate Palestinian terrorism. In return, he promised massive U.S. economic assistance and "American support for the creation of a provisional state of Palestine." He called on Israeli forces to withdraw from the occupied territories back to the positions they had held on September 28, 2000, when the Second Intifada began. He also demanded that "Israeli settlement activity in the occupied territories must stop." In addition, he expected Israel to lift restrictions impeding Palestinian economic development. Once these conditions had been met, the United States would work with the European Community (EC), Russia, the United Nations (UN), and other Arab states for a final peace settlement that would resolve outstanding issues dividing Israelis and Palestinians and "realize the vision of a Palestinian state." Many moderate Israelis and Palestinians welcomed Bush's proposals, although Israeli foreign minister Shimon Peres objected that it was unrealistic to expect the Palestinians to renounce the leadership of Arafat, who had been so closely identified with the Palestinian cause. Right-wing Israeli opponents of Bush's scheme claimed that it would effectively reward Palestinian terrorists with a state of their own, which would become a base for further attacks on Israel, while hard-line Palestinians demanded immediate Israeli withdrawal from all the occupied territories. These by now only too predictable responses neatly demonstrated why achieving a final peace settlement was such a difficult undertaking.

Primary Source

For too long, the citizens of the Middle East have lived in the midst of death and fear. The hatred of a few holds the hopes of many hostage. The forces of extremism and terror are attempting to kill progress and peace by killing the innocent. And this casts a dark shadow over an entire region. For the sake of all humanity, things must change in the Middle East.

It is untenable for Israeli citizens to live in terror. It is untenable for Palestinians to live in squalor and occupation. And the current situation offers no prospect that life will improve. Israeli citizens will continue to be victimized by terrorists, and so Israel will continue to defend herself. In the situation the Palestinian people will grow more and more miserable.

My vision is two states living side by side in peace and security. There is simply no way to achieve that peace until all parties fight terror. Yet, at this critical moment, if all parties will break with the past and set out on a new path, we can overcome the darkness with the light of hope. Peace requires a new and different Palestinian leadership, so that a Palestinian state can be born.

I call on the Palestinian people to elect new leaders, leaders not compromised by terror. I call upon them to build a practicing democracy, based on tolerance and liberty. If the Palestinian people actively pursue these goals, America and the world will actively support their efforts. If the Palestinian people meet these goals, they will be able to reach agreement with Israel and Egypt and Jordan on security and other arrangements for independence.

And when the Palestinian people have new leaders, new institutions and new security arrangements with their neighbors, the United States of America will support the creation of a Palestinian state whose borders and certain aspects of its sovereignty will be provisional until resolved as part of a final settlement in the Middle East.

In the work ahead, we all have responsibilities. The Palestinian people are gifted and capable, and I am confident they can achieve a new birth for their nation. A Palestinian state will never be created by terror. It will be built through reform, and reform must be more than cosmetic change, or a veiled attempt to preserve the status quo. True reform will require entirely new political and economic institutions, based on democracy, market economics and action against terrorism.

Today, the elected Palestinian legislature has no authority, and power is concentrated in the hands of an unaccountable few. A Palestinian state can only serve its citizens with a new constitution which separates the powers of government. The Palestinian parliament should have the full authority of a legislative body. Local officials and government ministers need authority of their own and the independence to govern effectively.

The United States, along with the European Union and Arab states, will work with Palestinian leaders to create a new constitutional framework and a working democracy for the Palestinian people. And the United States, along with others in the international community, will help the Palestinians organize and monitor fair, multiparty local elections by the end of the year, with national elections to follow.

Today, the Palestinian people live in economic stagnation, made worse by official corruption. A Palestinian state will require a vibrant economy, where honest enterprise is encouraged by honest government.

The United States, the international donor community, and the World Bank stand ready to work with Palestinians on a major project of economic reform and development. The United States, the EU, the World Bank, the International Monetary Fund are willing to oversee reforms in Palestinian finances, encouraging transparency and independent auditing. And the United States, along with our partners in the developed world, will increase our humanitarian assistance to relieve Palestinian suffering.

Today, the Palestinian people lack effective courts of law and have no means to defend and vindicate their rights. A Palestinian state will require a system of reliable justice to punish those who prey on the innocent.

The United States and members of the international community stand ready to work with Palestinian leaders to establish, finance, and monitor a truly independent judiciary.

Today, Palestinian authorities are encouraging, not opposing, terrorism. This is unacceptable. And the United States will not support the establishment of a Palestinian state until its leaders engage in a sustained fight against the terrorists and dismantle their infrastructure. This will require an externally supervised effort to rebuild and reform the Palestinian security services. The security system must have clear lines of authority and accountability and a unified chain of command.

America is pursuing this reform along with key regional states. The world is prepared to help.

Yet ultimately these steps toward statehood depend on the Palestinian people and their leaders. If they energetically take the path of reform, the rewards can come quickly. If Palestinians embrace democracy, confront corruption and firmly reject terror, they can count on American support for the creation of a provisional state of Palestine. With a dedicated effort, this state could rise rapidly, as it comes to terms with Israel, Egypt and Jordan on practical issues, such as security. The final borders, the capital and other aspects of this state's sovereignty will be negotiated between the parties, as part of a final settlement. Arab states have offered their help in this process, and their help is needed.

I've said in the past that nations are either with us or against us in the war on terror. To be counted on the side of peace, nations must act. Every leader actually committed to peace will end incitement to violence in official media and publicly denounce homicide bombings. Every nation actually committed to peace will stop the flow of money, equipment, and recruits to terrorist groups seeking the destruction of Israel—including Hamas, Islamic Jihad, and Hezbollah. Every nation actually committed to peace must block the shipment of Iranian supplies to these groups and oppose regimes that promote terror, like Iraq. And Syria must choose the right side in the war on terror by closing terrorist camps and expelling terrorist organizations.

Leaders who want to be included in the peace process must show by their deeds an undivided support for peace. And as we move toward a peaceful solution, Arab states will be expected to build closer ties of diplomacy and commerce with Israel, leading to full normalization of relations between Israel and the entire Arab world.

Israel also has a large stake in the success of a democratic Palestine. Permanent occupation threatens Israel's identity and democracy. A stable, peaceful Palestinian state is necessary to achieve the security that Israel longs for. So I challenge Israel to take concrete steps to support the emergence of a viable, credible Palestinian state.

As we make progress towards security, Israel forces need to withdraw fully to positions they held prior to September 28, 2000. And consistent with the recommendations of the Mitchell Committee, Israeli settlement activity in the occupied territories must stop.

The Palestinian economy must be allowed to develop. As violence subsides, freedom of movement should be restored, permitting innocent Palestinians to resume work and normal life. Palestinian legislators and officials, humanitarian and international workers must be allowed to go about the business of building a better future. And Israel should release frozen Palestinian revenues into honest, accountable hands.

I've asked Secretary Powell to work intensively with Middle Eastern and international leaders to realize the vision of a Palestinian state, focusing them on a comprehensive plan to support Palestinian reform and institution-building.

Ultimately, Israelis and Palestinians must address the core issues that divide them if there is to be a real peace, resolving all claims and ending the conflict between them. This means that the Israeli occupation that began in 1967 will be ended through a settlement negotiated between the parties, based on U.N. Resolutions 242 and 338, with Israeli withdrawal to secure and recognized borders.

We must also resolve questions concerning Jerusalem, the plight and future of Palestinian refugees, and a final peace between Israel and Lebanon, and Israel and a Syria that supports peace and fights terror.

All who are familiar with the history of the Middle East realize that there may be setbacks in this process. Trained and determined killers, as we have seen, want to stop it. Yet the Egyptian and Jordanian peace treaties with Israel remind us that with determined and responsible leadership, progress can come quickly.

As new Palestinian institutions and new leaders emerge, demonstrating real performance on security and reform, I expect Israel to respond and work toward a final status agreement. With intensive effort by all, this agreement could be reached within 3 years from now. And I and my country will actively lead toward that goal.

I can understand the deep anger and anguish of the Israeli people. You've lived too long with fear and funerals, having to avoid markets and public transportation, and forced to put armed guards in kindergarten classrooms. The Palestinian Authority has rejected your offered hand and trafficked with terrorists. You have a right to a normal life. You have a right to security, and I deeply believe that you need a reformed, responsible Palestinian partner to achieve that security.

I can understand the deep anger and despair of the Palestinian people. For decades you've been treated as pawns in the Middle East conflict. Your interests have been held hostage to a comprehensive peace agreement that never seems to come, as your lives get worse year by year. You deserve democracy and the rule of law. You deserve an open society and a thriving economy. You deserve a life of hope for your children. An end to occupation and a peaceful democratic Palestinian state may seem distant, but America and our partners throughout the world stand ready to help—help you make them possible as soon as possible.

If liberty can blossom in the rocky soil of the West Bank and Gaza, it will inspire millions of men and women around the globe who are equally weary of poverty and oppression, equally entitled to the benefits of democratic government.

I have a hope for the people of Muslim countries. Your commitments to morality and learning and tolerance led to great historical achievements, and those values are alive in the Islamic world today. You have a rich culture, and you share the aspirations of men and women in every culture. Prosperity and freedom and dignity are not just American hopes, or Western hopes. They are universal, human hopes. And even in the violence and turmoil of the Middle East, America believes those hopes have the power to transform lives and nations.

[. . .]

Source: George W. Bush, *Public Papers of the Presidents of the United States: George W. Bush, 2002,* Vol. 1 (Washington, DC: U.S. Government Printing Office, 2003), 1059–1062.

145. Quartet Joint Statement, July 16, 2002

Introduction

One of the results of U.S. secretary of state Colin Powell's Middle East peace mission of April 2002 was the foundation of the international coalition that would orchestrate the new process. After visiting the Middle East, he proceeded to Madrid and met representatives from the European Union (EU), the United Nations (UN), and Russia. Initially the group, christened the Quartet, planned to organize a Middle East peace conference, to begin in summer 2002. That gathering was not held, but representatives of the four sponsors met in New York in July 2002. They endorsed the prescriptions laid out in President George W. Bush's speech the previous month, including a commitment to the existence of two neighboring states, one Israeli and one Palestinian, and his demand for major Palestinian economic and political reforms, notably the creation of new democratic institutions and the holding of free elections in the near future. The International Task Force on Reform, comprising representatives from the Quartet group plus Japan, Norway, the World Bank, and the International Monetary Fund (IMF), had already been established to develop and implement a comprehensive reform program. The Quartet also endorsed a major overhaul of the Palestinian security apparatus. The Israelis were asked to relax the restrictions on the free movement of Palestinians, release frozen tax revenues, and "stop all new settlement activity." The Quartet called on both sides to renew dialogue with each other. Facilitating a Palestinian-Israeli settlement had clearly once again moved close to the top of the international agenda.

Primary Source

United Nations Secretary-General Kofi Annan, Russian Foreign Minister Igor Ivanov, U.S. Secretary of State Colin L. Powell, Danish Foreign Minister Per Stig Moeller, High Representative for European Common Foreign and Security Policy Javier Solana and European Commissioner for External Affairs Chris Patten met in New York today. The Quartet members reviewed the situation in the Middle East and agreed to continue close consultations, as expressed in the Madrid Declaration, to which the Quartet remains fully committed, to promote a just, comprehensive, and lasting settlement of the Middle East conflict. The Quartet expresses its support for the convening of a further international Ministerial meeting at an appropriate time.

The Quartet deeply deplores today's tragic killing of Israeli civilians and reiterates its strong and unequivocal condemnation of terrorism, including suicide bombing, which is morally repugnant and has caused great harm to the legitimate aspirations of the Palestinian people for a better future. Terrorists must not be allowed to kill the hope of an entire region, and a united international community, for genuine peace and security for both Palestinians and Israelis. The Quartet expresses once again its profound regret at the loss of innocent Israeli and Palestinian lives, and extends its sympathy to all those who have suffered loss. The Quartet members expressed their increasing concern about the mounting humanitarian crisis in Palestinian areas and their determination to address urgent Palestinian needs.

Consistent with President Bush's June 24 statement, the UN, EU and Russia express their strong support for the goal of achieving a final Israeli-Palestinian settlement which, with intensive effort on security and reform by all, could be reached within three years from now. The UN, EU and Russia welcome President Bush's commitment to active U.S. leadership toward that goal. The Quartet remains committed to implementing the vision of two states, Israel and an independent, viable and democratic Palestine, living side by side in peace and security, as affirmed by UN Security Council Resolution 1397. The Quartet members, in their individual capacity and jointly, pledge all possible efforts to realize the goals of reform, security and peace and reaffirm that progress in the political, security, economic, humanitarian, and institution-building fields must proceed together, hand-in-hand. The Quartet reiterates its welcome of the initiative of Saudi Arabia, endorsed by the Arab League

Beirut Summit, as a significant contribution towards a comprehensive peace.

To assist progress toward these shared goals, the Quartet agreed on the importance of a coordinated international campaign to support Palestinian efforts at political and economic reform. The Quartet welcomes and encourages the strong Palestinian interest in fundamental reform, including the Palestinian 100-Day Reform Program. It also welcomes the willingness of regional states and the international community to assist the Palestinians to build institutions of good government, and to create a new governing framework of working democracy, in preparation for statehood. For these objectives to be realized, it is essential that well-prepared, free, open and democratic elections take place. The new international Task Force on Reform, which is comprised of representatives of the U.S., EU, UN Secretary General, Russia, Japan, Norway, the World Bank and the International Monetary Fund, and which works under the auspices of the Quartet, will strive to develop and implement a comprehensive action plan for reform. The inaugural meeting of this Task Force in London [on] July 10 discussed a detailed plan including specific Palestinian commitments. It will meet again in August to review actions in areas including civil society, financial accountability, local government, the market economy, elections, and judicial and administrative reform.

Implementation of an action plan, with appropriate benchmarks for progress on reform measures, should lead to the establishment of a democratic Palestinian state characterized by the rule of law, separation of powers, and a vibrant free market economy that can best serve the interests of its people. The Quartet also commits itself to continuing to assist the parties in efforts to renew dialogue, and welcomes in this regard the recent high-level ministerial meetings between Israelis and Palestinians on the issues of security, economics and reform.

The Quartet agreed on the critical need to build new and efficient Palestinian security capabilities on sound bases of unified command, and transparency and accountability with regard to resources and conduct. Restructuring security institutions to serve these goals should lead to improvement in Palestinian security performance, which is essential to progress on other aspects of institutional transformation and realization of a Palestinian state committed to combating terror.

In this context, the Quartet notes Israel's vital stake in the success of Palestinian reform. The Quartet calls upon Israel to take concrete steps to support the emergence of a viable Palestinian state. Recognizing Israel's legitimate security concerns, these steps include immediate measures to ease the internal closures in certain areas and, as security improves through reciprocal steps, withdrawal of Israeli forces to their pre-September 28, 2000 positions. Moreover, frozen tax revenues should be released. In this connection, a more transparent and accountable mechanism is being put into place. In addition, consistent with the Mitchell Committee's recommendations, Israel should stop all new settlement activity. Israel must also ensure full, safe and unfettered access for international and humanitarian personnel.

The Quartet reaffirms that there must be a negotiated permanent settlement based on UN Security Council resolutions 242 and 338. There can be no military solution to the conflict; Israelis and Palestinians must address the core issues that divide them, through sustained negotiations, if there is to be real and lasting peace and security. The Israeli occupation that began in 1967 must end, and Israel must have secure and recognized borders. The Quartet further reaffirms its commitment to the goal of a comprehensive regional peace between Israel and Lebanon, and Israel and Syria, based upon Resolutions 242 and 338, the Madrid terms of reference, and the principle of land for peace.

The Quartet looks forward to upcoming consultations with the Foreign Ministers of Jordan, Egypt, Saudi Arabia, and other regional partners, and determines to continue regular consultation on the situation in the Middle East at the principals' level. The Quartet envoys will continue their work on the ground to support the work of the principals, to assist the Task Force on Reform, and to aid the parties in resuming a political dialogue in order to reach a solution to the core political questions.

Source: "Quartet Joint Statement," U.S. Department of State, http://www.state.gov/r/pa/prs/ps/2002/11882.htm.

146. Middle East Communiqué, September 17, 2002

Introduction

Meetings of the international Quartet, consisting of the United States, Russia, the European Union (EU), and the United Nations (UN), continued in the summer and fall of 2002 and moved swiftly in seeking to formulate a definite timetable, or road map, for a final Palestinian-Israeli settlement. Meeting again in New York in September 2002, the four principals issued a statement calling for "a concrete, three-phase implementation roadmap that could achieve a final settlement within three years." This plan would be detailed, and progress from one phase to the next "would be strictly based on the parties' compliance with specific performance benchmarks." The first stage, intended to last from then until mid-2003, would be marked by "comprehensive security reform" on both sides; "free, fair, and credible" Palestinian elections; and the withdrawal of Israeli forces from the occupied territories to their positions as of early September 2000. The second stage, during the remainder of 2003, would "creat[e] a Palestinian state with provisional borders based

upon a new constitution." The final phase, spanning all of 2004 and 2005, would be devoted to the negotiation of a permanent peace settlement based on UN Security Council Resolutions 242 and 338 with Israeli forces withdrawing from a Palestinian state to the safety of their own "secure and recognized borders." As before, the Quartet stated that "consistent with the recommendations of the Mitchell Commission, Israeli settlement activity in the occupied territories must stop." In addition, it called on both Israelis and Palestinians "to move quickly to ameliorate the sharply deteriorating humanitarian situation in the West Bank and Gaza." Palestinians were once again urged to reform their security system and move against terrorism, and Israelis were instructed to relax their barriers to free movement of persons in the occupied territories and in particular to allow representatives of international and humanitarian organizations unfettered access to these areas.

Primary Source

United Nations Secretary-General Kofi Annan, U.S. Secretary of State Colin Powell, Russian Foreign Minister Igor Ivanov, Danish Foreign Minister Per Stig Moeller, High Representative for European Common Foreign and Security Policy Javier Solana, and European Commissioner for External Affairs Chris Patten met today in New York and issued the following Communique:

Reaffirming their previous statements, the Quartet members reviewed developments since their last meeting, on July 16, 2002. They deplored and condemned the morally repugnant violence and terror, which must end. They agreed to intensify their efforts in support of their shared goal of achieving a final Israeli-Palestinian settlement based on their common vision, as *inter alia* expressed by President Bush, of two states, Israel and an independent, viable and democratic Palestine, living side by side in peace and security.

The Quartet will continue to encourage all parties to step up to their responsibilities to seek a just and comprehensive settlement to the conflict based on UN Security Council resolutions 242, 338, and 1397, the Madrid terms of reference, the principle of land for peace, and implementation of all existing agreements between the parties. The Quartet reaffirms the continuing importance of the initiative of Saudi Arabia, endorsed at the Arab League Beirut Summit, which is a vital part of the foundation of international efforts to promote a comprehensive peace on all tracks, including the Syrian-Israeli and Lebanese-Israeli tracks.

The Quartet is working closely with the parties and consulting key regional actors on a concrete, three-phase implementation roadmap that could achieve a final settlement within three years. Comprehensive security performance is essential. The plan will not succeed unless it addresses political, economic, humanitarian, and institutional dimensions and should spell out reciprocal steps to be taken by the parties in each of its phases. In this approach, progress between the three phases would be strictly based on the parties' compliance with specific performance benchmarks to be monitored and assessed by the Quartet.

The Quartet also supports, in preparation for establishment of a Palestinian state, efforts by the Palestinians to develop a constitution which ensures separation of power, transparency, accountability, and the vibrant political system which Palestinians deserve.

The plan will contain in its initial phase (2002–first half of 2003) performance-based criteria for comprehensive security reform, Israeli withdrawals to their positions of September 28, 2000 as the security situation improves, and support for the Palestinians' holding of free, fair, and credible elections early in 2003, based on recommendations established by the Quartet's International Task Force on Palestinian Reform. The first phase should include a ministerial-level meeting of the Ad Hoc Liaison Committee (AHLC) to review the humanitarian situation and prospects for economic development in the West Bank and Gaza and identify priority areas for donor assistance, including to the reform process, before the end of the year. The Quartet Principals will meet alongside the AHLC ministerial.

In the plan's second phase (2003), our efforts should focus on the option of creating a Palestinian state with provisional borders based upon a new constitution, as a way station to a permanent status settlement.

In its final phase (2004–5), the plan envisages Israeli-Palestinian negotiations aimed at a permanent status solution in 2005. Consistent with the vision expressed by President Bush, this means that the Israeli occupation that began in 1967 will be ended through a settlement negotiated between the parties and based on U.N. resolutions 242 and 338, with Israeli withdrawal to secure and recognized borders.

The Quartet welcomes the Task Force's report on the progress of the seven Reform Support Groups, and notes that a number of significant achievements, especially in the area of financial reform, have been realized in a short period of time under very difficult circumstances. Under the aegis of the Quartet, the Task Force will continue its work of supporting the Palestinians and the Palestinian Authority as they establish and prioritize reform benchmarks, particularly on the issues of elections, judicial reform, and the role of civil society.

Both the reform effort and the political process must include Israeli measures, consistent with Israel's legitimate security concerns, to improve the lives of Palestinians, including allowing the resumption of normal economic activity, facilitating the movement of goods, people, and essential services and lifting curfew and closures. Consistent with transparent and accountable Palestinian budget arrangements, the Quartet welcomes Israel's decision to transfer part of the Palestinian VAT and customs revenue that has been withheld since September 2000, and calls on Israel to continue this process and reestablish regular monthly revenue transfers to the Palestinian Ministry of Finance. And consistent with the recommendations of the Mitchell Commission, Israeli settlement activity in the occupied territories must stop.

The Quartet welcomes the report of UN Secretary-General's Personal Humanitarian Envoy Catherine Bertini as well as the latest UNSCO [United Nations Special Coordinator Office] report on the impact of closures. It calls on Israel and the Palestinians to recognize and act upon their respective responsibilities and to move quickly to ameliorate the sharply deteriorating humanitarian situation in the West Bank and Gaza. In particular, Israel must ensure full, safe and unfettered access for international and humanitarian personnel.

Reiterating the critical importance of restoring lasting calm through comprehensive performance on security, the Quartet calls on the Palestinians to work with the U.S. and regional partners to reform the Palestinian security services, strengthen policing and law and order for the civilian population, and fight the terror that has severely undermined the legitimate aspirations of the Palestinians. Israelis and Palestinians should reestablish security cooperation and reciprocal steps should be taken by Israel as the Palestinians work to combat terrorism in all its forms.

The Quartet will continue to discuss the timing and modalities of an international conference.

The Quartet also met and discussed these issues with the Foreign Ministers of Egypt, Jordan, Lebanon, Saudi Arabia, and Syria, as representatives of the Arab League Follow-up Committee, and with representatives of Israel and the Palestinian Authority. The Quartet looks forward to continuing consultations.

Source: "Middle East Quartet Communiqué of September 17, 2002," U.S. Department of State, http://www.state.gov/p/nea/rt/15207.htm.

147. George W. Bush, Draft Road Map to Israeli-Palestinian Peace, October 15, 2002

Introduction

By the fall of 2002 representatives of the Quartet international grouping consisting of the United Nations (UN), the United States, the European Union (EU), and Russia that sought to facilitate an Israeli-Palestinian settlement were publicly advocating a three-stage peace process whose objective was a final and permanent peace agreement and the creation of an independent Palestinian state. In October 2002 the U.S. State Department, with Quartet endorsement, issued a press release giving the specifics of this three-part program. The intention was that this would be completed by the end of 2005, at which point Israeli forces would have disengaged completely from Palestinian territory and an independent Palestinian state would exist. Progress from one stage to the next would be dependent on satisfying outside observers, through an unspecified "permanent monitoring mechanism," that "conditions [we]re appropriate to move on." Perhaps understandably, the first stage, supposed to cover the next nine months, was described in great detail. Specifics of the second and transitional phase, during which normal relations between the Palestinian authorities and Israel would be restored and a provisional state established, were also fairly full. The particulars of the third stage—the longest and most crucial stage and involving negotiations to conclude a permanent and final peace settlement and create a fully independent Palestinian state—were by far the most sketchy.

Primary Source

Elements of a Performance-Based Road Map to a Permanent Two-State Solution to the Israeli-Palestinian Conflict

The following are elements of a performance-based plan, under the supervision of the Quartet, with clear phases and benchmarks leading to a final and comprehensive settlement of the Israel-Palestinian conflict by 2005, as presented in President Bush's speech of 24 June, and welcomed by the EU, Russia and the UN in the 16 July and 17 September Quartet Ministerial statements. Such a settlement, negotiated between the parties, will result in the emergence of an independent, democratic Palestinian state living side by side in peace and security with Israel and its other neighbors. The settlement will end the occupation that began in 1967, based on the Madrid Conference terms of reference and the principle of land for peace, UNSCRs 242, 338 and 1397, agreements previously reached by the parties, and the Arab initiative proposed by Saudi Crown Prince Abdullah and endorsed by the Arab Summit in Beirut.

Phase I: October 2002–May 2003 (Transformation/Elections)
First Stage: October–December, 2002
Quartet develops detailed roadmap, in consultation with the parties, to be adopted at December Quartet/AHLC meeting.

Appointment of new Palestinian cabinet, establishment of empowered Prime Minister, including any necessary Palestinian legal reforms for this purpose.

PLC appoints Commission charged with drafting of Palestinian constitution for Palestinian statehood.

PA establishes independent Election Commission. PLC reviews and revises election law.

AHLC Ministerial launches major donor assistance effort.

Palestinian leadership issues unequivocal statement reiterating Israel's right to exist in peace and security and calling for an immediate end to the armed Intifada and all acts of violence against Israelis anywhere. All Palestinian institutions end incitement against Israel.

In coordination with Quartet, implementation of U.S. rebuilding, training and resumed security cooperation plan in collaboration with outside oversight board. (U.S.-Egypt-Jordan).

Palestinian security organizations are consolidated into three services reporting to an empowered Interior Minister.

Restructured/retrained Palestinian security forces and IDF counterparts begin phased resumption of security cooperation and other undertakings as agreed in the Tenet work plan, including regular senior-level meetings, with the participation of U.S. security officials.

GOI facilitates travel of Palestinian officials for PLC sessions, internationally supervised security retraining, and other PA business without restriction.

GOI implements recommendations of the Bertini report to improve humanitarian conditions, including lifting curfews and easing movement between Palestinian areas.

GOI ends actions undermining trust, including attacks in civilian areas, and confiscation/demolition of Palestinian homes/property, deportations, as a punitive measure or to facilitate Israeli construction.

GOI immediately resumes monthly revenue clearance process in accordance with agreed transparency monitoring mechanism. GOI transfers all arrears of withheld revenues to Palestinian Ministry of Finance by end of December 2002, according to specific timeline.

Arab states move decisively to cut off public/private funding of extremist groups, channel financial support for Palestinians through Palestinian Ministry of Finance.

GOI dismantles settlement outposts erected since establishment of the present Israeli government and in contravention of current Israeli government guidelines.

Second Stage: January–May 2003
Continued Palestinian political reform to ensure powers of PLC, Prime Minister, and Cabinet.

Independent Commission circulates draft Palestinian constitution, based on strong parliamentary democracy, for public comment/debate.

Devolution of power to local authorities through revised Municipalities Law.

Quartet monitoring mechanism established.

Palestinian performance on agreed judicial, administrative, and economic benchmarks, as determined by Task Force.

As comprehensive security performance moves forward, IDF withdraws progressively from areas occupied since September 28, 2000. Withdrawal to be completed before holding of Palestinian elections. Palestinian security forces redeploy to areas vacated by IDF.

GOI facilitates Task Force election assistance, registration of voters, movement of candidates and voting officials.

GOI reopens East Jerusalem Chamber of Commerce and other closed Palestinian economic institutions in East Jerusalem.

Constitution drafting Commission proposes draft document for submission after elections to new PLC for approval.

Palestinians and Israelis conclude a new security agreement building upon Tenet work plan, including an effective security mechanism and an end to violence, terrorism, and incitement implemented through a restructured and effective Palestinian security service.

GOI freezes all settlement activity consistent with the Mitchell report, including natural growth of settlements.

Palestinians hold free, open, and fair elections for PLC.

Regional support: Upon completion of security steps and IDF withdrawal to September 28, 2000 positions, Egypt and Jordan return ambassadors to Israel.

Phase II: June 2003–December 2003 (Transition)
Progress into Phase II will be based upon the judgment of the Quartet, facilitated by establishment of a permanent monitoring mechanism on the ground, whether conditions are appropriate to move on—taking into account performance of all parties and Quartet monitoring. Phase II starts after Palestinian elections and ends with possible creation of a Palestinian state with provisional borders by end of 2003.

International Conference: Convened by the Quartet, in agreement with the parties, immediately after the successful conclusion of Palestinian elections to support Palestinian economic recovery and launch negotiations between Israelis and Palestinians on the possibility of a state with provisional borders.

Such a meeting would be inclusive, based on the goal of a comprehensive Middle East peace (including between Israel and Syria, and Israel and Lebanon), and based on the principles described in the preamble to this document.

Other pre-Intifada Arab links to Israel restored (trade offices, etc.).

Revival of "multilateral talks" (regional water, environmental, economic development, refugees, arms control issues).

Newly elected PLC finalizes and approves new constitution for democratic, independent Palestinian state.

Continued implementation of security cooperation, complete collection of illegal weapons, disarmament of militant groups, according to Phase I security agreement.

Israeli-Palestinian negotiations aimed at creation of a state with provisional borders. Implementation of prior agreements, to enhance maximum territorial contiguity.

Conclusion of transitional understanding and creation of state with provisional borders by end of 2003. Enhanced international role in monitoring transition.

Further action on settlements simultaneous with establishment of Palestinian state with provisional borders.

Phase III: 2004–2005 (Statehood)
Progress into Phase III, based on judgment of Quartet, taking into account actions of all parties and Quartet monitoring.

Second International Conference: Convened by the Quartet, with agreement of the parties, at beginning of 2004 to endorse agreement reached on state with provisional borders and to launch negotiations between Israel and Palestine toward a final, permanent status resolution in 2005, including on borders, Jerusalem, refugees and settlements; and to support progress toward a comprehensive Middle East settlement between Israel and Lebanon and Syria, to be achieved as soon as possible.

Continued comprehensive, effective progress on the reform agenda laid out by the Task Force in preparation for final status agreement.

Continued sustained, effective security cooperation based on security agreements reached by end of Phase I and other prior agreements.

Arab state acceptance of normal relations with Israel and security for all the states of the region, consistent with Beirut Arab Summit initiative.

Source: Distributed by the Office of International Information Programs, U.S. Department of State, http://usinfo.state.gov.

148. Osama bin Laden, Letter to the American People [Excerpt], November 2002

Introduction

On September 11, 2001, 19 terrorists who belonged to the Al Qaeda network headed by the Islamic terrorist leader Osama bin Laden attacked the United States. Two hijacked civilian airliners flew into the twin towers of the World Trade Center in New York City; another hijacked airliner crashed into the Pentagon building in Washington, D.C., headquarters of the U.S. Department of Defense; and a fourth hijacked airliner crashed in a field in Shanksville, Pennsylvania, during an attempt by passengers to thwart the hijackers' plan. In all, close to 3,000 people were killed as a result of the attacks. Bin Laden, a fundamentalist Muslim militant from a wealthy Saudi family, had mounted several earlier attacks on U.S. military installations and other facilities elsewhere. He viewed the United States as the greatest enemy of Islam and was fanatically determined to wage a religious war, or jihad, against Americans and all allied with them. In several public statements, including the "Letter to the American People" published in Arabic on the Internet in 2002 and later translated into English, he enumerated what he viewed as U.S. threats and enmity toward Islam. Bin Laden cited what he considered to be the immoral and irreligious character of American life, which was an affront to Muslim principles. Foremost among U.S. offenses, however, he placed U.S. support for Israel, followed by its presence in the Persian Gulf and U.S. opposition to various Muslim governments and groups around the world. After the September 11 attacks, U.S. president George W. Bush quickly declared that waging a global war on terror wherever necessary was now by far the most significant U.S. foreign policy priority. The links that bin Laden drew between his organization's attacks on U.S. landmarks and other facilities and his adamant hostility toward Israel meant that the U.S. government and the American people were likely to view Palestinian and other terrorist operations against that country and its citizens and Israeli measures designed to repress them in the context of worldwide international efforts to combat the threat of armed Islamic militancy.

Primary Source

[. . .]

Some American writers have published articles under the title 'On what basis are we fighting?' These articles have generated a number of responses, some of which adhered to the truth and were based on Islamic Law, and others which have not. Here we wanted to outline the truth—as an explanation and warning—hoping for Allah's reward, seeking success and support from Him.

While seeking Allah's help, we form our reply based on two questions directed at the Americans:

(Q1) Why are we fighting and opposing you?

(Q2) What are we calling you to, and what do we want from you?

As for the first question: Why are we fighting and opposing you? The answer is very simple:

(1) Because you attacked us and continue to attack us.

    (a) You attacked us in Palestine:

        (i) Palestine, which has sunk under military occupation for more than 80 years. The British handed over Palestine, with your help and your support, to the Jews, who have occupied it for more than 50 years; years overflowing with oppression, tyranny, crimes, killing, expulsion, destruction and devastation. The creation and continuation of Israel is one of the greatest crimes, and you are the leaders of its criminals. And of course there is no need to explain and prove the degree of American support for Israel. The creation of Israel is a crime which must be erased. Each and every person whose hands have become polluted in the contribution towards this crime must pay its price, and pay for it heavily.

        (ii) It brings us both laughter and tears to see that you have not yet tired of repeating your fabricated lies that the Jews have a historical right to Palestine, as it was promised to them in the Torah. Anyone who disputes with them on this alleged fact is accused of anti-semitism. This is one of the most fallacious, widely-circulated fabrications in history. The people of Palestine are pure Arabs and original Semites. It is the Muslims who are the inheritors of Moses (peace be upon him) and the inheritors of the real Torah that has not been changed. Muslims believe in all of the Prophets, including Abraham, Moses, Jesus and Muhammad, peace and blessings of Allah be upon them all. If the followers of Moses have been promised a right to Palestine in the Torah, then the Muslims are the nation most worthy of this. When the Muslims conquered Palestine and drove out the Romans, Palestine and Jerusalem returned to Islam, the religion of all the Prophets, peace be upon them. Therefore, the call to a historical right to Palestine cannot be raised against the Islamic Ummah that believes in all the Prophets of Allah (peace and blessings be upon them) —and we make no distinction between them.

        (iii) The blood pouring out of Palestine must be equally revenged. You must know that the Palestinians do not cry alone; their women are not widowed alone; their sons are not orphaned alone.

    (b) You attacked us in Somalia; you supported the Russian atrocities against us in Chechnya, the Indian oppression against us in Kashmir, and the Jewish aggression against us in Lebanon.

(c) Under your supervision, consent and orders, the governments of our countries which act as your agents, attack us on a daily basis:

    (i) These governments prevent our people from establishing the Islamic Shariah, using violence and lies to do so.

    (ii) These governments give us a taste of humiliation, and places us in a large prison of fear and subdual.

    (iii) These governments steal our Ummah's wealth and sell them to you at a paltry price.

    (iv) These governments have surrendered to the Jews, and handed them most of Palestine, acknowledging the existence of their state over the dismembered limbs of their own people.

    (v) The removal of these governments is an obligation upon us, and a necessary step to free the Ummah, to make the Shariah the supreme law and to regain Palestine. And our fight against these governments is not separate from our fight against you.

(d) You steal our wealth and oil at paltry prices because of your international influence and military threats. This theft is indeed the biggest theft ever witnessed by mankind in the history of the world.

(e) Your forces occupy our countries; you spread your military bases throughout them; you corrupt our lands, and you besiege our sanctities, to protect the security of the Jews and to ensure the continuity of your pillage of our treasures.

(f) You have starved the Muslims of Iraq, where children die every day. It is a wonder that more than 1.5 million Iraqi children have died as a result of your sanctions, and you did not show concern. Yet when 3000 of your people died, the entire world rises and has not yet sat down.

(g) You have supported the Jews in their idea that Jerusalem is their eternal capital, and agreed to move your embassy there. With your help and under your protection, the Israelis are planning to destroy the Al-Aqsa mosque. Under the protection of your weapons, Sharon entered the Al-Aqsa mosque, to pollute it as a preparation to capture and destroy it.

(2) These tragedies and calamities are only a few examples of your oppression and aggression against us. It is commanded by our religion and intellect that the oppressed have a right to return the aggression. Do not await anything from us but Jihad, resistance and revenge. Is it in any way rational to expect that after America has attacked us for more than half a century, that we will then leave her to live in security and peace?!!

(3) You may then dispute that all the above does not justify aggression against civilians, for crimes they did not commit and offenses in which they did not partake:

(a) This argument contradicts your continuous repetition that America is the land of freedom, and its leaders in this world. Therefore, the American people are the ones who choose their government by way of their own free will; a choice which stems from their agreement to its policies. Thus the American people have chosen, consented to, and affirmed their support for the Israeli oppression of the Palestinians, the occupation and usurpation of their land, and its continuous killing, torture, punishment and expulsion of the Palestinians. The American people have the ability and choice to refuse the policies of their Government and even to change it if they want.

(b) The American people are the ones who pay the taxes which fund the planes that bomb us in Afghanistan, the tanks that strike and destroy our homes in Palestine, the armies which occupy our lands in the Arabian Gulf, and the fleets which ensure the blockade of Iraq. These tax dollars are given to Israel for it to continue to attack us and penetrate our lands. So the American people are the ones who fund the attacks against us, and they are the ones who oversee the expenditure of these monies in the way they wish, through their elected candidates.

(c) Also the American army is part of the American people. It is this very same people who are shamelessly helping the Jews fight against us.

(d) The American people are the ones who employ both their men and their women in the American Forces which attack us.

(e) This is why the American people cannot be innocent of all the crimes committed by the Americans and Jews against us.

(f) Allah, the Almighty, legislated the permission and the option to take revenge. Thus, if we are attacked, then we have the right to attack back. Whoever has destroyed our villages and towns, then we have the right to destroy their villages and towns. Whoever has stolen our wealth, then we have the right to destroy their economy. And whoever has killed our civilians, then we have the right to kill theirs.

The American Government and press still refuse to answer the question:

Why did they attack us in New York and Washington?

If Sharon is a man of peace in the eyes of Bush, then we are also men of peace!!! America does not understand the language of manners and principles, so we are addressing it using the language it understands.

(Q2) As for the second question that we want to answer: What are we calling you to, and what do we want from you?

(1) The first thing that we are calling you to is Islam.

(a) The religion of the Unification of God; of freedom from associating partners with Him, and rejection of this; of complete love of Him, the Exalted; of complete submission to His Laws; and of the discarding of all the opinions, orders, theories and religions which contradict the religion He sent down to His Prophet Muhammad (peace be upon him). Islam is the religion of all the prophets, and makes no distinction between them—peace be upon them all.

It is to this religion that we call you; the seal of all the previous religions. It is the religion of Unification of God, sincerity, the best of manners, righteousness, mercy, honour, purity, and piety. It is the religion of showing kindness to others, establishing justice between them, granting them their rights, and defending the oppressed and the persecuted. It is the religion of enjoining the good and forbidding the evil with the hand, tongue and heart. It is the religion of Jihad in the way of Allah so that Allah's Word and religion reign Supreme. And it is the religion of unity and agreement on the obedience to Allah, and total equality between all people, without regarding their colour, sex, or language.

(b) It is the religion whose book—the Quran—will remain preserved and unchanged, after the other Divine books and messages have been changed. The Quran is the miracle until the Day of Judgment. Allah has challenged anyone to bring a book like the Quran or even ten verses like it.

(2) The second thing we call you to, is to stop your oppression, lies, immorality and debauchery that has spread among you.

(a) We call you to be a people of manners, principles, honour, and purity; to reject the immoral acts of fornication, homosexuality, intoxicants, gambling, and trading with interest.

(b) We call you to all of this that you may be freed from that which you have become caught up in; that you may be freed from the deceptive lies that you are a great nation, that your leaders spread amongst you to conceal from you the despicable state to which you have reached.

(c) It is saddening to tell you that you are the worst civilization witnessed by the history of mankind:

(i) You are the nation who, rather than ruling by the Shariah of Allah in its Constitution and Laws, choose to invent your own laws as you will and desire. You separate religion from your policies, contradicting the pure nature which affirms Absolute Authority to the Lord and your Creator. You flee from the embarrassing question posed to you: How is it possible for Allah the Almighty to create His creation, grant them power over all the creatures and land, grant them all the amenities of life, and then deny them that which they are most in need of: knowledge of the laws which govern their lives?

(ii) You are the nation that permits Usury, which has been forbidden by all the religions. Yet you build your economy and investments on Usury. As a result of this, in all its different forms and guises, the Jews have taken control of your economy, through which they have then taken control of your media, and now control all aspects of your life making you their servants and achieving their aims at your expense; precisely what Benjamin Franklin warned you against.

(iii) You are a nation that permits the production, trading and usage of intoxicants. You also permit drugs, and only forbid the trade of them, even though your nation is the largest consumer of them.

(iv) You are a nation that permits acts of immorality, and you consider them to be pillars of personal freedom. You have continued to sink down this abyss from level to level until incest has spread amongst you, in the face of which neither your sense of honour nor your laws object. Who can forget your President Clinton's immoral acts committed in the official Oval office? After that you did not even bring him to account, other than that he 'made a mistake', after which everything passed with no punishment. Is there a worse kind of event for which your name will go down in history and [be] remembered by nations?

(v) You are a nation that permits gambling in all its forms. The companies practice this as well, resulting in the investments becoming active and the criminals becoming rich.

(vi) You are a nation that exploits women like consumer products or advertising tools calling upon customers to purchase them. You use women to serve passengers, visitors, and strangers to increase your profit margins. You then rant that you support the liberation of women.

(vii) You are a nation that practices the trade of sex in all its forms, directly and indirectly. Giant corporations and establishments are established on this, under the name of art, entertainment, tourism and freedom, and other deceptive names you attribute to it.

(viii) And because of all this, you have been described in history as a nation that spreads diseases that were unknown to man in the past. Go ahead and boast to the nations of man, that you brought them AIDS as a Satanic American Invention.

(ix)   You have destroyed nature with your industrial waste and gases more than any other nation in history. Despite this, you refuse to sign the Kyoto agreement so that you can secure the profit of your greedy companies and industries.

(x)   Your law is the law of the rich and wealthy people, who hold sway in their political parties, and fund their election campaigns with their gifts. Behind them stand the Jews, who control your policies, media and economy.

(xi)   That which you are singled out for in the history of mankind, is that you have used your force to destroy mankind more than any other nation in history; not to defend principles and values, but to hasten to secure your interests and profits. You who dropped a nuclear bomb on Japan, even though Japan was ready to negotiate an end to the war. How many acts of oppression, tyranny and injustice have you carried out, O callers to freedom?

(xii)   Let us not forget one of your major characteristics: your duality in both manners and values; your hypocrisy in manners and principles. All manners, principles and values have two scales: one for you and one for the others.

(d)   The freedom and democracy that you call to is for yourselves and for the white race only; as for the rest of the world, you impose upon them your monstrous, destructive policies and Governments, which you call the 'American friends'. Yet you prevent them from establishing democracies. When the Islamic party in Algeria wanted to practice democracy and they won the election, you unleashed your agents in the Algerian army onto them, to attack them with tanks and guns, to imprison them and torture them—a new lesson from the 'American book of democracy'!!!

(e)   Your policy on prohibiting and forcibly removing weapons of mass destruction to ensure world peace: it only applies to those countries which you do not permit to possess such weapons. As for the countries you consent to, such as Israel, then they are allowed to keep and use such weapons to defend their security. Anyone else who you suspect might be manufacturing or keeping these kinds of weapons, you call them criminals and you take military action against them.

(f)   You are the last ones to respect the resolutions and policies of International Law, yet you claim to want to selectively punish anyone else who does the same. Israel has for more than 50 years been pushing UN resolutions and rules against the wall with the full support of America.

(g)   As for the war criminals which you censure and form criminal courts for—you shamelessly ask that your own are granted immunity!! However, history will not forget the war crimes that you committed against the Muslims and the rest of the world; those you have killed in Japan, Afghanistan, Somalia, Lebanon and Iraq will remain a shame that you will never be able to escape. It will suffice to remind you of your latest war crimes in Afghanistan, in which densely populated innocent civilian villages were destroyed, bombs were dropped on mosques causing the roof of the mosque to come crashing down on the heads of the Muslims praying inside. You are the ones who broke the agreement with the Mujahideen when they left Qunduz, bombing them in Jangi fort, and killing more than 1,000 of your prisoners through suffocation and thirst. Allah alone knows how many people have died by torture at the hands of you and your agents. Your planes remain in the Afghan skies, looking for anyone remotely suspicious.

(h)   You have claimed to be the vanguards of Human Rights, and your Ministry of Foreign Affairs issues annual reports containing statistics of those countries that violate any Human Rights. However, all these things vanished when the Mujahideen hit you, and you then implemented the methods of the same documented governments that you used to curse. In America, you captured thousands [of] the Muslims and Arabs, took them into custody with neither reason, court trial, nor even disclosing their names. You issued newer, harsher laws.

What happens in Guantanamo is a historical embarrassment to America and its values, and it screams into your faces—you hypocrites, "What is the value of your signature on any agreement or treaty?"

(3)   What we call you to thirdly is to take an honest stance with yourselves—and I doubt you will do so—to discover that you are a nation without principles or manners, and that values and principles to you are something which you merely demand from others, not that which you yourself must adhere to.

(4)   We also advise you to stop supporting Israel, and to end your support of the Indians in Kashmir, the Russians against the Chechens and to also cease supporting the Manila Government against the Muslims in the Southern Philippines.

(5)   We also advise you to pack your luggage and get out of our lands. We desire for your goodness, guidance, and righteousness, so do not force us to send you back as cargo in coffins.

(6)   Sixthly, we call upon you to end your support of the corrupt leaders in our countries. Do not interfere in our politics

and method of education. Leave us alone, or else expect us in New York and Washington.

(7) We also call you to deal with us and interact with us on the basis of mutual interests and benefits, rather than the policies of subdual, theft and occupation, and not to continue your policy of supporting the Jews because this will result in more disasters for you.

If you fail to respond to all these conditions, then prepare to fight with the Islamic Nation. The Nation of Monotheism, that puts complete trust in Allah and fears none other than Him. . . . The Nation of honour and respect. . . . The Nation of Martyrdom; the Nation that desires death more than you desire life. . . . The Nation of victory and success that Allah has promised.

[. . .]

The Islamic Nation that was able to dismiss and destroy the previous evil Empires like yourself; the Nation that rejects your attacks, wishes to remove your evils, and is prepared to fight you. You are well aware that the Islamic Nation, from the very core of its soul, despises your haughtiness and arrogance.

If the Americans refuse to listen to our advice and the goodness, guidance and righteousness that we call them to, then be aware that you will lose this Crusade Bush began, just like the other previous Crusades in which you were humiliated by the hands of the Mujahideen, fleeing to your home in great silence and disgrace. If the Americans do not respond, then their fate will be that of the Soviets who fled from Afghanistan to deal with their military defeat, political breakup, ideological downfall, and economic bankruptcy.

This is our message to the Americans, as an answer to theirs. Do they now know why we fight them and over which form of ignorance, by the permission of Allah, we shall be victorious?

Source: "Bin Laden's 'Letter to America,'" November 24, 2002, Guardian Observer Worldview Extra, http://observer.guardian .co.uk/print/0,,4552895-110490,00.html.

149. Draft Palestinian Constitution [Excerpt], March 25, 2003

Introduction

From mid-2002, when President George W. Bush publicly urged Palestinian political reform as part of his new initiative for Middle East peace, the Palestinian Authority (PA) was under pressure from the United States to remodel its government on the lines of a democratic state based on separation of powers. The Quartet road map demanded this, and internally those Palestinians who resented

the dominance of outside Palestine Liberation Organization (PLO) members likewise sought greater transparency, accountability, and democracy in their government. In 1997 Palestinians had drawn up a basic law, but this had never been signed into effect. In 1999 the Palestinian National Council established a special committee to draft a constitution for the proposed Palestinian state. The first draft was published in February 2001, and a second was published in early March 2003. U.S. diplomats insisted that it be redrafted to include the position of prime minister, an office that they hoped would serve as a counterbalance to the long-term dominance of Yasser Arafat, PLO and PA chairman. On March 25 the PA issued the third and final draft constitution. The new document stated that Palestine was a "sovereign, independent republic . . . based upon its borders on the eve of June 4, 1967." Jerusalem was named as its capital. The official religion was Islam, although "Christianity and other monotheistic religions" were to be "equally revered and respected." The "principles of Islamic Shari'a" law were to be "a major source for legislation," but the right of members of other religions to conduct their civil affairs according to their own tenets was also guaranteed. Palestinians who had resided in "Palestine" before May 10, 1948, and their descendants were all guaranteed Palestinian nationality and had the right "to return to the Palestinian state." The constitution was based on liberal principles, promising all Palestinians, men and women alike, equality before the law and the same civil and political rights. Freedom of the press, the right to education, and freedom of religion, thought, expression, association, and assembly were all guaranteed; private property was protected by law; all citizens were entitled to employment; and all citizens enjoyed the right to strike and to take part in political activities. The powers of the president and prime minister were delineated, with the president as head of state exercising broad supervisory and ceremonial functions and with the prime minister "representing the government" and setting its agenda. Under considerable pressure from Great Britain and the United States, on March 7, 2003, President Arafat nominated the Palestinian Mahmoud Abbas, a strong opponent of the Second (al-Aqsa) Intifada violence, as prime minister of the PA.

Primary Source

CHAPTER ONE
GENERAL FOUNDATIONS OF THE STATE
Article (1)
The State of Palestine is a sovereign, independent republic. Its territory is an indivisible unit based upon its borders on the eve of June 4, 1967, without prejudice to the rights guaranteed by the international resolutions relative to Palestine. All residents of this territory shall be subject to Palestinian law exclusively.

Article (2)
Palestine is part of the Arab nation. The state of Palestine abides by the charter of the League of Arab States. The Palestinian people are

part of the Arab and Islamic nations. Arab unity is a goal, the Palestinian people hopes to achieve.

Article (3)
Palestine is a peace loving state that condemns terror, occupation and aggression. It calls for the resolution of international and regional problems by peaceful means. It abides by the Charter of the United Nations.

Article (4)
Jerusalem is the capital of the state of Palestine and seat of its public authorities.

Article (5)
Arabic and Islam are the official Palestinian language and religion. Christianity and all other monotheistic religions shall be equally revered and respected. The Constitution guarantees equality in rights and duties to all citizens irrespective of their religious belief.

Article (6)
The Palestinian flag, motto, seals, emblems, and national anthem shall be determined by law.

Article (7)
The principles of Islamic Shari'a are a major source for legislation. Civil and religious matters of the followers of monotheistic religions shall be organized in accordance with their religious teachings and denominations within the framework of law, while preserving the unity and independence of the Palestinian people.

Article (8)
The Palestinian political system shall be a parliamentarian representative democracy based on political pluralism. The rights and liberties of all citizens shall be respected, including the right to form political parties and engage in political activity without discrimination on the basis of political opinions, sex, or religion. The parties shall abide by the principles of national sovereignty, democracy and peaceful transfer of authority in accordance with the Constitution.

Article (9)
Government shall be based on the principles of the rule of law and justice. All authorities, agencies, departments, institutions and individuals shall abide by the law.

Article (10)
All activities of the Palestinian public authorities shall, in normal and exceptional circumstances, be subject to administrative, political, legal and judicial review and control. There shall be no provision of law which grants immunity to any administrative action or decision from judicial supervision. The state shall be bound to compensate for damages resulting from errors, and risks resulting from actions and procedures carried out by state officials in the pursuit of their duties.

Article (11)
The independence and immunity of the judiciary are necessary for the protection of rights and liberties. No public or private individual shall be immune from executing judicial rulings. Any act of contempt of the judiciary shall be punishable by law.

Article (12)
Palestinian nationality shall be regulated by law, without prejudice to the rights of those who legally acquired it prior to May 10, 1948 or the rights of the Palestinians residing in Palestine prior to this date, and who were forced into exile or departed there from and denied return thereto. This right passes on from fathers or mothers to their progeny. It neither disappears nor elapses unless voluntarily relinquished. A Palestinian cannot be deprived of his nationality. The acquisition and relinquishment of Palestinian nationality shall be regulated by law. The rights and duties of citizens with multiple nationalities shall be governed by law.

Article (13)
Palestinians who left Palestine as a result of the 1948 war, and who were denied return thereto shall have the right to return to the Palestinian state and bear its nationality. It is a permanent, inalienable, and irrevocable right.

The state of Palestine shall strive to apply the legitimate right of return of the Palestinian refugees to their homes, and to obtain compensation, through negotiations, political, and legal channels in accordance with the 1948 United Nations General Assembly Resolution 194 and the principles of international law.

Article (14)
Natural resources in Palestine are the property of the Palestinian people who will exercise sovereignty over them. The state shall be obligated to preserve natural resources and legally regulate their optimal exploitation while safeguarding Palestinian religious and cultural heritage and environmental needs. The protection and maintenance of antiquities and historical sites is an official and social responsibility. It is prohibited to tamper with or destroy them, and whoever violates, destroys, or illegally sells them shall be punishable by law.

Article (15)
The state strives to achieve a clean, balanced environment whose protection shall be an official and societal responsibility. Tampering with it is punishable by law.

Article (16)
The economic system in Palestine shall be based on the principles of a free market economy, and the protection of free economic activity within the context of legitimate competition. The law shall protect private property, which may not be expropriated or seized except for public benefit in accordance with the law, and in return

for a just compensation. Expropriation may only be carried out by judicial order. The state may establish public companies legally, without prejudice to the system of free market economy.

Article (17)

The state shall strive to promote social, economic and cultural growth and scientific development of the Palestinian people with due consideration to social justice and the provision of assistance to the more deserving, especially those who suffered during the national struggle.

Article (18)

The state of Palestine shall abide by the Universal Declaration of Human Rights and shall seek to join other international covenants and charters that safeguard human rights.

CHAPTER TWO
GENERAL RIGHTS, LIBERTIES AND DUTIES
Article (19)

Palestinians are equal before the law. They enjoy civil and political rights and bear public duties without discrimination. The term 'Palestinian' or 'Citizen' wherever it appears in the constitution refers to both, male and female.

Article (20)

Human rights and liberties are binding and must be respected. The state shall guarantee religious, civil, political, economic, social and cultural rights and liberties to all citizens on the basis of equality and equal opportunity.

Persons are not deprived of their legal competence, rights and basic liberties for political reasons.

Article (21)

Every Palestinian who has reached the age of eighteen years shall have the right to vote in accordance with the provisions of the law.

All those who bear Palestinian nationality shall have the right to enter presidential elections and/or House of Representatives membership and/or assume a ministerial or judicial position.

The law regulates age and other prerequisites to accede to those posts.

Article (22)

Women shall have their own legal personality and independent financial assets. They shall have the same rights, liberties, and duties as men.

Article (23)

Women shall have the right to participate actively in the social, political, cultural and economic aspects of life. The Law shall strive to abolish restraints that prevent women from contributing to the building of family and society.

The constitutional and legal rights of women shall be safeguarded; and any violation of those rights shall be punishable by law. The law shall also protect their legal inheritance.

Article (24)

Children shall have all the rights guaranteed by the "Charter of the Rights of the Arab Child".

Article (25)

The right to life is guaranteed by the Constitution.

Article (26)

Individuals shall have the right to personal safety. Physical or psychological torture of human beings, as well as their inhuman treatment and subjection to harsh, undignified and humiliating punishment is prohibited. Those who plan, perform, or take part in such actions, shall be deemed criminal and are punishable by law and their crime shall not lapse by prescription.

Confessions proven to be extorted under duress or serious threat shall not be considered proof of guilt. Those who carry out such actions will be prosecuted.

Article (27)

Scientific or medical experimentation on a human being without his prior legal consent is forbidden. No surgery, medical examination, or treatment shall be performed on a person, except in accordance with the law. The law shall govern the transplant of organs, cells and other, new scientific developments, consistent with legitimate, humanitarian purposes.

Article (28)

Every person has the right to freedom and personal safety. Such right may not be violated, except in cases and in accordance with procedures stipulated by law.

A person may not be arrested, searched, imprisoned or restrained in any way, except by order of a competent judge or public prosecutor in accordance with the law. This is to safeguard the security of the society. A person shall be immediately informed of the offense with which he is charged in a language he can understand and is henceforth entitled to a lawyer and shall be immediately brought before the competent judicial authority. The law shall define the conditions of provisional detention. Any person illegally arrested, imprisoned, or restrained shall be entitled to compensation.

Article (29)

The accused is innocent until proven guilty by a fair trial wherein he shall be afforded the guarantees of self defense.

The accused shall be granted all guarantees necessary for his self defense, *pro se*, or through the assistance of an attorney of his choice in a public hearing. If he cannot afford one, the court will appoint him a lawyer free of charge.

Article (30)
Detainees and those deprived of liberty shall be treated humanely and with dignity. In executing sentences, the basic global principles approved by the United Nations for the treatment of prisoners shall be considered. In the sentencing of minors and in the execution thereof, their reform, education and rehabilitation shall be considered.

Article (31)
Citizens shall have the right to choose their place of residence and to travel within the state of Palestine. No person may be denied the right to travel from Palestine except by a legally issued court order. Likewise a Palestinian may not be deported or prevented from returning to his country, and may not be extradited.

Article (32)
A foreign political refugee who legally enjoys the right of asylum may not be extradited. The extradition of ordinary foreign defendants shall be governed by bilateral agreements or international conventions.

Article (33)
Litigation is a right guaranteed to all by the state. Each individual shall have the right to resort to his natural judge to defend his rights and liberties, and to receive compensation for a violation thereof.

The law shall regulate the procedures for litigation in a manner that ensures a speedy disposition of cases without prejudice to the rights of litigants.

In the event of a judicial error, the state shall be obligated to compensate the damaged party. The law shall govern the conditions and procedures thereof.

Article (34)
There shall be no crime or punishment except as stipulated by law. No sentence shall be executed except by judicial order. Punishment shall be personal and the individual may not be punished more than once for the same offence. Collective punishment is prohibited. Parity shall be considered between crime and punishment. There can be no punishment except for acts committed after a law has come into effect. The law shall regulate, in non-criminal cases, the retroactivity of laws.

Article (35)
The private life of every person, including family matters, residences, correspondence and other means of private communication, shall be protected and may not be infringed upon except by court order and within the limits of the law. Any consequence of the violation of this Article is null and void, and those who are harmed as a result thereof shall be entitled to compensation.

Article (36)
Freedom of religion and religious practice is guaranteed by the Constitution.

The state shall guarantee access to holy shrines that are subject to its sovereignty. The state shall guarantee to followers of all monotheistic religions the sanctity of their shrines in accordance with the historic commitment of the Palestinian people and the international commitments of Palestine.

Article (37)
Freedom of thought shall be guaranteed. Individuals shall have the right to express their opinions and publicize them in writing, speech, art, or other means of expression within the provisions of the law.

The law may only apply minimal restrictions on the practice thereof so as to safeguard the rights and liberties of others.

Article (38)
The right to publish newspapers or other means of the media is universal and guaranteed by the constitution. Financial sources for such purposes shall be subject to legal control.

Article (39)
Freedom of the press, including print, audio, and visual media, and those working in the media, is guaranteed. The media shall freely exercise its mission and express different opinions within the framework of society's basic values, while preserving rights, liberties and public duties in a manner consistent with the rule of law.

The media may not be subject to administrative censorship, hindrance, or confiscation, except by court order in accordance with the law.

Article (40)
Journalists and other citizens shall have the right of access to news and information with transparency in accordance with the law.

Article (41)
Citizens shall have the right to live in an atmosphere of intellectual freedom; participate in cultural life; cultivate their intellectual and innovative talents; enjoy scientific and artistic progress; and protect their moral and material rights, which may be the product of scientific, artistic or cultural effort in a manner consistent with society's basic values and the rule of law.

Article (42)
Education is an individual and social right. Education is compulsory at least until the end of the elementary level. Education shall be guaranteed by the state in public schools, institutions, and other establishments until the end of the secondary level.

The law shall regulate the state's supervision of its performance and curricula.

Article (43)
Private education shall be respected, provided that schools, institutions and private educational centers abide by the plans and curricula adopted by the state. The law shall regulate the state's supervision of its curricula.

Article (44)
The state shall uphold the independence of institutions, universities and research centers that have a scientific purpose. The law shall regulate the supervision thereof in such a manner so as to safeguard the freedom of scientific research and innovation in all fields. The state shall, within its capabilities, strive to encourage, support and protect them.

Article (45)
The law shall regulate social security, disability and old age pensions, support to families of martyrs, detainees, orphans, those injured in the national struggle, and those requiring special care. The state shall guarantee them—within its capabilities—education, health and social security services and shall give them priority in employment opportunities in accordance with the law.

Article (46)
The state shall organize health insurance as an individual right and a public interest. It shall guarantee, within its capabilities, basic health care for the indigent.

Article (47)
Through a housing policy founded on collaboration of the state, private sector and banking system, the state shall seek to provide adequate housing to every citizen. In cases of war and natural disasters, the state shall also seek, within its capabilities, to provide shelter to the homeless.

Article (48)
The state shall guarantee family, maternal and child care. It shall care for adolescents and the youth. The law shall regulate children, mother and family rights in accordance with the provisions of international agreements and the 'Rights of the Arab Child' charter. In particular, the state shall seek to protect children from harm, harsh treatment, abuse, and from any work that would endanger their safety, health and education.

Article (49)
Public property shall be safeguarded and regulated by law so as to guarantee its protection and for it to serve the people's public interest. The law shall regulate the 'Waqf' [religious endowment's] organization and management of its properties and assets.

Article (50)
Private property is protected by law. General confiscation of private property is prohibited.

Confiscation of private property is allowed for public interest and in cases allowed for by law against fair compensation.

Law regulates real estate ownership by foreigners.

Article (51)
Employment is a right of all citizens. The state shall seek to provide work opportunities to the capable through its development and construction plan, with the support of the private sector. The law shall regulate work relations in such a manner so as to guarantee justice for all and provide for the protection and security of workers. Work may not be forcibly imposed on citizens. The law shall regulate adequate remuneration for compulsory work. Workers shall have the right to establish unions and professional associations at work.

Article (52)
The right to protest and strike shall be exercised within the limits of the law.

Article (53)
Citizens shall have the right to assume public office, on the basis of competence, merit and equal opportunity in accordance with the requirements of the law.

Article (54)
Based on constitutional rules and legal provisions, every citizen shall have the right to express his views in referenda and elections and run for election or nominate a person who meets electoral requirements.

Article (55)
All citizens shall have the right to partake, individually or collectively, in political activities, including:

The right to form political parties and/or subscribe thereto, and/or withdrawing therefrom in accordance with the law;
Formation of unions, societies, associations, fraternities, assemblies, clubs, and institutions and/or subscribe thereto and/or withdraw therefrom in accordance with the law.

The law shall govern the procedures for acquiring its legal personality.

Article (56)

Every individual shall have the right to organize private meetings in accordance with the law, and without the presence of the police. Every individual shall have the right to assemble and organize public meetings, and to demonstrate peacefully with others without bearing arms. The exercise of those two liberties may not be restrained except as mandated by law, consistent with measures acceptable in democratic society and constitutional rights and liberties.

Article (57)

Every individual shall have the right to address the public authorities, and to present petitions and grievances in writing.

Article (58)

Basic rights and liberties may not be suspended. The law shall regulate those rights and liberties that may be temporarily restricted in exceptional circumstances in matters related to public security and national safety purposes. The law shall penalize the arbitrary use of power and authority.

Article (59)

Any violation of the basic general rights and liberties guaranteed by the Constitution or the law, shall be considered a crime. All civil and criminal lawsuits arising as a result thereof shall not lapse by prescription. The state shall guarantee a just compensation for those who have been harmed.

Article (60)

An independent general organization shall be legally set up, composed of unofficial legal and political personalities who truly believe in the rights of the citizen and would volunteer for its defense.

The organization shall be concerned with monitoring the state of the rights and liberties of the citizens, for which purpose it shall have the competence to obtain official information responsibly and with transparency.

Its employees shall be responsible for any misuse of the information they obtain in matters other than those stipulated by their incorporating law.

The organization shall have the right to receive grievances from the citizens concerning the actions of the institutions of the state's authorities which illegally breach the rights and basic liberties of the citizen.

It shall have the right to suggest ways to improve the performance of the departments of the state with respect to protecting the rights and liberties of the citizens. It shall submit its proposals and reports on matters within its supervisory and developmental competence to the House of Representatives and the president of the state.

Article (61)

The state shall assume responsibility for the safety of persons and property. It protects the rights of every citizen within the state and abroad.

Article (62)

Defending the nation is a sacred duty and serving it is an honor for every citizen. It shall be regulated by law.

Individuals and groups may not bring or bear arms, nor may they illegally possess arms in violation of the provisions of the governing law.

Article (63)

The payment of taxes and general dues is a duty regulated by law.

CHAPTER THREE
PUBLIC AUTHORITIES
Article (64)

National sovereignty belongs to the people, who are the source of the authorities. They exercise their duties directly through referenda and general elections or through representatives of the electorate, within its three general powers: legislative, executive and judicial and by its constitutional institutions. No individual or group may claim for itself the right to exercise such powers.

Article (65)

The relationship between the three public authorities shall be based on equality and independence. They shall exercise their authority on the basis of relative separation with respect to their duties and mutual cooperation and oversight. No authority shall have the right to perform duties that have been attributed to another authority in accordance with constitutional rules.

Section One
Legislative Branch/House of Representatives
Article (66)

The House of Representatives shall assume legislative power. It shall endorse the general budget, which shall be prepared by the Cabinet. It shall supervise the actions of the executive branch in the manner specified by the Constitution.

Article (67)

The House of Representatives shall be composed of (150) individuals, representing the Palestinian people. They shall be elected according to the Constitution and election law. When running for candidacy to the House of Representatives, the provisions stated in this Constitution and the election law shall be observed. Candidates for the House of Representatives must be Palestinian.

Article (68)

Members of the House of Representatives are elected for five years and may be re-elected more than once. The term of the House of

Representatives may not be extended except in case of necessity and by virtue of a law ratified by two-thirds of the total number of the House of Representatives.

Article (69)
The seat of the House of Representatives shall be in Jerusalem, the capital of the State of Palestine. Its sessions may be held in different locations as per the request of the majority of the members of the House of Representatives.

[...]

The Consultative Council
Article (110)
The Consultative Council composed of one hundred and fifty independent members is established according to the Constitution. In its formation due consideration shall be given to the ratio of distribution of Palestinians in Palestine and abroad. The law shall regulate their election or appointment according to their countries of residence.

The president may appoint in the Consultative Council non-Palestinians who have distinguished themselves with noble services for the Palestinian cause.

Article (111)
The Consultative Council shall specialize:

—In the study of general strategic issues and submission of adequate advice.
—In making suggestions with relation to national rights, safety of the Palestinian soil and rights of Palestinians abroad.
—In discussion of constitutional amendments and giving opinion upon request.
—In whatever subject matters the president refers to the council concerning general policy in Arab and foreign affairs for the state of Palestine.
—In draft laws referred by the president concerning Palestinian expatriates.
—That which members of the council set for discussion on their agenda.

Article (112)
The Consultative Council shall send decisions and recommendations to the president of the state who shall order their publication in the official gazette, and to the Prime Minister and the speaker of the House of Representatives.

Section Two
The Executive Branch
First: The President of the State
Article (113)
The President of the State is the President of the Republic. He shall uphold the Constitution and the unity of the people. He shall guar-antee the continuity of the existence of the state and its national independence. He shall guarantee the proper functioning of the public authorities. He shall exercise his jurisdiction, and his responsibilities shall be determined pursuant to the provisions of the Constitution. Except those powers that are constitutionally attributed to the president of the State, the government's executive and administrative duties shall be the responsibility of the Cabinet.

Article (114)
The presidential candidate must bear Palestinian nationality exclusively, and be at least forty years of age, on the date of nomination. He must enjoy full civil and political rights.

Article (115)
The President shall be elected directly by the people for a five year term renewable once.

Article (116)
The elected president shall assume his duties immediately upon conclusion of his predecessor's term. Prior to exercising the duties of his office, the president shall take the following constitutional oath, before the House of Representatives and in the presence of the head of the supreme judicial council: "I swear by Almighty God to be faithful to the nation and its shrines, to the people and their national heritage, to respect the Constitution and the law, and to fully preserve the interests of the Palestinian people. May God be my witness".

[...]

Article (122)
After consultations with the representative parties, the president shall nominate the prime minister from the party that obtained the largest number of seats in the House of Representatives. If the formation of a government is impossible within a three week period, the President nominates a prime minister from the party that obtained the second highest number of seats at the House of Representatives and so on until a government is formed.

Article (123)
The president of the state shall ratify laws after their approval by the House of Representatives, within thirty days of their referral to him, and he orders their publication. The president of the state may object to a draft law that was approved by the House of Representatives, and may request its reconsideration accompanied by the reasons for his objection within thirty days of having received such draft law. If the mentioned legal time limit ends without ratifying the law or objecting to it, it would be considered effective and should be published in the official gazette. If the president of the state returns the law previously approved by the House of Representatives within the legal time limit, and such draft receives a second approval by the House of Representatives by a majority of two thirds of its members, it shall be considered a law and so promulgated.

Article (124)

The Speaker of the Council of Ministers, or the minister he appoints, shall negotiate international treaties, and inform the President of the State of the course of negotiations, which in turn have to be approved by the Council of Ministers and endorsed by the President. The treaties and agreements that burden the state treasury with expenses unaccounted for in the budget or burden the citizens with commitments in violation of the current laws may not be enforced unless and until the House of Representatives ratifies it, and approval by the president. Treaties that might affect the independence of the state or the integrity of its territory can only be approved by general public referendum.

Article (125)

In addition to the Presidential prerogatives, the President enjoys the following privileges:

— He heads, in exceptional cases, and during the State of Emergency, the Council of Ministers.
— He issues alone the decree for the nomination of the prime minister and the decree accepting the resignation of the government or considering it resigned. Other decisions and protocols have to be jointly signed by the prime minister, and the minister or ministers concerned. The prime minister co-signs with the president of the state decrees of law, decrees of re-evaluation of laws and decrees calling for exceptional meetings of the house of representatives.
— He addresses, when necessary, a non-debatable speech to the House of Representatives.
— He forwards drafts of laws approved by the council of ministers to the House of Representatives.
— He grants special pardons or reduction of sentences. Amnesty is by decree exclusively.
— He heads official receptions and grants state decorations by decree.

Article (126)

Upon the recommendation of the minister of foreign affairs, the president of the State shall appoint, and terminate the duties of, ambassadors and representatives of the state of Palestine to states, regional and international organizations. He shall receive the credentials of representatives of foreign states and representatives of regional and international organizations to the state of Palestine.

Article (127)

The president of the state is the supreme commander of the Palestinian national security forces which is headed by a concerned minister.

Article (128)

The president of the state may establish specialized advisory councils from qualified, specialized and experienced persons to participate in expressing opinion and to benefit from national capabilities.

The State of Emergency
Article (129)

The president of the state, with the approval of the prime minister and consultation with the Speaker of the House of Representatives, may declare a state of emergency if the security of the country is exposed to danger of war or natural disaster or siege threatening the safety of the society and continuity of operation of its constitutional institutions. The emergency measures must be necessary to restore public order, or the orderly functioning of the state's authorities, or confront disaster or siege, for a period not exceeding thirty days, renewable by approval of two thirds of all the members of the House of Representatives, with the exception of state of war. In all cases, any declaration of a state of emergency must specify the purpose thereof, and the region and time period covered thereby.

Article (130)

After the declaration of the state of emergency, the Council of Ministers may, if events necessitate the taking of speedy measures to confront situations that cannot be delayed, issue decrees that gain approval by the president within a period not exceeding fifteen days and then have the force of law. They are to be presented to the House of Representatives in its first meeting after the declaration of the state of emergency, or in the session to extend the state of emergency, whichever occurs first, to decide upon it, otherwise they lose their legal force retroactively. Should the House of Representatives not approve them, they shall cease to have legal effect, and the house would decide how to remedy its effects without any prejudice to material rights of third parties.

Article (131)

During a state of emergency it is forbidden to impose restrictions on basic rights and liberties, except to the extent necessary to safeguard public safety in the country. All decisions and actions taken by the council of ministers during the state of emergency shall be subject to judicial review. The competent courts will look into grievances within a period not exceeding three days.

Article (132)

Impeachment of the president of the state with high treason, breach of the Constitution or committing a felony shall be according to a suggestion by one-third of the total members of the House of Representatives. The decision to impeach may not be issued unless approved by a majority of two thirds of the total members of the House of Representatives. Upon the issuance of the decision to impeach, the president shall immediately cease performing his duties and shall be tried by the Constitutional Court.

Second: The Prime Minister
Article (133)

A precondition to be appointed prime minister or minister is to bear Palestinian nationality exclusively, to be at least thirty five years of age, enjoying his full civil and political rights.

Article (134)

The prime minister shall form the cabinet and when presenting his formed cabinet to the president of the state, he shall state which ministry is assigned to which minister. The prime minister shall present the members of his government and their program to the parliament to obtain its confidence.

Article (135)

If the prime minister fails to obtain the confidence of the House of Representatives, the government will be considered resigned, and the president shall resume consultation for the appointment of a new prime minister in accordance with Article (122) of the Constitution.

Article (136)

Neither the prime minister nor any minister before obtaining the confidence of the House of Representatives, performs his duties except [to] precede the duties in limited sense.

Article (137)

The prime minister shall preside over the activities of the government. Every minister shall be answerable to the Cabinet in accordance to the procedures as specified by the constitutional rules. The prime minister and the ministers are individually and jointly responsible before the House of Representatives for the actions of the government.

Article (138)

When making a ministerial change, or adding a minister or filling a vacancy for any reason whatsoever, the new ministers must be presented to the House of Representatives at the first session for a vote of confidence. If the change involves more than one third of the council of ministers, a vote of confidence on the whole cabinet must be taken. No minister may perform the duties of his office until he obtains confidence from the House of Representatives.

Article (139)

After obtaining the confidence, the prime minister and the ministers shall take the following oath before the president of the state and the House of Representatives in a joint session: "I swear by Almighty God to be faithful to the country, to uphold the rights of the people, nation and its interests, and to respect the Constitution and to fully carry out my duties. May God be my witness".

Article (140)

The prime minister practices the following competencies:

— He represents the government and speaks in its name, he is responsible for the implementation of the general policies set by the council of ministers.
— He submits the general policy of the government to the House of Representatives.

— He calls the council of ministers to meet, sets its agenda of which he informs the president of the state, he presides [over] its sessions except the ones attended by the president of the state.
— He oversees the work of the authorities and public institutions, coordinates between the ministers and gives general directives to ensure proper execution of work.
— He signs executive and organizational decrees.
— He exercises vigilance for the execution of laws, regulations, coordination of policies and governmental agendas.
— He approves higher level employment appointments per recommendations of the concerned minister in accordance with the basic laws of appointments in ministries and state administrations.
— He proposes draft laws.
— He promulgates laws that have been ratified by the House of Representatives after being endorsed by the president, or after being legally passed.
— Any other competence legally attributed to him.

[...]

Third: The Council of Ministers
(The Government)
Article (144)

The Council of Ministers shall be composed of a prime minister and the ministers, of which half of them at most shall be members of the House of Representatives.

Article (145)

The executive authority shall be entrusted with the council of ministers.

Article (146)

Upon the invitation of the prime minister, the council of ministers shall convene regularly. If need be, the president may attend and preside over the sessions of the council of ministers which he attends. Legal quorum for its convening is reached with two thirds of its members and decisions are reached by consent or by voting with a majority of the present as long as there is no text in violation of the constitution. The council of ministers practices its competencies in accordance with the provisions of the Constitution, and the regulations governing the activities of the government.

Article (147)

The council of ministers shall have the following competencies:

— Setting public policy, in the light of the ministerial program approved by the House of Representatives.
— Executing public policy as established, as well as laws and regulations, and ensuring compliance therewith, and proposing new draft laws.

—Preparing the draft general budget to be presented to the House of Representatives for approval.

—Organizing, governing and supervising the offices, agencies and institutions of the state at their various levels.

—Overseeing the performance of the ministries, departments, institutions and agencies and supervising their work.

—Discussing the proposals and plans of each ministry, and its policies in the area of exercising its powers.

—Approving the system of administrative formations.

—Issuance of organizational decrees and necessary regulations by law-implementing procedures, as well as supervisory regulations, and organization of public utilities and general welfare.

—Appointment of civil servants and military personnel, in accordance with and upon the recommendation of the concerned minister.

—Any other competencies granted pursuant to the provisions of the Constitution and the law.

Article (148)

The organizational regulation of the executive branch shall establish standing committees at the council of ministers. From among the chairpersons of those committees, two shall be selected as deputies to the prime minister.

Article (149)

The council of ministers shall issue the regulations necessary for the exercise of its powers.

The Ministers
Article (150)

The minister is the supreme administrative director of his ministry. He shall have the following competencies within the sphere of the ministry with which he is entrusted, under the supervision of the prime minister:

—Proposing the general policy for his ministry and overseeing its implementation after its adoption.

—Overseeing the course of work at the ministry and issuance of the necessary directives for the performance of his duties.

—Submitting to the council of ministers proposed laws related to his ministry.

—Implementing the general budget within the scope of his ministry according to the allocations approved for his ministry.

—Choosing employees and recommending them for appointment by the council of ministers.

—Delegating some of his administrative authority to the deputy minister or other senior officials in his ministry in accordance with the law.

—Chairing the administrative apparatus of his ministry.

—Supervising the implementation of laws and regulations related to his ministry.

—Any competence legally assigned to him.

[...]

Security Forces
Article (156)

The national defense forces shall be the property of the Palestinian people. They shall assume the task of protection and security of the Palestinians and defense of the state of Palestine. They are headed by a specialized minister and the head of the state is its supreme commander. Formation of armed groups outside the framework of the national defense forces is prohibited. The law shall regulate the general mobilization for the defense of the nation and the rights of the citizens.

Article (157)

The police is a civilian department, part of the ministry of the interior. It shall be legally organized to serve the people, defend the society, and exercise vigilance to maintain security, general order, and general morals. It shall perform its duty within the limitations defined by law, and with respect for all the rights and liberties set forth in this Constitution.

Public Administration
Article (158)

Appointment of civil servants and all persons working for the state and the conditions of their employment shall be according to the provisions of the law.

Article (159)

All that concerns civil service, including appointment, transfer, delegation, promotion and retirement, shall be regulated by law. The employees department, in coordination with the concerned governmental departments, shall strive to improve and develop the public administration, and offer advice on draft laws and regulations particular to the public administration and its employees.

[...]

Section Three
The Judicial Branch
Article (162)

The judicial branch shall be independent. It shall have original jurisdiction to perform the judicial function, and shall be entrusted with deciding all disputes and crimes. The law shall define the institutions of the judicial branch, and regulate their structure and the types of courts, and their levels, jurisdictions and procedures. Exceptional courts may not be formed.

Article (163)

A Supreme Judicial Council shall be entrusted with the affairs of the judicial institutions. [It] shall define the formation and jurisdictions of this council in a manner that ensures its equality and independence in cooperating with the other public authorities. This council shall be consulted on draft laws regulating judicial affairs. This council shall have the right to set its own internal regulation.

Article (164)

The president of the Supreme Judicial Council shall be appointed by a decision made by the head of the state according to the law, and approved by the House of Representatives. The law regulates the appointment of the members of the supreme judicial council and the preconditions they should meet.

[...]

Supreme Constitutional Court
Article (181)

A Constitutional Court shall be established by virtue of the Constitution to exercise its jurisdiction independently in order to preserve the legality of the work of state institutions. It shall be composed of nine judges appointed by the head of state and nominated by the council of ministers, and approved by the House of Representatives. The Court shall set its internal regulation to operational procedures. The judges shall be elected for one term of nine years that shall not be renewed or extended directly.

Article (182)

The judges of the Constitutional Court shall elect one of them as a president for the court for a three year term. The president of the Court and the judges in the Constitutional Court swear the legal oath before the president of the state, the speaker of the House of Representatives and the president of the Supreme Judicial Council at the same time before they start their duties.

[...]

Article (185)

The Constitutional Court shall examine the constitutionality of the following matters, pursuant to a request from the president of the state, or the Prime Minister, or the speaker of the House of Representatives, or ten members of the House of Representatives, or from the courts, the public prosecutor, or anyone whose constitutional rights have been violated:

— The constitutionality of laws before they are promulgated, whenever requested by the president of the state provided the request was submitted within 30 days of referring to the head of state for ratification and promulgation;

— Deciding disputes related to the constitutionality of laws, ordinances, regulations, measures and decisions issued by the president or the council of ministers which have the force of law;

— Interpretation of constitutional texts when a dispute arises over the rights, duties and competencies of the three branches,

and in case of a jurisdictional dispute between the head of state and the prime minister;

— Deciding problems that arise concerning the constitutionality of programs and activities of political parties and associations and the procedures of their dissolution and suspension and their conformity with the Constitution;

— The constitutionality of signing treaties and the procedures of their implementation, and nullification of all or some of its articles if it contradicts with the Constitution or an international treaty; and

— Any other jurisdictions assigned to it by the Constitution.

Article (186)

The Constitutional Court shall render void an unconstitutional law, regulation, ordinance or procedure, or end its effectiveness, as the case may be, and the conditions specified in governing its operation.

Article (187)

Judicial decisions of the Constitutional Court shall be final and may not be appealed in any manner and [are] binding on all government authorities and natural and legal persons.

[...]

Source: "Constitution of the State of Palestine, Third Draft, 7 March 2003, Revised in March 25, 2003," Constitution Committee of the Palestine National Council, 2003, http://www.jmcc.org.

150. Mahmoud Abbas, Inaugural Speech as Prime Minister [Excerpt], April 29, 2003

Introduction

By mid-2002, the dominance within the Palestinian Authority (PA) of Palestine Liberation Organization (PLO) officials appointed by Yasser Arafat, who chaired both organizations, had become the source of much resentment from local Palestinians in the occupied territories, who found their own government both corrupt and ineffective. The peace plans advanced by U.S. president George W. Bush and the Quartet consisting of the United States, Russia, the European Union (EU), and the United Nations (UN) also called for the democratization and wholesale reform of Palestinian institutions. The Israeli government would have liked to take the opportunity to eliminate Arafat from Palestinian political life, but the United States and other Quartet members considered him too prominent a figure to discard. Instead, they insisted on the inclusion in the draft Palestinian constitution of the post of prime minister, an executive who would head the government while the presidency, which Arafat would still fill, became more of a ceremonial office, its occupant serving as head of state. Under British and U.S. pressure, on March 7, 2003, Arafat nominated Mahmoud Abbas as the new prime minister. Abbas, a strong critic of the violence of the Second (al-Aqsa) Intifada who pledged himself to implement the Tenet Plan for a cease-fire, accepted the premiership later that month after waging a fierce battle with Arafat for control of cabinet appointments. Abbas also became interior minister with overall responsibility for security. A special session of the Palestinian Legislative Council held in Ramallah on April 29 approved Abbas's appointment. The new prime minister, who had been a key Palestinian negotiator in many past peace talks, delivered an inaugural speech in which he stated his intention of cracking down on terrorism and illegal weaponry and preserving public order. He urged political opponents to make their case through the press and the law and not to resort to violence. The Palestinians' foremost priority, he urged, should be the resumption and conclusion of peace talks aimed at ending the Israeli occupation and establishing a secure and independent Palestinian state within acceptable and contiguous boundaries. Abbas emphasized his government's commitment to implementation of the Quartet group's Road Map for Peace. Negotiations were, he stated, the only realistic way forward. Abbas condemned Israel's policies of expanding settlements in the occupied territories and around Jerusalem and of building walls within the occupied territories that, on the pretext of protecting Jewish areas, separated Palestinian communities from each other. Despite his commitment to talks, he called on Israel to end these practices, which were designed to sabotage any viable Palestinian state, and to cease military incursions into Palestinian territory and the imposition of restrictions on the movements of Palestinians. He also expressed his sympathy and solidarity for Iraq, where U.S. and British forces had just overthrown the government of Saddam Hussein, an old Palestinian ally. In defiance of Abbas's pledge to end terrorist tactics, a few hours after his inauguration a suicide bomber blew himself up in a nightclub in Tel Aviv, killing 3 Israelis and wounding more than 25. The next day, the Israel Defense Forces (IDF) quickly responded with a massive raid on Gaza. The two actions neatly indicated that neither side in the ongoing intifada wished to cooperate with Abbas's exhortations. He remained in power for only six months. In October 2003 he resigned, ascribing his decision to do so to inadequate support from Israel and the United States in the peace process and also to intransigence from within the Palestinian community.

Primary Source

[...]

I am filled with confidence and pride as I stand here before our elected Legislative Council, one of the expressions of the sovereignty of our people, and the constitutional reference for the government, and whose elected members are an integral part of our National Council that guards our political organization, the Palestine Liberation Organization.

I begin my speech by expressing all respect and esteem to the Palestinian people in every city, village and refugee camp in our home-land and in the Diaspora, to our resilient and struggling people of whom we are proud. We cherish this unlimited pride that has extended across several generations. This pride is exemplified in the hundreds of thousands of martyrs, injured and detainees who protect our national identity in spite of all attempts to destroy and annul our rights. We have preserved our inalienable rights and established our National Authority as an imperative step towards the establishment of our forthcoming independent state, with Jerusalem as its capital.

Our people, who have been steadfast throughout the past two and a half years during the courageous uprising against Israel's aggression, despite the killing and destruction in Jenin and its heroic camp, in Nablus, Tulkarm, Qalqilya, Hebron and all of our resistant cities, villages and camps in the West Bank and in Rafah, Khan Yunis, Dayr al-Balah, Gaza City, Beit Hanoun, Jabalya and in every part of our steadfast Strip. I specifically want to honor the families who have lost their loved ones, those who have suffered injuries, Palestinian political prisoners and those who have personally suffered. Palestinian accomplishments will always be indebted to the sacrifices of these heroes and to their families, people and homeland.

We are a highly-distinguished people and our energy has grown—in the eyes of the whole world—to be worthy of a genuine state that enjoys sovereignty like all other peoples and states: a modern and democratic state that will constitute a safe home to all Palestinians and an effective partner in building and supporting security and stability in the region. I believe that part of the responsibilities of the government should be to build the pillars of this state including the preparation for presidential, parliamentary and municipal elections, based on the Elections Law which we hope will be passed soon by your distinguished Council.

[...]

The root of our suffering and the source of our pain is the occupation and its detestable oppressive policies. We all commit to ending the occupation in all of its shapes and forms. This requires that we direct our main efforts to internal housekeeping while being committed to the provisions of the Basic Law adopted by the Palestinian Legislative Council and ratified by President Yasser Arafat. The government commits itself to abiding by the Law and enforcing it on all Palestinian institutions in order to ensure that in a short time there will be no violations of the Law and no signs of chaos or ambiguity in society. We will implement our Basic Law in a manner proving that we merit a state and will abide by its constitution. Our government will not allow for any violation of this Law.

The government is certain that internal organization cannot be achieved without a collective commitment to the principle of the rule of law. The rule of law will be meaningless without an independent, effective and impartial judiciary, and efficient legal institutions with a Ministry of Justice that supports the independence of the judiciary and an enforcement mechanism capable of implementing such provisions. The government promises to work side by side with the President and the Legislative Council to restructure the Higher Judiciary Council in accordance with the provisions of the Law and the Independence of the Judiciary. It also promises to improve the courts. It is committed to helping the courts overcome their gaps and perform their duties in the best manner. The government commits itself to work on the preparation of draft laws and regulations to complete the National Authority's body of laws. The judicial system is the real face of any society and the most accurate indicator of its civilization, progress and development. Accordingly, the government shall pay special attention to the judiciary.

Mr. President,

Ladies and Gentlemen,

The government will concentrate on the question of security. Our understanding of security is the security of Palestinian citizens in their homeland. We seek the security of the homeland for all sectors of society. Based on this understanding, the government endeavors to develop the security organs and apparatuses according to law. It will allocate special attention to the professional qualifications of the leaders and members of such security organs. It will tolerate no breach of discipline or violations of the law. The government will not allow—to the contrary it will strictly prevent—interference by the security forces in the lives, affairs and business of citizens unless within the limits permitted by the law. In this respect, the government will build upon the achievements of the previous government regarding the organization and responsibilities of the security apparatuses. These security arrangements give the Minister of the Interior wide jurisdiction, and provide him with the ability to control the internal situation and improve security performance.

The government understands that citizens' feeling of safety and security is the most important pillar of national resistance and is the most important requirement for growth and progress in all aspects of life for both individuals and the community. Therefore, the unauthorized possession of weapons, with its direct threat to the security of the population, is a major concern that will be relentlessly addressed. We aim to ensure that only legitimate weapons are used to preserve public order and implement the law. There will be no other decision-making authority except for the legitimate one—the Palestinian Authority. On this land and for this people, there is only one authority, one law, and one democratic and national decision that applies to us all.

It should be understood here that the rights of citizens to freely express themselves will not be jeopardized by any person or under any pretense or justification. Palestinians may hold any political views, and exercise such rights and freedoms in accordance with the law.

The government is aware of the importance of political opposition and is fully aware of the right of the opposition to strive to achieve power. In order to foster this, we call upon the opposition factions and forces to develop their institutions, frameworks and dialogues and to halt any incitement and negative campaigning. We call upon the opposition to make use of both the free press and the law to exercise its voice and to present its viewpoints. We also call on all sectors of Palestinian society to utilize the Political Party Law to revive internal political debate and enhance its effectiveness. I reconfirm here that our government will stand for pluralism within the framework of national unity in accordance with the law, but pluralism does not extend to security.

Within this framework, we will develop the most effective means of reaching an internal understanding aimed at ensuring the rights of all forces, parties and factions to exist and work. Here, I call upon all of you to partake in the election of representative institutions, particularly given that we have chosen elections as a non-revocable means to formulate and activate these organs.

Mr. President,

Ladies and Gentlemen, Members of the PLC,

The government understands the magnitude of our suffering and economic difficulties as a result of the continuation and escalation of Israeli measures. This suffering has led to an increase in poverty and unemployment rates with a major deterioration in economic indicators. This is a result of the enormous destruction of our infrastructure, our private property and sources of livelihood caused by the occupation. Palestinian citizens seek a glimmer of hope to eradicate their suffering and its destructive impact on their lives. The government pledges to address this economic situation by taking timely measures, within its capacities, to improve the living conditions mainly of the unemployed and other people living in extreme hardship until passage of the Social Security Law. The government will also work to restore the infrastructure that has been destroyed by the occupation. Within this framework, the government promises to launch an international effort to seek rehabilitation for the economic destruction caused by Israel's oppression, invasions, and killings.

The government will work to prepare a comprehensive national development plan (that includes Jerusalem) in which we will devote sufficient attention to the service and economic sectors and will provide necessary health, educational, cultural, media and agricultural services to citizens. The plan will be carried out in a professional and transparent manner. In this context, the government is keen to continue working with the private sector in order to enact and enforce legislation and regulations that will strengthen the market economy and develop the national economy and provide protection to investments and investors.

Moreover, the government will devote itself to the situation of Palestinian women, who constitute half of our population, and who play a major and effective role in our lives. We will also continue to work on the protection of the rights of children and families and develop the youth sector to ensure a better future for our people.

As regards the financial issue, the government will continue its efforts to implement the new fiscal policy and all the measures and arrangements as they were submitted to you by the Minister of Finance through the Budget Law. The fiscal policy reasserts our commitment to regulate the investments of the Palestinian Authority. These investments will be fully placed under the government's supervision and control so that all resources of the Palestinian Authority will be unified in the Ministry of Finance in accordance with international best practices in the administration of public funds.

The government will not allow—and will devise strict regulations to combat—abuse of personal positions in the exercise of trade and investment.

Public funds belong to the citizens and to the nation. Preserving public funds is a national and moral duty that will be exercised through institutions, laws, transparency and continuous supervision. In this context, the government will prosecute persons accused of corruption and embezzlement based on concrete evidence and pursuant to due process. The government is fully prepared to receive any complaints and supporting evidence in this regard, and to refer these to the competent authorities.

The government is fully aware of the problems facing our administrative structure and understands that it is necessary to quickly remedy this problem. It will continue to implement and develop its reform plan—in particular the reform plan adopted by the Legislative Council through a joint committee between the Council and the government and in cooperation with all relevant parties including civil society. The government will build the Ministerial Cabinet with professionalism and work ethics that will improve the work of all Executive Authority institutions in order to serve the public interest. One of the most important steps in this regard is the implementation of the financial and administrative components of the Civil Service Law. We will ensure that all civil servants (who number more than 120,000) are given guarantees for their present and future so that they have sufficient pension salaries upon the termination of their employment, in accordance with a comprehensive pension system that we hope to finalize in the coming few months.

The government will not allow for any sign of chaos, waste or duplication in our administrative structure and will therefore continue our efforts to restructure government ministries, institutions and agencies by merging and abolishing such organs as needed to allow them to best perform their tasks in serving the state and its citizens. All of this will be framed within a modern and comprehensive administrative law that the government will work to formulate in order to organize all aspects of the Executive Authority.

Mr. President,

Ladies and Gentlemen, Members of the PLC,

You may have noticed that I intentionally began this statement with the government's vision of the internal situation and the areas of major concern.

This is a message that we are conveying to Palestinian citizens who seek wide-scale reforms in all aspects of their lives and related to their rights.

However, the internal situation cannot be separated from the painful and political reality in which we live and encounter: the deplorable occupation and its accompanying colonization and oppressive policies that have caused us tremendous pain and suffering.

Once again, I reiterate that the military and colonizing occupation with its practices that include assassinations, detentions, checkpoints, sieges, demolition of homes and properties is the root of our suffering, has deepened our suffering and is the main source of our problems. The occupation impedes our growth and therefore ending the occupation in all of its forms and from all of the territories occupied since 1967, including our eternal capital Jerusalem, is our national priority that requires solidarity and unity among all Palestinian forces under the leadership of the Palestine Liberation Organization, the sole representative of our people authorized by the major Palestinian institutions, foremost among which are the National and Central Council, to negotiate and conclude agreements on behalf of the Palestinian people.

The government, which is part of our national political system, the PLO, is fully committed to the programs and decisions of our National and Central Councils on political and strategic levels.

We should translate our decades and generations of popular and revolutionary struggles into political achievements that will bring us closer to our goal of establishing our independent state (with Jerusalem as its capital) and resolving the question of our refugees on the basis of international law.

Based on our realistic and practical understanding of the contents, mechanisms and goals of our national struggle, our people fought with honor and undertook political initiatives with consciousness and seriousness.

Every means of struggle has its time, mechanisms and calculated return. Based on this, our people, through its legitimate leadership, has presented successive serious peace initiatives and has not hesitated to adopt peace as our strategic, irrevocable choice. The peace process has gone through essential failings and major deteriorations, to the point that we have now reached the most difficult stage of this bloody and escalating conflict. While we should learn from the lessons of the past, what we are living under does not cause us to lose hope in the benefits of peace, or to turn our backs on Arab and international initiatives that aim to achieve peace.

Before us, we have the Arab peace initiative that came out of the Summit in Beirut. This has formed a national consensus on the need to end the Arab-Israeli conflict peacefully and in accordance with international law. This initiative will ensure that our region goes from one of conflict to that of stability and normalized relations between all states. We also have before us the Roadmap as an international blueprint to aims to reach a permanent solution to the Palestinian question. The government is committed to the Palestinian leadership's official approval of this plan reached after an in-depth and thorough review of it. Nonetheless, I would like to mention a few points in this regard:

Israel is attempting to alter the Roadmap as we know it by entering into complicated negotiations and by outlining its own understanding of the clauses of this plan and its means of engaging in the plan.

Our engagement in this Roadmap will not be affected by Israel's attempts and we will not negotiate the Roadmap. The Roadmap must be implemented not negotiated. Therefore, the government supports the Palestinian leadership in asserting its refusal of the so-called Israeli amendments and calls upon the Quartet—author of this plan—to announce the Roadmap as we know it, as soon as possible and to guarantee and verify the implementation of each phase with an effective and guaranteed enforcement and monitoring mechanisms.

In this context, the government reconfirms the Palestinian commitment to the implementation of all of our obligations within the framework of this plan, whether it be on political or security levels. It is quite natural that we require Israel to fulfill its mutual obligations.

Yet, what we have outlined will be meaningless if Israel's policy of imposing facts on the ground continues. Settlements, which violate international law, continue to be the major threat to the creation of a Palestinian state with genuine sovereignty. Thus, settlements are the primary obstacle to any peace process.

Settlement expansion in and around Jerusalem, with its accompanying house demolitions, confiscation of land and property, (in addition to the economic, social, administrative and cultural strangulation in the lives of Palestinians and Israel's attempt to impose a permanent solution for this Holy City by means other than negotiations) will only lead to inflaming the conflict and destroying any chance for peace.

The construction of the so-called "separation" wall is a dangerous continuation of the colonization project. In addition to the confiscation of Palestinian citizens' lands and the cutting off of their sources of livelihood, the wall is an Israeli measure that is designed to annex large areas of land, to confiscate underground water, isolate our cities and villages and to encircle the city of Jerusalem. This is another attempt to destroy any chance for peace and destroy any possibility to reach a permanent and accepted solution to the Palestinian-Israeli conflict. The removal of the wall will be among the first issues that our government will address because, without its removal, Israel will effectively destroy the Roadmap and any other peace initiative.

Here, I would like to address the Israeli people and the Israeli government frankly and directly.

We want a lasting peace with you achieved through negotiations and on the basis of international law, to implement Security Council Resolutions 242 and 338, as well as signed agreements.

We denounce terrorism by any party and in all its shapes and forms both because of our religious and moral traditions and because we are convinced that such methods do not lend support to a just cause like ours, but rather destroy it. These methods do not achieve peace, to which we aspire.

We understand peace as a message of conscience and behavior based on mutual desire and recognition of rights with the goal of living in peace and security on the basis of equality.

As we extend our hand to you in peace, we reiterate that peace cannot be possible with the continuation of settlement activity. Peace will not be possible with the expropriation and annexation of land. The choice is yours: peace without settlements or a continuation of the occupation, subjugation, hatred and conflict.

To be clear, the Palestinian people will not accept anything less than the exercise of our right to self-determination and the establishment of our independent, sovereign state with Jerusalem as its capital; a genuine, contiguous state without any settlements, on all of the territories occupied in 1967.

I am quite certain that you realize the importance of the question of refugees, not only in the Palestinian-Israeli conflict, but also on Arab and regional levels as we are speaking of millions of Palestinian refugees around the world. Because you realize the importance of this issue, you placed it on the timetable of the permanent status negotiations.

Thus, a just, agreed upon, fair and acceptable solution to the refugee problem consistent with international law (particularly UN Resolution 194) will be the basis of peace and coexistence.

These are the fundamentals of any solution to the Palestinian-Israeli conflict and this will not be changed.

To the Arab population inside Israel, our people and our loved ones: I extend to you appreciation and respect for your continuous support to us in the Occupied Territories. I am certain that you will continue to play a positive role in Israeli politics, media and popular civic organization to strengthen and establish an Israeli public opinion that shares our commitment to a just political solution to the Palestinian-Israel conflict and to the establishment of an independent Palestinian state.

We do not ignore the sufferings of Jews throughout history. And in exchange, we hope that the Israelis will not turn their back to the sufferings of the Palestinians, which include displacement, occupation, colonization and continuous oppression of the Palestinians.

To the Israeli government, which advised us that we learn the lessons of Iraq, I say . . .

The Palestinian people are the ones who choose their leadership. The leadership decides its politics according to independent Palestinian choice. Our legitimacy is derived from the will of the people, which is embodied in national organizations.

Those who need to learn the lessons of war and its calamities are those who still believe that military might is capable of imposing political solutions and that implicit and explicit threats are capable of dissuading people from demanding their rights. I repeat, there is no military solution to our conflict. Our people do not accept threats and will not succumb to them. On the contrary, there is no alternative to a just and comprehensive political solution. Our people welcome peace, security and prosperity to all. We welcome a peace that guarantees Israel's withdrawal from all occupied Palestinian and Arab Territories in accordance with international law.

We have heard a lot of your desire for peace, but what we have witnessed from you is siege, assassinations, invasions, destruction and a continuation of settlements. We hope that your desire for peace will be translated into action.

[. . .]

Our hearts are filled with grief and pain because of what happened to our people in Iraq who throughout history have sacrificed for the Palestinian people. We hope for stability for our brothers and sisters in Iraq. We hope that the foreign occupation of their land will end. We hope that the reconstruction of their land will begin in the near future under an Iraqi government that represents the will of the Iraqi people and speaks on its behalf.

We understand what happened in Iraq is an expression of a new and straightforward policy vis-a-vis the Middle East, led unilaterally, to redraw the borders of the political map of the whole region. It is naive to assume that Palestine will not be affected by these turbulent developments, as it is only natural to feel concern for the impact and repercussions of the situation in Iraq on the Palestinian people and our cause.

We do not want to address this serious shift in policy with slogans and ardent mottos, but rather with sound logic and an understanding of our national aspirations in order to avoid losses or reduce the amount of such loss and to provide practical and realistic methods to achieve our goals.

[. . .]

The path of negotiations is our choice and the resumption of negotiations with Israel—under the much-appreciated auspices and sponsorship of the Quartet, and in close coordination with our brothers in Egypt, Jordan and Saudi Arabia—is a constant Palestinian demand.

All through the long negotiation process, there were criticisms of our performance in negotiations. However such criticisms do not nullify the fact that we have a rich accumulated experience from which we should benefit.

Therefore, our government will work side by side with the PLO Executive Committee and its Higher Negotiations Committee, under the direction of President Yasser Arafat, President of State and Palestinian Authority, Chairman of the PLO in order to restructure our negotiations framework and to allow the negotiations team to dedicate itself to this important, sensitive and vital task.

I thank our Arab brothers for their continued and constant support to our people and cause and confirm the government's commitment to the concerns of the Arab states and to the Charter of the Arab League and its decisions. We will continue to coordinate and cooperate with our brothers to consolidate Arab consensus.

The government will remain keen on developing our strategic relations with the rest of our friends in the world whom we thank for their support and who share our commitment to balanced international relations based on compliance with international law and UN resolutions. We also call upon the Security Council to fulfill its obligations in maintaining security and peace in our region and to ensuring the implementation of its resolutions in a fair and consistent manner, while also working to protect our people and to help us achieve independence and freedom.

[. . .]

Source: Mahmoud Abbas, "Speech to the Palestinian Legislative Council, April 29, 2003," Electronic Intifada, http://electronicintifada.net.

151. Road Map to Peace, April 30, 2003

Introduction

In May 2003, immediately after the inauguration of new Palestinian Authority (PA) prime minister Mahmoud Abbas, the U.S. government released the latest and fullest version of the Road Map to Peace drawn up by the Quartet grouping of the United States, Russia, the European Union (EU), and the United Nations (UN). The United States insisted that both Israel and the Palestinians accept the entire plan. Despite this stipulation, Israel accepted the plan but only with fourteen reservations of its own. The PA accepted the plan without reservations. The Road Map to Peace was supposed to offer a fairly precise schedule to end violence and terror; withdraw Israeli troops from Palestinian territory; establish a more democratic, open, and efficient government in Palestinian territory on principles to be enshrined in a new constitution; hold Palestinian elections; freeze new Israeli settlement activity in the occupied territories and remove illegal settlements; establish provisional borders for a Palestinian state; and hold an international peace conference to reach a final Palestinian-Israeli settlement establishing two states, Israel and a Palestinian state, that would accept each other's existence within mutually agreed boundaries. By early 2007, progress had been made in terms of Palestinian free elections and reforms, and a new constitution had been drafted. Israeli forces had withdrawn from Gaza, and some illegal settlements had been destroyed. Even so, the peace process had yet to progress beyond the first stage of the Road Map to Peace.

Primary Source

A PERFORMANCE-BASED ROADMAP TO A PERMANENT TWO-STATE SOLUTION TO THE ISRAELI-PALESTINIAN CONFLICT

The following is a performance-based and goal-driven roadmap, with clear phases, timelines, target dates, and benchmarks aiming at progress through reciprocal steps by the two parties in the political, security, economic, humanitarian, and institution-building fields, under the auspices of the Quartet [the United States, European Union, United Nations, and Russia]. The destination is a final and comprehensive settlement of the Israel-Palestinian conflict by 2005, as presented in President Bush's speech of 24 June, and welcomed by the EU, Russia and the UN in the 16 July and 17 September Quartet Ministerial statements.

A two state solution to the Israeli-Palestinian conflict will only be achieved through an end to violence and terrorism, when the Palestinian people have a leadership acting decisively against terror and willing and able to build a practicing democracy based on tolerance and liberty, and through Israel's readiness to do what is necessary for a democratic Palestinian state to be established, and a clear, unambiguous acceptance by both parties of the goal of a negotiated settlement as described below. The Quartet will assist and facilitate implementation of the plan, starting in Phase I, including direct discussions between the parties as required. The plan establishes a realistic timeline for implementation. However, as a performance-based plan, progress will require and depend upon the good faith efforts of the parties, and their compliance with each of the obligations outlined below. Should the parties perform their obligations rapidly, progress within and through the phases may come sooner than indicated in the plan. Non-compliance with obligations will impede progress.

A settlement, negotiated between the parties, will result in the emergence of an independent, democratic, and viable Palestinian state living side by side in peace and security with Israel and its other neighbors. The settlement will resolve the Israel-Palestinian conflict, and end the occupation that began in 1967, based on the foundations of the Madrid Conference, the principle of land for peace, UNSCRs 242, 338 and 1397, agreements previously reached by the parties, and the initiative of Saudi Crown Prince Abdullah—endorsed by the Beirut Arab League Summit—calling for acceptance of Israel as a neighbor living in peace and security, in the context of a comprehensive settlement. This initiative is a vital element of international efforts to promote a comprehensive peace on all tracks, including the Syrian-Israeli and Lebanese-Israeli tracks.

The Quartet will meet regularly at senior levels to evaluate the parties' performance on implementation of the plan. In each phase, the parties are expected to perform their obligations in parallel, unless otherwise indicated.

PHASE I: ENDING TERROR AND VIOLENCE, NORMALIZING PALESTINIAN LIFE, AND BUILDING PALESTINIAN INSTITUTIONS—PRESENT TO MAY 2003

In Phase I, the Palestinians immediately undertake an unconditional cessation of violence according to the steps outlined below; such action should be accompanied by supportive measures undertaken by Israel. Palestinians and Israelis resume security cooperation based on the Tenet work plan to end violence, terrorism, and incitement through restructured and effective Palestinian security services. Palestinians undertake comprehensive political reform in preparation for statehood, including drafting a Palestinian constitution, and free, fair and open elections upon the basis of those measures. Israel takes all necessary steps to help normalize Palestinian life. Israel withdraws from Palestinian areas occupied from September 28, 2000 and the two sides restore the status quo that existed at that time, as security performance and cooperation progress. Israel also freezes all settlement activity, consistent with the Mitchell report.

At the outset of Phase I:

—Palestinian leadership issues unequivocal statement reiterating Israel's right to exist in peace and security and calling for an immediate and unconditional ceasefire to end armed activity and all acts of violence against Israelis anywhere. All official Palestinian institutions end incitement against Israel.

—Israeli leadership issues unequivocal statement affirming its commitment to the two-state vision of an independent, viable, sovereign Palestinian state living in peace and security alongside Israel, as expressed by President Bush, and calling for an immediate end to violence against Palestinians everywhere. All official Israeli institutions end incitement against Palestinians.

SECURITY

—Palestinians declare an unequivocal end to violence and terrorism and undertake visible efforts on the ground to arrest, disrupt, and restrain individuals and groups conducting and planning violent attacks on Israelis anywhere.

—Rebuilt and refocused Palestinian Authority security apparatus begins sustained, targeted, and effective operations aimed at confronting all those engaged in terror and dismantlement of terrorist capabilities and infrastructure. This includes commencing confiscation of illegal weapons and consolidation of security authority, free of association with terror and corruption.

—GOI takes no actions undermining trust, including deportations, attacks on civilians; confiscation and/or demolition of Palestinian homes and property, as a punitive measure or to facilitate Israeli construction; destruction of Palestinian institutions and infrastructure; and other measures specified in the Tenet work plan.

—Relying on existing mechanisms and on-the-ground resources, Quartet representatives begin informal monitoring and consult with the parties on establishment of a formal monitoring mechanism and its implementation.

—Implementation, as previously agreed, of U.S. rebuilding, training and resumed security cooperation plan in collaboration with outside oversight board (U.S.-Egypt-Jordan). Quartet support for efforts to achieve a lasting, comprehensive cease-fire.

- All Palestinian security organizations are consolidated into three services reporting to an empowered Interior Minister.
- Restructured/retrained Palestinian security forces and IDF counterparts progressively resume security cooperation and other undertakings in implementation of the Tenet work plan, including regular senior-level meetings, with the participation of U.S. security officials.

—Arab states cut off public and private funding and all other forms of support for groups supporting and engaging in violence and terror.

—All donors providing budgetary support for the Palestinians channel these funds through the Palestinian Ministry of Finance's Single Treasury Account.

—As comprehensive security performance moves forward, IDF withdraws progressively from areas occupied since September 28, 2000 and the two sides restore the status quo that existed prior to September 28, 2000. Palestinian security forces redeploy to areas vacated by IDF.

PALESTINIAN INSTITUTION-BUILDING

—Immediate action on credible process to produce draft constitution for Palestinian statehood. As rapidly as possible, constitutional committee circulates draft Palestinian constitution, based on strong parliamentary democracy and cabinet with empowered prime minister, for public comment/debate. Constitutional committee proposes draft document for submission after elections for approval by appropriate Palestinian institutions.

—Appointment of interim prime minister or cabinet with empowered executive authority/decision-making body.

—GOI fully facilitates travel of Palestinian officials for PLC and Cabinet sessions, internationally supervised security retraining, electoral and other reform activity, and other supportive measures related to the reform efforts.

—Continued appointment of Palestinian ministers empowered to undertake fundamental reform. Completion of further steps to achieve genuine separation of powers, including any necessary Palestinian legal reforms for this purpose.

—Establishment of independent Palestinian election commission. PLC reviews and revises election law.

—Palestinian performance on judicial, administrative, and economic benchmarks, as established by the International Task Force on Palestinian Reform.

—As early as possible, and based upon the above measures and in the context of open debate and transparent candidate selection/electoral campaign based on a free, multi-party process, Palestinians hold free, open, and fair elections.

—GOI facilitates Task Force election assistance, registration of voters, movement of candidates and voting officials. Support for NGOs involved in the election process.

—GOI reopens Palestinian Chamber of Commerce and other closed Palestinian institutions in East Jerusalem based on a commitment that these institutions operate strictly in accordance with prior agreements between the parties.

HUMANITARIAN RESPONSE

—Israel takes measures to improve the humanitarian situation. Israel and Palestinians implement in full all recommendations of the Bertini report to improve humanitarian conditions, lifting curfews and easing restrictions on movement of persons and goods, and allowing full, safe, and unfettered access of international and humanitarian personnel.

—AHLC reviews the humanitarian situation and prospects for economic development in the West Bank and Gaza and launches a major donor assistance effort, including to the reform effort.

—GOI and PA continue revenue clearance process and transfer of funds, including arrears, in accordance with agreed, transparent monitoring mechanism.

CIVIL SOCIETY

—Continued donor support, including increased funding through PVOs/NGOs, for people to people programs, private sector development and civil society initiatives.

SETTLEMENTS

—GOI immediately dismantles settlement outposts erected since March 2001.

—Consistent with the Mitchell Report, GOI freezes all settlement activity (including natural growth of settlements).

PHASE II: TRANSITION—JUNE 2003–DECEMBER 2003

In the second phase, efforts are focused on the option of creating an independent Palestinian state with provisional borders and attributes of sovereignty, based on the new constitution, as a way station to a permanent status settlement. As has been noted, this goal can be achieved when the Palestinian people have a leadership acting decisively against terror, willing and able to build a practicing democracy based on tolerance and liberty. With such a leadership, reformed civil institutions and security structures, the Palestinians will have the active support of the Quartet and the broader international community in establishing an independent, viable, state.

Progress into Phase II will be based upon the consensus judgment of the Quartet of whether conditions are appropriate to proceed, taking into account performance of both parties. Furthering and sustaining efforts to normalize Palestinian lives and build Palestinian institutions, Phase II starts after Palestinian elections and ends with possible creation of an independent Palestinian state with provisional borders in 2003. Its primary goals are continued comprehensive security performance and effective security cooperation, continued normalization of Palestinian life and institution-building, further building on and sustaining of the goals outlined in Phase I, ratification of a democratic Palestinian constitution, formal establishment of office of prime minister, consolidation of political reform, and the creation of a Palestinian state with provisional borders.

—INTERNATIONAL CONFERENCE: Convened by the Quartet, in consultation with the parties, immediately after the successful conclusion of Palestinian elections, to support Palestinian economic recovery and launch a process, leading to establishment of an independent Palestinian state with provisional borders.

• Such a meeting would be inclusive, based on the goal of a comprehensive Middle East peace (including between Israel and Syria, and Israel and Lebanon), and based on the principles described in the preamble to this document.

• Arab states restore pre-intifada links to Israel (trade offices, etc.).

• Revival of multilateral engagement on issues including regional water resources, environment, economic development, refugees, and arms control issues.

—New constitution for democratic, independent Palestinian state is finalized and approved by appropriate Palestinian institutions. Further elections, if required, should follow approval of the new constitution.

—Empowered reform cabinet with office of prime minister formally established, consistent with draft constitution.

—Continued comprehensive security performance, including effective security cooperation on the bases laid out in Phase I.

—Creation of an independent Palestinian state with provisional borders through a process of Israeli-Palestinian engagement, launched by the international conference. As part of this process, implementation of prior agreements, to enhance maximum territorial contiguity, including further action on settlements in conjunction with establishment of a Palestinian state with provisional borders.

—Enhanced international role in monitoring transition, with the active, sustained, and operational support of the Quartet.

—Quartet members promote international recognition of Palestinian state, including possible UN membership.

PHASE III: PERMANENT STATUS AGREEMENT AND END OF THE ISRAELI-PALESTINIAN CONFLICT—2004–2005

Progress into Phase III, based on consensus judgment of Quartet, and taking into account actions of both parties and Quartet monitoring. Phase III objectives are consolidation of reform and stabilization of Palestinian institutions, sustained, effective Palestinian security performance, and Israeli-Palestinian negotiations aimed at a permanent status agreement in 2005.

—SECOND INTERNATIONAL CONFERENCE: Convened by Quartet, in consultation with the parties, at beginning of 2004 to endorse agreement reached on an independent Palestinian state with provisional borders and formally to launch a process with the active, sustained, and operational support of the Quartet, leading to a final, permanent status resolution in 2005, including on borders, Jerusalem, refugees, settlements; and, to support progress toward a comprehensive Middle East settlement between Israel and Lebanon and Israel and Syria, to be achieved as soon as possible.

—Continued comprehensive, effective progress on the reform agenda laid out by the Task Force in preparation for final status agreement.

—Continued sustained and effective security performance, and sustained, effective security cooperation on the bases laid out in Phase I.

—International efforts to facilitate reform and stabilize Palestinian institutions and the Palestinian economy, in preparation for final status agreement.

—Parties reach final and comprehensive permanent status agreement that ends the Israel-Palestinian conflict in 2005, through a settlement negotiated between the parties based on UNSCR 242, 338, and 1397, that ends the occupation that began in 1967, and includes an agreed, just, fair, and realistic solution to the refugee issue, and a negotiated resolution on the status of Jerusalem that takes into account the political and religious concerns of both sides, and protects the religious interests of Jews, Christians, and Muslims worldwide, and fulfills the vision of two states, Israel and sovereign, independent, democratic and viable Palestine, living side-by-side in peace and security.

—Arab state acceptance of full normal relations with Israel and security for all the states of the region in the context of a comprehensive Arab-Israeli peace.

Source: Distributed by the Office of International Information Programs, U.S. Department of State, http://www.state.gov.

152. Israeli Reservations on the Road Map to Peace, May 25, 2003

Introduction

In late May 2003 the government of Israel formally accepted the Road Map to Peace published by the Quartet at the end of April. When doing so, however, Israeli officials attached a list of fourteen reservations. These included stipulations that the Palestinian authorities must genuinely put a stop to all terrorist activities and disarm all terrorists so that terror and violence would come to a complete halt. Israel demanded the "emergence of a new and different leadership in the Palestinian Authority" and U.S. management of the monitoring mechanisms that supervised implementation of the Road Map to Peace. The "provisional Palestinian state" to be created under Stage Two of the peace plan was to be "fully demilitarized," could not undertake defense alliances or cooperation with outsiders, and would not control entry or exits across its own borders or its own air space. Israel insisted that all documents dealing with the creation of the provisional Palestinian state include clear references to "Israel's right to exist as a Jewish state," to which Palestinian refugees had no right of return, and that "issues pertaining to the final settlement," including the Israeli settlements in the occupied territories and the status of Jerusalem, be excluded from Stage Two negotiations for the provisional Palestinian state. Any peace settlement based on the Road Map to Peace should refer only to United Nations (UN) Security Council Resolutions 242 and 338 and not invoke any of the other peace initiatives mentioned in the peace plan. The withdrawal of Israel Defense Forces (IDF) to their September 2000 line was to be conditional upon "absolute

quiet" in the occupied territories. At best, Israeli cooperation with the peace plan was likely to be grudging and hedged around with stipulations, reservations, exceptions, and exclusions.

Primary Source

1. Both at the commencement of and during the process, and as a condition to its continuance, calm will be maintained. The Palestinians will dismantle the existing security organizations and implement security reforms during the course of which new organizations will be formed and act to combat terror, violence and incitement (incitement must cease immediately and the Palestinian Authority must educate for peace). These organizations will engage in genuine prevention of terror and violence through arrests, interrogations, prevention and the enforcement of the legal groundwork for investigations, prosecution and punishment. In the first phase of the plan and as a condition for progress to the second phase, the Palestinians will complete the dismantling of terrorist organizations (Hamas, Islamic Jihad, the Popular Front, the Democratic Front Al-Aqsa Brigades and other apparatuses) and their infrastructure, collection of all illegal weapons and their transfer to a third party for the sake of being removed from the area and destroyed, cessation of weapons smuggling and weapons production inside the Palestinian Authority, activation of the full prevention apparatus and cessation of incitement. There will be no progress to the second phase without the fulfillment of all above-mentioned conditions relating to the war against terror. The security plans to be implemented are the Tenet and Zinni plans. [As in the other mutual frameworks, the Roadmap will not state that Israel must cease violence and incitement against the Palestinians].

2. Full performance will be a condition for progress between phases and for progress within phases. The first condition for progress will be the complete cessation of terror, violence and incitement. Progress between phases will come only following the full implementation of the preceding phase. Attention will be paid not to timelines, but to performance benchmarks. (Timelines will serve only as reference points.)

3. The emergence of a new and different leadership in the Palestinian Authority within the framework of governmental reform: The formation of a new leadership constitutes a condition for progress to the second phase of the plan. In this framework, elections will be conducted for the Palestinian Legislative Council following coordination with Israel.

4. The Monitoring mechanism will be under American management. The chief verification activity will concentrate upon the creation of another Palestinian entity and progress in the civil reform process within the Palestinian Authority. Verification will be performed exclusively on a professional basis and per issue (economic, legal, financial) without the existence of a combined or unified mechanism. Substantive decisions will remain in the hands of both parties.

5. The character of the provisional Palestinian state will be determined through negotiations between the Palestinian Authority and Israel. The provisional state will have provisional borders and certain aspects of sovereignty, be fully demilitarized with no military forces, but only with police and internal security forces of limited scope and armaments, be without the authority to undertake defense alliances or military cooperation, and Israeli control over the entry and exit of all persons and cargo, as well as of its air space and electromagnetic spectrum.

6. In connection to both the introductory statements and the final settlement, declared references must be made to Israel's right to exist as a Jewish state and to the waiver of any right of return for Palestinian refugees to the State of Israel.

7. End of the process will lead to the end of all claims and not only the end of the conflict.

8. The future settlement will be reached through agreement and direct negotiations between the two parties, in accordance with the vision outlined by President Bush in his 24 June address.

9. There will be no involvement with issues pertaining to the final settlement. Among issues not to be discussed: settlement in Judea, Samaria and Gaza (excluding a settlement freeze and illegal outposts), the status of the Palestinian Authority and its institutions in Jerusalem, and all other matters whose substance relates to the final settlement.

10. The removal of references other than 242 and 338. A settlement based upon the Roadmap will be an autonomous settlement that derives its validity therefrom. The only possible reference should be to Resolutions 242 and 338, and then only as an outline for the conduct of future negotiations on a permanent settlement.

11. Promotion of the reform process in the Palestinian Authority: A transitional Palestinian constitution will be composed, a Palestinian legal infrastructure will be constructed and cooperation with Israel in this field will be renewed. In the economic sphere: International efforts to rehabilitate the Palestinian economy will continue. In the financial sphere: The American-Israeli-Palestinian agreement will be implemented in full as a condition for the continued transfer of tax revenues.

12. The deployment of IDF forces along the September 2000 lines will be subject to the stipulation of Article 4 (absolute quiet) and will be carried out in keeping with changes to be required by the nature of the new circumstances and needs created thereby. Emphasis will be placed on the division of responsibilities and civilian authority as in September 2000, and not on the position of forces on the ground at that time.

13. Subject to security conditions, Israel will work to restore Palestinian life to normal: promote the economic situation, cultivation of commercial connections, encouragement and assistance for the activities of recognized humanitarian agencies. No reference will be made to the Bertini Report as a binding source document within the framework of the humanitarian issue.

14. Arab states will assist the process through the condemnation of terrorist activity. No link will be established between the Palestinian track and other tracks (Syrian-Lebanese).

Source: "Israel's Response to the Road Map, May 25, 2003," Israeli Knesset, http://www.knesset.gov.il/process/docs/roadmap _response_eng.htm.

153. The Geneva Accord, Draft Permanent Status Agreement [Excerpt], October 2003

Introduction

Formal negotiations for a permanent status agreement under the provisions of the Road Map to Peace drawn up in 2002–2003 by the Quartet international group of the United States, the United Nations (UN), Russia, and the European Union (EU) did not take place. This did not prevent prominent Israeli and Palestinian leaders from holding informal talks designed to draft such a document, one its authors hoped might serve as a blueprint for the final agreement. During 2003, negotiations to this end were held between Israeli opposition politicians led by Yossi Beilin, the former Foreign Ministry diplomat who had quietly negotiated the 1993 Oslo Accords outside the official Madrid framework, and a Palestinian team headed by Yasser Abed Rabbo. In 1995 Beilin and new Palestinian prime minister Mahmoud Abbas had privately drafted a similar agreement that they had hoped would bring about full implementation of the later stages of the Oslo Accords. The new Geneva proposals contained compromises on some of the most contentious issues still dividing Israeli and the Palestinians. Of the 220,000 Jewish settlers in the West Bank, about half were likely to lose their homes to the Palestinian state and would have to leave, while the remainder would see their settlements incorporated into Israel. A corridor would link Gaza and the West Bank. Palestinian refugees would be compensated but would not be able to resettle in Israel. Jerusalem would be divided between Arabs and Jews, with each religious community retaining control of most of its own most sacred sites. An international committee would supervise implementation of the Geneva Accord. Palestine would be a nonmilitarized state but would possess internal security forces, and a multinational force would be responsible for protecting its "territorial integrity." Although the Geneva Accord was not in any sense an official document but instead an attempt by well-connected and influential private citizens to formulate a potential solution, the accord soon came to form part of the domestic and international discourse on a permanent and final peace settlement. U.S. secretary of state Colin Powell and UN secretary-general Kofi Annan met with the authors, who represented the moderate center among both Israelis and Palestinians. The Israeli government, led by hard-line Likud Party politician Ariel Sharon, condemned the accord, as did right-wing Zionists, but the Labor Party adopted certain portions of the accord as its own negotiating position. Palestinian Authority (PA) president and Palestine Liberation Organization (PLO) chairman Yasser Arafat gave them a tentative welcome, although many Palestinians deplored the abandonment of the right of Palestinian refugees to return to Israel, and groups such as Hamas, which refused to recognize Israel's existence, rejected the accord because the agreement accepted Israel's right to exist.

Primary Source

Preamble

The State of Israel (hereinafter "Israel") and the Palestine Liberation Organization (hereinafter "PLO"), the representative of the Palestinian people (hereinafter the "Parties"):

Reaffirming their determination to put an end to decades of confrontation and conflict, and to live in peaceful coexistence, mutual dignity and security based on a just, lasting, and comprehensive peace and achieving historic reconciliation;

Recognizing that peace requires the transition from the logic of war and confrontation to the logic of peace and cooperation, and that acts and words characteristic of the state of war are neither appropriate nor acceptable in the era of peace;

Affirming their deep belief that the logic of peace requires compromise, and that the only viable solution is a two-state solution based on UNSC Resolution 242 and 338;

Affirming that this agreement marks the recognition of the right of the Jewish people to statehood and the recognition of the right of the Palestinian people to statehood, without prejudice to the equal rights of the Parties' respective citizens;

Recognizing that after years of living in mutual fear and insecurity, both peoples need to enter an era of peace, security and stability, entailing all necessary actions by the parties to guarantee the realization of this era;

Recognizing each other's right to peaceful and secure existence within secure and recognized boundaries free from threats or acts of force;

Determined to establish relations based on cooperation and the commitment to live side by side as good neighbors aiming both separately and jointly to contribute to the well-being of their peoples;

Reaffirming their obligation to conduct themselves in conformity with the norms of international law and the Charter of the United Nations;

Confirming that this Agreement is concluded within the framework of the Middle East peace process initiated in Madrid in October 1991, the Declaration of Principles of September 13, 1993, the subsequent agreements including the Interim Agreement of September 1995, the Wye River Memorandum of October 1998 and the Sharm El-Sheikh Memorandum of September 4, 1999, and the permanent status negotiations including the Camp David Summit of July 2000, the Clinton Ideas of December 2000, and the Taba Negotiations of January 2001;

Reiterating their commitment to United Nations Security Council Resolutions 242, 338 and 1397 and confirming their understanding that this Agreement is based on, will lead to, and—by its fulfillment—will constitute the full implementation of these resolutions and to the settlement of the Israeli-Palestinian conflict in all its aspects;

Declaring that this Agreement constitutes the realization of the permanent status peace component envisaged in President Bush's speech of June 24, 2002 and in the Quartet Roadmap process;

Declaring that this Agreement marks the historic reconciliation between the Palestinians and Israelis, and paves the way to reconciliation between the Arab World and Israel and the establishment of normal, peaceful relations between the Arab states and Israel in accordance with the relevant clauses of the Beirut Arab League Resolution of March 28, 2002; and

Resolved to pursue the goal of attaining a comprehensive regional peace, thus contributing to stability, security, development and prosperity throughout the region;

Have agreed on the following:

Article 1—Purpose of the Permanent Status Agreement

1. The Permanent Status Agreement (hereinafter "this Agreement") ends the era of conflict and ushers in a new era based on peace, cooperation, and good neighborly relations between the Parties.

2. The implementation of this Agreement will settle all the claims of the Parties arising from events occurring prior to its signature. No further claims related to events prior to this Agreement may be raised by either Party.

Article 2—Relations between the Parties

1. The state of Israel shall recognize the state of Palestine (hereinafter "Palestine") upon its establishment. The state of Palestine shall immediately recognize the state of Israel.

2. The state of Palestine shall be the successor to the PLO with all its rights and obligations.

3. Israel and Palestine shall immediately establish full diplomatic and consular relations with each other and will exchange resident Ambassadors, within one month of their mutual recognition.

4. The Parties recognize Palestine and Israel as the homelands of their respective peoples. The Parties are committed not to interfere in each other's internal affairs.

5. This Agreement supercedes all prior agreements between the Parties.

6. Without prejudice to the commitments undertaken by them in this Agreement, relations between Israel and Palestine shall be based upon the provisions of the Charter of the United Nations.

7. With a view to the advancement of the relations between the two States and peoples, Palestine and Israel shall cooperate in areas of common interest. These shall include, but are not limited to, dialogue between their legislatures and state institutions, cooperation between their appropriate local authorities, promotion of non-governmental civil society cooperation, and joint programs and exchange in the areas of culture, media, youth, science, education, environment, health, agriculture, tourism, and crime prevention. The Israeli-Palestinian Cooperation Committee will oversee this cooperation in accordance with Article 8.

8. The Parties shall cooperate in areas of joint economic interest, to best realize the human potential of their respective peoples. In this regard, they will work bilaterally, regionally, and with the international community to maximize the benefit of peace to the broadest cross-section of their respective populations. Relevant standing bodies shall be established by the Parties to this effect.

9. The Parties shall establish robust modalities for security cooperation, and engage in a comprehensive and uninterrupted effort to end terrorism and violence directed against each other's persons, property, institutions or territory. This effort shall continue at all times, and shall be insulated from any possible crises and other aspects of the Parties' relations.

10. Israel and Palestine shall work together and separately with other parties in the region to enhance and promote regional cooperation and coordination in spheres of common interest.

11. The Parties shall establish a ministerial-level Palestinian-Israeli High Steering Committee to guide, monitor, and facilitate the process of implementation of this Agreement, both bilaterally and in accordance with the mechanisms in Article 3 hereunder.

Article 3: Implementation and Verification Group
1. Establishment and Composition
   (a) An Implementation and Verification Group (IVG) shall hereby be established to facilitate, assist in, guarantee, monitor, and resolve disputes relating to the implementation of this Agreement.
   (b) The IVG shall include the U.S., the Russian Federation, the EU, the UN, and other parties, both regional and international, to be agreed on by the Parties.
   (c) The IVG shall work in coordination with the Palestinian-Israeli High Steering Committee established in Article 2/11 above and subsequent to that with the Israeli-Palestinian Cooperation Committee (IPCC) established in Article 8 hereunder.
   (d) The structure, procedures, and modalities of the IVG are set forth below and detailed in Annex X. [Annex X not included in this printing.]

2. Structure
   (a) A senior political-level contact group (Contact Group), composed of all the IVG members, shall be the highest authority in the IVG.
   (b) The Contact Group shall appoint, in consultation with the Parties, a Special Representative who will be the principal executive of the IVG on the ground. The Special Representative shall manage the work of the IVG and maintain constant contact with the Parties, the Palestinian-Israeli High Steering Committee, and the Contact Group.
   (c) The IVG permanent headquarters and secretariat shall be based in an agreed upon location in Jerusalem.
   (d) The IVG shall establish its bodies referred to in this Agreement and additional bodies as it deems necessary. These bodies shall be an integral part of and under the authority of the IVG.
   (e) The Multinational Force (MF) established under Article 5 shall be an integral part of the IVG. The Special Representative shall, subject to the approval of the Parties, appoint the Commander of the MF who shall be responsible for the daily command of the MF. Details relating to the Special Representative and MF Force Commander are set forth in Annex X.
   (f) The IVG shall establish a dispute settlement mechanism, in accordance with Article 16.

3. Coordination with the Parties

A Trilateral Committee composed of the Special Representative and the Palestinian-Israeli High Steering Committee shall be established and shall meet on at least a monthly basis to review the implementation of this Agreement. The Trilateral Committee will convene within 48 hours upon the request of any of the three parties represented.

4. Functions

In addition to the functions specified elsewhere in this Agreement, the IVG shall:

(a) Take appropriate measures based on the reports it receives from the MF.
(b) Assist the Parties in implementing the Agreement and pre-empt and promptly mediate disputes on the ground.

5. Termination

In accordance with the progress in the implementation of this Agreement, and with the fulfillment of the specific mandated functions, the IVG shall terminate its activities in the said spheres. The IVG shall continue to exist unless otherwise agreed by the Parties.

Article 4—Territory

1. The International Borders between the States of Palestine and Israel

(a) In accordance with UNSC Resolution 242 and 338, the border between the states of Palestine and Israel shall be based on the June 4th 1967 lines with reciprocal modifications on a 1:1 basis as set forth in attached Map 1. [Map not included in this printing.]
(b) The Parties recognize the border, as set out in attached Map 1, as the permanent, secure and recognized international boundary between them.

2. Sovereignty and Inviolability

(a) The Parties recognize and respect each other's sovereignty, territorial integrity, and political independence, as well as the inviolability of each other's territory, including territorial waters, and airspace. They shall respect this inviolability in accordance with this Agreement, the UN Charter, and other rules of international law.
(b) The Parties recognize each other's rights in their exclusive economic zones in accordance with international law.

3. Israeli Withdrawal

(a) Israel shall withdraw in accordance with Article 5.
(b) Palestine shall assume responsibility for the areas from which Israel withdraws.
(c) The transfer of authority from Israel to Palestine shall be in accordance with Annex X.
(d) The IVG shall monitor, verify, and facilitate the implementation of this Article.

4. Demarcation

(a) A Joint Technical Border Commission (Commission) composed of the two Parties shall be established to conduct the technical demarcation of the border in accordance with this Article. The procedures governing the work of this Commission are set forth in Annex X.
(b) Any disagreement in the Commission shall be referred to the IVG in accordance with Annex X.
(c) The physical demarcation of the international borders shall be completed by the Commission not later than nine months from the date of the entry into force of this Agreement.

5. Settlements

(a) The state of Israel shall be responsible for resettling the Israelis residing in Palestinian sovereign territory outside this territory.
(b) The resettlement shall be completed according to the schedule stipulated in Article 5.
(c) Existing arrangements in the West Bank and Gaza Strip regarding Israeli settlers and settlements, including security, shall remain in force in each of the settlements until the date prescribed in the timetable for the completion of the evacuation of the relevant settlement.
(d) Modalities for the assumption of authority over settlements by Palestine are set forth in Annex X. The IVG shall resolve any disputes that may arise during its implementation.
(e) Israel shall keep intact the immovable property, infrastructure and facilities in Israeli settlements to be transferred to Palestinian sovereignty. An agreed inventory shall be drawn up by the Parties with the IVG in advance of the completion of the evacuation and in accordance with Annex X.
(f) The state of Palestine shall have exclusive title to all land and any buildings, facilities, infrastructure or other property remaining in any of the settlements on the date prescribed in the timetable for the completion of the evacuation of this settlement.

6. Corridor

(a) The states of Palestine and Israel shall establish a corridor linking the West Bank and Gaza Strip. This corridor shall:
   i.   Be under Israeli sovereignty.
   ii. Be permanently open.
   iii. Be under Palestinian administration in accordance with Annex X of this Agreement. Palestinian law shall apply to persons using and procedures appertaining to the corridor.
   iv. Not disrupt Israeli transportation and other infrastructural networks, or endanger the environment, public safety or public health. Where necessary, engineering solutions will be sought to avoid such disruptions.
   v.   Allow for the establishment of the necessary infrastructural facilities linking the West Bank and the Gaza Strip. Infrastructural facilities shall be understood to include, inter alia, pipelines, electrical and communications cables, and associated equipment as detailed in Annex X.
   vi. Not be used in contravention of this Agreement.

(b) Defensive barriers shall be established along the corridor and Palestinians shall not enter Israel from this corridor, nor shall Israelis enter Palestine from the corridor.

(c) The Parties shall seek the assistance of the international community in securing the financing for the corridor.

(d) The IVG shall guarantee the implementation of this Article in accordance with Annex X.

(e) Any disputes arising between the Parties from the operation of the corridor shall be resolved in accordance with Article 16.

(f) The arrangements set forth in this clause may only be terminated or revised by agreement of both Parties.

Article 5—Security

1. General Security Provisions

(a) The Parties acknowledge that mutual understanding and co-operation in security-related matters will form a significant part of their bilateral relations and will further enhance regional security. Palestine and Israel shall base their security relations on cooperation, mutual trust, good neighborly relations, and the protection of their joint interests.

(b) Palestine and Israel each shall:

  i. Recognize and respect the other's right to live in peace within secure and recognized boundaries free from the threat or acts of war, terrorism and violence;

  ii. refrain from the threat or use of force against the territorial integrity or political independence of the other and shall settle all disputes between them by peaceful means;

  iii. refrain from joining, assisting, promoting or co-operating with any coalition, organization or alliance of a military or security character, the objectives or activities of which include launching aggression or other acts of hostility against the other;

  iv. refrain from organizing, encouraging, or allowing the formation of irregular forces or armed bands, including mercenaries and militias within their respective territory and prevent their establishment. In this respect, any existing irregular forces or armed bands shall be disbanded and prevented from reforming at any future date;

  v. refrain from organizing, assisting, allowing, or participating in acts of violence in or against the other or acquiescing in activities directed toward the commission of such acts.

(c) To further security cooperation, the Parties shall establish a high level Joint Security Committee that shall meet on at least a monthly basis. The Joint Security Committee shall have a permanent joint office, and may establish such sub-committees as it deems necessary, including sub-committees to immediately resolve localized tensions.

2. Regional Security

(a) Israel and Palestine shall work together with their neighbors and the international community to build a secure and stable Middle East, free from weapons of mass destruction, both conventional and non-conventional, in the context of a comprehensive, lasting, and stable peace, characterized by reconciliation, goodwill, and the renunciation of the use of force.

(b) To this end, the Parties shall work together to establish a regional security regime.

3. Defense Characteristics of the Palestinian State

(a) No armed forces, other than as specified in this Agreement, will be deployed or stationed in Palestine.

(b) Palestine shall be a non-militarized state, with a strong security force. Accordingly, the limitations on the weapons that may be purchased, owned, or used by the Palestinian Security Force (PSF) or manufactured in Palestine shall be specified in Annex X. Any proposed changes to Annex X shall be considered by a trilateral committee composed of the two Parties and the MF. If no agreement is reached in the trilateral committee, the IVG may make its own recommendations.

  i. No individuals or organizations in Palestine other than the PSF and the organs of the IVG, including the MF, may purchase, possess, carry or use weapons except as provided by law.

(c) The PSF shall:

  i. Maintain border control;

  ii. Maintain law-and-order and perform police functions;

  iii. Perform intelligence and security functions;

  iv. Prevent terrorism;

  v. Conduct rescue and emergency missions; and

  vi. Supplement essential community services when necessary.

(d) The MF shall monitor and verify compliance with this clause.

4. Terrorism

(a) The Parties reject and condemn terrorism and violence in all its forms and shall pursue public policies accordingly. In addition, the parties shall refrain from actions and policies that are liable to nurture extremism and create conditions conducive to terrorism on either side.

(b) The Parties shall take joint and, in their respective territories, unilateral comprehensive and continuous efforts against all aspects of violence and terrorism. These efforts shall include the prevention and preemption of such acts, and the prosecution of their perpetrators.

(c) To that end, the Parties shall maintain ongoing consultation, cooperation, and exchange of information between their respective security forces.

(d) A Trilateral Security Committee composed of the two Parties and the United States shall be formed to ensure the implementation of this Article. The Trilateral Security Committee shall develop comprehensive policies and guidelines to fight terrorism and violence.

5. Incitement

(a) Without prejudice to freedom of expression and other internationally recognized human rights, Israel and Palestine shall promulgate laws to prevent incitement to irredentism, racism, terrorism and violence and vigorously enforce them.

(b) The IVG shall assist the Parties in establishing guidelines for the implementation of this clause, and shall monitor the Parties' adherence thereto.

6. Multinational Force

(a) A Multinational Force (MF) shall be established to provide security guarantees to the Parties, act as a deterrent, and oversee the implementation of the relevant provisions of this Agreement.

(b) The composition, structure and size of the MF are set forth in Annex X.

(c) To perform the functions specified in this Agreement, the MF shall be deployed in the state of Palestine. The MF shall enter into the appropriate Status of Forces Agreement (SOFA) with the state of Palestine.

(d) In accordance with this Agreement, and as detailed in Annex X, the MF shall:

   i.   In light of the non-militarized nature of the Palestinian state, protect the territorial integrity of the state of Palestine.

   ii. Serve as a deterrent against external attacks that could threaten either of the Parties.

   iii. Deploy observers to areas adjacent to the lines of the Israeli withdrawal during the phases of this withdrawal, in accordance with Annex X.

   iv. Deploy observers to monitor the territorial and maritime borders of the state of Palestine, as specified in clause 5/13.

   v.   Perform the functions on the Palestinian international border crossings specified in clause 5/12.

   vi. Perform the functions relating to the early warning stations as specified in clause 5/8.

   vii. Perform the functions specified in clause 5/3.

   viii. Perform the functions specified in clause 5/7.

   ix. Perform the functions specified in Article 10.

   x.   Help in the enforcement of anti-terrorism measures.

   xi. Help in the training of the PSF.

(e) In relation to the above, the MF shall report to and update the IVG in accordance with Annex X.

(f) The MF shall only be withdrawn or have its mandate changed by agreement of the Parties.

7. Evacuation

(a) Israel shall withdraw all its military and security personnel and equipment, including landmines, and all persons employed to support them, and all military installations from the territory of the state of Palestine, except as otherwise agreed in Annex X, in stages.

(b) The staged withdrawals shall commence immediately upon entry into force of this Agreement and shall be made in accordance with the timetable and modalities set forth in Annex X.

(c) The stages shall be designed subject to the following principles:

   i.   The need to create immediate clear contiguity and facilitate the early implementation of Palestinian development plans.

   ii. Israel's capacity to relocate, house and absorb settlers. While costs and inconveniences are inherent in such a process, these shall not be unduly disruptive.

   iii. The need to construct and operationalize the border between the two states.

   iv. The introduction and effective functioning of the MF, in particular on the eastern border of the state of Palestine.

(d) Accordingly, the withdrawal shall be implemented in the following stages:

   i.   The first stage shall include the areas of the state of Palestine, as defined in Map X, and shall be completed within 9 months. [Map X not included in this printing.]

   ii. The second and third stages shall include the remainder of the territory of the state of Palestine and shall be completed within 21 months of the end of the first stage.

(e) Israel shall complete its withdrawal from the territory of the state of Palestine within 30 months of the entry into force of this Agreement, and in accordance with this Agreement.

(f) Israel will maintain a small military presence in the Jordan Valley under the authority of the MF and subject to the MF SOFA as detailed in Annex X for an additional 36 months. The stipulated period may be reviewed by the Parties in the event of relevant regional developments, and may be altered by the Parties' consent.

(g) In accordance with Annex X, the MF shall monitor and verify compliance with this clause.

[...]

11. Law Enforcement

The Israeli and Palestinian law enforcement agencies shall cooperate in combating illicit drug trafficking, illegal trafficking in archaeological artifacts and objects of arts, cross-border crime, including theft and fraud, organized crime, trafficking in women and minors, counterfeiting, pirate TV and radio stations, and other illegal activity.

12. International Border Crossings

(a) The following arrangements shall apply to border crossings between the state of Palestine and Jordan, the state of Palestine and Egypt, as well as airport and seaport entry points to the state of Palestine.

(b) All border crossings shall be monitored by joint teams composed of members of the PSF and the MF. These teams shall prevent the entry into Palestine of any weapons, materials or equipment that are in contravention of the provisions of this Agreement.

[...]

13. Border Control

(a) The PSF shall maintain border control as detailed in Annex X.

(b) The MF shall monitor and verify the maintenance of border control by the PSF.

Article 6—Jerusalem

1. Religious and Cultural Significance

(a) The Parties recognize the universal historic, religious, spiritual, and cultural significance of Jerusalem and its holiness enshrined in Judaism, Christianity, and Islam. In recognition of this status, the Parties reaffirm their commitment to safeguard the character, holiness, and freedom of worship in the city and to respect the existing division of administrative functions and traditional practices between different denominations.

(b) The Parties shall establish an inter-faith body consisting of representatives of the three monotheistic faiths, to act as a consultative body to the Parties on matters related to the city's religious significance and to promote inter-religious understanding and dialogue. The composition, procedures, and modalities for this body are set forth in Annex X.

2. Capital of Two States

The Parties shall have their mutually recognized capitals in the areas of Jerusalem under their respective sovereignty.

3. Sovereignty

Sovereignty in Jerusalem shall be in accordance with attached Map 2. [Map 2 not included in this printing.] This shall not prejudice nor be prejudiced by the arrangements set forth below.

4. Border Regime

The border regime shall be designed according to the provisions of Article 11, and taking into account the specific needs of Jerusalem (e.g., movement of tourists and intensity of border crossing use including provisions for Jerusalemites) and the provisions of this Article.

5. al-Haram al-Sharif/Temple Mount (Compound)

(a) International Group

   i. An International Group, composed of the IVG and other parties to be agreed upon by the Parties, including members of the Organization of the Islamic Conference (OIC), shall hereby be established to monitor, verify, and assist in the implementation of this clause.

   ii. For this purpose, the International Group shall establish a Multinational Presence on the Compound, the composition, structure, mandate and functions of which are set forth in Annex X.

   iii. The Multinational Presence shall have specialized detachments dealing with security and conservation. The Multinational Presence shall make periodic conservation and security reports to the International Group. These reports shall be made public.

   iv. The Multinational Presence shall strive to immediately resolve any problems arising and may refer any unresolved disputes to the International Group that will function in accordance with Article 16.

   v. The Parties may at any time request clarifications or submit complaints to the International Group which shall be promptly investigated and acted upon.

   vi. The International Group shall draw up rules and regulations to maintain security on and conservation of the Compound. These shall include lists of the weapons and equipment permitted on the site.

(b) Regulations Regarding the Compound

   i. In view of the sanctity of the Compound, and in light of the unique religious and cultural significance of the site to the Jewish people, there shall be no digging, excavation, or construction on the Compound, unless approved by the two Parties. Procedures for regular maintenance and emergency repairs on the Compound shall be established by the IG after consultation with the Parties.

   ii. The state of Palestine shall be responsible for maintaining the security of the Compound and for ensuring that it will not be used for any hostile acts against Israelis or Israeli areas. The only arms permitted on the Compound shall be those carried by the Palestinian security personnel and the security detachment of the Multinational Presence.

   iii. In light of the universal significance of the Compound, and subject to security considerations and to the need not to disrupt religious worship or decorum on the site as determined by the Waqf, visitors shall be allowed access to the site. This shall be without any discrimination and generally be in accordance with past practice.

(c) Transfer of Authority

   i. At the end of the withdrawal period stipulated in Article 5/7, the state of Palestine shall assert sovereignty over the Compound.

ii. The International Group and its subsidiary organs shall continue to exist and fulfill all the functions stipulated in this Article unless otherwise agreed by the two Parties.

6. The Wailing Wall

The Wailing Wall shall be under Israeli sovereignty.

7. The Old City

(a) Significance of the Old City
  i. The Parties view the Old City as one whole enjoying a unique character. The Parties agree that the preservation of this unique character together with safeguarding and promoting the welfare of the inhabitants should guide the administration of the Old City.
  ii. The Parties shall act in accordance with the UNESCO World Cultural Heritage List regulations, in which the Old City is a registered site.
(b) IVG Role in the Old City
  i. Cultural Heritage
    1. The IVG shall monitor and verify the preservation of cultural heritage in the Old City in accordance with the UNESCO World Cultural Heritage List rules. For this purpose, the IVG shall have free and unimpeded access to sites, documents, and information related to the performance of this function.
    2. The IVG shall work in close coordination with the Old City Committee of the Jerusalem Coordination and Development Committee (JCDC), including in devising a restoration and preservation plan for the Old City.
  ii. Policing
    1. The IVG shall establish an Old City Policing Unit (PU) to liaise with, coordinate between, and assist the Palestinian and Israeli police forces in the Old City, to defuse localized tensions and help resolve disputes, and to perform policing duties in locations specified in and according to operational procedures detailed in Annex X.
    2. The PU shall periodically report to the IVG.
  iii. Either Party may submit complaints in relation to this clause to the IVG, which shall promptly act upon them in accordance with Article 16.

(c) Free Movement within the Old City

Movement within the Old City shall be free and unimpeded subject to the provisions of this article and rules and regulations pertaining to the various holy sites.

(d) Entry into and Exit from the Old City
  i. Entry and exit points into and from the Old City will be staffed by the authorities of the state under whose sovereignty the point falls, with the presence of PU members, unless otherwise specified.
  ii. With a view to facilitating movement into the Old City, each Party shall take such measures at the entry points in its territory as to ensure the preservation of security in the Old City. The PU shall monitor the operation of the entry points.
  iii. Citizens of either Party may not exit the Old City into the territory of the other Party unless they are in possession of the relevant documentation that entitles them to. Tourists may only exit the Old City into the territory of the Party which they possess valid authorization to enter.

(e) Suspension, Termination, and Expansion
  i. Either Party may suspend the arrangements set forth in Article 6.7.iii in cases of emergency for one week. The extension of such suspension for longer than a week shall be pursuant to consultation with the other Party and the IVG at the Trilateral Committee established in Article 3/3.
  ii. This clause shall not apply to the arrangements set forth in Article 6/7/vi.
  iii. Three years after the transfer of authority over the Old City, the Parties shall review these arrangements. These arrangements may only be terminated by agreement of the Parties.
  iv. The Parties shall examine the possibility of expanding these arrangements beyond the Old City and may agree to such an expansion.
(f) Special Arrangements
  i. Along the way outlined in Map X (from the Jaffa Gate to the Zion Gate) there will be permanent and guaranteed arrangements for Israelis regarding access, freedom of movement, and security, as set forth in Annex X.
    1. The IVG shall be responsible for the implementation of these arrangements.
  ii. Without prejudice to Palestinian sovereignty, Israeli administration of the Citadel will be as outlined in Annex X.

(g) Color-Coding of the Old City

A visible color-coding scheme shall be used in the Old City to denote the sovereign areas of the respective Parties.

(h) Policing
  i. An agreed number of Israeli police shall constitute the Israeli Old City police detachment and shall exercise responsibility for maintaining order and day-to-day policing functions in the area under Israeli sovereignty.
  ii. An agreed number of Palestinian police shall constitute the Palestinian Old City police detachment and shall exercise responsibility for maintaining order and day-to-day policing functions in the area under Palestinian sovereignty.
  iii. All members of the respective Israeli and Palestinian Old City police detachments shall undergo special training, including joint training exercises, to be administered by the PU.

iv. A special Joint Situation Room, under the direction of the PU and incorporating members of the Israeli and Palestinian Old City police detachments, shall facilitate liaison on all relevant matters of policing and security in the Old City.

(i) Arms

No person shall be allowed to carry or possess arms in the Old City, with the exception of the Police Forces provided for in this agreement. In addition, each Party may grant special written permission to carry or possess arms in areas under its sovereignty.

(j) Intelligence and Security
  i. The Parties shall establish intensive intelligence cooperation regarding the Old City, including the immediate sharing of threat information.
  ii. A trilateral committee composed of the two Parties and representatives of the United States shall be established to facilitate this cooperation.

8. Mount of Olives Cemetery
  (a) The area outlined in Map X (the Jewish Cemetery on the Mount of Olives) shall be under Israeli administration; Israeli law shall apply to persons using and procedures appertaining to this area in accordance with Annex X.
    i. There shall be a designated road to provide free, unlimited, and unimpeded access to the Cemetery.
    ii. The IVG shall monitor the implementation of this clause.
    iii. This arrangement may only be terminated by the agreement of both Parties.

9. Special Cemetery Arrangements

Arrangements shall be established in the two cemeteries designated in Map X (Mount Zion Cemetery and the German Colony Cemetery), to facilitate and ensure the continuation of the current burial and visitation practices, including the facilitation of access.

10. The Western Wall Tunnel
  (a) The Western Wall Tunnel designated in Map X shall be under Israeli administration, including:
    i. Unrestricted Israeli access and right to worship and conduct religious practices.
    ii. Responsibility for the preservation and maintenance of the site in accordance with this Agreement and without damaging structures above, under IVG supervision.
    iii. Israeli policing.
    iv. IVG monitoring.
    v. The Northern Exit of the Tunnel shall only be used for exit and may only be closed in case of emergency as stipulated in Article 6/7.
  (b) This arrangement may only be terminated by the agreement of both Parties.

11. Municipal Coordination
  (a) The two Jerusalem municipalities shall form a Jerusalem Coordination and Development Committee ("JCDC") to oversee the cooperation and coordination between the Palestinian Jerusalem municipality and the Israeli Jerusalem municipality. The JCDC and its sub-committees shall be composed of an equal number of representatives from Palestine and Israel. Each side will appoint members of the JCDC and its subcommittees in accordance with its own modalities.
  (b) The JCDC shall ensure that the coordination of infrastructure and services best serves the residents of Jerusalem, and shall promote the economic development of the city to the benefit of all. The JCDC will act to encourage cross-community dialogue and reconciliation.

[...]

12. Israeli Residency of Palestinian Jerusalemites

Palestinian Jerusalemites who currently are permanent residents of Israel shall lose this status upon the transfer of authority to Palestine of those areas in which they reside.

13. Transfer of Authority

The Parties will apply in certain socio-economic spheres interim measures to ensure the agreed, expeditious, and orderly transfer of powers and obligations from Israel to Palestine. This shall be done in a manner that preserves the accumulated socio-economic rights of the residents of East Jerusalem.

Article 7—Refugees
1. Significance of the Refugee Problem
  (a) The Parties recognize that, in the context of two independent states, Palestine and Israel, living side by side in peace, an agreed resolution of the refugee problem is necessary for achieving a just, comprehensive and lasting peace between them.
  (b) Such a resolution will also be central to stability building and development in the region.

2. UNGAR 194, UNSC Resolution 242, and the Arab Peace Initiative
  (a) The Parties recognize that UNGAR 194, UNSC Resolution 242, and the Arab Peace Initiative (Article 2.ii.) concerning the rights of the Palestinian refugees represent the basis for resolving the refugee issue, and agree that these rights are fulfilled according to Article 7 of this Agreement.

3. Compensation
  (a) Refugees shall be entitled to compensation for their refugeehood and for loss of property. This shall not prejudice or be prejudiced by the refugee's permanent place of residence.

[...]

4. Choice of Permanent Place of Residence (PPR)

The solution to the PPR aspect of the refugee problem shall entail an act of informed choice on the part of the refugee to be exercised in accordance with the options and modalities set forth in this agreement. PPR options from which the refugees may choose shall be as follows:

(a) The state of Palestine, in accordance with clause a below.
(b) Areas in Israel being transferred to Palestine in the land swap, following assumption of Palestinian sovereignty, in accordance with clause a below.
(c) Third Countries, in accordance with clause b below.
(d) The state of Israel, in accordance with clause c below.
(e) Present Host countries, in accordance with clause d below.
    i.   PPR options i and ii shall be the right of all Palestinian refugees and shall be in accordance with the laws of the State of Palestine.
    ii. Option iii shall be at the sovereign discretion of third countries and shall be in accordance with numbers that each third country will submit to the International Commission. These numbers shall represent the total number of Palestinian refugees that each third country shall accept.
    iii. Option iv shall be at the sovereign discretion of Israel and will be in accordance with a number that Israel will submit to the International Commission. This number shall represent the total number of Palestinian refugees that Israel shall accept. As a basis, Israel will consider the average of the total numbers submitted by the different third countries to the International Commission.
    iv. Option v shall be in accordance with the sovereign discretion of present host countries. Where exercised this shall be in the context of prompt and extensive development and rehabilitation programs for the refugee communities.

Priority in all the above shall be accorded to the Palestinian refugee population in Lebanon.

5. Free and Informed Choice

The process by which Palestinian refugees shall express their PPR choice shall be on the basis of a free and informed decision. The Parties themselves are committed and will encourage third parties to facilitate the refugees' free choice in expressing their preferences, and to countering any attempts at interference or organized pressure on the process of choice. This will not prejudice the recognition of Palestine as the realization of Palestinian self-determination and statehood.

6. End of Refugee Status

Palestinian refugee status shall be terminated upon the realization of an individual refugee's permanent place of residence (PPR) as determined by the International Commission.

7. End of Claims

This agreement provides for the permanent and complete resolution of the Palestinian refugee problem. No claims may be raised except for those related to the implementation of this agreement.

8. International Role

The Parties call upon the international community to participate fully in the comprehensive resolution of the refugee problem in accordance with this Agreement, including, inter alia, the establishment of an International Commission and an International Fund.

9. Property Compensation
(a) Refugees shall be compensated for the loss of property resulting from their displacement.
(b) The aggregate sum of property compensation shall be calculated as follows:
    i.   The Parties shall request the International Commission to appoint a Panel of Experts to estimate the value of Palestinians' property at the time of displacement.
    ii. The Panel of Experts shall base its assessment on the UNCCP records, the records of the Custodian for Absentee Property, and any other records it deems relevant. The Parties shall make these records available to the Panel.
    iii. The Parties shall appoint experts to advise and assist the Panel in its work.
    iv. Within 6 months, the Panel shall submit its estimates to the Parties.
    v.   The Parties shall agree on an economic multiplier, to be applied to the estimates, to reach a fair aggregate value of the property.
(c) The aggregate value agreed to by the Parties shall constitute the Israeli "lump sum" contribution to the International Fund. No other financial claims arising from the Palestinian refugee problem may be raised against Israel.
(d) Israel's contribution shall be made in installments in accordance with Schedule X. [Schedule X not included in this printing.]
(e) The value of the Israeli fixed assets that shall remain intact in former settlements and transferred to the state of Palestine will be deducted from Israel's contribution to the International Fund. An estimation of this value shall be made by the International Fund, taking into account assessment of damage caused by the settlements.

10. Compensation for Refugeehood

(a) A "Refugeehood Fund" shall be established in recognition of each individual's refugeehood. The Fund, to which Israel shall be a contributing party, shall be overseen by the International Commission. The structure and financing of the Fund is set forth in Annex X.

(b) Funds will be disbursed to refugee communities in the former areas of UNRWA operation, and will be at their disposal for communal development and commemoration of the refugee experience. Appropriate mechanisms will be devised by the International Commission whereby the beneficiary refugee communities are empowered to determine and administer the use of this Fund.

11. The International Commission

(a) Mandate and Composition

   i. An International Commission shall be established and shall have full and exclusive responsibility for implementing all aspects of this Agreement pertaining to refugees.

   ii. In addition to themselves, the Parties call upon the United Nations, the United States, UNRWA, the Arab host countries, the EU, Switzerland, Canada, Norway, Japan, the World Bank, the Russian Federation, and others to be the members of the Commission.

   iii. The Commission shall:

      1. Oversee and manage the process whereby the status and PPR of Palestinian refugees is determined and realized.

      2. Oversee and manage, in close cooperation with the host states, the rehabilitation and development programs.

      3. Raise and disburse funds as appropriate.

[…]

14. Reconciliation Programs

(a) The Parties will encourage and promote the development of cooperation between their relevant institutions and civil societies in creating forums for exchanging historical narratives and enhancing mutual understanding regarding the past.

(b) The Parties shall encourage and facilitate exchanges in order to disseminate a richer appreciation of these respective narratives, in the fields of formal and informal education, by providing conditions for direct contacts between schools, educational institutions and civil society.

(c) The Parties may consider cross-community cultural programs in order to promote the goals of conciliation in relation to their respective histories.

(d) These programs may include developing appropriate ways of commemorating those villages and communities that existed prior to 1949.

Article 8—Israeli-Palestinian Cooperation Committee (IPCC)

1. The Parties shall establish an Israeli-Palestinian Cooperation Committee immediately upon the entry into force of this agreement. The IPCC shall be a ministerial-level body with ministerial-level Co-Chairs.

2. The IPCC shall develop and assist in the implementation of policies for cooperation in areas of common interest including, but not limited to, infrastructure needs, sustainable development and environmental issues, cross-border municipal cooperation, border area industrial parks, exchange programs, human resource development, sports and youth, science, agriculture and culture.

3. The IPCC shall strive to broaden the spheres and scope of cooperation between the Parties.

[…]

Article 10—Sites of Religious Significance

1. The Parties shall establish special arrangements to guarantee access to agreed sites of religious significance, as will be detailed in Annex X. These arrangements will apply, inter alia, to the Tomb of the Patriarchs in Hebron and Rachel's Tomb in Bethlehem, and Nabi Samuel.

2. Access to and from the sites will be by way of designated shuttle facilities from the relevant border crossing to the sites.

[…]

Article 15—Palestinian Prisoners and Detainees

1. In the context of this Permanent Status Agreement between Israel and Palestine, the end of conflict, cessation of all violence, and the robust security arrangements set forth in this Agreement, all the Palestinian and Arab prisoners detained in the framework of the Israeli-Palestinian conflict prior to the date of signature of this Agreement, DD/MM/2003, shall be released in accordance with the categories set forth below and detailed in Annex X.

[…]

Article 16—Dispute Settlement Mechanism

1. Disputes related to the interpretation or application of this Agreement shall be resolved by negotiations within a bilateral framework to be convened by the High Steering Committee.

2. If a dispute is not settled promptly by the above, either Party may submit it to mediation and conciliation by the IVG mechanism in accordance with Article 3.

[…]

Source: "The Geneva Accord, Draft Permanent Status Agreement," Haaretz.com, http://www.haaretz.com/hasen/pages/ShArt .jhtml?itemNo=351461.

154. United Nations General Assembly Resolution Condemning the Israeli Security Barrier [Excerpt], October 21, 2003

Introduction

By June 2001, the growing number of Israeli civilian deaths due to suicide bombings by Palestinians who crossed into Israel from the West Bank had generated a popular movement to construct a continuous security fence, or barrier, that would seal off Palestinian from Israeli territories and prevent further terrorist attacks. Construction of portions of the barrier began in 2002. It generally constituted three parallel concrete fences, the two outer ones, begun in 2002, fortified with barbed wire with patrol roads in between them and reinforced by an antivehicle ditch on the West Bank side plus strips on either side. Standard features included observation posts and automatic sensors. Israeli soldiers controlled gates in the wall. Legal challenges meant that sections of the fence were rerouted. In some places the barrier followed the 1949 armistice line (Green Line), but other sections diverged substantially from that line to include numerous West Bank Israeli settlements. In some areas, secondary walls completely enclosed and isolated particular enclaves. At the beginning of 2007, the barrier fence plan as authorized by the Israeli government was approximately 436 miles (703 kilometers) long, with 58.4 percent already constructed, 8.96 percent under construction, and around 33 percent still to be built. Opponents of the barrier charged that it was intended not merely to exclude potential terrorist attacks but also to promote permanent Israeli annexation of areas within the West Bank by establishing "facts on the ground" in the shape of nonnegotiable territorial barriers that discouraged Palestinian settlement within the barrier. Negotiating the wall and associated checkpoints also caused considerable hardship to those Palestinians who worked in Israel but lived in the occupied territory. At Syria's initiative, in 2003 the United Nations (UN) General Assembly passed a nonbinding resolution condemning the construction of the fence as contravening international law and calling on Israel to cease building and dismantle those portions already constructed. The resolution charged that the construction of this barrier "could prejudice future negotiations and make the two-State solution physically impossible to implement." At U.S. insistence, the resolution as passed did not refer the matter to the International Court of Justice; included strong condemnations of terrorist actions, especially suicide bombings; and called on the Palestinian Authority (PA) to act forcefully to prevent further violence. The resolution also reiterated UN opposition to further Israeli settlement activities and called on Israel to renounce depor-

tations, attacks, and murders of Palestinians. The resolution had no impact on Israeli determination to continue building the barrier.

Primary Source

[...]

Illegal Israeli actions in Occupied East Jerusalem and the rest of the Occupied Palestinian Territory

The General Assembly,

Recalling its relevant resolutions, including resolutions of the tenth emergency special session,

Recalling also Security Council resolutions 242 (1967) of 22 November 1967, 267 (1969) of 3 July 1969, 298 (1971) of 25 September 1971, 446 (1979) of 22 March 1979, 452 (1979) of 20 July 1979, 465 (1980) of 1 March 1980, 476 (1980) of 30 June 1980, 478 (1980) of 20 August 1980, 904 (1994) of 18 March 1994, 1073 (1996) of 28 September 1996 and 1397 (2002) of 12 March 2002,

Reaffirming the principle of the inadmissibility of the acquisition of territory by force,

Reaffirming its vision of a region where two States, Israel and Palestine, live side by side within secure and recognized borders,

Condemning all acts of violence, terrorism and destruction,

Condemning in particular the suicide bombings and their recent intensification with the attack in Haifa,

Condemning also the bomb attack in the Gaza Strip which resulted in the death of three American security officers,

Deploring the extrajudicial killings and their recent intensification, in particular the attack yesterday in Gaza,

Stressing the urgency of ending the current violent situation on the ground, the need to end the occupation that began in 1967, and the need to achieve peace based on the vision of two States mentioned above,

Particularly concerned that the route marked out for the wall under construction by Israel, the occupying Power, in the Occupied Palestinian Territory, including in and around East Jerusalem, could prejudice future negotiations and make the two-State solution physically impossible to implement and would cause further humanitarian hardship to the Palestinians,

Reiterating its call upon Israel, the occupying Power, to fully and effectively respect the Fourth Geneva Convention of 1949,

Reiterating its opposition to settlement activities in the Occupied Territories and to any activities involving the confiscation of land, disruption of the livelihood of protected persons and the de facto annexation of land,

1. *Demands* that Israel stop and reverse the construction of the wall in the Occupied Palestinian Territory, including in and around East Jerusalem, which is in departure of the Armistice Line of 1949 and is in contradiction to relevant provisions of international law;

2. *Calls upon* both Parties to fulfil their obligations under relevant provisions of the Road Map; the Palestinian Authority to undertake visible efforts on the ground to arrest, disrupt, and restrain individuals and groups conducting and planning violent attacks; the Government of Israel to take no actions undermining trust, including deportations and attacks on civilians and extrajudicial killings;

[...]

Source: United Nations General Assembly Official Records, 58th Sess., A/ES-10/L.15, October 21, 2003. http://www.jewishvirtual library.org.

155. United Nations Security Council Resolution 1515, November 19, 2003

Introduction

By late 2003 the prospects for further implementation of the steps laid out in the Road Map to Peace put forward so enthusiastically by the Quartet of the United Nations (UN), the United States, Russia, and the European Union (EU) 18 months earlier seemed bleak. In October 2003 the new Palestinian Authority (PA) prime minister, Mahmoud Abbas, resigned after a mere 6 months in office, and terrorist activities seemed ever more entrenched within the Palestinian territories. Israel had responded by constructing a security fence that was likely to further complicate the future situation in the West Bank occupied territories. Seeking to reenergize the Road Map peace process, the UN Security Council passed a resolution introduced by Russia calling on all parties involved to cease all acts of violence, terrorism, and destruction and return to the Road Map process and live up to their obligations under it. While the Road Map's sponsoring powers were undoubtedly willing to heed this appeal, in Israel and the Palestinian territories it largely fell on deaf ears.

Primary Source

The Security Council,

Recalling all its previous relevant resolutions, in particular resolutions 242 (1967), 338 (1973), 1397 (2002) and the Madrid principles,

Expressing its grave concern at the continuation of the tragic and violent events in the Middle East,

Reiterating the demand for an immediate cessation of all acts of violence, including all acts of terrorism, provocation, incitement and destruction,

Reaffirming its vision of a region where two States, Israel and Palestine, live side by side within secure and recognized borders,

Emphasizing the need to achieve a comprehensive, just and lasting peace in the Middle East, including the Israeli-Syrian and Israeli-Lebanese tracks,

Welcoming and encouraging the diplomatic efforts of the international Quartet and others,

1. *Endorses* the Quartet Performance-based Roadmap to a Permanent Two-State Solution to the Israeli-Palestinian Conflict (S/2003/529);

2. *Calls on* the parties to fulfil their obligations under the Roadmap in cooperation with the Quartet and to achieve the vision of two States living side by side in peace and security;

3. *Decides* to remain seized of the matter.

Source: United Nations Security Council Official Records, 03-62185 (E)S.C. Res. 1515, November 19, 2003, http://daccessdds.un.org/doc/UNDOC/GEN/N03/621/85/PDF/N0362185.pdf?OpenElement.

156. Ariel Sharon, Address at the Fourth Herzliya Conference [Excerpt], December 18, 2003

Introduction

With the process set out in the Road Map to Peace apparently bogged down as the Second (al-Aqsa) Intifada continued, Israeli prime minister Ariel Sharon took the decisive step of announcing that Israel intended to withdraw completely from Gaza and hand it over to Palestinian control. In December 2003 Sharon announced in a public speech that while he sought a final peace accord with the Palestinians under the peace plan, he was not prepared to make any peace settlement while terrorist activities against Israel continued. With the approval and collaboration of the United States, Israel would, however, take unilateral action to withdraw all Israeli forces and settlers from Gaza, which formed part of the territory of the Palestinian Authority (PA), and return it to full Palestinian control. Withdrawing Israeli troops from Gaza would reduce the potential for friction between Israelis and Palestinians. Israeli forces would be redeployed along a security line that might or might not constitute the final border between Israel and a Palestinian state but was defensible under existing conditions. Given terrorist threats to Israel's security, in tandem with the Disengagement Plan Israel would also accelerate the construction of the security fence separating Israel from the West Bank. Sharon warned that the Palestinians would receive less under the Disengagement Plan than they would have under the Road Map to Peace and claimed that he would have greatly preferred to have resumed the negotiations anticipated under the Road Map scheme. Some critics nonetheless later alleged that Sharon's motive in launching this initiative was to delay further progress on the broader peace process aimed at a final status agreement until a later date, as he was not prepared to accept a Palestinian state that had not firmly renounced terrorist activities against Israel. The passage of United Nations (UN) Security Council Resolution 1515 one month earlier had been one attempt to revitalize that peace process. Concentration on disengagement from Gaza would allow Sharon to defer any other initiative and avoid the prospect of an unstable Palestinian state on Israel's border that would provide a haven for terrorist activities against Israel.

Primary Source

[. . .]

I know that there is sometimes a tendency to narrow all of Israel's problems down to the political sphere, believing that once a solution is found to Israel's problems with its neighbors, particularly the Palestinians, the other issues on the agenda will miraculously resolve themselves. I do not believe so. We are facing additional challenges, which must be addressed: the economy, educating the young generation, immigrant absorption, enhancement of social cohesion and the improvement of relations between Arabs and Jews in Israel.

Like all Israeli citizens, I yearn for peace. I attach supreme importance to taking all steps, which will enable progress toward resolution of the conflict with the Palestinians. However, in light of the other challenges we are faced with, if the Palestinians do not make a similar effort toward a solution of the conflict I do not intend to wait for them indefinitely.

Seven months ago, my Government approved the Roadmap to peace, based on President George Bush's June 2002 speech. This is a balanced program for phased progress toward peace, to which both Israel and the Palestinians committed themselves. A full and genuine implementation of the program is the best way to achieve true peace. The Roadmap is the only political plan accepted by Israel, the Palestinians, the Americans and a majority of the international community. We are willing to proceed toward its implementation: two states, Israel and a Palestinian State, living side by side in tranquility, security and peace.

The Roadmap is a clear and reasonable plan, and it is therefore possible and imperative to implement it. The concept behind this plan is that only security will lead to peace. And in that sequence. Without the achievement of full security within the framework of which terror organizations will be dismantled it will not be possible to achieve genuine peace, a peace for generations. This is the essence of the Roadmap. The opposite perception, according to which the very signing of a peace agreement will produce security out of thin air, has already been tried in the past and failed miserably. And such will be the fate of any other plan which promotes this concept. These plans deceive the public and create false hope. There will be no peace before the eradication of terror.

The government under my leadership will not compromise on the realization of all phases of the Roadmap. It is incumbent upon the Palestinians to uproot the terrorist groups and to create a law-abiding society, which fights against violence and incitement. Peace and terror cannot coexist. The world is currently united in its unequivocal demand from the Palestinians to act toward the cessation of terrorism and the implementation of reforms. Only a transformation of the Palestinian Authority into a different authority will enable progress in the political process. The Palestinians must fulfill their obligations. A full and complete implementation will at the end of the process lead to peace and tranquility.

We began the implementation of the Roadmap at Aqaba, but the terrorist organizations joined with Yasser Arafat and sabotaged the process with a series of the most brutal terror attacks we have ever known.

Concurrent with the demand from the Palestinians to eliminate the terror organizations, Israel is taking and will continue to take steps to significantly improve the living conditions of the Palestinian population: Israel will remove closures and curfews and reduce the number of roadblocks; we will improve freedom of movement for the Palestinian population, including the passage of people and goods; we will increase the hours of operation at international border crossings; we will enable a large number of Palestinian merchants to conduct regular and normal economic and trade relations with their Israeli counterparts, etc. All these measures are aimed at enabling better and freer movement for the Palestinian population not involved in terror.

In addition, subject to security coordination, we will transfer Palestinian towns to Palestinian security responsibility.

Israel will make every effort to assist the Palestinians and to advance the process.

Israel will fulfill the commitments taken upon itself. I have committed to the President of the United States that Israel will dismantle unauthorized outposts. It is my intention to implement this commitment. The State of Israel is governed by law, and the issue of the outposts is no exception. I understand the sensitivity; we will try to do this in the least painful way possible, but the unauthorized outposts will be dismantled. Period.

Israel will meet all its obligations with regard to construction in the settlements. There will be no construction beyond the existing construction line, no expropriation of land for construction, no special economic incentives and no construction of new settlements.

I take this opportunity to appeal to the Palestinians and repeat, as I said at Aqaba: it is not in our interest to govern you. We would like you to govern yourselves in your own country. A democratic Palestinian state with territorial contiguity in Judea and Samaria and economic viability, which would conduct normal relations of tranquility, security and peace with Israel. Abandon the path of terror and let us together stop the bloodshed. Let us move forward together towards peace.

We wish to speedily advance implementation of the Roadmap towards quiet and a genuine peace. We hope that the Palestinian Authority will carry out its part. However, if in a few months the Palestinians still continue to disregard their part in implementing the Roadmap then Israel will initiate the unilateral security step of disengagement from the Palestinians.

The purpose of the Disengagement Plan is to reduce terror as much as possible, and grant Israeli citizens the maximum level of security. The process of disengagement will lead to an improvement in the quality of life, and will help strengthen the Israeli economy. The unilateral steps which Israel will take in the framework of the Disengagement Plan will be fully coordinated with the United States. We must not harm our strategic coordination with the United States. These steps will increase security for the residents of Israel and relieve the pressure on the IDF and security forces in fulfilling the difficult tasks they are faced with. The Disengagement Plan is meant to grant maximum security and minimize friction between Israelis and Palestinians.

We are interested in conducting direct negotiations, but do not intend to hold Israeli society hostage in the hands of the Palestinians. I have already said we will not wait for them indefinitely.

The Disengagement Plan will include the redeployment of IDF forces along new security lines and a change in the deployment of settlements, which will reduce as much as possible the number of Israelis located in the heart of the Palestinian population. We will draw provisional security lines and the IDF will be deployed along them. Security will be provided by IDF deployment, the security fence and other physical obstacles. The Disengagement Plan will reduce friction between us and the Palestinians.

This reduction of friction will require the extremely difficult step of changing the deployment of some of the settlements. I would like to repeat what I have said in the past: In the framework of a future agreement, Israel will not remain in all the places where it is today. The relocation of settlements will be made, first and foremost, in order to draw the most efficient security line possible, thereby creating this disengagement between Israel and the Palestinians. This security line will not constitute the permanent border of the State of Israel, however, as long as implementation of the Roadmap is not resumed, the IDF will be deployed along that line. Settlements which will be relocated are those which will not be included in the territory of the State of Israel in the framework of any possible future permanent agreement. At the same time, in the framework of the Disengagement Plan, Israel will strengthen its control over those same areas in the Land of Israel which will constitute an inseparable part of the State of Israel in any future agreement. I know you would like to hear names, but we should leave something for later.

Israel will greatly accelerate the construction of the security fence. Today we can already see it taking shape. The rapid completion of the security fence will enable the IDF to remove roadblocks and ease the daily lives of the Palestinian population not involved in terror.

In order to enable the Palestinians to develop their economic and trade sectors, and to ensure that they will not be exclusively dependent on Israel, we will consider, in the framework of the Disengagement Plan, enabling in coordination with Jordan and Egypt the freer passage of people and goods through international border crossings, while taking the necessary security precautions.

I would like to emphasize: the Disengagement Plan is a security measure and not a political one. The steps which will be taken will not change the political reality between Israel and the Palestinians, and will not prevent the possibility of returning to the implementation of the Roadmap and reaching an agreed settlement.

The Disengagement Plan does not prevent the implementation of the Roadmap. Rather, it is a step Israel will take in the absence of any other option, in order to improve its security. The Disengagement Plan will be realized only in the event that the Palestinians continue to drag their feet and postpone implementation of the Roadmap.

Obviously, through the Disengagement Plan the Palestinians will receive much less than they would have received through direct negotiations as set out in the Roadmap.

According to circumstances, it is possible that parts of the Disengagement Plan that are supposed to provide maximum security to the citizens of Israel will be undertaken while also attempting to implement the Roadmap.

Ladies and Gentlemen,

My life experience has taught me that for peace, as well as for war, we must have broad consensus. We must preserve our unity, even in the midst of a difficult, internal debate.

In the past three years, the Palestinian terrorist organizations have put us to a difficult test. Their plan to break the spirit of Israeli society has not succeeded. The citizens of Israel have managed to step into the breach, support each other, lend a helping hand, volunteer and contribute.

I believe that this path of unity must be continued today. Whether we will be able to advance the Roadmap, or will have to implement the Disengagement Plan, experience has taught us that, together, through broad national consensus, we can do great things.

Let us not be led astray. Any path will be complicated, strewn with obstacles, and obligate us to act with discretion and responsibility. I am confident that, just as we have managed to overcome the challenges of the past, we will stand together and succeed today.

[. . .]

> **Source:** Ariel Sharon, "Address by Prime Minister Ariel Sharon at the Fourth Herzliya Conference, December 18, 2003," Israel Ministry of Foreign Affairs, http://www.mfa.gov.il/MFA.

157. The Revised Disengagement Plan [Excerpt], June 6, 2004

Introduction

The Israeli plan for disengagement from Gaza, approved by the Israeli cabinet in June 2004, was comprehensive. The plan's basic assumption was that in any future final status agreement, no Israeli settlements or territory would be left in Gaza, making complete withdrawal the most practical option. Relocation from Gaza would reduce Israeli friction with Palestinians there and remove the burden of responsibility for the Palestinians from Israel. A timetable for withdrawal was set out and was expected to be completed by the end of 2005. The Gaza Strip would remain demilitarized, but Israel reserved its right to intervene there. Israel intended to continue to control the borders of Gaza and to remove all Israeli residents and buildings from the area. Similar arrangements also applied to a small portion of northern Samaria, in the West Bank, that was also covered by the Disengagement Plan. Israel would also move the existing corridor for passage between Gaza and the West Bank southward in order to facilitate easier and more extensive transit arrangements. Israelis who were relocated from Gaza would be rehoused and would receive compensation. The arrangements for the removal of all Israeli settlers in Gaza were among the most politically controversial. In the second half of August 2005, Sharon ordered the removal of 9,485 protesting diehard Jewish residents from 21 settlements in Gaza and 4 settlements in northern Samaria. Israeli soldiers with bulldozers demolished all buildings in those settlements. Conservative rabbis pronounced formal curses on Sharon, begging the Angel of Death to kill him. Disengagement was nonetheless completed more than three months ahead of schedule on September 11, 2005, when the last Israeli soldier left and the border fence between Gaza and Israel was closed. Despite being fiercely attacked by members of his own Likud Party, Sharon's decision to abandon Gaza was generally popular with Israelis. The episode was a striking demonstration of Sharon's readiness to take forceful action against diehard Israeli settlers if he thought this appropriate and implied that he might in the future be prepared to endure similar political heat if a genuine final status peace settlement was offered.

Primary Source

Addendum A—Revised Disengagement Plan—Main Principles
1. Background—Political and Security Implications
The State of Israel is committed to the peace process and aspires to reach an agreed resolution of the conflict based upon the vision of US President George Bush.

The State of Israel believes that it must act to improve the current situation. The State of Israel has come to the conclusion that there is currently no reliable Palestinian partner with which it can make progress in a two-sided peace process. Accordingly, it has developed a plan of revised disengagement (hereinafter—the plan), based on the following considerations:

One. The stalemate dictated by the current situation is harmful. In order to break out of this stalemate, the State of Israel is required to initiate moves not dependent on Palestinian cooperation.

Two. The purpose of the plan is to lead to a better security, political, economic and demographic situation.

Three. In any future permanent status arrangement, there will be no Israeli towns and villages in the Gaza Strip. On the other hand, it is clear that in the West Bank, there are areas which will be part of the State of Israel, including major Israeli population centers, cities, towns and villages, security areas and other places of special interest to Israel.

Four. The State of Israel supports the efforts of the United States, operating alongside the international community, to promote the reform process, the construction of institutions and the improvement of the economy and welfare of the Palestinian residents, in order that a new Palestinian leadership will emerge and prove itself capable of fulfilling its commitments under the Roadmap.

Five. Relocation from the Gaza Strip and from an area in Northern Samaria should reduce friction with the Palestinian population.

Six. The completion of the plan will serve to dispel the claims regarding Israel's responsibility for the Palestinians in the Gaza Strip.

Seven. The process set forth in the plan is without prejudice to the relevant agreements between the State of Israel and the Palestinians. Relevant arrangements shall continue to apply.

Eight. International support for this plan is widespread and important. This support is essential in order to bring the Palestinians to implement in practice their obligations to combat terrorism and effect reforms as required by the Roadmap, thus enabling the parties to return to the path of negotiation.

2. Main Elements
A. The process:
[...]

3.1 The Gaza Strip
1) The State of Israel will evacuate the Gaza Strip, including all existing Israeli towns and villages, and will redeploy outside the Strip. This will not include military deployment in the area of the border between the Gaza Strip and Egypt ("the Philadelphi Route") as detailed below.

2) Upon completion of this process, there shall no longer be any permanent presence of Israeli security forces in the areas of Gaza Strip territory which have been evacuated.

3.2 The West Bank
3) The State of Israel will evacuate an area in Northern Samaria (Ganim, Kadim, Sa-Nur and Homesh), and all military installations in this area, and will redeploy outside the vacated area.

4) Upon completion of this process, there shall no longer be any permanent presence of Israeli security forces in this area.

5) The move will enable territorial contiguity for Palestinians in the Northern Samaria area.

6) The State of Israel will assist, together with the international community, in improving the transportation infrastructure in the West Bank in order to facilitate the contiguity of Palestinian transportation.

7) The process will facilitate normal life and Palestinian economic and commercial activity in the West Bank.

3.3 The intention is to complete the planned relocation process by the end of 2005.

B. The Security Fence:
The State of Israel will continue building the Security Fence, in accordance with the relevant decisions of the Government. The route will take into account humanitarian considerations.

3. Security Situation Following the Relocation
One. The Gaza Strip:
1) The State of Israel will guard and monitor the external land perimeter of the Gaza Strip, will continue to maintain exclusive authority in Gaza air space, and will continue to exercise security activity in the sea off the coast of the Gaza Strip.
2) The Gaza Strip shall be demilitarized and shall be devoid of weaponry, the presence of which does not accord with the Israeli-Palestinian agreements.
3) The State of Israel reserves its fundamental right of self-defense, both preventive and reactive, including where necessary the use of force, in respect of threats emanating from the Gaza Strip.

Two. The West Bank:
1) Upon completion of the evacuation of the Northern Samaria area, no permanent Israeli military presence will remain in this area.
2) The State of Israel reserves its fundamental right of self-defense, both preventive and reactive, including where necessary the use of force, in respect of threats emanating from the Northern Samaria area.
3) In other areas of the West Bank, current security activity will continue. However, as circumstances require, the State of Israel will consider reducing such activity in Palestinian cities.
4) The State of Israel will work to reduce the number of internal checkpoints throughout the West Bank.

4. Military Installations and Infrastructure in the Gaza Strip and Northern Samaria
In general, these will be dismantled and evacuated, with the exception of those which the State of Israel decides to transfer to another party.

5. Security Assistance to the Palestinians
The State of Israel agrees that by coordination with it, advice, assistance and training will be provided to the Palestinian security forces for the implementation of their obligations to combat terrorism and maintain public order, by American, British, Egyptian, Jordanian or other experts, as agreed therewith.

No foreign security presence may enter the Gaza Strip and/or the West Bank without being coordinated with and approved by the State of Israel.

6. The Border Area Between the Gaza Strip and Egypt (Philadelphi Route)

The State of Israel will continue to maintain a military presence along the border between the Gaza Strip and Egypt (Philadelphi Route). This presence is an essential security requirement. At certain locations, security considerations may require some widening of the area in which the military activity is conducted.

Subsequently, the evacuation of this area will be considered. Evacuation of the area will be dependent, inter alia, on the security situation and the extent of cooperation with Egypt in establishing a reliable alternative arrangement.

If and when conditions permit the evacuation of this area, the State of Israel will be willing to consider the possibility of the establishment of a seaport and airport in the Gaza Strip, in accordance with arrangements to be agreed with Israel.

7. Real Estate Assets

In general, residential dwellings and sensitive structures, including synagogues, will not remain. The State of Israel will aspire to transfer other facilities, including industrial, commercial and agricultural ones, to a third, international party which will put them to use for the benefit of the Palestinian population that is not involved in terror.

The area of the Erez industrial zone will be transferred to the responsibility of an agreed upon Palestinian or international party.

The State of Israel will explore, together with Egypt, the possibility of establishing a joint industrial zone on the border of the Gaza Strip, Egypt and Israel.

8. Civil Infrastructure and Arrangements

Infrastructure relating to water, electricity, sewage and telecommunications will remain in place.

In general, Israel will continue, for full price, to supply electricity, water, gas and petrol to the Palestinians, in accordance with current arrangements.

Other existing arrangements, such as those relating to water and the electro-magnetic sphere shall remain in force.

9. Activity of Civilian International Organizations

The State of Israel recognizes the great importance of the continued activity of international humanitarian organizations and others engaged in civil development, assisting the Palestinian population.

The State of Israel will coordinate with these organizations arrangements to facilitate their activities.

The State of Israel proposes that an international apparatus be established (along the lines of the AHLC), with the agreement of Israel and international elements which will work to develop the Palestinian economy.

10. Economic Arrangements

In general, the economic arrangements currently in operation between the State of Israel and the Palestinians shall remain in force. These arrangements include, inter alia:

One. The entry and exit of goods between the Gaza Strip, the West Bank, the State of Israel and abroad.

Two. The monetary regime.

Three. Tax and customs envelope arrangements.

Four. Postal and telecommunications arrangements.

Five. The entry of workers into Israel, in accordance with the existing criteria.

In the longer term, and in line with Israel's interest in encouraging greater Palestinian economic independence, the State of Israel expects to reduce the number of Palestinian workers entering Israel, to the point that it ceases completely. The State of Israel supports the development of sources of employment in the Gaza Strip and in Palestinian areas of the West Bank, by international elements.

11. International Passages

a. The International Passage Between the Gaza Strip and Egypt
  1) The existing arrangements shall continue.
  2) The State of Israel is interested in moving the passage to the "three borders" area, south of its current location. This would need to be effected in coordination with the Government of Egypt. This move would enable the hours of operation of the passage to be extended.

b. The International Passages Between the West Bank and Jordan: The existing arrangements shall continue.

12. Erez Crossing Point

The Erez crossing point will be moved to a location within Israel in a time frame to be determined separately by the Government.

13. Conclusion

The goal is that implementation of the plan will lead to improving the situation and breaking the current deadlock. If and when there is evidence from the Palestinian side of its willingness, capability and implementation in practice of the fight against terrorism, full cessation of terrorism and violence and the institution of reform as required by the Road Map, it will be possible to return to the track of negotiation and dialogue.

[. . .]

> **Source:** "The Cabinet Resolution regarding the Disengagement Plan," Israel Ministry of Foreign Affairs, http://www.mfa.gov.il/MFA.

158. Advisory Opinion of the International Court of Justice, Legal Consequences of the Construction of a Wall in the Occupied Palestinian Territory [Excerpt], July 9, 2004

Introduction

Palestinians in the occupied territories deeply resented Israel's construction of the barrier wall separating them not just from Israel itself but also from Israeli settlements in the occupied territories. In 2004 the Palestinian Authority (PA) brought the matter before the International Court of Justice and claimed that the security fence represented an Israeli attempt to annex portions of the West Bank. The Israeli government refused to appear before the court, merely submitting an advisory opinion that the International Court had no jurisdiction in the matter. The International Court nonetheless found in the Palestinians' favor and ruled not merely that construction of the wall was illegal if it encompassed any territory beyond Israel's June 1967 borders but also that Israeli settlements in the occupied territories were illegal. The International Court demanded the demolition of the wall, compensation for those affected, and a return to the peace process set out in the Quartet's Road Map to Peace. Israel simply ignored the judgment. Opposition from the United States to this decision ensured that the issue of enforcement of this judgment was not brought before the United Nations (UN) Security Council. In 2005 the Israeli High Court ruled that construction of the fence was not in itself illegal, although diversions of its route might in certain cases be justified.

Primary Source

[. . .]

119. The Court notes that the route of the wall as fixed by the Israeli Government includes within the "Closed Area" . . . some 80 per cent of the settlers living in the Occupied Palestinian Territory. Moreover, it is apparent . . . that the wall's sinuous route has been traced in such a way as to include within that area the great majority of the Israeli settlements in the occupied Palestinian Territory (including East Jerusalem).

120. As regards these settlements, the Court notes that Article 49, paragraph 6, of the Fourth Geneva Convention provides: "The Occupying Power shall not deport or transfer parts of its own civilian population into the territory it occupies." That provision prohibits not only deportations or forced transfers of population such as those carried out during the Second World War, but also any measures taken by an occupying Power in order to organize or encourage transfers of parts of its own population into the occupied territory.

In this respect, the information provided to the Court shows that, since 1977, Israel has conducted a policy and developed practices involving the establishment of settlements in the Occupied Palestinian Territory, contrary to the terms of Article 49, paragraph 6, just cited.

The Security Council has thus taken the view that such policy and practices "have no legal validity". It has also called upon "Israel, as the occupying Power, to abide scrupulously" by the Fourth Geneva Convention and:

"to rescind its previous measures and to desist from taking any action which would result in changing the legal status and geographical nature and materially affecting the demographic composition of the Arab territories occupied since 1967, including Jerusalem and, in particular, not to transfer parts of its own civilian population into the occupied Arab territories" (resolution 446 (1979) of 22 March 1979).

The Council reaffirmed its position in resolutions 452 (1979) of 20 July 1979 and 465 (1980) of 1 March 1980. Indeed, in the latter case it described "Israel's policy and practices of settling parts of its population and new immigrants in [the occupied] territories" as a "flagrant violation" of the Fourth Geneva Convention.

The Court concludes that the Israeli settlements in the Occupied Palestinian Territory (including East Jerusalem) have been established in breach of international law.

121. Whilst the Court notes the assurance given by Israel that the construction of the wall does not amount to annexation and that the wall is of a temporary nature . . . , it nevertheless cannot remain indifferent to certain fears expressed to it that the route of the wall will prejudge the future frontier between Israel and Palestine, and the fear that Israel may integrate the settlements and their means of access. The Court considers that the construction of the wall and its associated régime create a "fait accompli" on the ground that could well become permanent, in which case, and notwithstanding the formal characterization of the wall by Israel, it would be tantamount to de facto annexation.

122. The Court recalls moreover that, according to the report of the Secretary-General, the planned route would incorporate in the area between the Green Line and the wall more than 16 per cent of the territory of the West Bank. Around 80 per cent of the settlers living in the Occupied Palestinian Territory, that is 320,000 individuals, would reside in that area, as well as 237,000 Palestinians. Moreover, as a result of the construction of the wall, around 160,000 other Palestinians would reside in almost completely encircled communities....

In other terms, the route chosen for the wall gives expression in loco to the illegal measures taken by Israel with regard to Jerusalem and the settlements, as deplored by the Security Council.... There is also a risk of further alterations to the demographic composition of the Occupied Palestinian Territory resulting from the construction of the wall inasmuch as it is contributing . . . to the departure of Palestinian populations from certain areas. That construction, along with measures taken previously, thus severely impedes the exercise by the Palestinian people of its right to self-determination, and is therefore a breach of Israel's obligation to respect that right.

[. . .]

141. The fact remains that Israel has to face numerous indiscriminate and deadly acts of violence against its civilian population. It has the right, and indeed the duty, to respond in order to protect the life of its citizens. The measures taken are bound nonetheless to remain in conformity with applicable international law.

142. In conclusion, the Court considers that Israel cannot rely on a right of self-defence or on a state of necessity in order to preclude the wrongfulness of the construction of the wall. . . . The Court accordingly finds that the construction of the wall, and its associated régime, are contrary to international law.

143. The Court having concluded that, by the construction of the wall in the Occupied Palestinian Territory, including in and around East Jerusalem, and by adopting its associated régime, Israel has violated various international obligations incumbent upon it . . . , it must now, in order to reply to the question posed by the General Assembly, examine the consequences of those violations.

[. . .]

149. The Court notes that Israel is first obliged to comply with the international obligations it has breached by the construction of the wall in the Occupied Palestinian Territory.... Consequently, Israel is bound to comply with its obligation to respect the right of the Palestinian people to self-determination and its obligations under international humanitarian law and international human rights law. Furthermore, it must ensure freedom of access to the Holy Places that came under its control following the 1967 War....

150. The Court observes that Israel also has an obligation to put an end to the violation of its international obligations flowing from the construction of the wall in the Occupied Palestinian Territory....

151. Israel accordingly has the obligation to cease forthwith the works of construction of the wall being built by it in the Occupied Palestinian Territory, including in and around East Jerusalem. Moreover, in view of the Court's finding (see paragraph 143 above) that Israel's violations of its international obligations stem from the construction of the wall and from its associated régime, cessation of those violations entails the dismantling forthwith of those parts of that structure situated within the Occupied Palestinian Territory, including in and around East Jerusalem. All legislative and regulatory acts adopted with a view to its construction, and to the establishment of its associated régime, must forthwith be repealed or rendered ineffective, except in so far as such acts, by providing for compensation or other forms of reparation for the Palestinian population, may continue to be relevant for compliance by Israel with the obligations referred to in paragraph 153 below.

152. Moreover, given that the construction of the wall in the Occupied Palestinian Territory has, inter alia, entailed the requisition and destruction of homes, businesses and agricultural holdings, the Court finds further that Israel has the obligation to make reparation for the damage caused to all the natural or legal persons concerned....

153. Israel is accordingly under an obligation to return the land, orchards, olive groves and other immovable property seized from any natural or legal person for purposes of construction of the wall in the Occupied Palestinian Territory. In the event that such restitution should prove to be materially impossible, Israel has an obligation to compensate the persons in question for the damage suffered. The Court considers that Israel also has an obligation to compensate, in accordance with the applicable rules of international law, all natural or legal persons having suffered any form of material damage as a result of the wall's construction.

[. . .]

Source: "Legal Consequences of the Construction of a Wall in the Occupied Palestinian Territory, Advisory Opinion of 9 July 2004," International Court of Justice, http://www.icj-cij.org/.

159. Mahmoud Abbas, Inaugural Speech as President of the Palestinian Authority [Excerpt], January 15, 2005

Introduction

Longtime Palestine Liberation Organization (PLO) and Palestinian Authority (PA) president Yasser Arafat died in the fall of 2004, opening the way for new movement in the peace process. Mahmoud Abbas, leader of the Fatah group within the PLO who had served six rather ineffective months as PA prime minister in 2003, was the front-runner to succeed Arafat. Abbas, chairman of the PLO Executive Committee, was a moderate who favored an end to violence and resumption of the stalled Quartet Road Map to Peace. He was also a strong supporter of greater democracy and constitutional reform within the PA. During the 1990s Abbas had been one of the PLO's chief negotiators with Israel. In January 2005 in elections largely boycotted by Hamas, the Palestinian group that staunchly opposed any recognition of or compromise with Israel and was pledged to the destruction of the Israeli state, Abbas was elected PA president, winning 62 percent of the vote. Israeli forces had, however, detained or restricted the movements of some of his rivals, and the Abbas campaign had virtually monopolized Palestinian television coverage of the election. In his inaugural speech, Abbas nonetheless celebrated the fact that democratic elections had been held and the rule of law upheld within the Palestinian territories. He urged the resumption of negotiations under the Quartet's peace plan to bring about the final creation of a Palestinian state, one committed to coexistence with Israel, and called for an end to the Second (al-Aqsa) Intifada and the renunciation by Palestinians of the use of violence and terror against Israeli targets. He also demanded that Israel show its good faith by ending "assassinations, the siege on our towns, arrests, land confiscations, settlement activity and the separation wall."

Primary Source

[. . .]

As I address you today, I am full of pride over the Palestinian people's exceptional democratic achievement. Our people have stood in the face of the occupation to say—first and foremost to ourselves but also to the whole world—that no matter how great the challenges may be, we will not give up on our national project. . . . That no matter how many obstacles may stand in our way, we will not be deterred from advancing our democratic process. The winner in these elections is the great Palestinian people who have created this democratic epic and who will safeguard it.

[. . .]

This is a historic day in our national process, and I say to all our people who voted: you have kept the flame of democracy alive, and all my thanks and gratitude go to you. I pledge to exert all of my efforts to implement the program according to which I was elected, and to continue on the path towards achieving our national goals.

My thanks and appreciation also go to all those who worked to make the election campaign a success, my brothers in the FATAH movement all over Palestine, and to all political forces, organizations, institutions, movements and individuals who spared no effort to defend our national democratic program. This program now has the widest public support.

To all the other candidates, I say: we highly appreciate your efforts in making the democratic process a success. You have my pledge to encourage and guarantee the active role of all of our political forces and strands, and to protect the freedom of expression in accordance with the law.

For even if our opinions may differ, we share one national cause, and even if our judgments may diverge, we defend one goal. We will make sure that we work together to achieve the national goals to which we all aspire.

Today, the results of the elections are final, and our great people have passed this important test. I stand before you as the President and representative of the whole Palestinian people to say: we will continue consolidating national unity. We will deepen dialogue with all the active forces in our nation, and we will remain devoted to strengthening the unity of our society and institutions. We will also continue on the path of Yasser Arafat to achieve just peace—the peace of the brave for which he had always worked, and to which he dedicated all his life and efforts.

[. . .]

And I salute all of our people, particularly the residents of Jerusalem—the capital of our independent state. You have proven to the whole world your national commitment, determination to move forward, and commitment to our national goals and democratic choice. Your turnout exceeded all expectations, and you overcame difficulties, obstacles, and hardships.

- —The people have spoken for the end of occupation and the democratic choice—for the continuation and consolidation of development and reform in all its forms,
- —The people have voted for the rule of law, order, pluralism, the peaceful transfer of authority, and equality for all,
- —The people have chosen just peace, ending the occupation, and coexistence based on equality and international legitimacy.

Ladies and Gentlemen,

This year is the year of Palestinian elections—presidential, legislative, and municipal elections. Let us muster our national efforts to further extend the election process to all civil organizations, trade unions, and political forces and factions so as to rejuvenate our domestic political life.

The greatest challenge before us, and the fundamental task facing us is national liberation. The task of ending the occupation, establishing the Palestinian state on the 1967 borders, with Jerusalem as its capital, and reaching a just and agreed solution to the refugee problem on the basis of international legitimacy [resolutions], first and foremost [the UN General Assembly] resolution 194 (of 1949) and the Beirut Arab Summit Resolution [in 2002].

To achieve these national goals, we will remain committed to the PLO's strategic choice: the choice of achieving just peace and our national goals through negotiations. The path to these goals is what we and the world have agreed upon in the Road Map. We have repeatedly stated that we are committed to our responsibilities in the Road Map. We will implement our obligations as a matter of Palestinian national interest. In return, Israel has to implement its obligations.

In the last few days, a number of incidents took place. We condemn these actions, whether by the Israeli occupation forces or the reactions of some Palestinian factions. This does not help bring about the calm needed to enable a credible, serious peace process. We are seeking a mutual ceasefire to end this vicious circle.

Our hand is extended towards an Israeli partner for making peace. But partnership is not through words but rather deeds. It is through ending assassinations, the siege on our towns, arrests, land confiscations, settlement activity and the separation wall. Partnership cannot be achieved by dictation, and peace cannot be reached by partial or interim solutions. Peace can only be achieved by working together to reach a permanent status solution that deals with all of the outstanding issues, and which turns a new page on the basis of two neighboring states.

I would like to stress here that we are fully prepared to resume permanent status negotiations, and that we are politically ready to reach a comprehensive agreement over all of the issues.

From this forum, and on this day, I say to the Israeli leadership and to the Israeli people: we are two peoples destined to live side by side, and to share this land between us. The only alternative to peace is the continuation of the occupation and the conflict. Let us start implementing the Road Map, and—in parallel—let us start discussing the permanent status issues so that we can end, once and for all, the conflict between us.

From this forum, I call upon all concerned international actors, particularly the Quartet, to play a direct role in guaranteeing the implementation of the Road Map. You must ensure that we do not re-enter the labyrinth of preconditions that preclude progress in implementation. You must ensure that we do not get stuck in the maze of long-term partial or interim solutions designed to delay reaching a just and comprehensive solution.

As we at the Palestinian Authority express our readiness to implement all of our Road Map obligations, we expect all other parties to implement theirs. It is not reasonable that only we are required

to take action while settlements continue, or while the Wall expands within Palestinian land to separate Palestinian from Palestinian, and to destroy the livelihoods of hundreds of thousands of our people, or while closures, the siege, arrests, and other violations continue against our people, spreading despair, frustration, and loss of hope.

Today, it is up to the world to give our people hope, and it is up to the world not to repeat the same mistakes that sabotaged many initiatives and positive efforts in the past. In particular, I direct this call to all of the leaders of the Quartet members, and to all those committed to re-launching the peace process, and particularly to the US as the main player in this context.

Welcoming Palestinian democracy and supporting it is important, but this support will remain deficient if it is not shored up with efforts to end all aspects of the occupation so that this democracy may continue and thrive.

I also call upon the international community to take the necessary measures to implement the decision of the International Court of Justice, this decision that condemned the racist separation wall as illegal and called for its removal.

Brothers and Sisters,

Palestinians at the Homeland and in the Diaspora,

Ending the occupation was and will remain at the top of our national Palestinian agenda, but it is not the only priority. I can find no justification for ignoring the rest of our national issues under the pretext that we are an occupied people. The same proud Palestinian spirit that has struggled to ensure recognition of our just cause must guide us in dealing with our domestic agenda.

For decades, Palestinians have been a beacon of creativity and achievement, a light that has shone with talent and skill over the whole world. It is our duty to continue faithfully working in the same spirit and with the same determination to build an enlightened, civilized society that will be—both in its official and civil parts—a democratic example to be followed, and a basis for a bright outlook for our future generations.

I believe that we all agree that the first step towards building our society lies in establishing the rule of law. Only then will our people enjoy safety and security, only then will we be able to truly develop our institutions of governance and our political system, and only then will we achieve development and economic prosperity and make progress in social, cultural, and other fields.

The rule of law is embodied in one authority and one legal weapon in the hands of this authority, within the framework of political pluralism and the peaceful periodic transfer of authority. We all have the right to differ, and we all have the right to present our case to the people through the ballot box, but no-one has the right to by-pass the will of the people or to take law into their own hand in the service of their own agenda. Let law and democracy remain the only method of dealing with all aspects of our domestic concerns.

We have started the process of reform, and we will—God willing—continue. Reforming and developing the judiciary, security and government agencies, and continuing the development of our financial and economic system, and establishing a new mechanism for cooperation between the public and private sectors are prerequisites for enabling the National Authority to play its role in serving the Palestinian people. But more than that, they are also a duty so as to establish the foundations of the Palestinian state to which we aspire. It is our duty, whether in the Authority, opposition, or civil society not to allow the occupation to derail us from this path, or internal chaos to sabotage this process.

We will work to establish close cooperation between the various institutions of the Palestinian Authority—the legislative, judicial and executive authorities—while respecting their separation and distinct role in accordance with the Basic Law. This should become the solid foundation and the established tradition of our political life, so as to develop our political system and to preserve its vitality.

We will exert all of our efforts to revitalize the PLO institutions and to activate its national role as the sole legitimate representative of our people. This will intensify our efforts to serve our people in the Diaspora. The PLO must assume its leading role in supporting the National Authority, in emphasizing the unity of Palestinian decision, and in protecting the National Program of 1988 and the Palestinian Declaration of Independence.

[. . .]

Today, I address the families of our revered martyrs to assure you that we will remain faithful to their memory and committed to protecting the future of their children. We will continue to care for the injured and the handicapped, and all of those affected by the violations of the occupation, whether home demolitions, the destruction of agricultural facilities, and all other forms of collective punishment.

I also address my brothers the prisoners and detainees to assure them that their cause will remain at the forefront of our efforts and will figure high on all levels. Opening the path of freedom before them is a noble purpose that we will do our utmost to achieve. We will also protect our fugitives and deportees, and we will absorb them and guarantee their future.

I have been throughout my [career on] field visits to the refugee camps here in the homeland and in Syria, Lebanon, and the Arab World. I have met our people who have entrusted us with their

national aspirations and daily concerns. These will remain a central part of our own concerns. While we reject involuntary settlement outside the homeland, we must guarantee that our people—wherever they are—enjoy the best standards of living, through cooperation with our brothers in the host countries.

[. . .]

Source: Mahmoud Abbas, "Inauguration of Palestinian President Mahmoud Abbas, 15 January, 2005," Electronic Intifada, http://electronicintifada.net.

160. Mahmoud Abbas, Transcript of Speech regarding Cease-Fire Agreement in Sharm al-Sheikh, Egypt [Excerpt], February 8, 2005

Introduction

Less than a month after he was sworn in as president of the Palestinian Authority (PA), Mahmoud Abbas met Israeli prime minister Ariel Sharon at Sharm al-Sheikh in Egypt. The two men announced a cease-fire agreement between all Israelis and Palestinians and expressed their hopes that this accord would facilitate the resumption of peace negotiations along the lines laid out in the stalled Road Map to Peace guidelines. Admitting that the exceedingly difficult issues of the status of Jerusalem, refugees, and settlements still required resolution, Abbas proclaimed that it was "high time that . . . the long decades of suffering and pain would stop" so that Palestinians could live a normal life. He hoped that "the language of negotiations will replace the language of bullets and cannons." He then moved forcefully to crack down on Palestinians who disregarded this new cease-fire. A few days later, when Palestinian gunmen attacked isolated Israeli settlements in defiance of the truce, Abbas summarily dismissed some of his security officials for their failure to prevent the attacks. He responded equally sharply when Israeli soldiers shot three unarmed Palestinian boys in April, charging that this was a deliberate effort to sabotage the cease-fire and demanding that Israel's government take serious action to punish the troops involved. When Abbas visited U.S. president George W. Bush at the White House in May 2005, Bush applauded his crackdown on violence and terrorism, promised U.S. support for an independent Palestinian state, and offered the PA $50 million in economic aid, the first such assistance that the U.S. government had paid directly to the Palestinians. The cease-fire lasted until June 2006, when militant Palestinians linked to the extremist Hamas political grouping, then locked in dispute with Abbas over their governmental role, broke the truce with renewed attacks on Israeli civilians.

Primary Source

[. . .]

We have agreed with Prime Minister Ariel Sharon to cease all acts of violence against the Israelis and against the Palestinians wherever they are. Tranquility and quiet that will be witnessed and in our land, starting today, is the beginning for a new era. The beginning of peace and hope, [is] what [was] announced today in addition to being the implementation of the first article of the road map that was established by the quartet. It is also a step—and a basic step, an important step that provides a new opportunity for restoring the peace process and its momentum, so that the Palestinian and the Israeli peoples restore hope and confidence in the possibility for achieving peace.

I believe that we all understand our big responsibilities and joint responsibilities to consolidate this opportunity and to development. This can be achieved through an urgent work of restoring the spirit of partnership and reciprocity [so as] to avoid unilateral steps.

And we have, starting this very moment, to protect what we have already announced, to provide the suitable mechanisms toward implementation. What we agree on today is just the beginning of a process of bridging the gap and difference among all of us.

We differ on several issues. And this may include settlements, the release of prisoners, the wall closing institutions in Jerusalem. We will not be able to solve all of these issues today, but our positions towards these issues are clear and firm. Intensifying our efforts will lead us to implementing another obligation on the road map, which is resuming the negotiations of the final status in order to end the Israeli occupation that started in 1967, of the Palestinian territory and solving all of the issues pertaining to the final status, Jerusalem, refugees, settlements and other issues which were kept for the final status and negotiations according to the terms of reference in the road map, mentioned in the road map.

Mr. President, His Majesty, Mr. Prime Minister, just less than one month ago the Palestinian people went to the ballot boxes for the presidential elections, which were held after the departure of President Yasser Arafat. In this remarkable democratic practice, the Palestinian people embodied through these elections their setting to the just peace that will put an end to dictates of war, violence and occupation. Peace that means the establishment of a Palestinian state, or the state of—the democratic state of independent Palestine along[side] the State of Israel, as mentioned in the road map plan.

Here in the city of Sharm el-Sheikh, the city of peace, we renew on behalf of the Palestine Liberation Organization, and the Palestinian Authority, our adherence to the terms of reference of the peace process and to the resolutions of international legitimacy and all the resolutions endorsed by the PLO, the Palestinian government, and the government of Israel, and the road map as well.

And also I assert our interest in respecting all our obligations and implementing all our commitments. And will save no effort whatever to protect this newborn opportunity of peace, that is provided through what we have already declared here today. We hope that our brothers in the Arab Republic of Egypt and the Hashemite Kingdom of Jordan, we hope that they will continue their good efforts as well as we hope that the quartet, the international quartet, will resume its responsibilities to achieve acceleration of progress on the Palestinian/Israeli [track] while reviving a peace process, as well, on the Syrian and Lebanese track, [treating both] tracks as one.

It is high time that the Palestinian people restore their freedom and independence. It is high time that the decades, the long decades of suffering and pain would stop. It is high time that our people enjoy peace and their right to live a normal life, just like all other peoples in the world under the sovereignty of law, under one authority and one weapon and with political pluralism.

We look forward to that day and hope it will come as soon as possible in order that the language of negotiations will replace the language of bullets and cannons; and in which neighborhood and livelihood will prevail instead of the war; and in order to provide our grandsons and our future generations, Palestinian and Israelis, a different tomorrow, a promising tomorrow.

This is a new opportunity. A new opportunity of peace is won today in the city of peace. Let us all pledge to protect this opportunity in order to see that the wish of peace becomes a true and daily fact in this region.

[...]

Source: "Transcript of Mahmoud Abbas' Speech at Egypt Summit," CNN.com, http://edition.cnn.com/2005/WORLD/meast/02/08/transcript.abbas/index.html. Courtesy of CNN.

161. Talia Sasson, Conclusion of Report on Illegal Outposts [Excerpt], March 8, 2005

Introduction

The expansion of Israeli settlements in the occupied territories and their future after the establishment of a Palestinian state was among the most contentious and acrimonious issues requiring resolution before any final Palestinian-Israeli peace settlement could be reached. Under the 1993 Oslo Accords, Israel undertook to establish no further settlements in the West Bank and to cease expanding those already in existence. For much of that decade, however, government officials had sanctioned and even encouraged the establishment of additional settlements. Under the Quartet's Road Map to Peace of 2002–2003, Israel would evacuate all settlements— often known as outposts because they masqueraded as outlying sections of existing settlements—established after March 21, 2001, together with those founded without authorization before that date. It was not even clear precisely how many outposts existed, in part because even when they were destroyed, settlers often quickly re-established them and because there were no centralized records regarding them. In March 2005 Talia Sasson, who had previously headed the State Prosecution Criminal Department, prepared a report for the prime minister's office that detailed a pattern of illegal establishment of settlements, frequently on land whose ownership was dubious, with collusion, encouragement, and secret funding from various government ministries "in blatant violation of the law." Even though her data were probably incomplete, Sasson identified at least 24 unauthorized outposts established since March 2001, 71 that had come into existence before then, and 10 whose foundation date was uncertain. The process of creating such unauthorized settlements was, she added, still "profoundly under way." Many of Sasson's findings were an open secret, but their appearance as an official report—even though the government only published a summary—created a sensation. Somewhat ironically, in the late 1990s Prime Minister Ariel Sharon, for whom the report was prepared, had actively encouraged such activities, something that Sasson forbore to mention. Her report made it clear that for more than a decade Israeli officials had blatantly ignored many of their government's international commitments on settlements, a deficiency that undercut many of their own complaints that the Palestinians had failed to honor their own pledges. Sasson recommended that Sharon consider instituting criminal proceedings against those involved, but the prime minister largely ignored her report, merely establishing a ministerial committee to study it and make further recommendations. Despite the international embarrassment they represented, the Israeli government was not prepared to pay the political cost of implementing forcible evacuations of illegitimate outposts.

Primary Source

[...]

The reality revealed is difficult.

For years Israeli governments have dismantled of their roles, not formally but in fact, and left the scene for the executive echelon. Instead of the government deciding on establishing settlements in Judea, Samaria and Gaza, others took its place, beginning in the mid nineties:

The "engine" behind a decision to establish outposts are regional councils in Judea, Samaria and Gaza, settlers and activists, imbued with ideology and motivation to increase Israeli settlement in the Judea, Samaria and Gaza territories. Some of the officials working in the Settlement Division of the World Zionist Organization, and in the Ministry of Construction & Housing, cooperated with them to promote the unauthorized outposts phenomenon. These actions were apparently inspired by different Ministers of Housing in the relevant times, either by overlooking or by actual encouragement and support, with additional support from other Ministries, initiated either by officials or by the political echelon of each Ministry.

The result was that the executive echelon, so to speak, became the deciding echelon, with no authorization, contrary to government resolutions, bearing no political or public responsibility, which by nature of things rests upon the political echelon.

All of this with massive financing by the State of Israel, with no appropriate transparency, no criteria.

The establishment of unauthorized outposts violates standard procedure, good governing rules, and is an especially bold ongoing law violation.

Furthermore, the State authorities speak [with] two voices. Sometimes grant, and sometimes prevent. Rules have become flexible. One hand builds outposts, the other invests money and force to evacuate them.

These actions were not done by individuals only. The problem is State and public authorities took part in breaking the law. They are the ones who financed construction without a resolution by the political echelon, contrary to government resolutions, with no legal planning status, sometimes not on State owned land, sometimes on private Palestinian property or on survey land.

State authorities and public authorities broke the laws, regulations and rules made by the State.

The IDF, which has sovereignty in Judea, Samaria and Gaza, and is responsible for peace and security, and the Israeli police, which is responsible for law enforcement in these territories—both fail to stand up to their missions. Law enforcement bodies cannot act against State authorities breaking the law. They cannot handle a mixed message, that the outposts are illegal but encouraged by the authorities.

The security concept, that wherever there is an Israeli person—IDF will be there to protect him, resulted in a very sad reality. Therefore, any settler who places his home wherever he chooses, even if unauthorized and against the law—gains the protection of the army. The outcome is that the settlers are the ones who set the army's deployment in the territories, not the army. Everyone is king. In order to protect one outpost, forces must be taken out of other places. The forces are not unlimited, and so the security level drops down.

The protection supplied by IDF to unauthorized outposts, its mere existence there, drags it unwillingly to give its "seal" to unauthorized outposts.

And as if all this is not enough, the law enforcement tools in Judea, Samaria and Gaza are lacking. The security legislation does not support law enforcing bodies with the necessary tools to handle law violations regarding unauthorized outposts. Long-needed legislation was not done, even though the bodies involved are well aware of it. A certain change appears, maybe, in the last few months.

The State of Israel is a democratic state. This is what the Declaration of Independence and the Basic Laws teach us. This is the glue that sticks all its citizens together, allows them to live together in one political entity.

Democracy and the rule of law are two inseparables. One cannot exist without the other.

The reality drawn up in this opinion shows that all of these deeds seriously endanger the principle of the rule of law. Even though the outposts are built in the Judea, Samaria and Gaza territories and not in Israel, the settlers and the authorities who take part in their establishment are Israeli. A continuing, bold, institutionalized law violation undermined the rule of law. When law violations become standard behavior they tend to spread into other areas.

The Jewish settlement in the Judea, Samaria and Gaza territories is a matter in great dispute in Israel. Some support it passionately, others oppose it. Settlement policy in the Judea, Samaria and Gaza territories should be decided on by an elected government.

But any government policy must obey the law. All officials and politicians are governed by law.

The actions described are not a matter of political view. It is a matter of law enforcement, a question of the rule of law.

In order to maintain the democratic regime of Israel, urgent measures must be taken to change the reality I have described. It can no longer be accepted. It must be reformed, and I believe you have the power to do so.

I therefore suggest to implement my recommendations.

[…]

Source: "Summary of the Opinion Concerning Unauthorized Outposts," Israel Ministry of Foreign Affairs, http://www.mfa.gov.il/MFA.

162. Ariel Sharon, Speech at the United Nations Assembly [Excerpt], September 15, 2005

Introduction

A few days after the completion of Israel's disengagement from Gaza, Prime Minister Ariel Sharon addressed the United Nations (UN). His speech was brief and somewhat unspecific but, particularly given his past record as a hard-liner, was also relatively moderate and tactful. Recalling his lengthy career in the military, Sharon urged the Palestinians to seek "reconciliation and compromise" and "embark on the path which leads to peace and understanding between our people." Describing eloquently and emotionally just how much the territory of Israel meant to him personally and how difficult he would find it to relinquish any of its soil to others, he nonetheless declared that the Palestinians were "also entitled to freedom and to a national, sovereign existence in a state of their own." He called upon the Palestinians to end policies tolerating the use of terrorist tactics and the incitement of hatred against Israel. Sharon emphasized that Israel would defend itself in whatever ways were necessary and praised the security fence for its role in protecting Israelis and saving lives. He also stressed that he would not compromise on "the right of the State of Israel to exist as a Jewish state, with defensible borders, in full security and without threats and terror." Having established his hard-line credentials, however, he urged Palestinian leaders to seize the "window of opportunity" that implementation of the Disengagement Plan in Gaza now offered for resuming progress under the Road Map to Peace and working toward peace that would benefit both Palestinians and Israelis. Sharon's speech was tough but not bombastic in tone and, by making few specific demands or pledges, left room for maneuver on peace terms. Tactfully, he omitted any mention of the anarchy that broke out in Gaza immediately after the Israeli disengagement, even though this might have been used to cast doubt on Palestinian fitness for self-rule. He also forbore to complain that Hamas candidates were running for office in Palestinian elections even though, under the Oslo Accords, the party's opposition to making peace with Israel or accepting Israel's existence should have excluded it from the polls. Given his past record as a military hawk, Sharon might have had the credentials to move for a compromise peace settlement with the Palestinians and simply ride out conservative Israeli opposition to this. Already in his late seventies, he could move decisively and take risks for peace with few worries about the impact on his political future. In early January 2006, however, Sharon suffered a massive stroke that left him incapacitated, and after three months the Israeli cabinet declared him incompetent to continue in office. If a window of opportunity for Palestinian-Israeli peace genuinely existed, Sharon would not be the one to open it.

Primary Source

My friends and colleagues, heads and representatives of the UN member states,

I arrived here from Jerusalem, the capital of the Jewish people for over 3,000 years, and the undivided and eternal capital of the State of Israel.

[…]

I stand before you at the gate of nations as a Jew and as a citizen of the democratic, free and sovereign State of Israel, a proud representative of an ancient people, whose numbers are few, but whose contribution to civilization and to the values of ethics, justice and faith, surrounds the world and encompasses history. . . .

I was born in the Land of Israel, the son of pioneers—people who tilled the land and sought no fights—who did not come to Israel to dispossess its residents. If the circumstances had not demanded it, I would not have become a soldier, but rather a farmer and agriculturist. My first love was, and remains, manual labor: sowing and harvesting, the pastures, the flock and the cattle.

I, as someone whose path of life led him to be a fighter and commander in all Israel's wars, reach out today to our Palestinian neighbors in a call for reconciliation and compromise to end the bloody conflict, and embark on the path which leads to peace and understanding between our peoples. I view this as my calling and my primary mission for the coming years.

The land of Israel is precious to me, precious to us, the Jewish people, more than anything. Relinquishing any part of our forefathers' legacy is heartbreaking, as difficult as the parting of the Red Sea. Every inch of land, every hill and valley, every stream and rock, is saturated with Jewish history, replete with memories.

The continuity of Jewish presence in the Land of Israel never ceased. Even those of us who were exiled from our land, against their will, to the ends of the earth—their souls, for all generations, remained connected to their homeland, by thousands of hidden threads of yearning and love, expressed three times a day in prayer and songs of longing.

The Land of Israel is the open Bible, the written testimony, the identity and right of the Jewish people. Under its skies, the prophets of Israel expressed their claims for social justice, and their eternal vision for alliances between peoples, in a world which would know no more war. Its cities, villages, vistas, ridges, deserts and plains preserve as loyal witnesses its ancient Hebrew names. Page after page, our unique land is unfurled, and at its heart is united Jerusalem, the city of the Temple upon Mount Moriah, the axis of the life of the Jewish people throughout all generations, and the seat of its yearnings and prayers for 3,000 years. The city to which we pledged an eternal vow of faithfulness, which forever beats in every Jewish heart: "If I forget thee, O Jerusalem, may my right hand forget its cunning!"

I say these things to you because they are the essence of my Jewish consciousness, and of my belief in the eternal and unimpeachable right of the people of Israel to the Land of Israel. However, I say this here also to emphasize the immensity of the pain I feel deep in my heart at the recognition that we have to make concessions for the sake of peace between us and our Palestinian neighbors.

The right of the Jewish people to the Land of Israel does not mean disregarding the rights of others in the land. The Palestinians will always be our neighbors. We respect them, and have no aspirations to rule over them. They are also entitled to freedom and to a national, sovereign existence in a state of their own.

This week, the last Israeli soldier left the Gaza Strip, and military law there was ended. The State of Israel proved that it is ready to make painful concessions in order to resolve the conflict with the Palestinians. The decision to disengage was very difficult for me, and involves a heavy personal price. However, it is the absolute recognition that it is the right path for the future of Israel that guided me. Israeli society is undergoing a difficult crisis as a result of the Disengagement, and now needs to heal the rifts.

Now it is the Palestinians' turn to prove their desire for peace. The end of Israeli control over and responsibility for the Gaza Strip allows the Palestinians, if they so wish, to develop their economy and build a peace-seeking society, which is developed, free, law-abiding, transparent, and which adheres to democratic principles. The most important test the Palestinian leadership will face is in fulfilling their commitment to put an end to terror and its infrastructures, eliminate the anarchic regime of armed gangs, and cease the incitement and indoctrination of hatred towards Israel and the Jews.

Until they do so—Israel will know how to defend itself from the horrors of terrorism. This is why we built the Security Fence, and we will continue to build it until it is completed, as would any other country defending its citizens. The Security Fence prevents terrorists and murderers from arriving in city centers on a daily basis and targeting citizens on their way to work, children on their way to school and families sitting together in restaurants. This Fence is vitally indispensable. This Fence saves lives!

The successful implementation of the Disengagement Plan opens up a window of opportunity for advancing towards peace, in accordance with the sequence of the Roadmap. The State of Israel is committed to the Roadmap and to the implementation of the Sharm El-Sheikh understandings. And I hope that it will be possible, through them, to renew the political process.

I am among those who believe that it is possible to reach a fair compromise and coexistence in good neighborly relations between Jews and Arabs. However, I must emphasize one fact: there will be *no* compromise on the right of the State of Israel to exist as a Jewish state, with defensible borders, in full security and without threats and terror.

I call on the Palestinian leadership to show determination and leadership, and to eliminate terror, violence and the culture of hatred from our relations. I am certain that it is in our power to present our peoples with a new and promising horizon, a horizon of hope.

Distinguished representatives,

As I mentioned, the Jewish people have a long memory. We remember events which took place thousands of years ago, and certainly remember events which took place in this hall during the last 60 years. The Jewish people remember the dramatic vote in the UN Assembly on November 29, 1947, when representatives of the nations recognized our right to national revival in our historic homeland. However, we also remember dozens of harsh and unjust decisions made by the United Nations over the years. And we know that, even today, there are those who sit here as representatives of a country whose leadership calls to wipe Israel off the face of the earth, and no one speaks out.

The attempts of that country to arm itself with nuclear weapons must disturb the sleep of anyone who desires peace and stability in the Middle East and the entire world. The combination of murky fundamentalism and support of terrorist organizations creates a serious threat that every member nation in the UN must stand against.

I hope that the comprehensive reforms which the United Nations is undergoing in its 60th anniversary year will include a fundamental change and improvement in the approach of the United Nations, its organizations and institutions, towards the State of Israel.

My fellow representatives,

Peace is a supreme value in the Jewish legacy, and is the desired goal of our policy. After the long journey of wanderings and the hardships of the Jewish people; after the Holocaust which obliterated one third of our people; after the long and arduous struggle for revival; after more than 57 consecutive years of war and terror which did not stop the development of the State of Israel; after all this— our heart's desire was and remains to achieve peace with our neighbors. Our desire for peace is strong enough to ensure that we will achieve it, only if our neighbors are genuine partners in this longed-for goal. If we succeed in working together, we can transform our plot of land, which is dear to both peoples, from a land of contention to a land of peace—for our children and grandchildren.

[...]

Source: Ariel Sharon, "Statement of Israel, 2005 UN World Summit," United Nations, http://www.un.org/webcast/summit2005/statements15.html.

163. United Nations Security Council Resolution 1680, May 17, 2006

Introduction

Lebanon was a small country surrounded by larger neighbors including Israel, Syria, and Iran, all of which sought to manipulate Lebanon's turbulent factional politics to their own advantage. From 1976 until 2005 Syrian troops controlled much of Lebanon, while Israeli forces held a security zone in southern Lebanon from 1982 until 2000 when they withdrew behind the Blue Line, which demarcated the border between the two countries. The weakness of Lebanon's government also impelled anti-Israeli militia groups, first the Palestine Liberation Organization (PLO), whose leaders moved there after their expulsion from Jordan in 1971 until Israeli attacks forced them to leave in 1982, and then the Islamic Shiite Hezbollah group, to use it as a base from which to launch assaults against Israel. Israel briefly invaded Lebanon in 1978 in the hope of removing Palestinian forces there and launched a more successful war against Palestinian positions in 1982. In February 2005 the assassination, probably with Syrian and Hezbollah collusion, of popular Lebanese ex-prime minister Rafik Hariri sparked huge popular demonstrations against the presence of Syrian and Hezbollah forces in the country and demands that Lebanon's own government be allowed to run a unified country on democratic principles. Even though Syria and Hezbollah mounted large counterdemonstrations, the events highlighted the presence of Syrian troops in Lebanon, encouraging popular and international calls for their removal. In 2004 United Nations (UN) Security Council Resolution 1559 had called for an end to Syria's occupation of Lebanon and the disarming of all militia forces, including Hezbollah. Under substantial international pressure Syria withdrew its forces in late April 2005, although Hezbollah and other militias still failed to disarm. Sections of Lebanon's border with Syria also remained unclearly defined. Seeking to encourage the restoration of control of the country to Lebanon's own government, in May 2006 the UN Security Council therefore passed a further resolution urging the full implementation of the provisions of Resolution 1559 on disarming all militias within Lebanon and negotiations between Syria and Lebanon to delineate clearly the border between them. The UN also called on Syria and other countries to interdict the unauthorized movement of armaments into Lebanese territory. These UN resolutions had little concrete impact on the situation, as the parties involved failed to observe them. One month later, the use of such weaponry by the still active Hezbollah militia to attack Israel would provoke a small but fierce Israeli military operation against Lebanon.

Primary Source

The Security Council,

Recalling all its previous resolutions on Lebanon, in particular resolutions 1559 (2004), 425 and 426 (1978), resolution 520 (1982) and resolution 1655 (2006), as well as the statements of its President on the situation in Lebanon, in particular the statements of 18 June 2000 (S/PRST/2000/21), of 19 October 2004 (S/PRST/2004/36), of 4 May 2005 (S/PRST/2005/17) and of 23 January 2006 (S/PRST/2006/3),

Reiterating its strong support for the territorial integrity, sovereignty and political independence of Lebanon within its internationally recognized borders,

Noting positively that further significant progress has been made towards implementing in full all provisions of resolution 1559 (2004), in particular through the Lebanese national dialogue, but noting also with regret that other provisions of resolution 1559 have not yet been fully implemented, namely the disbanding and disarming of Lebanese and non-Lebanese militias, the extension of the control of the Government of Lebanon over all its territory, the strict respect of the sovereignty, territorial integrity, unity and political independence of Lebanon, and free and fair presidential elections conducted according to the Lebanese constitutional rules, without foreign interference and influence,

Noting with concern the conclusion of the Secretary-General's report (S/2006/248) that there had been movements of arms into Lebanese territory for militias over the last six months,

Expressing full support for the Lebanese National Dialogue and commending all Lebanese parties for its conduct and for the consensus reached in this context on important matters,

Having heard the Prime Minister of Lebanon's address to the Security Council on 21 April 2006 (S/PV.5417),

1. *Welcomes* the third semi-annual report of the Secretary-General to the Security Council of 18 April 2006 on the implementation of resolution 1559 (2004) (S/2006/248);

2. *Reiterates* its call for the full implementation of all requirements of resolution 1559 (2004);

3. *Reiterates also* its call on all concerned States and parties as mentioned in the report, to cooperate fully with the Government of Lebanon, the Security Council and the Secretary-General to achieve this goal;

4. *Strongly encourages* the Government of Syria to respond positively to the request made by the Government of Lebanon, in line with the agreements of the Lebanese national dialogue, to delineate their common border, especially in those areas where the border is uncertain or disputed and to establish full diplomatic relations and representation, noting that such measures would constitute a significant step towards asserting Lebanon's sovereignty, territorial

integrity and political independence and improving the relations between the two countries, thus contributing positively to the stability in the region, and urges both parties to make efforts through further bilateral dialogue to this end, bearing in mind that the establishment of diplomatic relations between States, and of permanent diplomatic missions, takes place by mutual consent;

5. *Commends* the Government of Lebanon for undertaking measures against movements of arms into Lebanese territory and calls on the Government of Syria to take similar measures;

6. *Welcomes* the decision of the Lebanese national dialogue to disarm Palestinian militias outside refugee camps within six months, supports its implementation and calls for further efforts to disband and disarm all Lebanese and non-Lebanese militias and to restore fully the Lebanese Government's control over all Lebanese territory;

7. *Reiterates* its support to the Secretary-General and his Special envoy in their efforts and dedication to facilitate and assist in the implementation of all provisions of resolution 1559 (2004);

8. *Decides* to remain seized of the matter.

Source: United Nations Security Council Official Records, 06-35177 (E), S.C. Res. 1680, May 17, 2006, http://daccessdds.un.org.

164. National Conciliation Document of the Prisoners [Excerpt], June 28, 2006

Introduction

In January 2006 candidates of the extremist Hamas political party, which supported the destruction of Israel, won 76 out of 132 seats in the Palestinian legislature, whereas the more moderate Fatah won only 43 seats. The result appeared to threaten the continuation of the process under the Road Map to Peace guidelines drawn up during 2002–2003. For more than a year, negotiations were in progress between Hamas and moderate Palestinian Authority (PA) president Mahmoud Abbas, head of Fatah, who was determined that the election results should not sabotage his ongoing efforts for a lasting peace settlement that would establish an independent Palestinian state. Abbas sought to make the inclusion of Hamas in a coalition Palestinian government conditional on that organization's renunciation of violence and acceptance of Israel's right to exist. In May 2006 a document appeared that quickly became a rallying point for Palestinian peace advocates. Five Palestinian prisoners held in Israeli jails, each from a different Palestinian organization, including the hard-line Hamas and Islamic Jihad, drafted a document that they hoped would serve to reconcile the conflicting Palestinian viewpoints. The 18-point document called on all Palestinian groups to work together and form a national unity government in order to achieve the objective of an independent Palestinian state. The first point of the program anticipated that the territorial basis of such a state would be the territories that Israel had occupied in 1967, a definition that was interpreted as recognizing the right of Israel to exist. Likewise, the third and seventh points referred to "negotiations and diplomacy" as appropriate strategies for accomplishing this objective together with "resistance by various means," the details of which were left unspecified. In their fifteenth point, the authors proclaimed that "our national interest necessitates reassessing our means of struggle in order to find the best methods of resisting the occupation." Although less than forthright, the prisoners' document could therefore be interpreted as one that called for acceptance of Israel's existence and at least left open the possibility of relying on peaceful methods rather than violent struggle to achieve this. The document won wide circulation among Palestinians, especially those who deplored the fratricidal conflicts among the various Palestine Liberation Organization (PLO) factions, which caused numerous deaths and injuries during 2006. Abbas hoped to make a slightly revised version, that was issued in June 2006, the basis of a territory-wide referendum but failed to accomplish this, and the two original Hamas and Islamic Jihad signatories repudiated the document after it became politicized. Israeli president Ehud Olmert, however, characterized the charter as unrealistic since it demanded that Israel withdraw from all territory occupied in 1967 and allow Palestinian refugees to return to Israel. The Mecca Accords that the feuding Fatah and Hamas parties signed in February 2007 specifically endorsed the Prisoners' Document. The National Reconciliation Document, as it was known, was evidence of a growing consciousness among Palestinians that their bitter internal divisions greatly vitiated their own effectiveness as they tried to win and create an independent state.

Primary Source

[...]

Based on the high sense of historical national responsibility and in light of the dangers facing our people and based on the principle saying that rights don't fall by law of limitations, and on the basis of no recognition of the legitimacy of occupation and for the sake of reinforcing the internal Palestinian front and [to] maintain and protect the national unity and the unity of our people in the homeland and in the Diaspora and in order to confront the Israeli scheme that aims to impose the Israeli solution and to blow up the dream and right of our people in establishing their independent state with full sovereignty; this scheme that the Israeli government intends to execute in the next phase based on concluding the apartheid wall and the Judaization of Jerusalem and expansion of the Israeli settlements and the seizure of the Jordan Valley and the annexation of large areas from the West Bank and blocking the path in front of our people in exercising their right in return.

In Order to maintain the accomplishments of our people throughout this long struggle and out of loyalty to our martyrs, prisoners and our injured and given that we are still in a phase of liberation, this necessitates that we formulate a political strategy. Therefore, with the goal of making our comprehensive national dialogue a success, based on the Cairo Declaration and coupled with the urgent need for unity and solidarity, we put forth this document (the national conciliation document) to our people, President Mahmoud Abbas (Abu Mazen), the PLO leadership, Prime Minister Ismail Hanieh, the Council of Ministers, the Speaker and members of the PNC, the Speaker and members of the PLC, all Palestinian forces and factions, all nongovernmental and popular organizations and institutions and to the popular leadership of the Palestinians in the homeland and in the Diaspora.

This document is being put forth as a complete package and the introduction is part of it:

1—The Palestinian people in the homeland and in the Diaspora seek and struggle to liberate their land and remove the settlements and evacuate the settlers and remove the apartheid and annexation and separation wall and to achieve their right to freedom, return and independence and to exercise their right to self-determination, including the right to establish their independent state with al-Quds al-Shareef as its capital on all territories occupied in 1967, and to secure the right of return for refugees to their homes and properties from which they were evicted and to compensate them and to liberate all prisoners and detainees without any discrimination and all of this is based on the historical right of our people on the land of our forefathers and based on the UN Charter and international law and legitimacy in a way that does not affect the rights of our people.

2—To speed up efforts to achieve that which was agreed on in Cairo in March 2005 pertaining to the development and reactivation of the PLO and the participation of all forces and factions in it according to democratic principles that reinforce the status of the PLO as the sole legitimate representative of the Palestinian people wherever they are in a manner that meets with the changes on the Palestinian arena and in a manner that consolidates the authority of the PLO to assume its responsibilities in leading our people in the homeland and the Diaspora. The PLO should also be the body that mobilizes the people in defending their national, political and humanitarian rights in the various fora and circles and in the international and regional arenas. Furthermore, our national interest stipulates the formation of a new Palestinian National Council before the end of 2006 in a manner that secures the representation of all Palestinian national and Islamic forces, factions and parties and all sectors of our people through elections, where possible, according to proportional representation, and through agreement where it is not possible to hold elections according to mechanisms set up by the Higher Committee resulting from the Cairo Dialogue. The PLO therefore, will remain a broad front and framework and a comprehensive national coalition and the higher political reference for all the Palestinians in the homeland and in the Diaspora.

3—The right of the Palestinian people to resist and to uphold the option of resistance of occupation by various means and focusing resistance in territories occupied in 1967 in tandem with political action, negotiations and diplomacy whereby there is broad participation from all sectors in the popular resistance.

4—To formulate a Palestinian plan aimed at comprehensive political action; to unify Palestinian political discourse on the basis of the Palestinian national goals as mentioned in this document and according to Arab legitimacy and international legitimacy resolutions that grant justice to the Palestinian people maintaining their rights and constants to be implemented by the PLO leadership and its institutions, and the PNA represented in president and government, the national and Islamic factions, the civil society organizations and public figures. This is aimed at mobilizing Arab, Islamic and international political, financial, economic and humanitarian support and solidarity with our people and the PNA and to gain support for the right of our people to self-determination, freedom, return and independence; furthermore, it is aimed at confronting Israel's plan to impose any unilateral solution on our people and to confront the oppressive siege.

5—To protect and support the PNA since it is the nucleus of the future state and was born of the struggle and sacrifices of the Palestinian people; to stress that higher national interests call for respecting the "Basic Law" of the PNA and the effective laws and for respecting the responsibilities and authorities of the president elected according to the will of the Palestinian people through free, honest and democratic elections.

It also calls for respecting the responsibilities and authorities of the government granted by a vote of confidence from the PLC which came through free and honest and democratic elections and stresses the importance and need for creative cooperation between the presidency and the government; there should be joint action and regular meetings between them to achieve and reinforce cooperation and integration according to the provisions of the Basic Law and the higher national interests; and for the need for comprehensive reforms in PNA institutions, especially the judiciary whereby the judiciary authority should be respected at all levels, its rulings implemented so as to reinforce the rule of the law.

6—To work on forming a national unity government that secures the participation of parliamentary blocs and political forces interested in participating on the basis of this document and the joint program to upgrade the Palestinian situation at the local, Arab, regional and international levels. Their goal is also to implement the reform program and develop the national economy and encourage investment and fight poverty and unemployment and provide the best possible care for the sectors that carried the burden of steadfastness, resistance and the Intifada and who were the victims of the Israeli aggression. In particular, this refers to the families of martyrs, prisoners and injured and the owners of demolished homes and properties, destroyed by the occupation, and the unemployed and graduates.

7—Administration of the negotiations falls within the jurisdiction of the PLO and the President of the PNA, which will be on the basis of adhering to Palestinian national goals as mentioned in this document on condition that any agreement must be presented to the new PNC for ratification or a general referendum to be held in the homeland and the Diaspora through organizing the referendum.

8—Liberation of the prisoners and detainees is a sacred national duty that must be assumed by all Palestinian national and Islamic forces and factions, the PLO and the PNA represented in President and government, the PLC and all resistance forces.

9—Stressing the need to double our efforts to support and care for the refugees and defend their rights and work on holding a popular conference representing the refugees that would create commissions to carry out duties towards the refugees and to stress the right of return; the international community should also be pressured to implement Resolution 194 which stipulates the right of refugees to return and to be compensated.

10—To work on forming a unified resistance front called the "Palestinian Resistance Front" to lead and engage in resistance against the occupation and to unify and coordinate resistance action and work on defining a unified political reference for the front.

11—To cling to the principles of democracy and to hold regular, general, free and honest democratic elections according to the law for the presidency, the PLC and the local and municipal councils and trade unions and federations and to respect the principle of a peaceful and smooth transfer of authority and to stress the principle of separation of authorities; the Palestinian democratic experience should be protected and any democratic choice and its results respected; furthermore, there should be respect for the rule of the law, public and fundamental freedoms, freedom of the press and equality among the citizens in rights and duties without discrimination; the achievements of women should be respected and further developed and promoted.

12—To reject and denounce the oppressive siege against the Palestinian people being led by the US and Israel and to call on the Arabs at the popular and official levels to support the Palestinian people, the PLO and the PNA and to call on the Arab governments to implement the political, financial, economic, and media decisions of the Arab summits that support the Palestinian people and their national cause; to stress that the PNA is committed to the Arab consensus and to joint Arab action that supports our just cause and the higher Arab interests.

13—To call on the Palestinian people to strive for unity and solidarity, to unify their ranks and to support the PLO and PNA represented in president and government; to endorse the people's steadfastness and resistance in the face of Israeli aggression and siege and to reject any interference in internal Palestinian affairs.

14—To denounce all forms of division that could lead to internal strife; to condemn the use of weapons in settling internal disputes and to ban the use of weapons among the people; to stress the sanctity of Palestinian blood and to adhere to dialogue as the sole means of resolving disagreements. There should be freedom of expression through the media, which also applies to any party in opposition to the authority and its decisions in accordance with the law; adherence to the right to peaceful protest and to organize marches, demonstrations and sit-ins on condition that they be peaceful and unarmed and do not attack the property of citizens or public property.

15—The national interest necessitates the need to find the best means of allowing our people and their political forces in the Gaza Strip to participate in the battle for freedom, return and independence while bearing in mind the new situation in the Gaza Strip as true elevation and power for the steadfastness of our people and on the basis of using the struggle methods of resisting the occupation while taking into consideration the higher interests of our people.

16—The need to reform and develop the Palestinian security system in all its branches in a modern manner that allows them to assume their responsibilities in defending the homeland and people and in confronting the aggression and the occupation; their duties also include maintaining security and public order, enforcing laws, ending the state of security chaos and lawlessness, ending the public show of arms and parades and confiscating any weapons that harm the resistance and distort its image or those that threaten the unity of Palestinian society; there is also a need to coordinate and organize the relationship between the security forces and the resistance and organize and protect their weapons.

17—To call on the PLC to continue issuing laws that regulate the work of the security apparatus in its various branches and to work towards issuing a law that bans the exercise of political and partisan action by members of the security services whereby they are required to abide by the elected political reference as defined by the law.

18—To work on expanding the role and presence of international solidarity committees and peace-loving groups that support our people in their just struggle against the occupation, settlements and the apartheid wall both politically and locally; to work towards the implementation of the International Court of Justice ruling at The Hague pertaining to the dismantlement of the wall and settlements and their illegitimate presence.

Signed by:

Fatah—PLC member Marwan Barghouthi, Fatah Secretary
Hamas—Sheikh Abdul Khaleq al-Natsheh—Higher Leading Commission
Islamic Jihad Movement—Sheikh Bassam al-Sa'di
PFLP—Abdul Rahim Mallouh—member of PLO Executive Committee and Deputy General Secretary of the PFLP
DFLP—Mustafa Badarneh

Note: Islamic Jihad expressed reservations on the item pertaining to the negotiations

Source: "The Full Text of the National Conciliation Document of the Prisoners, June 28, 2006," Jerusalem Media & Communication Centre, http://www.jmcc.org/documents/prisoners.htm.

165. United Nations Security Council Resolution 1701, August 11, 2006

Introduction

Neighboring Lebanon's lengthy history, from 1971 onward, of providing a safe haven for anti-Israeli guerrilla forces, first the Palestine Liberation Organization (PLO) and then the radical Islamic Hezbollah group, provoked several military interventions on Israel's part and an occupation of southern Lebanon that lasted from 1982 until 2000. Even after Israel's withdrawal, sporadic Hezbollah Katyusha rocket and mortar attacks on northern Israeli continued from the area, causing some civilian deaths and provoking occasional retaliatory Israeli air raids against Hezbollah positions. On July 12, 2006, Hezbollah forces crossed into Israel, where they killed three soldiers and abducted two others, whom they took back to Lebanon. An initial Israeli rescue attempt was unsuccessful, leaving five more soldiers dead. Israel then launched massive air strikes and artillery attacks on targets in Lebanon, together with a ground invasion, and imposed a naval and air blockade on the country. Hezbollah and Israeli forces engaged each other, and Hezbollah launched major rocket strikes against northern Israel. As a result of the attacks 975,000 Lebanese and 300,000 Israelis fled. The conflict caused around 1,100 Lebanese deaths, mostly civilians, while Hezbollah probably lost around 500 fighters. In addition, 119 Israeli soldiers died, and another 400 were injured. United Nations (UN) officials eventually brokered a partial cease-fire agreement under which Lebanese government forces would replace Hezbollah militia groups in southern Lebanon and Israeli troops would withdraw. Three days before the cease-fire came into effect, the UN Security Council unanimously passed the rather lengthy Resolution 1701, which laid out the terms of such a settlement. A UN Interim Force in Lebanon (UNIFIL) was deployed in Lebanon to keep the peace. The cease-fire negotiations represented only part of a broader UN effort to restore stable government within Lebanon and exclude foreign influence that had gained momentum since the assassination in February 2005 of former Lebanese prime minister Rafik Hariri, a death in which Syria and Hezbollah were widely believed to have been implicated. Israel welcomed the cease-fire resolution under whose terms Lebanese and UN forces would supplant Hezbollah units in southern Lebanon, a development that Israeli officials hoped would permanently cripple Hezbollah influence and operations in the region.

Primary Source

The Security Council,

Recalling all its previous resolutions on Lebanon, in particular resolutions 425 (1978), 426 (1978), 520 (1982), 1559 (2004), 1655 (2006), 1680 (2006) and 1697 (2006), as well as the statements of its President on the situation in Lebanon, in particular the statements of 18 June 2000 (S/PRST/2000/21), of 19 October 2004 (S/PRST/2004/36), of 4 May 2005 (S/PRST/2005/17), of 23 January 2006 (S/PRST/2006/3) and of 30 July 2006 (S/PRST/2006/35),

Expressing its utmost concern at the continuing escalation of hostilities in Lebanon and in Israel since Hizbollah's attack on Israel on 12 July 2006, which has already caused hundreds of deaths and injuries on both sides, extensive damage to civilian infrastructure and hundreds of thousands of internally displaced persons,

Emphasizing the need for an end of violence, but at the same time emphasizing the need to address urgently the causes that have given rise to the current crisis, including by the unconditional release of the abducted Israeli soldiers,

Mindful of the sensitivity of the issue of prisoners and *encouraging* the efforts aimed at urgently settling the issue of the Lebanese prisoners detained in Israel,

Welcoming the efforts of the Lebanese Prime Minister and the commitment of the Government of Lebanon, in its seven-point plan, to extend its authority over its territory, through its own legitimate armed forces, such that there will be no weapons without the consent of the Government of Lebanon and no authority other than that of the Government of Lebanon, *welcoming also* its commitment to a United Nations force that is supplemented and enhanced in numbers, equipment, mandate and scope of operation, and *bearing in mind* its request in this plan for an immediate withdrawal of the Israeli forces from southern Lebanon,

Determined to act for this withdrawal to happen at the earliest,

Taking due note of the proposals made in the seven-point plan regarding the Shebaa farms area,

Welcoming the unanimous decision by the Government of Lebanon on 7 August 2006 to deploy a Lebanese armed force of 15,000 troops in South Lebanon as the Israeli army withdraws behind the Blue Line and to request the assistance of additional forces from UNIFIL as needed, to facilitate the entry of the Lebanese armed forces into the region and to restate its intention to strengthen the Lebanese armed forces with material as needed to enable it to perform its duties,

Aware of its responsibilities to help secure a permanent ceasefire and a long-term solution to the conflict,

Determining that the situation in Lebanon constitutes a threat to international peace and security,

1. *Calls for* a full cessation of hostilities based upon, in particular, the immediate cessation by Hizbollah of all attacks and the immediate cessation by Israel of all offensive military operations;

2. Upon full cessation of hostilities, *calls upon* the Government of Lebanon and UNIFIL as authorized by paragraph 11 to deploy their forces together throughout the South and *calls upon* the Government of Israel, as that deployment begins, to withdraw all of its forces from southern Lebanon in parallel;

3. *Emphasizes* the importance of the extension of the control of the Government of Lebanon over all Lebanese territory in accordance with the provisions of resolution 1559 (2004) and resolution 1680 (2006), and of the relevant provisions of the Taif Accords, for it to exercise its full sovereignty, so that there will be no weapons without the consent of the Government of Lebanon and no authority other than that of the Government of Lebanon;

4. *Reiterates* its strong support for full respect for the Blue Line;

5. *Also reiterates* its strong support, as recalled in all its previous relevant resolutions, for the territorial integrity, sovereignty and political independence of Lebanon within its internationally recognized borders, as contemplated by the Israeli-Lebanese General Armistice Agreement of 23 March 1949;

6. *Calls on* the international community to take immediate steps to extend its financial and humanitarian assistance to the Lebanese people, including through facilitating the safe return of displaced persons and, under the authority of the Government of Lebanon, reopening airports and harbours, consistent with paragraphs 14 and 15, and *calls on* it also to consider further assistance in the future to contribute to the reconstruction and development of Lebanon;

7. *Affirms* that all parties are responsible for ensuring that no action is taken contrary to paragraph 1 that might adversely affect the search for a long-term solution, humanitarian access to civilian populations, including safe passage for humanitarian convoys, or the voluntary and safe return of displaced persons, and *calls on* all parties

to comply with this responsibility and to cooperate with the Security Council;

8. *Calls for* Israel and Lebanon to support a permanent ceasefire and a long-term solution based on the following principles and elements:
— full respect for the Blue Line by both parties;
— security arrangements to prevent the resumption of hostilities, including the establishment between the Blue Line and the Litani river of an area free of any armed personnel, assets and weapons other than those of the Government of Lebanon and of UNIFIL as authorized in paragraph 11, deployed in this area;
— full implementation of the relevant provisions of the Taif Accords, and of resolutions 1559 (2004) and 1680 (2006), that require the disarmament of all armed groups in Lebanon, so that, pursuant to the Lebanese cabinet decision of 27 July 2006, there will be no weapons or authority in Lebanon other than that of the Lebanese State;
— no foreign forces in Lebanon without the consent of its Government;
— no sales or supply of arms and related materiel to Lebanon except as authorized by its Government;
— provision to the United Nations of all remaining maps of land mines in Lebanon in Israel's possession;

9. *Invites* the Secretary-General to support efforts to secure as soon as possible agreements in principle from the Government of Lebanon and the Government of Israel to the principles and elements for a long-term solution as set forth in paragraph 8, and *expresses* its intention to be actively involved;

10. *Requests* the Secretary-General to develop, in liaison with relevant international actors and the concerned parties, proposals to implement the relevant provisions of the Taif Accords, and resolutions 1559 (2004) and 1680 (2006), including disarmament, and for delineation of the international borders of Lebanon, especially in those areas where the border is disputed or uncertain, including by dealing with the Shebaa farms area, and to present to the Security Council those proposals within thirty days;

11. *Decides,* in order to supplement and enhance the force in numbers, equipment, mandate and scope of operations, to authorize an increase in the force strength of UNIFIL to a maximum of 15,000 troops, and that the force shall, in addition to carrying out its mandate under resolutions 425 and 426 (1978):
(a) Monitor the cessation of hostilities;
(b) Accompany and support the Lebanese armed forces as they deploy throughout the South, including along the Blue Line, as Israel withdraws its armed forces from Lebanon as provided in paragraph 2;

(c) Coordinate its activities related to paragraph 11 (b) with the Government of Lebanon and the Government of Israel;
(d) Extend its assistance to help ensure humanitarian access to civilian populations and the voluntary and safe return of displaced persons;
(e) Assist the Lebanese armed forces in taking steps towards the establishment of the area as referred to in paragraph 8;
(f) Assist the Government of Lebanon, at its request, to implement paragraph 14;

12. Acting in support of a request from the Government of Lebanon to deploy an international force to assist it to exercise its authority throughout the territory, *authorizes* UNIFIL to take all necessary action in areas of deployment of its forces and as it deems within its capabilities, to ensure that its area of operations is not utilized for hostile activities of any kind, to resist attempts by forceful means to prevent it from discharging its duties under the mandate of the Security Council, and to protect United Nations personnel, facilities, installations and equipment, ensure the security and freedom of movement of United Nations personnel, humanitarian workers and, without prejudice to the responsibility of the Government of Lebanon, to protect civilians under imminent threat of physical violence;

13. *Requests* the Secretary-General urgently to put in place measures to ensure UNIFIL is able to carry out the functions envisaged in this resolution, *urges* Member States to consider making appropriate contributions to UNIFIL and to respond positively to requests for assistance from the Force, and *expresses* its strong appreciation to those who have contributed to UNIFIL in the past;

14. *Calls upon* the Government of Lebanon to secure its borders and other entry points to prevent the entry in Lebanon without its consent of arms or related materiel and *requests* UNIFIL as authorized in paragraph 11 to assist the Government of Lebanon at its request;

15. *Decides* further that all States shall take the necessary measures to prevent, by their nationals or from their territories or using their flag vessels or aircraft:
(a) The sale or supply to any entity or individual in Lebanon of arms and related materiel of all types, including weapons and ammunition, military vehicles and equipment, paramilitary equipment, and spare parts for the aforementioned, whether or not originating in their territories; and
(b) The provision to any entity or individual in Lebanon of any technical training or assistance related to the provision, manufacture, maintenance or use of the items listed in subparagraph (a) above;
except that these prohibitions shall not apply to arms, related material, training or assistance authorized by the Government of Lebanon or by UNIFIL as authorized in paragraph 11;

16. *Decides* to extend the mandate of UNIFIL until 31 August 2007, and *expresses its intention* to consider in a later resolution further enhancements to the mandate and other steps to contribute to the implementation of a permanent ceasefire and a long-term solution;

17. *Requests* the Secretary-General to report to the Council within one week on the implementation of this resolution and subsequently on a regular basis;

18. *Stresses* the importance of, and the need to achieve, a comprehensive, just and lasting peace in the Middle East, based on all its relevant resolutions including its resolutions 242 (1967) of 22 November 1967, 338 (1973) of 22 October 1973 and 1515 (2003) of 18 November 2003;

19. *Decides* to remain actively seized of the matter.

Source: United Nations Security Council Official Records, 06-46503 (E), S.C. Res. 1701, August 11, 2006, http://daccessdds.un.org/doc/UNDOC/GEN/N06/465/03/PDF/N0646503.pdf?OpenElement.

166. The Iraq Study Group Report, Executive Summary [Excerpt], December 2006

Introduction

In March 2006 as the situation in Iraq and the Middle East appeared increasingly problematic, the U.S. Congress appropriated $1 million in funding for a full-scale bipartisan expert study of the situation in Iraq and the Middle East. The study group was cochaired by former Republican secretary of state James A. Baker III and former Democratic congressman Lee Hamilton Jr., each of whom was widely respected within both political parties. The group's terms of reference were wide-ranging: to explore the entire Iraqi situation—economic, political, strategic, and military—and its broader regional and international context and to make recommendations for the future. To considerable fanfare, the report was issued in December 2006. Highly critical of past U.S. policies in Iraq and the region, the document warned that the situation in Iraq was precarious and that unless it took decisive and immediate action to limit the damage, the United States might well be facing a major foreign policy disaster. The report did not confine itself to the situation in Iraq, which the authors argued could only be considered and resolved in the broader Middle East context. Among the outstanding regional issues that had to be addressed were the continuing Arab-Israeli impasse, the volatile situation in Lebanon, and Syrian sponsorship of extreme Palestinian and Arab groups that sought to overthrow Israel and destabilize the Middle East. The report therefore recommended "a renewed and sustained commitment by the United States to a com-

prehensive Arab-Israeli peace on all fronts," an effort that would also utilize the good offices of Russia, the European Union (EU), and the United Nations (UN). This would involve two tracks: one to bring about the final establishment of separate and independent Israeli and Palestinian states that could coexist in relative harmony, and the other to persuade Syria to cease supporting the radical Hezbollah in Lebanon and its attacks on Israeli territory and personnel, in return for which Israel would return the Golan Heights to Syria. In response to the report, U.S. secretary of state Condoleezza Rice showed new interest in brokering an understanding between Israel and leaders of the Palestinian Authority.

Primary Source

[. . .]

The United States cannot achieve its goals in the Middle East unless it deals directly with the Arab-Israeli conflict and regional instability. There must be a renewed and sustained commitment by the United States to a comprehensive Arab-Israeli peace on all fronts: Lebanon, Syria, and President Bush's June 2002 commitment to a two-state solution for Israel and Palestine. This commitment must include direct talks with, by, and between Israel, Lebanon, Palestinians (those who accept Israel's right to exist), and Syria. . . .

From Section II, "A New Way Forward", Part A— "The External Approach: Building an International Consensus"
1. The New Diplomatic Offensive
Iraq cannot be addressed effectively in isolation from other major regional issues, interests, and unresolved conflicts. To put it simply, all key issues in the Middle East—the Arab-Israeli conflict, Iraq, Iran, the need for political and economic reforms, and extremism and terrorism—are inextricably linked. In addition to supporting stability in Iraq, a comprehensive diplomatic offensive—the New Diplomatic Offensive—should address these key regional issues. By doing so, it would help marginalize extremists and terrorists, promote U.S. values and interests, and improve America's global image. . . .

4. The Wider Regional Context
The United States will not be able to achieve its goals in the Middle East unless the United States deals directly with the Arab-Israeli conflict.

There must be a renewed and sustained commitment by the United States to a comprehensive Arab-Israeli peace on all fronts: Lebanon, Syria, and President Bush's June 2002 commitment to a two-state solution for Israel and Palestine. This commitment must include direct talks with, by, and between Israel, Lebanon, Palestinians (those who accept Israel's right to exist), and particularly Syria—which is the principal transit point for shipments of weapons to Hezbollah, and which supports radical Palestinian groups.

The United States does its ally Israel no favors in avoiding direct involvement to solve the Arab-Israeli conflict. For several reasons, we should act boldly:

- There is no military solution to this conflict.
- The vast majority of the Israeli body politic is tired of being a nation perpetually at war.
- No American administration—Democratic or Republican—will ever abandon Israel.
- Political engagement and dialogue are essential in the Arab-Israeli dispute because it is an axiom that when the political process breaks down there will be violence on the ground.
- The only basis on which peace can be achieved is that set forth in UN Security Council Resolutions 242 and 338 and in the principle of "land for peace."
- The only lasting and secure peace will be a negotiated peace such as Israel has achieved with Egypt and Jordan. This effort would strongly support moderate Arab governments in the region, especially the democratically elected government of Lebanon, and the Palestinian Authority under President Mahmoud Abbas.

RECOMMENDATION 13: There must be a renewed and sustained commitment by the United States to a comprehensive Arab-Israeli peace on all fronts: Lebanon and Syria, and President Bush's June 2002 commitment to a two-state solution for Israel and Palestine.

RECOMMENDATION 14: This effort should include—as soon as possible—the unconditional calling and holding of meetings, under the auspices of the United States or the Quartet (i.e., the United States, Russia, European Union, and the United Nations), between Israel and Lebanon and Syria on the one hand, and Israel and Palestinians (who acknowledge Israel's right to exist) on the other. The purpose of these meetings would be to negotiate peace as was done at the Madrid Conference in 1991, and on two separate tracks—one Syrian/Lebanese, and the other Palestinian.

RECOMMENDATION 15: Concerning Syria, some elements of that negotiated peace should be:

- Syria's full adherence to UN Security Council Resolution 1701 of August 2006, which provides the framework for Lebanon to regain sovereign control over its territory.
- Syria's full cooperation with all investigations into political assassinations in Lebanon, especially those of Rafik Hariri and Pierre Gemayel.
- A verifiable cessation of Syrian aid to Hezbollah and the use of Syrian territory for transshipment of Iranian weapons and aid to Hezbollah. (This step would do much to solve Israel's problem with Hezbollah.)
- Syria's use of its influence with Hamas and Hezbollah for the release of the captured Israeli Defense Force soldiers.

- A verifiable cessation of Syrian efforts to undermine the democratically elected government of Lebanon.
- A verifiable cessation of arms shipments from or transiting through Syria for Hamas and other radical Palestinian groups.
- A Syrian commitment to help obtain from Hamas an acknowledgment of Israel's right to exist.
- Greater Syrian efforts to seal its border with Iraq.

RECOMMENDATION 16: In exchange for these actions and in the context of a full and secure peace agreement, the Israelis should return the Golan Heights, with a U.S. security guarantee for Israel that could include an international force on the border, including U.S. troops if requested by both parties.

RECOMMENDATION 17: Concerning the Palestinian issue, elements of that negotiated peace should include:

- Adherence to UN Security Council Resolutions 242 and 338 and to the principle of land for peace, which are the only bases for achieving peace.
- Strong support for Palestinian President Mahmoud Abbas and the Palestinian Authority to take the lead in preparing the way for negotiations with Israel.
- A major effort to move from the current hostilities by consolidating the cease-fire reached between the Palestinians and the Israelis in November 2006.
- Support for a Palestinian national unity government.
- Sustainable negotiations leading to a final peace settlement along the lines of President Bush's two-state solution, which would address the key final status issues of borders, settlements, Jerusalem, the right of return, and the end of conflict.

[. . .]

Source: James A. Baker, Lee H. Hamilton, Lawrence S. Eagleburger, et al., *The Iraq Study Group Report,* United States Institute of Peace, http://www.usip.org/isg/iraq_study_group_report/report/1206/index.html.

167. Mahmoud Abbas, Message to Ismail Haniyeh, February 7, 2007

Introduction

In January 2006 the Palestinian party Hamas won a majority of votes in general elections held throughout the territory under the jurisdiction of the Palestinian Authority (PA). According to its charter, Hamas was officially committed to the destruction of the State of Israel and declined to accept any peace settlement that left Israel in existence. Fearing that the election results would derail the peace process, Israeli leaders and the international community greeted them with shock and consternation. Mahmoud Abbas, PA president since January 2005 and leader of the Palestine Liberation Organization (PLO) mainstream Fatah faction, was, by contrast, a strong supporter of continuing peace negotiations with Israel under the Road Map to Peace guidelines, whose ultimate objective was the existence of two neighboring states, Palestinian and Israeli, that could live in peace with each other behind secure and recognized boundaries. After Hamas's victory, Abbas refused to allow Hamas leaders to hold key ministries in the PA or form part of a coalition government including both Fatah and Hamas leaders unless they first endorsed the Road Map to Peace guidelines and the peace process as set out in the 1993 Oslo Accords. Over the next year Abbas and Hamas engaged in lengthy negotiations, as Abbas put various forms of public pressure on Hamas to accept the commitments to United Nations (UN) Security Council Resolutions 242 and 338 accepting the existence of Israel that the PLO had already made. These included threats by Abbas to call a territory-wide Palestinian referendum on peace or to hold new elections. In June 2006 Hamas broke the ceasefire agreement with Israel that Abbas had brokered in early 2005 and resumed attacks on Israelis in retaliation for an incident in which several civilians died on a beach in Gaza. In February 2007 leaders of Hamas and Fatah met in the Muslim holy city of Mecca, Saudi Arabia, and signed an agreement whereby Hamas agreed to "respect international resolutions and the agreements signed by the Palestine Liberation Organization," in return for which Hamas would hold more cabinet ministries than any other Palestinian party, including the post of prime minister. Among the commitments that Hamas agreed to accept were those of the National Reconciliation Document, also known as the Prisoners' Agreement. The lengthy impasse over the selection of the Palestinian government was one of several reasons that throughout 2006 the peace process was stalled.

Primary Source

In my capacity as the head of the Executive Committee of the Palestine Liberation Organization and the president of the Palestinian Authority:

a) I designate you to form the upcoming Palestinian government within the time specified under the basic law [five weeks].
b) After forming the government and presenting it to us, it should be presented to the Palestinian Legislative Council for a vote of confidence.
c) I call upon you as the head of the upcoming Palestinian government to commit to the higher interests of the Palestinian people, to preserve its rights and to preserve its achievements and to develop them, and to work in order to achieve its national goals as was approved by the Palestine National Council, the clauses of the Basic Law and the National Reconciliation Document.

Based on this, I call upon you to respect international resolutions and the agreements signed by the Palestine Liberation Organization [referring to peace accords with Israel].

Under the agreement, Hamas will hold nine ministries in the Cabinet, including the prime minister's post. Fatah will hold six, and other factions will hold four. Fatah will name independents as foreign minister and two state ministers without portfolio. Hamas will name independents as interior minister, planning minister and a state minister without portfolio.

> **Source:** Mahmoud Abbas, "Mecca Accord for Palestinian National Unity Government, 8 February, 2007," Electronic Intifada, http://electronicintifada.net.

168. Program of the Palestinian Authority National Unity Government [Excerpt], March 17, 2007

Introduction

In February 2007 representatives of Hamas, which had won a majority of seats in the January 2006 Palestinian Authority (PA) elections, and Fatah, the Palestinian grouping to which President Mahmoud Abbas belonged, finally reached agreement on the formation of a national unity government. Until that time, European powers and the United States had refused to deal with or provide aid directly to the Palestinian government until Hamas, officially committed to the destruction of Israel, agreed to accept previous international agreements concluded by Palestinian representatives, including the 1991 Oslo Accords recognizing Israel's right to exist. The February 2007 Mecca Accord between Hamas and Fatah, brokered by the Saudi government, remained ambivalent on this subject. The following month, the new national unity government issued a platform stating that peace, security, and stability in the region "depend[ed] on ending the Israeli occupation of the Palestinian territories" and affirming its intention to "work with the international community" to this end. The platform also affirmed that "resistance is a legitimate right of the Palestinian people," a statement that the Israeli Foreign Ministry promptly condemned as an affirmation of continued Palestinian support for "violence and terrorism." The platform then stated, notwithstanding this stance, that the Palestinians hoped to reach "a reciprocal truce" with Israeli forces if the latter would abandon their repressive measures against Palestinians, including "assassinations, arrests, incursions and home demolition and leveling of lands," and restore Palestinian freedom of movement. Any final agreement that the PA's president, at this point the conciliatory Abbas, might reach with Israel was to be ratified either by the Palestinian National Council or by a general referendum among all Palestinians. The platform also affirmed the right of Palestinian refugees to return to their former homes in Israel. In a friendly gesture toward Israel, the platform also stated that the new government would seek to encourage the captors of a kidnapped Israeli soldier held in Lebanon since the previous summer to return their prisoner to Israel. The Palestinian national platform clearly represented a compromise between the various parties, but many feared that it only papered over their differences. The Israeli government decried not just its failure to condemn violence and forthrightly accept Israel's right to exist and the United Nations (UN) Security Council resolutions to that effect but also its endorsement of the right of return to Israel of Palestinian refugees. The United States also demanded almost immediately that the new Palestinian government clearly renounce violence, recognize Israel, and accept existing peace agreements. On March 17, 2007, the Palestinian assembly, 41 of whose 132 members, including 37 Hamas representatives, were then residing in Israeli jails, voted 83–3 in favor of the new government and its platform. Many observers, however, cynically believed that Israel and the United States would make every effort to provoke the collapse of the new Palestinian government in the hope that this would force fresh parliamentary elections upon the PA and that these in turn would put less radical and militant Palestinian elements in power. The Mecca Accord and the PA National Unity government it established were short-lived. In June 2007 the Fatah-Hamas coalition broke down when bitter fighting between the two Palestinian factions erupted in Gaza. Hamas forces won control of Gaza, capturing eight armored combat vehicles and many thousands of guns that had originally belonged to the PA. Fatah, meanwhile, retained power on the West Bank, where President Abbas dissolved the national government and declared a state of emergency. Most governments and international organizations were willing to deal with the West Bank Palestinians while largely ignoring Hamas in Gaza. With Hamas representatives no longer included in the PA government, international donors, including the United States and the European Union (EU), resumed direct aid to the PA after the West Bank government had jettisoned its Hamas members, while Israel handed over previously frozen tax payments. The division of the Palestinian territories between the two rival Palestinian groups placed additional obstacles and complications in the path of efforts to reach a lasting Israeli-Palestinian settlement.

Primary Source

[…]

The Palestinian people have lived for more than 60 years under the yoke of dispersion, deprivation and eviction and suffered due to occupation all kinds of suffering and oppression and aggression while our people marked a long process of struggle, resistance, perseverance, and resilience through which they sacrificed hundreds of thousands of martyrs and injured and prisoners and gave the best examples of sacrifice and self denial and giving and clinging to their rights and constants moving through important historical phases until we reached the phase of the national unity government (the eleventh government). This government was born after many efforts exerted by the loyal members of our people who worked day and night to reach a reconciliatory vision and common denominators that gather all Palestinians under one umbrella.

This government came as a fruit of the positive spirit and mutual confidence that resulted in solving all issues in the various fields and this government is one of the major and leading results of the blessed Mecca Agreement under the sponsorship of the Saudi King Abdul Aziz. The national unity government is the culmination of a long series of Palestinian dialogues where Egypt and Syria had a leading role in sponsoring these dialogues and following them up with appreciated efforts by several brotherly Arab countries and the Arab and Islamic organizations. It also reflects the devotion and loyalty to the long process of martyrs and the pains of the prisoners and injured, mainly the major martyrs the late president Yasser Arafat and Sheikh Imam Ahmad Yaseen and Leader Abu Ali Mustafa and leader Fathi al-Shiqaqi and leader Abdul Abbas.

Based on the national conciliation document and in light of the letter of commissioning, the national unity government will work at all levels in a manner that achieves the higher interests of the Palestinian people in the following manner:

First: At the political level

1—The government affirms that the key to security and stability in the region depends on ending the Israeli occupation of the Palestinian territories and recognizing the right to self determination of the Palestinian people; the government will work with the international community for the sake of ending the occupation and regaining the legitimate rights of the Palestinian people so that we can build a solid basis for peace, security and prosperity in the region.

2—The government shall abide to protect the higher national interests of the Palestinian people and protect their rights and preserve and develop their accomplishments and work on achieving their national goals as ratified by the resolutions of the PNC meetings and the Articles of the Basic Law and the national conciliation document and the resolutions of the Arab summits and based on this, the government shall respect the international legitimacy resolutions and the agreements that were signed by the PLO.

3—The government shall abide by rejecting the so called state with temporary borders because this idea is based on taking away from the legitimate rights of the Palestinian people.

4—To cling to the right of the Palestinian refugees and right of return to their lands and properties.

5—To work diligently for the sake of liberating the heroic prisoners from the Israeli occupation prisons.

6—To confront the measures of the occupation on the ground in terms of the assassinations, arrests, and incursions. The government shall grant special importance to the city of Jerusalem to confront the Israeli policies pertaining to the people, lands and holy sites of Jerusalem.

7—To consolidate the relations with the Arab and Islamic countries and open up and cooperate with the regional and international surrounding on the basis of mutual respect.

Second: At the level of the occupation

1—The government affirms that peace and stability in the region depends on ending all forms of occupation of the Palestinian territories and removing the apartheid wall and settlements and halt of the Judaization of Jerusalem and policies of annexation and restore the rights to their owners.

2—The government affirms that resistance is a legitimate right of the Palestinian people as granted by the international norms and charters; our Palestinian people have the right to defend themselves in [the] face of any Israeli aggression and believes that halting resistance depends on ending the occupation and achieving freedom, return and independence.

3—Despite this, the government, through national conciliation, will work on consolidating the calm and expanding it to become a comprehensive reciprocal truce happening at the same time between both sides and this should be in return for Israel halting its occupation measures on the ground in terms of assassinations, arrests, incursions and home demolition and leveling of lands and the digging works in Jerusalem and it should work on removing the check-points and reopening the crossings and lifting all the restrictions on movement and the release of prisoners.

4—The government affirms what came in the national conciliation document on the issue of the administration of the negotiations which is the jurisdiction of the PLO and the President of the PNA on the basis of clinging to the Palestinian national goals and towards achieving these goals, so that any offer on any final agreement should be presented to the new Palestinian National Council for ratification or to hold a general referendum to have the Palestinian people inside and abroad and to have a law that organizes this referendum.

5—The government shall support the exerted efforts and shall encourage the relevant parties to accelerate and end the case of the Israeli soldier in the context of an honorable prisoners exchange deal.

Third: At the security level

The national unity government realizes the internal difficult conditions and believes that its top priority at the coming phase is to control the current security conditions and in order to achieve this, the government shall depend in its program on the following:

1—To form a higher national security council that represents the terms of reference to all security services and the framework that organizes their work and define their policies, and

request from the PLC to finalize the law pertaining to the national security higher council.

2—To structure the security services and build them on [a] professional basis and work to provide their needs and reduce the partisan considerations and move them away from political polarizations and conflicts and consolidate in them the loyalty to the homeland and to have them abide by executing the decisions of their political leadership and to make sure that the personnel working in these services commit themselves to the tasks commissioned to them.

3—To work on activating the laws that have been ratified by the PLC with regard to the security institution.

4—To set up a comprehensive security plan to end all forms of chaos and security chaos and aggressions and protect and prevent any bloodshed and honor of families and funds and public and private properties and control the weapons and provide security to the citizen and work on ending the oppression inflicted on the people through the rule of the law and support the police to perform its duties in the best manner.

Fourth: At the legal level

1—The government shall work in full cooperation with the judicial authority to secure the reform and activation and protection of the judicial apparatus with all its institutions in a manner that can enable it to perform its duties in the context of achieving justice and fighting corruption and abiding by the rule of the law and implement the law with transparency and integrity on everybody without any interference from any party.

2—The government affirms that it shall work according to the Basic Law which organizes the relations between the three authorities on the basis of separating between the authorities and respect the authorities granted to the Presidency and to the government according to the law and order.

3—The government shall assist Mr. President in performing his various duties and will make sure to cooperate fully with the Presidency institution and the constitutional institutions and work with the PLC and the juridical authorities towards developing the Palestinian political system on the basis of having a unified strong national authority.

Fifth: At the level of the Palestinian values system

1—The eleventh government shall abide by consolidating national unity and protect social peace and consolidate the values of mutual respect and adoption of the language of dialogue and end all forms of tension and consolidate the culture of tolerance and protection of the Palestinian blood and ban internal fighting.

2—The government affirms the unity of the Palestinian people inside and abroad and shall work to have the participation of the Palestinian people abroad in all matters pertaining to the Palestinian affairs.

3—The government shall seek to consolidate national conciliation and towards achieving comprehensive national conciliation through forming a higher national commission under the sponsorship of the presidency and the government to be formed from the PLC and the factions and the well known figures and legal experts and scholars. The aim of this commission is to end the blood problems between the factions and families and assess the damage caused to the properties and institutions and work on solving these problems.

4—The government shall work on reinforcing the principle of citizenship through equality in rights and duties and equal opportunities and consolidate social justice in appointments and recruitments in the various ministries and institutions and end all forms of political favoritism in civil and security recruitments.

5—The government affirms its respect for the principle of political pluralism and protection of public freedoms and [shall] reinforce the values of Shura and democracy and protect human rights and consolidate the principle of justice and equality and protect the free press and freedom of expression and abide by [the] peaceful transfer of power and authorities and conclude the elections at the local councils within the next six months God willing.

6—The government shall abide by providing a dignified life to the Palestinian citizen and provide the requirements of life and social welfare and meet the health needs and develop the health facilities and expand health insurance and improve the situation of the hospitals and clinics and work on tackling the phenomena of poverty and unemployment through providing job opportunities and development projects and social securities and the social welfare program; the government shall grant special care to the education and higher education and shall encourage scientific research and provide its needs.

7—To care for the sectors of laborers, farmers, fishermen and the sectors of youths and women so that women can assume the status they deserve based on their sacrifices and to secure to them participation in the decision making process and to contribute to the building process in all institutions and ministries and at the various fields.

Sixth: The economic situation

1—The government shall work on ending the siege imposed on our Palestinian people through the programs and relations and to activate the regional and international frameworks to alleviate the suffering of our Palestinian people.

2—The government shall give priority to upgrade and advance the national economy and encourage the economic and trade sectors with the Arab and Islamic world and encourage economic and trade relations with the European Union and the rest of the world.

3—To move to protect the consumer and encourage the private sector and provide the proper climate for its activities and lay down sound rules for government work and its official institutions and the institutions of the private sector and end monopoly. The government shall work on providing the proper climate and protection and stability of investment projects.

4—The government shall work on respecting the principles of free economy in a manner that meets with our values and norms and in a manner that serves Palestinian development and protect the private sector and encourage investment and fight unemployment and poverty and reinforce the productive economic sectors and reconstruct the infrastructure and develop the industrial zone and the housing and technology sectors.

Seventh: The field of reform

1—The government which adopts the reform strategy affirms to your respectful council and to the people who granted us their esteemed confidence that we will remain faithful and the citizen shall feel this in the work of the government—God willing—through real achievements on the ground in the areas of administrative and financial reforms and will cooperate with the PLC on issuing laws that reinforce reform and that fight corruption and will look into the structures and methods of work in a manner that guarantees efficacy of work and performance in the ministries and their abidance by the law.

2—The government shall work on meeting the urgent needs of the citizen in the various fields through planning and initiatives and in defining the priorities of spending and rationalizing spending and in launching initiatives and innovative ideas and maintaining the highest degrees of credibility and transparency.

3—Within the context of reform, the government shall seek to fight corruption and reinforce the values of integrity and transparency and refrain from abusing public funds and we will give the matter of administrative development a social dimension and societal culture that establishes a new concept and formulate a Palestinian societal strategy for administrative development and to develop a sound working mechanism based on the principles of modern administration which can assist in implementing this strategy according to the requirements and needs of Palestinian society.

Eighth: International relations

At the time when our government stresses on its Arab and Islamic depth, it shall work on establishing sound and solid relations with the various world countries and with the international institutions, including the UN and the Security Council and the international regional organizations, in a manner that assists [in] reinforcing world peace and stability. The European Union has offered lots of assistance to our Palestinian people and supported our people's right to freedom and independence and the EU has had serious standpoints in launching criticism to the Israeli occupation policies; therefore, we are interested in solid ties with the EU and we expect from it a larger role in exerting pressure on the occupation authorities to respect human rights as stipulated by the international charters, to withdraw its troops from the occupied Palestinian Territories and halt all and repeated aggressions against our people. The government seeks to develop relations with the countries with permanent membership in the Security Council, mainly Russia and China, and Japan and the African and Asian countries in a manner that secures the just rights of our people and at the same time, the government calls on the United States Administration to reconsider its unjust positions towards the Palestinian cause and calls on the need to respect the choice of the Palestinian people as realized and translated in the national unity government.

Source: "The Program of the National Unity Government," Jerusalem Media & Communication Centre, http://www.jmcc.org/politics/pna/nationalgovprog.htm.

Categorical Index

Events

Groups and Organizations

Technologies, Objects, and Artifacts

Treaties, Plans, and Other Documents

Other

Index